CIVIL JUSTICE IN CRISIS

CIVIL JUSTICE IN CRISIS

Comparative Perspectives of Civil Procedure

EDITED BY

ADRIAN A. S. ZUCKERMAN

CONSULTANT EDITORS

SERGIO CHIARLONI
University of Turin, Italy

PETER GOTTWALD
University of Regensburg, Germany

OXFORD
UNIVERSITY PRESS

OXFORD
UNIVERSITY PRESS

Great Clarendon Street, Oxford OX2 6DP

Oxford University Press is a department of the University of Oxford.
It furthers the University's objective of excellence in research, scholarship,
and education by publishing worldwide in

Oxford New York

Athens Auckland Bangkok Bogotá Buenos Aires Calcutta
Cape Town Chennai Dar es Salaam Delhi Florence Hong Kong Istanbul
Karachi Kuala Lumpur Madrid Melbourne Mexico City Mumbai
Nairobi Paris São Paulo Singapore Taipei Tokyo Toronto Warsaw

and associated companies in Berlin Ibadan

Oxford in a registered trade mark of Oxford University Press
in the UK and certain other countries

Published in the United States
by Oxford University Press Inc., New York

British Library Cataloguing in Publication Data

Data available

Library of Congress Cataloging in Publication Data

Civil justice in crisis: comparative perspectives of civil procedure/
edited by Adrian Zuckerman; consultant editors, Sergio Chiarloni,
Peter Gottwald.
p. cm.
Includes index.
1. Civil procedure. 2. Civil procedure (International law).
3. Conflict of laws–Civil procedure. 4. Justice, Administration of.
5. Court congestion and delay. 6. Courts. I. Zuckerman, A. A. S.
II. Chiarloni, Sergio. III. Gottwald, Peter, 1944– .
K2205.C58 1999   99–27813
347'.05–dc21

ISBN 0-19-829833-1

1 3 5 7 9 10 8 6 4 2

Typeset in Baskerville
by J&L Composition Ltd., Filey, North Yorkshire
Printed in Great Britain
on acid-free paper by
Bookcraft Ltd., Midsomer Norton, Somerset

Preface

There is a widespread perception that the administration of civil justice is failing to meet the needs of the community. This perception seems to persist across national and cultural frontiers. It is present in many different countries, both within the common law and civil law legal systems. Access to justice is so adversely affected by high litigation costs and long delays that in quite a few countries the courts no longer provide an adequate venue for seeking the protection of rights or for resolving disputes. It is no exaggeration to say that many systems of civil justice experience a crisis of some kind.

Most countries have responded by adopting various measures to address the pressing problems faced by their systems. There seems to be a truly global trend to reform the administration of civil justice. However, while legislatures, practising lawyers, and academics are familiar with the difficulties within their own respective systems, there is limited knowledge of what happens elsewhere. This collection of essays aims to redress this position so that those interested in the reform of civil justice may obtain a broader perspective. After all, the problems of high costs and excessive delays are the same, wherever they occur, and even the solutions are not that different.

Thirteen countries were chosen to be included in this volume, representing both common law and civil law systems. They are: Australia, Brazil, England, France, Greece, Germany, Holland, Italy, Japan, Portugal, Spain, Switzerland, and the United States of America. In each case, an essay was commissioned from a local civil procedure expert to present the country's system of civil justice.

Each essay begins with a general outline of the national civil justice system. Thus, quite apart from the question of reform, the essays aim to provide the raw material for comparative studies of civil procedure. Each essay then moves on to describe the practical operation of the national system, its strengths and weaknesses, and the steps that have been taken, or are proposed, to improve the system. Finally, each essay concludes with an assessment.

The essays aim to provide as much statistical information as is available, so that the reader may get some idea about the size of the court system, the length of delays, and the cost of litigation in each country. Unfortunately, the availability of data varies greatly between countries. In some ample information is available; in others very little. The temptation to construct comparative statistical tables has been resisted because of the risk of making misleading comparisons. For instance, most countries can provide some figures about the number of judges, but what is included in these figures varies considerably: judicial statistics in one country may include all judges, but in another they may exclude lay judges (such as the English magistrates) or specialist judges (such as judges of industrial tribunals). The same goes for the number of lawyers; the English figures may include all lawyers, but the Italian figures will exclude notaries and the conveyancing profession, who would be included in the English statistics. Nevertheless, the statistics available for each country should provide readers with an opportunity to form a fairly good idea about the operation of the various systems.

The study of different systems will help those involved in reform to learn how others have approached the problems, what solutions have been tried, and with what success. The first chapter in the book tries to provide a general comparative perspective. It offers parameters of civil justice or criteria of reasonable provision of justice. It draws attention to the main themes of the different national essays and to the sources of the difficulties. Finally, it highlights the general trends, such as the move towards judicial control of civil litigation. The second chapter, written by Professor Leubsdorf, gives a historical and rather gloomy perspective of the reform of civil procedure, particularly in common law countries. These two introductory chapters are followed by national accounts.

As many of the contributors are not native English speakers, considerable editorial work was involved in preparing the essays for publication. Sue Gibbons and Paul Michalik of University College, Oxford, provided invaluable assistance with the editorial task. If deficiencies of style still remain, it is not for lack of effort on their part.

Lastly, thanks are due to Professor Chiarloni and Professor Gottwald, who were involved with the project from the start and whose wise counsel helped to bring it to a successful conclusion.

A.A.S.Z.
University College, Oxford
April 1999

Contents

List of Contributors

Adrian A. S. Zuckerman, Fellow of University College, Oxford, England

Professor John Leubsdorf, School of Law, Rutgers University, Newark, NJ, USA

Professor Richard L. Marcus, Horace O. Coil ('57) Chair of Litigation, Hastings College of the Law, University of California, USA

Paul Michalik, Lecturer in Law, University College, Oxford, England

The Honorable Justice Geoffrey Davies, Judge of Appeal, Court of Appeal, Queensland, Australia

Professor Peter Gottwald, Faculty of Law, University of Regensburg, Germany

Professor Yukiko Hasebe, Faculty of Law, Gakushuin University, Tokyo, Japan

Professor Sergio Chiarloni, Faculty of Law, University of Turin, Italy

Professor Loïc Cadiet, Faculty of Law, University of Panthéon-Sorbonne, Paris, France

Professor Sergio Bermudes, Faculty of Law, Pontifical Catholic University, Rio de Janeiro, Brazil

Professor K. D. Kerameus, Faculty of Law, University of Athens, Director of Hellenic Institute of International and Foreign Law, Athens, Greece

Professor Stelios Koussoulis, Faculty of Law, University of Athens, Greece

Professor Ignacio Díes-Picazo Giménez, University of San Pablo CEU, Madrid, Spain

Professor Maria Manuel Leitão Marques, Conceição Gomes, and João Pedroso, Centre for Social Studies, Faculty of Economics, University of Coimbra, Portugal

Professor Erhard Blankenburg, Faculty of Law, Vrije University, Amsterdam, the Netherlands

Professor Isaak Meier, Faculty of Law, University of Zurich, Switzerland

Part I
Parameters of Civil Justice

1

Justice in Crisis: Comparative Dimensions of Civil Procedure

Adrian A. S. Zuckerman

1. THE DIMENSIONS OF JUSTICE

All systems of procedure seek to do justice. So much we can take for granted as regards each of the systems discussed in this volume. It is also obvious that different systems of procedure employ different methods for achieving this goal. Whether the differences between systems are small or great, a comparison is inevitably called for. We look at each other in order to measure ourselves. But like any other form of assessment, this too requires some parameters, some common denominator by which we can measure and compare.

Accordingly, the first purpose of this opening essay is to develop such a set of parameters. It will be argued that justice has three dimensions by which it is measured. Unfortunately, these three dimensions are not entirely complementary. As we shall see, at times they pull in different directions and call for compromises. Compromise, therefore, is an inescapable feature of any system of justice.

Once this conceptual framework has been set out, attention will be given to individual procedures. The purpose of this analysis is not to grade the different procedures in some order of preference. Such ordering, it will become apparent, would be largely meaningless, if not altogether arbitrary. Rather, the purpose of the analysis will be to draw attention to how different systems of procedure seek to achieve the goals of justice and what compromises or sacrifices are made in the attempt to do so. This last point is perhaps the most instructive aspect of a comparison of systems, for it draws attention to the fact that what lies behind different methods of doing justice is really a difference in priorities. It is the priority given to this or that objective of justice which shapes the procedures with which we end up.

The dimension of truth: rectitude of decision

In all systems of procedure doing justice means arriving at decisions which give the parties before the court what is legally due to them. In order to do justice, then, the court has to determine the true facts and then correctly apply the law

Sue Gibbons, of University College, Oxford, has rendered invaluable assistance with the preparation of this paper.

to them. In Bentham's terminology, the purpose of procedure is rectitude of decision, which requires the correct application of the law to the true facts.[1]

While rectitude of decision, or truth, is the aim of civil procedure, it is acknowledged that our procedures are not perfect. There are always limitations to the ability of procedure to achieve rectitude of decision. A system of procedure can strive to determine what happened in the past and to apply the law precisely, but it cannot guarantee that errors will never occur. It is the mark of legal procedures that, while the criterion of justice is external to the procedure (i.e. the true facts, the correct law), the procedure itself cannot always achieve a perfect correspondence between individual decisions and this criterion, as Rawls observed.[2] Accordingly, a procedure may be just even if individual decisions arrived at by this procedure are sometimes erroneous.

We cannot expect perfect justice but we can and should expect a just procedure. The question therefore arises: what is a just procedure? Since rectitude of decision is, as we have seen, the most basic requirement, a system of procedure must take sufficient steps to arrive at decisions that are correct in fact and in law. A procedure in which the courts do not even try to get at the truth is manifestly an unjust procedure, because it fails in its main task of giving those who seek the courts' help what is due to them by right. We can, therefore, take it for granted that all procedures seek to achieve rectitude. Yet not all procedures are necessarily just. To be just we have to be satisfied that the system of procedure produces results which are broadly correct.

Although it is a perfectly simple requirement of justice that a legal procedure should, by and large, produce correct results, it is extremely difficult to assess the extent to which this requirement is fulfilled in any given system of procedure. The criterion of what is true or false is, of course, independent of the legal procedure. For instance, whether the plaintiff delivered the goods as stipulated by his contract with the defendant is a simple question about factual reality that the procedure must discover. At the same time it is very difficult to determine whether a judgment determining this issue is correct or not. We do not have a super-test for testing the factual accuracy of individual judgments.[3] All we possess is the legal procedure that we have devised. Our confidence in the conformity of individual decisions with fact and law is simply a function of whether we are satisfied that the measures adopted by the procedure are adequate to secure a reasonable level of rectitude of decision.

Most, if not all, procedural requirements are concerned to secure rectitude of decision, including the requirements of procedural justice. Measures such as the right to be heard or the right to an impartial tribunal are dictated by the desire

---

[1] *Principles of Judicial Procedure*, in *Collected Works of Jeremy Bentham*, ed. Bowring (1938–43), vol. ii. See also W. Twining, *Theories of Evidence: Bentham & Wigmore* (1985).

[2] J. Rawls, *A Theory of Justice*, 85–6.

[3] If such a test were available, we might be tempted to adopt it as our procedure for deciding cases.

for rectitude of decision.[4] Of course, the appearance of justice is also important, but it does not alter the fact that at the foundation of procedure lies the objective of getting at the truth. This objective lies behind the entire procedural organization. Rules such as those dealing with notice of commencement of proceedings, with the definition of the issues between the parties, with the obtaining of evidence, and with the calling of witnesses are all designed to facilitate the correct determination of fact and of law. It is not the aim of this collection of essays to examine in detail the procedures of different countries. However, we cannot analyse the dimension of rectitude of decision without some understanding of the procedural tools employed by different systems.

There is one more observation that needs to be made about rectitude of decision. A partial or prejudiced judge could distort the truth or the application of the law and thus undermine rectitude of decision. But it is not only judges who could distort rectitude of decision: procedures too could do so since, as we have seen, procedures are imperfect and liable to some mistakes. Given that there is always a risk of error, justice demands that this risk should be equally distributed between different litigants. A procedure which imposed a higher risk of error on a certain class of litigants would fail to treat those litigants with equal concern and regard. Being treated as equals is a basic requirement of justice. It is not suggested that plaintiffs and defendants are treated equally *vis-à-vis* each other. Clearly they are not, because one is bound to win whereas the other will lose. The requirement of treating litigants as equals means that none of them is discriminated against in procedural terms. It means that none of them is given preferential treatment compared with the others. It means that one litigant is not subjected to a higher risk of error compared with the others. In short, it means that all are equal before the law in the sense that the rules of procedure will not distort the correct application of the law to the true facts in favour of one litigant.

It follows that the first feature of a just procedure is that it should not interfere with the court's ability to get to the truth in a way which favours one litigant over the other. In some situations it may be felt that a completely equal procedural treatment is not practicable. For instance, provision needs to be made for situations where, at the end of the trial, there is doubt as to whether the plaintiff or the defendant is in the right. Anglo-American systems solve this problem by holding that the plaintiff must prove his case on the balance of probabilities. If at the end of the trial the judge is in doubt, the judge must reject the plaintiff's claim. Obviously, in these systems plaintiffs carry a slightly higher risk of error than defendants do. But we can also say that respect for the

---

[4] Rectitude of decision will dictate these measures regardless of whether or not they may be regarded as justified independently of the objective of arriving at the truth. For instance, the right to be heard may be considered as deserving of respect regardless of whether it leads to more factually correct judgments. But the fact remains that the right to be heard is a requirement of rectitude too, because without hearing the parties affected the court is less likely to arrive at the truth.

principle of treating litigants as equals is shown by keeping the difference in the risk distribution to the minimum compatible with the need to have a tie-break rule.

The time dimension

There are further dimensions of justice which, while having no direct bearing on rectitude of decision, have a powerful influence on both the justice of the system and on individual outcomes. These are time and cost.

In one sense the passage of time is not a separate dimension but a factor influencing rectitude of decision. Delay may induce error by allowing evidence to disappear or deteriorate. In a dispute which turns on the reliability of witness testimony, the longer the time that is allowed to elapse before the trial (or before the taking of the testimony), the greater the probability that memories will fade. Indeed, if a long enough time passes, the witnesses may die or disappear altogether. Inasmuch as the system of procedure has to minimize the risk of error, it has to ensure that adjudication takes place while the evidence is still fresh. However, it should be remembered that time may contribute to error not only where a decision is delayed but also where it is hurried. A judgment given in haste, without allowing adequate time for the collection of evidence and the preparation of argument, could also run a high risk of error.

Beyond this connection between time and accuracy of decisions, there is a further dimension, which is independent of rectitude of decision. Time may erode the utility of a judgment regardless of its correctness. With the passing of time a point will come beyond which delay will, with increasing acceleration, undermine the practical utility of judgment. A decision in a dispute between two litigants may correctly apply the law to the true facts and yet come too late to be of practical use to the winning litigant. Suppose that a person intends to travel abroad to attend an important event. He applies for a passport but is refused. He applies to court for an order directing the appropriate government department to issue him with a passport. If a judgment cannot be given before the planned trip, a later judgment recognizing the applicant's right to a passport will be incapable of redressing his grievance. Similarly, a system that makes victims of road accidents wait thirty years for compensation fails to take reasonable steps to redress their wrongs. It follows that a decision may be unjust not because it is incorrect in law or in fact, but because it comes too late to put things right. It is this idea that is conveyed by the aphorism 'justice delayed is justice denied' or in the Latin saying *venter non patitur dilationem* (the stomach brooks no delay). A procedure that systematically allows delays to undermine the utility of vindicating judgments, by robbing them of practical usefulness, cannot be said to be a just procedure.

We may refer to this aspect of delay as the incremental effect of delay, indicating the increasing disutility of a remedy over the course of time. In some situations the disutility of delay may not be incremental but may occur at once as a result of some event. In the example concerning the denial of a passport, once the reason for the trip had gone, little could be done to put things right. We may refer to this type of disutility as complete disutility.

In the same way that a just procedure cannot be wholly indifferent to the truth, so it cannot be wholly indifferent to delay which undermines the practical utility of judgments. Putting things right is one of the objects of the legal process. Therefore, justice demands that judgments should be given at a time when they can still remedy the wrong or, if the wrong has not yet taken place, at a time when the wrong may still be prevented. A correct judgment which comes too late to do good to the person who has been wronged is not much better than a judgment that erroneously denies that person his right. Timely justice is therefore a dimension of justice just as much as the correct application of the law to the true facts is a dimension of justice.

The cost dimension

Cost has several aspects which are closely bound up with the dimension of truth, or rectitude of decision. When we discussed the dimension of rectitude of decision earlier, we observed that all legal procedures are imperfect in the sense that they cannot guarantee absolute rectitude in all decisions. There are of course degrees of imperfection; some systems are better than others in this respect. We could confidently say that, for example, the replacement of trial by battle with a system of rational assessment of evidence was an improvement. Clearly, the level of correct decisions produced by the system as a whole is a function of the adequacy of the procedures employed for determining facts and deciding law. The better a procedure is designed to achieve these aims, the higher the proportion of correct decisions is likely to be. We may therefore say that rectitude of decision is a function of the quality of the procedure adopted.

Procedural quality is to some extent a function of the resources that we are prepared to invest in procedure. A system which suffers from inadequate resources is likely to have inferior procedural quality, and is liable to produce decisions of low rectitude value. Suppose, for example, that a country refused to allocate significant resources to procedure, that judges were appointed but not paid, and that no court facilities were provided. The judges in such a system would either be of inadequate standard or would have few incentives to invest time and effort in reaching correct decisions. It is probable that such a system would provide decisions of low rectitude value.

Of course, there are other factors that influence rectitude of decision, such as the rationality of the process and the integrity of the judges. Nevertheless, it is the case that, everything else being equal, the more resources we invest in procedural facilities, the higher their quality is likely to be and the greater their contribution to rectitude of decision.

This last observation gives rise to the question of whether a well-ordered state is under an obligation to provide the most accurate civil procedure no matter how much it costs. Put differently, are citizens entitled to claim that the state should provide them with the best possible procedures for the protection of their rights, no matter how much such procedures may cost? Most people would agree that it would be absurd to say that we are entitled to the best legal procedure regardless of expense, when we cannot reasonably claim the best possible health service or the best possible transport system. But, as we have just seen, it would be equally absurd to say that the state need not provide any resources in order to achieve rectitude of decision. Since neither of these extremes is sustainable, what we can reasonably claim for procedure lies somewhere between the extremes. As Dworkin has observed, we are entitled to expect procedures which strive to provide a reasonable measure of protection of rights, commensurable with the general resources that the community has, and relative to the other public facilities that the community needs to provide.[5]

Once it is accepted that the obligation to allocate resources to the administration of civil justice is not absolute and boundless, we must also accept that the choice of procedure must involve compromises.[6] A country that cannot afford a limitless investment in the administration of justice must achieve a compromise, whereby the resources invested in procedure are affordable and, at the same time, sufficient to achieve a reasonable degree of quality. It follows that, in devising a system of procedure, the legislature has a considerable scope for choice between different ways of balancing rectitude of decision against cost.

All systems of procedure are forced to balance available resources against the ideal of optimal rectitude. It follows that, when we come to look at different procedural systems, we will need to consider how different systems set out to strike this balance, and whether they are thought to cater adequately for the needs of their communities. We may refer to this aspect of cost as the global cost aspect, denoting the financial support given by the community to the administration of justice. In most systems demands are made for more resources. This is natural. But it is also legitimate to ask whether it is justified to require the taxpayer to invest vast sums of money in the administration of civil justice, when justice may be bought more cheaply, if a little less accurately. The global aspect

---

[5] R. Dworkin, *A Matter of Principle* (1985), ch. 3. For a purely economic approach see: R. Posner, 'An Economic Approach to Legal Procedure and Judicial Administration' (1973) 2 Journal of Legal Studies 399, and Posner, *Economic Analysis of the Law* (3rd edn., 1986).

[6] See: Jolowicz, 'On the Nature and Purposes of Civil Procedural Law', in I. Scott (ed.), *International Perspective on Civil Justice* (1990), 27; Walker, Lind, and Tyler, 'The Relationship between Procedural and Distributive Justice' (1979) 65 Virginia L. Rev. 1401; W. Twining, 'Alternative to What? Theories of Litigation, Procedure and Dispute Settlement in Anglo-American Jurisprudence: Some Neglected Classics' (1993) 56 MLR 380. The tensions between quality and economy and between speed and accuracy are discussed in Zuckerman, 'Quality and Economy in Civil Procedure: The Case for Commuting Correct Judgments for Timely Judgments' (1994) 14 OJLS 353.

raises, therefore, questions of the relationship between the investment of resources and the performance of the system as a whole.

There is, however, a further aspect to cost. It concerns not the performance of the system as a whole, but the relationship between cost and individual justice. We have seen that the aim of civil procedure is to protect and enforce legal rights. It follows that all citizens whose rights are threatened or infringed are entitled to receive protection and assistance from the courts. Put differently, it is not enough that a system tries to achieve rectitude of decision, it must also enable those who wish to enforce or defend their rights a reasonable opportunity to do so. A system which, for example, denies certain sections of the community the opportunity to enforce or defend their rights in the courts deprives these sections of justice. Access to justice is, therefore, a fundamental civic or constitutional right recognized by all civilized societies.

Yet, even though the right of access to courts is universally recognized as a requirement of justice, the practical implications of this right are less widely discussed. Several factors are involved here. At the most basic level we need to consider the direct and immediate cost of initiating or defending proceedings in a court of law. In most systems of procedure litigants are expected to pay court fees. So, the first question is whether entry fees constitute an obstacle to access to the courts; whether those who could not afford those sums are denied access to the courts. All the national systems discussed in this volume accept that it is unjust to deny access to the courts through the imposition of high court fees. But different systems employ different methods of providing access to those who cannot afford the entry fees.

When we discuss the cost of access to justice, we need to bear in mind two important considerations. First, each system is required to make a policy decision about whether the system of civil justice should be financed primarily by its users, the litigants, through realistic court fees or, alternatively, whether the system should be principally financed by the taxpayer. Second, it has to be remembered that low litigation costs tend to encourage litigation. The more litigation there is, the more the taxpayer will have to pay in order to maintain the system. Alternatively, if resources are not increased in line with the volume of litigation, the more litigation there is, the longer delays will be. Accordingly, the relationship between cost and access is a complicated relationship which different systems address in different ways.

There is a further and even more troublesome aspect of the relationship between costs and individual justice. It concerns not the direct effect of cost on access, but the indirect effect that cost may have on the dispensation of justice between opposing litigants. This indirect effect may take different forms. A system that allows access to all may still discriminate against the poor if it leaves them without adequate legal representation. In theory, it is possible to imagine systems in which lay litigants can effectively present their cases without the assistance of lawyers. But this is not usually the position. Accordingly, the first question to consider in this regard is whether a given procedural system enables lay litigants to represent themselves effectively. More particularly, we should ask whether legal representation enhances the procedural advantage of the individual litigant. Indeed, in some systems legal representation is obligatory. Where, as in most procedures, legal representation is advantageous, we shall have to consider how the system caters for those who cannot afford to employ lawyers.

The availability of public assistance for legal representation gives rise to complex questions of justice. For the question is not just about public assistance, but also about how personal means affect one's ability to protect one's interests in court. In particular, we shall have to consider whether superior financial resources enable richer litigants to obtain unfair advantages *vis-à-vis* poorer litigants. A number of factors have a bearing on this question. We shall have to examine whether and how litigants can recover their costs when they have obtained judgment against their opponents. We shall also have to look at the methods by which clients are charged for legal representation. If the cost of litigation is both high and unforeseeable, as it is in some legal systems, then parties with large financial resources may have an advantage when litigating against persons of limited means. This is because persons of limited means would be reluctant to run the risk of losing and having to pay large and unpredictable costs to their opponents. In such a system the possession of large financial resources could well enable the rich to obtain an unfair advantage over their poorer opponents.

It will have become clear that considerations of cost are involved in the assessment of procedural justice in a number of ways. The amount of public resources devoted to procedure influences the global level of rectitude of decision. Court fees and other costs affect individual access to justice. Lastly, high and unpredictable litigation costs could give unfair procedural advantage to the richer litigant over the poorer litigant.

Assessment, comparison, and reform: a three-dimensional enterprise

It will have become clear that measuring the success of procedures in doing justice calls for a complex judgment. It is not enough to ask whether the system produces correct judgments. We have also to ask how timely judgments are, because a judgment given too late may amount to a denial of justice even though it involves a correct application of the law to the true facts. Cost too is relevant to the assessment of procedural systems. The resources available to the system will influence its global level of rectitude of decision. Cost will affect access to justice and, lastly, high litigation costs may enable rich litigants to acquire a procedural advantage against their opponents.

Each of these aspects is clearly relevant to the assessment of any system of civil justice. Each procedural system discussed in this volume has devised methods for attempting to achieve justice in all its dimensions, though none of them is fully realizable. There is no perfect rectitude of decision, justice cannot be dispensed instantly without some delay, and justice cannot be absolutely free of cost constraints. Each system has had to balance the competing demands and strike a compromise. As in any compromise of this kind, some aspects of justice will suffer while others may benefit from certain procedural arrangements.

It follows that, when we come to look at the different systems, we should not merely compare how particular aspects of procedure are treated by different systems. For such a comparison may well be of little use. For example, compulsory discovery of documents is a central feature of Anglo-American systems, but is absent from continental codes. It might be tempting to say that the former systems make a greater contribution to rectitude of decision, because discovery tends to bring out more relevant evidence and therefore leads to greater factual accuracy of judgments. But such a conclusion would be superficial because discovery has its own disadvantages. There is considerable concern in Anglo-American systems about the negative cost implications of discovery. In a significant proportion of cases in which discovery is seriously employed, the cost of the process exceeds its benefits. High litigation cost adversely affects access to justice by deterring litigants of limited means. Accordingly, a comparison of the Anglo-American and the continental systems has to take into account not just the rectitude dimension of discovery but also its cost dimension. When both dimensions are taken into account, we may well decide that what continental systems lose in rectitude they gain through increased access to justice.

A comparison of systems calls therefore for a holistic approach; that is, for an assessment of systems as a whole. Each individual system needs to be judged by reference to the three-dimensional justice criteria that have been outlined. However, we have to be clear about the limitations of such a comparative approach. A three-dimensional investigation may reveal the strengths and weaknesses of individual systems, but it will not necessarily tell us which system is better. Just because a procedure gives greater weight to rectitude of decision does not mean that it is better than a different system which sacrifices rectitude for the sake of delivering quicker and more timely judgments. As we have seen, the mere fact that discovery is a good method of obtaining the truth is not a conclusive argument for importing discovery into a system that prefers to keep down costs. Each system of procedure has its own preferences when it comes to making choices between the different dimensions of justice.

It does not follow, however, that a comparison of systems is useless. By looking at other systems we can evaluate different ways of resolving conflicts between competing demands of justice. English lawyers, for example, believe that no expense should be spared in the search for the truth. They believe that placing a limit on the costs charged by lawyers will result in an unacceptable deterioration in the truth quality of judicial decisions. Yet other systems, such as the German procedure, may show that an acceptable level of rectitude of decision can be achieved at a reasonable and predictable cost.

The purpose of this volume is not to offer a comprehensive evaluation of procedures, but to provide the raw materials for making comparison and evaluation. Each chapter is written from within a given procedure. Each chapter explores the strengths and weakness of a national system of procedure. As systems can only be improved from within, it is for those interested in assessing their own procedures to make comparisons. The purpose of the rest of this chapter is to draw attention to the state of affairs in the different countries included in this book and to the ways that different systems try to accommodate the three dimensions of justice.

2. A COMPARATIVE PERSPECTIVE

The incidence of crisis

A sense of crisis in the administration of civil justice is by no means universal, but it is widespread. Most countries represented in this book are experiencing difficulties in the operation of their system of civil justice. Whether the difficulties take the form of exorbitant costs or of excessive delays, they have serious implications. As we have seen, cost can place access to justice beyond the reach of citizens with limited means. Delays may render access to justice useless. Each of these phenomena may have many and varied ramifications for the social fabric. A denial of justice to the poor contributes to deprivation and social alienation. Delays can render the judicial protection of rights ineffectual, reduce the value of rights, adversely affect economic activity, and lead to economic distortions. Of course, there are always cost implications to justice, as we have observed, and there are inevitable delays. But no society can remain indifferent when cost and delay reach proportions that threaten the justice system as a whole.

In England, the cost and delay involved in civil litigation have been a source of concern for some time now.[7] The cost of litigation is not only high, but also unpredictable and often disproportionate. Indeed, it is possible for the costs to each party to exceed the value of the subject matter in dispute. The urgency of the situation may be inferred from the attempts that the British government is currently making to reform the administration of civil justice in order to reduce costs.

---

[7] *Report of the Review Body on Civil Justice* (1988), Cm. 394. For a discussion see T. M. Swanson, 'A Review of the Civil Justice Review: Economic Theories behind the Delays in Tort Litigation' [1990] Current Legal Problems 185. The Bar Council and the Law Society set up the Heilbron–Hodge Committee which produced a report on the subject: *Civil Justice on Trial: The Case for Change* (June 1993).

The situation is not much better in other common law countries. In Australia there has been a huge increase in the volume and complexity of litigation, especially over the last four or five decades. The present system simply cannot cope. It is too labour intensive, too costly, and too slow. As in England, the strain of the legal aid budget has proved insupportable. As a result, Australia has seen a drastic reduction in the availability of legal aid.

In the United States the position is more complex. The cost of litigation is certainly high but the social consequences are somewhat softened by the system of contingency fees. Yet this system has itself led to serious problems. Lawyers' interest in taking up contingency fee actions is stimulated by the prospect of high punitive damages awards. But the level and frequency of such awards have caused much alarm, with the result that a number of state legislatures have passed legislation designed to reduce the availability of punitive damages or to limit their extent.

In most civil law countries the state of the administration of justice is a source for concern. In France there has been an explosion in the volume of litigation and a substantial increase in delays. Costs are also worrying. Although these problems are not as serious as in some other continental countries, the French system seems to suffer from low public confidence; a majority of the population see civil justice as being too difficult to attain, too expensive, and unequal. Moreover, judges and lawyers share the public's sense of dissatisfaction.

In Italy the problem of delay is acute. Ordinary litigants may need to wait as much as ten years to obtain a final resolution of their disputes. The Italian civil process, Professor Chiarloni points out, is largely useless to citizens who seek justice. As an Italian Senate Committee acknowledged, the mechanism of the civil process has been replaced by 'a complex celebration of obscure and often indecorous rituals'[8] which delay justice. The party in the wrong may hide behind the extremely long duration of the process to avoid responsibility.

In Portugal the administration of civil justice is incapable of responding in reasonable time to the demands for the protection of rights. Its poor performance has undermined the credibility of the judicial system as a means for resolving disputes. The Spanish system is so beset by anachronistic complexity that it has become a veritable jungle of localized rules and special proceedings, all of which put pressure on resources and contribute to delays. Brazil seems to suffer from all possible ills. The civil process is complex, antiquated, and lengthy, the costs to litigants are high, and the resources allocated to the administration of justice are inadequate.

Some civil law countries have fared better. In Japan the rate of litigation is very much lower than most other developed countries. In the 1980s the Japanese system was subject to fierce criticisms which were followed by a series of reforms, culminating in a new Code of Civil Procedure which came into

---

[8] See *Rivista trimestrale di diritto e procedura civile* (1986), 318 ff.

effect in 1998. In Germany the system has been working relatively well, but reform is needed in a number of areas, such as limiting the right of appeal. Of all the countries reviewed in this volume, only Holland presents a truly positive picture. Overall, the Netherlands experiences a lower volume of litigation and fewer problems with court congestion than its neighbours do. This enviable situation is due to the fact that the legal profession and the social institutions have found solutions to the problems by developing alternatives to the court process that work better and faster at less cost to the people involved in legal disputes.

It would appear, therefore, that most systems experience serious problems in the administration of civil justice. In every country represented here efforts have been made to improve the benefits that the administration of civil justice provides for the community. The varying measures taken in different countries are suggestive not only of different problems but also of different perceptions of cause and effect and of different priorities.

Before looking at the position in individual countries, it is important to note that reform has as long a history as civil procedure itself. Civil procedure systems are means to an end. They have always been judged by reference to their objectives. Since no system is perfect, there has always been some pressure to achieve improvement. However, the history of reform is not encouraging. Every system has been through many changes, some of them quite fundamental. But, more often than not, as Professor Leubsdorf points out in the next chapter, the reforms have failed to achieve their objectives. It has proved difficult to simplify the civil process, at least in the long run. It has proved difficult to shorten the duration of proceedings. Above all, it has proved difficult to cut the cost of litigation. Whatever the nature of the problems that a given procedure suffers from, they appear to be hard to solve.

All the same, the fact that there are systems which perform better than others, coupled with the fact that in all systems there is a willingness to consider solutions for the old problems, offer some ground for optimism. Certainly, it makes it worth our while to look at the state of civil justice in different countries.

England

The cost of litigation in England can be very high indeed, far higher than in any civil law country. This is due to a number of factors.

First, traditionally parties to litigation have had considerable freedom in determining the intensity and duration of the litigious activity, especially during the pre-trial preparations. Accordingly, where it is in the interest of one or other of the parties, or, indeed, the lawyers, to complicate and protract the process, there has been considerable scope for doing so.

Second, the loser in litigation has to pay the winner's costs. Given that success brings with it not only the sum claimed but also the expenses laid out in securing judgment, a litigant who believes that an increase in the amount spent on litigation will increase his chances of success has a very good reason for progressively raising his stakes. Once one party increases the stakes, the opponent feels compelled to follow suit for fear that by using inferior procedural devices—be it a less celebrated lawyer or a less qualified expert—he will compromise his chances of success and run a greater risk of having to pay the other party's costs as well as losing the subject matter in dispute. Indeed, a point may come where the parties have reason to persist with investment in litigation not so much for the sake of securing a favourable judgment on the merits, as for the purpose of recovering the money already expended in the dispute, which may well outstrip the value of the subject matter in issue.[9]

The third factor is connected with the method of paying for legal services. Generally speaking, lawyers are paid by the hour, regardless of outcome and without an upper limit. The hourly fees vary considerably and can range between £80 and £300 per hour or even more. Inevitably, this system of remuneration provides an incentive to lawyers to protract and complicate litigation.

In his Report on Access to Justice, Lord Woolf MR drew attention to the abundance of satellite litigation and to 'the tendency of parties at present to make numerous interlocutory applications. These are generally of a tactical nature which may be of dubious benefit even to the party making the application and which may not be warranted by the costs involved.'[10] Procedural litigation is both expensive and largely unproductive. Yet it is fuelled by the factors that have just been listed.

In England even a simple dispute which proceeds with uncommon speed can absorb vast sums of money.[11] Since legal fees are not subject to an upper limit, litigants must be prepared for unlimited expenditure when they embark on litigation. As a result, serious litigation is open only to the very rich and to the very poor, who are supported by publicly funded legal aid.

Professor Hazel Genn carried out a survey of costs in the High Court for the Lord Woolf Inquiry.[12] She found a lack of proportionality between the value of

---

[9] Cf. *Hanlon* v. *The Law Society* [1981] AC 124, 142.

[10] *Access to Justice: Final Report* (HMSO, 1996), ch. 7, para. 23.

[11] *Symphony Group plc* v. *Hodgson* [1993] 4 All ER 143. An action to enforce a covenant in restraint of trade against an employee whose annual salary was about £10,000, in which the plaintiffs issued a writ, secured an interlocutory injunction, and obtained final judgment, all in just nine weeks, cost the winning plaintiffs in excess of £100,000. The procedure which consumed these sums involved the following steps. The writ was issued on 11 May 1992 in the High Court and on the same day the plaintiffs obtained an *ex parte* injunction. A statement of claim was served the following day. The interlocutory injunction was considered *inter partes* on 15 May, when it was continued until trial and speedy trial was directed. Pleadings were closed and discovery completed by the time trial started on 22 June. The hearings lasted eight days, culminating in a 31-page judgment delivered on 6 July 1992.

[12] *Access to Justice: Final Report*, annex III. See also costs statistics in the annual reports of the Legal Aid Board.

claims and the costs incurred in prosecuting them, especially at the lower end of the scale. Amongst cases with a value of less than £12,500, in 31 per cent the costs to the successful party alone were between £10,000 and £20,000, with a further 9 per cent incurring costs in excess of £20,000. These figures look even worse if one remembers that about half of the cases surveyed were concluded with a consent order and only one quarter by judgment. Amongst claims with a value of between £12,500 and £25,000, costs as a percentage of claim-value ranged from 41 per cent for personal injury cases to 96 per cent among Official Referees' cases (i.e. disputes concerning building contracts).[13] This level of expenditure means that the legal system is simply too expensive and too inefficient to provide a meaningful forum for dispute resolution in common-place litigation.

The duration of proceedings in England is considerable. The average time from commencement of proceedings to judgment in the High Court is 161 weeks in London and 195 weeks outside London. The comparable data for the county court are 70 and 90 weeks respectively.

A serious attempt is being made to reform the system. A new set of Civil Procedure Rules came into effect in April 1999. While the changes made to the basic structure of procedure are modest, the changes in the philosophy of procedure and the approach to its operation are far reaching.

Two such changes deserve special notice. The first concerns the control over the litigation process; the second is concerned with the philosophy of procedure. As already noted, the main defect of English civil procedure is thought to be an excess of litigation activity. To reduce this activity the new rules place the control of litigation in the hands of the courts. This is a radical departure from the previous system, under which the parties and their lawyers were free to control the duration and intensity of the pre-trial process and, to some extent, of the trial itself. From now on the courts will decide these matters. There will be strict timetables and economical processes for simple disputes. For the more complex disputes the courts will determine the procedural steps that parties will be required or permitted to take and their timetables.

In exercising this control over litigation the courts will be guided by a new philosophy of procedure. Under the old philosophy, the main function of the courts was to do justice on the merits; that is, to decide cases on the basis of the true facts and the correct law, and not on procedural grounds. This is of course true of all procedures. But in England the 'justice on the merits' approach was taken to override all other procedural arrangements. It was considered in-

---

[13] It is also to be borne in mind that the survey was conducted on the basis of bills submitted for taxation (i.e. bills submitted for court approval by the winning parties seeking to recover their costs from their opponents). Many disputes are settled without reference to taxation. It is reasonable to assume that settlement costs are also very high. According to practitioners, it is not unknown for a dispute concerning a builder's bill of £12,000, which is settled, to generate legal fees of more than half that amount per party.

appropriate to dismiss a claim or a defence on the ground of non-compliance with the procedural rules. Thus, no matter how much a party neglected the procedural requirements, no matter how late the party was in fulfilling a procedural duty, the court would forgive the defect in order to decide the case on its true merits. The result was that conformity with the rules became largely optional, and parties and their lawyers could protract and complicate the litigation process virtually at will.

The justice on the merits philosophy assumes that, as long as the court reaches a decision which is in accordance with the facts and the law, justice has been done; nothing else matters. But other things do matter. Delay may be so extensive as to rob the eventual judgment of any practical usefulness. More important still, high and unpredictable costs deter aggrieved persons from prosecuting their rights in the courts. Even those who are able to start proceedings are at times compelled to withdraw with an unfavourable settlement. For the high cost of litigation enables rich litigants to force poorer opponents to accept compromises which are not dictated so much by the merits as by the inability of the poorer litigants to finance expensive litigation.

Those who have been content with a system which places substantive justice above matters of mere procedure have been equally content with a situation whereby justice is denied in whole or in part to large sections of the population, through lack of practicable access. Yet there is nothing universal or timeless about the justice on the merits philosophy. It represents a particular choice: offering justice with no expense spared to the few who can afford it. But there are other choices that can be made, choices which proceed on the assumption that undue expense and delay too amount to a denial of justice.

Whereas the justice on the merits philosophy gives precedence to rectitude of decision over considerations of timely justice and reasonable costs, a new balance between the three dimensions of justice is adopted by the new English Civil Procedure Rules. For the first time the rules spell out the overriding objectives of the civil process (in Part 1.1):

(a) ensuring that the parties are on an equal footing;
(b) saving expense;
(c) dealing with the case in ways which are proportionate —

    (i)   to the amount of money involved;
    (ii) to the importance of the case;
    (iii) to the complexity of the issues; and
    (iv) to the financial position of each party;

(d) ensuring that it is dealt with expeditiously and fairly;
(e) allotting to it an appropriate share of the court's resources, while taking into account the need to allot resources to other cases.

Implicit in these objectives is a new philosophy: a philosophy of distributive justice. This new philosophy has a number of components. First, it accepts that the resources of the administration of civil justice are finite, just as are the resources of all other public services. Accordingly, the new philosophy holds that these resources must be justly distributed amongst all those seeking or needing justice. Second, a just distribution of these resources must take into account the character of individual cases, so that individual cases get no more than a reasonable allocation of court time and attention. The notion of proportionality is invoked here. The allocation of court resources, and the investment of time and money, must bear a reasonable relation to the difficulty, complexity, value, and importance of the case in hand. Third, time and cost are relevant considerations in the allocation of resources; justice may be bought at too high a price, and justice delayed is justice denied. The fourth and last component of the new philosophy is judicial responsibility. The courts' responsibility extends beyond doing justice in individual cases. They are responsible for the administration of civil justice as a whole, for the resources of the system, and for their fair and just distribution.

Australia

The Australian system of civil justice is similar to that in England, and so are the problems faced by Australians. In many cases the costs of going to trial are disproportionate to the amount in dispute. For parties of average means the prospect of losing, and having to pay the opponent's costs, is so serious that they cannot afford to take the risk. The total costs payable by the losing party often exceed the judgment sum. In all except very large cases, costs are unacceptably high in proportion to the amount involved, and more than most citizens can afford to pay. The duration of Australian proceedings is roughly similar to that of English proceedings, but there are considerable variations between different states.

As in England, the Australian litigation process is labour intensive. The pre-trial process is not complicated, but it can involve much lawyer activity, including court hearings. Two related features of the system make it so. One is the adversarial imperative; that is, the tendency of litigants, and particularly their lawyers, to see the opponent as the enemy who must be defeated. The other feature is the perceived need to leave no stone unturned; that is, the habit of litigants to employ every procedural means available and to spare no cost in an attempt to defeat the opponent. Against the background of party control over the pace and shape of litigation, these two features combine to encourage unnecessary expenditure of time and cost and, at times, cause unfairness to the weaker party through a war of attrition.

Such excessive litigious activity is influenced by economic factors. As in England, one of the more influential factors is the system by which lawyers receive an hourly remuneration. Therefore, the more protracted the case, the more the lawyers earn.

To reverse these factors, Justice Davies points out, lawyers and judges must accept a new concept of a just dispute resolution. This concept involves greater frankness between disputants, it is less adversarial, and it accepts that costs, the rights of others, and the public interest are relevant considerations. Justice Davies's analysis spells out much that is implicit already in the new English rules. More disputes should be resolved earlier by processes other than court proceedings. Reforms have been made and proposed to encourage more summary adjudication of specific issues, leaving only the more complex issues to be dealt with by the full trial process. It is proposed to allow only the courts, not parties, to obtain expert evidence.

As in England, Australia is moving towards judicial control over litigation. There too we can see the emergence of a new culture of adjudication. Judges are far more proactive in the conduct of proceedings before them. They are far more ready to dictate to the parties which procedural steps need to be taken and the time limits for performing them.

New rules are being introduced to achieve procedural economy. In Queensland the rules now limit discovery to only those documents which are directly relevant. This change in the discovery rules appears to have substantially reduced the cost of discovery, without a noticeable increase in judgment error. In New South Wales, entitlement to discovery is also limited. A discovery notice may only require production of documents referred to in pleadings, affidavits, or witness statements, or where the total number of documents is no more than fifty. Discovery in respect of entire classes of documents will only be ordered upon application, and then only in respect of truly relevant documents.

Both in England and Australia there is now less emphasis on orality than in the past. Justice Davies is of the view that it should be possible in all cases for pre-trial procedural questions to be determined entirely in writing. He believes that each party should have the right to elect, in any such proceeding, to give evidence and to make submissions entirely in writing.

USA

Although litigation costs in the USA can be as high as in England and Australia, the position there is somewhat different because there is no general rule that the winner in litigation pays the loser's costs. By and large, there is no cost-shifting rule in the USA. The winning litigant is not entitled to recover its attorneys' fees from the loser. Although some costs (e.g. docket fees and photocopying costs) are usually recoverable, these are typically minuscule compared to attorneys' fees. Costs therefore constitute a considerable concern. This situation is particularly resented by the party (often a defendant) who must expend considerable sums to compile information for its adversary through the discovery process.

The absence of customary recovery of attorneys' fees stands as a high barrier to litigants of limited means, who cannot afford to spend the very considerable amounts of money needed to fund litigation. The position is, however, somewhat ameliorated by the possibility of contingency fee agreements. Under this system, if the plaintiff's case fails, the lawyer is paid nothing. But, if the plaintiff's case succeeds, the lawyer is entitled to take a substantial proportion of any award recovered by the plaintiff. It should be stressed that contingency fee representation is virtually non-existent outside of personal injury litigation. It should also be borne in mind that defendants must always pay for their legal representation. American lawyers, like their counterparts in England and Australia, charge by the hour.

The American legislatures are fully aware that this state of affairs impedes access to justice. Accordingly, to facilitate access in some categories of litigation, special statutory cost-shifting provisions have been introduced, for example in the areas of employment discrimination and environmental litigation.

In the United States, unlike in any other common law country, civil cases may still be tried by a jury. Juries may determine the amount to be awarded to the plaintiff and may even award punitive damages. The prospect of recovering large awards operates as an incentive for lawyers to take up contingency fee cases. Since the lawyers take a portion of the awards, they have an incentive to secure the highest awards possible. In 1991, the President's Council on Competitiveness, headed by the then Vice President, reported that the USA had 'become a litigious society' in which 'litigation necessarily exacts a terrible toll on the U.S. economy'. In that recession-plagued time, the report cited an estimate that 'the average lawyer takes $1 million a year from the country's output of goods and services'. Several states have attempted to reduce the scope of punitive damages.[14]

There are many reasons why American litigation costs are high. Discovery, interrogatories, and other document requests can require very large expenditure, perhaps even more than in England and Australia.

In the USA delays vary greatly from state to state and even between different courts within the same state. The American Bar Association adopted goals for reducing civil litigation delay in 1984. It recommended that 90 per cent of all cases should be completed within one year, and that all should be cleared within two. However, these goals have not been met. A 1991 study of thirty-nine urban state trial courts, for example, found very considerable differences in the degree to which the courts approached satisfying the ABA standards regarding delay. None had met either standard, but some were close. In twelve of the courts, at least 90 per cent of cases were concluded within two years of filing, and in one of those only 1 per cent of cases were two years old. On the other hand, in three

---

[14] *BMW of North America, Inc. v. Gore*, 116 S. Ct. 1589 (1996), 1618–20 (appendix to dissenting opinion of Ginsburg J.) and L. L. Schlueter and K. R. Redden, *Punitive Damages* (3rd edn., 1995).

courts more than 50 per cent of cases lasted over two years, and in one of those 96 per cent of cases lasted more than one year.

A reassessment of the philosophy of litigation and of the function of the judiciary has been taking place in the United States. The liberal ethos underlying much of the procedural superstructure has not gone unchallenged or unmodified. The main ingredient for civil justice reform is shifting of the control of litigation from the parties to the judiciary. However, on the evidence so far it is difficult to assess the success of the new strategy of judicial case management with confidence. There are indications that early case management shortens the duration of litigation, but does not necessarily reduce overall costs. It also seems that discovery time limits reduce both delays and costs.

There is reason to believe that judges can bring about improvement by taking a more active interest in their civil cases. Faced with growing demands on their time and stable or shrinking resources, judges can be expected to continue trying to control litigation. The trend in the USA definitely points in this direction.

France

It is not easy to assess the situation of the French administration of justice. For a long time now there has been an upward increase in the volume of litigation. This trend has accelerated considerably in the last twenty years. The resources of the system have not, however, increased at the same pace. In the middle of the last century, France had about 6,000 judges for a population of 37 million. The size of the judiciary is approximately the same today, although the population is now 58 million. Yet, as we shall shortly see, as far as the duration of proceedings is concerned, the situation is not bad. At the same time, however, public opinion suggests dissatisfaction with the system. In a 1991 survey, 97 per cent of the persons surveyed considered litigation to be too slow, and 85 per cent thought it to be too difficult; 84 per cent regarded it as too costly; 83 per cent believed it to be unequal. In 1995, a survey conducted by the Ministry of Justice showed that the system of justice came last in the ranking of public services. Similar public opinions were reflected in a 1997 survey.

Not only is the duration of proceedings in France fairly reasonable, but in the *tribunaux de grande instance* the average case duration has even diminished from 10 months in 1991 to 8.8 months in 1996. The average duration of cases before the *tribunaux d'instance* has increased. Average duration has gone from 4.5 months in 1991 to 5 months in 1995 for ordinary proceedings. However, these figures conceal great variations, because they include cases adjudicated in summary proceedings. In contested ordinary proceedings adjournments are common and may greatly delay the resolution of a dispute, so that the path to a first instance judgment may be considerably longer than the average figures suggest. Statistics suggest an increase in the average time taken between a full hearing on the merits and delivery of judgment across the first instance jurisdictions. The backlog of appeals has been growing, with the average appeal duration increasing from 13.9 months in 1991 to 15.6 months in 1996. Recent forecasts suggest that the appeal system will probably be paralysed by the year 2000.

Recovery of litigation costs in France is, at best, partial. The winner has a right to recover court fees, witness fees, and the like (all of which are fixed by law) from the loser. By contrast, lawyers' fees, which normally represent the bulk of litigation costs, are not recoverable as of right. Lawyers are free to negotiate their fees with clients. Hourly billing is fairly common, and lawyers may even charge part of their fees as contingency fees. The court does, though, have discretion to order the loser to pay the fees paid by the winner to his lawyers. However, French courts are reluctant to order full recovery of these costs. Although the general level of lawyers' fees is not as high as in common law countries, many regard the cost of litigation as excessive, and see this as an obstacle to access to the court.

To secure access to the courts, some households carry litigation costs insurance. Insured parties are free to choose their lawyers, but they do not have complete freedom in the choice of the procedure to be followed.

Over the years there have been considerable pushes to reform the system of civil procedure, especially in 1958 and in 1977. Two particular trends are notable in the reform movement. The first is a tendency to move more and more types of proceedings to specialized courts or judges. Some specialist courts provide a fairly good service to the community, while others are less successful. The second tendency is one of moving from party freedom in the conduct of litigation towards court control. Traditionally, French procedure was very liberal, giving the parties a large measure of control over the pace and depth of the process. Recent reforms have been directed at curbing this freedom. The trial is still considered to 'belong to' the parties, but the judge is given extended powers including: powers to control the progress of litigation; power to order investigative measures and production of documents; and the power to take into account matters not raised by the parties. The new regime is aimed at promoting co-operation between the judge and the parties in the litigation process.

At the same time, efforts have been made to simplify the procedure and remove unnecessary complications. The emphasis is on flexibility designed to facilitate better management of judicial time, so that the time invested in individual cases is in proportion to their real need. Summary procedures are employed wherever possible. Different tracks have been designed to cater for cases with different needs, with different timetables. Judges of varying degrees of specialization (*juge de la mise en état, juge-rapporteur, conseiller rapporteur, conseiller de la mise en état*) operate these tracks. The use of single judges is developing.

Although much has been done in recent years to improve the administration of civil justice, success has been limited. As a result, fresh proposals have recently been put forward. These have been resisted by the legal profession, whose self-interested objections proved a stumbling block to past reforms. Nevertheless, a new reform project on justice has been tabled in Parliament. It involves strengthening the *conseils départementaux de l'aide juridique* (departmental councils for legal aid), increasing the monetary limits of the lower first instance court, the *tribunaux d'instance,* and some further expansion of ADR.

It remains to be seen whether these new ideas will bring with them significant improvements. However, in Professor Cadiet's view, without the will and the ability to resist self-interested pressure groups, little can be achieved in this area.

Italy

The duration of civil proceedings in Italy is measured in years rather than months. Although the average duration of first instance proceedings is 3.3 years, the appeal process can stretch the final resolution of disputes by several more years. Sadly, it is not uncommon for plaintiffs to be forced to wait 10 years for final judgment.

Only a small proportion of actions ends in a judgment on the merits. Most are abandoned. Thus, in 1994, of 1,080,933 concluded cases, only 376,546 proceedings (about 35 per cent) ended in a decision on the merits. This is chiefly due to the excessive delays. Many litigants would rather accept a disadvantageous settlement, however unfair, than wait for years to have their claims heard.

Procedural complexity is a major problem; yet the majority of those who operate the justice system favour the slow bureaucratic stages of ordinary proceedings. Lawyers tend to run cases more for their own convenience than for the benefit of their clients or the system as a whole. There is a large number of lawyers, most of whom must make what income they can out of handling large volumes of cases in low-value fields. The very survival of lower- and lower-middle-level practitioners depends on them being able to conduct lengthy and complicated proceedings and inflate costs. This, in turn, contributes to the judicial burden. The present system also serves the interests of upper- and upper-middle-level practitioners. The Italian written proceedings, lacking in deadlines and allowing for extensive adjournments, allow bigger law firms to engage in extensive litigious activity with a relatively small number of employees.

These factors explain the fierce opposition of most Italian lawyers to any innovations designed to reduce complexity and delays. There have been a number of attempts to improve the situation, but they have had very modest success. It seems that the problems are so deeply rooted in the practices and culture of the legal profession that only a radical cultural change could begin to bring about an improvement. Unfortunately, there is no sign of such a change taking place.

Car accident cases make up nearly one-third of the civil cases which are dealt with in ordinary proceedings. But it often serves the interest of insurance companies to drag out litigation. A situation in which proceedings to enforce even small claims are disproportionately costly and lengthy serves the interests of insurers. The knowledge that it will be too expensive to fight the insurance claim all the way through the court system contributes to the burdens on individual plaintiffs. Plaintiffs often prefer to settle on unfair terms rather than wait for years, and spend huge sums of money, to get their full awards.

This situation prompted the legislature, in 1969, to empower the courts to award interim payments to road accident victims, on account of a final judgment in their favour. But the conditions for applications for interim payments are too strict: the victim must be shown to be in financial need, and serious fault must be shown on the part of the driver. As a result, few interim payment orders are made, and the situation has hardly improved as a result of this legislation.

Judges, who in Italy are civil servants, also bear a responsibility for the state of the administration of justice. Law graduates become judges by way of a public examination. Once admitted to the judiciary they enter a bureaucratic culture lacking in a tradition of excellence and hard work. Excessive importance is given to formalities. Judges seem to prefer demonstrating their ability by engaging in complex legal questions, instead of concentrating on the real merits of the cases before them. They prefer a written handling of cases to establishing personal contact with the parties.

Even the *Corte di Cassazione*, the Italian Supreme Court, which oversees the uniform interpretation of the law throughout Italy, is malfunctioning. The number of appeals with which it deals is so large that it is no longer able to provide a uniform and authoritative interpretation of the law.

Not all litigants are obstructed by delays. Some areas of procedure function well. While normal proceedings can last for years, there is a fast and efficient procedure for recovering debt. Further, rich litigants, such as companies, can refer their cases to arbitration and thus obtain swift resolution, at a price.

On a more hopeful note, there is an increasing willingness on the part of the judiciary to acknowledge the problems. The *Consiglio Superiore della Magistratura* (the body which governs the judiciary) has recently denounced the poor service given by the courts. Further, there is an increasing number of groups of local judges who club together to organize their case management better so that they can offer more effective and efficient service.

Lawyers too are beginning to appreciate that they risk losing clients because delays make litigation pointless. Even so, the introduction of the 1995 Code of Civil Procedure was only accomplished after many delays caused by stiff opposition from lawyers. The profession objected to the introduction of strict timetables designed to control the progress of litigation and to measures aimed at combating dilatory practices.

Sadly, the history of reform does not inspire confidence in the future. At the end of the nineteenth century, under the 1865 Code, the administration of civil justice was conducted quite efficiently by comparison to present standards.

Paradoxically, the 1942 Code, although inspired by modern ideas of procedure, permitted the progressive decay of the administration of justice to levels which are intolerable in a civilized country.

It is not enough to improve procedures, Professor Chiarloni says; a change of attitudes and culture would be necessary to bring improvement to the administration of civil justice in Italy. Deep changes in the organization of both the legal profession and the judiciary are called for, as well as improvements in the relationship between the two branches of the profession. Above all, the negative incentives which affect both lawyers and judges must be reversed.

Spain

Spain seems to suffer from several ills. Civil procedure is still dominated by the antiquated code of 1881, with the result that civil litigation is cumbersome, complex, and liable to be hampered by procedural technicalities. Furthermore, the process is largely written and largely dominated by the lawyers. The judges, who have limited powers to control the progress of litigation, are bombarded by motions and interlocutory applications, which delay and sometimes frustrate altogether a fair determination of disputes.

Although it has been apparent for a long time that the multitude of procedural laws and their complexity impede the efficient operation of the administration of civil justice, little has been done to rectify this. Indeed, such changes as have been introduced have made matters worse because of their piecemeal nature.

Court fees were abolished in 1986 as a measure against corruption. Previously, the payment of court fees seems to have provided an opportunity for the payment of bribes to court officials.

Representation in the courts requires the employment of two kinds of lawyers—the *abogado* and the *procurador*—each of whom has to be paid by the client. Lawyers are free to charge what they choose; though there are minimum scales to prevent competition at too low a level. As in most other European countries, contingency fees are outlawed.

A new Civil Procedure Bill (December 1997) is being proposed. It represents an attempt to simplify the Spanish civil procedure. The Bill is clearly inspired by the adversarial principle. It endeavours to reduce the number of judgments given on the basis of procedural rather than substantive points. The courts will be given powers to exercise control over the litigation process. Judges will be able to give directions to ensure that the majority of procedural prerequisites are complied with. A general rule is to be introduced, allowing procedural defects to be rectified. A sustained effort is to be made to limit appeals. First instance interlocutory decisions will not be appealable. Final judgments will be liable to appeal only upon establishing good cause. In an attempt to remove some of the temptation to appeal, the new rules will allow for first instance judgments to be enforced pending an appeal.

Portugal

In Portugal, as in most other countries, there has been an enormous increase in the number of actions commenced in the courts. The volume of litigation more than doubled between 1986 and 1996. Until 1986 the number of pending cases increased far faster than the number of new actions commenced. But, since 1986, there has been an improvement in disposal rates.

In Portugal 65 per cent of first instance actions are disposed of within one year and a further 22 per cent within a further year. However, one should bear in mind that the vast majority of actions are disposed of without full trial on the merits. Indeed, only 17 per cent of actions go all the way to trial. We may assume that the 11.7 per cent of actions that last longer than two years are those that go to trial. Of these, 7.7 per cent are determined within a further year and the rest take longer. These figures do not take into account the period of appeal. The majority of appeals are disposed of within one year. It follows that the period from commencement to final disposal after appeal could take three years or more in contested actions.

In the public view, the Portuguese system of justice is incapable of responding, in reasonable time, to the demand for protection of rights. Excessive and unnecessary formalism in the law of procedure is responsible for delay in many types of action. But delay is also caused through the failings of those involved in the administration of justice (judges, lawyers, administrators) and by the intentional procrastination of interested parties. Investigations into the causes of court inefficiencies found that poor performance by judges and administrative staff was a significant contributing factor to the problem of delay.

Portuguese experience illustrates the complexity of the task of improving the administration of justice. Sometimes a measure introduced to increase efficiency may actually diminish it. For example, some courts have benefited from the appointment of temporary or auxiliary judges in order to help with the backlog of cases. However, since this was not accompanied by a commensurate increase in the number of court support staff, matters became even worse, since the existing support staff could not cope with the increased load.

In Portugal, as in Germany, court fees are fixed as a proportion of the value of the dispute and relate to the stage that the dispute has reached. A minimum scale governs lawyers' fees, but lawyers are free to charge higher amounts, though it is unethical for their fees to exceed the value of subject matter in dispute. Charging by the hour is uncommon and contingency fees are altogether forbidden. The costs of litigation are recoverable from the loser, but in practice only a small proportion of lawyers' fees is recoverable. If we take into account all the litigation costs, resort to the courts is very expensive indeed. For individuals, or one-time players, the cost of litigation presents a powerful obstacle to access to the court. In the main, only large claims are brought to court.

Portugal, as we have just observed, suffers from poor organization of the courts and from considerable procedural complexity. Attempts have been made to improve both the organizational aspects of the administration of justice and to simplify the process. Certain kinds of litigious activity have been taken out of the courts altogether. But the results have been mixed. In particular, a new summary procedure for recovering debt has failed to deliver the hoped-for improvements.

In 1997, the new Code of Civil Procedure came into effect, considerably altering the relationship between litigants and the courts through the establishment of the co-operation principle. Judges now have a duty to compensate for the omissions of the litigants, in furtherance of the principle of the discovery of the truth. The judges protested against this reform because it meant a substantial increase in their work and responsibility.

Brazil

In Brazil there is an enormous variation in the duration of first instance and appeal proceedings between different parts of the system. In some regions the average duration of first instance proceedings is between two and three years, but in others it can take very much longer. Most courts experience huge backlogs. At least 25 per cent of actions filed are not processed at all, but simply sit in the courts. In north-eastern and northern states actions may crawl for years and years and not be tried.

Although appeal is normally only by leave, the volume of applications for leave is enormous. Most losing parties try to appeal as a means of putting off the enforcement of the judgment. As a result, much of the time of the appellate courts is taken by applications for leave, even though the great majority of them are denied.

The loser in litigation must pay the winner's costs. Lawyers are free to charge whatever they can persuade their clients to agree to pay. Generally, lawyers calculate their fees on the basis of a number of factors: the amount of work which they are required to do; the value of the subject matter; the professional status and prestige of the law firm. They may charge up to 20 per cent of the value of the subject matter. For instance, in a lawsuit for the collection of a debt of $US1 million, a lawyer might charge an initial fee of $US30,000, plus a contingent fee of 10 per cent of what the client recovers, reduced by any costs recovered from the losing party. In a simple lawsuit for the collection of a debt, about 50 per cent of the fees are likely to be recovered from the losing debtor. In other types of cases, the percentage will vary between 5 per cent and 20 per cent. Lawyers' fees will, generally speaking, end up amounting to 10 per cent of the value of the subject matter. Litigation lawyers, particularly large firms, might prefer to charge by the hour. However, there is resistance to paying hourly fees for litigation work, because of clients' fears that lawyers will protract or complicate cases if they are paid in this way.

The state of the Brazilian administration of civil justice reflects the complexity of the social and political conditions of this vast and variable country. Three types of problems can be identified. First, there is a shortage of well-educated and properly trained lawyers and judges. Second, the administration of justice is poorly equipped for dealing with the volume of litigation that enters the courts. Many tasks are performed manually which, in more developed systems, are automated or simply obsolete. Every new piece of paper is actually sewn to the file of the case with needle and thread, and there are few, if any, document reproduction facilities.

Third, numerous laws, some of them quite antiquated, govern civil procedure. This aggravates the problem of disparity in the interpretation of the law which, in turn, creates uncertainty and further complexity. One of the problems faced when a new procedural law comes into effect in Brazil is the very strong conservatism of those in charge of the administration of justice, who seek to apply the new rules according to obsolete principles. Professor Bermudes suggests that at the root of the problems lie not complex and difficult procedures, but the unhelpful attitudes of those who operate the procedures and the deep infrastructural flaws of the court system.

In recent years attempts have been made to improve the civil process, with some limited success. The procedure has been somewhat simplified. Summary judgment is now easier to obtain. Indeed, efforts have been made to ensure that litigation is conducted in a speedy and effective manner. However, litigation costs remain so high that a large proportion of the population has no access to justice at all, and cannot therefore benefit from such improvements as have been achieved.

Greece

In Greece, 63 per cent of final decisions given by courts of first instance are delivered within one year from the commencement of proceedings. However, this figure conceals great variations. For instance, the time from the initial hearing of a case, before the three-member district court, until the final decision is rendered may be two or three years. Furthermore, since first instance judgments are not final and may not be enforced before the appeal procedures have been exhausted, the great majority of first instance decisions are appealed, so that the final disposition is considerably longer.

As elsewhere, lawyers have considerable influence over the length of litigation. Lawyers are known to employ delaying tactics by requesting postponements. Parties are entitled to seek postponements in certain circumstances, but only for up to two months, or to the earliest possible trial date thereafter. Although the reason for seeking a postponement should be scrutinized by the court before postponement is granted, in practice first-time requests are usually granted virtually automatically. In this way, the progress of the trial may be significantly delayed, particularly since courts tend to grant postponements even longer than two months because they are overloaded with cases.

Generally speaking, the cost of litigation in Greece is low and courts rarely order full payment of the expenditure incurred. Fees for legal representation in litigation are charged as a small percentage of the value of the subject matter. The system is similar to the German system of fees. Lawyers are allowed to negotiate higher fees, and even contingency fees are allowed. But a contingency fee may not exceed 20 per cent of the value of the subject matter in dispute. The legal profession benefits from effective procedures to recover fees due to lawyers from their clients. The Attorneys Code contains a provision whereby clients must pay 10 per cent of the fee due in advance. However, this provision has been recently held to be unconstitutional.

As a rule, the winner in litigation is entitled to recover costs from the loser. But the court may depart from this rule in certain situations. For instance, where the winner unreasonably commenced proceedings, or was guilty of falsehood, the court may order the winner to pay the loser's costs. Interestingly, the court has discretion to make no order of costs where there is some doubt about the correctness of the judgment, thus letting each party bear its own costs.

Greek civil procedure suffers from an excess of unmeritorious claims, and from an unacceptable rate of appeals (the vast majority of first instance judgments are appealed). Only limited efforts have been made to improve matters. Proposals that conciliation should be a precondition to litigation have been defeated by the lawyers' organizations. Although appeals are too frequent, the legislature is reluctant to restrict appeals.

The history of reform since the Code of Civil Procedure (1967) shows that many procedural changes have either resulted in increased complexity or have had only short-lived impact. For example, changes to the appeal system have actually delayed the final resolution of disputes. There have been some limited improvements. For instance, default judgments may no longer be set aside as a matter of right and without giving good cause.

Litigation costs have never been a means for avoiding court overloading in Greece. On the contrary, the trend seems to have been for costs to remain low, in order to facilitate access to the courts. Some have argued in favour of increasing court fees to reflect to some extent the cost of the administration of justice, and as a means of moderating the volume of unmeritorious litigation, particularly at appeal level. However, the legislature has shown no interest in such proposals and the lawyers' organizations are firmly opposed to the idea, as one would expect. Overall, well-entrenched and cherished judicial and professional traditions have stood in the way of sensible reform proposals.

Japan

Three countries stand out as being relatively well served by their systems of civil justice. Japan is one of them. However, a word of caveat is called for when one looks at the Japanese system. Litigation volumes in Japan are much lower than in other developed countries. Indeed, there is considerable cultural hostility to litigation and a strong preference for keeping disputes out of the public arena.

The Japanese civil procedure is strongly influenced by the German system. However, as far as litigation costs are concerned, the Japanese system has also seen American influence. Court fees are recoverable, but not the cost of legal representation. Time charging is permitted, but lawyers are normally paid a fixed fee, representing a percentage of the value of the claim, as in Germany. The fixed fee is in two parts. One is payable regardless of outcome; the other is contingent on winning the action.

On the face of it, the Japanese system is impressively efficient. In the great majority of actions, judgments are given at first instance within a year. Appeals from the senior first instance court, the district court, run at a rate of between 20 and 25 per cent. Appeals from judgments of the junior first instance court, the summary court, are rare. The rate of second appeals is higher.

Litigants may appeal as of right against first instance judgments, on issues of both law and fact. There is a right to a second appeal on questions of law only. Even though an appeal suspends the execution of judgment, the rate of appeals against first instance decisions of the district court is moderate by comparison to some other countries. Furthermore, even where such appeals take place, a final resolution is reached in less than twenty months from the commencement of proceedings. Appeals to the Supreme Court, the highest authority in the land, are considered to be too numerous and measures have been taken to limit the right of appeal to this court.

It would appear that although the volume of cases entering the system every year has been showing a steady increase, the number of cases disposed of within the year has increased in tandem. Thus, the number of actions started every year tends to be almost the same as the number of actions disposed of within the year. In a substantial proportion of cases litigants represent themselves (in 58 per cent of district court cases at least one litigant is a litigant in person; the rate goes up to 99 per cent in summary proceedings).

Behind these encouraging data lurk some problems concerning access to justice. The number of attorneys, Professor Hasebe suggests, is too small. In 1997, there were approximately 13 attorneys for every 100,000 people. It is extremely difficult to qualify as a practising lawyer. Candidates have to pass the exceptionally difficult National Bar Examination, in which the success rate has traditionally been a mere 2 per cent to 3 per cent. In 1998, for example, just 812 out of 30,568 candidates passed the examination. Their average age was nearly 27. As the lawyers are concentrated in the large cities, people in rural areas have great difficulty finding lawyers. Even in large cities, it is necessary to have friends or relatives who are lawyers, or at least who know lawyers, in order to obtain legal services. Owing to the scarcity of practising attorneys and their monopoly, citizens have no choice of legal representatives. Incompetent attorneys survive because they have no competition.

The restrictive practices of attorneys affect the conduct of civil proceedings. First, the rate of litigants in person is substantial, as we have noted. Judges are expected to intervene to assist litigants in person where necessary, but this is not always satisfactory.

The civil justice system was subject to criticism in 1980s, on the grounds that it was slow, expensive, and hardly comprehensible to the ordinary person. After extensive debate, a new Code of Civil Procedure was enacted in 1996 and came into effect in January 1998. The aim of the reforms was to offer ordinary citizens plain and accessible civil justice. The main changes are: the establishment of pre-trial procedures for identifying genuine issues; the improvement of the devices for obtaining evidence; the introduction of a small claims procedure; and the restriction of appeals to the Supreme Court.

Looked at from the outside, there is no doubt that the Japanese system operates far better than most of its counterparts. But such a conclusion fails to accord sufficient respect to the wishes and expectations of those served by the system in Japan. As outsiders we may envy the Japanese efficiency in processing actions. But the desire of Japanese citizens for easier access to legal services, and, indeed, for better access to justice, cannot be dismissed as unimportant.

Germany

It may come as a surprise to many common lawyers, but the German system is largely adversarial. German civil procedure is influenced by a liberal conception of the role of the parties and the state. The liberal idea of procedure holds that party freedom should be restricted as little as possible. However, this idea has come under strain with the increase in the burden of caseloads.

By comparison to most other European countries, whether having common law or civil law systems, the German system performs extremely well. In Germany both court fees and lawyers' litigation fees are fixed by law. Both types of fees are calculated as a small proportion of the value of the subject matter in dispute (the percentage fee decreases with the increase in the value of the dispute). The cost of litigation in Germany appears cheap indeed by comparison to common law countries. Furthermore, unlike in most other countries reviewed in this volume, there is a high degree of public confidence in, and satisfaction with, the administration of civil justice.

In all courts litigation is concluded within a reasonable time. Before the regional courts of first instance in 1996 38.9 per cent of proceedings were dealt with within three months; 26.5 per cent within six months; 21.7 per cent within twelve months; and a further 9.6 per cent within twenty-four months. The average duration of all regional court proceedings, from filing to final settlement or final decision, was 6.5 months. In the local courts in 1996, 48.2 per cent of cases were dealt with within three months; 28.5 per cent within six months; and 17.5 per cent within twelve months. The average duration of all local court proceedings, from filing to final settlement or final decision, was 4.6 months. But 4 per cent lasted more than three years. These figures are impressive, in the light of the very high volumes of litigation in German.

Litigation costs in Germany are modest, especially when compared to the costs in common law countries. Furthermore, litigation costs are predictable since both court fees and lawyers' fees are fixed as a small and decreasing proportion of the value of the disputes. This predictability of costs has fostered a thriving market in litigation cost insurance. A substantial proportion of German households are insured in respect of traffic accidents and private liability (excluding divorce and family matters). Almost one-fifth of all litigation is financed by insurance, at least on one side.

Nevertheless, the system suffers from some weaknesses. Foremost amongst them is the high volume of litigation, which places strains on the court system. In some areas of Germany backlogs are building up and the progress of cases may be held up unnecessarily, despite efforts to improve the administration of the courts.

Within the European Union, Germany has by far the highest number of judges per capita of population. However, the total number of judges has been constant for years. The number of lawyers admitted has grown considerably in recent years (an estimated 5 per cent increase per year). Court fees cover scarcely 50 per cent of system costs. There is an ongoing debate about raising costs in order to discourage unmeritorious litigation. But, so far, no method has been worked out of achieving this goal without, at the same time, reducing access to justice.

Three areas offer scope for reducing the burden on the courts. The first of these concerns appeals. The rate of appeals in Germany is high; nearly 50 per cent of first instance judgments of the regional courts are appealed (the rate of appeal from local courts' judgments, in relation to which the right of appeal is more limited, is lower). Furthermore, since appeals may be against findings of facts at first instance, the appeal process imposes a great burden on the appellate jurisdictions. Proposals have been put forward to limit the grounds for appeal; in particular, to limit the right of appeal against findings of fact. These proposals have met with opposition, especially from practitioners, who regard appeals as an important source of income. Many believe that any serious procedural reform is doomed to failure due to the conservatism of the legal culture.

The second area in which there is scope for easing the courts' burden is that of alternative dispute resolution. While ADR has become fashionable, conciliation proceedings are not popular. It is thought that the courts themselves offer sufficient mediation and settlement opportunities. Besides, German litigants prefer to entrust their disputes to the judiciary, whom they trust and respect.

A third area in which improvements are possible has to do with stricter adherence to the procedural rules and to the timetables. The trend is to insist on timely adherence to procedural duties, and restrict the scope for delaying tactics, particularly on appeal. There is an emphasis on the need to handle litigation more efficiently.

Holland

The Dutch system operates well. When litigants have to refer their disputes to court, they find the courts accessible in the sense that they can obtain a resolution within a reasonable time and at a reasonable cost. Equally importantly, Dutch citizens are offered other effective ways of resolving their disputes so that court proceedings are really reserved for disputes that are either important or intractable.

A single judge, before whom legal representation is mandatory, hears first instance cases. As far as the duration of proceedings is concerned, there is a big difference between local courts (*kantongerecht*), with an average duration of 133 days for an opposed case to reach final judgment, and district courts (*rechtbank*), where the corresponding average is 626 days. On appeal, an average of only 25 per cent of cases are determined within nine months, and only two-thirds are terminated within two years. Summary procedures (*kort geding*) count their average duration in terms of weeks. *Kort geding* make up 12 per cent of the civil caseload.

Some interesting experiments to reduce delays are under way. Some district courts, in co-operation with local lawyers, offer parties the possibility of choosing an abbreviated procedure. If the plaintiff and the defendant are prepared to put forward their case in full at the outset, the court will undertake either to get the parties to agree an early settlement or, failing that, to arrive at a final judgment within six to eight months. Initial evaluation of this procedure indicates that 89 per cent of the cases adopting this procedure produce a final judgment within eight months. However, the proportion of disputes adopting this procedure is small. This is due to the fact that those who are willing to adopt such a co-operative attitude will also be the parties most willing to settle.

Court fees are related to the value of the dispute. On their part, lawyers charge an hourly fee. The hourly fee is moderate, by the standards of the common law countries. An appropriate two-hourly fee for an attorney might be Dfl. 360. The winner in litigation is entitled to recover the court fees from the loser and also his or her lawyers' fees, unless the court orders otherwise. For small claims, the costs can easily exceed the value of the dispute, a fact that leads many litigants to seek alternative methods of dispute resolution.

About 15 per cent of all Dutch households hold policies for legal expenses insurance. In Germany, the comparable figure is more than half of all households. Most insurance policies exclude family law and tax matters from the coverage. Dutch legal expense insurers take an active role in avoiding the high litigation costs which neighbouring German or Belgian insurance companies have to pay.

Dutch legal insurance companies handle the legal problems of their clients in-house first. When they get involved in a dispute, insured persons first contact their insurance companies, not their lawyers. As the legal profession does not have a monopoly on the giving of legal advice, Dutch insurance companies can advise their policyholders on their disputes. Indeed, they manage to negotiate a settlement in 96 per cent of disputes. Advocates are consulted only *after* such legal first aid has been exhausted, and only when court litigation is seriously threatened.

The Dutch pattern of litigation avoidance is impressive, when one considers that the Netherlands provides generous legal aid. Furthermore, as out-of-court procedures handle disputes more informally and less adversarially, it is easier for Dutch citizens to obtain some assistance with their disputes. In addition, there is a solid layer of small partnerships and solo lawyers offering reasonable services to the public. Since lawyers' monopoly is not as strong as in other countries, lawyers have to compete with the legal services given by trade unions and other organizations, such as insurance companies. If the government's present plans become law, the privilege of representing parties in court might be extended to a number of salaried lawyers. According to these plans, in-house lawyers and the staff lawyers of legal aid bureaux, trade unions, and legal insurance companies will be given rights of audience. Since such salaried lawyers are often highly specialized in certain fields of law, the change could well have far-reaching effects for lawyers in private practice.

The Dutch system has developed a number of processes for expediting court proceedings or for avoiding them altogether. Recent changes in divorce proceedings, as well as the innovative use of the preliminary injunction procedure, *kort geding*, provide prominent examples of the ways in which the Dutch system has managed to avoid an overwhelming caseload.

Technically, the *kort geding* is the procedure for a preliminary injunction, but it has developed, largely informally, into a type of summary proceeding. The *kort geding* rarely requires more than one oral hearing. The parties present their respective cases during the hearing. The proceedings are informal enough for the judge to indicate to the parties what their chances of success in a full action are likely to be. The oral hearing very often ends in a settlement between the parties. Where settlement is not reached, a decision is often given immediately after the public hearing. On average, cases in *kort geding* are terminated within six weeks from start to finish. Even though they remain free to do so, few parties initiate ordinary proceedings afterwards.

Speedy procedures are available for debt recovery. The bailiffs (*deurwaarders*) are the key agents in Dutch debt enforcement. Dutch bailiffs can combine business as private debt collectors with the public function of summoning debtors to court and, ultimately, executing judgments. Judicial proceedings are used only as a last resort. The mere threat of court action is normally sufficient to secure some agreement on payment.

As in most European countries, divorce in the Netherlands must be by judicial decision. However, the procedure can be very simple. Unless one of the parties objects, or the Council for Child Protection claims that children will be adversely affected, the decision can be taken on the basis of written documents. In 25 per cent of cases, the parties handle their divorce on the basis of a pre-court agreement negotiated with the help of only one lawyer. If, as announced, Parliament ends the practitioners' monopoly on rights of audience in district courts, divorce mediators could become serious competition for lawyers. In reaction to this proposal, lawyers are now developing mediation skills so that they can compete for divorce business.

Consumer associations have developed practices of handling complaints by direct negotiation, campaigning publicly on major issues, and occasionally taking a test case to court. Their main impact is achieved by publicity. Many service industries, such as travel agencies, cleaners, the textile industry, and car repair garages, have installed complaint boards to take up the bulk of cases. Such boards are usually set up with tripartite representation, including industrial representatives and consumer organizations, with a neutral person chairing.

When one looks at the variety of dispute resolution facilities available in Holland one can see why the Dutch have been successful in keeping their judiciary small and the court system so efficient.

Switzerland

One of the more interesting features of Swiss civil procedure is that the majority of judges, whether justices of the peace or district court judges, are lay judges, i.e. persons without legal qualifications. Only the presiding judges in the district court and the judges of the higher courts have legal qualifications. Furthermore, judges are elected for limited periods of office.

Caseloads have remained generally stable over the last few years. Litigation seems to be fairly expeditiously concluded. In proceedings before a single judge the vast majority of cases are concluded within three months (83 per cent) and only 2 per cent last more than a year. In the district court (a three-judge court) about 75 per cent of cases are concluded in six months. Ordinary appeals are concluded within six months in 60 per cent of the cases and 13 per cent last more than a year. But the proportion of appeals lasting more than one year has increased. In 1997 26 per cent of all the judgments were appealed to the cantonal high court in Zurich. In the same year 33 per cent of the judgments were attacked by an appeal to the Federal Court.

In general, civil proceedings cannot be commenced without first attending a settlement hearing before a justice of the peace. Accordingly, the rate of settlement is quite high, ranging between 44 per cent and 72 per cent in the district court, depending on the type of case.

As the above account suggests, proceedings are expedited within a reasonable time. But this is mainly true of the canton of Zurich. In some cantons the position is less satisfactory. There are problems, however, inside the judicial organization, in that the quality is not even. Some judges find it difficult to handle complex cases, and judges who are promoted tend to leave behind a backlog of unfinished cases. However, the judiciary is increasingly aware of the importance of efficient case management.

Going to court in Switzerland is very expensive. The losing party, who also has to pay the winner's legal costs, can face large bills. For instance, the losing party in an action concerning Sw. Frs. 100,000 will face a bill of Sw. Frs. 90,000 if the case goes all the way to appeal.

The principal problems of the Swiss system lie in the very high cost of litigation and in the complexity of the remedies. There are too many remedies and their scope is often extremely difficult to distinguish. Professor Meier observes that it would be better to create a new and simplified remedy system within a new federal code for procedural law.

The Legal Aid Story

The position of legal aid in the different countries surveyed in this volume deserves special consideration.

As we have already noted, the function of the civil process is to protect rights. The courts can only protect the rights of those litigants who have succeeded in beating a path to the courts. Yet, traversing this path almost inevitably involves some cost: court fees and lawyers' fees, as well as other incidental expenses, such as expert and witness fees. If the assistance of the courts were denied to those who cannot afford the cost of litigation, the poor would be denied the courts' protection and, therefore, their legitimate rights. None of the systems reviewed here is willing to accept such a denial of justice. Every system makes some provision for enabling poor people to obtain access to the courts. However, their success in doing so varies greatly, as we shall presently see.

England

Traditionally, the aim of the English legal aid system has been a lofty one. It has aimed not only to provide the poor with a basic legal service, but to grant to the poor a level of legal services sufficient to ensure that they are not at a disadvantage compared with their richer opponents. By aiming to match the legal services given to the poor to those affordable by the rich, the level of legal aid services was from the start determined by the general standards of litigation practices.

To qualify for legal aid, a person's income must be below a certain level and a lawyer must certify that the case has legal merit, in the sense that the lawyer would advise an unaided person in the position of the party concerned to proceed with the case. An application is then made to the Legal Aid Board, which is run by representatives of the legal profession.

The Legal Aid Board pays the aided person's lawyer's bills in the usual way, just as if the legally aided person were paying them personally. Where the legally aided person wins the case, the Legal Aid Board is entitled to the money recovered by way of costs from the loser. The Board also has a charge over any money or property recovered or preserved in the proceeding, to cover any excess of legal aid money paid out over and above the amount recovered from the losing party through costs. However, if the aided person loses, the Legal Aid Board is not obliged to pay the costs incurred by winner. This can give the legally aided party a strong advantage in negotiating settlement with a non-legally aided opponent, because the opponent will know that he will never recover his costs if the litigation proceeds.

This system of legal aid removes considerations of cost-efficiency from the minds of those in control of litigation funded by the Legal Aid Board, allowing costs to grow out of all reasonable proportion to the amounts at stake. Lawyers have an incentive to certify that the case is worth pursuing, even if it is not. And, because the budget of the Legal Aid Board has traditionally been unlimited, they have had an incentive to protract and complicate proceedings. It is well known that many legal aid cases are pursued in circumstances in which no privately funded litigant would persist with litigation.

According to the Lord Chancellor's Department, the legal aid expenditure in 1990–1 was some £682 million. But by 1997 it had increased by 115 per cent to £1.478 billion. Lawyers' fees consume 90 per cent of the legal aid bill. Civil legal aid alone cost £634 million in 1997–8. The total cost of the civil court service in the same financial year is estimated to amount to only £319.8 million.

There seems to be a coincidence between the availability of funds and lawyers' income. Over the past twenty years there has been a marked shift toward increased reliance by the profession on income generated from litigation work. In 1975–6 contentious work accounted for £141 million, or 22 per cent, of solicitors' gross income.[15] By 1984–5 contentious work represented 32 per cent of gross income.[16] By 1992 it had risen again to 40 per

---

[15] Non-matrimonial civil work represented £78 million or 12% and legal aid work £39 million or 6%. Royal Commission on Legal Services (1978), Cmnd. 7468, ii. 494.

[16] Of which two-thirds was referable to non-matrimonial civil litigation. Law Society, Special Committee on Remuneration (1986), vol. ii, table 24.

cent.[17] Glasser has calculated that the gross income that solicitors derive from non-matrimonial civil cases has increased nineteen times in twenty years.[18] He concludes 'that professional incomes and the size of firms do seem to have increased substantially and to have been funded, to some considerable extent, by the increase in litigation over the last two decades'.[19]

The relentlessly increasing demands for legal aid support presented the government with an unpalatable dilemma: it must keep paying up without limit; or, alternatively, it must cut its support for the poor.[20] It chose the latter course and cut down eligibility to legal aid.[21] Over the last four years, the number of people helped by legal aid has fallen by 9 per cent. Yet total legal aid spending has continued to rise nonetheless. Since 1990–1, the cost of each case to the Legal Aid Board has grown by 53 per cent in real terms, when adjusted for inflation. Accordingly, fewer people are now assisted, at a much greater cost per person. The legal aid scheme costs every taxpayer £57 per annum. The contraction of eligibility threatens to leave ever-larger sections of the population worse off than before the introduction of the legal aid system, for, in the meantime, costs have increased in real terms.

Legal aid has now reached a level far greater than the spending on the courts themselves, amounting to £1.6 billion in the present financial year. This vast budget largely represents direct payments to the legal profession. Such a level of expenditure is clearly unsustainable. It is now clear that a system whereby the level of publicly funded services is governed by what the affluent are used to purchasing for themselves, rather than by what the taxpayer can afford, was destined to break down.

The reform of the legal aid system which is now under way in England is in large measure a sign of despair at the inability of the administration of civil justice to come to grips with the underlying problem of rising costs. The government has put forward a number of proposals. First, legal aid will be withdrawn from most money claims and will be replaced by rules allowing lawyers to take cases on a conditional fee basis. The idea is that those with reasonable money claims will be able to find lawyers who will take the risk of receiving no fee if the plaintiff loses, in the hope of obtaining a higher fee than normal if the plaintiff wins.

[17] Centre for Interfirm Comparison, quoted by R. Smith, *The Future of the Legal Profession* (Legal Action Group publication, 1995), 7.

[18] C Glasser, 'Solving the Litigation Crisis' (1994) Litigator, No. 1.

[19] Ibid. One has to distinguish here between increase in volume and increase in unit cost. As the statistics cited earlier show, there has been an increase in unit cost as well as in volume.

[20] For analysis of the problems and proposals for reform see: A. Gray, 'The Reform of Legal Aid' (1994) 10 Oxford Review of Economic Policy 51.

[21] Households in Great Britain entitled to civil legal aid on income grounds alone fell from 81% to 41%; Home Affairs Committee, *5th Report: Legal Aid: The Lord Chancellor's Proposals* (1992–3), HC 517, 41; see also *41st Legal Aid Annual Report* (1993–4), HC 462, 11. See also; C. Glasser, 'Legal Aid: Decline and Fall' (1986) Law Society Gazette, 19 Mar., 839; 'Legal Aid Eligibility' (1988) Law Society Gazette, 9 Mar., 11. The Civil Legal Aid (General) (Amendment) Regulations 1994.

There will still be areas of litigation where legal aid will be available. However, the government is determined to put an end to the unlimited hourly fee system. Instead, it will nominate groups of franchised firms of solicitors who will provide legal services to litigants eligible for legal aid at fixed cost. The government is also proposing to put an overall limit on the legal aid expenditure.

Australia

Similar pressures on legal aid have resulted in drastic reduction in the legal aid provision in Australia.

USA

The government offers little assistance to people of limited means who want a lawyer for a civil case. Until the 1960s, there was no substantial governmental assistance for representation in civil litigation. In the 1960s, the federal government created a system of legal aid offices supported by tax dollars to provide free representation for those who met the very low income criteria. In the 1970s, this effort was shifted to a government-supported independent corporation, the Legal Services Corporation. During the 1980s, President Reagan tried to terminate funding for the Legal Services Corporation. Although that did not happen, Congress has increasingly limited the range of activities which are supported by legal aid. In short, the available funding for impoverished litigants is very limited.

Poor plaintiffs with personal injury claims are normally able to find a lawyer on a conditional fee basis. In essence, these lawyers underwrite the litigation by investing their time with no assurance of being paid, and they often bear the out-of-pocket expenses as well. Further, there are a number of fee-shifting statutes, in areas such as employment discrimination, which can ease access to court for the poor.

France

The state provides assistance with litigation costs to those with modest means. Eligibility is determined by monthly income. Those persons with an income below F. Frs. 4,848 per month are entitled to full legal aid, whereas persons with an income above that but below F. Frs. 7,273 are entitled to partial legal aid assistance. These are fairly low limits, leaving much of the low-income middle classes outside the scheme and without access to justice. A divorce petition, for example, involving no complications or appeal, costs approximately the equivalent of the minimum monthly wage, about F. Frs. 7,000.

The scope of legal aid is wide. It is given before all courts: civil; administrative; criminal; disciplinary; contentious and non-contentious; to plaintiff or defendant; for all or part of the trial, including interviews in police stations and proceedings for the enforcement of judgments. Legal aid is available for legal advice and assistance in respect of out-of-court proceedings (non-contentious administrative proceedings or conciliation proceedings before certain commissions, such as that dealing with the affairs of over-indebted households).

Between 1991 and 1997, the general budget of the Ministry of Justice rose from F. Frs. 18.17 billion (1.42 per cent of the general budget of the state) to F. Frs. 23.90 billion, an increase of roughly 31 per cent. The total amount of sums distributed in legal aid rose from F. Frs. 367.72 million to F. Frs. 1072.21 million, an increase of 191 per cent.

Italy

Article 24 of the Italian Constitution gives citizens the right to take legal action in the courts in order to protect their rights. Further, it requires the state to provide legal aid for those who cannot afford the expense of court proceedings. However, in practice the Italian state fails to provide adequate assistance to the poor in this regard. The criteria of eligibility for legal aid are so stringent that very few are able to benefit. Legal aid today is available only to those who earn less than £3,500 a year. It is accordingly not surprising that the public expenditure on legal aid in Italy is less than one-hundredth of that in England.

Spain

Spain's legal aid system was reformed in 1996. The reform extended the right to free legal assistance to those persons whose annual income is lower than double the minimum wage. In exceptional cases assistance may be granted to persons whose annual income is between double and four times the minimum wage; although in such cases the assistance may be limited in certain respects.

When full legal aid is granted, it covers all the legal costs, including lawyers' fees. The lawyers are paid at a fixed rate. However, the rate is so low (24,000 pesetas for representing a party for an entire litigation process) that the standard of service provided under the legal aid scheme is poor.

Portugal

Legal aid may provide needy litigants with the entire cost of litigation, both in respect of court and lawyers' fees.

The power to grant legal aid is vested in the judge who is in charge of the case. When a lawyer is needed, the judge requests a nomination from the District Board of the Lawyers' Association. The lawyers are paid by the state, in accordance with a schedule. As a rule, lawyers appointed are either trainees or lawyers embarking on their careers. Consequently, legal aid does not work very well.

Brazil

Only litigants who can show that they are unable to meet the litigation costs are granted relief, by being allowed the privilege of 'gratuity'. The system of public defenders is still very inefficient. In many states it does not operate at all, or it exists only by way of token public legal assistance to persons most in need. Legal aid is therefore meagre.

Greece

Parties who show that they cannot pay the costs of litigation and that they have a reasonable case may be granted assistance in respect of court fees and lawyers' fees. At the request of the party concerned, the court will certify assistance and appoint a lawyer. At the end of the proceedings orders of costs are made in the normal way. But orders of costs will not be enforceable against legally aided litigants unless their financial circumstances improve.

Where the court has granted the benefit of legal aid, lawyers are expected to offer *pro bono* work. They will only be paid if their client recovers the costs from the opponent. Not surprisingly, the system of legal aid does not work well. This is due to the restrictive interpretation developed by the case law, the reluctance of the parties to appear as destitute, and above all the unwillingness of lawyers to undertake *pro bono* work.

Japan

Legal aid is available for citizens with inadequate means. The Japan Association of Legal Aid administers the legal aid scheme. However, the budget is so tight that eligibility is very limited. In addition, the assisted person must repay the costs, whether he or she recovers money through the action or not. The insufficiency of legal aid discourages claimants of modest means from embarking on litigation.

Germany

Legal aid is granted where the applicant has a case which can reasonably be expected to result in a favourable decision. The power to grant legal aid resides with the judge in the case. Once applicants have disclosed their financial circumstances, the courts are relatively generous in granting legal aid. Where legal representation is obligatory, a lawyer is assigned to the aided party. Where legal representation is not compulsory, a legally aided party is assigned a lawyer if a lawyer represents the opposing party, or if legal representation seems necessary.

Lawyers assigned to legally aided parties receive a lower remuneration. However, the system of remuneration is otherwise the same as in normal proceedings; i.e. payment in three tranches according to the stage that the litigation has reached. No official statistics exist on a federal level. The official figures for Bavaria are, however, likely to reflect the general trend. From these figures, it appears likely that the number of grants has generally continued to increase in the last few years. In 1996, Bavarian local courts granted legal aid in 9,224 general civil cases (a 9.5 per cent increase on 1995) and in 38,254 family cases (15.4 per cent more than 1995). Bavarian regional courts (in first instance matters) granted legal aid for 1,973 civil cases (7.6 per cent more than 1995). In 1996, the total Bavarian spending on assigned lawyers was approximately DM 64.6 million (15.8 per cent more than 1995), and in 1997 a total of about DM 73 million was spent (a 13 per cent rise). It is estimated that the total annual expenditure on legal aid of the Federation and the *Länder* is approximately DM 500 million at present.[22]

Holland

Almost half of all Dutch households are eligible for legal aid. Roughly two-thirds of these have to pay contributions, starting from Dfl. 50 and increasing up to Dfl. 1,200 per case. Lawyers' fees are paid by Legal Aid Councils according to a fixed fee scheme. Where hourly fees are allowed under the legal aid scheme, they are set at around Dfl. 125 (privately paid attorneys charge two to three times that amount).

Austerity policies in the 1990s led to a sharp reduction in eligibility, and the contributions payable by middle-income persons were raised. When the level of eligibility dropped to 40 per cent of all Dutch households in 1994, the government corrected its regulations in order to raise it again to about 50 per cent. Government spending on legal aid in 1995 was Dfl. 207 million in respect of civil cases, Dfl. 73 million for criminal cases and Dfl. 91 million for legal aid bureaux/councils.

3. THE EMERGENCE OF A NEW LANDSCAPE

Symptoms and trends

This survey of different national systems shows why the dissatisfaction with the administration of justice is so widespread. The usefulness of going to court to claim or defend one's rights is impaired, to a greater or lesser extent, by long delays and high costs. The survey suggests that in virtually all the countries represented in this volume efforts have been made to improve matters. A number of trends are noticeable in the struggle with the ills of delay, cost, and access to justice.

In virtually all the countries surveyed there has been a steady, sometime sharp, increase in the volume of litigation entering the courts. Many factors have contributed to this trend: increasing credit facilities and housing problems; increasing divorce rates; increasing social and labour mobility; and, above all, improvements in education, in the dissemination of information, and a far greater willingness to insist on one's rights.

The rising volume of litigation has created in some countries great backlogs

---

[22] Roughly £171 million, or $US286 million.

of cases and has caused protracted delays. In some systems it has also been accompanied by a substantial increase in the cost of litigation. It should, however, be remembered that these problems are not new; indeed they have been present in the different systems for the best part of the last fifty years. Before examining the solutions that are being offered at present, we would do well to look at the history of procedural reform and see what lessons may be learned from past experiments.

In all the reviewed systems efforts have been made periodically to improve the administration of civil justice. These efforts have been directed at different aspects of litigation. Measures have been adopted to simplify the rules and the structure of civil proceedings. Attempts have been made to persuade litigants to resolve their disputes otherwise than by court proceedings. In many countries improvements were introduced in court administration, and in most the number of judges and of support staff was increased. Yet, notwithstanding the persistent reform efforts, the problems of delay and cost have proved intractable in most systems. Indeed, on occasion reform has made matters worse. In Italy, for example, the quality of litigation services has fallen following procedural modernization. A similar complaint is made about the Greek procedure. All this lends support to Professor Leubsdorf's view that, overall, the benefits of the reform of civil procedure have been disappointing.

However, there are also encouraging signs which give some reason for optimism. First, there are three notable exceptions to the general picture of inefficiency: Japan, Germany, and, above all, Holland. We can hope to derive some beneficial lessons from the operation of these systems. Second, when we look at the variety of the causes of the problems, we discover certain persistent contributory factors which may be capable of being reversed. Lastly, we can observe in certain systems a willingness to address these factors in an innovative and determined way.

While the cost of litigation is a source of complaint in most countries, it is clear that cost levels are far higher in common law countries. The possibility that the cost to each party may not just exceed the value of the subject matter in dispute, but even surpass it by a large margin, is virtually unknown in civil law countries, except perhaps in very low-value disputes. At the same time, delays of the magnitude experienced in a few civil law countries are alien to the common law countries.

There is a far greater diversity of efficiency and performance amongst civil law systems than amongst common law systems. Amongst civil law systems we have at one extreme Holland, Germany, and Japan, which provide their citizens with a reasonable service, and, at the other extreme, systems such as Italy with an abysmal record. This diversity is particularly striking when we compare countries which share similar procedural arrangements. Holland's procedural code is derived from the French code, yet the Dutch administration of justice seems to cater better for the needs of its citizens. Similarly, the Greek procedural arrangements are derived from the German system, yet the latter inspires far greater confidence in the community.

The obstructive influence of lawyers' vested interest

There is one notable factor which makes a substantial contribution to both high costs and excessive delays: the economic interest of the legal profession. Where, as in England, lawyers are paid by the hour, they have an interest in complicating and protracting litigation, for the more demanding the litigation process, the more the parties' lawyers earn. In Italy lawyers are not paid by the hour, but by keeping a large number of cases which progress slowly they are able to increase their income.

The experience of the German system, which, as we have seen, is one of the most satisfactory, provides a telling example of the influence that financial incentives have on legal practice. In Germany litigation costs are fixed and are payable in three tranches, depending on the stage reached in the process. The first tranche is payable upon commencement of proceedings, the second for the preliminary hearing, and the third after the taking of evidence at the trial. It was found that cases that could have been settled early tended to go all the way to trial. In order to counteract this tendency the law was changed, giving lawyers the right to recover two fee tranches if the case settled before the preliminary hearing. In this way the German system manages to encourage early settlements. But, even in Germany, areas of negative incentives remain. For instance, the high rate of appeals is blamed, to a large extent, on lawyers' incentives. Lawyers who have already made the investment of time and effort in preparing for first instance proceedings will tend towards appeal, from which they can gain extra income for little extra preparation.

In every country where efforts have been made to expedite the litigation process in ways which threatened lawyers' economic interests, the legal profession has strongly resisted reform attempts and, on the whole, managed to defeat the proposals. This is true even in Germany, where the legal profession has strongly resisted the curtailment of the right of appeal for fear of losing income. In England, for example, the legal profession has been largely successful in opposing the introduction of fixed cost litigation. In Italy the legal profession has strongly resisted the introduction of strict timetables for the conduct of litigation.

Almost every country has a similar story to tell. It is remarkable how in each country the legal profession has opposed attempts to simplify and expedite the civil process, or efforts to introduce cost-reducing measures. It is equally remarkable how reluctant legislatures have been to redress the imbalance between the economic interests of the legal profession and those of the public. As we have seen, neither in common law countries nor in civil law countries has there been a sustained campaign to reverse the economic incentives that lawyers have to protract and complicate the civil process. The power of the legal profession to maintain structures that serve their economic interests is great in every country.

There have been some attempts to change the incentive system. In England, a fixed cost regime is being introduced for the fast-track procedure, involving claims of up to £15,000. Furthermore, England is moving away from the hourly fee system of remunerating lawyers towards conditional fee agreements, under which lawyers are paid nothing if the plaintiff fails to recover. It is doubtful whether this particular proposal will have the desired effect, but it is at least an indication that the lawmaker is aware of the problem. In Germany, where lawyers receive fixed costs for litigation work, incentives for settlement have been created, as we noted earlier. However, such moves are few and far between.

Only Holland has managed to achieve a satisfactory balance between the interests of the legal profession and those of the users of the administration of justice. Lawyers are free to charge what they wish and normally charge by the hour. Nevertheless, litigation costs are moderate and delays are minimal. The reason for this satisfactory state of affairs has to do with the fact that there is far greater competition in the provision of legal services in Holland. Legal advice may be given by persons and organizations other than lawyers. Insurance companies offer their clients dispute settlement services and, very soon, lawyers who are employed by companies and other organizations will even be able to represent their employers in the courts. The fact that lawyers do not have a complete monopoly over legal advice and dispute settlement services has had two effects. First, it has kept down the cost of litigation. Second, it has prompted the legal profession to develop skills and services which compete favourably with other providers of services.

One of the clearest conclusions of the survey is that, unless the incentives possessed by the legal profession to complicate and protract civil litigation are reversed, and unless the profession's monopoly is weakened, the system of justice will continue to provide poor service to the community.

The general failure of legal aid strategies

There appear to be three strategies for affording access to the courts to poor persons who cannot afford the cost of litigation. Each of them seems to be problematic.

The first strategy operated in England until recently. The legal aid scheme was designed to offer the poor the same level of legal services that rich litigants would adopt at their own expense. Legal aid lawyers were paid like non-legal aid lawyers; they were paid an hourly fee, regardless of outcome and without an upper limit. The temptation created by this system was such that the cost of the scheme rose at a great rate. In the end the system proved intolerably expensive and it is now in the process of being abolished.

In its place the government is introducing a new scheme, which adopts a mixture of measures. The first measure is that of abolishing legal aid altogether in respect of monetary claims, leaving plaintiffs to find lawyers willing to represent them on a conditional fee basis. This proposal represents the second strategy used for dealing with the problem: providing no assistance at all to the poor, but hoping that market forces will come to their aid. This is the strategy current in the USA. The strategy works well for plaintiffs with strong monetary claims, such as claims in respect of personal injury, in which recovery is highly probable. Such plaintiffs can find lawyers willing to take the risk of losing their fees, in the event that the plaintiffs fail to recover, for the benefit that they will derive if the plaintiffs win.

However, this strategy does not assist plaintiffs with non-monetary claims, or with weak claims, nor does it help defendants. Poor litigants in this category would remain without access to justice if the system did nothing to help them. But the British government is also proposing to retain some form of legal aid for such litigants. To that extent, the first strategy will continue to operate, for such legally aided litigants will receive services comparable to those employed by privately funded litigants. To discourage unacceptable exploitation such as under the traditional scheme, the government is proposing to adopt cost-reducing strategies in order to keep a lid on the budget.

This brings us to the third strategy available for dealing with the legal aid problem. Under this strategy the legal costs of the poor are subsidized by the state only partially; the legal profession is expected to provide the rest of the subsidy. This is the strategy adopted in Germany, Holland, Spain, Portugal, and Greece. However, where the main burden of the subsidy falls on lawyers, as in Greece and Spain, the poor are left with no meaningful assistance. Where the main burden of the strategy falls on the state, the system tends to show the same strains as the first strategy of full state subsidy, as the Dutch experience shows.

The problems encountered by legal aid provision in different countries reflect, by and large, the more general problems of access to justice in those countries. In England the old legal aid provision was defeated by the exorbitant costs of English litigation. The cost of litigation in England is simply unaffordable, even by the taxpayer. In the USA the poor face the same problems that middle-class people do: they cannot afford to litigate unless they have a claim that attracts the services of contingency fee lawyers. In Italy, Spain, Portugal, Greece, and Brazil, the state provides such low support for the poor that they are effectively denied access to justice.

It is mainly in Germany and Holland that poor litigants can still have decent access to the courts. But then, these are the very systems which provide reasonable access to justice to the rest of the community. This suggests that the solution to the problem of the poor is indivisible from the provision of reasonable legal services to the community as a whole. It is only in countries that have found a sensible balance between the three dimensions of justice—truth, time, and cost—that the poor can be secure in their access to justice.

The universal assertion of judicial control

One of the most persistent beliefs is the view that, as a whole, civil law procedures are inquisitorial or judge-controlled, whereas common law procedures are adversarial and party-controlled. This view is certainly wrong at the level of theory. Continental procedures are largely oral and judges are meant to leave the initiative over the civil process to the parties. Civil law procedures, as the contributors to this volume explain, are dominated by a liberal philosophy of party autonomy. However, as Professor Blankenberg observes, the practice is not as absolute as the theory suggests. Both orality and party control are more limited in civil law systems. Judges lead the hearings on the basis of a file that contains all the documents submitted by the parties. This offers judges the opportunity to control the process and to encourage the parties to settle. Even so, there is a widespread perception in civil law countries that parties have too great a scope to protract and complicate the civil process, to the detriment of the efficient operation of the administration of justice.

The clearest trend emerging from the different national accounts is a general tendency towards judicial control of the civil process. Both common law countries and civil law countries display a shift towards the imposition of a stronger control by judges over the progress of civil litigation. In virtually all the systems reviewed here there is a perception that, when the process of litigation is left to the parties and their lawyers, its progress is impeded by narrow self-interest. Such self-interest may be that of recalcitrant defendants bent on exhausting and tormenting their plaintiffs or that of self-interest of lawyers determined to enhance their own incomes.

The contemporary dominant view is that the disruptive self-interest of parties and their lawyers can only be kept at bay by an active judiciary that directs the litigation process and is able to prevent disruptive tactics. The USA has been leading the trend amongst common law countries. A culture of managerial judges is now well established there. In England and Australia the move towards judicial control is more recent, but it is equally dramatic. New arrangements give judges unprecedented powers over the litigation process, its intensity, and its pace. Not only are the common law systems adopting a more interventionist judicial approach, they also display a marked move away from orality.[23] This is to be expected, for control cannot be exercised without a prior understanding by judges of the dispute and its ramifications. Such advance understanding can only be gained from written materials.

---

[23] A. A. S. Zuckerman, 'English Civil Procedure: The Shift away from Party Control and Orality', ZZP (Zeitschrift für Zivilprozessrecht)-International (1996).

A similar trend is reported from the great majority of civil law countries. In France, Spain, Portugal, Italy, and even in Japan and in Germany, moves are afoot to strengthen the judicial supervision of the litigation process.

The emergence of a new philosophy of procedure and adjudication

The move towards judicial domination of the civil process represents more than a change in the mechanics of litigation. It involves the development of a new philosophy of procedure. The new philosophy is most clearly elaborated in the new Civil Procedure Rules in England, where the idea of proportionality is spelt out. According to this idea, the procedure adopted for resolving a given dispute should be proportionate to the value, importance, and complexity of the dispute. A further idea expressed by the English rule is the idea of distributive justice. This requires that the limited resources of the administration of justice should be justly and fairly distributed between all those who require access to justice, and not just the individual litigants before the court.

These ideas are fairly widespread throughout the systems discussed here. The Portuguese code of civil procedure contains a principle of procedural economy similar to that adopted by the English rules. In France, where the traditional theory was that the civil process belongs to the parties, the judiciary now has extensive powers to control civil litigation. The ideas of flexibility and proportionality exemplified in recent French developments are not much different from those adopted by the new English rules. A similar comment may be made about recent trends in Spain and in Japan.

A reappraisal of the balance between truth, time, and cost

The ideas of proportionality and a just distribution of procedural resources require a reassessment of the balance which every procedural system strikes between rectitude of decision, the duration of proceedings, and their cost. There is now a widespread acceptance that improvements in the operation of justice may require different priorities to be adopted and new compromises to be made. Several general trends are indicative of such acceptance.

In many civil law systems there is a right to appeal by way of a rehearing. These systems recognize the right of litigants to have their dispute retried by a different court. The right to a retrial is an expression of the commitment to rectitude of decision. It represents the willingness of the system to have at least one more adjudication in order to reduce the risk of an erroneous outcome. Indeed, in order to avoid mistakes, the first instance judgment is not enforceable before the appeal procedure has been exhausted, in many of these countries.

However, in almost all the countries which allow for such appeals the cost–time benefits of such arrangements are being reassessed. For, while a second hearing may reduce the risk of error, it also involves delays and costs which render the overall benefit negative. Hence, there is now widespread pressure to restrict the right to such appeals. In some countries appeals as of right have been replaced with appeals by leave. In others the right of appeal has been limited to appeals on questions of law. Even in countries, such as Germany, where no changes have taken place, there is pressure to move in the same direction.

It should be noted that the idea of procedural economy is not new. All procedures employ some sort of economical or summary process for certain type of disputes. For instance, the recovery of debt accounts for a substantial proportion of litigation in all countries. Since claims for debt are generally straightforward, most countries have developed cost-efficient summary procedures for debt recovery. Examples include *Mahnbescheid* in Germany, and *injonction de payer* in France. Similar procedures exist in Italy and Holland. Such procedures allow creditors to make out their claims by simply presenting evidence of a contract and a statement that payment is overdue. These procedures are quick, cheap, and painless for plaintiffs, especially as debtors rarely contest such claims. In England such claims are usually resolved by default or summary judgment.

While, as we have just observed, the idea of summary procedures is old, the tendency to extend their use is more widespread nowadays. In England an abbreviated fast-track procedure has been created for claims up to £15,000. In France increasing use is made of the *référé* procedure. In Holland there is a more frequent use of the *kort geding*. Japan and Italy too are experimenting with new summary procedures. All this is indicative of a readiness to sacrifice some measure of rectitude of decision in order to achieve a more timely resolution of disputes and lower costs.

Dealing with the increase in litigation resulting from better access

Improvements in efficiency may have undesirable side effects. As the German experience shows, low litigation costs and a fairly efficient system of processing claims can stimulate litigation and increase the burden on the courts. We have seen that in several systems, such as in Germany and Greece, some argue that court fees should be increased in order to deter unmeritorious litigation. It would, however, be a mistake to assume that high costs, or, indeed, lengthy delays, are appropriate measures for keeping down the volume of litigation. High litigation costs operate unfairly against the poorer sections of the community. Using high access cost as a moderating factor is, therefore, offensive to the principle that all are equal before the law. Using delay as a tactic for deterring litigation is also objectionable, since it not only creates economic inefficiency but also involves a denial of protection for the rights of those who are entitled to protection.

The experience of the Dutch system shows that it is possible to operate a relatively quick and relatively cheap system of civil justice and, at the same time, avoid the scourges of excessive litigation volumes, delays, and high costs. Overall, the Netherlands experiences less court litigation and fewer problems with court congestion than its neighbours. This is so not because there is no demand for litigation in Holland, but because the legal profession and various social institutions have created a variety of processes that, overall, work better and faster at less cost to the disputant than in other countries.

As we have observed, Dutch citizens can obtain legal advice and dispute settlement services from sources other than lawyers. Lawyers have learnt to compete with these providers by offering effective dispute resolution services of their own. Court action is undertaken only when it is the most efficient way to proceed with the dispute in hand. This leaves the courts relatively free to concentrate on the cases that really require judicial attention. Even in this last category, settlements may be possible, and are encouraged by the ability of the judges to urge them. Finally, the availability of the quick and simple *kort geding* procedure has proved to be a very popular and effective way to deal with a wide range of cases which need the decision of a judge, but which do not require the exploration of a full-blown trial process.

Investment in staff and administration

A recurring complaint is that courts are understaffed and short of other resources. These may well be important factors. However, there is a growing recognition that, before asking the taxpayer to assume an even greater burden in paying for the administration of civil justice, we should try and find out whether there are other factors contributing to the duration of proceedings.

In England and Australia the litigation process is labour intensive. As already noted, while the pre-trial process is not complicated, it can involve much lawyer activity and court hearings. This litigious activity is not dictated by the rules, but is at times a result of party choice and of a culture of excessive adversariness. We should try to find ways of curbing the appetite for unproductive procedural activity, before we expand the number of judges and of support staff.

This is not to say, however, that increased investment in the administration of justice is never justified. Clearly, little progress can be made to improve the efficiency of civil justice in Brazil so long as the courts lack the most basic equipment for running an effective administration. At the same time, it is clear that investment alone is not enough. More than just a large and well-equipped court system is required in order to provide access to justice in reasonable time and at an affordable cost.

Conclusion

The objective of a system of civil litigation is easy to define: deciding disputes in accordance with the law and on the basis of the true facts, or, in other words, returning judgments which enforce the substantive rights of the litigants. However this objective, which is common to all modern systems of civil justice, cannot be entirely and perfectly obtainable. Mistakes whether in the application of the law or in the determination of facts, cannot be completely avoided. Nor can justice be rendered instantaneously, without any delay, and at zero cost. Accordingly, justice is relative: it varies in rectitude of decision, in the time that it takes to be provided, and in the cost that is involved.

The systems discussed in this volume vary, therefore, not in their central objective but in the way that they seek to provide correct decisions within a reasonable time and at an affordable cost. Although excessive delay and high cost have serious adverse effects on the efficacy of the system of justice, they have been persistent in most civil justice systems for a very long time. Every country boasts a long history of attempts to reduce delay and cost, yet few have been even moderately successful in reaching a sensible balance.

Notwithstanding the cultural divides between different systems (not just between common law and civil law systems but even within each of these groups), there seem to be emerging some general approaches to the problems. Foremost amongst them is the general trend towards judicial control of the litigation process. The assertion of judicial control seems to go hand in hand with a new philosophy of distributive justice in procedure.

According to this idea, the function of the courts is not only to decide cases according to the law and the facts, but also to ensure that the limited resources of the system of civil justice are justly distributed between all those seeking justice. Accordingly, judges must ensure that the resources given to individual disputes are proportionate to the complexity and importance of each dispute. In so doing judges must take into account not only the interests of the litigants before the court, but also the interests of all others waiting in the queue. The aim of judicial control is, therefore, to avoid unnecessary cost and delay and ensure that the court resources are economically managed. This philosophy of distributive justice brings to the administration of civil justice the practical considertions of cost-effectiveness and of efficient management of public resources, which play an important part in the provision of most other public services.

However, the problems of excessive delays and high cost have not been entirely due to a flawed philosophy of procedure or to the lack of judicial control of litigation. There have been other powerful contributing factors. One such factor has been the economic interest of the legal profession. In England and other common law countries, where legal services are paid by the hour, lawyers have had a strong economic interest in lengthening the process. In Germany, where litigation costs are fixed, the high rate of appeals is partly due to the fact that appeals offer lucrative returns to lawyers. In all the countries represented in this volume the legal profession has tended to resist measures designed to simplify the litigation process, or to speed it up or to reduce its cost.

It is not suggested that all the ills of the administration of civil justice are caused by forensic practices. At the same time, it can hardly be denied that the practices of the legal profession do exert an important influence. It seems fairly clear that, unless some of these practices change, little improvement is likely to be brought about by active court management, even if it is guided by a new and progressive philosophy of distributive justice. To some extent this is widely acknowledged. Indeed, many of the essays echo the need for a change in the culture of litigation. But changes do not come about simply because they are advocated. They come about in response to social and economic incentives. The desire to bring about a cultural change is widespread, but the will to address the socio-economic factors that lie at the root of the present problems seems to be lacking.

2

The Myth of Civil Procedure Reform

John Leubsdorf

Most lawyers in the United States emerge from law school in the grip of a myth. In the beginning, the myth runs, there was common law pleading, and it was very bad. Parties exchanged almost interminable series of pleadings—from declaration to surrebutter and beyond—in expensive and unsuccessful attempts to filter out invalid claims and defences without holding trials. Plaintiffs could not join related claims; defendants could not assert more than one defence; and advocates argued about how to fit claims into an incoherent medieval system of forms of action.

After this had gone on for 500 years, God said, 'let Bentham be' and all was light. Over the opposition of greedy conservative lawyers, an enlightened English public won legislation culminating in the Judicature Acts of 1873 and 1875. In the United States, the Field Code of 1848 initiated similar reforms, which the Federal Rules of Civil Procedure of 1938 consummated. As a result, cases were decided on their merits, without wasteful technicalities, and justice was done until 1975, when civil litigation somehow became even more expensive and time-consuming than under the common law.

Even today, many first-year law students find much of this story in their books[1] or hear it in their civil procedure classes. Most teachers realize that it is an oversimplification,[2] but it furnishes too useful an organizing perspective to discard. Indeed, it is hard to survey common law procedure and its replacements at all without students hearing this as a narrative of progress. Most never learn or soon forget most of the necessary qualifications, bringing the myth into their lives as lawyers and judges. The forms of action we have buried, but we keep on digging them up to show how rotten they were.

The myth of past reform impedes present reform. If we believe that we have already emerged from darkness into light, we are less likely to seek further illumination. The historical narrative that structures our understanding of civil procedure functions as a justification for the status quo.

I appreciate the assistance of Stephen Burbank, Aviam Soifer, Stephen Subrin, Stephen Yeazell, and Adrian Zuckerman. This essay is dedicated to Benjamin Kaplan, who taught me legal history under guise of employing me as a research assistant.

[1] e.g. R. H. Field, B. Kaplan, and K. M. Clermont, *Materials for a Basic Course in Civil Procedure* (7th edn. 1997), 386–480; J. J. Cound, J. A. Friedenthal, A. R. Miller, and J. E. Sexton, *Civil Procedure: Cases and Materials* (7th edn. 1997), 446–92; F. James, Jr., G. C. Hazard, Jr., and J. Leubsdorf, *Civil Procedure* (4th edn. 1992), 11–22, 137–49, 464–91.

[2] e.g. S. N. Subrin, 'How Equity Conquered Common Law: The Federal Rules of Civil Procedure in Historical Perspective' (1987) 135 U. Pa. L. Rev. 909.

How false is the myth? I do not know, and doubt that anyone else does either. Little historical research has been done, and some of it is dated and tendentious. We have no answers to most of the relevant questions. I will try to ask, but not answer, some of those questions here. My hope, of course, is that this will inspire someone else to do the work.

1. WHAT IS THE GOAL?

How could we decide whether today's civil procedure is an improvement on the common law system? We can try to assess the relative fairness of any given part of the systems—say, the rules governing jury selection—although our judgment of what is fair will inevitably arise from our own culture, including our own procedural system. Judging the relative fairness of systems taken as wholes is still more problematic: what constitutes procedural fairness is by no means obvious. Should the standard be enforcement of the substantive law, convenient dispute resolution, litigant satisfaction, social cohesion, controlled exercise of state power, or some combination of these factors?[3]

The rise of the alternative dispute resolution movement, fostering scepticism about the wonders of litigation, underscores the difficulty of agreeing on a standard for appraising procedural systems. According to that movement, what we should be trying to assess is all of society's methods for settling disputes, of which civil litigation constitutes only a part. Furthermore, some might claim, civil procedure should be shaped not just to adjudicate some disputes on their legal merits, but to encourage most disputants to resolve their disputes in a more co-operative and flexible way.[4] Neither the common law nor the current United States (or English) system was designed to fulfil this ideal, and neither does so very well. Trying to compare their relative lack of success faces formidable obstacles, both conceptual and practical.

Comparing different procedural systems in different nations also demonstrates that, although we proceduralists often speak as though we face problems that are primarily practical, we actually disagree radically about the goals of procedural systems. In France, for example, civil cases are tried by judges passing on a written record, with little use of compulsion to obtain evidence and frequent resort to court-appointed experts to help resolve many factual disputes.[5] In the

---

[3] e.g. R. Dworkin, 'Principle, Policy, Procedure', in *A Matter of Principle* (1985), 72; C. R. Farina, 'Conceiving Due Process' (1991) 3 Yale JL & Feminism 189; J. Mashaw, 'Administrative Due Process: The Quest for a Dignitary Theory' (1981) 61 BUL Rev. 885; R. Summers, 'Evaluating and Improving Legal Processes: A Plea for "Process Values"' (1974) 60 Cornell L. Rev. 1.

[4] e.g. C. Menkel-Meadow, 'The Trouble with the Adversary System in a Postmodern, Multicultural World' (1996) 38 Wm. & Mary L. Rev. 5; J. Resnik, 'Many Doors? Closing Doors? Alternate Dispute Resolution and Adjudication' 10 Ohio St. J. on Disp. Resol. 211; F. E. Sander, 'Varieties of Dispute Processing' (1976) 70 FRD 111.

[5] J. Vincent and S. Guinchard, *Procédure civile* (24th edn., 1996).

United States, juries hear many civil cases, live witnesses present most proof (filtered by a complex law of evidence), parties use elaborate pre-trial procedures to look for evidence, and an adversary culture encourages the use of privately retained experts who as a result are widely distrusted. Although it would oversimplify to claim that each system succeeds in embodying its culture's ideals—both are widely criticized by those who encounter them—two such divergent approaches could scarcely arise from identical goals.

Bypassing for the moment the debate about goals, we might fix on three fairly trite criteria for appraising a procedural system: the cost of litigation; the time needed to resolve disputes; and the accuracy with which the system finds the facts and applies the law. As we have seen, some will question these criteria: those, for example, who see litigation less as law enforcement and more as dispute resolution might replace accuracy by litigant satisfaction.[6] And the three criteria sometimes conflict. Making procedure speedier and cheaper might well make it less accurate[7] even though keeping it slower and more expensive will not necessarily make it more accurate.

Applying these criteria calls for statistical analysis of the caseload, which has not been forthcoming in the existing assessments of the great reforms of the nineteenth and twentieth centuries. Rather, law teachers focus, as is our wont, on odd cases that expose a procedural system's problems. At least five American civil procedure casebooks published during the last decade feature *Scott* v. *Shepherd*,[8] a case most of whose charm resides in its freakish facts, and whose discussion emphasizes the complexity and arbitrariness of common law pleading—which, admittedly, could be pretty complex and arbitrary. That judges had a hard time deciding which forms of action embraced liability for a re-thrown firecracker says nothing about the common law's ability to handle routine cases without procedural wrangling. In fact, *Scott* and its progeny may well show that the courts were able to fit the new tort of negligence into common law procedure without undue trouble.[9]

Unfortunately, even granted the willingness to appraise a system in its typical working, it is virtually impossible to assess accuracy, short of readjudicating a sample of cases with enough thoroughness to guarantee almost total correctness. One might investigate what percentage of cases in a given system were decided on procedural grounds, as did one influential article;[10] but many procedural decisions reflect the merits. Dismissal of a case for want of an essential allegation,

---

[6] See J. W. Thibaut and L. Walker, *Procedural Justice: A Psychological Analysis* (1975); T. R. Tyler, 'Citizen Discontent with Legal Procedures: A Social Science Perspective on Civil Procedure Reform' (1997) 45 Am. J. Comp. L. 871.

[7] A. A. S. Zuckerman, 'Quality and Economy in Civil Procedure: The Case for Commuting Correct Judgments for Timely Judgments' (1994) 14 Ox. J. Leg. Stud. 353; see J. Kakalik *et al.*, *Just, Speedy, and Inexpensive? An Evaluation of Case Management under the Civil Justice Reform Act* (1997).

[8] 96 Eng. Rep. 525 (1773).

[9] M. J. Prichard, *Scott* v. *Shepherd and the Emergence of the Tort of Negligence* (1976) (Selden Society Lecture).   [10] C. B. Whittier, 'Notice Pleading' (1918) 31 Harv. L. Rev. 501.

for example, may occur either because of a lawyer's incompetence or because the matter to be alleged is in fact absent. On the other hand, what appears to be a ruling on the merits may be warped by procedural problems, for example a rule obstructing access to evidence.[11]

Deleting the accuracy criterion leaves us with speed and cheapness, which are relatively measurable but tell us only part of what we would like to know. Emphasizing the difficulty of appraising and comparing procedural systems, however, leads us toward renouncing all possibilities of purposeful reform. If we do not know what we are seeking, or cannot tell when we have found it, we might as well stay in the present system, whatever it may be. Let us therefore assume for the moment that we have somehow cut the Gordian knot and proceed to some more empirical questions about common law procedure and its successors.

2. WHAT ARE WE COMPARING?

The myth's comparison between the bad old days and the brave new world assumes that each of these constitutes a single procedural system. Of course, that is not so.

The pre-reform system included Chancery and other equity courts as well as the common law courts. As everyone knows, equity procedure differed strikingly from common law procedure. It allowed broad joinder of parties and claims, the parties provided sworn evidence, pre-trial discovery was available, evidence was reduced to writing, and cases were decided by judges. In some periods, at least, equity was believed to be far more lengthy and expensive than common law procedure.

Common law procedure itself varied among the different courts, in ways that sometimes made a big difference for litigants despite the seemingly minor and technical nature of the variations. The court of King's Bench, for example, lost more than half its business between 1465 and 1525, but then recovered. Reportedly its lawyers, clerks, and judges, presumably to swell their own incomes, developed new ways of compelling defendants to appear that attracted plaintiffs.[12] (Similar enforcement problems are still important today,[13] but receive little attention from civil procedure experts or reformers.)

As this example shows, common law procedure did not remain unchanged between the thirteenth and the nineteenth century. Neither did the society around it. We should obviously not assume that the common law was equally adequate or inadequate at all times.

---

[11] To do it justice, Whittier's article responded to this objection. Ibid., at 510–12.

[12] M. Blatcher, *The Court of King's Bench, 1450–1550: A Study in Self-Help* (1978). But see C. W. Brooks, *Pettyfoggers and Vipers of the Commonwealth* (1986), 79–101.

[13] D. L. Chambers, *Making Fathers Pay* (1979).

The few attempts to examine the working of the common law system show marked differences at different periods. C. W. Brooks concludes that, in the late sixteenth and early seventeenth centuries, litigation was 'quite within the financial reach of a large number of customers'.[14] He estimates that a King's Bench or Common Pleas suit for £100 that went to trial would cost the plaintiff a total of between £6 and £8 which, if successful, he would recover from the defendant. (Compare a 1975 survey reporting median damage awards for contested cases of £3,748 and median cost awards of £806.[15]) A dramatic rise in litigation during this period—by 1640, the business of the most popular courts was fourteen times as great as it had been fifty years before—testifies to the accessibility of the courts. So does the fact that more than two-thirds of the litigants were below the ranks of gentleman.[16] These statistics tell us little about the speed of litigation or the quality of the result—although they do suggest that conditions were not so bad as to discourage plaintiffs—but they do indicate that the cost of common law litigation at this time was less than we might have surmised.

Clinton Francis's study of common law litigation around the beginning of the nineteenth century paints a very different picture.[17] He describes costs—for both parties added together—amounting to six or seven times the recovery. (These costs, reflecting increased lawyer and court fees, may well have been responsible for the huge drop in civil litigation between 1680 and 1750.[18]) As a result, plaintiffs did not sue unless they had such a strong case, typically one based on written evidence of indebtedness, as virtually to ensure that they would prevail and recover their costs. For such plaintiffs, however, the threat that the defendant would have to pay the costs as well as the sum due made litigation a highly effective way to collect debts. Consequently, the growth of a credit economy brought about huge increases in the number of suits brought in the early nineteenth century. This was a different procedural world from that of the Elizabethans, yet both used 'common law procedure'.

Needless to say, common law procedure in the United States diverged markedly from the English system in any of its phases, as well as in its social context. No colony or state ever recreated the English system in its full complexity, and each introduced various changes through legislation or practice.[19] There is

---

[14] Brooks, *Pettyfoggers and Vipers*, at 101.
[15] D. Barnard, *The Civil Court in Action* (1977) (1975 study), 168 n. 1. English litigation today is no doubt at least as expensive as it was in 1975. *Access to Justice: Final Report* (London: HMSO, 1996).
[16] Brooks, *Pettyfoggers and Vipers*, at 48–63, 101–7, 281–3.
[17] C. W. Francis, 'Practice, Strategy, and Institution: Debt Collection in the English Common-Law Courts, 1740–1840' (1986) 80 Nw. UL Rev. 807.
[18] C. W. Brooks, *Lawyers, Litigation and English Society since 1450* (1998), at 27–62, 91–5.
[19] R. W. Millar, *Civil Procedure of the Trial Court in Historical Perspective* (1952), 39–42; *The Papers of Daniel Webster, Legal Papers*, i: *The New Hampshire Practice*, ed. Alfred S. Konefsky and Andrew J. King (1982), 63–5, 260–95; *The Papers of John Marshall*, ed. Charles F. Hobson (1987), v, pp. xxxiii–li.

no reason to believe that the speed, expense, or accuracy of litigation coincided with those of contemporary litigation in England.

On the post-reform side, we again encounter not one but a variety of systems, each of which has changed over the years. Recent studies by Stephen Subrin, Stephen Yeazell, and Robert Bone, for example, show that the Field Code of 1848 can by no means be reduced to a halfway stop between the common law and the Federal Rules of Civil Procedure. Field wanted to bind judges with rules, while the Federal Rules expand judicial discretion; Field preserved the narrow scope of the common law lawsuit almost unchanged, while the Federal Rules adopt broad equity principles of joining parties and claims; Field stressed accurate pleading, while the Federal Rules downgraded pleading but emphasized pre-trial discovery.[20] We cannot dismiss in advance the possibility that these contrasts affected the speed, cost, and accuracy of litigation. And both the Field Code and the Federal Rules were implemented in many different jurisdictions, each with its own characteristics. The Code system did not necessarily work the same way in New York as it did in Montana, and recent years have witnessed a proliferation of idiosyncratic local rules in the federal trial courts.[21]

Notwithstanding the influence of the Field Code on the English reforms, and the English reforms on the Federal Rules, large differences likewise separate the English and Federal Rules systems. Indeed, considering how the House of Lords has spoken of discovery practice under the Federal Rules, many English practitioners might be startled by the suggestion that the two systems are similar.[22] The differences between the English and United States rules on legal fees, only slightly diminished by England's recent legalization of partially contingent fees in certain cases, could scarcely fail to affect the cost of litigating in the English and Federal Rules systems.[23] England's traditional division of functions between barristers and solicitors and its abolition of jury trial in virtually all civil cases are only two of the other significant divergences between the systems.

---

[20] Subrin, 'How Equity Conquered Common Law'; S. N. Subrin, 'David Dudley Field and the Field Code: A Historical Analysis of an Earlier Procedural Vision' (1988) 6 L. & Hist. Rev. 311; S. N. Subrin, 'Charles E. Clark and his Procedural Outlook: The Disciplined Champion of Undisciplined Rules', in P. Petruck, *Judge Charles Edward Clark* (1991), 115; S. C. Yeazell, 'The Misunderstood Consequences of Modern Civil Process' 1994 Wis. L. Rev. 631; R. G. Bone, 'The Boundaries of a Dispute: Conceptions of Ideal Lawsuit Structure from the Field Code to the Federal Rules' (1989) 89 Colum. L. Rev. 1.

[21] E. Chemerinsky and B. Friedman, 'The Fragmentation of the Federal Rules' (1995) 46 Mercer L. Rev. 757; S. N. Subrin, 'Federal Rules, Local Rules, and State Rules: Uniformity, Divergence and Emerging Procedural Patterns' (1989) 137 U. Pa. L. Rev. 1999; J. B. Oakley and A. F. Coon, 'The Federal Rules in State Courts: A Survey of State Court Systems of Civil Procedure' (1986) 61 Wash. L. Rev. 1367.   [22] e.g. *British Airways Board* v. *Laker Airways, Ltd.* [1985] AC 58.

[23] See E. A. Snyder and J. W. Hughes, 'The English Rules for Allocating Legal Costs: Evidence Confronts Theory' (1990) 6 JL Econ. & Org. 345 (Florida's shift to English rule of fee recovery in medical malpractice cases increased litigation expense).

3. WHO SOUGHT OR RESISTED REFORM?

The traditional story is that, starting in the nineteenth century, a public enlightened by Jeremy Bentham rose up and overthrew the old system, led by a few reformers like David Dudley Field and opposed by most of the bar.[24] Because this genealogy vouches for the scope and virtue of the resulting changes, it provides important support for the myth of procedural reform. Many would not accept the myth so easily if they believed, for example, that the procedural reform movement (like the contemporary 'tort reform' movement in the United States) emanated from a cabal of corporations. Although the traditional story undoubtedly contains some truth, it badly needs re-examination.

In the parallel field of evidence law reform, recent historical scholarship has reduced, without eliminating, Bentham's role. Before Bentham wrote, the law was already moving in directions he espoused. Even long after he wrote, many of his proposals met with no success. Other factors affected change, for example religious concerns in the case of the reform of the oath requirement in England, and in the United States concerns about testimony by freed slaves in the case of allowing parties to actions to testify.[25]

Similar points can be made about Bentham and civil procedure. More than a century before Bentham wrote, Commonwealth law reformers called for changes that he took up, such as county courts, court officials paid by salary rather than by litigants' fees, and simplified pleadings.[26] Bentham's scheme for basing procedure on the model of a father's family tribunal was more distinctive, but no one followed it. And his preference for broad judicial discretion in procedural matters foreshadowed the Federal Rules but not at all the Field Code.[27]

Whether the bar's greedy conservatism was the main obstacle to reform—as Bentham and succeeding reformers claimed—is another question deserving

---

[24] C. M. Hepburn, *The Historical Development of Code Pleading* (1897), 71–88, 174–84; C. S. C. Bowen, 'Progress in the Administration of Justice during the Victorian Period', in *Select Essays in Anglo-American Legal History* (1907), i. 516; E. R. Sunderland, 'The English Struggle for Procedural Reform' (1920) 39 Harv. L. Rev. 725 (the classic account, by one of the drafters of the Federal Rules of Civil Procedure); T. W. Shelton, 'The Drama of English Procedure' (1931) 17 Virg. L. Rev. 215 (by a persistent and influential advocate of federal court rulemaking); M. I. Zagday, 'Bentham on Civil Procedure', in G. W. Keeton and G. Schwarzenberger, *Jeremy Bentham and the Law* (1948), 68; C. W. Everett, 'Bentham in the United States of America', ibid. 185; C. E. Clark, *Handbook of the Law of Code Pleading* 12–45 (2nd edn. 1947); Millar, *Civil Procedure of the Trial Court*, at 43–64; L. M. Friedman, *A History of American Law* (2nd edn. 1985), 144–50, 391–403. Some of these sources omit components of the myth, for example the claim that the bar opposed reform.

[25] C. Allen, *The Law of Evidence in Victorian England* (1997); G. Fisher, 'The Jury's Rise as Lie Detector' (1997) 107 Yale LJ 575.

[26] N. L. Matthews, *William Sheppard, Cromwell's Law Reformer* (1984), 148–68; D. Veall, *The Popular Movement for Law Reform, 1640–1660* (1970), at 167–99. On 18th-century reformers, see S. C. Yeazell, 'Default and Modern Process', in William Gordon, *Legal History in the Making* (1991), 125; D. Lemmings, 'Blackstone and Law Reform by Education: Preparation for the Bar and Lawyerly Culture in Eighteenth-Century England' (1998) 16 L. & Hist. Rev. 211, 216–22.

[27] G. J. Postema, *Bentham and the Common Law Tradition* (1986), 344–57; sources cited nn. 2, 20 above.

reconsideration. Outside the realm of procedure, scholars dispute whether solicitors stymied reform of English land law, or on the contrary promoted it.[28] R. W. Kostal's engrossing study of law and English railways finds lawyers at work (to their own profit) on both sides of every conflict.[29] Thus, although many English lawyers undoubtedly opposed many procedural reforms,[30] and although self-interest influenced their opposition, that may not be the whole story.

It is certainly not the whole story of the adoption of the Rules Enabling Act of 1934[31] and the Federal Rules of Civil Procedure that it spawned. The American Bar Association—then a far more conservative and elitist organization than it is now—was the main proponent of the Act. Its main opponent was Senator Thomas Walsh of Montana, himself a lawyer by training, but better known as a liberal legislator. This line-up apparently reflects support by conservatives for federal judges, whose discretion the Federal Rules expanded, and who were then considered a bulwark against progressive legislation and tort plaintiffs.[32] It may also indicate that many lawyers correctly foresaw that the Federal Rules would be a boon for lawyers.

Whether lawyerly self-interest or conservatism was a major obstacle to the Field Code has not, to my knowledge, been investigated. Some lawyers no doubt feared the worst from the new regime,[33] but it is hard to see what grounds they had for fear. On the contrary, the Code confirmed that lawyers could charge clients any fee the client would accept, while reducing the fees payable to court officials, who were placed on salaries.[34] Lawyers probably absorbed some of the money thus liberated; perhaps the costs of litigation dropped, attracting more clients. Whatever occurred, and whatever lawyers may have feared, there is no reason to expect that the Code lowered lawyer incomes any more than did the Federal Rules. Perhaps we should postulate a law of the conservation of expense, under which whatever savings a reform may produce are promptly gobbled up by one or another portion of the litigation community.

This is not the only instance of lawyer opposition to changes that ultimately enriched the bar. Many although not all English professionals resisted the creation of the county courts in 1846, although that innovation led to increased

---

[28] Compare A. Offer, *Property and Politics, 1870–1914* (1981) with J. S. Anderson, *Lawyers and the Making of English Land Law, 1832–1940* (1992).

[29] R. W. Kostal, *Law and English Railway Capitalism, 1825–1875* (1994).

[30] Francis, 'Practice, Strategy and Institution'; Sunderland, 'The English Struggle for Procedural Reform'. [31] 28 USC § 2072 (as amended).

[32] S. B. Burbank, 'The Rules Enabling Act of 1934' (1982) 130 U. Pa. L. Rev. 1015; Subrin, 'How Equity Conquered Common Law'. E. A. Purcell, Jr., *Litigation and Inequality: Federal Diversity Jurisdiction in Industrial America, 1870–1958* (1992) describes the efforts of corporate defendants to remove tort suits into the federal courts.

[33] *The Diary of George Templeton Strong*, ed. A. Nevins and M. Thomas, i (1952), 324, 328 (predicting disaster for the bar).

[34] J. Leubsdorf, 'Toward a History of the American Rule on Attorney Fee Recovery' 47 L. & Contemp. Probs. (winter 1984), at 9, 16–22.

litigation and more judgeships for barristers.[35] During the New Deal, elite lawyers in the United States opposed the growth of administrative agencies that ultimately enriched their firms, whether from miscalculation, advocacy of their clients' interests, commitment to an ideal of judicial lawmaking, or reluctance to associate with the Jewish and Catholic lawyers who were already involved in administrative law.[36]

As an explanation for the slowness of change, lawyer greed is at once too easy and too feeble to be accepted without careful proof. Because of public suspicion of lawyers, reformers from Bentham to the present have delighted to claim that the bar's self-interest motivates resistance to their proposals.[37] In some instances, for example opposition to proposed limits on legal fees, self-interest is indeed likely to predominate. Even when the profession responds to proposals that do not directly target its income, lawyers surely consider what will be good for them. That the claim of self-interest is often valid, however, does not establish its truth in any specific instance. Perhaps it is worth adding that, the more we accept self-interest as the explanation for all human behaviour, the more likely it is to govern our own actions.

Lawyers usually find ways to profit from the status quo, but they also usually profit from changes—if only because lawyers are needed to propose, resist, explain, and litigate about new law. Lawyers are good at profiting from the law, whatever it may be. And a change that reduces profits in one way may increase them in another, so that lawyers often disagree with other lawyers about whether a proposal would be good or bad for the bar. The interests of one segment of the profession may conflict with those of another. In addition, as recent studies claim, professionals seek prestige as well as profit,[38] and promoting reform might increase the bar's prestige. Ultimately, because few non-lawyers interest themselves in legal procedure, procedural changes are unlikely to occur without the support of at least part of the bar. (The present head of the leading American anti-lawyer organization HALT is himself a lawyer.[39])

Two subgroups of the bar, judges and law teachers, further complicate the picture. Some judges helped write and promote the Federal Rules—which increase the power of judges—but some nineteenth-century judges in both England and the United States were accused of sabotaging legislative reforms by reading them narrowly.[40] Bentham, of course, regarded judges as well as

---

[35] Brooks, *Lawyers, Litigation and English Society*, at 103–7.

[36] R. Shamir, *Managing Legal Uncertainty: Elite Lawyers in the New Deal* (1995); N. S. Zeppos, 'The Legal Profession and the Development of Administrative Law' (1997) 72 Chi.-Kent. L. Rev. 1119.

[37] See A. A. S. Zuckerman, 'Lord Woolf's Access to Justice: Plus ça change . . .' (1996) 59 Mod. L. Rev. 773.

[38] e.g. M. J. Osiel, 'Lawyers as Monopolists, Aristocrats, and Entrepreneurs' (1990) 103 Harv. L. Rev. 2009; S. Haber, *The Quest for Authority and Honor in the American Professions, 1750–1900* (1991).

[39] W. R. Fry, 'New Laws, or a New Breed of Lawyers?', Washington Post, 25 Feb. 1996, at C11.

[40] On the role of judges, see Yeazell, 'The Misunderstood Consequences of Modern Civil Process'; Shelton, 'The Drama of English Procedure'; authorities cited n. 32 above. On judicial resistance to the Code, see *McFaul* v. *Ramsey*, 61 US 523 (1858); J. N. Pomeroy, *Code Remedies* (5th edn., 1929), 7–21, 48–9, 63–8, 619–20, 678–83.

lawyers as the enemy,[41] which makes it more difficult to view him as the progenitor of reforms that consecrated judicial rulemaking.

As for law teachers, they seem to have wielded little influence on nineteenth-century reforms; and while some United States professors were major shapers of the Federal Rules, many were still inculcating common law pleading into the 1930s and even after.[42] So it seems that in United States law schools the myth of procedural reform did not definitively vanquish its mirror image, the myth of the good old days, until surprisingly recently.

Who then, other than lawyers and an occasional philosopher, helped to propose or oppose the great procedural reforms? We do not know. Merchants, manufacturers, and bankers are worth investigating, because during the first half of the nineteenth century the great bulk of civil litigation was brought by business creditors against their debtors.[43] (The surge in tort suits came much later.[44]) Creditor interests might have been powerful and organized enough to push for reforms that, they hoped, would make collection suits cheaper and faster. Conceivably, they did so sooner in the United States than in England—where the major reforms did not occur until the 1870s—because the English system of attorney fee recovery made expensive suits a deadly weapon against defendants for plaintiffs with strong cases, or because English creditors first sought not to reform the central courts but to avoid them by establishing county courts and promoting arbitration.[45] That would still leave us wondering why debtor interests—which were often powerful, at least in the United States, where they helped write the civil jury into the Constitution—did not block reform.[46]

Accident sometimes sets the course of change.[47] David Dudley Field's brother Stephen, later a justice of the United States Supreme Court, migrated to California in 1848 and served in the judiciary committee of its legislature,

[41] J. Bentham, *Rationale of Judicial Evidence*, ed. J. S. Mill, iv (1827), 13–62.

[42] M. B. McManamon, 'The History of the Civil Procedure Course: A Study in Evolving Pedagogy' (1998) 30 Ariz. St. LJ 397, 411–33.

[43] Francis, 'Practice, Strategy, and Institution'; Brooks, *Lawyers, Litigation and English Society*, at 78, 109–10; R. A. Silverman, *Law and Urban Growth* (1981), 27–30.

[44] R. E. Bergstrom, *Courting Danger* (1992); L. M. Friedman and R. V. Percival, 'A Tale of Two Courts: Litigation in Alameda and San Benito Counties' (1976) 10 L. & Soc'y Rev. 267.

[45] H. W. Arthurs, 'Special Courts, Special Law: Legal Pluralism in Nineteenth Century England', in G. Rubin and D. Sugarman (eds.), *Law, Economy and Society, 1750–1914: Essays in the History of English Law* (1984), 380, 385–7; R. B. Ferguson, 'The Adjudication of Commercial Disputes and the Legal System in Modern England' (1980) 7 Brit. JL & Soc'y 141. As Paul Carrington has reminded me, seeing creditor interests behind the Field Code contradicts the traditional view linking it to Jacksonian Democrats and the codification movement.

[46] C. W. Wolfram, 'The Constitutional History of the Seventh Amendment' (1973) 57 Minn. L. Rev. 639, 673–705. In recent years, institutional defendants have mobilized to seek procedural and substantive legislation impeding plaintiffs, with some success. See J. Leubsdorf, 'Class Actions at the Cloverleaf' (1997) 39 Ariz. L. Rev. 453. E. G. Thornburg, 'Giving the "Haves" a Little More: Considering the 1998 Discovery Proposals' (1999) SMUL Rev. 229.

[47] See A. Watson, *Legal Transplants* (1974).

which then adopted his brother's Code. The California precedent in turn influenced other western states. About fifteen territories adopted variants of the Code soon after they acquired legislatures, probably because that was a way to set up a procedural system without much work, and because a Code was easier for lawyers in new communities to find and use than a library of common law precedent.[48]

4. WHAT DIFFERENCE DID REFORM MAKE?

The question I have been circling is whether the Field Code, the Judicature Acts, or the Federal Rules of Civil Procedure actually made civil procedure faster, cheaper, or more accurate.

Although little has been done to answer this question, court and other records should make before-and-after studies possible. These could cover speed, and at least in England—where courts tax costs that include legal fees—expense as well. Even in the United States, investigating whether suits for various sums were filed and brought to trial should yield information on the costs of litigation.

Just to stir things up, let me propose a counter-myth: the great reforms had little or no impact on the speed or cost of the average civil action. That is because, in any system, most cases are simple ones, concerning small sums, that settle or are otherwise resolved without much ado.[49] Ironically, Charles Clark was well aware of this when he drafted the Federal Rules, having recently finished one of the first statistical studies of civil litigation.[50] (Of course, although most cases settle, the procedural rules affect the size, timing, and expenses of the settlement.) Often—although that may not be true of the major remakings we are considering—procedural reform simply puts the seal of legislation on changes that many judges are already implementing.[51] Even when reformers introduce something new, it is hard to know in advance (or even afterward) what effects the innovation actually has.

Although this counter-myth is almost pure speculation, a bit of evidence supports it in the case of the Federal Rules and their impact on delay. In 1938, when the Rules came into effect in the federal courts, the average time from filing to disposition for civil actions had been declining for thirty years. It ranged between three and four years between 1900 and 1910, dropped sharply

---

[48] C. B. Swisher, *Stephen J. Field: Craftsman of the Law* (1963), 2–22, 53–5; Hepburn, *The Historical Development of Code Pleading*, at 93–113.

[49] B. G. Garth, 'Two Worlds of Civil Discovery: From Studies of Cost and Delay to the Markets in Legal Services and Legal Reform' (1998) 39 BCL Rev. 597.

[50] J. H. Schlegel, *American Legal Realism and Empirical Social Science* (1995), 82–8; C. Baar and S. Flanders, 'False Start? Charles Clark and the Quantitative Study of Judicial Administration', in P. Petruck, *Judge Charles Edward Clark*, i (1991).

[51] J. Resnik, 'Changing Practices, Changing Rules: Judicial and Congressional Rulemaking on Civil Juries, Civil Justice, and Civil Judging' (1997) 49 Alabama L. Rev. 133.

to about two years in 1920, and continued to decrease thereafter. The procedural system had not changed markedly during these decades, but administrative improvements had been implemented. The Federal Rules brought no significant change. The slow decline continued until 1942, when the average was less than one year. After that, it rose still more slowly, hovering around one year until 1980.[52]

These suggestive figures do not establish that the Federal Rules had no impact on court delay: they might have counteracted other trends tending to increase or decrease delay.[53] Because the Rules led to a sharp drop in the percentage of cases going to trial,[54] they may have reduced delay for some cases by promoting pre-trial disposition while increasing it for others. The figures tell us nothing about cost, although it is hard to believe that much saving resulted from a system that radically expanded pre-trial discovery, and under which the sum of the parties' expenses and those of the court system comes close to the amount recovered.[55] The reforms may have been governed by a law of the conservation of complexity: simplifying pleading freed lawyers, judges, and scholars to elaborate other procedural devices.

Investigations focusing on just some of the Federal Rules innovations provide a bit more evidence for the counter-myth. William Glaser's study of pre-trial discovery found that cases in which discovery occurred were less likely to settle before trial, took longer from filing to disposition, and had longer trials than comparable cases without discovery, and that this occurred without increasing lawyers' and clients' satisfaction with the outcome.[56] That was in the 1960s, when there were fewer complaints of abusive discovery practices than there are today. During the same period, Maurice Rosenberg found that compulsory pre-trial conferences did not promote or speed settlement or reduce trial time, although they seemed to improve the quality of trials.[57]

Such studies and more recent experiences have left some scholars in the United States sufficiently sceptical to doubt the wisdom of frequent procedural

[52] D. S. Clark, 'Adjudication to Administration: A Statistical Analysis of Federal District Courts in the Twentieth Century' (1981) 55 S. Cal. L. Rev. 64. The median time to disposition has stayed relatively low since 1980, although there has been much concern over those cases that take much longer. C. E. Johnson, 'Rocket Dockets: Reducing Delay in Federal Civil Litigation' (1997) 85 Calif. L. Rev. 225.

[53] For this and other problems, see M. Rosenberg, 'The Federal Rules of Civil Procedure in Action: Assessing their Impact' (1989) 137 U. Pa. L. Rev. 2197.

[54] Yeazell, 'The Misunderstood Consequences of Modern Civil Process', at 632–9.

[55] D. M. Trubek *et al.*, 'The Cost of Ordinary Litigation' (1983) 31 UCLAL Rev. 72; see J. Kakalik *et al.*, *Variations in Asbestos Litigation Compensation and Expenses* (1984); A. Conard *et al.*, *Automobile Accident Costs and Payments* (1964).

[56] W. Glaser, *Pretrial Discovery and the Adversary System* (1968); see also Columbia University Project for Effective Justice, *Field Survey of Federal Pretrial Discovery* (1968).

[57] M. Rosenberg, *The Pretrial Conference and Effective Justice* (1964). See generally Symposium, Empirical Studies of Civil Procedure, 51 L. & Contemp. Probs. (summer and autumn 1988).

changes.[58] In the most recent incident, Congress enacted the Civil Justice Reform Act of 1990[59] to institute a massive trial of different judicial case management techniques in a number of district courts. Guess what. The changes had little effect on delay, cost, or attorney satisfaction, although they did raise the possibility that one package of measures—early case management, setting the trial schedule early, and cutting the time allowed for discovery— might save time without increasing expenses.[60] Meanwhile, Lord Woolf has proposed that England adopt case management techniques bearing some resemblance to those whose success in the United States has been so questionable.[61] So perhaps the Federal Rules and the managerial activism they fostered[62] have indeed been successful, if one views them from far enough away.

That leaves us with the Field Code and the English reforms, the effects of which remain virtually unstudied—although there are tantalizing hints that the Judicature Acts were followed by a rise in costs and a decline in filings.[63] In the United States, criticism of the Federal Rules system and its many recent supplements has become so intense in the scholarly world as to suggest that at any moment a movement to return to the Field Code might materialize. Of course, that will not happen, and even the most critical scholars are, in the last analysis, too attached to much of the Federal Rules system to propose a total overhaul. (Some alternative dispute resolution proponents, however, may be prepared to do so.) In any event, research on the effects of the Code and English systems would be of great scholarly interest, and perhaps even of practical importance.

5. IS IT ALL POINTLESS?

This essay may seem to carry the conservative message that no reform makes a difference. That is not my intention. I believe that many procedural changes do make many differences, some good and some bad.

---

[58] See S. B. Burbank, 'Ignorance and Procedural Law Reform: A Call for a Moratorium' (1993) 59 Brooklyn L. Rev. 841; L. Walker, 'Perfecting Federal Civil Rules: A Proposal for Restricted Field Experiments', 51 L. & Contemp. Probs. (summer and autumn 1988), at 67. For a guarded but more optimistic appraisal, see R. L. Marcus, 'Of Babies and Bathwater: The Prospects for Procedural Progress' (1993) 59 Brooklyn L. Rev. 761 (1993).   [59] 28 USC §§ 471–82.

[60] J. S. Kakalik *et al.*, *Just, Speedy, and Inexpensive? An Evaluation of Judicial Case Management under the Civil Justice Reform Act* (Federal Judicial Center, 1997); Symposium, Evaluation of the Civil Justice Reform Act (1997) 49 Ala. L. Rev. 1.

[61] *Access to Justice*, at 14–102; R. L. Marcus, '"*Déjà Vu* All Over Again"? An American Reaction to the Woolf Report', in A. A. S. Zuckerman and R. Cranston, *The Reform of Civil Procedure: Essays on 'Access to Justice'* (1995), 219.

[62] e.g. J. Resnik, 'Managerial Judges' (1982) 96 Harv. L. Rev. 376; R. L. Marcus, 'Malaise of the Litigation Superpower' in this volume.

[63] Brooks, *Lawyers, Litigation and English Society*, at 106, 108; Zuckerman, 'Lord Woolf's Access to Justice', at 779–80.

The point is that, without careful investigation, it is hard to tell what change will make what difference. Given the difficulty of prediction and the tendency of reformers to claim, and often to believe, that their favourite reforms will 'secure the just, speedy, and inexpensive determination of every action',[64] it is all too easy for the latter end of our commonwealth to forget the beginning. Those of us in the United States who have seen one trendy change succeed another during recent decades—attempts to reduce the diversity of local rules followed by directives for their proliferation,[65] harsh measures against baseless pleadings instituted and then diluted,[66] discovery limited while compulsory disclosure makes its debut,[67] class actions turned from a means to assert claims into a means to extinguish them[68]—find it hard to believe that all changes labelled 'reform' necessarily move in a desirable direction.[69] It would be nice to believe that these various changes constitute a series of experiments and that we are now learning from experience.

In the case about which I know most, I believe that the introduction of the Federal Rules of Civil Procedure probably did increase accuracy without fostering delay, although very likely at the cost of added expense. Increased accuracy was the goal of many of the rulemakers' innovations, notably expanded pre-trial discovery[70] and replacement of the pleadings by summary judgment as the main method of eliminating baseless claims and defences before trial.

The benefits of the Federal Rules were probably greatest for disputed cases affecting many parties in which crucial facts lie hidden in one party's files and complex equitable relief is appropriate. Although complex litigation of this sort had occurred previously,[71] the Federal Rules made it far more practicable. The modern civil rights or antitrust or environmental suit would be virtually inconceivable under the Field Code. It is no coincidence that, although some drafters of the Rules might have been distressed by such suits and their social con-

---

[64] Fed. R. Civ. P. 1. See P. Johnston, 'Problems in Raising Prayer to the Level of Rule: The Example of Federal Rule of Civil Procedure 1' (1995) 75 BUL Rev. 1325.

[65] P. D. Carrington, 'A New Confederacy? Disunionism in the Federal Courts' (1996) 45 Duke LJ 929.

[66] Compare the 1983 with the 1993 amendments to Fed. R. Civ. P. 11; C. Tobias, 'The 1993 Revision of Federal Rule 11' (1994) 70 Indiana LJ 171. In 1995, Congress reinstated some of the 1983 rule for securities fraud class actions. 15 USC §§ 77z-1 (a) (c), 78u-4 (a) (c).

[67] Symposium, Recent Changes in the Rules of Pretrial Fact Development (1994) 46 Fla. L. Rev. 1; T. E. Willging *et al.*, *Discovery and Disclosure Practice, Problems, and Proposals for Change* (Federal Judicial Center, 1997).

[68] J. C. Coffee, Jr., 'Class Wars: The Dilemma of the Mass Tort Class Action' (1997) 95 Colum. L. Rev. 1343; Symposium, Mass Tortes: Serving up Just Deserts (1995) 80 Cornell L. Rev. 811. But see *Amchem Products* v. *Windsor*, 117 S. Ct. 2231 (1997).

[69] Procedure, of course, is not the only arena in which many political groups have sought to wrest the banner labelled 'reform' from its former holders, as witness, for example, 'welfare reform' and 'tort reform'. See Alliance for Justice, *Justice for Sale: Shortchanging the Public Interest for Private Gain.*

[70] S. N. Subrin, 'Fishing Expeditions Allowed: The Historical Background of the 1938 Federal Discovery Rules' (1998) 39 BCL Rev. 691.

[71] T. E. Eisenberg and S. C. Yeazell, 'The Ordinary and the Extraordinary in Institutional Litigation' (1980) 93 Harv. L. Rev. 465.

sequences, the drafters were predominantly elite lawyers concerned with big cases. On the other hand, the Code (also drafted by an elite lawyer) may have been at least as cheap, quick, and accurate as the Rules in resolving the relatively small debt collection cases that were the bread and butter of the court system when the Code was written. Perhaps the rise of more complex tort litigation is what led to its demise.[72]

Ultimately, our judgement of a procedural system should go beyond its average speed, cheapness, and accuracy. We should think about what suits we want it to foster or discourage. We should think about how its procedures will affect litigants and others. We should recognize it as part of the governmental system, wielding powers that must be properly allocated and controlled. Very likely concerns such as these greatly influenced the creators of past and present procedural systems, however loudly they may have proclaimed their desire to make lawsuits cheaper, speedier, and more accurate. The most firmly implanted myth of procedural reform may be that we can talk usefully about it as simply an effort to increase judicial efficiency, without talking about our visions of procedural and social justice.

---

[72] Lord Woolf has proposed different procedures for cases involving small and large sums (*Access to Justice*). In the United States, scholars have questioned the Federal Rules ideal of transsubstantive procedure applicable to all kinds of cases, but so far the main deviations from that ideal have come from legislation implementing congressional hostility to securities fraud, prison reform, and other litigation. Leubsdorf, 'Class Actions at the Cloverleaf'.

Part II
Common Law Countries

3

Malaise of the Litigation Superpower

Richard L. Marcus

America is the litigation superpower, or at least it seems to think it is. It berates itself for having more lawyers, more laws, and more lawsuits than any other place on earth. As a consequence of this self-perception, over the last generation it has periodically flailed itself for these supposed national characteristics. A prime example of this sort of overstatement is a 1991 report by the President's Council on Competitiveness, headed by the Vice-President, declaring that the USA had 'become a litigious society' in which 'litigation necessarily exacts a terrible toll on the U.S. economy'.[1] In that recession-plagued time, the report cited an estimate that 'the average lawyer takes $1 million a year from the

The views expressed herein are entirely my own and do not reflect the views of any other person or organization. I owe a great debt to Faye Jones of the Hastings Law Library for helping me gather data and sources for this essay. I am also indebted to Karen Cannata and Kathleen Shih of the Judicial Council of California for assistance in obtaining and interpreting data on the California state courts. I am also indebted to Tom Willging of the Federal Judicial Center for assistance in identifying and locating statistical information on the federal court system. No doubt there are errors, particularly about numbers, but those are mine alone.

[1] *Agenda for Civil Justice Reform in America* (1991), 1.

country's output of goods and services'.[2] The report proceeded to forecast dire consequences for the US economy unless American litigation was changed a great deal, but no such dramatic changes have occurred. Given the current relative prosperity of the American economy, these rumblings of discontent seem almost quaint. In large measure, this sort of outburst reaction to civil litigation reflects an ideological attitude toward substantive outcomes perceived as unfair or inappropriate. It is not based on a careful evaluation of reliable information. But it is a real force in this country.

A related reaction is that American litigation is not only unduly protracted and expensive, but uniquely so. It may be that the readers of this volume will be able to come to some comparative judgment about the validity of that self-perception by comparing hard and soft data from the various essays our editors have collected. For present purposes it suffices to recognize that American judges have been preoccupied with these concerns long enough and pervasively enough to invite the parody depicted in the cartoon beginning this essay. Indeed, one might well call this the American century in terms of energetic tinkering with civil procedure to try to cope with issues of cost and delay.

The century began with the clarion call of Roscoe Pound, who in 1906 confronted a resistant and conservative American Bar Association with an attack on its smug acceptance of the shortcomings of American civil justice.[3] About a third of the way through the century, America embarked on the experiment of the Federal Rules of Civil Procedure, which embraced reduced reliance on pleadings to decide cases and broadened discovery to escape supposedly unjust and technical outcomes prevalent under the prior arrangement. Whether or not one accepts Professor Leubsdorf's suggestion that this description of procedural progress depicts a myth,[4] it does seem rather clear that the reformers had a genuine faith that they were making positive contributions.[5]

By the end of the second third of the century, that enthusiasm had begun to be supplanted by misgivings about what the reformers had wrought. Much of this concern depended on the sort of uneasiness about outcomes that under-girded the 1991 report of the Commission on Competitiveness. But a related strand of reforming thought focused directly on the topics of this collection— the cost and delay of civil litigation. Hence, for the last third of the century the

---

[2] See *Agenda for Civil Justice Reform in America* (1991), 1.

[3] Pound, 'The Causes of Popular Dissatisfaction with the Administration of Justice', 29 Rep. of the ABA 395 (1906). Contemporary reports indicate that those gathered in the hall were not entirely receptive to Pound's call for reform. Thirty years later, however, Dean Wigmore said that it 'struck the spark that kindled the white flame of high endeavor, now spreading through the entire legal profession'. Wigmore, 'Roscoe Pound's St. Paul Address of 1906', 20 J. Am. Jud. Soc. 176, 176 (1936). In 1976, Chief Justice Warren Burger called Pound's speech 'the first truly comprehensive critical analysis of American Justice'. Burger, 'Agenda for 2000 A.D.: A Need for Systemic Antici-pation', 70 FRD 83, 83 (1986).

[4] See Leubsdorf, 'The Myth of Civil Procedure Reform', in this volume.

[5] See, e.g., Resnik, 'Failing Faith', 53 U. Chi. L. Rev. 494 (1986).

general focus of innovation in American civil procedure has been on minimizing these two features of litigation. This process is ongoing, and it is a moving target imbued with the ideological freight that attends the simultaneous debate about litigation outcomes themselves.

The moving target of American reform to cope with cost and delay provides the backdrop for this essay. It begins with a basic primer on the relatively elaborate apparatus available for civil litigation in America, and follows that with a sampler of statistical information about American civil litigation. It then provides a somewhat more expansive historical overview of the procedural reform efforts of the past, focusing principally on the procedures used in the US federal courts, as a prelude to profiling problems of cost of delay and the legal retrenchment that has occurred in recent years. After separate consideration of case management, it closes with some reflections on prospects and portents.

1. THE AMERICAN LITIGATION MACHINE(S)

The USA is a big country, in terms of geographical size, population, and economy, so one might expect it to have a large litigation apparatus. But one would not necessarily anticipate the variety, intricacy, and superfluity of the American system simply by looking at the sort of size data just mentioned. From an early time, one could say that America was over-lawyered and over-judged.[6] But efficiency was not necessarily an important consideration, and there were certainly others that bulked large in creating the current array of litigation possibilities.

At a basic level, there is structural superfluity. At any location in this country, there exist parallel local and federal judicial systems. The federal court system consists of ninety-four district courts throughout the nation, superintended by twelve geographical and one specialized intermediate appellate courts[7] and ultimately overseen by one Supreme Court. Simultaneously, there is in each place in this country a set of local courts, usually state courts.[8] In that local court

---

[6] For example, in 1906 Pound used the following illustration: 'England and Wales, with a population in 1900 of 32,000,000, employ for their whole civil litigation ninety-five judges, that is, thirty-seven in the Supreme Court and House of Lords and fifty-eight county judges. Nebraska, with a population in 1900 of 1,066,000, employs for the same purpose one hundred and twenty-nine.' Pound, 'The Causes of Popular Dissatisfaction', at 414.

[7] The twelve geographical intermediate courts are organized by 'circuits' consisting of several states or, in one instance, of the District of Columbia. The subdivision of these circuits to create more circuits is occasionally done, and occasionally politically controversial. At this time, for example, Congress has directed the appointment of a commission to study whether to subdivide the Ninth Circuit, the largest, and report back to Congress by December 1998. The specialized court of appeals is the Court of Appeals for the Federal Circuit, which hears appeals from district courts around the country in patent and copyright matters.

[8] In the District of Columbia, the Commonwealth of Puerto Rico, and in Guam, the local court system is not a state court system. It is nevertheless separate from and parallel to the US district court in that location.

system there may be a variety of types of courts, but one will be a court of 'general jurisdiction'. Federal courts, by way of contrast, are courts of 'limited jurisdiction', in that they can only hear cases because the litigants come from different states and are accordingly of 'diverse citizenship',[9] or because the plaintiff's claim arises under federal law.[10]

There is a lot of federal law, but many more topics are not governed by federal law. As to those topics, state law controls, even in federal court.[11] Federal courts—even the United States Supreme Court—are in no position to decide that a state law is wrong.[12] To the contrary, state law is ultimately the exclusive preserve of state supreme courts, and they may diverge considerably in an array of topics. On occasion, those who are perturbed by this diversity of state treatments of similar questions may try to persuade Congress to impose a single legal rule,[13] but that is rare. As a consequence, there is in America a cacophony on a variety of issues central to civil litigation on which the judiciaries in most other countries speak with a single voice. Indeed, this circumstance is often touted as a virtue, providing the country with 'laboratories' to experiment with new legal regimes.

The significance of these arrangements for an appreciation of civil litigation in America is that litigants often can make choices about the legal regime under which their case will proceed, subject to relatively relaxed jurisdictional constraints. The country has a welter of choice of law rules to cope with these problems, also governed by state law (and hence differing from state to state) and also binding on the federal courts.[14] But the federal courts have their own procedural regime—the Federal Rules of Civil Procedure—to enliven the potential mix.

This plethora of litigation opportunities means that in high stakes litigation multiple and parallel efforts may occur, and that generalizations about simpler litigation are difficult. With that caveat, one can observe that generally American jurisdictions have a trial level court that affords litigants an extended opportunity to prepare for a single-event trial, after which a disappointed litigant may appeal to an intermediate appellate court and ask that the decision be reversed due to a mistake of the trial court judge. Under the 'final judgment'

---

[9] See 28 USC § 1332.   [10] See 28 USC § 1331.

[11] See *Erie RR Co. v. Tompkins*, 304 US 64 (1938) (requiring a federal court to follow state law unless valid federal law governs the point).

[12] A state law can be struck down as unconstitutional if its application violates a provision of the federal Constitution. In addition, Congress can invalidate state law by enacting provisions to govern a topic (called 'pre-emption'). Both the federal constitution and valid enactments of Congress must be applied in state court as well as federal court under the supremacy clause of the federal Constitution.

[13] A recent example is the effort to get Congress to pass national products liability legislation that would pre-empt state law and replace it with a single national standard. See below text accompanying n. 185.   [14] See *Klaxon Co. v. Stentor Elec. Manuf. Co.*, 313 US 487 (1941).

rule in place in most jurisdictions,[15] there is no opportunity for appeal until the proceedings are entirely done in the trial court. Moreover, under the 'harmless error' doctrine,[16] mistakes by the trial court are not a ground for reversal unless they caused a substantial harm. Accordingly, unlike some other systems, American cases are principally under the domination of the trial court, which is the only court that interacts with most litigated matters.[17] This circumstance is important in connection with efforts to energize these trial court judges to take active control of their cases to reduce cost and delay.

Most American litigation therefore stays in the trial court where it starts. If there is a ground for federal court jurisdiction and the plaintiff chooses to sue in federal court, the case will remain there and can be appealed only if it reaches final judgment. If there is no ground for suing in federal court, the case will usually remain in the state trial court until all trial court proceedings are finished.[18] Because most cases do not lead to a final judgment, they end where they start. Should the case lead to a final judgment, the loser has a right to one appeal to the intermediate appellate court of the judicial system in which the case was filed.[19] Thereafter, an unsatisfied litigant can usually ask the supreme court of that court system to review the case, but the decision whether to hear that appeal rests with the supreme court.[20] A litigant who has lost on a federal ground in a state court can, after exhausting all appeals through the state court system, ask the United States Supreme Court to review the resolution of that federal issue.[21]

Against this structural background, there is considerable similarity about how lawsuits are handled in the various American courts. The variations, and the issues that attend them, form the stuff of much American reform of this century.[22] For present purposes, however, a sketch should suffice.

The plaintiff initiates suit by filing a complaint alleging that the defendant has taken certain actions that provide a basis for relief in plaintiff's favour in court.[23] Ordinarily this means that the plaintiff accuses the defendant of

---

[15] e.g. 28 USC § 1291. There are some exceptions to this requirement for a final judgment before appeal in the federal system. See, e.g., 28 USC § 1292 (interlocutory appeals allowed for rulings on preliminary injunctions and in cases where the district judge certifies the order for immediate appeal); Fed. R. Civ. P. 23 (f) (new provision added in 1998 permitting immediate appeal to court of appeals of rulings granting or denying class action status). In addition, some states deviate more aggressively from the requirement of a final judgment as a prerequisite to appeal. See, e.g., Cal. Code Civ. Proc. § 418.10 (c) (requiring that a defendant who has objected to personal jurisdiction seek immediate review of a decision rejecting that objection or waive the personal jurisdiction issue).

[16] e.g. Fed. R. Civ. P. 61.

[17] For a theoretical contrast between this sort of arrangement—labelled the 'reactive' state—and an arrangement stressing more active direction from the appellate level, see M. Damaska, *Two Faces of Justice and State Authority* (1986).

[18] If the plaintiff files in state court but could have sued in federal court, the defendant can usually remove the case to federal court, and it will proceed there as though originally brought there. See 28 USC § 1441 (a).   [19] e.g. 28 USC § 1291.

[20] e.g. 28 USC § 1254.   [21] 28 USC § 1257.

[22] See below text accompanying nn. 88–102.   [23] See Fed. R. Civ. P. 3; 8 (a) (2).

committing some wrong specified in the complaint, although under some circumstances a potential litigant accused of a wrong can force the matter into court by suing for a declaratory judgment that its conduct has not been wrongful.[24] The responding party then has available a number of challenges to the court selected by the plaintiff—on the ground that suit was filed in a court lacking jurisdiction of the subject matter of the case,[25] or that it was filed in the wrong geographical location due to lack of personal jurisdiction[26] or improper venue.[27] In addition, the defendant can attack the suit on the merits by arguing that it should be dismissed because it fails to state a claim,[28] or that a demurrer should be sustained because the complaint fails to state a cause of action.[29] Failing to obtain dismissal, the defendant files an answer admitting or denying the allegations of the complaint and raising any matters of affirmative defence it claims apply.[30] If some of these grounds of defence are legally unjustified, the plaintiff may move to strike them,[31] and if the answer asserts no legally valid ground for defence on its face the plaintiff may move for judgment on the pleadings.[32] The defendant can also assert a counter-claim against the plaintiff,[33] and can bring in new parties as third party defendants under some circumstances.[34] Either such manœuvre permits the party named in the defendant's claim to react with motions, an answer, a counter-claim, or a third party claim of its own. Once the initial pleadings are completed, there is broad opportunity to amend, to add claims and parties not included initially.[35]

As this process is unfolding, the plaintiff may be able to obtain immediate relief under extraordinary circumstances by either seeking a preliminary injunction or asking the court to attach assets as security for the judgment the plaintiff hopes to obtain in the suit.[36] Before those remedies can be obtained, the defendant is usually given notice and an abbreviated opportunity to respond.[37]

Decisions on the pleadings occur only in a small proportion of cases, so there is ordinarily a period of discovery during which the parties are entitled to force each other and non-parties to divulge information that may have a bearing on the suit. At any time during this process, or even before it is under way, either

---

[24] See 28 USC §§ 2201; 2202.   [25] e.g. Fed. R. Civ. P. 12 (b) (1).

[26] e.g. Fed. R. Civ. P. 12 (b) (2). There is an extensive body of law on personal jurisdiction in America. State laws limit the reach of their courts' jurisdiction, and those limitations are generally applicable in federal court. See Fed. R. Civ. P. 4 (k) (1). In addition, the due process clause of the federal Constitution provides grounds for rejecting jurisdiction in some cases. Unless the defendant properly raises this objection, however, it is lost. See Fed. R. Civ. P. 12 (h) (1).

[27] See Fed. R. Civ. P. 12 (b) (3); cf. 28 USC § 1391.   [28] e.g. Fed. R. Civ. P. 12 (b) (6).

[29] e.g. Cal. Code Civ. Proc. § 430.10 (e).   [30] See Fed. R. Civ. P. 8 (b) and (c).

[31] Fed. R. Civ. P. 12 (f).   [32] Fed. R. Civ. P. 12 (c).   [33] Fed. R. Civ. P. 13.

[34] Fed. R. Civ. P. 14 (allowing defendant to assert third party claim for indemnity against non-party).

[35] See Fed. R. Civ. P. 15 (a) (leave to amend 'shall be freely given when justice so requires').

[36] See Fed. R. Civ. P. 64; 65.

[37] e.g. *Connecticut* v. *Doehr*, 501 US 1 (1991) (due process requirements for notice and a right to be heard before defendant's house is attached even though the attachment in no way interfered with his use of the house).

side can file a motion for summary judgment supported by evidentiary materials it claims show that it should be entitled to judgment.[38] Ordinarily this motion is filed by the party that will not have the burden of proof at trial, and usually it thrusts onto the other party the obligation to show it has enough evidence to justify holding a trial, but governing standards call for denying the motion unless there is no reasonable doubt about the proper outcome of a trial.[39]

Unless summary judgment entirely disposes of a case,[40] the only route for decision is trial. In most American courts, there is a constitutional right to trial by jury in suits for money,[41] but that can be lost if not asserted in the right way at the right time.[42] Whether or not there is a jury, the heart of the trial is presentation of evidence. Unlike some other countries, an American trial is usually a single continuous event, and American rules of evidence customarily require live testimony by available witnesses.[43] The parties have extensive power to subpoena witnesses to obtain their testimony at trial,[44] and witnesses often appear willingly even when beyond the subpoena power.

As will be reported below, trials are relatively infrequent events, and resolutions by judicial decision are also. Should a claimant obtain a judgment, however, that judgment is entitled to full faith and credit throughout the country[45] and can be enforced anywhere the defendant has assets by relatively simple procedures.[46] Flexible procedures also exist to assist the judgment creditor in enforcing the judgment, including discovery for that purpose.[47] In most jurisdictions, the judgment creditor can obtain a stay against enforcement of the judgment only by filing a motion and posting a bond.[48]

In sum, the American system of civil procedure affords both plaintiffs and defendants many opportunities to present their positions and aspires to a non-technical resolution of suits on their merits. As stated in Rule 1 of the Federal Rules of Civil Procedure, the courts aspire to provide 'the just speedy and inexpensive determination of every action'.

---

[38] See, e.g., Fed. R. Civ. P. 56.

[39] On occasion, the party opposing summary judgment can put off a decision on the ground that it needs more time to do investigation or discovery to gather evidence. See Fed. R. Civ. P. 56 (f).

[40] An important possibility is partial summary judgment, which may winnow a multi-claim case down to one or two claims. Cf. Fed. R. Civ. P. 56 (d).   [41] e.g. US Const., amend. VII.

[42] See Fed. R. Civ. P. 38 (b).

[43] For a discussion, see Marcus, 'Completing Equity's Conquest? The Future of Trial under the Federal Rules of Civil Procedure', 50 U. Pitt. L. Rev. 725 (1989).   [44] See Fed. R. Civ. P. 45.

[45] See 28 USC § 1738.   [46] See 28 USC § 1963.   [47] e.g. Fed. R. Civ. P. 69.

[48] e.g. Fed. R. Civ. P. 62 (d); cf. *Pennzoil Co. v. Texaco, Inc.*, 481 US 1 (1987) (federal court may not enjoin enforcement of state court judgment despite defendant's claim that it is unable to satisfy state court requirement of bond).

2. STAKING THE CLAIM TO SUPERPOWER STATUS:
A STATISTICAL PROFILE OF AMERICAN LITIGATION

In some ways, the American legal system is awash in data.[49] That, indeed, is part of the problem, for straight-line projections of numerical trends can be employed to support doomsday scenarios, as by the presidential commission cited at the beginning of this essay. Accordingly, one who presents such data, particularly profiling trends over time, risks contributing to the tenor of crisis. On another level, data collection and presentation presents a peculiar challenge in this country because its legal system is decentralized and diffuse, as outlined in the first section above. The federal and many or most of the state judicial systems have data collection efforts that annually have produced varying quantities of numerical information about their activities over recent decades.

One who seeks to convey these data must necessarily be selective, and to recognize that the data do not necessarily capture what the observer wants. This essay will attempt to provide some indication of the numerical features of American litigation, focusing largely on two legal systems that have considerable recent experience with civil justice reform—the federal courts and the courts of the state of California. Rather than using these numbers as springboards for prognosis, it intends only to indicate the breadth of American litigation and the consequent difficulty of generalization.[50]

The traditional starting point is the largest raw number, the number of civil actions commenced. This is the sort of information regularly cited by alarmists as evidence of impending doom.[51] At the national level, for 1993 state courts reported the filing of 14,600,000 civil actions (excluding domestic relations matters).[52] Broken down by state or locality, these data showed considerable variation in level of litigation. In raw numbers the range is from a high of

---

[49] For those anxious to go beyond published data, selective mining of some court-generated data can be done at http://teddy.law.cornell.edu:8090/questata.htm.

Published studies often announce that they offer unparalleled access to data. See, e.g., J. Goerdt, C. Lomvardias, and G. Gallas, *Reexamining the Pace of Litigation in 39 Urban Trial Courts* (1991), 1 ('this report presents the most broadly based analysis of the pace of litigation and its correlates that has ever been undertaken'); J. Kakalik, M. Selvin, and N. Pace, *Averting Gridlock: Strategies for Reducing Delay in the Los Angeles Superior Court* (1990), 6 (study is 'unique in its use of a wealth of empirical data combined in new ways'); J. Goerdt, *Examining Court Delay* (1989), 3 (the 'largest national database ever compiled regarding the pace of litigation in urban America'); M. Selvin and P. Ebener, *Managing the Unmanageable: A History of Civil Delay in the Los Angeles Superior Court* (1984), pp. iii–iv ('by far the largest store of evidence ever compiled on the history of delay in a major court').

[50] Throughout, and particularly with the statistics about the California state court system, there is a problem selecting the most suitable category for information on raw filings. For example, should family law actions be counted? An effort has been made to make sensible choices, but it may occasionally be true that the categories differ from one chart to another, so that these raw numbers do not seem to correspond. [51] e.g. *Agenda for Civil Justice Reform*, at 1.

[52] B. Ostrom and N. Kauder, *Examining the Work of State Courts* (1993), 11 (repr. 1995). The authors also note that this figure means that, as a matter of numbers, state courts handle 98 per cent of the country's civil litigation.

1,615,417 filings in California to a low of 15,305 in Montana.[53] In terms of filing rates, the range is from a high of 20,321 filings per 100,000 population to a low of 1,167 per 100,000 population.[54] Obviously it is difficult to generalize confidently about a nation with legal systems encompassing such a range simply in numerical terms.

For the two jurisdictions upon which we focus, a breakdown over time seems useful to provide some sense of numerical growth. Thus, the civil filings in the federal court system and the California courts over time have grown as shown in Table 3.1. Although the numbers permit some assessment of an order of magnitude, they must be approached cautiously, for equally important is the mix of cases. In California, for example, a study of the largest court, the Superior Court of Los Angeles, found that the mix of cases changed greatly from the beginning of this century, when it was mainly contract cases, to the 1970s, when it was mainly personal injury cases.[55] In the federal court system, the civil docket of the 1930s involved a very different mix of cases, also emphasizing contract actions, from the docket of the 1990s, in which the largest category in terms of raw filings consists of prisoner and civil rights suits.[56]

The number of judges is also large and growing. Nationwide, the state courts had in 1995 8,848 judges of courts of general jurisdiction.[57] In total general jurisdiction trial level judges, this ranged from 881 in Illinois to 16 in Maine.[58] In number of such judges per 100,000 population, it ranged from 10.21 in the District of Columbia to 1.10 in South Carolina.[59] For purposes of a general feel of the dimensions, the data in Table 3.2 are useful. These data must also be viewed with care, for the category 'judge' can be expanded, and has been expanded. In the federal system, Congress in 1968 added magistrate judges, who numbered 495 in 1995 and disposed that year of 511,039 'matters',[60] exercising lesser powers than life-tenured district judges.[61] There were also 326

---

[53] Note that these figures evidently include actions in California municipal courts, which are not included in the figures below on growth of filings in California superior courts.

[54] B. Ostrom and Kauder, *Examining the Work of State Courts*, at 12. The highest filing rate was in the District of Columbia, the nation's capital. The lowest was in the state of Tennessee. If it is of interest, the number of filings and rate per 100,000 population for the highest and lowest rates of filing are as shown in App. 3.1.

[55] Selvin and Ebener, *Managing the Unmanageable*, at 14. The authors note that this shift reflects 'relatively consistent patterns of litigation' noted by many such studies.

[56] In 1960, prisoner and civil rights cases were 3.1 per cent of filings in the district courts. R. Posner, *The Federal Courts: Challenge and Reform* (2nd edn. 1996), 57. In 1995, these categories had grown to 34.7 per cent of district court filings. Ibid. at 60–1.

[57] Ostrom and Kauder, *Examining the Work of State Courts*, at 7.   [58] Ibid.

[59] Ibid. See also App. 3.2 for a listing of the five jurisdictions in the highest and lowest numbers of judges per 100,000 population.

[60] *Long Range Plan for the Federal Courts*, table 1. As set forth in that table, the breakdown for these judicial officers and their work is shown in App. 3.3. The Third Circuit summed up the view of many judges in 1989: 'Given the bloated dockets that district courts have now come to expect as ordinary, the role of the magistrate in today's federal judicial system is nothing less than indispensable.' *Government of the Virgin Islands* v. *Williams*, 892 F. 2d 305, 308 (3d Cir. 1989), cert. denied, 495 US 949 (1990).   [61] See 28 USC § 636 (detailing powers of magistrate judges).

Table 3.1. *Number of civil filings, federal and California court systems*

Year	Federal system	California superior courts
1995	239,013	852,722
1990	217,879	669,722
1980	168,789	532,550
1970	87,321	150,638
1960	59,284	96,154
1950	54,622	46,935
1940	34,734	32,337

Sources: Judicial Conference of the United States, *Long Range Plan for the Federal Courts* (1995), table 3; Judicial Council of California, Reports, 1940–95.

Table 3.2. *Number of judges, federal and California court systems*

Year	Federal district judges	Federal appellate judges	California trial judges	California appellate judges
1995	649	167	789	88
1990	575	156	789	88
1980	516	132	487	59
1970	401	97	416	48
1960	245	68	302	21
1950	224	65	203	21
1940	191	57	162	18

Sources: *Long Range Plan for the Federal Courts*, table 6; California Judicial Council Reports, 1940–97; K. Arnold, *California Courts and Judges: Analysis* (7th edn. 1997), ii. 13–14.

federal bankruptcy judges in 1995, presiding over a system that had 939,935 filings and 962,333 terminations in 1993.[62] In the California system, there are also 'court commissioners' who preside over certain matters such as discovery disputes. At the same time, there have been trends that reduce the total number of judges by excluding persons previously included. Fifty years ago, for example, California had a significant number of officials know as 'justices of the peace', often people without formal legal training. In the 1970s, these positions were eliminated and the responsibilities shifted to judges with legal training.

Nationally, the number of lawyers is large and growing, as illustrated by

---

[62] *Federal Judicial Workload Statistics* (1993), 5–7.

Table 3.3. A similar trend exists for the state of California.[63] The status 'lawyer' may mean quite different things in different countries. In the USA, rules regarding unauthorized practice of law are applied with some rigour to those providing services that may, in other countries, be done by people not called lawyers. For example, much drafting and debt collection and other out-of-court activity that may be done by non-lawyers elsewhere must be done by attorneys in the USA.[64] As a consequence, it is hardly true that all American lawyers spend the bulk of their time on litigation; the subcategory 'litigator' is the name for those who work on court cases. This category comprises a large proportion of all lawyers,[65] and a growing one.

Providing concrete information about what these lawyers and judges do with these cases is more difficult than providing raw numbers of filings. One thing that can be said with confidence is that most civil cases do not actually go to trial. In twenty-seven states for which 1993 data were reported, the rate of jury trials averaged 1.2 per cent as a percentage of dispositions, ranging from 5.8 per cent (South Dakota) to 0.3 per cent (District of Columbia and Kansas).[66] The rate of court trials averaged 6.4 per cent and varied from 19.2 per cent (Indiana) to 0.2 per cent (District of Columbia).[67] In general, it is thought that the frequency of trial has been falling[68] as illustrated by Table 3.4 showing the percentage of cases that go to trial in the federal system.[69]

The decline in the trial rate in federal courts over the past half century may not be so pronounced as it seems if one takes into account the substantial number of filings in recent years in categories in which a trial would be very unlikely to occur. Prisoner cases, for example, have come to constitute a substantial proportion of all civil filings, but almost never go to trial. If one excluded all categories of cases in which trials are extremely unlikely, the trend

---

[63] Active membership in the state bar of California has grown as shown in App. 3.4.

[64] For a description of the increasingly broad monopoly of lawyers in America effected by restrictions on 'unauthorized practice of law' in the last century, see C. Wolfram, *Modern Legal Ethics* (1986), § 15.1.1.

[65] In the American Bar Association, for example, the Section of Litigation is the largest section with 60,000 members, nearly twice as large as the next largest section. This number is more useful as a measure of the relative importance of litigation than as a measure of the number of litigators in the country. Membership in the ABA, much less the section, is far from universal, and it is wise to recognize that the proportion of all litigators who belong to the Section of Litigation is relatively small.   [66] Ostrom and Kauder, *Examining the Work of State Courts*, at 14.

[67] Ibid.

[68] Yeazell, 'The Misunderstood Consequences of Modern Civil Process', 1994 Wis. L. Rev. 631, 633 (in 1990, only 4.3% of civil cases filed in federal court resulted in trials, a decline of almost 80% in rate of trial from the pre-1938 period); Galanter and Cahill, ' "Most Cases Settle": Judicial Promotion and Regulation of Settlements', 46 Stan. L. Rev. 1339, 1342 (1994) (asserting that percentage of cases that reached trial declined from 11% in 1961 to 4% in 1991).

[69] Based on information found in table C-5 of the Annual Report of the Director, Administrative Office of the United States Courts, 1970–97. For 1950 and 1960, the information is taken from tables C-2 and C-5 providing the totals for eighty-six districts (not including the District of Columbia and territorial courts). For similar data on the rate of trial in the California state courts, see Table 3.5 and App. 3.5.

Table 3.3. *Number of lawyers in the USA, and ratio of lawyers to population*

Year	No. of lawyers	Population/lawyer ratio
2000	1,005,842	267/1
1995	896,172	290/1
1988	723,189	340/1
1980	542,205	403/1
1971	355,242	418/1
1960	285,933	627/1
1951	221,605	695/1

Source: From B. Curran and C. Carson, *The Lawyer Statistical Report: The Legal Profession in the 1990s* (1996), 1.

Table 3.4. *Number of trials as a percentage of total civil filings in federal court system*

Year	Total cases	No. of trials	% tried
1997	187,185	6,235	3.33
1990	173,834	8,158	4.69
1980	133,394	9,490	7.11
1970	80,598	7,791	10.35
1960	48,625	4,979	10.23
1950	54,240	5,020	9.26

Source: See n. 69.

might not be so pronounced, although one would have to do the same thing with the figures for earlier eras as with recent figures.[70]

Although the great bulk of cases do not go to trial, it would be misleading to say that the remainder are 'settled'. A 1990 study by RAND showed that in Los Angeles Superior Court some 60 per cent of civil cases settled.[71] There is no ready method for counting such cases from the records kept by most courts, except by some sort of elimination, and even that is uncertain since a case listed as decided in official data might be settled after judgment in return for willingness to forgo an appeal. Some proportion of the cases are simply abandoned. According to 1993 data on fifteen states, the default rate averaged 31.3 per cent

---

[70] Note that the figures for frequency of trial in the California state courts found in App. 3.5 vary substantially by case type.   [71] Kakalik, Selvin, and Pace, *Averting Gridlock*, at 27.

of all dispositions and varied from 4.1 per cent (Virginia) to 50 per cent (Nebraska).[72] Another category may be dismissed on non-merits grounds such as lack of jurisdiction.

The number of federal court cases that are resolved on the merits through judicial action short of trial is not reliably available, but probably considerably exceeds the number resolved by trial. Although the US Supreme Court has on occasion made it appear impossible to obtain a dismissal on the pleadings,[73] in fact it appears that dismissals are obtained in some 3 per cent to 6 per cent of cases.[74] To this number must be added a considerable (but unobtainable) number of cases in which pleadings motions resolve important claims or issues but not the entire case. Summary judgment dispositions are similarly difficult to pin down in the federal system. For a long time district judges supposedly feared that granting summary judgment was an invitation to reversal, but in 1986 the Supreme Court appeared to invite broader use of summary judgment.[75] Since then, the number of grants of summary judgment in the federal system has almost certainly increased, and their fate on appeal has improved.[76] As with dismissals, this number would include cases only partially adjudicated on summary judgment and thereafter settled. In sum, although the great bulk of civil filings do not lead to a judgment on the merits, the trial rate is only a small proportion of all cases strongly affected or resolved by judicial decision.

In the California state court system, the attitude toward summary judgment

---

[72] Ostrom and Kauder, *Examining the Work of State Courts*, at 15.

[73] See *Conley v. Gibson*, 355 US 41, 45–6 (1957) (complaint should not be dismissed for failure to state a claim 'unless it appears beyond doubt that the plaintiff can prove no set of facts in support of his claim that would entitle him to relief').

[74] See Willging, 'Use of Rule 12 (b) (6) in *Two Federal District Courts* (1989), 5–8 (describing a 1975 study showing a 6% dismissal rate and a 1988 study showing a 3% rate); C. Wright, *Law of Federal Courts* (5th edn. 1994), 462 (citing 1962 study showing dismissals in fewer than 2% of all filed cases). A 1998 article by Judge Patricia Wald reports that in 1996 42% of the terminations in the district court of the District of Columbia were by dismissal. Wald, 'Summary Judgment', at 60, 76 Texas L. Rev. 1897, 1915 (1998).

[75] *Celotex Corp. v. Catrett*, 477 US 317, 327 (1986) ('Summary judgment procedure is properly regarded not as a disfavored procedural shortcut, but rather as an integral part of the Federal Rules as a whole').

[76] See W. Schwarzer, A. Hirsch, and D. Barrans, *The Analysis and Decision of Summary Judgment Motions* (1995), 4 n. 13 ('Statistical analysis indicates that the rate of affirmance of summary judgments is similar to the overall rate of affirmance in civil cases'). A 1995 study by the Federal Judicial Center regarding another rule, for example, noted that some 15% of the cases in the sample used were disposed of by a motion for summary judgment. J. Shapard, *Likely Consequences of Amendments to Rule 68, Federal Rules of Civil Procedure* (1995), 4. In 1996–7, 22% of the terminations in the district court of the District of Columbia were by summary judgment. Wald, 'Summary Judgment', at 1915. Judge Wald summarized the situation as follows: 'What almost everyone in the academic and legal communities agreed on was that the Supreme Court had moved summary judgment out of left field and onto first base, where it began shortening the innings by taking out runners before they could even begin to make the rounds. From 1986 to the present, summary judgment has remained on first base and, some would say, it is getting progressively better at tagging runners out.' Ibid., at 1914–15.

has officially followed the US Supreme Court.[77] Nevertheless, summary judgment appears still to be very rare compared to trial and other grounds for disposition of cases, as demonstrated by Table 3.5. These numbers do not directly connect, in that cases tried in 1994–5 were almost certainly not filed during that same year, but the raw numbers should give a good sense of the relative importance of different types of judicial action in terminating cases. A more detailed breakdown by types of cases is provided in Appendix 3.5.

Although an appeal usually cannot be taken until final judgment is entered, the number of appeals has been rising. In 1990, the Federal Courts Study Committee characterized this circumstance in the federal system as an 'appellate caseload crisis'[78] based on the very considerable growth in number of appeals.[79] As tabulated in 1995, total appeals in the federal system were as shown in Table 3.6.

Explaining this growth in appellate caseload has proved somewhat controversial. The Federal Courts Study Committee posited a generalized increase in likelihood to appeal in civil cases.[80] But a 1995 study by the Federal Judicial Center found that conclusion over-broad.[81] This study recognized that 'the true rate of appeal cannot be determined',[82] but using estimates found that for most types of cases the rate of appeal had not changed significantly in the period 1977–92. Excluding prisoner cases and three other categories of cases, the study found that the rate of appeal held steady through the period 1977–93 at around 9 per cent.[83]

In prisoner cases, however, there was a very considerable rise in the estimated rate of appeals; for prisoner civil rights cases that rate rose from 8 per cent in 1977 to 20.5 per cent in 1987, and in other prisoner suits the rate rose from 13.99 per cent to 26.98 per cent in the same decade.[84] During the same period, prisoner civil rights cases had come to constitute a larger proportion of the district courts' dockets,[85] so this development had a sort of double whammy effect on the appellate courts because of the great increase in the rate of appeals in these cases.

Despite the increased caseloads, the federal appellate courts seem to have managed to dispose of their cases with some dispatch. During the 1990s, the median time from filing of notice of appeal to disposition by the appellate court

---

[77] See *Union Bank* v. *Superior Court*, 31 Cal. App. 4th 573, 590 (1995) (holding that the practice under the California summary judgment provision should essentially be the same as under *Celotex Corp.* v. *Catrett*, 477 US 317 (1986)).   [78] *Report of the Federal Courts Study Committee* (1990), 109.

[79] Ibid., at 109–10. As compiled by that committee, the rate of appealing in all cases (not just civil cases) was on the rise (see App. 3.6).   [80] *Long Range Plan for the Federal Courts*, table 4.

[81] C. Krafka, J. Cecil, and P. Lombard, *Stalking the Increase in the Rate of Federal Civil Appeals* (1995).

[82] Ibid., at 4. The problem is that although the number of notices of appeal can be determined with accuracy, the number of appealable orders cannot. The study instead relied on estimates of the number of appealable orders to derive estimated rates of appeal.

[83] Ibid., at 29, fig. 8. The other types of cases excluded were non-prisoner civil rights cases, social security appeals, and government benefit repayment cases.

[84] Ibid., at 10, table 3. The report also singled out non-prisoner civil rights cases, but the change in rate of appeals for these was not so substantial.   [85] See ibid., table 2.

Table 3.5. *Number of civil filings, dismissals for lack of prosecution, summary judgments, and trials in California court system*

Year	Filings	Dismissals for lack of prosecution	Summary judgments granted	Trials
1994–5	203,710	20,418	1,575	25,785
1989–90	225,468	35,545	1,756	16,007
1984–5	235,719	25,231	2,033	19,446
1979–80	175,080	6,450	1,445	21,127

Source: Based on unpublished data provided by the Judicial Council of California, for which I am indebted.

Table 3.6. *Number of appeals in federal court system*

Year	Total appeals	Criminal appeals	Prisoner appeals	Other appeals
1995	49,671	10,023	14,488	25,160
1990	40,898	9,493	9,941	21,464
1980	23,200	4,405	3,675	15,120
1970	11,662	2,660	2,440	6,562
1960	3,899	623	290	2,986
1950	2,830	308	286	2,236
1940	3,505	260	65	3,180

Source: *Long Range Plane for the Federal Courts*, table 4, p. 15.

has been around eleven months,[86] a reasonable figure given that a substantial part of it is occupied preparing the record on appeal and the briefs. One can cavil, however, about some of the short cuts the appellate courts have used to keep up with their increased workload—particularly the unpublished decision.[87]

3. US STRATEGIES FOR COPING WITH LITIGATION PRIMACY: AMERICAN CIVIL JUSTICE REFORM IN THE TWENTIETH CENTURY

This century has involved waves of reform of American civil litigation that were introduced at the outset, and now can be explored in somewhat more detail. Of

[86] See App. 3.7.

[87] For critical commentary on this practice, see Robel, 'The Myth of the Disposable Opinion: Unpublished Opinions and Government Litigants in the United States Courts of Appeals', 87 Mich. L. Rev. 946 (1987); Reynolds and Richman, 'An Evaluation of Limited Publication in the United States Court of Appeals: The Price of Reform', 48 U. Chi. L. Rev. 573 (1981); Reynolds and Richman, 'The Non-precedential Precedent: Limited Publication and No-Citation Rules in United States Courts of Appeals', 78 Colum. L. Rev. 1167 (1978).

necessity, however, this overview can only scratch the surface of a complicated series of developments. In a legal system as intricate as this one, all generalizations will misdescribe some circumstances. To some extent, the trends described below counteract one another. Ultimately, they offer a background for the case management movement that is the subject of the next section.

3.1. The open access tradition

Perhaps the most confident impulse, and the one that flowed from Pound's exhortations, was to remove impediments to resolution on the merits. Pound's evidence of failings in the American system centred on the tendency to decide cases on matters of pleading or procedure.[88] Whether or not his characterization of existing circumstances was accurate,[89] it had powerful supporters. One mid-century American observer posited 'rigidity to flexibility as a law of procedural progress': '[W]ith increasing stability of the courts and growing confidence in their justice, judicial discretion becomes by degrees a surrogate of the old supremacy of form, and there is progression from rigidity to flexibility in the rules of procedure.'[90] Certainly this impulse animated the framers of the Federal Rules of Civil Procedure. As Professor Subrin demonstrated a decade ago, the orientation of those rules was toward the relaxed aspiration of equity for perfect justice, and away from the more rigid and confining ways of the common law tradition.[91] This orientation had at least three pertinent features.

First, it relaxed the limitations on who could become a party to a lawsuit, which had formerly seemed on occasion unduly rigid. As eventually established by 1966 amendments to the rules, the orientation eschewed legal categorizations and became essentially functionalist.[92] This orientation coincided with pressures on the limitations on standing to sue[93] and generally facilitated what came to be known as 'public law' litigations asserting constitutional or related claims.[94] In some ways, it received its highest expression in the 1966 amendment to the class action rule,[95] which allowed actions on behalf of large

---

[88] See Pound, 'The Causes of Popular Dissatisfaction', at 405–6, 410–11.

[89] Consider the questions raised in Prof. Leubsdorf's contribution to this collection ('The Myth of Civil Procedure Reform') on this point.

[90] R. Millar, *Civil Procedure in the Trial Court in Historical Context* (1952), 5–6.

[91] Subrin, 'How Equity Conquered Common Law: The Federal Rules of Civil Procedure in Historical Perspective', 135 U. Pa. L. Rev. 909 (1987).

[92] e.g. Fed. R. Civ. P. 20 (allowing joinder of all whose claims arise out of 'the same transaction, occurrence, or series of transactions or occurrences').

[93] For a discussion, see Chayes, 'Foreword: Public Law Litigation and the Burger Court', 96 Harv. L. Rev. 4 (1982).

[94] The classic description of this phenomenon is Chayes, 'The Role of the Judge in Public Law Litigation', 89 Harv. L. Rev. 1281 (1976). Somewhat carried away by the significance of the developments he was describing, Chayes urged that '[p]erhaps the dominating characteristic of modern federal litigation is that lawsuits do not arise out of disputes between private parties about private rights. Instead, the object of the litigation is the vindication of constitutional or statutory policies.' Ibid., at 1284.   [95] Fed. R. Civ. P. 23.

numbers of people whose claims arose out of similar circumstances. In the 1970s, these devices were used with some frequency to challenge large institutions, often governmental, on grounds of discrimination or unsafe conditions. In the 1990s, these devices have been employed to 'settle' large numbers of personal injury and other product liability claims. Altogether, public law litigation appeared to represent a more vigorous presence of litigation than had characterized earlier eras in American history.[96]

The second change was in the area of pleading. Eschewing the common law pleading strictures and a body of law under code pleading that was regarded as restrictive, the Federal Rules sought to curtail scrutiny of cases at the pleading stage.[97] In part, this was viewed as a way to save time, as sustained demurrers were regarded as pyrrhic victories that simply delayed proceeding to the merits of the case. Beyond that, it was intended to prevent frustration of meritorious claims by undue emphasis on pleading niceties. Altogether, it contributed to an attitude that plaintiffs could not be successfully defeated at the pleading stage. There was a debate about the extent to which a plaintiff was officially authorized to file a suit based upon a suspicion (rather than proof) of wrongdoing.

For present purposes, however, the most important development was the third—a 'discovery revolution'.[98] Although borrowing aspects of discovery practices that obtained elsewhere, the framers of the federal rules fashioned a package of unprecedented breadth and flexibility. As expanded by amendments culminating in 1970, these rules allowed very great latitude to parties seeking to unearth information. Interrogatories and document requests could be directed to all parties, and depositions could be scheduled by a simple notice, with a subpoena to the witness if not a party.

The reason for canvassing these developments is that they could be seen to establish a benchmark for access to the courts consistent with what I have previously called the 'liberal ethos'.[99] As an idealized vision, these rules' reluctance to cut off claims early and emphasis on exhuming all possibly pertinent information seem perfectly calculated to ensure access to the courts. To a greater or lesser extent, the states moved in the same general direction; many of them adopted rules modelled on the Federal Rules.[100] It has even been urged that these rules also have shaped the substantive law.[101] At least,

---

[96] But see Eisenberg and Yeazell, 'The Ordinary and the Extraordinary in Institutional Litigation', 93 Harv. L. Rev. 465 (1980) (arguing that older English cases offered parallels to contemporary American litigation).

[97] See generally Marcus, 'The Revival of Fact Pleading under the Federal Rules of Civil Procedure', 86 Colum. L. Rev. 433 (1986).

[98] Subrin, 'Fishing Expeditions Allowed: The Historical Background of the 1938 Federal Discovery Rules', 39 Bos. Col. L. Rev. 691 (1998).

[99] See Marcus, 'The Revival of Fact Pleading'.

[100] See generally Oakley and Coon, 'The Federal Rules in State Court: A Survey of State Court Systems of Civil Procedure', 61 Wash. L. Rev. 1367 (1986).

[101] See Friedenthal, 'A Divided Supreme Court Adopts Discovery Amendment to the Federal Rules of Civil Procedure', 69 Calif. L. Rev. 806, 818 (1981): '[O]ver the years developments in areas

they underwrote the private enforcement of law that is a hallmark of the American legal scene.[102]

We turn next to issues of delay and cost, which might dim the rosy picture presented in the idealized vision, and then to efforts to recalibrate that vision in light of those concerns. Although these strands may be analytically separate, they are closely related in the public and political reality of America.

3.2. Justice delayed

In the eyes of many, '[d]elay is the most significant single problem affecting the civil justice system'.[103] The American Bar Association adopted goals for reduction of civil litigation delay in 1984—that 90 per cent of all cases be completed within one year and that all be cleared within two.[104] As somewhat detailed below, there has been effort to achieve this objective. But it is useful to explore reasons for doubting that 'delay' should be viewed as the bogeyman of procedure. Much as it has a pejorative sound, the term has no inherent content. Compare a university that operates on a system using nine-week quarters with one using fourteen-week semesters. Does the latter inflict 'delay' on its students because each course takes half as long again to complete according to the calendar? So long as each offers basically the same number of hours of instruc-

---

such as products liability, employment discrimination, and consumer protection have been the result at least partly of broad-ranging discovery provisions. For example, lawyers would not have pushed in the courts and in the legislatures for expanded causes of action hinged on proof that defendants knew or should have known of a product's danger, if such proof were normally unavailable. The ability of plaintiff attorneys to obtain a corporate defendant's records, to depose corporate employees, and to send searching interrogatories has had a substantial impact on particular areas of law, and is one important factor in the dramatic increase in cases filed.' For cautious questioning of some of these conclusions, see Marcus, 'Discovery Containment Redux', 39 Bos. Col. L. Rev. 747, 749–53 (1998).

[102] See Higginbotham, 'Foreword to Symposium on Evaluation of the Civil Justice Reform Act', 49 Ala. L. Rev. 1, 4–5 (1997): 'The revolution in procedure wrought by the changes of the 1938 rules has served us well for an extraordinary period of time. Over the years access to the power federal engine of discovery has become central to a wide array of social policies. Congress has elected to use the private suit, private attorneys general as an enforcing mechanism for the anti-trust laws, the securities laws, environmental laws, civil rights and more. In the main, the plaintiff in these suits must discover his evidence from the defendant. Calibration of discovery is calibration of the level of enforcement of the social policy set by Congress.'

[103] American Bar Association, *Defeating Delay: Developing and Implementing a Court Delay Reduction Program* (1986), 1.

[104] These standards were developed by the National Conference of State Trial Judges and adopted by the ABA House of Delegates at its 1984 annual meeting. Ibid., at 2–3. Section 2.52 of the standards provides as follows for general civil cases: '90% of all civil cases should be settled, tried or otherwise concluded within 12 months of the date of case filing; 98% within 18 months of such filing; and the remainder within 24 months of such filing except for individual cases in which the Court determines exceptional circumstances exist and for which a continuing review should occur.' Ibid., at 179.

tion, the question is not 'delay' but whether the learning process is facilitated by a more compressed coverage of that number of class hours.[105]

Courts are not universities, but a similar difficulty exists in considering delay in litigation. At the pre-trial phase, one confronts a welter of statutes of limitation, indicating that a claim is not considered 'delayed' if it is not filed for some time, often several years. Once suit is filed, the American system is designed to require considerable pre-trial activity. The plaintiff is not required to have the evidence in hand on filing suit, nor to provide the defendant with a precise description of the circumstances on which the claim is based. Broad discovery would seem by definition to take some time, and it may yield information prompting a reformulation of the suit and the addition of new parties. Of itself, then, the passage of some time is not necessarily a bad thing.[106]

There may even be senses in which delay is a good thing. Should the suit relate to circumstances that are in a state of flux—such as the medical consequences of plaintiff's injury—there may be reasons to prefer deferring final resolution. Moreover, somewhat counter-intuitively, there is reason to think that those parties most likely to be upset about delay—personal injury plaintiffs—do not attach great importance to it.[107] Surely there is some truth to the old saw that the defendant is always willing to put off the day of judgment. Systemically, it might be said that delay could have advantages in fostering settlement.

Balanced against these considerations are very real issues about frustrating the ability of litigants anxious to obtain decisions because there is no opportunity in

---

[105] Posner made a similar point when he was a law professor: 'Thus far we have assumed, with the judicial administrators, that court delay is a bad thing and should be the focus of attention by court reformers. In fact delay is an omnipresent feature of social and economic life; in the judicial system as in the restaurant industry, it would be surprising indeed if the optimal amount of delay were zero. Since court delay does not involve the same costs as waiting in line for a table at a restaurant . . . and since some interval is necessary to prepare a case and defense thereto, some delay must be optimal; on the other hand long delays may be highly inefficient. . . . And the costs of delay must not only be measured, but also balanced against the costs of shortening the court queue.' R. Posner, *Economic Analysis of Law* (2nd edn., 1977), § 21.10, at 456. This point seems to have been dropped from the third and fourth editions of this book, published after Posner became a judge.

[106] Those who gather data on delay sometimes acknowledge this point: 'Although much has already been written about the pace of litigation, it is important to reiterate the distinction between "delay" and the "pace" of litigation. "Pace" is simply the time it takes to proceed from the filing of a complaint to the issuance of a verdict or judgment. At the court level, which is the focus of this study, the pace of civil litigation is measured by the median court. . . . "Delay," however, is case-specific; it is any time beyond that which is reasonable for obtaining a just resolution of a case. Naturally, what constitutes delay is determined by the nature of a particular case. At the aggregate or court level, however, the ABA disposition time standards provide a useful and widely accepted tool with which to determine the degree to which courts are concluding civil cases within a reasonable time period.' Goert, Lomvardias, and Gallas, *Reexamining the Pace of Litigation*, at 36.

[107] See E. Lind, R. MacCoun, P. Ebener, W. Felsteiner, D. Hensler, J. Resnik, and T. Tyler, *The Perception of Justice: Tort Litigants' Views of Trial, Court-Annexed Arbitration and Judicial Settlement Conferences* (1989), 77: 'Case delay did affect the litigants' attitudes, but what mattered was not the absolute delay but rather the litigants' personal evaluations of whether the delay was reasonable. Further, the litigants' evaluations of delay showed no relationship to the actual duration of the case. Apparently some delays seem reasonable to litigants while others do not.'

an overcrowded court to obtain one. Certainly there are instances in which this is true. For example, Los Angeles Superior Court has on occasion delayed parties ready for trial as long as five years,[108] a circumstance that even prompted the Los Angeles Bar Association to sue the state of California in federal court claiming that underfunding of the court caused the delay and deprived litigants of their constitutional rights.[109] It may be that the ABA guidelines, as a generalization, accurately capture what should customarily be sufficient for the completion of all cases, but it need not be true that exceeding them represents a serious deficiency.

Even clamour about delay from litigants may not be compelling evidence that the problem is serious. In an in-depth 1984 study of Los Angeles Superior Court, RAND researchers were somewhat bemused to find that there had been vociferous lobbying to curtail 'delay' in the early 1930s, when it rose to a six-month wait for trial.[110] From the perspective of delay in the 1980s, of course, that figure excites envy, although it is true that the time to trial in Los Angeles Superior Court dropped to one month in the mid-1930s. Absent extreme circumstances like the five-year lag time afflicting Los Angeles in the 1980s, it is uncertain how much weight to attach to such durational figures.

More to the point, there is at least considerable uncertainty about why delays occur, and some likely candidates are not necessarily the offenders. The above study of Los Angeles Superior Court noted, for example, that although logic would indicate that a rising civil caseload would correlate to increased delay, from 1970 to 1982 the caseload per judge fell while the delay to trial sky-rocketed.[111] A 1978 study of an array of courts suggested that 'local legal culture' was a primary source of differences in the pace of litigation.[112] Others have found it similarly difficult to be precise on causes or cures for delay.

A 1991 study of thirty-nine urban state trial courts, for example, found very considerable differences among them in the degree to which they approached satisfying the ABA standards regarding delay. None had met either standard, but some were close. In twelve of the courts, at least 90 per cent of cases were concluded within two years of filing, and in one of those only 1 per cent of cases were two years old.[113] On the other hand, in three courts more than 50 per cent of cases lasted over two years, and in one of those 96 per cent of cases lasted more than one year.[114] Overall, comparing these courts yielded some insights

---

[108] Kakalik, Selvin, and Pace, *Averting Gridlock*, at 12.

[109] *Los Angeles County Bar Ass'n v. Eu*, 979 F. 2d 697 (9th Cir. 1992) (upholding summary judgment granted to defendants on ground that state statute prescribing number of superior court judges did not unconstitutionally deprive litigants of access to the courts).

[110] Kakalik, Selvin, and Pace, *Averting Gridlock*, at 19. The authors report also that when the lag time rose to eight months in 1927 there were dire warnings that this would bring the legal system into disrepute.   [111] Ibid., at 40, fig. 2.8.

[112] T. Church, A. Carlson, J. Lee, and T. Tan, *Justice Delayed: The Pace of Litigation in Urban Trial Courts* (1982).

[113] Goerdt, Lomvardias, and Gallas, *Reexamining the Pace of Litigation*, at 37, fig. 3.1.

[114] Ibid.

on the features of a court system that exhibited fast or slow case processing, but these indicia do not seem particularly helpful in designing ways to cope with delay. One feature that correlated with long processing time was type of case; tort cases generally take longer than contract cases, but this was not universally true.[115] The presence or absence of a jury trial did not correlate to duration of case.[116] In general (but not invariably), the larger the population of the locality and the larger the number of judges the longer the case duration.[117] Filings per judge did not correlate to speed of disposition, but the number of dispositions per judge did.[118] Obviously these factors offer little in the way of prescription; one cannot solve problems of delay by excluding tort cases or reducing the population of the area, and subdividing populous areas to reduce the number of judges per court is likely to magnify other problems.

The only clear direction from the 1991 study was one that deals with matters addressed below—case management procedures and an individual calendar system were more typical of courts with rapid case completion than courts with long case duration.[119] But a comparison of available data on these courts from a decade earlier showed diverse comparisons, with increased case duration more typical than decreased case duration.[120]

One additional factor stands out, however. It might be called a problem of priorities. To some extent, the judicial system's ability to process cases is a zero-sum game; as resources are used for one case they are not available for another. If a certain type of case is assured priority, that guarantee can easily have a disproportionate impact on other types of cases. In most courts, criminal cases are understandably granted priority. Thus, in the study of thirty-nine state trial courts, the researchers found that the presence, or a large increase, of felony cases (particularly drug-related cases) corresponded to delays in civil cases.[121] A 1990 study of Los Angeles Superior Court offered graphic evidence of that phenomenon: between 1970 and 1987, the average judge time per civil case dropped from 77 minutes to 44 minutes, while the judge time per criminal case rose from 73 minutes to 114 minutes.[122] 'Criminal cases are only 16 percent of all cases filings but consume nearly half the available judges. . . . This is because the average criminal case requires five times as much judicial work as does the average civil case.'[123]

---

[115] Ibid., at 44–5; 47–9.   [116] Ibid., at 45.   [117] Ibid., at 43, table 3.3.
[118] Ibid., at 42.
[119] Ibid., at 47. Summarizing such research results by others, another group of researchers said: 'The findings of these analyses are remarkably consistent. The researchers found, first, that the pace of litigation is *not* associated with factors such as the court's size, the jurisdiction's population, the jury trial rate, or the presence or absence of alternative dispute resolution (ADR) procedure. Second they found that speedy case disposition *is* associated with active judicial case management.' Kakalik, Selvin, and Pace, *Averting Gridlock*, at 61 (emphasis in original).
[120] Goerdt, Lomvardias, and Gallas, *Reexamining the Pace of Litigation*, at 56–7. For generally similar results, see the earlier survey by the same organization of court delay, Goerdt, *Examining Court Delay*.
[121] Goerdt, Lomvardias, and Gallas, *Reexamining the Pace of Litigation*, at 64–5.
[122] Kakalik, Selvin, and Pace, *Averting Gridlock*, at 47.   [123] Ibid., at 50.

For more than a decade, America has been pursuing a strategy for reducing crime that involves increased prosecutions and longer incarceration. A number of states have adopted 'three strikes' laws providing mandatory and very long sentences for those convicted of three felonies, although most have not evidently used these laws too frequently.[124] Coupled with the priority afforded criminal cases and other commitments of courts to non-civil matters,[125] this prospect casts a shadow over expeditious processing of civil cases in American courts.

3.3. Cost

Whether or not the orientation of American procedure has tended toward delay, it certainly could lead to heightened costs in its aspiration to do perfect justice. As Professor Subrin has cogently observed:

In some ways, we in the legal community have reached a position similar to the medical community. The search for perfect and complete justice, like the search for perfect health, left unrestrained, leads to excesses of time and expense that society cannot or will not afford. In both the practice of medicine and the practice of law, when the goal to do everything possible to have the best result is combined with the profit motive of the professionals, costs are likely to continue to rise, absent other controls.[126]

The cost of American litigation is hence a matter of enduring importance.[127]

For more than a quarter of a century, the customary method of billing used by many American lawyers has indeed given them a profit motive to run up costs, for they bill by the hour. This circumstance has made it possible for law firms to hire large numbers of young law graduates to handle litigation. As some have said of civil discovery, 'It's quite attractive to make sure you leave no stone unturned, particularly if you get paid by the stone.' But it bears emphasis that cost increases may not be inexorable. To the contrary, in mid-1998 the *Wall*

---

[124] See Reske, 'Hardly Hardball', ABAJ (Dec. 1996), at 26 (reporting that three strikes law is used frequently only in California, where 15,000 had already been sentenced under a provision providing a sentence of twenty-five years to life for a third conviction of one of the over 500 felonies recognized by the state).

[125] Thus, a newspaper article recounted the impact on two federal district courts, one in southern California and the other in southern Texas, of increased enforcement of immigration restrictions. In the California court, there was a 43% increase in such cases in a year, and a lawyer said that '[o]ur federal court has been reduced to something like a state traffic court, with immigration and marijuana cases'. Palermo, 'Border Cases Overrun Courts', Nat. LJ, 27 Oct. 1997, at A6.

[126] Subrin, 'Uniformity in Procedural Rules and the Attributes of a Sound Procedural System: The Case for Presumptive Limits', 49 Ala. L. Rev. 79, 89 (1997).

[127] See, e.g., Levin and Collier, 'Containing the Cost of Litigation', 37 Rutgers L. Rev. 219 (1985).

Street Journal reported in a first-page story that during the 1990s American lawyers' fees had stayed constant or declined.[128]

The cost pressure may nonetheless be compounded in discovery, because very often the cost is borne by the adversary. Interrogatories or document requests may be cheap to draft but very expensive to respond to. Document production, in particular, may require large amounts of time to ensure that requested materials are being made available and to avoid the risk that privileged items mistakenly are turned over, thereby waiving the privilege.[129] Repeatedly, there have been complaints that the American system makes substantial settlements cheaper than the large cost of litigating.

The customary allocation of costs does little to prevent this from happening. Under the American rule, the winning litigant does not recover its attorneys' fees from the loser. Although some costs (e.g. docket fees and photocopying costs) are usually recoverable,[130] these are typically minuscule compared to attorneys' fees.[131] Costs therefore constitute a considerable concern. This concern may seem most galling to a party (often a defendant) required to expend considerable sums to compile information for its adversary. One might argue in favour of a rule requiring the party seeking discovery to internalize this cost,[132] but that would run counter to the access-promoting current attitude undergirding the relaxed pleading and discovery apparatus in American courts.

On the other hand, the absence of customary recovery of attorneys' fees stands as a high barrier to litigants of limited means. Given the scale of litigation common in American courts, it is said that many have often been priced out. There is a significant number of instances in which the prevailing party is allowed to recover attorneys' fees due to an applicable statutory exception to the American rule,[133] but even in such instances there can be considerable litigation about what is a 'reasonable' fee. The government offers little assistance to people of limited means who want a lawyer for a civil case. Until the 1960s, there was no substantial governmental assistance for representation in civil litigation. In the 1960s, the federal government created a system of legal

---

[128] Felsenthal and Barrett, 'Not So Fast: It Only Seems Like Legal Fees Are Still Skyrocketing', Wall St., 27 May 1998, at A1. In this, the legal profession may be following the path of the medical profession: 'The cutback in legal spending mirrors the course of health-care costs, whose growth has also subsided after years in which they were often described in the same breath as lawyers' fees. In both cases, despite a lot of talk about political reform, change has been driven by market pressure.' Ibid., at A10. But these developments have not quelled political attacks on lawyers: 'The broad impact of such changes has gone virtually unnoticed by critics of the profession, many of whom continue to demand stringent fee caps and other legislative reforms.' Ibid., at A1.

[129] See generally Marcus, 'The Perils of Privilege: Waiver and the Litigator', 84 Mich. L. Rev. 1605 (1986). [130] e.g. Fed. R. Civ. P. 54 (d).

[131] See 28 USC § 1920 (listing costs that are recoverable).

[132] See Cooter and Rubinfeld, 'Reforming the Discovery Rules', 84 Geo. LJ 61 (1996) (making such a proposal).

[133] See *Marek* v. *Chesny*, 473 US 1, at 44–51 (1985) (listing federal fee-shifting statutes); Note, 'State Attorney Fee Shifting Statutes: Are We Quietly Repealing the American Rule?', 47 Law & Contemp. Probs. 320 (winter 1984).

aid offices supported by tax dollars to provide free representation for those who met the income criteria (very low). In the 1970s, this effort was shifted to a government-supported independent corporation, the Legal Services Corporation. During the 1980s, President Reagan tried to terminate funding for the Legal Services Corporation. Although that did not happen, Congress has increasingly limited the range of activities governmentally supported legal aid can provide.[134] In short, the available funding for impoverished litigants is very limited.[135]

The one exception to this generalization is litigation involving serious personal injuries. America has a relatively vibrant personal injury bar that will take such cases on contingency and charge no fees except out of the proceeds.[136] In essence, these lawyers underwrite the litigation by investing their time with no assurance of being paid, and they often front the out-of-pocket costs as well.

The consequence of these rules and practices is that the cost of litigation is a matter of serious concern. It could enable those with unjustified claims or defences to club their opponents into submission. It could also preclude a considerable number of claimants from ever reaching court. Undoubtedly the existence of fee-shifting statutes has somewhat ameliorated the latter problem (upon which it is premised), but equally undoubtedly the decline of subsidized legal assistance has exacerbated it as well.

Determining the incidence of exclusion due to litigation cost is not possible, and assessing the risk that cost will be used as a club is difficult. Because there is no consistent gathering of information on litigation cost (as might occur if winners customarily recovered from losers), there are limited data about the general level of expenditure. Undoubtedly there are instances of enormous expenditures on litigation, but some data indicate that the general level is not, at least in the eyes of lawyers, particularly high. Most agree that discovery is the largest culprit in driving up costs, but the most recent data on discovery cost paint a mixed picture. A 1997 survey by the Federal Judicial Center sought to determine the costs of discovery in recently closed cases in federal courts. The researchers excluded cases that they expected would be unlikely to have discovery (about half the average district court's civil docket).[137] Even in the

---

[134] See, e.g., Reuben, 'Keeping Legal Aid Alive', ABAJ (Nov. 1996), at 20; Roberts, 'Poverty Law Braces for Painful Cuts', Nat. LJ, 18 Nov. 1996.
[135] One illustration of the extent of this problem is the current IOTLA controversy. Many state bars hit upon a money-raising technique to help support legal services for the poor: since lawyers often hold funds for their clients without paying them interest, the states ordered the lawyers to put the funds into interest-bearing accounts and pay over the interest to funds that supported legal services for low-income persons. Eventually, this practice generated some $100 million annually in revenue, but the interest was held to be private property under the US Constitution, meaning that the requirement that it be used to support legal services for the poor may be an illegal taking of private property. *Phillips* v. *Washington Legal Foundation*, 118 S. Ct. 1925 (1998).
[136] For background, see Karsten, 'Enabling the Poor to Have their Day in Court: The Sanctioning of Contingency Contracts, A History to 1940', 47 DePaul L. Rev. 231 (1998).
[137] T. Willging, J. Shapard, D. Stienstra, and D. Miletich, *Discovery and Discovery Practice, Problems, and Proposals for Change* (1997), 58 (about 55 per cent of civil cases excluded from consideration).

remaining portion of the caseload, they found that the median expenditure per side for discovery, as a percentage of the stakes in the litigation, was 3 per cent, which seems a relatively modest proportion.[138] At the 95th percentile, however, the expenditures were 32 per cent of the amount at stake.[139] More than half of the lawyers said that the discovery expenses were about right, and of the remainder more said they were too low than said they were too high.[140] Depending on the type of case, the discovery costs could vary greatly in high-intensity litigation, but otherwise seemed relatively consistent.[141] Although the spending in some high-cost cases therefore was high, the overall cost of discovery did not seem alarming.[142] But these costs did seem unnecessary to the lawyers in many instances, sometimes to a startling degree.[143] It is not at all clear, however, what one could do about this situation by rule or statute.

A final cost factor deserves mention—the cost of the court system itself. Litigants pay a filing fee in the USA, but this amount does not come close to supporting the court system,[144] which is paid for by tax dollars. Of course, the amount of court time a given case uses up varies greatly, but that customarily does not affect the fees charged the litigants. Occasionally there are efforts to quantify the cost of operation of the court system. For instance, a district judge recently concluded that the appropriate figure was $1,750 per hour for a judge's time.[145] Whatever the figure, this amount affects access to court only in that it constitutes a subsidy and constrains the appointment of more judges. Some have urged that the cost should be passed along to court users,[146] or at least some of them,[147] but this idea has nowhere caught on in America in any significant way.

---

[138] Ibid., at 17, table 6.   [139] Ibid.   [140] Ibid., at 18, table 8.

[141] Ibid., at 38, table 29 (see App. 3.8).

[142] Note that the above figures do not include client costs, which have thus far proven impossible to measure.

[143] Attorney estimates of the percentage of discovery expenses that were incurred unnecessarily are shown in App. 3.9.

[144] In a US district court, the filing fee charged a plaintiff for instituting a civil action is $150. 28 USC § 1914 (a). Other fees are charged according to a schedule adopted by the Judicial Conference of the United States for various other things such as making copies and searching records. There is no fee for the initial appearance of a defendant. In superior courts of the State of California, the fee for initiating an action is $185. Cal. Gov't Code § 26820.4. Each defendant is required to pay $182 for its initial appearance. Ibid., § 26826.

[145] *Specialized Plating, Inc. v. Federal Environmental Services, Inc.*, 975 F. Supp. 397 (D. Mass. 1997). In 1990, RAND seemingly thought that the appropriate figure for an hour of judge time in Los Angeles Superior Court was about $400. See Kakalik, Selvin, and Pace, *Averting Gridlock*, at 32. In 1982, RAND Corp. estimated the cost per hour of federal court time at $600. J. Kakalik and A. Robyn, *Costs of the Civil Justice System: Court Expenditures and Processing Tort Cases* (1982), 49.

[146] See R. Posner, *Economic Analysis of Law* (4th edn. 1992), § 21.12 (arguing that overuse of the courts is due to the fact that users do not have to pay the cost of the courts and suggesting that judicial time be rationed by price).

[147] During the deliberations of the Federal Courts Study Committee, Judge Posner, a member of the Committee, proposed that it recommend that court access fees be charged corporate litigants at levels sufficient to support the operation of the court system. This idea was scotched by a majority of the Committee. See Motz, 'A Federal Judge's View of Richard A. Posner's *The Federal Courts: Challenge and Reform*', 73 Notre Dame L. Rev. 1029, 1038–9 (1998) (describing the debate over user fees in the deliberations of the Federal Courts Study Committee).

3.4. The backlash: procedural retrenchment and substantive retreat

The liberal ethos that underlies much of the American procedural super-structure has not gone unchallenged or unmodified. Accordingly, this survey of the condition of civil litigation in the USA would not be complete without considering the retrenchment that has occurred from the most dramatic embrace of the mid-century ideal. For the last two decades, the main direction of change has been to cut back on the most aggressive expansion of procedure and to retreat from pro-plaintiff shifts in substantive law. Both types of developments deserve mention because they both form important ingredients of the impulse toward civil justice reform in the USA.

3.4.1. Retrenching on the Liberal Ethos in Procedure

From the outset, there were fault lines in the liberal ethos; the relaxed attitude it adopted toward pleading, in particular, excited opposition among judges anxious to insist that plaintiffs include more specifics in their complaints.[148] Notwithstanding, the general trend of rulemaking was toward greater relaxation until 1970, when comprehensive revision of the discovery rules produced the high-water point for the liberal ethos. All agree that the climate for relaxation cooled during the 1970s and that the urge to retrench emerged. An early target of this urge was the revised class action of Rule 23, as amended in 1966. Previously class actions had been available only in relatively limited circumstances. The 1966 amendment was functional in orientation, and permitted a class action on the ground that the various claims presented 'common questions' and that a class suit would be 'superior' to individual litigation. This change opened the door to using class actions in a much larger variety of cases. Celebrated by some as offering exhilarating possibilities,[149] the 1966 amendment was quickly condemned as authorizing 'legalized blackmail'.[150] There seemed to be a spate of ill-conceived class actions that some judges authorized without sufficient care.[151]

---

[148] For a review of these events, see Marcus, 'The Revival of Fact Pleading', at 445.

[149] The Reporter of the Advisory Committee on Civil Rules admitted that 'I am exhilarated, not depressed, by experimentation which spies out carefully the furthest possibilities of the new Rule.' Kaplan, 'A Prefatory Note', 10 BC Indus. & Comm. L. Rev. 497, 500 (1969). Later he admitted to being aware of the prospect for a backlash: '[O]ne could foresee that [the Rule] would apply particularly in certain substantive fields such as securities fraud, and, with no great flight of imagination, one might predict that the working of the rule must bring about changes of substance . . . . [I]t did not escape attention at the time that it would open the way to assertion of many, many claims that otherwise would not be pressed; so the rule would stick in the throats of establishment defendants.' Kaplan, 'Comment on Carrington', 137 U. Pa. L. Rev. 2125, 2126–7 (1989).

[150] Handler, 'The Shift From Substantive to Procedural Innovations in Antitrust Suits: The Twenty-Third Annual Antitrust Review', 71 Colum. L. Rev. 1, 9 (1971).

[151] These developments are chronicled in Miller, 'Of Frankenstein Monsters and Shining Knights: Myth, Reality, and the "Class Action Problem"', 92 Harv. L. Rev. 664 (1979).

More pervasive, however, was criticism of the broad discovery possible under the rules.[152] In 1976, a conference called to commemorate the seventieth anniversary of Pound's speech calling for reform[153] prompted the American Bar Association's Section of Litigation to propose that the scope of discovery be narrowed, that the number of interrogatories be limited to thirty, and that the rules require the judge to convene a discovery conference on request of any party to consider controls on discovery in the case.[154] Although it initially proposed amendments to the rules to do all three things,[155] the Advisory Committee on Civil Rules eventually decided on a more moderate set of changes,[156] which were condemned as inadequate by three Justices of the Supreme Court.[157]

In 1981 the Advisory Committee returned to the fray, proposing further amendments calculated to address concerns about improper litigation behaviour. As discussed in the next section,[158] it wrote some judicial management into the rules. In addition, it directed the judge to limit discovery if it was disproportionate.[159] Finally, it rewrote Rule 11, regarding the representations a lawyer makes by signing a complaint or other paper filed in court, to strengthen this self-policing by the bar and direct judges to impose sanctions on those who violated its terms. Previously Rule 11 had essentially called for good faith in filings, and it had not been employed very often, but the amended rule said that signing filings certified that they were 'well grounded in fact' and 'supported by existing law or a good faith argument for the extension, modification or reversal of existing law'. It also required the court to sanction lawyers who violated the new certification requirements.

The proportionality provision seems to have made no palpable difference in practice,[160] but the Rule 11 amendment produced a firestorm of protest by

---

[152] For a more extensive review of the events described below, see Marcus, 'Discovery Containment Redax', at 753–68. [153] See Pound, 'The Causes of Popular Dissatisfaction'.

[154] See ABA Section of Litigation Special Committee on Discovery Abuse, 'Report to the Bench and Bar', 92 FRD 151 (1977).

[155] See 'Preliminary Draft of Proposed Amendments to the Federal Rules of Civil Procedure', 77 FRD 613 (1978).

[156] 'Proposed Amendments to the Federal Rules of Civil Procedure', 80 FRD 222 (1979).

[157] See 'Amendments to the Federal Rules of Civil Procedure', 85 FRD 521, 523 (1980) (Powell J, dissenting from adoption of amendments) ('acceptance of these tinkering changes will delay for years the adoption of genuinely effective reforms'). [158] See below text accompanying nn. 192–7.

[159] See Fed. R. Civ. P. 26 (b) (2) which at present reads: 'The frequency or extent of use of the discovery methods otherwise permitted under these rules and by any local rule shall be limited by the court if it determines that: (i) the discovery sought is unreasonably cumulative or duplicative, or is obtainable from some other source that is more convenient, less burdensome, or less expensive; (ii) the party seeking discovery has had ample opportunity by discovery in the action to obtain the information sought; or (iii) the burden or expense of the proposed discovery outweighs its likely benefit, taking into account the needs of the case, the amount in controversy, the parties' resources, the importance of the issues at stake in the litigation, and the importance of the discovery in resolving the issues.'

[160] See C. Wright, A. Miller, and R. Marcus, *Federal Practice & Procedure*, viii. (2nd edn., 1994), § 2008.1 at 121.

those who claimed that it operated to cut off claims disfavoured by judges and silence the plaintiffs' bar.[161] Alarmed, the Advisory Committee in 1990 issued an unprecedented 'call' for comment on the rule and ideas for revising it.[162] Eventually the rule was amended in 1993 to make sanctions discretionary rather than mandatory and to provide other procedural protections for those confronting sanctions requests.[163] Again there was dissent on the Supreme Court, this time on the ground that the changes would render the revised rule 'toothless'.[164]

The year 1993 saw other important changes to the rules as well. Most notable was an effort to curtail the cost and delay that attend discovery by requiring initial disclosure of 'core materials' by both sides early in the case and without the need for formal discovery requests.[165] When originally proposed, the initial disclosure idea provoked 'a flood of objections unprecedented in fifty plus years of judicial rule-making'.[166] Momentarily deterred by the reaction, the Advisory Committee resolutely proceeded with a revised initial disclosure requirement[167] that was adopted over dissent by the Supreme Court and almost removed from the eventual amendments package by Congress owing to a legislative logjam that prevented the matter from coming to a vote in the Senate.[168] In addition,

---

[161] See Marcus, 'Of Babies and Bathwater: The Prospects for Procedural Progress', 59 Brooklyn L. Rev. 761, 794–800 (1993); Burbank, 'The Transformation of American Civil Procedure: The Example of Rule 11', 137 U. Pa. L. Rev. 1925 (1989).

[162] See 'Call for Written Comments on Rule 11 of the Federal Rules of Civil Procedure and Related Rules', 131 FRD 335 (1990).

[163] Thus, the rule now allows a 'safe harbour' period after service of a sanctions motion during which the party accused may withdraw the offending paper or assertion without punishment. In addition, the amended rule says that sanctions must be limited to the amount needed to deter future misconduct and not calibrated according to the asserted costs incurred by the 'victim'.

[164] See 'Amendments to the Federal Rules of Civil Procedure', 146 FRD 401, 507 (Scalia J, dissenting).

[165] For a review of these events, see Marcus, 'Of Babies and Bathwater', at 805–12.

[166] Pelham, 'Judges Make Quite a Discovery; Litigators Erupt, Kill Plan to Reform Federal Civil Rules', Legal Times, 16 Mar. 1992, at 1.

[167] Fed. R. Civ. P. 26 (a) (1) provides that 'a party shall, without awaiting a discovery request, provide to other parties' the following: '(A) the name and, if known, the address and telephone number of each individual likely to have discoverable information relevant to disputed facts alleged with particularity in the pleadings, identifying the subjects of the information; (B) a copy of, or a description by category and location of, all documents, data compilations, and tangible things in the possession, custody, or control of the party that are relevant to disputed facts alleged with particularity in the pleadings; (C) a compilation of any category of damages claimed by the disclosing party, making available for inspection and copying as under Rule 34 the documents or evidentiary material . . . on which such computation is based, including materials bearing on the nature and extent of injuries suffered, and (D) for inspection and copying . . . any insurance agreement under which any person carrying on an insurance business may be liable to satisfy part or all of a judgment which may be entered in the action or to indemnify or reimburse for payments made to satisfy the judgment.' As can be seen from (A) and (B) above, part of the compromise in this provision is a retreat from the broadest relaxation of pleading requirements; the disclosure obligation only applies with regard to matters 'alleged with particularity'.

[168] The House of Representatives passed a bill to remove initial disclosure, but the measure never got to a vote in the Senate: 'The United States House of Representatives voted unanimously to

the 1993 amendments made a number of other changes to contain discovery. They set a numerical limit on depositions[169] and interrogatories[170] and also tightened up limitations on conduct during depositions.[171] The amendments also bolstered the obligation to supplement discovery and disclosure responses,[172] and added a provision for relatively automatic exclusion of materials not turned over when they should have been.[173]

The 1993 package of amendments was not the end of the process. In October 1996, the Advisory Committee inaugurated a comprehensive review of the discovery provisions to consider further changes. In part, this move was precipitated by divergence among various districts in handling initial disclosure, for the compromise that was adopted in 1993 permitted district courts to 'opt out' of the national rule. Beyond that, it was prompted as well by ongoing concern that discovery problems had not been solved by the 1993 package of amendments. This process of re-examination is ongoing,[174] and has yielded yet another set of proposed amendments.[175]

Another strand needs to be added to the mix: the class action rule has again come to occupy centre stage. From prompting controversy after the 1966 amendments, the class action rule lapsed into relative tranquillity for some time once courts began to take a more careful attitude toward it. Indeed, a decade ago it was said that class actions were 'dying'.[176] But reports of the death of the class action were premature, and interest in it was rekindled by efforts to deal with mass torts. Enterprising lawyers and innovative judges hit on class actions as a method to wrap up otherwise protracted and dispersed product liability and related litigation.[177] This innovation prompted the first

---

derail the Committee's proposal and substitute one of its own. The House bill was brought before the Senate Judiciary Committee on the day before adjournment when that committee was acting under a rule requiring unanimity. When Senator Metzenbaum objected to the House bill, that killed it. And so Rule 26 became law as the result of its support by a single Senator voting against a unanimous House, a House that would have been joined by an almost unanimous Senate if the matter had even reached the Senate floor. The final vote was thus one Senator against the world, with the one Senator prevailing.' Carrington and Apanovich, 'The Constitutional Limits of Rule-making: The Illegitimacy of Mass-Tort Settlements Negotiated under Rule 23', 39 Az. L. Rev. 462, 485 (1997).   [169] Fed. R. Civ. P. 30 (a) (2) (A) (ten depositions per side).

[170] Fed. R. Civ. P. 33 (a) (twenty-five interrogatories per party).

[171] Fed. R. Civ. P. 30 (d) (requiring that objections to questions be concise and non-suggestive, and also forbidding instructions that the witness not answer except in very limited circumstances).

[172] See Fed. R. Civ. P. 26 (e).   [173] Fed. R. Civ. P. 37 (c) (1).

[174] I serve as Special Reporter to the Advisory Committee in connection with this review of the discovery rules.

[175] See 'Proposed Amendments to the Federal Rules of Civil Procedure', 181 FRD 18, 25–70 (1998). Among other things, the proposed changes include narrowing automatic disclosure to favourable material, retracting the scope of attorney-managed (but not court-ordered) discovery, and adopting a presumptive limit on the duration of a deposition. These proposals have been examined in a series of public hearings. The earliest they could take effect is 1 Dec. 2000.

[176] Martin, 'The Rise and Fall of the Class Action Lawsuit', NY Times, 8 Jan. 1988, at B7.

[177] For a review of these issues, see Marcus, 'They Can't Do That, Can They? Mass Tort Reform Via Rule 23', 80 Cornell L. Rev. 858 (1995).

formal proposals to amend the class action rule since the 1966 changes,[178] and consideration of these changes is ongoing as well.[179]

Altogether, these changes represent a retrenchment on the liberal ethos, but not a rejection of it. Some criticize the trend as abandoning the objective of access to court,[180] and that surely is the objective of some proponents of change. On balance, however, the current situation is perhaps better viewed as an effort at recalibration.

3.4.2. *Substantive Retrenchment*

Outside the realm of procedural rules, the most aggressive advances of post-war American substantive law have stopped and, in some instances, there has been a partial retreat. Although these changes often rely on shaky or plainly incorrect empirical foundations,[181] they also form a part of the landscape of access to justice in the USA, as they redefine what is accepted as 'justice'. Moreover, on occasion the 'reformers' use procedural means to accomplish their ends.

A large variety of ideas has been advanced under the heading of 'tort reform'. The presumption of these reformers that tort litigation needs considerable change is debatable, but it is not debatable that the reform impulse has wrought changes. Academics who follow actual court decisions have announced that the pro-plaintiff sweep that may have characterized the legal developments of the 1960s and 1970s has ended.[182] State legislatures have responded to objections to tort litigation with a variety of measures such as caps on recoveries for pain and suffering, requirements that professional malpractice plaintiffs first present their claims to expert boards for review, and other measures that are designed to curtail access to a civil justice system labelled as too plaintiff-friendly.[183] In addition, there have been efforts to enhance the power of judges to review jury awards and cut them back.[184]

---

[178] See 'Preliminary Draft of Proposed Amendments to the Federal Rules', 167 FRD 523, 559–60 (1996).

[179] One proposed amendment, to permit interlocutory appellate review of class action determinations, has been adopted. Others are still under consideration, and a Mass Torts Working Group has been formed involving representatives of various rulemaking committees to consider comprehensive procedural changes to deal with mass torts. There have also been a number of proposals in Congress to alter class action practice by statute.

[180] e.g. Weinstein, 'After Fifty Years of the Federal Rules of Civil Procedure: Are the Barriers to Justice Being Raised?', 137 FRD U. Pa. L. Rev. 1901 (1989).

[181] For a recent effort to undo the effects of unjustified broadsides about tort litigation in America, see Galanter, 'Real World Torts: An Antidote to Anecdote', 55 Md. L. Rev. 1093 (1996).

[182] Henderson and Eisenberg, 'The Quiet Revolution in Products Liability: An Empirical Study of Legal Change', 37 UCLA L. Rev. 479 (1990) (describing 'a significant turn in the direction of judicial decision-making away from extending the boundaries of product liability and toward placing significant limitations on plaintiffs' rights to recover for product-related injuries').

[183] See generally M. Rahdert, *Covering Accident Costs: Insurance, Liability and Tort Reform* (1995).

[184] See, e.g., *Gasperini v. Center for Humanities, Inc.*, 116 S. Ct. 2211 (1996) (holding that federal court must apply New York tort reform measure that calls for reduction of award to plaintiff if the award 'deviates materially from what would be reasonable compensation').

A similar legislative impulse has been felt in the federal Congress. Repeatedly there have been efforts to supplant state law entirely by adoption of federal products liability legislation.[185] Adopted legislation has attempted to curtail supposedly undesirable features of civil litigation with a package of substantive and procedural components. Most prominently, in 1995 Congress adopted the Private Securities Litigation Reform Act over the President's veto.[186] This Act revises the treatment of a number of issues pertinent to substantive securities law. It also includes protective provisions designed to alter the handling of such cases by changing what would normally be regarded as procedural matters. Thus, it provides a heightened pleading standard,[187] and directs that the plaintiff be allowed no discovery if the defendant files a motion to dismiss unless that motion is denied.[188] Responding to concerns that securities fraud class actions have permitted lawyers to take over litigation using 'figurehead plaintiffs',[189] the Act directs an elaborate notice procedure upon the filing of a securities fraud class action designed to ensure that person 'most capable of adequately representing the interests of class members' be appointed lead plaintiff, which is presumed to be the person with the largest financial stake.[190] Congress has also adopted legislation altering the handling of prisoner suits.[191]

What all this serves to emphasize is that civil litigation reform is a multifaceted endeavour in America, and that similar concerns may be advanced in many different ways and places. Nevertheless, the main ingredient for civil justice reform is probably still judicial action, and the principal ingredient in that effort by judges has been some form of managerial judging, to which we turn.

4. JUDGES *ÜBER ALLES*:
THE RISE OF MANAGERIAL JUDGING

Until the last generation, American judges were considerably less active than their counterparts in many other countries. By design or tradition, they

---

[185] For a recent report on the status of this legislative effort, see Holdman, 'Product Liability Compromise May Unravel in Senate', SF Recorder, 8 July 1998, at 1.

[186] Private Securities Litigation Reform Act of 1995, 109 Stat. 737 (1995). For analyses of this legislation, see Symposium, Securities Litigation: The Fundamental Issues, 39 Az. L. Rev. 491–737 (1996).

[187] See 15 USC § 78u-4 (b); Weiss, 'The New Securities Fraud Pleading Requirement: Speed Bump or Road Block?', 39 Az. L. Rev. 675 (1996).

[188] 15 USC § 77z-1 (b). The Act further directs that potential discovery materials be preserved during the pendency of such a motion. See ibid., § 77z-1 (b) (2).

[189] See Weiss and Beckerman, 'Let the Money Do the Monitoring: How Institutional Investors Can Reduce Agency Costs in Securities Class Actions', 104 Yale LJ 2053 (1995).

[190] 15 USC § 78u-4 (a) (3) (B).

[191] See Prison Litigation Reform Act of 1995, Pub. L. 104–34 §§ 801–10, 110 Stat. 1321–66 (1996). Among other things, this legislation imposes limitations on the remedies available in prison conditions litigation, imposes additional limits on *in forma pauperis* suits by prisoners, expands grounds for dismissing prisoner suits, and directs that any compensation ordered in such cases be paid directly to crime victims if a restitution order is in effect directing such payment.

generally left the handling of litigation to the lawyers and the parties until the case was ready for trial. Largely because of concerns about delay and cost, that generalization is not true of federal judges, and increasingly not true in state courts either. Because case management is such a basic change in the activities of judges, and because it may be exported to some other judicial systems,[192] it deserves separate treatment.

4.1. Federal court case management: bottom-up development

The ultimate origins of case management go back to state court practices in Michigan, but the principal contemporary developments have come from the federal courts. The history is extensively chronicled elsewhere,[193] so the present treatment can hit a few points.

The origin was the emergence of the single calendar system in the 1960s, under which federal judges were assigned responsibility for a given case upon filing. Partly due to concerns about cost and duration of litigation, judges in metropolitan areas began to insist that lawyers report to them early in the case about what was contemplated, and then to enter orders regulating the development of the case. This activity grew for over a decade and emerged as the Advisory Committee's preferred method of dealing with criticisms of civil litigation in the late 1970s. At the same time that it was declining to narrow the scope of discovery,[194] the Committee also began work on ways to institutionalize case management nationwide.[195]

The upshot was the very substantial amendment of Rule 16 of the Federal Rules of Civil Procedure in 1983. Pursuant to this amendment, except as to categories of cases exempted as inappropriate the district judge was required to enter an order early in the case limiting the time to complete discovery and joinder of parties, and authorized to enter orders regarding a variety of other topics covering virtually the gamut of litigation activities.[196] Coupled with exhortation to take control of civil cases that were included in new judge seminars, this rule was designed to require some case management and foster more.

In 1990, Congress lent its own support to case management by adopting the Civil Justice Reform Act, which targeted cost and delay in federal civil litigation

---

[192] See, e.g., *Access to Justice: Final Report to the Lord Chancellor on the Civil Justice System in England and Wales* (1996), 14–102 (advocating adoption of case management somewhat modelled on American experience).

[193] For a recent and exhaustive treatment, see Resnik, 'Changing Practices, Changing Rules: Judicial and Congressional Rulemaking on Civil Juries, Civil Justice, and Civil Judging', 49 Ala. L. Rev. 133, 152–88 (1997).   [194] See above text accompanying nn. 155–6.

[195] For a description of this development, see Marcus, 'Discovery Containment Redux', at 760–4.

[196] In 1993 the list of authorized topics was expanded to make sure that nothing had been left out.

and endorsed case management to solve the problems.[197] The Act directed each of the ninety-four district courts to appoint an advisory group and develop a plan for the district. Over the ensuing several years, these plans included a variety of provisions, including some that seemed directly contrary to national rules.

The CJRA ended by its own terms in December 1997. By then many courts had incorporated provisions that began in CJRA plans into their local rules. The end of the CJRA experiment is one of the reasons the Advisory Committee on Civil Rules has again turned its attention to the discovery rules, for the experiment may have produced experience that supports changing some of those rules. Up to this point, however, the federal case management movement has been a bottom-up effort. The stimulus for the 1983 amendments to the national rules was prompting from judges excited by their own experiences with case management. The CJRA was similarly premised on a 'bottom-up' approach to innovation. The time has come to assess the results.

4.2. The California experience: reform from the top down

As mentioned above, civil case delay in some urban superior courts in California reached critical proportions in the mid-1980s.[198] But the courts themselves may have been limited in their responses. Few if any had an individual calendar system, and in general court operations in California state courts were more closely directed by the legislature than federal court operations are overseen by Congress.

The initiative therefore fell to the legislature, which in 1986 adopted the Trial Court Delay Reduction Act.[199] As a report on this experiment required by the legislature recognized, 'California is the only state in which the decision to introduce a delay reduction program came from the legislature and not the Judiciary.'[200] This Act added a number of provisions that came to be known as Fast Track to the state Government Code[201] (not the Code of Civil Procedure) regarding timely handling of all litigation. This legislation looked something like

---

[197] Civil Justice Reform Act of 1990, PL 101–650, 104 Stat. 5089. In § 102 of the Act, Congress found that 'it is necessary to achieve a method of consultation so that individual judicial officers, litigants, and litigants' attorneys who have developed techniques for litigation management and delay reduction can effectively and promptly communicate those techniques to all participants'. It also observed that 'an effective litigation management and cost and delay reduction program should incorporate' several principles: '(A) the differential treatment of cases that provides for individualized and specific management according to their needs, complexity, duration, and probable litigation careers; (B) early involvement of a judicial officer in planning the progress of a case, controlling the discovery process, and scheduling hearings, trials, and other litigation events; (C) regular communication between a judicial officer and attorneys during the pretrial process; and (D) utilization of alternative dispute resolution programs in appropriate cases.'

[198] See above text accompanying nn. 108–10.   [199] Cal. Stats. 1986, ch. 1335.

[200] Judicial Council of California, *Prompt and Fair Justice in the Trial Courts* (1991), 'Introduction' at 2.

[201] Cal. Gov't Code §§ 68600–20.

the CJRA, which was adopted by Congress four years later. It directed the California Judicial Council to adopt standards for timely disposition of cases, with a presumption in favour of the American Bar Association standards.[202]

As originally adopted, the Act directed the creation of a number of pilot delay reduction programmes and directed the judges involved in these programmes 'to actively manage the processing of litigation from the commencement to disposition, and to compel attorneys and litigants to prepare and resolve all litigation without delay'.[203] It also authorized local courts to establish requirements for completion of various stages of litigation even if these requirements were inconsistent with California Rules of Court or imposed shorter time limits than those provided in the California Code of Civil Procedure.[204] To reduce delay, the Act also provided judges enforcing such a programme with 'all the powers to impose sanctions authorized by law, including the power to dismiss actions or strike pleadings'.[205]

In 1990, the legislature revised the Act and expanded it state-wide. But it also significantly changed its operation. It removed the former authority to shorten state-wide due dates for certain actions and for sanctions against transgressors. It also directed courts to develop programmes of differentiated case management,[206] put minimum time limitations into the statute, and guaranteed the parties the right to extend these time periods.[207] Thus, unlike the federal experience, in California the legislature initiated, and then took control of much of the substance of, the case management programme

4.3. Does case management work?

The effectiveness of such a programme is, of course, a central concern. At a general level, as we have seen, experience in a number of state courts indicated that case management practices seemed to relate to reduced case disposition time.[208] At the same time, the whole concept of judicial management has come under vigorous attack in this country on the ground that it improperly deprives litigants of control of their cases without assuring corresponding systemic advantages.[209] As I wrote three years ago in connection with the possible

---

[202] Cal. Gov't Code § 68603 (b). For the ABA standards, see above n. 104.

[203] This was contained in Gov't Code § 68608 as adopted in 1986. See 1986 Cal. Stats. ch. 1335 § 1. This provision was changed in 1990.

[204] Gov't Code § 68612. As noted below, this provision was removed in 1990.

[205] Ibid., § 68609. As noted below, this provision was removed in 1990.

[206] Cal. Gov't Code § 68603 (c).

[207] See Gov't Code § 68616, which provides that local time limitations cannot (*a*) require service of the complaint sooner than sixty days after filing of the actions and guarantees the plaintiff more time on a showing that service could not be effected within sixty days or (*b*) require service of responsive pleadings sooner than thirty days after service of the complaint and guarantees the parties the right to stipulate a fifteen-day extension; and (*c*) guarantees the parties the right to agree to an additional thirty-day continuance.   [208] See above text accompanying nn. 119–20.

[209] See, e.g., Resnik, 'Managerial Judges', 96 Harv. L. Rev. 374 (1982).

adoption of a case management programme in England, the degree of effectiveness of the programme remained unproved.[210]

The completion of the CJRA experiment in the federal courts offers further information, but still somewhat uncertain conclusions. As directed by Congress, a comprehensive study was undertaken by an outside investigator, the RAND Corporation, of the operation of the implementation of the Act in the ten courts Congress designated as 'pilot' districts in which certain measures had to be implemented and ten 'comparison' districts chosen to resemble the pilot districts.

The RAND study produced a mountain of data and some relatively straightforward conclusions. First, the researchers found that early case management works in shortening the duration of litigation, and that it was most effective in that regard if it was coupled with early setting of a trial date.[211] But there was a cloud with this silver lining: because lawyers had to perform tasks under the court's direction, early case management also resulted in significantly increased costs. In the words of the RAND researchers, '[t]hese results debunk the myth that reducing time to disposition will necessarily reduce litigation costs'.[212] The explanation for this finding was that in some cases lawyers would undertake tasks they would not have undertaken had the pace of the case not been pressed by the court; it was not just a question of doing more work sooner, but of doing more work overall. The only purely good news, from the perspective of the RAND researchers, was that setting a discovery schedule with a short time for discovery both advanced disposition and reduced litigation costs.[213] Thus, their prescription was for the court to engage in early case management and set a trial date as soon as possible, and to impose an early discovery cutoff, thereby recouping the added cost that would otherwise attend the imposition of early case management.

Lest this 'good news' be carried too far too fast, it should be added that the Federal Judicial Center also examined the effect of discovery cutoffs in its 1997 survey of discovery in recently closed federal cases drawn from around the nation. Unlike RAND, the FJC found that discovery cutoffs had no substantial relationship to case duration or total litigation costs.[214] The FJC explained this difference on two grounds: First, it studied cases from across the entire country and not just twenty districts. Second, it used case-specific information rather than district-wide means to determine the effects of this management practice.

Not surprisingly, the California experience has not been studied as intensively

---

[210] Marcus, '"Deja Vu All Over Again"? An American Reaction to the Woolf Report', in A. Zuckerman and R. Cranston (eds.) *Reform of Civil Procedure* (1995), at 219, 232–5.

[211] J. Kakalik, T. Dunworth, L. Hill, D. McCaffrey, M. Oshiro, N. Pace, and M. Vaiana, *Just, Speedy, and Inexpensive? An Evaluation of Case Management under the Civil Justice Reform Act* (1997), 12.

[212] Ibid.   [213] Ibid., at 16.

[214] Memorandum from Tom Willging, Federal Judicial Center, to Advisory Committee on Civil Rules, 23 Feb. 1998, at 3 (on file with Rules Committee Support Office, Washington, DC).

as the federal CJRA experiment. But before launching its Fast Track programme state-wide, the California legislature did receive a report on a study
that concluded that the Act had 'fundamentally changed the way California
trial courts operate. In just three years, judges have taken control of their
calendars and have significantly improved the pace of civil litigation.'[215] The
study found considerable numerical evidence of accelerated dispositions in the
courts required to implement these techniques.[216] But even these supporters
noted that, due to the new methods '[t]he pace of litigation had quickened,
putting pressure on everyone in the system from court administrators to court
clerks to judges'.[217]

The anecdotal reports indicate mixed results from this extra work. From the
judicial side, the returns are very positive in expedited completion of litigation.[218] But that was only half the story. Court officials exulted that Fast Track
improved the way lawyers practised law by reducing the amount of time they
had to work on the case. Lawyers often condemned the new programme as
unduly rigid and time-conscious, asserting that their lives were being dominated
by a computer operated from the clerk's office.[219] They also argued (in keeping
with RAND's findings about cost) that the proliferation of activities required by

---

[215] Judicial Conference of California, *Prompt and Fair Justice*, at 1.

[216] The summary of these results was: '*Case processing time improved dramatically*: In 1990, 90 percent
or more of case dispositions were achieved within two years of filing in all nine mandatory pilot
courts. In 1987, it was taking more than three years from filing to disposition for 90 percent or more
of cases in seven of the nine mandatory pilot courts. For the cases disposed most quickly (the fastest
50 percent), all nine mandatory pilot courts showed improvement; four pilot courts cut their median
time to disposition in half. *Trial time for jury trials is shorter*: Seven of the nine mandatory pilot courts
cut the length of jury trials, and five now complete at least half of their jury trials in one week. Four
mandatory pilot courts completed over 90 percent of their program jury trials in two court weeks or
less, in contrast to 1987, when no court completed 90 percent of its jury trials within two court
weeks. This is a result of trial management techniques used by the judges. *Pending cases are younger*:
Five of the nine mandatory pilot courts cut in half the percentage of cases pending more than two
years. In all nine mandatory pilot courts, the age of cases pending was substantially less than cases
pending before the program began.' Ibid., at 7.   [217] Ibid., at 5.

[218] See, e.g., Bray, 'Statewide System Forces Local Courts to Speed Up', LA Times, 14 Nov. 1993,
at B1 (reporting that in Ventura County, where matters formerly languished for up to five years, they
make it to court with unprecedented speed); Maharaj, 'Civil Justice is Speedier in Courts These
Days', LA Times, 26 Oct. 1993, at B1 (reporting that in Orange County, cases get to trial in
seventeen months, compared to three to five years previously, that a similar change has occurred in
Los Angeles County, where cases are being heard in eighteen months, and that in San Diego County
the new system has 'worked like a charm'); Peters, 'Fast Track a Success, But More Counsel Losing
Faith', Amer. Lawyer, 2 Apr. 1991, at 1 (case processing time dropped dramatically in the courts
targeted by the pilot programme); Hearn, '"Fast Track" Has Helped Provide Speedier Trials', San
Diego Union-Tribune, 10 Dec. 1990, at B1 (in San Diego County some 95% of all civil cases are
resolved within twenty-four months, compared with the 'lumbering old days' when it took fifty-two
months to resolve 90% of filings).

[219] Bray, 'Stateside System'; Peters, 'Fast Track a Success' (lawyers objected to 'inflexible rules
and deadlines, an inordinate emphasis on speed; arbitrary and rigid judges'); Hearn, '"Fast Track"
Has Helped Provide Speedier Trials' ('Under the fast track system, the judges usurped control, and
their most powerful weapon was a computer—ever spewing forth filing dates, fines and court
appearances').

the court increased the cost of litigation. In short, they felt that they were being run ragged by a computer operated from the clerk's office.

These complaints seem to explain the compromise measure adopted in 1990 when the legislature was called upon to decide whether to continue Fast Track in effect; the limitations placed on local requirements provided some protection for lawyers and the removal of the sanctions provision also provided protection against more serious results due to failure to comply with scheduling requirements. These effects are ironically illustrated by an article written by a California court administrator complaining about the effects of the changes made by the legislature in 1990.[220] In her view, the time assurances built into the revised legislation that guarantee lawyers some latitude in handling of their cases undercut its purpose because it became difficult or impossible to determine in an automated way whether the lawyers had violated a deadline:

The legislation . . . made efficient case tracking extremely difficult by imposing a set of labyrinthine time standards apparently designed to increase rather than decrease the time to disposition. A case-tracking quagmire resulted from the various delays produced by permitting attorneys to: (1) stipulate to an additional 15 days for filing a responsive pleading; (2) agree to a single continuance of 30 days; (3) avoid appearing at any type of court-ordered conference for at least 30 days following the service of the first responsive pleadings, or not sooner than 30 days after the expiration of a stipulated continuance; and (4) escape referral to arbitration for at least 210 days after filing a complaint, exclusive of any stipulated 30-day continuance.[221]

Thus, the computer could not easily continue to dominate the lawyers' lives.

The California Supreme Court has also put some brakes on Fast Track by holding that a court could not dismiss a case as a sanction for a lawyer's failure to comply with the Act's requirements.[222] In that personal injury case, the court clerk served a notice on the plaintiff's lawyer for failure to comply with a local requirement to serve the complaint within sixty days, and later the clerk directed counsel to appear for a status hearing and serve an explanation for his failure to serve within the time limits. When counsel did not appear at the hearing because he was in trial in another county, the judge fined him $50 and *sua sponte* set the matter over for hearing on the court's motion to dismiss. At that hearing, the judge imposed a further sanction and continued the matter one more time with a warning that if the case were not at issue by that continued date it would be dismissed. By that time, several defendants had been served, but the case was still not at issue and another judge dismissed the action without prejudice. Since the statute of limitations had run, the plaintiff appealed.

Although one might conclude that the trial court had been relatively

---

[220] Goodman, 'Effective Case Monitoring and Timely Dispositions: The Experience of One California Court', 76 Judicature 254 (1993). The author is identified as a staff analyst for planning and research services at the superior court described in the article.
[221] Ibid., at 256. [222] *Garcia v. McCutchen*, 16 Cal. 4th 469 (1997).

accommodating, the Supreme Court held that dismissal was barred by a statute saying that penalties should not be imposed on parties for the failure of lawyers to comply with local rules.[223] In doing so, it emphasized that delay reduction is only one goal among many: '[defendants] are incorrect in suggesting that either the 1986 Act or the current Act directs that the goal of delay reduction take precedence over all other considerations.'[224] The court also noted that at the time it adopted the Fast Track legislation, the legislature also recognized that cases should be decided on their merits if possible.[225]

In sum, the returns are mixed on case management.

5. REFLECTIONS ON PROCEDURAL IMPROVEMENT

Whether or not '[t]he history of procedure is a series of attempts to solve the problems created by the preceding generation's procedural reforms',[226] the above recent history should chasten ambitious reformers. The American litigation system is exceedingly complicated and resilient, as reformers have discovered. Changes that are expected to have major effects may turn out not to make an impact. Thus, the 1983 imposition of a proportionality principle in discovery[227] was thought by its drafters to be a dramatic shift but had no results. Similarly, the enormously controversial initial disclosure provisions added in 1993[228] did not have the sort of effects that either the proponents or detractors predicted. To the contrary, although the existence of desirable impacts remains somewhat contested,[229] all agree that the sort of major changes promised by some, and feared by others, did not occur. On a different level, the adoption of limits on securities fraud litigation by Congress in 1995 has not necessarily had

---

[223] Cal. Code Civ. Proc. § 575.2 (b): 'It is the intent of the Legislature that if a failure to comply with these rules is the responsibility of counsel and not of the party, any penalty shall be imposed on counsel and shall not adversely affect the party's cause of action or defense thereto.'

[224] 16 Cal. 4th at 479.

[225] Former Cal. Gov't Code § 68601 (c) (repealed in 1990): 'Cases filed in California's trial courts should be resolved as expeditiously as possible, consistent with the obligation of the courts to give full and careful consideration to the issues presented, and consistent with the right of parties to adequately prepare and present their cases to the courts.'

[226] Resnik, 'Tiers', 57 S. Cal. L. Rev. 837, 1030 (1984).

[227] See above text accompanying nn. 159–60.

[228] See above text accompanying nn. 165–8.

[229] Thus, the RAND study of the CJRA found no firm evidence that the types of disclosure practised in the districts it studied had a statistically significant measurable positive impact on duration or cost of litigation. Kakalik, Hensler, McCaffrey, Oshiro, Pace, and Vaiana, 'Discovery Management: Further Analysis of the Civil Justice Reform Act Evaluation Data', 39 Bos. Coll. L. Rev. 613, 657–62 (1998). But this study did not examine the actual 1993 amendment, and a 1997 study by the Federal Judicial Center did find that when that provision was applied and had an effect, it was generally the effect desired by its framers. See Willging *et al.*, *Discovery*, at 26–7. RAND has recognized that 'the "empirical" story of the effects of Rule 26 (a) (1) [the 1993 initial disclosure provision] remains to be told'. Kakalik *et al.*, 'Discovery Management', at 659.

the effects desired, and one result supposedly has been an increase in filings in state courts.[230]

All of this is not to say that the American reform effort had no effect whatsoever. Hard though it may be to sustain the more ambitious claims for the effects of relaxed procedure,[231] it does seem clear that the American brand of relatively open access to court and to broad discovery lies at the heart of much enforcement of public law.[232] To 'reform' away from these central tenets, therefore, implicates very substantial concerns. The reformer has a very limited latitude in which to work without coming up against a basic reconfiguration of the country's legal arrangements.[233] If by reform one implies confidence in the final solution of problems, then that will not happen. But an incrementalist perspective nevertheless permits a variety of observations.

Judicial capacity will continue to be a pressing concern. Much of the empirical scholarship on caseload growth and other issues of judicial capacity has been designed to defuse misuse of other data to support ideological positions such as those embraced by the President's Council on Competitiveness. The growth of case filings does not really support America's self-image as an over-litigious nation, but it is a legitimate concern. Particularly at the appellate level,[234] caseload growth is a matter of concern.[235] Already in some urban state trial courts the overload of judicial work often becomes large, and some sympathetic observers see the same situation becoming true in the federal courts.[236] Simply to announce that there should be more judges is unlikely to carry sufficient

---

[230] See Brownlie, 'Federal Preemption as a Possible Response to a New Challenge: Securities Class Actions in State Court', 34 Cal. Western L. Rev. 493, 493–4 (1998) ('Perhaps the most surprising result [of the adoption of the federal Act] has been a shift of case filings from claims under federal law brought in federal courts to claims under state law in state courts—where the changes in federal law have not been embraced'). Although there is some debate about the significance of this rise of state court filings, Congress reacted to this development by adopting the Securities Litigation Uniform Standards Act of 1998, Pub. L. 105–353, 112 Stat. 3227 (1998), which pre-empts all state court suits covered by the Act.

[231] See above n. 101 and accompanying text (asserting that broadened discovery caused the substantive law to change). [232] See above n. 102.

[233] Cf. Zuckerman, 'Lord Woolf's Access to Justice: Plus ça change . . .', 59 Mod. L. Rev. 773, 795–6 (1996) (suggesting that in England only the overhaul of the system of litigation finance can consequentially effectively address the problem of litigation cost).

[234] See above nn. 78–87 and accompanying text.

[235] To date, American appellate courts have responded to caseload growth in a number of innovative ways, such as adopting programmes of alternative dispute resolution, and of depublication, under which a substantial proportion of decisions are not published and therefore not available to be cited as precedent.

[236] e.g. Kastenmeier and Geyh, 'The Case in Support of Legislation Facilitating the Consolidation of Mass-Accident Litigation: A View from the Legislature', 73 Marquette L. Rev. 535, 545 (1990) ('Arguments advanced as recently as the mid-1980s that the problem of federal court congestion is illusory, even if valid when made, are all but indefensible today'). For a recent example, see 'Testimony Shows Increasing Workload is Straining Judiciary's Resources', Third Branch, July 1998, at 1 ('An increasing workload is driving a Judiciary-wide need for resources').

weight, even if there were not potential disadvantages to unlimited expansion of the judiciary.[237]

The problem of priorities will not go away. As noted above, one prime source of delays in civil litigation is the priority given to criminal and some other matters.[238] For those who disagree with the policy behind increased emphasis on criminal prosecution and long incarceration, the solution to the problems thus created is easy: reverse the policy. But that is not a choice available to the rulemakers or the courts, and the legislative branch and executive branch legitimately hold sway on this point. Absent the unexpected willingness to fund unlimited expansions of the judiciary to accommodate all civil cases as well, therefore, the risk of displacement by matters having higher priority will remain.

Judges will continue to exercise control over litigation. Despite the absence of hard evidence that various forms of case management have desirable consequences,[239] there is sufficient basis for confidence that judges can bring about improvement by taking more interest in their civil cases. Faced with potentially growing demands on their time and stable or shrinking resources, judges can be expected to continue to be active in trying to control litigation. Although arguments can be made about the importance of leaving parties in control of their litigation,[240] the general American reality in connection with case management is that the choice is between freedom for lawyers and authority for judges. By and large, the objectors to judicial case management have been lawyers who formerly had unrestrained latitude to control their cases. Moreover, many lawyers welcome the involvement of the judge and support more rather than less judicial supervision.

There is a choice to be made about the form of case management. Accepting the idea of case management does not necessarily dictate its content. One model is individual tailoring for each case. Not only is this time-consuming,[241] it also

---

[237] An underlying tension is the desire of some to restrain the growth of the federal judiciary. The Federal Courts Study Committee, for example, cautioned that it would be desirable to avoid having the life-tenured federal judiciary expand beyond 1,000. Although that is in some ways an arbitrary number, the unlimited growth of the institution has potential negative effects. Indeed, the size of a trial court is one of the factors that was cited as contributing to delay at the trial level. See above text accompanying n. 117.   [238] See above text accompanying n. 121.

[239] See above text accompanying nn. 208–25. Ultimately RAND concluded that judicial management only constituted a 5% factor in the amount of time lawyers spent on cases. See Kakalik, Dunworth, Hill, McCaffrey, Oshiro, Pace, and Vaiana, *Just, Speedy, and Inexpensive?*, at 211.

[240] See, e.g., Walker, Lind, and Thibaut, 'The Relation between Procedural and Distributive Justice', 65 Va. L. Rev. 1401 (1978) (arguing that empirical research shows that parties prefer procedures that give them personal control over litigation choices).

[241] 'Case-by-case management developed because the transaction costs of procedural rules with broad attorney latitude were too high. As a result of federal local rules and state experimentation, the judiciary has already demonstrated that it thinks the transaction costs of ad hoc case-by-case management are also too high. Judges are already turning to formal limitations and definitions in order to reduce transaction costs.' Subrin, 'Federal Rules, Local Rules, and State Rules: Uniformity, Divergence, and Emerging Procedural Patterns', 137 U. Pa. L. Rev. 1999, 2049 (1989).

offers individual judges great latitude that many find disquieting.[242] The alternative is to rely on pattern or form case management procedures. This alternative has potential drawbacks also, as litigants whose cases are pigeonholed inappropriately may incur additional costs to get reclassified or fail to escape the patterned fate.

To some extent, the resolution of this choice depends on whether the case management is developed bottom up or imposed from above; change from above is more likely to be of the cookie-cutter, or one-size-fits-all, variety. The choice also raises issues of local autonomy; should local conditions control the handling of case management? In the federal system, the variations among district courts in caseloads and types of cases (particularly the level of criminal filings) would make it difficult or impossible to devise specific controls without dislodging important interests of many courts. But the more dispersed the task of developing the controls, the more they are likely to diverge depending on the individual preferences of judges (and therefore raise the concerns about discretion mentioned above).

6. CONCLUSION

The images invoked at the beginning of this essay are basically wrong. Whether or not it is the litigation superpower, America is not threatened with devastation by runaway civil litigation. Neither are judges approaching their task like fry cooks at McDonald's. But the underlying questions focus directly on the concerns of this collection and illustrate the difficulties that await the reformer, and these problems remain on or near the political front burner.[243]

For two decades, Americans have been asking themselves whether there is not a better way to handle civil litigation. Improvement is always possible, of course, but if the question really is whether a procedural shift can cause a metamorphosis, the probable answer is that it cannot without dislodging so much else that the entire role of litigation in society would need to be recalibrated. That might be worthwhile, but it would discard a great deal of advantage that the country has reaped from the basic orientation it has developed. Continuing with the system we have is going to mean that the problems will persist, and perhaps some of them will get worse, but the advantages will probably remain as well. Until a reformer arrives with authority to effect such a basic shift, procedural tinkering will continue to involve tinkering with many of the same tactics that have been used in the past.

---

[242] For an extensive examination of this topic, see Resnik, 'Managerial Judges'.

[243] 'In the two presidential debates of October, 1996, the need for civil litigation reform was mentioned four times.' Parness and Leonetti, 'Expert Opinion Pleading: Any Merit to Special Certificates of Merit?', 1997 BYUL Rev. 537, 538.

Richard L. Marcus

Appendix 3.1
Rate of civil filings per 100,000 population
(top five and bottom five jurisdictions)

State	Total filings	Per 100,000 pop.
DC	117,456	20,321
Maryland	867,564	17,474
Virginia	1,094,280	16,858
New Jersey	779,625	9,895
Utah	128,619	6,915
Maine	34,949	2,821
Montana	15,305	1,824
Nevada	20,120	1,449
Pennsylvania	171,516	1,424
Tennessee	59,498	1,167

Source: Ostrom and Kauder, *Examining the Work of State Courts.*

Appendix 3.2
Number of general jurisdiction judges
per 100,000 population
(top five and bottom five jurisdictions)

State	No. of judges per 100,000 population
District of Columbia	10.21
Illinois	7.53
Iowa	6.57
Missouri	5.90
Kansas	5.89
Utah	2.10
Mississippi	1.51
Maine	1.29
North Carolina	1.20
South Carolina	1.10

Note: The District of Columbia, Illinois, and Iowa have all cases heard by general jurisdiction courts, while other states have some heard by courts of limited jurisdiction.

Source: Ostrom and Kauder, *Examining the Work of State Courts.*

Appendix 3.3
Number of US magistrate judges, and number of 'matters' resolved by them

Year	Full time	Part time	Civil and criminal matters disposed of
1975	143	322	255,061
1980	210	263	280,151
1985	277	179	426,440
1990	329	146	450,565
1995	416	79	511,039

Source: Long Range Plan for the Federal Courts, table 1.

Appendix 3.4
Number of lawyers in California

Year	Membership of the California state bar
1995	120,267
1988	93,054
1980	64,840
1971	32,956

Source: Supplement to Curran and Carson, *The Lawyer Statistical Report*.

Appendix 3.5

Number of civil filings, dismissals for lack of prosecution, summary judgments, and trials, in California court system, by type of case

	Personal injury— motor vehicle	Personal injury— other	Eminent domain	Other civil complaints
1995–6				
Filings	47,554	32,038	1,232	122,886
Lack pros.	7,831	4,023	66	8,498
Sum. jdgt.	147	372	8	1,048
Trial	2,163	2,043	175	21,404
1989–90				
Filings	82,866	39,167	1,957	101,478
Lack pros.	10,981	7,053	49	17,462
Sum jdgt.	171	428	24	1,133
Trial	2,036	2,086	185	11,700
1984–5				
Filings	63,929	48,406	1,319	121,865
Lack pros.	5,764	3,277	36	16,154
Sum. jdgt.	75	137	8	1,813
Trial	1,649	1,670	168	15,959
1979–80				
Filings	53,733	29,538	2,509	89,300
Lack pros.	1,762	1,062	45	3,581
Sum jdgt.	99	218	2	1,126
Trial	2,021	2,043	363	16,700

Source: Based on unpublished data provided by the Judicial Council of California, for which I am indebted.

Appendix 3.6

Rate of appeal in federal court system as a percentage of district court terminations

Year	Dist. ct. terminations	Appeals filed	% of terminations appealed
1989	277,790	36,125	13.0
1985	306,987	29,606	9.6
1975	148,298	13,925	9.4
1965	97,556	5,512	5.7
1955	97,554	3,049	3.1
1945	91,655	2,168	2.4

Note: A 1995 study by the Federal Judicial Center raised doubts about the conclusion that there was a general increase in the frequency of appeals. See text accompanying nn. 81–3.

Source: V. Flanagan, 'Appellate Court Caseloads: A Statistical Overview', table 3 (14 Sept. 1989), in *Working Papers and Subcommittee Reports of Federal Courts Study Committee*, ii.

Appendix 3.7

Median duration of appeals, from filing of notice of appeal to disposition on the merits, in federal court system

Year	Duration of appeals[a]
1997	11.4 months
1996	10.4 months
1995	10.4 months
1994	10.5 months
1993	10.3 months
1992	10.6 months

[a] Median durations for appeals from the filing of the notice of appeal to disposition on the merits.

Source: *Federal Court Management Statistics* (1997), at 30.

Appendix 3.8

Discovery expenses per client by type of case

Case type	95th % ($)	Median ($)	10th % ($)
Tort	88,000	6,600	750
Civil rights	58,000	5,700	490
Contract	64,000	4,000	300
Other	300,000	4,000	400

Note: In the 'other' category, patent, securities, trademark, and antitrust cases stood out as having high discovery expenses.

Source: Willging *et al.*, *Discovery*.

Appendix 3.9

Attorney estimates of percentage of discovery expenses per client incurred unnecessarily because of problems in discovery

	All respondents (%)	Plaintiff attorneys (%)	Defence attorneys (%)
95th %	58	75	50
Median	13	15	10
15th %	2	2	2

Source: T. Willging *et al.*, *Discovery*, at 22, table 12.

4

Justice in Crisis:
England and Wales

Paul Michalik

1. INTRODUCTION

It is well recognized that the existing system of civil procedure in England and Wales is beset by excessive costs, delay, and complexity. For example, litigation is very expensive, and it is generally impossible to predict the probable costs of an action accurately in advance. Cases can take many years to be heard, due to unchecked party delays and backlogs within the system. Complexity within the procedural laws compounds both cost and delay, not least by protracting litigation and widening the range of potential matters in dispute between the parties.

These three interdependent factors of cost, delay, and complexity significantly impair access to justice in this country for the majority of the population. In order to redress this problem, over the past decade several reforms have been suggested. The most far-reaching reform proposals are contained in a report by Lord Woolf MR, entitled *Access to Justice*.[1] As a result of Lord Woolf's comprehensive review, a number of substantial procedural reforms are currently being introduced.

This essay will describe the existing system of civil procedure in England and Wales,[2] and identify the changing procedural principles that have underpinned English procedure over the past century.[3] It will identify the key problems associated with cost and delay, drawing on available statistical information.

This essay was prepared in close consultation with the editor, Mr Adrian Zuckerman, whose advice and assistance proved absolutely invaluable. Significant help was also given by Ms Sue Gibbons, whose editorial skill contributed greatly to the essay's final shape. All errors and omissions, however, remain entirely the responsibility of the named author.

[1] Lord Woolf, *Access to Justice: Interim Report* (London: HMSO, 1995); *Access to Justice: Final Report* (London: HMSO, 1996).

[2] For ease of reference, hereafter 'England' and 'English' will be used to refer to both England and Wales.

[3] This commentary is necessarily incomplete. Detailed information about English procedural rules in force, together with a comprehensive commentary, may be found in the so-called 'Green' and 'White' books, which contain the County Court Rules (CCR) and Rules of the Supreme Court (RSC) respectively. As at the time of writing, the most recent *Green Book* is Thompson *et al.* (eds.), *County Court Practice 1998* (London: Butterworths, 1998). The latest *White Book* is Scott *et al.* (eds.), *Supreme Court Practice 1999* (London: Sweet & Maxwell, 1998).

Finally, it will describe the proposed reforms, and consider the extent to which these reforms are likely to reduce the problems associated with cost, delay, and complexity.

2. THE ENGLISH SYSTEM OF CIVIL PROCEDURE

The English system of civil procedure applies throughout England and Wales.[4]

2.1. The hierarchy of the courts

The English courts serve the civil and criminal justice needs of a population of 51.8 million people.[5] There are two main courts of original civil jurisdiction: the county court (for smaller or simpler cases); and the High Court (for larger or more complex cases). Above these courts sit the Court of Appeal and the House of Lords, both purely appellate courts.

2.2. The county court

The county court forms the lowest tier of the civil jurisdiction. There are about 240 county courts, each having a regional jurisdiction.[6]

County court jurisdiction used to be limited to cases having a maximum value of £5,000. However, this restriction was abolished, and today the county court has a theoretically unlimited jurisdiction. Nevertheless, the High Court and County Courts Jurisdiction Order 1991 provides a general presumption that, where the value of an action exceeds £50,000, the action should be transferred to the High Court. Conversely, the same Order presumes in favour of the county court deciding those cases where the amount claimed is less than £25,000. In between these two values, cases can be allocated to either court, depending on their complexity and importance. The idea is that the more complex and important cases of middling value should at least have a chance to be heard and decided in the higher court. However, the county courts alone have jurisdiction in personal injury claims with a value of £50,000 or less.

The county court's equity jurisdiction is limited in most cases to £30,000,

---

[4] The Scottish system is based not on the English common law, but on the Roman/Dutch civil law. It comprises a very different procedure, applied by a hierarchy of courts which is different from that in England except at the final appeal level. Northern Ireland, although part of the United Kingdom (with England, Wales, and Scotland), also operates its own procedure and own courts up to the level of final appeal. However, unlike Scotland, in Northern Ireland civil procedure is based on the English common law model, and is much closer to that in force in England and Wales. This report will deal only with the civil procedure of England and Wales.

[5] Office of National Statistics website. Population figures given are the latest published, and relate to 1995: see http://www.statistics.gov.uk/stats/ukinfigs/pop.htm.

[6] *Judicial Statistics: England and Wales for the Year 1997* (London: HMSO, 1998), 35.

with the possibility in some cases of extending this figure by agreement.[7] In addition, for cases of the lowest value (under £3,000), the county court operates a separate small claims court.[8]

2.3. The High Court

A case may be brought before the High Court by filing a claim in any one of about 130 district registries, or in the Central Office in London. The High Court has no upper limit to its original jurisdiction.

The High Court is divided into three major divisions: Chancery; Queen's Bench; and Family. This division allows for a certain amount of judicial specialization. Several specialist courts also exist within the High Court, including a Commercial Court, Patents Court, Official Referee's Court, Companies Court, and an Admiralty Court.[9]

The Queen's Bench division deals with claims for common law as opposed to equitable remedies (e.g. debt; damages; recovery of land or goods). Thus, the Queen's Bench division hears most claims based in contract or tort. It also has responsibility for all judicial reviews of administrative actions, admiralty, and commercial cases.

The Chancery division deals with claims for primarily equitable remedies, including cases involving: sale of land; mortgages; trusts; estates; insolvency; probate; intellectual property; and company matters. In practice, there is a good deal of overlap between the judicial business of the Queen's Bench and the Chancery divisions.

The Family division deals with all matrimonial cases.

2.4. Appeals

Each first instance court also hears some appeals. Both the High Court and the county courts have judges of at least two types, one junior to the other. The more junior judge handles interlocutory or procedural matters, and trials where a relatively low amount is at stake. The more senior judge hears full trials. In the county court, the junior type of judge is known as a district judge, and the senior type of judge is called the circuit judge. In the High Court, the more junior judge is called either a master or a district judge (who will also act as the district judge in the local county court). The more senior judge is known as a High Court judge.

The basic rule is that decisions of the more junior judge in each court may be

---

[7] County Courts Act 1984, ss. 23 and 24, and County Courts Jurisdiction Order 1981.
[8] County Courts Act 1984, s. 64 and CCR Ord. 19—the Small Claims Arbitration procedure. This is discussed further below.
[9] For more detail, see Sime, *A Practical Approach to Civil Procedure* (3rd edn. London: Blackstone Press Ltd., 1997), 20–2.

appealed to the more senior judge in the same court. Procedural questions are decided by junior judges in interlocutory hearings. Thus, procedural appeals are heard initially by a senior judge of the same court.

Appeals against final decisions of the senior judges in either court go to the Court of Appeal. The Court of Appeal also hears further appeals from interlocutory appeals decided by the senior judges in the two lower courts. The House of Lords hears further appeals from final decisions of the Court of Appeal, or appeals direct from the High Court in cases of special importance.

2.5. The stages in the English civil process

The typical English civil action involves several stages, divided roughly into pre-trial, trial, and post-trial proceedings. The ordinary case goes through the following stages.

2.5.1. Pre-trial

1. Commencement: court action is commenced by the issue and service of proceedings.
2. Pleadings: the plaintiff's statement of claim is answered by the defendant's statement of defence. Comparison between these formal statements of the parties' positions should define the issues for trial.
3. Directions: in modern practice, directions as to how to progress the case must be sought from the court within one month of the close of pleadings, unless automatic directions apply.
4. Discovery: the process by which the documentary evidence is revealed.
5. Interlocutory applications: these may be brought at any time, but it is usual for non-urgent interlocutory applications to be brought after discovery, when the evidence is known and the case is taking its final shape.
6. Exchange of witness statements: the oral evidence which each party proposes to call from the witnesses is shown to the other side.
7. Setting down: once the case is ready to proceed to trial, the plaintiff must apply to the court to 'set it down', or to fix a date, for trial.

2.5.2. Trial

8. Trial: the court hears evidence and legal argument and decides the case.

2.5.3. Post-trial

9. Taxation of costs: the winning party is usually entitled to have his or her legal bills paid by the loser. Unless the loser agrees, the bills are 'taxed' by a taxing officer of the court to ensure that they are reasonable.
10. Execution of judgment: the court's execution procedures are designed to enable the winner to enforce the judgment.

2.6. Pre-trial/trial distinction

English law makes a sharp distinction between pre-trial procedures and trial. The substance of the claim is only investigated at trial. Before trial, pre-trial interlocutory applications are made to prepare the case for determination at trial. Nothing done before the trial is of final effect insofar as the substantive merits of the case are concerned.

In practice, a significant amount of pre-trial activity involves curing procedural defects. If the parties miss a deadline, or are required by the rules to obtain the court's permission before undertaking a procedural step that they wish to take, an interlocutory application must be made.

Before the trial, the case is in the hands of the parties. They are responsible for gathering information and preparing the case. Traditionally, none of the available procedures was compulsory. Pre-trial procedural applications are brought as and when the parties see fit. By contrast, at trial the judge has control over the procedure. An English trial is a single, continuous event, involving the presentation of oral evidence and arguments by the parties, usually through legal representatives. A trial will not be adjourned without very good reason. However, the judge's control does not extend to the content of the trial. He or she cannot direct what evidence should be presented or what arguments should be raised. These matters are exclusively for the parties to decide.

2.7. Commencement of proceedings in the High Court

The High Court procedure appears to have been designed to ensure that the plaintiff[10] need not take steps to advance his case unless this is shown to be necessary. Thus, proceedings are commenced by the plaintiff filing in court and serving on the defendant a 'writ of summons'. Although the court must stamp the writ before it can be served, service is effected by the plaintiff himself, and the court has no involvement. The writ calls on the defendant to give notice of whether or not she intends to defend the plaintiff's claim, which is very briefly outlined in his writ.

The defendant has fourteen days from receiving the writ to file an acknowledgement with the court that the writ has been served. The court sends a copy of this document to the plaintiff. The defendant's acknowledgement must indicate whether or not she intends to contest the plaintiff's claim.[11] Where no acknowledgement is made, or the acknowledgement does not indicate that

---

[10] In an effort to use gender-balanced language, without resorting too often to the clumsiness of 'he or she', all plaintiffs and applicants are treated as male, and all defendants and respondents are treated as female.

[11] Such an acknowledgement does not constitute a submission to the jurisdiction of the court, which the defendant may also contest.

the defendant will contest the claim, the plaintiff may obtain judgment in default of a defence.

2.8. High Court pleadings

At the option of the plaintiff, the writ may be accompanied by a 'statement of claim'. This document is the detailed formal exposition of the plaintiff's claim, which, together with the defendant's reply to it (the 'statement of defence'), defines the issues and arguments for the trial before the court.

If the statement of claim was not already served with the writ, the plaintiff must serve it on the defendant within fourteen days of the date on which the defendant files her acknowledgement of service in court. Subsequently, the defendant has either fourteen days from the date of service of the statement of claim, or twenty-eight days from the date of service of the writ (whichever is the longer), to serve the plaintiff with her statement of defence. Note that service of documents is undertaken by the parties themselves, usually by sending the documents through the post or by delivering them (or having them delivered) personally to the other party.

The defendant's statement of defence may be accompanied by any counter-claim that the defendant wishes to make against the plaintiff. Finally, the plaintiff has another fourteen days to file a defence to the defendant's counter-claim, or reply to her statement of defence, if desired. Once this stage has been reached, the pleadings are considered to be closed. As we will see below, the timetable set by the automatic directions begins to run from the close of pleadings. Once again, where no defence is received from the defendant, the plaintiff can obtain a default judgment.

2.9. Commencement and pleadings in the county court

The commencement procedure follows similar lines in the county court, with modifications designed to make it easier for litigants who are not represented by lawyers. For example, the county court itself takes responsibility for serving all documents, and relies exclusively on the post. Many county court documents are in the shape of forms. These are more or less self-explanatory, and can be completed simply by inserting the relevant details in the spaces provided on the forms.

To commence his claim, the plaintiff must complete the form for a summons and the form for giving particulars of his claim. These are equivalent to the High Court writ and statement of claim. Both must be prepared and given to the county court, which then stamps them and mails them to the defendant by way of service.

The court includes a blank form on which the defendant may give details of any defence. The defendant can complete this form and mail it back to the court if she wishes to contest the plaintiff's claim. Any letter or other document from the defendant opposing the plaintiff's claim will also be taken as sufficient to amount to a 'defence'. In the absence of other pleadings (such as a reply by the plaintiff, or a counter-claim by the defendant), the pleadings are closed once the defence is received.

2.10. Small claims in the county court

Money claims for less than £3,000 are automatically sent by the county court to 'arbitration' as soon as a defence is received. Although called 'arbitration', such hearings in fact proceed before a judicial officer of the county court. They are private and informal. Any documents relied on, and any expert reports, must be exchanged beforehand. Evidence is not given on oath, and the normal rules of evidence do not apply. There are low, fixed maximum sums which may be claimed by the winner as 'costs'. Unlike costs recoverable in other courts, these do not include the expenses of employing a legal representative. Instead, a fixed amount, ranging from £27.50 to £73.50, is recoverable, together with certain direct expenses.[12] All of these factors make the small claims process accessible to ordinary people, giving litigants access to an informal, inexpensive forum where they need not be legally represented.

However, the small claims procedure is only available in very modest cases. All other claims must proceed via the full civil procedure.

2.11. Directions

Under modern practice, in order to streamline the conduct of cases and ensure that they are fully prepared before they are due to be heard, it is compulsory to obtain judicial directions as to how each case should proceed. In county court cases in which automatic directions do not apply, a pre-trial conference will be called by the court. In the High Court, the plaintiff is obliged to take out a summons for directions within one month of the close of pleadings.[13] The directions hearing which follows from the plaintiff's application is intended to facilitate judicial control over the pre-trial process.

In most cases in the county court, and in High Court personal injury cases (except those brought in admiralty or involving medical negligence), a standard set of directions will automatically apply, unless the court is specifically asked to vary it.[14]

---

[12] CCR Ord. 19, r. 4 and Ord. 38, app. B.
[14] CCR Ord. 17, r. 11 and RSC Ord. 25, r. 8.

[13] RSC Ord. 25, r. 1.

The automatic directions require:

		High Court	County court
(a)	Discovery of documents by exchange of lists	14 days	28 days
(b)	Inspection of documents	21 days	35 days
(c)	Exchange of expert reports	14 weeks	10 weeks
(d)	Exchange of witness statements	14 weeks	10 weeks
(e)	Setting down/request for hearing	6 months	6 months
(f)	Photos/sketch plan submitted for agreement	Before trial	Before trial
(g)	Police accident book submitted for agreement	Before trial	Before trial

(Time limits are measured from the close of pleadings, except in (f) and (g) above.)

Under these directions, the parties must be ready to ask the court to set a trial date within six months of the close of the pleadings. (Close of pleading is usually fourteen days after service of the defence.) We will see below how far this expectation is fulfilled in the typical case.

In the county court, the potential for party delay is subject to an outer limit. If the plaintiff fails to request a date for trial within fifteen months of the close of pleadings, the case is automatically struck out without further warning.[15]

Where no automatic directions apply, the court will design specific directions suitable to the needs of each case, after hearing from the parties as to what those needs are. The directions will cover broadly the same matters as the automatic directions, together with anything else that must be done to prepare the case for trial.

2.12. Judgment in default of a defence

A high proportion of cases filed in the English courts are determined by judgment in default. Where no defence is received within the time allowed, the plaintiff may apply for judgment to be entered against the defendant.[16]

A default judgment is final where the claim is for a certain, or ascertainable, sum of money (a liquidated claim) or for the possession of land. A final default judgment may be enforced immediately. Where this is not the case, an interlocutory judgment is given, holding the defendant liable for 'damages to be assessed and costs'. A further hearing must be held, to determine the amount for which the defendant is liable, before the interlocutory judgment becomes final and enforceable.

After judgment has been entered, a defendant who can show that she has

---

[15] CCR Ord. 17, r. 11 (9). Note that the courts may reinstate actions automatically struck out, thereby undermining the sanctioning effect of the rule: *Rastin* v. *British Steel plc* [1994] 1 WLR 732.

[16] CCR Ord. 9 and RSC Ord. 13. Not all claims are amenable to default judgment. Those which are include: actions for a sum of money and no other remedy in the county court (called 'default actions'); other county court actions (called 'fixed date actions') except those to which automatic directions do not apply; and High Court actions where the writ claims only common law remedies.

some reasonable excuse for failing to respond to the proceedings within the time allowed, and that she has a defence which ought to be heard, may have the default judgment set aside. Where a default judgment was irregularly obtained, as where the proceedings were not served properly, the defendant may have it set aside as of right.

2.13. Summary judgment

Where the plaintiff believes that the defendant has no reasonable or arguable defence, he may make an application for summary judgment.[17] The application must be supported by one or more affidavits substantiating the plaintiff's belief that his claim is just and that the defendant has no reasonable or arguable defence. The defendant may file affidavits in reply, giving her version of the evidence.

At the hearing, the judge will hear legal argument and submissions as to the effect of the affidavit evidence. Taking the evidence in the most favourable light to the defendant's case, the judge will assess whether or not there is a reasonably arguable defence which deserves the chance to be heard at a full trial. If there is not, the judge will grant the plaintiff's application for summary judgment. Summary judgment is final and enforceable unless appealed. Alternatively, the judge may refuse summary judgment in whole or in part, if there is a reasonably arguable defence.

If summary judgment is refused, the judge will grant the defendant leave to defend. This may be subject to conditions. Usually, conditions are imposed where the defence is weak but the court cannot be persuaded that it has no chance of succeeding. The most common condition is that the defendant must pay into court the sum claimed by the plaintiff. If the judge decides that the summary judgment application ought never to have been brought, he or she will simply dismiss the plaintiff's application, and may order the plaintiff to pay the costs of the application immediately.

2.14. Discovery

Discovery is the process by which each side gains access to relevant documents in the hands of the other party. It is a two-stage process. First, each party lists all of the documents which it has, or has had, in its possession, which are potentially relevant to the case. Secondly, the other side is given an opportunity to inspect the documents listed as discoverable. This process of locating, reviewing, listing, inspecting, and copying documents can be extremely time-consuming, especially

---

[17] RSC Ord. 14 and CCR Ord. 9, r. 14. Summary judgment is not available in certain prohibited cases, such as: claims for libel, slander, malicious prosecution, and false imprisonment; admiralty actions *in rem*; probate matters; small claims cases; actions against the Crown; and certain cases having their own specific summary procedure.

in major commercial cases where there may be rooms full of potentially relevant files.

Discovery lies at the heart of the evidence-gathering processes in the English system. Failure to disclose a relevant document is a serious ethical offence, punishable by striking out of the claim, or a fine or imprisonment for contempt of court.[18]

The existence of all relevant documents must be disclosed; but not all such documents must be revealed for inspection. Certain types of documents are 'privileged' and need not be shown to the other side. The most important category of privilege is legal professional privilege. This privilege covers documents passing between clients and their lawyers which give or seek legal advice, or documents between clients or their lawyers and third parties which were created for the dominant purpose of preparing or conducting litigation. Other important categories of privilege are public interest immunity (which protects certain sensitive government papers from disclosure in the public interest) and self-incrimination privilege (covering documents which tend to incriminate the party concerned).

Privileged documents must be enumerated on the list of discoverable documents provided to the other party, with a brief description of the grounds upon which privilege is claimed. This enables the opponent to challenge the claim to privilege in respect of a particular document, if she thinks that it is not justified. Unless the court rejects the claim, documents for which privilege is claimed can legitimately be withheld from inspection.[19]

The unprivileged documents which have been disclosed for inspection are available to either party for use as evidence at the trial.

2.15. Interlocutory applications

Interlocutory applications are requests made to the court during the pre-trial stage of proceedings. *Inter alia*, they may be brought to obtain a decision on a point which needs to be decided by the court before trial; an interim remedy; or permission to take certain steps for which leave of the court is necessary under the rules. In practice, many interlocutory applications are brought to obtain the court's forgiveness for procedural failings by the parties or to cure defects in procedure.

2.16. The lack of procedural discipline in the English system

It might appear that the directions system outlined above creates a tough timetable which should eliminate delay. Yet, directions have had only a limited

---

[18] RSC Ord. 24, r. 16 (1) and (2); CCR Ord. 14, r. 10.

[19] Note that mere confidentiality alone is not sufficient reason to withhold discoverable documents: *Alfred Crompton Amusement Machines Ltd.* v. *Customs & Excise Comrs (No. 2)* [1974] AC 405, 433; *Science Research Council* v. *Nassé* [1980] AC 1028, 1065.

effect. They have certainly not eliminated the problems that they were designed to address. The reasons for this lie in the traditional English approach to procedural discipline, and, specifically, in the fact that interlocutory applications may be made to the court to forgive breaches of the procedural rules and to excuse delays.

Before the late nineteenth century, procedural discipline was exceptionally rigorous. Parties were required to get every element of their case exactly right, including the precise words to be used. Any mistake risked the claim being dismissed or the defence struck out. In the late nineteenth century, the Judicature Acts of 1873 and 1875 reformed the courts, abolishing this formalism. A new spirit of liberality was inaugurated, which has since become firmly established at the heart of English civil procedure.

The new liberal regime was expounded in two late nineteenth-century cases concerning late amendment of pleadings, which are still regularly referred to today. In the first case, Brett MR said:[20]

However negligent or careless may have been the first omission, and however late the proposed amendment, the amendment should be allowed if it can be made without injustice to the other side. There is no injustice if the other side can be compensated in costs.

In the second case, Bowen LJ endorsed this emphasis, explaining:[21]

[T]he object of the courts is to decide the rights of parties, and not to punish them for mistakes they make in the conduct of their cases by deciding otherwise than in accordance with their rights . . . I know of no kind of error or mistake which, if not fraudulent or intended to overreach, the court ought not to correct, if it can be done without injustice to the other party. Courts do not exist for the sake of discipline, but for the sake of deciding matters in controversy . . . It seems to me that as soon as it appears that the way in which a party has framed his case will not lead to a decision of the real matter in controversy, it is as much a matter of right on his part to have it corrected, if it can be done without injustice.

Under the rules of court, no procedural irregularity is automatically fatal to proceedings. Instead, the court has discretion to cure procedural defects and allow cases to continue. RSC Order 2, rule 1 provides:

1 (1) Where . . . there has . . . been a failure to comply with . . . these rules . . . the failure shall be treated as an irregularity and shall not nullify the proceedings. . . .

1 (2) . . . [T]he court may, on the ground that there has been such a failure . . . and on such terms as to costs or otherwise as it thinks just, set aside . . . any step taken . . . or . . . allow such amendments . . . and . . . make such order . . . as it thinks fit.

---

[20] *Clarapede & Co.* v. *Commercial Union Association* (1883) 32 WR 262, 263.
[21] *Cropper* v. *Smith* (1884) 26 Ch. D. 700, 710–11.

RSC Order 3, rule 5 deals expressly with the extension and abridgement of time limits:

5 (1) The Court may, on such terms as it thinks just, by order, extend or abridge the period within which a person is required or authorised by these rules, or by any judgment, order or direction, to do any act, in any proceedings.

5 (2) The Court may extend any such period as is referred to in paragraph (1) although the application for extension is not made until after the expiration of that period.

When requested to do so, the courts almost always forgive delays and cure procedural defects. The only exception is where amending errors would prejudice the opponent in a way for which costs could not compensate her. Having said this, English courts generally assume that costs can compensate for almost any possible prejudice.[22]

This liberal approach, which has dominated English civil procedure for the last 100 years or so, gives priority to achieving substantive justice on the merits over procedural justice. However, by relaxing procedural discipline and giving primacy to doing justice on the merits, it has diminished the power of the rules and timetables to curb party delays.

There is a fundamental tension between, on the one hand, the need to ensure that the rules of court are respected and complied with, so that the court can function; and, on the other hand, the fact that courts exist to decide disputes on their merits, and should eschew technicality wherever possible. However, as Zuckerman has noted, neither principle (formalism or liberalism) can be given supremacy.[23] If justice on the merits were always to be pursued, and failure to comply with time limits were always excused, the rules of court would lose their authority. Vice versa, if failing to comply with a time limit were always fatal, justice would be lost in technicality.

The tension between these two principles can only be resolved by the exercise of discretion in each case. The inevitable result is uncertainty. Unfortunately, such uncertainty can only be resolved by further litigation. One party must apply for a court order. There must be a hearing and a decision, which creates the possibility of one or more appeals. Paradoxically, the desire to give priority to substance over procedure has itself created immense scope for swamping the resolution of substantive disputes in wasteful procedural litigation.

In his report entitled *Access to Justice*, Lord Woolf noted the abundance of satellite litigation and 'the tendency of parties at present to make numerous interlocutory applications. These are generally of a tactical nature which may be of dubious benefit even to the party making the application and which may not be warranted by the costs involved.'[24]

---

[22] Although note that this assumption has recently been questioned: *Grovit* v. *Doctor* [1997] 1 WLR 640, per Lord Woolf MR.

[23] Zuckerman, 'Dismissal for Delay: The Emergence of a New Philosophy of Procedure' (1998) 17 CJQ 223.　　　　[24] Woolf, *Access to Justice: Final Report*, ch. 7, para. 23.

This proliferation of procedural or 'satellite' litigation has had undesirable consequences for the administration of civil justice as a whole. First, the more procedural litigation that takes place in any case, the fewer court resources are left for other cases, and the more delay that is generated. Secondly, procedural litigation renders the cost of litigation high and unpredictable. As a result, the majority of the population, who cannot afford to commit considerable, or potentially unlimited, financial resources to litigation, are denied access to justice.

Ironically, as purely procedural litigation has burgeoned, the English system has increasingly come to manifest the very ills that the liberalizing reforms were meant to cure. While emphasizing substantive justice to the individual litigants before the court, it is indifferent to the adverse systemic effects which the liberal approach produces. The giving of priority to substance over procedure seriously impairs the courts' ability to deliver justice to other litigants waiting to have their cases heard, and potential litigants in society at large.

2.17. Interim and provisional relief: injunctions

Interim relief is available in the form of interlocutory injunctions. An injunction is a binding command from the court directing a party to do something, or to refrain from doing something, pending trial.

Interim relief by way of interlocutory injunction is available where one party's ordinary freedom to act would undermine irreparably the benefit that the other party could otherwise expect from his right to have his action or defence tried and vindicated in court. If the payment of damages after trial would properly compensate the affected party, then the harm is not irreparable, and no injunction will be granted. The court will only grant an injunction if restraining the other party is necessary in order to minimize irreparable harm.

The party who seeks an interlocutory injunction must give an undertaking as to damages. This is an undertaking given to the court that, if the injunction is granted but it later turns out to have been unjustified, the applicant will pay to the respondent damages for any harm which the injunction has caused her, as the court may think fit. The undertaking as to damages is intended to protect the party affected by an interlocutory injunction. Should the defendant suffer loss from an unjustified interlocutory injunction, then the undertaking ensures that this harm is repaired, as far as repair can be made by an award of damages.

The position is more complex where both sides claim that they will suffer irreparable harm pending trial: the applicant if the injunction is withheld; and the respondent if it is granted. Where neither party can be adequately compensated by the payment of damages after judgment, the courts' approach is to minimize the irreparable harm suffered. The judge will compare the magnitude of the irreparable harms arising to each party, discounted by the likelihood of each party's success, and grant or withhold the injunction according to which course of action is less harmful.[25]

An injunction must be applied for, like any other pre-trial order, by way of an interlocutory application. Such applications must usually be made with notice to the other party. However, in special circumstances of urgency, or where notice to the other party might allow her to frustrate the purpose of the application, an *ex parte* procedure is available. This procedure contains two safeguards to protect the absent party. The applying party has a duty of utmost good faith. She must disclose all information which might affect the court's decision, including information detrimental to her own case. She must also draw the court's attention to any arguments against the issue of the injunction on which she can foresee that the respondent might wish to rely. A court order issued in response to an *ex parte* application is provisional only, and will be reviewed at an *inter partes* hearing as soon as one can be arranged.

2.17.1. Mareva *injunctions*

The *Mareva* injunction is a special form of urgent, *ex parte*, interim relief. It is designed to prevent a defendant from gathering up her assets and taking them out of the country, or otherwise hiding or dissipating them, for the purpose of frustrating execution of judgment. It should be understood that security for judgment is not normally available in the English system. However, where the court is persuaded that the defendant is likely to act deliberately so as to undermine the judgment which the plaintiff might obtain, a *Mareva* injunction may be ordered.

First, the plaintiff must show that he has a good arguable case for obtaining judgment against the defendant. Secondly, he must show good grounds for suspecting that the defendant would put her assets beyond the reach of the court if she were to be informed of the commencement of proceedings against her in the normal way. Where both elements can be shown, the *Mareva* injunction is available as an *ex parte* order even before proceedings are commenced.

A *Mareva* injunction forbids the defendant from dealing with her assets, up to an amount sufficient to cover the plaintiff's claim, otherwise than in the normal course of her business. It binds all those with notice of it, including banks who hold funds for the defendant. Such banks are under a duty to prevent the defendant from withdrawing her money, in violation of the injunction. At the *inter partes* review, the order will usually be restructured, to allow the defendant maximum financial freedom consistent with protecting the plaintiff's rights against evasion of the court's jurisdiction.

---

[25] *American Cyanamid v. Ethicon* [1975] AC 396.

2.17.2. Anton Piller *injunctions*

The *Anton Piller* order also protects against abuse of the process of the court. In this case, however, its purpose is to prevent the destruction of evidence. Again, it is an *ex parte* order, obtainable before service.

Anton Piller orders are available where there is reason to believe that the defendant might destroy or hide relevant evidence if she receives notice of the commencement of proceedings against her in the normal way. Such an order requires the defendant to allow the plaintiff's lawyers access to her premises, where there is reason to believe that evidence in favour of the plaintiff's case may be found there. The plaintiff's lawyers must be permitted to enter the premises, search for evidence, and seize and secure anything relevant which is found there.

2.17.3. Interim payment

Traditionally, the English courts had no mechanism for granting interim payments on account of an eventual judgment. However, interim awards of damages have recently been made available by statutory reform.

A plaintiff can now make an interlocutory application for an order directing the defendant to make an interim payment to the plaintiff on account of final judgment.[26] The plaintiff must persuade the court that the trial will inevitably result in the plaintiff receiving an award of 'a substantial sum' in damages from the defendant. The amount paid is subject to adjustment, once the final judgment is given and the defendant's true liability is known.

2.18. Exchange of witness statements

Traditionally, the first and only time that each party heard the witnesses of their opponent was at trial. This was a function of the principle of orality, which has historically underpinned English procedure. This principle accounts for the English system's tradition of a single, continuous trial at which evidence and legal argument are presented orally to the judge. However, in practice, this principle led to a distinct possibility of 'trial by ambush', wherein one side might be defeated by an unexpected point which could have been answered had fair notice been given. To avoid 'trial by ambush', recent changes to the rules of court require parties to give advance notice of the evidence which they intend to call, by providing written witness statements to the other side in advance of trial.[27]

A timetable for the exchange of witness statements is incorporated into the

---

[26] RSC Ord. 29, rr. 9–18, and CCR Ord. 13, r. 12.

[27] The rules regarding the exchange of witness statements have developed since the Civil Evidence Act 1968. Since 1988, the procedure has been extended to apply in all divisions of the High Court and in the county courts. The current legislative framework is set out in: s. 5, Courts and Legal Services Act 1990; RSC Ord. 38, r. 2A; and CCR Ord. 20, r. 12A.

directions given by the court. The exchange is almost invariably simultaneous, to prevent the possibility of one party taking advantage of her foreknowledge of the other party's case, by tailoring her evidence accordingly. The automatic directions provide for simultaneous exchange to occur before the expiry of ten weeks from the close of pleadings in the county court, or fourteen weeks in the High Court.

By a practice direction of the High Court, written witness statements now replace oral examination-in-chief in all cases, unless the court orders otherwise.[28] In the county court there is no general rule, but judges usually follow the High Court practice. Cross-examination follows orally in the usual way.[29]

2.19. Setting down

Once the interlocutory procedures are completed, the case is ready for trial. It is the plaintiff's responsibility to inform the court that the case is ready, and to ask that provision should be made on the court calendar for it to be heard. This is done by applying to the court to have the case 'set down' for trial.

In the High Court, on an application to set down, the plaintiff must lodge with the court the 'case bundle'. This comprises all of the important papers representing the case so far. Two copies are lodged. One is for the judge, and the other becomes the court record. (The High Court does not keep its own file of the papers in each case.) The bundle must contain: the writ; the pleadings; any interrogatories together with the answers given; all interlocutory orders other than orders as to time; a statement of the value of the claim; a note estimating the expected length of trial and indicating which court list is appropriate; notice of any grant of legal aid; and, in district registries, a certificate of readiness.

The High Court enters the case on the appropriate list, according to its type. Subsequent allocation, from these lists to particular judges for hearing, is not made by random assignment, as is the case in some systems. The allocation of cases to particular judges is made by a senior judge, as a matter of discretion, taking into account the nature of the case. This enables a certain allowance to be made for varying levels of judicial experience and specialization.

Rather than allocating each case a fixed appointment for hearing, the bulk of cases are simply heard in turn according to their position on the list. Parties must watch the progress of their case up the list as other cases are heard or withdrawn. The court notifies the parties when their case is set down, and again when it reaches the point at which it is likely to be heard the next day. Where there are good reasons for a case to be given a fixed appointment for hearing,

---

[28] *Practice Direction (Civil Litigation: Case Management)* [1995] 1 WLR 262.

[29] In cases where oral examination-in-chief is held, counsel are prohibited from asking any questions of their own witnesses which are designed to elicit evidence which is not included in the witnesses' statements, without permission of the court: RSC Ord. 38, r. 2A (7) (b).

such as the involvement of witnesses who must travel internationally, or numerous expert witnesses with crowded diaries, the court may grant a fixture for a set date instead.

In the county court, this process is called making an application for a fixture. The county court does not use a list system, but, instead, fixes a specific hearing date for each case. This is done at the directions hearing, if one is held. Where automatic directions apply, a date is set upon application by the plaintiff.

In both courts, the applicable directions will provide for a time limit within which the plaintiff must apply to the court to have the case set down, or a fixture allocated. The automatic directions provide for this to be done within six months of the close of pleadings. In the county court, a long-stop provision means the case will automatically be struck out if no application for a fixture is made within fifteen months.

2.20. Trial

As already seen, an English trial is a single continuous event. It was traditionally an entirely oral procedure, with oral evidence and argument. In modern practice, written witness statements are exchanged, which will ordinarily stand as witnesses' evidence-in-chief, in substitution for oral examination by the party calling the witness.

As trial approaches, the evidential documents to be put before the court must be made up into a second bundle. This bundle must contain: exchanged witness statements; disclosed expert reports; contemporaneous correspondence; and any other documents on which any party will rely. The court will usually order that this bundle also contain: a skeleton of each party's argument; a list of the legal authorities that each party will rely on; and a chronology of the relevant events. Once again, two copies must be filed in court, at least two days before the trial.

At trial, the witnesses are called by each party in turn, and their evidence is given under oath. Note that the parties themselves may give evidence as witnesses. The witnesses swear to tell the truth. Lying under oath constitutes the crime of perjury.[30] The plaintiff presents his case first. Witness statements may be read aloud or simply taken as read. Each witness's evidence is tested by oral cross-examination before the court. The defendant must challenge any part of the plaintiff's evidence which she does not accept. Any positive case which a party intends to make, and which conflicts with the evidence-in-chief of a witness in the stand, must be put to the witness for reaction and comment. Finally, the judge may ask questions of the witness, limited to those necessary to ensure that she has properly understood the witness's evidence. The defendant's witnesses are then called, and a similar oral procedure is followed.

---

[30] Perjury Act 1911.

Witnesses may be compelled to testify in court by a *subpoena ad testificandum*, and may be compelled to produce documents or evidence in their possession (provided that the material is not privileged) by a *subpoena duces tecum*. Any witness who fails to appear after being served with a subpoena is liable to punishment for contempt of court. Where a witness is not co-operative, and must be subpoenaed, it is probable that no witness statement will have been obtained. In this case, a statement of the witness's expected evidence must be prepared and exchanged.

Legal argument follows the evidence, in each party's closing address. Where the defendant has called evidence, she starts the legal argument, leaving the plaintiff with the last word. Where the defendant calls no witnesses of her own, the plaintiff must close his case first. After the completion of legal argument, the judge may deliver an immediate decision. In more complicated matters, however, judgment is usually reserved for further consideration, and is delivered later, in written form.

2.21. Costs and taxation

Under the English system, the loser is usually ordered to pay to the winner the costs incurred in fighting the case. This is called the 'indemnity' rule. These costs include lawyers' fees, experts' fees, the expenses of other witnesses, and the fees charged by the court for access to its procedures. By far the most significant charge is the lawyers' fees. A plaintiff is considered to have won his case if he has had an order made in his favour against the defendant, even if it might not have been all that he sought.

2.21.1. Legal fees

Lawyers' fees are not subject to regulation. Solicitors generally charge by the hour according to a scale, agreed with their clients, which takes into account the seniority of the lawyers doing the work. Traditionally, barristers accepted cases for an agreed fee, determined according to the complexity and importance of the case. However, there is a growing trend amongst members of the bar to adopt hourly charges. The barrister's fee, or hourly rate, is agreed with the solicitor, who is the barrister's employer, not with the client.

2.21.2. Taxation of costs

The indemnity rule obligation only indemnifies the winner against costs reasonably incurred. The losing party has a general right to have the winner's bills assessed for their reasonableness, in the light of the issues at stake, their seriousness, and what is reasonable practice in the conduct of litigation. This process is called 'taxation of costs'. The loser can require the winner to submit his bill of costs to the taxing office of the court, which will assess its reasonableness.

The party to whom costs are awarded must prepare a detailed bill of costs.

This bill must make all the relevant background of the case clear to the taxing officer. A brief narrative must be included, describing the issues, the relevant circumstances, when instructions were received, and when the matter ended. The status of each lawyer for whom fees are claimed should be indicated, along with their rates of payment. The bill should then list all relevant events in the action, in chronological order, with dates and amounts claimed in respect of each event. These amounts will include all direct expenses and fees incurred.

Legal fees claimed are divided into three parts. First, a basic fee is claimed for the time actually spent. This is calculated as an hourly rate, varying with the seniority of the lawyer concerned. The average of solicitors' basic hourly rates ranges from about £60 to £80 per hour outside of London, up to £100 per hour in London firms, or even £170 per hour in firms in the city of London (London's financial district).[31] The hourly rate is intended to represent direct cost to the firm (i.e. salaries and overheads). Secondly, the basic fee is increased for general care and conduct of the file. This mark-up is intended to provide the firm with its element of profit. Mark-ups range from 50 per cent in the ordinary case to 100 per cent in complex cases.[32] This produces effective hourly rates between one and a half times and twice the basic rates. The most expensive firms will be charging in excess of £300 per hour. Finally, sums claimed for travelling and waiting time (usually billed at lower hourly rates) must be set out separately.

The bill of costs, and any supporting documents relevant to proving the work which was done on the file, and the need for that work to be done, must be lodged in the taxing office of the court. Once these papers are lodged, the other party is served with the bill. Under the 'standard basis' of taxation, the taxing officer applies a double test of reasonableness in taxing the bill: first, was it reasonable in the circumstances to do the work done; and, secondly, was the charge made for that work reasonable? After the hearing (if there is one),[33] the

---

[31] See for example rates allowed in *Jones* v. *Sec. of State for Wales* [1997] 2 All ER 507 (£100 per hour too high in Reading—£75 substituted, with 70 per cent mark-up); *Truscott* v. *Truscott* [1998] 1 All ER 82 (£95 per hour allowed for non-city London firm), and *KPMG Peat Marwick McLintock* v. *HLT Group Ltd.* [1995] 2 All ER 180 (survey showed average City of London rates in 1991–2 as £171.26, compared to average Holborn/Westminster rates (i.e. rates in other areas of central London outside the international financial district) of £108.74.

[32] Readers should note: (1) these rates are the basic rates allowed, and are subject to mark up of between 50 per cent and 100 per cent, giving overall hourly rates in the city of London of between about £255 and £340 per hour (as at 1991); (2) the rates are those allowed on taxation, dealing in many cases with work done several years ago; contemporary rates will inevitably be higher; (3) the rates allowed reflect the court's assessment of the rough average cost of litigation in the area concerned, and may well be below those charged by any individual firm; (4) discussions with litigators at present practising in the city of London indicate that, although still often required for taxation purposes, most firms have all but abandoned the mark-up method of charging, and simply charge their own clients an hourly rate, varying according to the firm, the client, and the file, of anything up to £400 per hour at the highest end of the market.

[33] The taxing office may make a provisional taxation, without hearing from either party. If this is done, the parties are given notice of the amount proposed to be allowed. They then have fourteen days to request a hearing on the taxation if they wish to challenge the proposed amount.

party entitled to costs amends the bill to show the allowed sums, pays the taxing fee, and lodges the amended bill with the taxing office for the issue of a certificate showing the taxed costs allowed.

The taxation may be appealed. In the first instance, the taxing officer's decision may be reviewed by another taxing officer, or district judge. Further review is available before a judge. In such cases, the judge often sits with experienced members of the profession as assessors. Appeal from the judge's review lies to the Court of Appeal.

Taxation only limits the sum that the loser must reimburse to the winner by way of costs. The winner must still pay the full fee to his lawyer. In practice, this typically leaves the winner bearing about one-third of his own legal costs.

2.21.3. Court fees

Court fees are also included in recoverable costs. These are charged to the party who initiates a particular procedure. Recently, court fees were restructured, so that the scale of fees payable depends on the size of the claim. For example, High Court commencement fees range from £100 on a claim of up to £10,000, to £500 on a claim for more than £100,000 or where no monetary limit is specified.[34]

This reform represented an attempt to use a price mechanism to ration court services, and to make the Court Service self-funding. The scheme has been successful, as far as raising the revenue to pay for the Court Service is concerned. Provisional results for the 1997–8 financial year suggest that civil court fees collected totalled 102.1 per cent of the total cost of running the civil courts.[35] However, judicial review proceedings were brought to test the legality of the scheme.[36] The Court of Appeal was unhappy that no provision had been made to preserve the right of access to justice for the very poor. They held that any future exercise of the power to set court fees must take into account the need to allow a right of access to all, including the very poor.

2.21.4. Special cases

The obligation to pay costs is not invariable. In litigation over a fund, such as a deceased's estate, costs will often be ordered to be paid out of the fund itself for all parties concerned.

The court retains discretion to order that the parties should each bear their own costs, or even that the winner should pay some or all of the costs of the loser. This discretion is exercised against parties who deliberately inflate costs or who indulge in wasteful or abusive procedural tactics. In certain circumstances, the court may also order that a party's lawyer must pay costs personally. Such a

---

[34] Supreme Court Fees Order 1980 (as amended in 1996).
[35] *Court Service: The Annual Report 1997–1998* (London: Stationery Office, 1998), 13.
[36] *R. v. The Lord Chancellor, ex p. Witham* [1998] 2 WLR 849.

'wasted costs order' will be made where the lawyer acted improperly, unreasonably, or negligently, and that conduct caused the applicant to incur unnecessary costs.[37]

2.21.5. Legal aid

Legal aid is available to poor persons for the conduct of civil cases. Companies cannot be legally aided. A lawyer must certify that the case has legal merit, in the sense that she would advise an unaided person in the position of the party concerned to proceed with the case.

The applicant for legal aid must have a disposable income[38] and disposable capital[39] below the upper limits set by the Legal Aid Board. Legal aid may be granted free, in which case the aided person pays nothing towards their case, or with contributions. Whether contributions will be required depends upon the applicant's disposable income and disposable capital.

The qualifying thresholds for disposable income and capital are low. They are regularly adjusted by regulations. At the time of writing, civil legal aid is available to those with a yearly disposable income of £7,777 or less.[40] Legal aid can nevertheless be refused to an applicant who qualifies on grounds of low income, if her disposable capital exceeds £6,750, and it appears that she is able to afford the proceedings without aid. In personal injuries claims, slightly more generous levels of £8,571 yearly disposable income, and £8,560 disposable capital, apply. Contributions are required from any applicant whose yearly disposable income exceeds £2,625 per year, or whose disposable capital exceeds £3,000.

Where aid is granted, the Legal Aid Board pays the aided person's lawyer's bills in the usual way, just as if the legally aided person were paying them herself. Where the legally aided person wins the case, the Legal Aid Board is entitled to the money recovered by way of costs from the loser. The Board also has a charge over any money or property recovered or preserved in the proceeding, to cover any excess of legal aid money paid out over and above the amount recovered from the losing party through costs. By contrast, the 'indemnity rule' does not apply against legally aided parties. Thus, where an aided person loses, her opponent will not be awarded any costs. This can give a

---

[37] Supreme Court Act 1981, s. 51 (6); *Ridehalgh* v. *Horsefield* [1994] 3 All ER 848.

[38] 'Disposable income' is calculated excluding: income tax, National Insurance payments (social security), and council tax (local taxes); allowances for dependants (up to £1,580 per annum each); maintenance paid for family members not living in the same household; housing costs (water, repairs, rent, mortgage payments on a house of up to £100,000 equity value); work-related expenses (including child care); certain state benefits received (e.g. disability living allowance); and other discretionary allowances (e.g. school fees).

[39] 'Disposable capital' is calculated excluding: up to £100,000 of the equity value of the applicant's house; the value of clothes, furniture, tools, trade equipment; and capital of up to £35,000 in the case of pensioners relying on income from capital.

[40] Civil Legal Aid (Assessment of Resources) Regulations 1989, as amended by the Civil Legal Aid (Assessment of Resources) (Amendment) Regulations 1998.

legally aided party a strong advantage in negotiating settlement with a non-legally aided opponent, because the opponent will know that he will never recover his costs if the litigation proceeds.

The blank cheque nature of the existing legal aid system removes considerations of cost-efficiency from the minds of those in control of litigation funded by the Legal Aid Board, allowing costs to grow out of all reasonable proportion to the sums at stake in smaller claims. It is therefore not surprising that the civil legal aid system is currently undergoing substantial review.

2.21.6. Payment into court

To obtain some protection from liability for costs, the defendant can make a 'payment into court'.[41] She must pay into court a sum that she is willing to pay to the plaintiff to settle the case, and notify the plaintiff that she has done so. If the plaintiff withdraws the money from court, the case is at an end. If instead he proceeds with the case, but at trial fails to recover more than the amount paid in, he must pay both his own costs and the costs which the defendant incurred from the time of her payment in.

The system of payment in thus puts pressure on plaintiffs to accept settlement offers made by defendants. Even where a payment in is less than what the plaintiff hopes to recover at trial, there is great pressure to avoid the risk of becoming liable for the defendant's costs.

2.22. Execution

Numerous execution procedures are available to help recover money which is owed under a judgment. The judgment debtor may be summoned into court and examined under oath to discover what assets or resources she has available. Once her assets are identified, these may be seized and sold. Chattels are taken under a writ of *fieri facias* in the High Court, or an order for execution in the county court. Land or chattels may be charged with the judgment debt, and subsequently sold by order of the court if payment is not forthcoming. Sums of money due to the debtor may be made subject to a garnishee order, requiring them to be paid to the judgment creditor instead. The debtor's earnings may be made subject to periodic deductions by an order for the attachment of earnings.

The county court and the High Court share jurisdiction over these different measures according to the amount at stake. It is sometimes necessary to have the judgment of one court transferred into the other for enforcement. For example, although the county court's jurisdiction has no upper limit, any execution against goods for an amount in excess of £5,000 can only be brought in the High Court. Conversely, any High Court judgment for less than £2,000

---

[41] RSC Ord. 22 and CCR Ord. 11.

sought to be executed against the judgment debtor's goods must be transferred into the county court.

3. COST AND DURATION OF PROCEEDINGS

The English system of civil procedure is sophisticated, flexible, and wide-ranging. Yet, it is much criticized as arcane, overly complicated, and expensive to operate. To evaluate these criticisms, it is instructive to consider the available statistical evidence concerning the cost and duration of civil proceedings in England.

In 1997, a large number of civil cases were commenced in the English courts. As Table 4.1 shows, a significant majority of cases were brought in the county court. Indeed, new county court cases outnumbered new High Court cases by more than twelve to one.

Very few of the cases started in any court proceed all the way to judgment after a full trial. Figures are available for the London Queen's Bench division of the High Court, sitting in the Royal Courts of Justice. Dispositions during the year may be compared with new cases filed during the year, although, naturally, many of the cases disposed of during the year will have been commenced in previous years (see Table 4.2).

Of all cases disposed of by court order, only 960 out of 11,664, or 8.2 per cent, were decisions reached after full trials. By far the most significant proportion of the cases decided by court order ended in default judgment (83.5 per cent). Of the 4,077 cases which were set down for trial, 2,987 (73.2 per cent) collapsed or settled before trial. Even greater numbers must have settled or collapsed before reaching the stage of being set down.

3.1. Analysing case duration

Waiting time can be divided, by and large, into two periods. The first is the time between filing the action and setting it down for trial. The length of this period is more or less within the control of the parties. It is used to prepare the case, and ends when the parties are ready for trial. (The case will not be set down for trial until the plaintiff believes that the case is ready, and makes application to the court for setting down.) What is required to make a case ready for trial is determined by the parties' procedural choices, the extent to which they co-operate, and the nature of the case. Such matters as the number and type of interlocutory applications, the amount of discovery, and the time dedicated to any settlement negotiations all contribute to this delay. If the parties co-operate, this delay can be minimized.

This preparatory period is subject to timetable directions issued by the court. In those cases where automatic directions apply, these directions 'allow' no

Paul Michalik

Table 4.1. *Actions commenced in English courts 1997*

High Court	
New Actions for trial	
Chancery division	38,360
Queen's Bench division	121,446
Family division	370
Total (new actions)	160,176
Appeals set down[a]	
Chancery division	182
Queen's Bench division	
Judicial review (for leave)	3,848
Judicial review (hearing)	1,285
Cases stated	184
Miscellaneous others	592
Family division	36
Total (appeals)	6,127
Total new High Court business	166,303
County courts	
Plaints	2,209,135
Insolvency matters	
Bankruptcy petitions	18,065
Companies winding-up petitions	1,092
Family matters	
Adoption applications	3,343
Divorce, nullity, and separation	165,332
Total new county court business	2,396,967

[a] The High Court hears appeals as set out in the text above. The High Court also conducts judicial review cases where procedures applied by subordinate tribunals are tested for legality. If judicial review is sought, leave of the High Court must be granted in a separate application, before the actual review is conducted. The case stated procedure involves appeals on questions of law raised in lower courts which are brought into the High Court for authoritative decisions. The lower court states the facts as it has found them, and the High Court decides what the legal effect of the facts should be.

Source: Judicial Statistics: England and Wales for the Year 1997 (London: HMSO, 1998), tables 2.1, 3.1, 4.2, 5.1, 1.12, 1.13, 1.14, 1.15, 1.16. Statistics available count appeals set down for hearing, not all appeals commenced.

more than six months before a hearing must be sought or setting down requested. The practice, however, is very different.

The second period of delay is the time between applying to the court to set the matter down for trial, and the date when trial commences. As described

Table 4.2. *Disposition of cases during 1997 in the Queen's Bench division at the Royal Courts of Justice in London*

Total writs and originating summonses issued	23,411
Cases ending by court order without trial or consent	
Default judgments	9,748
Summary judgments	956
Total	10,704
Trials	
Cases set down for trial	4,077
Trials held	1,090
Judgments given	960
Total dispositions (trial and non-trial)	11,664

Source: Judicial Statistics 1997, tables 3.2, 3.3, and 3.5.

above, in the High Court, upon setting down, the case is entered into a list of cases of the relevant type, and advances up the list, as each case before it is heard, until it takes its turn.[42] In the county court, a fixed date is allocated. In either court, the period between setting down and the hearing is within the court's control. Except where the case reaches the head of the list or the allocated date for trial and, due to party default, cannot proceed, there is nothing that the parties can do to extend or shorten this period.

Available figures are divided between these two periods of party and court delay respectively. Average figures for the Queen's Bench division of the High Court and for county courts may be taken by way of example. As Table 4.3 demonstrates, civil waiting times are too long. The six-month period before setting down envisaged by the automatic directions, which apply in most county court cases, would allow for a delay of twenty-six weeks. Yet, the average delay before setting down in the county courts is more than double this.

The automatic striking out provision in the county court comes into effect fifteen months (about sixty-four weeks) after the close of pleadings, if the plaintiff makes no application for a hearing. Depending on the promptness of service, pleadings should close only a few weeks after commencement of the proceeding. It appears that the average county court case outside of London comes very close to being struck out.

By contrast, the average criminal defendant waits only twelve weeks between committal for trial and trial in the criminal court system. Fifty-five per cent of

---

[42] For more details, see Sime, *A Practical Approach to Civil Procedure,* 378–80.

Table 4.3. *Average waiting times (in weeks)*

	Average time commencement to setting down	Average time setting down to trial	Average time commencement to trial
High Court—Queen's Bench			
Royal Courts (London)	120	41	161
Others (outside London)	154	41	195
County court			
London courts	53	17	70
Other courts	65	26	91

Source: *Judicial Statistics 1997*, tables 3.8 and 4.16.

criminal defendants wait less than eight weeks, and 76 per cent wait less than sixteen.[43]

Party delay up until setting down may be a result of the parties' own choices, and thus, to some extent, their own responsibility. But to have to wait almost another year after setting down before trial is an indictment of the English civil justice system.

3.2. Appeals

Published judicial statistics concerning appeals are not particularly comprehensive, nor are they well chosen to illustrate the primary concerns of caseload, cost and delay. In the official publication *Judicial Statistics* for 1997, no figures are given for the time taken in the purely appellate courts to dispose of appeals. Only selected figures are presented to illustrate caseload. The statistics in Table 4.4 do not shed much light on the problem of delay. The Court of Appeal appears to have dealt with more cases in 1997 than the number of new cases filed, which may have reduced its backlog. This appears to be the result of a decline in new business being filed in that court. The compilers of *Judicial Statistics* note that, from 1996 to 1997, the number of appeals in the Court of Appeal declined by eighty-nine, and the number of applications for leave fell by 6 per cent. They attribute this to extensions in the leave to appeal requirements, which mean that fewer cases can be brought to the Court of Appeal without leave first being obtained.

Nevertheless, problems of cost and delay plague the appeals courts. In 1996, the average time between setting down and finally disposing of the fastest 70 per cent of appeals to the Court of Appeal was fourteen months. The slowest 30 per cent of appeals took much longer. As at the end of 1996, some appeals had been

---

[43] *Judicial Statistics 1997*, table 6.15.

Table 4.4. *Appeal numbers 1997*

	Set down or presented	Disposed of
House of Lords		
Applications for leave[a]	237	220
Appeals[b]	72	57
Court of Appeal		
Interlocutory appeals	609	841
Final appeals	1,106	1,255

Note: In certain circumstances, leave of the court is required before an appeal can be brought. This table shows numbers for both applications for leave to appeal and actual appeals brought in the House of Lords, and for interlocutory and final appeals set down and heard in the Court of Appeal.

[a] All civil applications for leave, from England and Wales, Scotland, and Northern Ireland, including 27 Divisional Court matters, and two 'leapfrog' appeals from the High Court.

[b] All civil appeals presented, from England and Wales, Scotland, and Northern Ireland, including five Divisional Court matters, and one Northern Ireland Divisional Court matter, and four 'leapfrog' appeals from the High Court.

Source: *Judicial Statistics 1997*, tables 1.3, 1.4, 1.9, and 1.10.

awaiting hearing for more than five years. Where there is a demonstrated need for urgency, an individual case can be heard very quickly in the Court of Appeal. However, the great majority of cases wait far too long.[44]

3.3. Causes of delay

Litigation in England takes too long. It is impossible to believe that any but the smallest number of High Court cases really demand more than two years' attention before they are ready to be set down. Yet, Table 4.3 shows a mean preparation time for High Court cases outside of London much closer to three years than to two. Parties and their lawyers habitually fail to progress their cases in a timely way. The most important cause of delay between commencement and setting down for trial is dilatory behaviour on the part of litigants and their lawyers.

In addition, Table 4.3 shows that a mean delay of another forty-one weeks occurred in 1997 after Queen's Bench cases were given into the hands of the court for trial dates to be set. Thus, on average, about another ten months will pass, while cases further up the ready list take it in turns to be heard, before a

---

[44] Bowman, *Review of the Court of Appeal (Civil Division): Report to the Lord Chancellor* (London: Court of Appeal (Civil Division) Review, 1997). See also the summary published at http://www.open.gov. uk/lcd/civil/bowman/bowfr.htm.

case comes on for trial. This delay is caused when the court has failed to decide all of the cases set down in any given period, and the backlog has accumulated to such a degree that hearings cannot be given to all parties who want one at any given time. This represents a failure of the court system to provide sufficient resources, or to use the resources provided efficiently enough. Either more hearing time must be provided, or the courts must become significantly more efficient at using the hearing time available.

Interestingly, Table 4.3 shows a marked difference in the county courts. There, party-controlled waiting time is much shorter. More than a year still passes, even in the fastest county courts (those in London). However, the mean time during which cases are in party hands while being prepared for trial is less than half of the mean time taken in the High Court. This might be expected, as the county courts are intended to handle cases of lesser complexity and lower value. Also, plaintiffs presumably take some notice of the provision automatically striking out cases after fifteen months if no hearing is requested.

The court delay is also much shorter in the county court. But, unlike the High Court, which has a uniform forty-one week mean time from setting down to trial, the county court shows a significant discrepancy between London and provincial courts. In the county court, the mean time before hearing is nine weeks longer outside London. London and provincial High Courts are able to achieve equivalent mean performances. This indicates that there is potential to improve the situation in the provincial county courts.

3.4. The courts' reaction to delay

Most judges and court staff are anxious to improve the situation regarding delay, so that the courts can offer a useful, timely service. Most of the proposed solutions to the problems of delay have involved giving the courts greater powers to supervise and control the party preparation period, using case management techniques.

To this end, it has become standard practice to apply some form of judicial directions in each case, to set a court-imposed timetable for preparation. This directions process has been outlined above. However, as also noted above, directions have not been a great success. Parties frequently fail to comply with timetabling directions. The traditional liberality of the English approach to procedural discipline is completely at odds with a system which relies on judicial case management.

As can be seen from the sixty-five week mean time in 1997 between commencement and application for a hearing in the county court (Table 4.3), the parties will go right to the limit of any procedural freedom that they are allowed.[45] One

---

[45] Sixty-five weeks is very close to the automatic striking-out deadline of fifteen months from the close of pleadings.

important reason for this is the fact that the available sanctions are weak and ineffective. Under the liberal approach, outlined above, the only sanction usually applied is an order to pay the 'costs thrown away'. Yet an order of costs can only be made on the application of the aggrieved party, and must be fought out like any other interlocutory application. Interlocutory applications can further delay progress of the case until they are finally settled, possibly upon appeal. A party who is already concerned about delay may well be unwilling to delay matters further by dragging her opponent into court to argue about the delay and to fight for a small award of costs.

The sanction of costs thrown away is not especially punitive. Default due to inactivity does not tend to generate a great deal of cost. In a world where lawyers charge by the hour, inactivity is one thing which is free. Even orders of costs which are intended to sanction party misbehaviour are not usually payable until after trial and final judgment. Such small items as a punitive order for costs on an interlocutory application tend to get lost, as the sum involved is tiny compared to the whole cost of the proceeding. The party who was ordered to pay punitive costs may herself be the overall winner. Moreover, most proceedings end in settlement. In such cases, there is no winner, and hence no entitlement to costs except as agreed between the parties. Neither party has an interest in reviving the proceeding to enforce an order for costs on an interlocutory application.

Judicial efforts to control delay have generally been ineffective to date. It is difficult to change parties' behaviour through sanctions, and especially difficult to do so when the sanctions available are weak, and themselves inevitably involve more satellite litigation.

3.5. The cost of litigation

Litigation in England costs too much. This is clearly demonstrated by a study commissioned by Lord Woolf's Access to Justice Working Party. That study, conducted by Professor Hazel Genn, examined the cost of civil litigation. Professor Genn's full report is published as an annex to the Woolf Report, and a summary of its main findings appears as annex III to Lord Woolf's final report.

3.5.1. The Genn study: the taxing office and lawyers' bills

The data for Professor Genn's study were obtained from the Supreme Court Taxing Office, which collected comprehensive information about bills submitted for taxation between 1990 and 1995. In the majority of cases that proceed to trial, the winner receives his taxed costs from the loser. Most settlements reached before judgment acknowledge this reality by including an agreement about taxed costs. Thus, the taxing office receives and taxes bills paid by the winner to his own lawyers in a wide range of cases, including many which settle before trial (see Table 4.5).

Table 4.5. *Median taxed costs allowed by category of case and value, showing median % when costs represented as % of claim value*

	Up to £12,500 inclusive		£12,501–£25,000		£25,001–£50,000		£50,001–£100,000		£100,001–£250,000		Over £250,000		Overall median	Overall mean
	Cost (£)	%	Cost (£)	%	Cost (£)	%	Cost (£)	%	Cost (£)	%	Cost (£)	%		
Medical negligence	10,482	137	12,464	57	15,655	46	24,982	33	35,936	21	76,011	12	15,531	29,380
Personal injury	7,099	135	8,006	41	10,474	28	14,881	22	18,688	13	64,435	13	12,134	19,382
Professional negligence	9,440	135	9,688	54	13,250	43	27,524	41	34,208	27	78,904	15	14,834	32,866
Official referees	12,245	158	19,696	96	17,272	48	34,355	53	43,865	31	133,805	19	19,320	35,844
Breach of contract	8,882	138	7,774	46	13,405	32	14,993	21	14,632	12	31,610	5	Not given	Not given
Chancery	7,316	119	11,150	62	13,434	40	10,757	17	9,421	8	11,906	2	Not given	Not given
Queen's Bench	6,693	154	7,751	44	10,677	33	9,912	14	8,876	5	16,199	3	Not given	Not given
Commercial	6,187	174	10,907	54	13,522	27	20,262	38	27,537	16	26,503	2	Not given	Not given
Bankruptcy/ Companies Court	6,785	115	7,050	39	5,748	18	9,015	15	16,592	10	13,042	1	Not given	Not given

Note: The allowed costs represent about two-thirds of the actual costs incurred only by the winner. Some costs will have been disallowed on taxation. The losing party or parties will each have spent some money (perhaps less, perhaps more) on their own costs. The percentage figure (costs ÷ value × 100) is calculated for each case, and the median percentage for the value category is shown. Again, the costs figure treated is only the costs allowed on taxation, not even the total winner's costs, let alone the total costs for all parties to the case.

Source: Woolf, *Access to Justice: Final Report*, 'Survey of Litigation Costs: Annex III', tables 3 and 4.

The bills of only one side (the winning side) are examined by the taxing office. For simplicity, we may assume that both sides have invested roughly equally in the case.[46] The Genn study makes it very clear that aggregate costs exceed the value of the sum in issue in a very high proportion of smaller claims. Indeed, in a significant number of claims up to £12,500, the taxed costs alone (i.e. about two-thirds of the cost incurred by the winning side) exceeded the sum in issue.

To put this into perspective, 42 per cent of all individual taxpayers in the United Kingdom have an annual income of less than £10,000.[47] A proposal to introduce a minimum wage has focused on an hourly minimum of £3.60 per hour, giving a gross annual wage (at forty hours per week) of £7,488. While £12,500 (the lowest category of claim value used in the Genn Report) is only a small sum in the context of claims brought in the High Court, it is a very significant amount of money compared to the sum that an ordinary working person in England might handle in a year. Yet, to recover such a sum through litigation appears to require the investment of a similar sum, and involves the risk not only that the amount claimed will not be recovered, but also that around two-thirds of the costs incurred by the other side will have to be paid as well. This triples the potential loss.

The percentage figure relating the amount awarded as costs by the taxing office to the amount recovered (the percentage figure in Table 4.5) gives a rough guide to the economic efficiency of the proceedings. A low percentage figure indicates that the money spent on costs was well invested given the rewards to be expected from the claim. The low percentage figures for the highest value categories of claims of almost all sorts seems to indicate that litigating over very large sums of money in England is both cost-efficient and sensible. On average, a win returns good value for money, and the extra costs of a loss are not great compared to the potential rewards.

However, in every type of claim below £12,500, the median amount recovered as costs by the winner exceeded the amount in issue. Every percentage figure in the 'Up to £12,500' column is over 100 per cent. At 174 per cent, costs awarded in the median 'small' commercial case were close to double the amount at issue. Applying our rough rule of thumb (that awarded costs approximate two-thirds of the amount actually spent by the winner), this 174 per cent of the claim figure represents 261 per cent of the claim value actually being spent by the winning party alone. Assuming that the loser spent the same amount, around five times as much money would have been spent fighting a

---

[46] This assumption is not entirely accurate. Plaintiffs' costs are typically higher, as the burden of actively progressing litigation usually falls more heavily on plaintiffs. Also, if a higher investment in legal services makes a litigant more likely to win, the taxing office will tend to see only the higher of the two sides' expenditure.

[47] Data from the Survey of Personal Incomes, Board of Inland Revenue, published in a table entitled *Distribution of Income Liable to Assessment for Tax, 1995–96*, available on the Office of National Statistics website at http://www.statistics.gov.uk/statbase/xsdataset.asp?B2=Display+All.

small commercial case of median efficiency as was actually at stake. This represents extreme economic inefficiency. It is economically irrational to spend £2.50 for every £1.00 recovered. No rational system should tolerate the waste represented by £5.00 being spent to sort out who takes home £1.00. (This is for the case of *median* efficiency. The worst case does not bear thinking about.)

The indemnity rule removes the incentive for parties to economize on procedure, because each party expects to win and recover costs from the loser. Disputes do not proceed to trial unless both parties hold such a view. Thus, each party has an incentive to continue spending, even to spend £2.50 for each £1.00 expected return or more, as each party believes that he or she is spending the enemy's money. Beyond a certain point, the original claim becomes unimportant compared to the liability for costs invested in the litigation so far.[48]

This potentially open-ended liability for the other party's costs is a strong deterrent to litigation. People with limited means simply cannot afford to run the risk. Even those who can potentially afford to pay the large sums required may be unwilling to enter into litigation to defend their rights, given the uncertainty as to costs. Most people are risk averse, in the sense that they will avoid situations where the outcome is uncertain, even if they could afford the maximum expected loss. Potential outcomes from litigation range from winning the claim and recovering the money lost plus costs, to losing the claim and becoming liable for two sets of legal fees of an unpredictable amount. Risk-averse people simply will not go to court.

A more rational system would allow for litigation to be conducted efficiently, so that the costs of the case are known in advance, and are proportionate to the amount at issue in the proceeding. Removing the intimidating risk of enormous cost liability, and replacing it with an assurance that, whatever the costs might be, they will be no more than is proportionate to the sum at stake, is an essential precondition of making litigation accessible.

As it is, there is little chance of small cases being efficiently dealt with in England. A claim cannot be brought unless the plaintiff has legal aid or independent wealth, or the claim is small enough and simple enough to come within the county court's small claims arbitration procedure, and is brought by a party who is confident enough to act for himself rather than employing a lawyer.

3.5.2. *Legal aid*

The English courts' budget is funded through the Lord Chancellor's Department. Table 4.6 shows the Department's funding for legal aid and court and judicial services over the last five financial years, together with current year's

---

[48] Zuckerman has described this 'vicious circle' effect of spiralling costs in 'A Reform of Civil Procedure: Rationing Procedure Rather than Access to Justice' (1995) 22 Journal of Law and Society 155.

Table 4.6. *Summary of government spending on courts and legal aid—actual and budgeted* (£ million)

	1992–3 (actual)	1993–4 (actual)	1994–5 (actual)	1995–6 (actual)	1996–7 (actual)	1997–8 (estimated)	1998–9 (planned)
Lord Chancellor's Department							
Total legal aid	1,090	1,212	1,301	1,389	1,478	1,560	1,602
Includes Civil legal aid[a]	463	544	602	643	671	634	
Court service[b] (includes cost of civil courts where known)[c]	816	813	862	842	762	730 (319.8)	665 (325)
Total	1,905	2,025	2,163	2,231	2,240	2,290	2,266
Northern Ireland Court Service	43	37	50	55	53	55	47

[a] Unpublished figures provided by the Court Service, in response to author's direct enquiry.
[b] These figures include a sum for the cost of the Public Trust Office's executive agency.
[c] *Court Service: The Annual Report 1997–1998* (London: Stationery Office, 1998), 56.

Source: The Lord Chancellor's and Law Officers' Departments Departmental Report: The Government's Expenditure Plans 1998–1999, http://www.open.gov.uk/lcd/deprep/index.htm.

estimated spending and planned spending for the next budget cycle. These figures show total legal aid spending (combined civil and criminal provision) and also separate out civil legal aid provision.

By far the largest part of the British government's spending on civil justice comprises legal aid. Although the costs of providing the court system have diminished over the last five years, the costs of legal aid have grown out of control. Legal aid has now reached a level of more than double the spending on the courts themselves. This money largely represents direct payments to the legal profession, which are planned to reach more than £1.5 billion in 1999.

According to the Lord Chancellor's Department,[49] net legal aid expenditure in 1990–1 was only some £682 million. By 1997, it had increased by 115 per cent to £1.478 million. Lawyers' fees consume 90 per cent of the legal aid bill. Civil legal aid alone cost £634 million in 1997–8. The total cost of the civil court service in the same financial year is estimated to amount to only £319.8 million.[50]

---

[49] Lord Chancellor's Department report on a speech given by the Lord Chancellor, Lord Irvine of Lairg, unveiling his plans for the civil justice and legal aid systems in his keynote address to the Solicitors' Annual Conference in Cardiff on 18 Oct. 1997. This report is available at http://www.open.gov.uk/lcd/speeches/1997/speechfr.htm.
[50] *Court Service: The Annual Report 1997–1998*, 56.

Over the last four years, the number of people helped by legal aid has fallen by 9 per cent. This is due to government efforts to save money, which have seen steady reductions in eligibility levels. Yet total legal aid spending has continued to rise nonetheless. This is because average civil legal aid payments have increased by more than 43 per cent over the same period. The increase in the fees charged per case has been so great that the savings brought about by the reduction in eligibility are more than overtaken. Accordingly, fewer people are now assisted, at a much greater cost per person. Since 1990–1, the cost of each case to the Legal Aid Board has grown by 53 per cent in real terms, when adjusted for inflation. The legal aid scheme costs every taxpayer £57 per annum. At such levels, the present system of legal aid is quite clearly unsustainable.

4. REFORM OF CIVIL PROCEDURE

4.1. The need for reform: specific illustrations

As the statistics show, problems associated with cost, delay and complexity are manifest under the present system. Before turning to the reforms proposed, it is worth pausing to consider specific cases which illustrate just how acute these problems can become in practice.

As *Symphony Group* v. *Hodgson*[51] demonstrates, even simple disputes, heard and decided within a very short timeframe, can consume substantial sums of money. Symphony Group sued Hodgson, a former employee, to enforce a restraint of trade clause in his employment contract. Hodgson's annual salary had been approximately £10,000. Symphony Group brought the action, secured an interlocutory injunction, and obtained final judgment, all within just nine weeks. Yet, it spent over £100,000 in the process. To this sum must be added both the cost of Hodgson's defence, which was funded by legal aid and may have been of a similar magnitude, and the systemic costs associated with administering justice (including paying judges, clerks, and other court staff, and providing courtrooms, buildings, and offices).

The imposition of tight timetables (for example, via judicial directions[52]) is often assumed to be an effective method for preventing procedural waste and reducing cost. But, as *Symphony Group* illustrates, a quick case is not necessarily an inexpensive one. Even in straightforward cases heard expeditiously costs may rise out of all proportion to the subject matter.

The law reports are replete with examples of how complicated, and thus how

---

[51] *Symphony Group plc* v. *Hodgson* [1993] 4 All ER 143.
[52] The automatic directions which apply in the county court, and to High Court personal injury actions, may have reduced delay. However, the fixed timetable for pre-trial matters has certainly not eliminated delay, as discussed in the procedural discipline section above. There also appears to have been little or no effect on the cost of proceedings.

costly and protracted, civil litigation can become. It is not unknown for disputes over as preliminary and purely technical a matter as whether proceedings have been properly commenced to be appealed all the way to the House of Lords.[53] Every such case represents hundreds of thousands of pounds being spent on purely satellite litigation, which does not advance the determination of the substantive dispute by one iota. An egregious example is *Barclays Bank of Swaziland v. Hahn*.[54] There, the defendant sought to evade service of the writ by leaving England shortly after arriving, without visiting his English home where the writ had been sent. An ambiguity in the rules allowed the parties to dispute the validity of service through three levels of court, before the House of Lords finally ruled on whether the proceedings had been brought at all. Similar patterns exist in respect of other procedural disputes.[55]

A sophisticated litigant with sufficient means can easily manipulate these avenues for satellite litigation, so that proceedings become too expensive for the other party to pursue. Delay is one very effective method for achieving this end. Under the existing system, delay tends to create more delay, which inexorably drives up costs. For, *inter alia*, delay produces the need to seek an extension of time from the court, which requires an interlocutory hearing, which in turn creates the possibility of interlocutory appeals. A sophisticated party may well use delay and complexity as tactical weapons, to increase costs and force the opponent to settle the case on advantageous terms. As only about 2 per cent of civil cases filed in court each year proceed all the way to judgment, there is clearly ample scope for such abuse.

The removal of the financial limit over the county court's jurisdiction, as discussed above, was intended to reduce costs by allowing more cases to be heard in the county court. However, the reform has not produced significant savings. Certain savings are possible: lawyers generally charge lower hourly rates for county court work; and, as solicitors enjoy rights of audience in the county court, barristers need not be engaged. Overall, however, these savings are not substantial. Aside from the small claims arbitration procedure, county court procedures are similar to High Court procedures, and are essentially just as costly to invoke. Moreover, the minimum hourly rate that solicitors can realistically charge may still generate costs out of proportion to the value of many claims, simply because many hours of work may still be needed, to get to grips with the facts and the law, even where the value at stake is small. The amount of work needed to prepare a claim or defence depends on its complexity,

---

[53] See e.g. *Dagnell v. JL Freedman & Co. (a firm)* [1993] 2 All ER 161; *Kenneth Allison Ltd. v. AE Limehouse & Co.* [1991] 4 All ER 500; *Norglen Ltd. v. Reeds Rains Prudential Ltd.* [1998] 1 All ER 218. See also Zuckerman, 'A Reform of Civil Procedure: Rationing Procedure Rather than Access to Justice' (1995) 22 Journal of Law and Society 155.

[54] *Barclays Bank of Swaziland Ltd. v. Hahn* [1989] 2 All ER 398.

[55] See e.g. *Re Jokai Tea Holdings Ltd.* [1992] 1 WLR 1196; *Costellow v. Somerset CC* [1993] 1 WLR 256; *Roebuck v. Mungovin* [1994] 2 WLR 290 (extension of time and dismissal for want of prosecution); *Easton v. Ford Motor Co. Ltd.* [1993] 1 WLR 1511 (amendment of pleadings).

not on its value. Just as much work can be required to prosecute or defend a complicated £5,000 claim as may be needed for a complicated £500,000 claim.

Wilkinson v. *Kenny*,[56] an action for possession of land, epitomizes how acute these problems of cost, complexity, and delay can become, even in routine county court cases. Although the case concerned 'a simple straightforward dispute crying out for summary determination', it rapidly got derailed by 'applications being made for this, applications being made for that, various orders for this, orders for that, hearings in relation to this, hearings in relation to that, all of them of course increasing costs'.[57]

4.2. The Woolf Report

Over the past decade or so, a number of reforms have been proposed in an attempt to make civil justice more economical, efficient, and accessible. Several changes to county court procedure resulted from the 1988 report of the Civil Justice Review Body.[58] These included abolishing the monetary limit on the court's jurisdiction; adopting certain judicial case management techniques, including automatic directions and automatic striking out after fifteen months; and granting limited rights of audience to solicitors to overcome the barristers' monopoly. As we have seen, the effect of these reforms has been modest. However, the review triggered a more fundamental debate, which paved the way for the radical proposals in the Woolf Report.

In 1994, a comprehensive and far-reaching reform of civil justice began. The Lord Chancellor appointed Lord Woolf, one of England's most senior judges, to review existing rules and procedures, gather evidence and opinion from civil justice professionals and commentators, and identify effective ways to cut costs, reduce the complexity of the rules, and remove unnecessary distinctions of practice and procedure between the courts. Lord Woolf's interim report was published in June 1995. After consultation, his final report was published in July 1996. In his reports, Lord Woolf makes over 300 recommendations for change.

According to Lord Woolf, the main cause of unpredictable and dispro-portionate cost, undue delay, and procedural complexity is the uncontrolled adversarial culture of litigants and their lawyers. Traditionally, the English system allowed parties to control the pace and extent of litigation, especially at the pre-trial stage, with minimal judicial supervision. As a result, parties have been free to subvert the available procedures to serve their own personal ends. This has engendered an unduly partisan, combative litigation culture. The complexities in the rules have given lawyers and litigants ample opportunities to indulge in wasteful, costly practices.

---

[56] *Wilkinson* v. *Kenny* [1993] 3 All ER 9; see also Zuckerman, 'A Reform of Civil Procedure: Rationing Procedure Rather than Access to Justice' (1995) 22 Journal of Law and Society 155.

[57] *Wilkinson* v. *Kenny* [1993] 3 All ER 9, 11, per Sir Thomas Bingham MR.

[58] Report of the Review Body on Civil Justice (Cmnd. 394, 1988).

Because he identifies the underlying source of the system's woes as a deeply ingrained adversarial culture, for Lord Woolf nothing short of a total change of culture can ever produce significant change. Accordingly, the linchpin of the Woolf Report is judicial case management. Under Woolf's case management scheme, judges are responsible for controlling litigation at all stages, so that parties cannot indulge 'their worst excesses'. Judges and administrative court staff ensure that proportionality is maintained between the importance and complexity of a dispute, and the procedural means employed, and costs incurred, in its resolution.

In addition, Lord Woolf proposes that 'pre-action protocols' should extend a measure of control over the pre-commencement phase of certain types of disputes (e.g. personal injury cases). Such protocols should detail how parties and their lawyers are expected to conduct themselves before a case is commenced, and indicate how long the steps expected of them should take.

The Woolf Report recommends three principal mechanisms to achieve proportionality and predictability and, thereby, reduce cost, delay, and complexity. The first is a threefold system of standardized procedural 'tracks' for cases to follow, depending upon their value and complexity. The second is restricting recoverable costs. The third is the unification and simplification of the rules of court.

The three standardized tracks formulated in the Woolf Report are a 'small claims track', a 'fast track', and a 'multi-track'. The rationale behind having different track assignments is to limit the available procedures (and, in some cases, the recoverable costs), in proportion to the value and complexity of individual cases. The following summary details the key features of each track, as its operation is envisaged in the Woolf Report.

The small claims track is intended for all actions up to £3,000 (except personal injury cases where the threshold is £1,000). These claims follow an informal procedure, similar to that under the present system of small claims arbitration in the county court.

The 'fast track', which Lord Woolf describes as civil procedure 'without frills', is designed for all actions between £3,000 and £10,000 in value (or £1,000 and £10,000 for personal injury cases) which are not especially complex. Cases on this track are governed by standard directions creating a tight timetable (normally of no more than thirty weeks from commencement to trial), with automatic penalties for non-compliance. Key features of the fast track include the following:

(a) Discovery of documents (renamed 'disclosure') is limited. Normally, a party need only disclose the documents on which she intends to rely, and any which materially undermine her case or advance her opponent's case ('standard disclosure').

(b) Expert evidence is limited, and under the court's complete control.

Parties are encouraged to rely on a single, jointly appointed expert. Only written expert evidence is permitted, preferably from a single expert. Experts may not give oral evidence, but may be asked questions in writing.

(c) Only limited oral evidence from witnesses of fact is permitted. Written witness statements, in the form of succinct summaries of witnesses' evidence, must be exchanged prior to trial. These statements may be supplemented orally at trial where necessary, with the court's permission.

(d) Trial takes place on a fixed date, at a fixed time, with a fixed duration. Trials are ordinarily limited to three hours, but may take up to a day. Judgment will normally be given orally at the end of the trial, and written reasons will follow later where necessary.

(e) Recoverable costs are standardized to encourage economy. A low, fixed sum is recoverable by the winner from the loser, instead of the indemnity against taxed costs presently available. Unless the party and the lawyer agree otherwise in writing, the fees the lawyer can charge are also limited to the same low, fixed sum.

The 'multi-track' is intended for all actions over £10,000, and any others that are unusually complex or important. While the multi-track is similar to the existing procedure, the power to control the pace and conduct of litigation is vested in a procedural judge and the trial judge, rather than in the parties and their lawyers. The multi-track has the following key features:

(a) Uncomplicated actions worth over £10,000 are dealt with under a standardized multi-track procedure. This procedure is similar to the existing automatic directions approach, but with limited discovery, a shorter timetable, and potentially limited trial time.

(b) For more complex actions, the full spectrum of procedures is available. The procedural steps permitted by the judge, and the directions made, are tailored to suit the individual requirements of each case.

(c) A compulsory 'case management conference' takes place before a procedural judge, shortly after the defence has been received. Its purpose is to set an agenda for the case before significant costs are incurred. The procedural judge identifies the issues to be resolved in the litigation, and gives directions governing the pre-trial steps. These directions must address the extent of disclosure (discovery) required, the scope of any expert evidence, and the time limit for completing the pre-trial procedure.

(d) Once the case management conference directions have all been carried out, the trial judge conducts a 'pre-trial review' conference. This normally takes place eight to ten weeks before trial. Its purpose is to narrow the issues as far as possible, prepare a statement of the issues to be tried, and set a programme, timetable, and budget for trial. The witnesses to be called to give oral evidence are identified.

(e) At both conferences, judges must actively encourage settlement by way of alternative dispute resolution (ADR). Parties must indicate their costs incurred to date, and their estimated costs for proceeding to trial.

(f) Full taxed costs are available. However, costs are taxed according to a new overall criterion: what is reasonable to both parties to the taxation. This is intended to allow an objective appraisal of what would have been a reasonable overall sum for each case, not simply what is a reasonable sum for the work actually done.

The Woolf Report exhorts litigants to embrace a 'new ethos' of co-operation. Lord Woolf's hope is that greater co-operation will lead to earlier settlements, thus reducing cost and delay. He therefore seeks to make litigation the dispute resolution option of last resort, and calls for public funding to extend beyond the provision of court services to support ADR.

In order to encourage settlement, and to balance the advantages which a defendant can obtain by making a payment into court under the present rules, Lord Woolf proposes that both plaintiffs and defendants should be able to make 'offers to settle'. Like payments into court, offers to settle will have consequences in terms of liability for costs if they are not accepted. Where a party who rejects an opponent's offer to settle subsequently achieves a less favourable result at trial, he or she will be liable for all of the costs of the proceeding from the point at which the offer was made.

Rule 1 of the new unified draft Civil Proceedings Rules sums up the essence of Lord Woolf's proposals. Rule 1 provides that the 'overriding objective' of the rules is 'to enable the courts to deal with cases justly'. 'Just' dealing, in this context, includes ensuring that, as far as possible: the parties enjoy procedural equality of arms; expense is saved; procedures used are proportionate to a case's importance, value, complexity, and the financial resources of the parties; delay is avoided; and each case consumes an appropriate share of the court's resources, bearing in mind the need to provide resources to other cases as well.

4.3. Responses to the Woolf Report

As at the time of writing, Lord Woolf's proposals have been accepted by the English government with some modification. As adopted, the upper limit of the small claims track will be £5,000, and the fast track £15,000. A lower limit of £50,000 will be placed on the High Court's jurisdiction, to push smaller cases into the county court. New unified rules for the courts of first instance are currently being drafted, together with the necessary amending legislation. The reformed system is due to be introduced on 26 April 1999.[59]

---

[59] Those interested in following the progress of implementation of the English government's civil justice reforms should visit the Lord Chancellor's Department website, where six-monthly progress reports are available: see http://www.open.gov.uk/lcd/civil/cjustfr.htm.

Despite this positive response from government, the Woolf Report has not gone uncriticized. One outspoken critic is Professor Zander.[60] *Inter alia*, Zander criticizes Woolf's front-loading of costs since most cases settle in any event; disputes the supposed causal relationship between adversarial freedom and cost, delay, and complexity; and predicts that case management will increase rather than decrease costs, due to systemic expenses associated with increased judicial intervention and satellite litigation flowing from case management decision appeals. More fundamentally, Zander opposes Woolf's shift away from the traditional liberal approach to procedural discipline, whereby technicality is eschewed in favour of substantive justice. He notes the inherent conflict underlying procedural rules. He believes that the level of procedural discipline which the Woolf reforms anticipate will be unsustainable. Judges will resist being so harsh in individual cases.[61] Zander therefore opposes Woolf's re-orientation towards judicial case management, strict timetables, and sanctions for non-compliance.

Zander calls for the utmost caution in implementing reform. This would require maintaining the status quo until conclusive evidence indicates the best way forward. However, ample evidence already demonstrates the urgent need to improve matters. The status quo simply cannot be sustained.

In contrast to Zander, Zuckerman criticizes the Woolf reforms for being insufficiently radical.[62] Zuckerman argues that the proposed reforms will be ineffective because they leave the underlying framework of incentives unchanged. Hourly fees, indemnity costs, the current system of legal aid, and the inability of lay clients to assess whether their lawyers' procedural decisions represent value for money, all conspire to encourage lawyers and their clients to invest disproportionate resources into litigation. Hourly billing in particular encourages lawyers to spend more time on litigation than may be warranted, especially as the winning party in multi-track cases can still expect to recover most of his costs from the loser. In addition, solicitors may be sued for negligence if they fail to do all that the 'reasonable solicitor' would have done in a given case. The reasonable solicitor standard is that of a very careful solicitor indeed. Accordingly, even lawyers who are concerned about cost and delay may still feel pressured to take unnecessary procedural steps to avoid later censure.

---

[60] Zander, 'Forwards or Backwards for the New Lord Chancellor' (1997) 16 CJQ 208.

[61] Zander's critique of Woolf relies in particular on a study conducted during the 1990s evaluating case management in the USA by the RAND corporation. This material consists of three reports and an executive summary, authored by Kakalik *et al.* and published separately by RAND, Santa Monica, Calif. The three reports are: *Implementation of the Civil Justice Reform Act in Pilot and Comparative Districts*; *An Evaluation of Judicial Case Management under the Civil Justice Reform Act*; and *An Evaluation of Mediation and Early Neutral Evaluation under the Civil Justice Reform Act*. The executive summary is entitled *Just, Speedy and Inexpensive? An Evaluation of Judicial Case Management under the Civil Justice Reform Act*. The RAND study has recently been criticized. Accordingly, Zander's critique of Woolf based on the RAND study's findings is similarly open to question.

[62] Zuckerman, 'Lord Woolf's Access to Justice: Plus ça change . . .' (1996) 59 MLR 773.

The only Woolf recommendation which touches upon these incentive concerns is the introduction of fixed costs in the fast track. However, this reform is too limited to bring about significant change. It is limited to fast track cases, and does not govern costs as between solicitors and their own clients, if there is agreement otherwise.

As Zuckerman points out, if these incentives are not suppressed by stern and credible sanctions, they will inevitably undermine the reformed system. The system will simply revert back to its current form, exhibiting the same problems of cost, delay, and complexity.

Yet consistent application of stern and credible sanctions is a foreign concept to judges trained in the traditional, liberal English model. To date, judges have proven reluctant to use their existing powers to curb party excesses and punish culpable delays.[63] The recent introduction of automatic striking out and judicial directions provides a clear example. After an initial period of strictness, judges are once again tending to reinstate cases which fall foul of the automatic striking-out provision.[64] The same effect is noticeable in the case law concerning existing case management directions.[65] Not even Lord Woolf himself is always prepared to be unjust in an individual case *pour encourager les autres.*[66] Clearly, conferring even more extensive case management powers on judges will achieve nothing unless a substantial change in judicial philosophy is brought about. Given past experience, it is doubtful whether such a change is possible, especially with the rapidity which the Woolf reforms demand.

Overall, there are numerous reasons to doubt whether the Woolf reforms will achieve substantial improvements in terms of cost, delay, and complexity. In addition to the concerns already noted, two more warrant mention. First, given the failure of previous exhortations to litigants to exercise procedural restraint, there is little reason to believe that Lord Woolf's call for a 'new ethos' will produce any better results. Secondly, the new system is still too complex. The draft unified rules are nowhere near sufficiently simplified. In the interests of limiting the scope for interlocutory disputes, the Woolf system places each proceeding under judicial management. Judges will decide many matters which are currently left to the parties. Yet every judicial decision made in a case carries with it the potential for satellite litigation to erupt, if the dissatisfied party chooses to appeal.

A better, more realistic alternative to the Woolf reforms would be to constrain the underlying incentives by limiting party choice, not through judicial

---

[63] See e.g. *Department of Transport* v. *Chris Smaller (Transport) Ltd.* [1989] AC 1197, 1207, where the House of Lords expressly held that dismissal for want of prosecution should not be used to punish litigants or deter delay.   [64] *Rastin* v. *British Steel plc* [1994] 2 All ER 641.
[65] *Pereira* v. *Beanlands* [1996] 3 All ER 528.
[66] See Zander, 'Forwards or Backwards for the New Lord Chancellor' (1997) 16 CJQ 208, discussing the cases (all on late submission of evidence): *Beachley Property* v. *Edgar* [1996] The Times, 18 July; *Letpak* v. *Harris* [1996] The Times, 6 Dec.; *Mortgage Corp.* v. *Sandoes* [1996] The Times, 27 Dec.

discipline, but through greater simplification. Complicated procedures cannot be used if they do not exist. The creation of a new summary procedure, to be applied to every case, would be one beneficial way forward. Zuckerman has previously proposed such an option.[67]

4.4. Other reforms

Four further reform initiatives deserve mention. Reforms are proposed, or in place, for: the civil division of the Court of Appeal; the legal aid system; the way in which lawyer's fees are calculated; and the incorporation of the European Convention for the Protection of Human Rights and Fundamental Freedoms into English law. The reforms to legal aid and lawyer's fees are interdependent, and will be discussed together below.

4.4.1. Civil appeals

First, as part of its integrated programme of civil justice review (which includes introducing the Woolf reforms), the Lord Chancellor's Office has appointed a committee, chaired by Sir Jeffrey Bowman, to review the civil division of the Court of Appeal. The Bowman Committee reported in November 1997,[68] recommending systematic changes to civil appeals. These changes are intended to work in conjunction with the particular changes recommended by the Woolf Report to the first instance jurisdiction. The Bowman Committee's recommendations are a mixture of detailed proposals ready for implementation, and general plans for further investigation. *Inter alia*, requirements for leave to appeal are to be extended to all cases, except those directly impinging on personal liberty or concerning child abduction. One level of appeal will become the normal maximum. Interlocutory or procedural appeals will be discouraged, and should be dealt with swiftly and locally where allowed. The Court of Appeal will adopt a programme of judicial case management with tight time limits to manage its caseload. The proposed reforms have been adopted by the government, and are incorporated into the Access to Justice Bill 1998, introduced into the House of Lords on 2 December 1998. The Bill also contains important provisions designed to enact the government's proposed legal aid and lawyers' fee reforms.

4.4.2. Legal aid

Accepting the recommendations made in a report by Sir Peter Middleton,[69] the government intends to overhaul completely the system under which legal aid is

---

[67] Zuckerman, 'A Reform of Civil Procedure: Rationing Procedure Rather than Access to Justice' (1995) 22 Journal of Law and Society 155.

[68] Bowman, *Report of the Review Committee into the Court of Appeal (Civil Division)*. For a summary of the recommendations see http://www.open.gov.uk/lcd/civil/bowman/bowfr.htm.

[69] Middleton, *Review of Civil Justice and Legal Aid* (London: Lord Chancellor's Department, 1997). The report is published on the internet at http://www.open.gov.uk/lcd/middle/middfr.htm.

provided. The Access to Justice Bill 1998 creates a new Legal Services Commission. The Commission will be responsible for providing two distinct services, which will replace the existing system of criminal and civil legal aid. The Criminal Defence Service will provide advice and assistance to those facing criminal investigation by the police, or who are facing criminal charges in court. The Community Legal Service will take responsibility for providing civil and family law services to the less well-off. It is intended that the Commission will arrange the provision of these services by contracting directly with the lawyers who work for legal aid, both by way of contracting for bulk provision of services and by direct employment of its own lawyers. It is expected that allowing direct contracting will enable the Commission to take control over the legal aid budget, and will create the necessary conditions for price competition to help reduce overall costs. Such reforms should also help to redress the incentive on lawyers for legally aided litigants to complicate proceedings. Where lawyers provide bulk services, on the basis of a fixed fee per case, instead of individual services, paid for by hours worked, the incentive is for swift and streamlined case processing, rather than for manœuvre and delay. Eligibility levels for free or partly-funded legal assistance are also under review.

4.4.3. Conditional fees

Thirdly, other fee structures which better enable people to afford to litigate are also being explored. In particular, the use of conditional fee agreements (no win, no fee) was recently legalized for personal injury cases, for human rights cases before the European Court of Human Rights, and in insolvency matters.[70] In practice, such agreements have only been of significance in personal injury cases. The Access to Justice Bill 1998 seeks to expand their availability, and to make them even more attractive.

Under these arrangements, as they presently stand, a lawyer agrees with an intending plaintiff not to charge any fee unless the case is successful. If the client wins, the lawyer charges a fee calculated on the usual basis (the 'basic fee'), together with a percentage 'uplift' of up to 100 per cent. The lawyer and client agree in advance on what the percentage uplift will be. The rationale for allowing an uplift is to reflect the risk that the lawyer accepts of not being paid at all. In most cases, uplifts agreed are far less than the allowable maximum of 100 per cent. They are normally 50 per cent or less, and are commonly subject to a voluntarily accepted overriding limit, for example that the uplift will not exceed 25 per cent of the damages awarded.[71]

The uplift is calculated as a percentage of the lawyer's hourly fee to his own

---

[70] From 5 July 1995, under the Courts and Legal Services Act 1990, s. 58; and the Conditional Fee Agreements Order 1995 and the Conditional Fee Agreements Regulations 1995.

[71] Oral statement of the Lord Chancellor to the House of Lords, introducing the Lord Chancellor's Department Discussion Paper on Conditional Fees: http://www.open.gov.uk/lcd/laid/lacon2fr.htm. Only the uplift portion of the fee is usually subject to the limit.

client, not as a percentage of the taxed costs payable by the loser. Thus, the lawyer will receive roughly two-thirds of his basic fee from the losing party, paid as taxed costs; while roughly one-third of his basic fee, plus the uplift, will be paid by his own client. In practice, this means that a sum of up to 133 per cent of the basic fee will be taken from the damages award (i.e. the uplift of up to 100 per cent of the basic fee, and the portion of the basic fee not paid by the defendant). As we have seen, fees can be very high in relation to sums recovered. The 25 per cent overriding limit on the uplift, which the Law Society urges all practitioners to adopt voluntarily, is often a significant limit on the amount that the lawyer will receive.[72]

As noted above, conditional fees are currently lawful in only three categories of case: personal injury; human rights; and insolvency. They are expressly prohibited in criminal and family cases. The Access to Justice Bill 1998 seeks to extend this, in furtherance of the government's policy that the normal method of funding any claims by a poor plaintiff for a sum of money should be the conditional fee agreement, and should not be legal aid.[73] The Bill cuts down the prohibition, so that family cases dealing purely with financial or property matters may also be funded by a conditional fee agreement.

A conditional fee arrangement suits a poor plaintiff, because it means that, if the claim is unsuccessful, there is no legal fee to pay. Although the losing plaintiff will usually be liable for the winning defendant's costs, litigation insurance can be used to cover this. Appropriate insurance products are available, with typical premiums for simple personal injury cases of £155 or less.[74] (In more complicated medical negligence cases, the insurance premium would be much higher. In really difficult cases it may cost as much as £15,000 for cover of up to £100,000.) If the plaintiff wins, the losing defendant pays the taxed portion of the conditional fee costs, as usual. For any remainder owing to the plaintiff's lawyer, the fruits of the judgment are available. While beneficial for plaintiffs, conditional fees are not so suitable for dealing with the position of defendants. Also, they do nothing to improve the overall economic efficiency of litigation.

The Access to Justice Bill 1998 proposes two further changes to the law about conditional fee agreements. These changes are intended to make such agreements more suitable for funding the defence of a claim. The uplift sum is to become fully recoverable from the losing party as costs, as is any insurance premium paid. The intention is that a winning defendant will be able to pass the full cost (albeit taxed) of her defence under the conditional fee agreement to the losing plaintiff, and will not be faced with the liability to pay the uplift sum

---

[72] See Underwood, *No Win No Fee: No Worries* (Birmingham: CLT Professional Publishing Ltd., 1998), 29.

[73] *Access to Justice with Conditional Fees* (Mar. 1998), published on the internet at http://www.open.gov.uk/lcd/consult/leg-aid/laconfr.htm.

[74] Underwood, *No Win No Fee: No Worries*, 29.

herself, without a pool of damages available to pay it out of. In the event that the plaintiff is not of sufficient means, nor sufficiently insured, to meet the burden of paying his own lawyers, plus the defendant's lawyers, plus the uplift, the defendant will still face a substantial costs burden. Presumably it is expected that the developing sophistication of the legal expenses insurance market in England will respond to the market need for policies to cover such contingencies.

4.4.4. Legal aid reform in the light of conditional fee agreements

The Access to Justice Bill 1998 represents the cutting edge of government thinking on the reform of legal aid. It will put into practice the system described in the discussion paper entitled *Access to Justice with Conditional Fees*, adopting the mechanism of the conditional fee agreement as the preferred method for providing access to justice for poor plaintiffs and poor defendants in the context of monetary claims.[75] Legal aid funding will be withdrawn from claims for the payment of sums of money, replacing government funding of litigation with funding effectively advanced by the plaintiff's lawyers, and underwritten by insurance.

The conception is a sound one. Where other methods are available to ensure that poor people can obtain access to justice, there is no need for a massive public subsidy to be made available. In the case of claims for sums of money, conditional fees can allow access to justice. Those who wish to prosecute such claims, but who are without the means to pay their own lawyer, will be able to persuade their lawyer to enter into a conditional fee agreement, if the claim is a good one. If the lawyer expects to win, he will be willing to prosecute the claim for the payment of his usual fee, plus uplift, at the end of the case. He will accept the minor risk that there will be no fee, if the case is lost.

Under such an arrangement, the legal profession, rather than the government, funds the litigation. Cases with a poor chance of success will not be brought, as lawyers will not invest in cases which they expect to lose, and for which they can expect to earn no fee. This in turn should have beneficial consequences in reducing the congestion of the civil courts and the resulting delay.

The ambit of legal aid will thus become very restricted. The funds available will be targeted towards cases where there are no realistic alternative methods for funding, such as where the impecunious party is a defendant, or where the claim is not for the payment of a sum of money. Under the scheme described in the discussion paper, cases where legal aid will remain available to the poor will include housing matters, social security entitlements, and judicial review.

Targeting of available legal aid money, and control of legal aid expenditure, will be pursued through the increased use of contracting by the legal aid authorities, as noted above. This will end the demand-fed nature of the current

---

[75] *Access to Justice with Conditional Fees.*

legal aid system, allowing the authorities to exercise greater control over their budgets and over the services that they obtain for each pound spent.

The government also plans to tighten the merits test, so as to ensure that fewer unsuccessful cases are brought at public expense. In the future, the government plans to use legal aid funding to promote cases which ought to be brought in the public interest, but which are not economical for the individuals affected to bring themselves. Public legal aid funds will have a role to play as purchaser of 'public good' litigation.

4.5.5. The ECHR

Finally, an entirely separate reform may have its own part to play in future debate on English civil procedure. Under the Human Rights Act 1998, all but one of the substantive rights provisions in the European Convention for the Protection of Human Rights and Fundamental Freedoms (ECHR) is to be made directly enforceable under English law. Although the Act has received royal assent, the substantive rights provisions have not as yet been brought into force. When they do take effect, it will be unlawful for any public authority (which includes the courts) to act in contravention of any person's convention rights. Convention rights include the right contained in article 6 (1) of the ECHR to a fair and public hearing, within a reasonable time, by an independent and impartial tribunal established by law. This right applies in both civil and criminal matters. It remains to be seen exactly what effect this will have on English civil procedure. However, given the European Court of Human Rights' existing jurisprudence condemning systemic backlogs,[76] it is probable that ongoing delays before trial in the English civil courts will soon be tested for their reasonableness under the Act.

4.5. Alternative dispute resolution

Alternative dispute resolution (ADR) is of great interest to reformers. As we have seen, the Woolf Report recommends public support for ADR services. ADR has the potential to divert large numbers of cases out of the court system, thereby relieving the congestion which causes excessive court (as opposed to party) delay.

4.5.1. Arbitration

In England, ADR in the form of arbitration is of particular significance to major commercial parties, and is common in the fields of shipping, construction, insurance, and international trade. Because formal arbitration is the ADR option most like ordinary court proceedings, it is particularly suitable for these big money disputes. Parties can arrange arbitration proceedings to take place at

---

[76] See e.g. *Unión Alimentaria Sanders SA* v. *Spain* (1990) 12 EHRR 24.

the time and location most convenient for them. They can choose an arbitrator who is experienced in their particular type of dispute. The arbitrator's decision is binding, and can be enforced (if necessary) through the courts.

Arbitration has most of the advantages of litigation, but without the courts' delay. Yet it is expensive. Arbitration is accordingly a suitable way to accelerate disputes which could be litigated economically in court. It is not a suitable alternative for parties who are seeking an alternative to litigation because the cost of litigating is disproportionate to the value of their case.

Note that the county court small claims procedure, although called 'arbitration', is not truly a form of ADR. It is simply a less formal division of the county court.

4.5.2. ADR and pre-action protocols

As the Woolf Report observes, the vast majority of cases settle. Therefore, the primary object of the court system is not necessarily to prepare every case for trial. Rather, it should be to bring each case as quickly as possible to the point at which the parties and their lawyers can reach a fair settlement.

Part of the thrust of the Woolf reforms is to encourage out-of-court settlements, by requiring the early preparation of cases. This enables the parties to assess the alternatives available to them properly, in the light of a realistic assessment of their respective likely results at trial. To this end, 'pre-action protocols' are being developed for different types of claims, such as personal injury, motor accident, and medical negligence claims, and for expert evidence.[77]

These protocols will set out statements of good practice in the conduct of negotiations before the beginning of litigation, including speedy co-operation with requests for information, and the preparation of joint expert reports where appropriate. By creating an expectation of pre-commencement co-operation, backed up by judicial power to impose sanctions in the litigation on parties who fail to comply with relevant protocols, Lord Woolf hopes to accelerate the preparation of cases. Parties will be able to gather better information earlier, without having to resort to the courts for discovery orders. This, it is hoped, will result in earlier settlements through ADR on the basis of information openly shared by both sides. The key belief underpinning Woolf's pre-action protocols is that earlier investigation of the merits of a case allows for better negotiation, and earlier and more satisfactory settlements.

4.5.3. ADR and judicial case management

Several features of Lord Woolf's judicial case management scheme promote ADR. Pre-action protocols themselves represent the extension of judicial case

---

[77] Civil Justice Reform Progress Report (July 1998), which is published on the internet at http://www.open.gov.uk/lcd/civil/progr2fr.htm.

management powers into the time before litigation is commenced, with a view to encouraging settlement. Secondly, while the Woolf Report does not recommend making the referral of cases to ADR compulsory, or giving judges power to refer cases to ADR against parties' wishes, it supports the courts encouraging parties to refer their disputes to ADR where this might be beneficial.[78] This is achieved by requiring parties to attend pre-trial conferences and directions hearings. At those hearings, presiding judges must confirm with the parties' legal representatives that the possibility of ADR has been canvassed with the parties. In addition, Lord Woolf recommends that legal aid funding should be extended to legal advice and assistance aimed at achieving resolution of a dispute without resort to court action, and by using ADR. Information about ADR will be available at all courts.

The Central London County Court is currently undertaking a pilot mediation scheme, offering the services of a mediator to the parties to any dispute which is too large for the existing small claims procedure (over £3,000).[79] Reference to mediation is entirely voluntary, but the scheme has wider beneficial consequences. It draws the attention of all litigants to ADR alternatives, and it promotes ADR by way of mediation as a cost-effective alternative to full county court proceedings.

5. CONCLUSION: THE PRESENT STATE OF AFFAIRS

The English civil justice system is in desperate need of reform. The system is unacceptably expensive for all but the largest of claims. The time taken for cases to reach trial and judgment is commonly measured in years rather than months. The system is unduly complex, which in turn increases costs and delays. All of these factors put litigation out of the reach of the majority of the population. As a result, the civil justice system has little or no relevance to all but the very poor, who can obtain legal aid, and the very rich, who can afford the expense and potential risk of a crippling liability for costs. Clearly, the system fails to provide what the English public should be able to expect from it—fair, economical, and timely access to justice.

To remedy this situation, the English government is in the process of reforming the system in almost every respect. The Woolf reforms are intended to inaugurate a 'new legal landscape' in order to redress the problems of cost, delay, and complexity. To this end, the rules of court are being rewritten and

---

[78] Lord Woolf addresses ADR in detail in ch. 18 of his interim report. Although he does not resile from his interim conclusions on ADR, there is no equivalent chapter in his final report which is more tightly linked to his terms of reference. Both interim and final reports are available on the internet at http://www.open.gov.uk/lcd/civil/reportfr.htm.

[79] See the outline by Judge Butter QC, published on the Lord Chancellor's Department's website at: http://www.open.gov.uk/lcd/civil/adrpilfr.htm.

procedures substantially revised. The appeal system is under review. Legal aid will change fundamentally under legislation now before Parliament.

The publication of this essay will come only after the Big Bang of 26 April 1999, when the new unified rules of court are due to come into effect. At this stage, it is impossible to say what effects the reforms will have in practice, positive or negative. However, as discussed above, there seems little reason to expect significant or lasting improvement.

Yet the reformers' intentions are admirable. They have not been afraid to take radical steps, including the complete restructuring of legal aid and the wholesale adoption of a novel judicial case management philosophy. If the Woolf reforms do fail to fix the existing problems, there is every reason to believe that those in charge of the process of reform will continue to search for workable alternatives. Indeed, this is essential. At present, England has no suitable civil justice system for dealing economically with cases of medium value. If the major (and, some would say, the only) task of government is to protect individual rights and liberties, then the English system is failing in a large part of its task. Urgent steps must be taken to ensure that civil justice is accessible to all who reasonably require it.

5

Civil Justice Reform in Australia

G. L. Davies

1. INTRODUCTION

The civil justice system in Australia is derived from and remains substantially similar to that in England. Moreover, notwithstanding a federal system, it has remained substantially similar in all its various state and federal jurisdictions. Indeed, until the last decade or so, it had remained virtually unchanged for about a century notwithstanding that, especially over the last four or five decades, there has been a huge increase in the volume and complexity of litigation and in the classes of litigants.[1] Whereas, at the turn of the century, it was, in the main, men of property and a few corporations who litigated, now almost everyone is a potential litigant. This has been due substantially to social changes and legislative initiatives in social welfare and economic regulation.

Our present system of dispute resolution cannot cope with this increase in the number and classes of litigants and in the complexity of litigation. The system is too labour intensive for that. And because it is too labour intensive it is too costly; in most cases in our system the costs of those that go to trial are disproportionate to the amount or value in dispute and, for the losing party of average means, they may be ruinous.[2] Reducing the cost of dispute resolution must therefore be the primary objective of civil justice reform.[3]

There are, however, two concerns which must be addressed about the consequences of reforms aimed at reducing the labour intensiveness of dispute resolution. The first is that they may bring with them an increased risk of error; in particular that some relevant fact may be overlooked or its significance not fully appreciated. That does not mean that reforms of this kind should not proceed; on the contrary, as I shall endeavour to show, I think they must if cost is to be substantially reduced. But it is necessary to appreciate that cost reduction

I acknowledge with thanks the diligent work of my former associate Mr Andrew Tuch in the preparation of this essay, especially the graphs.

[1] Coopers & Lybrand W. D. Scott, 'Report on a Review of the New South Wales Court System', May 1989, p. 69 (hereinafter 'Coopers & Lybrand').

[2] Cf. G. Brennan, 'Key Issues in Judicial Administration' (1997) 6 JJA 138 at 139; see also Law Reform Commission of Victoria, 'Access to the Law: The Cost of Litigation', Issues Paper, May 1990, 1.

[3] Cost is also the principal cause of complaints against lawyers in Australia. About one-half of the 11,000 complaints made to the New South Wales Legal Services Commissioner against lawyers in that state in 1994–5 was about costs: Office of the Legal Services Commissioner (NSW) Annual Report, 1994–5.

may come at the risk of greater error in judgment[4] and a new balance between the objectives of reducing cost and reducing error risk may have to be accepted.

The second is that, whilst it may be true that, in some cases, requiring additional expenditure at specific stages may reduce the total cost of resolution of a dispute, great care must be taken before introducing additional requirements into an already too labour intensive system. Two aspects of this, in particular, must be borne in mind. One is that reforms which reduce the labour intensiveness of complex cases may in fact increase it in simple cases.[5] The second is that too much concentration, early in the litigation process, on reforms designed to simplify or otherwise shorten the trial may pay too little regard to the facts that almost all disputes resolve before trial[6] and that, of those that do not, by far the greater percentage of costs is incurred in the pre-trial phase.

Excessive delay is also a consequence of the labour intensiveness of our system and reduction of that delay should also be an objective of civil justice reform. Delay may, of itself, increase cost, both directly and indirectly. It may do so directly because the longer a case runs the more it will cost; essential tasks tend to be repeated and marginally relevant ones undertaken. Indirectly, client resources which could be utilized in income-earning activities may be tied up for longer in litigation and income-earning opportunities may be forsaken because of the length or uncertainty of result of the litigation. It may also have an emotional cost.

Delay may also affect the reliability of the result. Memories become less reliable and reconstruction tends to replace recollection. Moreover witnesses with no interest in the outcome tend to cease to recall relevant events or conversations and some witnesses disappear or die.

If we accept, as I think we must, that advocating substantial increases in court resources is a futile exercise,[7] delay reduction must be sought by other means. But the effect of delay reduction measures on cost and fairness must be borne in mind.[8]

High cost or long delay may also lead to unfairness to a poorer litigant or to one whose interests are otherwise best served by a speedy resolution; and the laissez-faire approach of our system permits this possibility to be exploited. Reduced reliability of result because of delay may also cause that result to be unfair. Moreover fairness, in a publicly funded dispute resolution system,

---

[4] Whether it does in fact result in greater error in most cases may be doubted. I discuss this further below.

[5] Judicial case management may be an example of this. I discuss this at s. 4.2 below.

[6] Well over 90% of actions commenced are settled before trial; submissions made by the Law Council of Australia to the Senate Cost of Justice Inquiry, Dec. 1989, 50 (hereinafter 'Submissions of LCA'); Coopers & Lybrand, 121. Given that many disputes resolve before litigation commences the percentage of disputes which go to trial must be very small indeed.   [7] See n. 94.

[8] Some of the discussion of the advantages of judicial case management focuses on delay reduction without fully considering its costs consequences. See s. 4.2 below.

involves more than merely the interests of the parties to a dispute; the interests of others may be affected by delay.[9]

I shall attempt to demonstrate the correctness of those propositions in this essay the main object of which is to discuss what I consider to be the main defects in our existing civil justice system and how they are being or should be remedied.[10] But first I need to describe our existing system and say a little about its history.

2. THE CIVIL JUSTICE SYSTEM IN AUSTRALIA

2.1. The inherited civil justice system

Subject to limitations which are not relevant to the present discussion,[11] the law of England became, upon the foundation of the Australian colonies, the law of those colonies. The Supreme Courts of those colonies which, within their territories, were courts of general jurisdiction, were invested with the common law and equitable jurisdictions of English courts.[12] Similarly the English practice rules were adopted as the rules of colonial Supreme Courts although, for periods varying among the colonies, and in some cases the states after 1901, the procedures in law and equity remained separate. The close control exercised by England over its colonies, including by the right of appeal from Supreme Courts to the Privy Council, ensured that neither in substance nor procedure did the law depart from that in England.

Upon Federation in 1901 the colonial Supreme Courts became state Supreme Courts and were also invested with federal jurisdiction.[13] After the establishment of the High Court of Australia in 1903 appeal lay from those courts to it. But there remained an alternative appeal from those courts to the Privy Council and an appeal by leave lay from the High Court to the Privy

---

[9] These include potential litigants waiting in line, those who are deterred from seeking to vindicate their rights because of the perception of cost and delay, those who are indirectly affected by the outcome of litigation, and the public who bear some of its cost.

[10] The views expressed here have been developed from those expressed by me in previous papers, the published ones, in chronological order, being: 'The Survival of the Civil Trial System: A Judicial Responsibility' (1989) 5 Aust. Bar Rev. 277; 'Some Proposed Changes in Civil Procedure: Their Practical Benefits and Ethical Rationale' (1993) 3 JJA 111, also in S. Parker and C. Sampford (eds.), *Legal Ethics and Legal Practice: Contemporary Issues* (Oxford: Clarendon Press, 1995), at 127; 'Reforming the Civil Litigation System: Streamlining the Adversarial Framework' (1995) 25 QLSJ 111; 'A Blueprint for Reform: Some Proposals of the Litigation Reform Commission and their Rationale' (1996) 5 JJA 201; and 'Justice Reform: A Personal Perspective' (1997) 15 Aust. Bar Rev. 109.

[11] See for example *Mabo v. Queensland [No.2]* (1992) 175 CLR 1.

[12] As well as with jurisdiction in ecclesiastical matters, insolvency, matrimonial causes, and criminal jurisdiction.

[13] Civilly by a combination of s. 77 (iii) of the Commonwealth of Australia Constitution and s. 39 (2) of the Judiciary Act 1903 (Cth.).

Council. The Privy Council was removed from the Australian system of courts by a series of enactments between 1968 and 1986.[14]

Except for some limited kinds of matters which, even at first instance, had to be heard in the High Court of Australia, the state Supreme Courts continued to have and exercise jurisdiction in almost all federal matters, that is matters arising under Acts of the Commonwealth Parliament, until 1975 when their matrimonial causes jurisdiction became vested in a new Family Court of Australia. Then in 1976 the Federal Court of Australia was established to hear and determine matters arising under other Commonwealth Acts. The result is that jurisdiction in civil cases came to be shared by state courts and the Federal Court of Australia,[15] though until 1987 the jurisdiction of the Federal Court was limited to matters arising under Commonwealth Acts and state Supreme Courts, during that period, generally did not have jurisdiction in respect of such matters. That unsatisfactory situation, which resulted in many sterile jurisdictional disputes, was then remedied by joint state and Commonwealth cross-vesting legislation[16] in consequence of which, speaking generally, where the Federal Court is hearing a federal matter it can also hear and determine a related non-federal matter and where a state Supreme Court is hearing a non-federal matter it can also hear and determine a related federal matter.[17]

2.2. The civil courts in Australia and the system they administer

As appears from what I have said, at the apex of the system is the High Court of Australia as the ultimate court of appeal. Beneath that are the state Supreme Courts as courts of general jurisdiction and the Federal Court, initially with jurisdiction limited to matters arising under federal legislation but later, as I have said, with more extensive accrued jurisdiction. In both cases, like the High Court of Judicature in England, they exercise both original and appellate jurisdiction. Although the way in which trial and appellate jurisdiction is divided in each of those courts is not uniform it is convenient to take as examples the Supreme Courts of Queensland, New South Wales, and Victoria.[18] In each of those courts, somewhat like the High Court of Judicature in England, the court is divided into a Court of Appeal and a Trial Division, the Court of Appeal hearing appeals from the Trial Division. In each of the states there are also two inferior courts, a Magistrates' Court[19] with jurisdiction up to

---

[14] Privy Council (Limitation of Appeals) Act 1968 (Cth.); Privy Council (Appeals from the High Court) Act 1975 (Cth.); Australia Acts 1986.

[15] Leaving aside matrimonial causes which are beyond the ambit of this essay.

[16] Jurisdiction of Courts (Cross-vesting) Act 1987 (Cth.) and corresponding state legislation.

[17] s. 4.

[18] In the Supreme Courts of the three less populous states and in the Federal Court, the appellate court is constituted by a bench of three judges of the Court, there being no separate Court of Appeal. [19] Known in some states as a Local Court.

approximately $50,000 and a District Court[20] with jurisdiction up to approximately $250,000. Appeals from decisions of the Magistrates' Court lie to the District Court. Appeals from the District Court and the Supreme Court lie to the Court of Appeal and decisions of state Courts of Appeal and their federal equivalent lie only by leave of the High Court to that Court.[21] The result is that state Courts of Appeal and their federal equivalent are, for the most part, final Courts of Appeal. Generally less than 1 per cent of matters heard by those courts go on appeal to the High Court of Australia.[22]

Appointments to the judiciary of the Supreme Courts, the Federal Court, and District Courts are generally from the practising profession, for the most part from the bar of those states where the profession is divided. Magistrates, who are almost all legally qualified, are also increasingly being appointed from the practising profession.

Over the last twenty years or so the Australian common law has tended to move away from United Kingdom common law.[23] The same has tended to occur in procedural law although here, except for case management, the changes have been more recent. As I mentioned earlier, until the course of the last decade or so, the procedural systems in Australian courts remained virtually unchanged. Indeed the only substantial change, before the last decade or so, in civil procedure has been the virtual abolition of the civil jury. It was eliminated by statute in respect of most claims for damages for personal injury and by choice in most other kinds of actions.[24]

Even with recent changes, referred to below, our procedural system remains a predominantly adversarial one; that is, one in which the conduct of litigation, at least up to the part of trial, is left substantially in the hands of the parties (or more accurately, their lawyers). The procedure is designed to concentrate the judicial function into one continuous hearing, evidence is elicited by the parties, not the judge, and sanctions for non-compliance with rules are generally imposed on the party in default only at the request of the opposite party. Its

---

[20] Known in Victoria as the County Court. Tasmania has no intermediate court.

[21] In general terms, leave is only granted if an appeal raises an issue of significant public interest.

[22] AGPS, High Court of Australia, Annual Report 1995–6 (1996), part III, 44–53; Court of Appeal, Queensland, Annual Report 1996, tables 2 and 12.

[23] This reflects formal removal of judicial ties to England (see n.14 above) and the recent High Court tendency to afford less weight to precedents of the Privy Council (*Viro* v. *The Queen* (1978) 141 CLR 88), the House of Lords, and the English Court of Appeal (*Parker* v. *The Queen* (1963) 111 CLR 610 at 632; *Cook* v. *Cook* (1986) 162 CLR 376 at 390). For merely one example of this divergence, consider the High Court decisions concerning unconscionable conduct, starting in 1983 with *Commercial Bank of Australia* v. *Amadio* (1983) 151 CLR 447, *Taylor* v. *Johnson* (1983) 151 CLR 422, and *Legione* v. *Hateley* (1983) 152 CLR 406 and culminating in *Louth* v. *Diprose* (1992) 175 CLR 621, and contrast the House of Lords' decisions in *Scandinavian Trading Tanker Co. AB* v. *Flota Petrolera Ecuatoriana* [1983] 2 AC 694 and *National Westminster Bank plc.* v. *Morgan* [1985] AC 686. For other comparisons, see J. Toohey, 'Towards an Australian Common Law' (1990) 6 Aust. Bar Rev. 185 at 193–6.

[24] By 1959 less than 1% of civil trials in Queensland were by jury: B. McPherson, *The Supreme Court of Queensland 1859–1960* (Sydney: Butterworths, 1989), at 392.

main features are a joinder of issues by pleadings, mutual documentary but not oral disclosure, interlocutory skirmishes, a climatic trial in which generally the evidence and submissions are mainly oral, and a costs order against the losing party. Other features are a huge attrition rate between commencement and trial, adjudication of some cases summarily, and, more recently, alternative dispute resolution.[25]

Appeals are generally heard and determined on the written record of the trial evidence.

2.3. The extent of litigation in Australia, delay, and cost

The current population of Australia is approximately 18,532,247[26] of whom approximately 13,303,492[27] are adults. In the 1996–7 year 799,400 actions were commenced.[28] There are delays in finalizing actions at all levels but particularly at the middle (District or County Court) level (see Fig. 5.1). There are also delays in finalizing appeals[29] notwithstanding that appeals are decided on the written record of the trial with little or no contest on findings of primary fact by the trial judge, hearing times have been substantially reduced in some courts of appeal[30] by permitting extensive written submissions well in advance of the hearing date with oral argument being confined to elaboration or addition to, but not repetition of, the written submissions, and some appeals are presented entirely in writing.

There are very few statistics in Australia on costs. But it is plain that, in all except very large cases, they are an unacceptably high proportion of the amount or value involved and, in all cases, more than most can afford to pay. A survey conducted in the County Court of Victoria in 1988 is revealing in this respect. It showed that the average costs awarded to a successful party were 58 per cent of the damages awarded. When the unsuccessful party's own costs were added, the total costs payable by that party often exceeded the amount of the judgment.[31]

Delay is, in part, caused by insufficiency in the number of judges and support staff. Governments in Australia, federal and state, have been reluctant to appoint sufficient judges. Take, for example, the New South Wales Court of Appeal. When it was established in 1966, it consisted of the Chief Justice, the President

---

[25] Referred to in detail later.
[26] *Australian Demographic Statistics*, June Quarter 1997, Australian Bureau of Statistics Catalogue No. 3101.0.
[27] *1996 Census of Population and Housing: Selected Social and Housing Characteristics—Australia*, Australian Bureau of Statistics Catalogue No. 2015.0.
[28] For the distribution of those among states and among courts see Table 5.1.
[29] See Figs 5.2 and 5.3, and Tables 5.2 and 5.3. The delays are worst in New South Wales. See M. Clarke, 'Delay Reduction in the New South Wales Court of Appeal' (1996) 6 JJA 87.
[30] For example Queensland and, to a lesser extent, other states.
[31] M. Sargent, 'The Litigation Costs System in Victoria: Indemnifying or Ineffectual?' (1988) 62 Law Institute Journal 379.

G. L. Davies

Table 5.1. *Civil actions commenced and their distribution among courts*

(*a*) Number of civil actions started 1996–7 ('000)

	NSW	Vic.	Qld.	WA	SA	ACT	NT	Cth.	Total
Supreme Court/									
Federal Court	10.4	4.5	4.2	2.9	1.6	1.4	0.4	17.3	42.7
District/County									
Court	10.9	9.2	6.7	5.8	2.8	—	—	—	35.4
Magistrates' Court	279.2	208.1	114.3	58.7	43.8	9.7	7.4	—	721.2
TOTAL	300.5	221.8	125.3	67.4	48.2	11.1	7.8	17.3	799.4

Note: Measured as the number of matters commenced by filing originating process. No figures are available for Tasmaia.

(*b*) Proportion of civil lodgements per court level, 1996–7 (%)

	NSW	Vic.	Qld.	WA	SA	ACT	NT	Total
Supreme Court/								
Federal Court	3.5	2.0	3.4	4.3	3.4	12.2	5.1	5.3
District/County								
Court	3.6	4.1	5.4	8.6	5.8	—	—	4.4
Magistrates' Court	92.9	93.8	91.2	87.1	90.8	87.8	94.9	90.2
ALL COURTS	100.0	100.0	100.0	100.0	100.0	100.0	100.0	100.0

and six judges of appeal. There were then 48 judges from whose decisions appeals could be brought. By 1997 there were 115 such judges but only two additional judges on the Court of Appeal; that is, more than a 100 per cent increase in the number of judges from whom appeals lie but only a 20 per cent increase in the size of the Court of Appeal. An even more dramatic statistic is that the number of appeals increased between 1978 and 1995 from 199 to 551. A similar, if less dramatic comparison can be made between general population increase (leaving aside the fact referred to earlier that a much greater proportion of the population are now potential litigants) and increase in the number of trial judges.

There is a danger, to which I shall refer later, that some cost reduction reforms, such as encouraging an increase in the written content of evidence and argument, may simply transfer delay from the period between commencement of proceedings and hearing to that between hearing and judgment, unless it is appreciated that, if this is done, judges require more time, out of court, in which to read, analyse, and write.

(a)

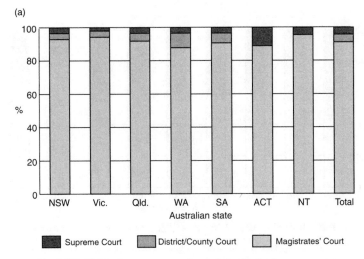

Fig. 5.1(*a*) Civil actions commenced and their distribution among states

(b)

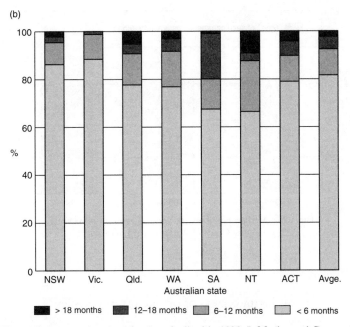

Fig. 5.1(*b*) Average duration of actions finalized in 1996–7, Magistrates' Court only
Note: Duration is measured as the time from lodgement date to the finalization date. The finalization date is identified as either: (1) adjudicated suit finalization, in which a judgment is entered on the record, including ratification by the court of a settlement out of court; or (2) non-adjudicated suit finalization (includes death of the defendant or plaintiff (where this is relevant), withdrawal by the plaintiff, settlement out of court (where the court has not been notified officially of the settlement but has classed the dispute as finalized or no longer pending), and expiration of time).

(a)

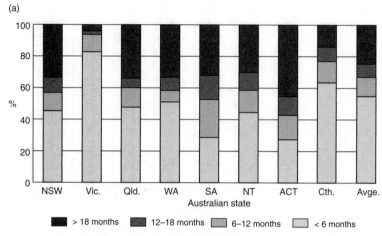

Fig. 5.2(*a*) Delays in hearings in intermediate appellate courts

(b)

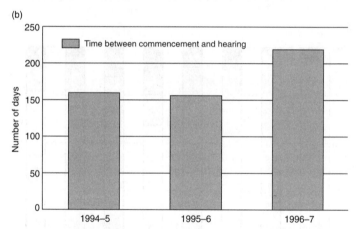

Fig. 5.2(*b*) Median time between commencement and hearing,
Queensland Court of Appeal, in graphical form

3. THE DISADVANTAGES OF OUR TRADITIONAL SYSTEM

The main reason why our traditional procedural system causes excessive cost and delay is that it is too labour intensive. There are two related features of our system which make it so labour intensive. One of these I have called the adversarial imperative; the compulsion which each party, and particularly that party's lawyer, has to see the other as the enemy who must be

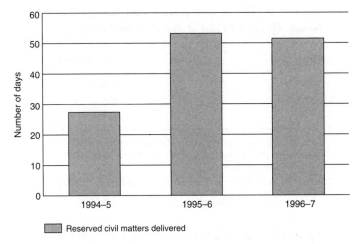

Fig. 5.3. Median time between hearing and delivery of judgment,
Queensland Court of Appeal, in graphical form

defeated.[32] The system is designed along the lines of trial by battle. Legal education and professional ethical rules also contribute to this. The other related feature is the perceived need to leave no stone unturned. This may have an altruistic motive, a desire to achieve perfect justice, but it is also strongly motivated by the adversarial imperative. It also has a practical cause because if one side leaves a stone unturned and the other does not the first may lose the case and the client may then sue the lawyer. Together these features encourage the contesting of too many issues, the discovery of too many documents, and a huge amount of duplicated work by opposing lawyers. So does the existing costs system in which lawyers generally charge by time spent on items of work completed rather than on the total amount of work which should be completed for the efficient and fair resolution of a dispute.

I think that our traditional system has been too adversarial in six main respects, each of which tends to increase costs and some of which may cause unfairness between parties of unequal means. The first of these is that the desire to win is antithetical to a willingness to contest only the real issues and to disclose relevant information to the other side, particularly if either is likely to help the opponent. The second is that the focus on winning often obscures the advantages of an agreed solution. The third is that the emphasis on resolution by ultimate trial obscures the advantages of, and provides few opportunities for,

---

[32] 'The object of the parties is always victory, not abstract truth': O. Dixon, *Jesting Pilate* (Melbourne: Law Book Co., 1965), at 16; war is, in my view, a better analogy these days than the 'sporting theory of justice': R. Pound, 'The Causes of Popular Dissatisfaction with the Administration of Justice' (1906) 29 ABA Rep. 395 at 404.

Table 5.2. *Median time between commencement and hearing, Queensland Court of Appeal, in table form*

Year	Civil matters
1994–5	158.5
1995–6	156
1996–7	217

Note: Median time (in days) between commencement and hearing for all civil matters heard during the relevant year (whenever commenced).

Source: Supreme Court of Queensland Annual Report 1996–7, table 8, at 27.

Table 5.3. *Median time between hearing and delivery of judgment, Queensland Court of Appeal, in table form*

Year	Civil matters
1994–5	27
1995–6	53
1996–7	51

Note: Median time (in days) between hearing and delivery of reserved judgments where reserved judgments were delivered in the relevant year (whenever commenced).

Source: Supreme Court of Queensland Annual Report 1996–7, table 9, at 28.

resolving a dispute before then. The fourth is that the adversarial imperative tends to make advocates of the witnesses. The fifth is that the system permits a richer litigant, by engaging better lawyers and incurring greater expenditure of labour, to obtain an unfair result. And the sixth is that, by leaving the pace and shape of litigation entirely to the parties, it permits unnecessary expenditure of time and cost and may cause unfairness. I should explain briefly what I mean by each of these factors which, to some extent, overlap.

3.1. The system discourages the limiting of issues and the disclosure of unfavourable information

Our traditional system of pleading allows, and the adversarial imperative encourages, each party to allege facts generally rather than with particularity, to deny generally all allegations which it is not in the party's interests to admit, and even to deny specifically facts known to be true.[33] By making general rather than specific allegations a party may avoid the risk, however slight, that a specific fact, which later turns out to be important, has not been alleged. And by denying all the opponent's allegations a party may require the opponent to prove facts which are known to be true or of marginal relevance but which may not be easily proved.[34] By such tactics the parties are playing a very expensive game rather than getting to the real issues in dispute.

Whilst our system remains one in which no stone may be left unturned and no point on which the other side could possibly fail should be conceded, and in which the lawyer who advises otherwise is at risk, it will remain too costly. The system must require that only the real issues between the parties be disputed.

The traditional discovery process allows, and the adversarial imperative encourages, excessive expenditure of time in searching through the opponent's disclosed documents, concealment of the more relevant (or damaging) documents in a mass of marginally relevant ones, and abuse of the process by oppressive over-discovery. There is, however, a curious ambivalence in our system with respect to the disclosure of information. It requires disclosure of all documentary evidence, favourable or unfavourable; indeed, far too much of it.[35] So that, in a case which turns substantially on documentary evidence, each party may be more than fully informed of the evidence of the other. Yet there is no obligation at all to disclose oral evidence. So that, in the majority of cases which turn substantially on oral evidence, each party may take the other by surprise.[36]

3.2. The system obscures the advantages of an agreed solution

These advantages are obvious enough. An agreed solution is generally cheaper than a trial. It can be moulded to achieve an outcome which the parties desire and which is in their best interests rather than being bound by rules to a fixed result. It is more conducive to an amicable resumption of a former relationship between the parties whether personal or business. And often parties are happier with a solution which they have chosen and over which they have some control than with one imposed on them.[37] Yet our system still encourages the view that one party is right and the other is wrong; that one must win and the other must lose.

---

[33] *Myers* v. *Elman* [1940] AC 282 at 292, 316, 333.

[34] Curiously, professional ethical rules do not preclude this.

[35] In Queensland until 1994 when the *Peruvian Guano* test ((1882) 11 QBD 55) was abandoned in favour of one requiring disclosure only of documents directly relevant to an allegation in issue. See the text at n. 71.

[36] Interrogatories and witness statements have both, for reasons to which I refer later, been limited and generally unsatisfactory exceptions to this.

[37] See e.g. E. Lind *et al.*, 'In the Eye of the Beholder: Tort Litigants' Evaluation of their Experiences in the Civil Justice System' (1990) 24 L. & Soc'y Rev. 953 at 972, 976.

It is true, of course, that the vast majority of cases settle.[38] But experience has also shown that far too many of these settle at too late a stage to result in a substantial saving in time or cost.

My point is that more cases would be resolved by agreement and many more of those which are so resolved would be resolved sooner, if the means of assisting parties to reach an agreement were as much an institutionalized part of our system as are the means of litigating. That does not involve merely making mediation available within that system. It also involves a change in legal culture; a more ready acceptance of a belief that both parties may 'win' from an agreed solution.

3.3 It provides too few opportunities for adjudication otherwise than by a full trial

Our system focuses on the trial as the main event. The common assumption is that, if a dispute is not settled, it will be resolved at, and only at, an ultimate trial. That assumption is not an unreasonable one under the existing system because there are few opportunities for adjudication, even of specific issues, otherwise than by trial of an action.

It should not necessarily follow, in my view, from the need for adjudication, that there must be a trial in the traditional sense with all that that involves. Litigants should, in all cases, be given choices of quicker and cheaper, even if less perfect, means of adjudication and, in smaller cases, where the cost of a full trial may exceed or be an unacceptably high proportion of the amount involved, quicker and cheaper adjudication should be the rule rather than the exception.

In a system such as ours, in which the issues to be contested tend to be determined by the party who desires to be least specific and the gathering of evidence on those issues is left entirely to the parties, the cheaper and simpler the means of adjudication are, the greater is the risk of error. The imposition of greater obligations on the parties to identify relevant issues and disclose relevant evidence, favourable and unfavourable, is therefore an essential part of providing cheaper and simpler means of adjudication.

It is not sufficient, given the existing legal culture, merely to provide alternative means of adjudication. Lawyers must be encouraged to use them, including encouragement by fee incentives; because if lawyers do not want to use them, their clients, on the whole, will not do so.

---

[38] In a recent study of civil matters conducted in New South Wales (District and Supreme Courts) and Victoria (County and Supreme Courts), 83% of New South Wales matters and 92% of Victorian matters settled before verdict: D. Worthington and J. Baker, 'The Costs of Civil Litigation: Current Charging Practices', Civil Justice Research Centre, Dec. 1993, at 55.

3.4. It tends to make advocates of the witnesses

There is no doubt that, in our system in which each party's lawyer obtains statements from the witnesses whom the party intends to call, most witnesses, at least unconsciously, adopt sides. They see themselves as giving evidence for one side or the other. The presumption that any witness is giving evidence neutrally is foreign to our thinking. I do not mean to imply by that that most witnesses are dishonest or even that they consciously colour their evidence to favour the party who calls them; it is rather that our system tends to give them an unconscious bias which often makes them, in varying degrees, advocates for the party who calls them.

More than a decade ago Professor Langbein made my point quite graphic-ally. I think what he said then is worth repeating:

The European jurist who visits the United States and becomes acquainted with our civil procedure typically expresses amazement at our witness practice. His amazement turns to something bordering on disbelief when he discovers that we extend this sphere of partisan control to the selection and preparation of experts. . . .

At the American Trial Bar, those of us who serve as expert witnesses are known as 'saxophones'. This is a revealing term, as slang often is. The idea is that the lawyer plays the tune, manipulating the expert as though the expert were a musical instrument on which the lawyer sounds the desired notes. I sometimes serve as an expert in trust and pension cases and I have experienced the subtle pressures to join the team—to shade one's views, to conceal doubt, to overstate nuance, to downplay weak aspects of the case that one has been hired to bolster. Nobody likes to disappoint a patron; and beyond this psychological pressure is the financial inducement. Money changes hands upon the rendering of expertise, but the expert can run his meter only so long as his patron litigator likes the tune. Opposing counsel undertakes a similar exercise, hiring and schooling another expert to parrot the contrary position. The result is our familiar battle of opposing experts. The more measured and impartial an expert is, the less likely he is to be used by either side.

At trial, the battle of experts tends to baffle the trier, especially in jury courts. If the experts do not cancel each other out, the advantage is likely to be with the expert whose forensic skills are the more enticing.[39]

The battle of experts is a common experience in our system. That is not to suggest that they give dishonest evidence. But given a range of permissible views, the realistic assumption is that the expert will give evidence at the end of that range which most accords with his or her client's contentions; otherwise the witness generally would not be called. This encourages the practice of 'shopping' for favourable experts.

Often there is more than one expert called on each side of one question and each is subjected to extensive cross-examination. The end result in such a case

---

[39] J. Langbein, 'The German Advantage in Civil Procedure' (1985) 52 U. Chi. L. Rev. 823 at 835–6; see also (1988) 82 NWUL Rev. 763.

may be a huge expenditure of time, a crippling expenditure of cost,[40] and a judge, or still worse a jury, having no relevant expertise, left to decide the question. To add to the problem, the increasing complexity of scientific and technical evidence has meant that there is now a good deal of expert evidence that is quite beyond the capacity of most judges to understand.[41]

The risk of partisan evidence is at least as great in respect of witnesses giving evidence of facts. Like the expert referred to by Professor Langbein, they also feel the pressure to join the team.

3.5. It advantages the richer litigant

We all know that all lawyers are not equal in ability and that generally those who are perceived to be better command higher fees. So the richer litigant can afford the better lawyer. That litigant can also afford to pay for more time to be spent on the preparation of his or her case. Up to a point, which is well beyond the means of most, the more time and money spent by a litigant on the preparation of his or her case, the greater is the chance of winning. The unfairness of these consequences can, to some extent, be lessened by changes to the existing system.

In the first place, any change which reduces cost also reduces the advantage of the richer litigant. Consequently any measures which lessen any of the first four of the above factors are likely to lessen this one because they are all likely to reduce cost. Secondly, any measure which overcomes the first of the above factors, by requiring disclosure of relevant but unfavourable evidence, is likely to make the contest more even by giving to the poorer litigant some of the benefit of the evidence-gathering resources of the richer litigant.[42] Thirdly, as the richer litigant can afford the more persuasive expert, and more experts, any proposal which reduces that advantage will produce a fairer result.

---

[40] Little research has been conducted in Australia on the cost of expert witnesses as a component of litigation costs. However the Australian Institute of Judicial Administration (AIJA), in its study on the cost of civil litigation in the District Court of Queensland and the County Court of Victoria, found that medical reports and medical experts at trial accounted for a significant proportion of the total costs of litigation. In Victoria expert witnesses accounted for 27% of the cost of cases settled at the pre-trial conference and 16% of the cost of cases that went to verdict. The comparable figures for Queensland were 10% and 15%: P. Williams et al., The Cost of Civil Litigation before Intermediate Courts in Australia (Australian Institute of Judicial Administration, Melbourne 1992), at 72.

[41] See the recent concern expressed by the New South Wales Branch of the Australian Medical Association in 'Tort Law Reform in New South Wales' (1997), at para. 17.3.

[42] Curiously, this seems to be the main criticism made of a proposal, referred to below, that the obligation of disclosure should, in a limited way, extend to oral as well as written evidence. But it is put in a different way: it is said that a lazy or incompetent litigant or lawyer will reap the advantage of the work done by his or her more diligent and capable opponent.

3.6. It permits the parties to dictate the shape and pace of litigation[43]

There remain, among litigation lawyers, some who still think it a party's right to 'put the other side to proof'; which is a euphemism for raising every possible obstacle in the opponent's path in the hope that he or she will trip on one of them and fail. Those people also generally think that it should be left entirely to the parties, which often in reality means the party who least wants the litigation to reach the point of judgment, to determine its pace.

Those beliefs can affect all stages of an action from pleadings through discovery and preparation for trial to the trial itself. And their implementation can result in a war of attrition in which a skilfully advised party can prolong the pre-trial period and the trial itself to such an extent as to cause the opponent to give up in financial exhaustion. When that occurs, and it undoubtedly does, it brings the system, and those who work in it, into disrepute.

Fortunately there are now many who believe that that should not be allowed to continue and that both the pace and shape of litigation should, to some extent, be controlled by the courts. Indeed that has been the impetus for case management,[44] which blossomed in this country more than a decade ago and which now flourishes in almost all higher jurisdictions. It has also been the impetus for the introduction of rules permitting judges to exercise greater control over the conduct of trials and for a number of other changes to which I shall also refer.

These systemic defects must be remedied if costs and unfairness between parties of unequal means are to be substantially reduced. But it is implicit, I think in what I have said so far, that the mind-set of lawyers, their clients, and even the judiciary must also change if systemic changes are to be effective in causing practical change. And, for reasons which I advance below, the existing system of charging fees must also change. I shall discuss these changes in the following part.

4. HOW OUR SYSTEM HAS BEEN AND MUST BE CHANGED

One defect in reforms implemented during the past decade is that they have been piecemeal. That is not a criticism of the reformers. It is an almost inevitable aspect of reform of this kind. There will always be opposition to it, some of it quite strong and influential. No one likes changing the way they do things; and the longer we have done things in a particular way, the more opposed we will be to changing it. Moreover effective civil justice reform

---

[43] By shape I mean the definition of issues in dispute and the way in which they may be proved.
[44] I shall use this term to describe not only the management of individual cases but the management of the overall flow of cases, sometimes called 'caseflow management'.

must make dispute resolution cheaper and that means that, from every dispute, the lawyers will earn a little less. In Australia the legal profession is now overcrowded and the average income of lawyers is very much less than it was a decade ago. All of this makes comprehensive reform difficult. So it has been piecemeal reform or none at all. But it is important not to lose sight of the overall objective. My own view, and the rationale of many of the reforms of my own Commission[45] has been that, in order to achieve cheaper, quicker, and fairer[46] justice, each of four specific objects must be achieved, at least in part. They are:

1. more disputes must be resolved earlier and by a process other than litigation;[47]
2. the litigation process must be simplified and accelerated, the complexity of the process being more closely related to the complexity of, and the amount or value involved in, the dispute;
3. the system for fixing lawyers' costs must change. Costs must be more closely related to the amount of work which should be performed, or best practice, than to the amount of work actually done or the time actually spent; and they must be more predictable; and
4. the mind-set of lawyers, judges, and litigants must change. The battle-ground atmosphere should change to one of co-operation, at least to the extent of limiting issues in dispute, disclosing relevant information, oral or written, favourable or unfavourable, and perceiving and utilizing the advantages of an agreed solution. Lawyers (and through them their clients) must be made aware of the advantages of, and encouraged to use, simpler, even if less perfect, adjudication. All of this may require some loss of control by parties and their lawyers in the resolution of disputes. Lawyers should also appreciate that they can perform a useful role in dispute prevention. And they should appreciate that the best interests of their clients may not always be achieved by the pursuit of perceived legal rights.

There are, in addition, two further objects which, in my view, should be pursued and which, if pursued, will make our system cheaper, quicker, and fairer, but which are beyond the scope of this essay. The first is the simplification of substantive law which has become and continues to become increasingly complex, especially in those areas of law in which standards of conduct are substantially governed by statute. There has been talk of simplification in specific areas,[48] but little action. Although I do not favour some of the more

---

[45] Litigation Reform Commission of Queensland.
[46] I explain later what I mean by fairness.
[47] By litigation I mean the traditional process leading to and including the trial of an action.
[48] Corporations law and taxation law.

extreme suggestions for simplification of substantive law[49] there is, in my view, considerable scope for this. The second is the increased use of information technology in all aspects of dispute resolution.[50] I shall, however, mention in passing some aspects of this.

In stating the objects in this way I do not mean to imply that the function of courts in civil dispute resolution is merely to resolve disputes between parties. They also perform an important role in the definition and development of the law and in demonstrating its effectiveness. But I do not think that the achievement of these objects will detract from courts' performance of that role.

I turn now to a discussion of the ways in which those objects are being achieved, or how it has been proposed they should be achieved, in various jurisdictions in Australia. I should however, preface my discussion with a reminder that, as I am discussing a federal system in which reforms have been made and are being proposed in the Federal Court, six Supreme Courts, and at least some of five District Courts and six Magistrates' Courts, I intend to be selective rather than comprehensive.

4.1. Resolution earlier and otherwise than by litigation

I need hardly justify seeking to resolve more disputes by a process cheaper than litigation. When one has regard to the risk of losing with the likely consequence of paying two sets of costs, most litigation is beyond the means of most prospective litigants. And notwithstanding recent and proposed reforms it will remain beyond the means of many. Moreover in all cases, other than those involving very large sums of money, costs are an unacceptably high proportion of the amount involved.[51] Hence the need to provide cheaper alternatives.

I have already mentioned the advantages of an agreed solution. But because some disputes and some disputants are not amenable to such a solution, cheaper adjudicated solutions should also be provided.

There are at least two reasons why dispute resolution should also be quicker. The first is that the longer a dispute remains unresolved the costlier its resolution tends to become: direct costs tend to increase with time as necessary tasks may be repeated and unnecessary or marginally necessary tasks may be undertaken; for an income-earning litigant time spent in dispute resolution or preparing for it is likely to result in lost income; and there may be an emotional cost. The second is that the longer a dispute remains unresolved the less accurate an adjudicated solution is likely to be and the more difficult it will be to resolve it by agreement; adversarial attitudes harden, memories fade, and costs often become more important than the amount involved.

---

[49] See for example R. Epstein, *Simple Rules for a Complex World* (Cambridge, Mass.: Harvard UP, 1995).   [50] See generally R. Susskind, *The Future of Law* (Oxford: Clarendon Press, 1996).
[51] See n. 38; D. Worthington and J. Baker, 'The Cost of Civil Litigation: Current Changing Practices', Civil Justice Research Centre, Dec. 1993, 24, 49.

At least in theory, in our existing system the more time and money expended in resolving a dispute the closer its adjudication will come to achieving justice according to law. More specifically it should, but by no means always does, result in the parties and the court being more fully informed of the relevant contentions, facts, and opinions.

Notwithstanding those aspects of our system, to which I have already referred, which work against that theoretical result, there is a risk, which is cause for some concern, that quicker and cheaper resolution of a dispute, whether by agreement or adjudication, may be achieved before the parties or the adjudicator are fully informed as to either relevant facts or applicable law. I shall return later to that concern. In the meantime, in the context of resolving disputes without litigation, the following points may be made.

The first is that, to some extent, that concern may be allayed by ensuring that, as much as possible, subject to my second point, issues are defined and relevant information exchanged before any such resolution takes place. The second is that, in determining what is a fair resolution between the parties to a dispute, including the precise definition of issues and the mutual disclosure of relevant information, costs are a relevant factor; if the cost of ensuring precision in the definition of issues and the mutual disclosure of all relevant information is beyond the means of the parties or grossly disproportionate to the amount involved, its expenditure may be pointless. And the third is that, provided parties know what their legal rights are, alternative resolution may offer them an informed choice of a solution which is interest based rather than rights based; that is, one which promotes their best future interests notwithstanding that it may not accord with their strict legal rights.

Notwithstanding the obvious advantages of an agreed resolution of a dispute, the systemic factors which I have mentioned and other factors such as pride or greed or wronged feelings often impede a party's rational appreciation of the likely financial consequences of litigation and, often more importantly, the consequences which it will have on that party's wider interests and future relationship with the other. It is not sufficient therefore merely to provide the means by which parties may be assisted to an agreed resolution. They and their lawyers must be encouraged to use them. The same may be said of cheaper and more expeditious means of adjudication. Moreover it is not sufficient that the means of assisting parties to an agreed resolution or the means of obtaining a cheaper and quicker adjudication be provided to parties to existing litigation. They should be provided, and their use encouraged, before litigation commences.

I have so far avoided the use of the terms mediation or alternative dispute resolution (ADR). Different groups of people define them in different ways. I propose to define and use mediation broadly to mean assisting parties to a dispute to an agreed resolution of it. That embraces a range of activities from, at one end, merely keeping the peace while encouraging the parties to discuss their dispute through to, at the other end, pointing out to each party the strengths and weaknesses of his or her case, commenting on each's likely prospects of success, and even suggesting possible solutions. And I shall use ADR to embrace mediation and all adjudicated resolution otherwise than by trial.

For about two decades mediation has been offered in Australia, outside the court system, by mediators some of whom have received accreditation from bodies specializing in providing such service. During the last decade it has also become increasingly available within court systems. There is nothing incompatible between mediation provided outside the court system and mediation within the court system. The first is, of course, entirely voluntary and, if that is what the parties want, it will often provide the most satisfactory resolution. It also has the advantage of being available to disputants before litigation commences. It is commonly used in the resolution of large commercial disputes and there is now a large body of skilled persons, many of them former judges, offering their services as mediators for cases of this kind.

There are obvious advantages in offering mediation within the court system. Despite criticisms[52] of it, because of the public respect for our judicial system many parties to disputes are more likely to have confidence in a mediation which is part of that system than one which is arranged privately. That confidence, and the authority of the court to compel parties to discuss the possibility of resolution by agreement, are important in overcoming reluctance which parties may feel about becoming involved in compromise discussions.

In some courts[53] mediation is provided by persons within the court system who are not judges. In others[54] the mediator is not a government employee but is selected by the judge, if the parties do not agree upon one, from a panel of skilled mediators kept by the court. The former system has the advantage of cheapness, the mediation service being provided as part of the court services. The latter has the advantage, at least in some cases, of a mediator whose skill and standing will enable otherwise reluctant parties to see the advantages of an agreed solution, often by being made to see the disadvantages to them of a more confrontational approach. But this system is more expensive for the parties than the other because the parties must pay the mediator.

Within some systems[55] the judge has power to require parties to a dispute to engage in mediation, even over the objection of all of them. That is a useful power to have because it may overcome the loss of face which is sometimes perceived to be a consequence of agreeing to mediate; and it may overcome any

---

[52] See for example L. Street in 'The Courts and Mediation: A Warning' (1993) 67 ALJ 491 and a response of M. Pearlman in 'Mediation' (1993) 67 ALJ 941.
[53] For example the Supreme Court of Western Australia.
[54] For example the Supreme and District Courts of Queensland and New South Wales.
[55] For example the Queensland and Victorian system. A less authoritarian approach is to reward those who submit their dispute to mediation with an early trial date if mediation fails.

initial emotional reluctance to mediate where anger or pride is involved or simply where adversarial attitudes have become entrenched.

Because mediation should be available to parties before litigation has commenced, and because of the perceived advantages of mediation within the court system, that system should plainly be available to parties to a dispute before litigation has commenced. That requires legislative change, and draft legislation has been produced in at least one state[56] to achieve that.

There is one important qualification which should be made about the advantages of mediation. It assumes equality of bargaining power whereas often that is not the case. Indeed inequality of bargaining power is endemic to certain classes of litigation; for example, personal injury actions and actions for debt. In almost all of these cases one party is an individual who is a first-time litigant; the other is a corporation, an insurer, or a financier, who is a repeat litigant. The former has an emotional interest in the outcome of the litigation; the latter only an economic one. To the former, the risk of having to pay the other's costs threatens bankruptcy; the latter has its costs publicly subsidized by tax deductibility.

In some cases inequality of bargaining power can be eliminated or at least reduced by a competent mediator. But in many cases, including those to which I have just referred, for mediation to be fair some systemic changes are necessary. Many insurers and financiers are becoming more, not less, adversarial. The changes must be effective to change that mind-set; otherwise the risk of unfairness in mediation of these cases will remain. I shall discuss possible systemic changes in this respect later.

Not all disputes can be resolved by mediation. Some will require a trial and a court judgment. But there are many disputes which, though they cannot be resolved by mediation, can and should be resolved by some adjudicatory process which is cheaper and quicker than a trial. There is also a procedure, now common to several jurisdictions in Australia, which, though in form one of adjudication, is in reality one which merely assists parties to reach an agreed resolution.

This process, which I shall call case appraisal,[57] permits a judge to order parties to submit their dispute to the appraisal of an experienced lawyer, selected by the judge from a court panel. The appraiser may appraise the dispute in whatever form he or she chooses, the only requirements being that it be, on the one hand, expeditious and cheap and, on the other, sufficiently thorough to enable the appraiser to reach a decision, without reasons, on the likely result of the case if it were to go to court. This would often be done by reading the pleadings, the principal documents, and the statements of the principal witnesses and listening to or reading short addresses from counsel.

---

[56] Queensland.

[57] That is its name in Queensland. It goes by other names in other states.

But it may in some cases include some limited cross-examination. The appraiser's decision, which must be given within a limited time, may be accepted by the parties, in which case it becomes a judgment of the court. If, however, one party does not accept it, he or she may elect to proceed to trial but with the added risk that, if that party does not do better at trial, he or she will pay the further costs of the other party. This process, although it appears to have been successful when used, has not been widely used. Judges have been reluctant to compel parties to engage in case appraisal and lawyers have been disinclined to recommend it. Plainly however it offers considerable cost savings to litigants.

This process would be even more beneficial if it were offered to disputants before litigation has commenced, and legislation has been drafted in one state[58] for achieving this. But it requires much greater recognition by judges and practitioners of the cost burden of litigation and of the saving which such a process can achieve.

There are variations of this process in Australia including allowing it, by consent, to be combined with a mediation; that is that the appraiser would attempt first to mediate a solution and, only if that failed, to give a decision having the above effect.[59] There is also one, to which the parties must agree, in which the appraiser's decision is final, subject to appeal, by leave, on a question of law.[60]

An offer to settle, under most Australian systems, has cost consequences for the offeree who rejects it. If the offeree does no better at trial he or she is ordinarily obliged to pay the costs of the offeror incurred after the offer was made. A fair offer will therefore often either resolve a dispute or protect the offeror from the risk of incurring substantial further costs.

For more than two decades in Australia there have been small claims tribunals, generally with a jurisdiction of up to about $5,000, having jurisdiction to determine civil disputes in a summary and informal way; without pleadings, without rules of evidence, without lawyers, and by a mixture of mediation and investigatory adjudication. These have worked reasonably well though they impose considerable burdens on the adjudicator who, in most cases, is a magistrate. They have the obvious advantages that they are cheap and expeditious. However, for them to be also reasonably fair requires the exercise of considerable skill and industry on the part of the magistrate for he or she is performing, in part, the work which the parties' lawyers would perform, generally adducing the documentary evidence and calling and examining the relevant witnesses, though allowing the parties limited rights of cross-examination, mediating where possible, and adjudicating where mediation fails. Curiously no thought seems to have been given to any system of training magistrates in these multiple skills.

---

[58] Queensland.   [59] New South Wales.   [60] South Australia.

The extension of such a procedure, although with some modifications, to all matters within the jurisdiction of Magistrates' Courts,[61] by agreement of the parties or at the Magistrate's discretion upon the request of one party, has been proposed.[62] Plainly such an informal and quick procedure with no or minimal involvement of lawyers has considerable cost advantages with, at least in simpler cases with proper training of magistrates, minimal risk of unfairness. In the absence of such a procedure, at least in our current system, costs in such cases will remain an unacceptably high proportion both of the amount involved and, generally, of the means of the parties. There is no reason why such a procedure could not be extended to the District Court at least in respect of those matters, such as personal injury actions or small contract disputes, where resolution is likely to turn entirely on questions of fact. It is mainly in those two Courts (and even more so in actions in the Federal Court where the amount or value involved does not exceed the monetary limits of those Courts) that costs tend to be an unacceptably high proportion of the amount or value involved[63] and where, consequently, very much less labour intensive procedures are needed. Although the present proposal envisages that no costs would be recoverable by the successful party there is much to be said for an exception permitting recovery of costs where a claim or defence has been unreasonably made or maintained.

No research has been conducted in Australia with a view to ascertaining whether ADR is more successful in some kinds of disputes than in others. But common sense suggests that cases in which the parties have been in a continuing relationship, business or personal, and it is in the interest of at least one of them to maintain that continuity, and cases, such as personal injury disputes arising from motor vehicle or workplace accidents, where the law is fairly stable and disputes are mainly factual and in more or less standard form, are likely to be amenable to ADR.

Reforms have also been made and proposed to encourage the more frequent summary adjudication of specific issues in a dispute where the whole of it cannot be resolved expeditiously. It is often the case that the resolution of one of several issues between parties to a dispute will result in resolution of the whole dispute. This may occur for a number of reasons, not all of them legal ones. The issue may be of paramount importance to the parties, irrespective of its legal importance in the dispute. The parties, or one of them, may, rightly or wrongly, perceive that the determination of that issue is a true indication of how other issues will be determined. Or its determination may reveal to one or both sides aspects of the case which they had not previously appreciated. For these reasons there is considerable advantage in encouraging applications for the

---

[61] Generally up to about $50,000.
[62] Proposed amendment to the Magistrates Courts Act 1921 (Qld.) by the Queensland Litigation Reform Commission.   [63] See the survey referred to in n. 38.

determination of specific issues in advance of trial and even in permitting judges to determine such issues summarily whether a party requests that course or not.

One such reform has been a rule empowering judges, at any interlocutory hearing including an application for summary judgment, to decide any issue of law or fact finally, whether or not requested to do so, even though it will not result in judgment. General powers to try issues separately have long existed in most jurisdictions but, in the past, these have been little used. This has been due partly to a reluctance on the part of lawyers to seek their use and partly to a reluctance by judges to use them, resulting in a narrow construction being given to them. A more ready perception of the advantages of such a procedure, both by litigation lawyers and judges, is necessary for their more frequent use. It is hoped that this and also proposed reforms empowering judges to give judgment on part of a claim, define and limit issues to be tried to those which remain genuinely in dispute and which are reasonably arguable, and make orders for interim payment and payment into court, will encourage lawyers and judges to see and use the advantages of summary resolution of specific issues.

As I mentioned earlier, questions involving expert opinion create difficulties for courts. Due to scientific and technological advances there is an increasing number of questions the comprehension of which, let alone their resolution, is beyond the capacity of most judges. Contradictory opinions by partisan experts exacerbate the problem. One solution proposed[64] has been to require, with limited exceptions, all expert evidence to be obtained by the court rather than by the parties though, where the parties can agree upon an expert, the court would ordinarily appoint that expert. This requires considerable modification to the existing system and to the adversarial imperative. But that is not a sufficient objection to what now seems to me to be a necessity. The proposal would enable the court to obtain an expert opinion or, if there is a recognized range of or difference in views, more than one, the experts in such case being required to prepare a joint report stating where they agree, where they disagree, and why. They would then, if necessary, confer with the judge, no doubt in the presence of the parties, in order to inform the judge more fully.

Such a scheme would require legislation enabling parties to a dispute to have a court expert appointed and an opinion obtained even before litigation commences because, in many disputes, expert opinion is required well before litigation commences. Nor would such a scheme necessarily always exclude party-appointed experts, though the calling of such experts should be the exception rather than the rule. But it is not hard to imagine cases in which, because of their knowledge of facts which can no longer be verified, the evidence of party-appointed experts may be necessary.

Where, pursuant to such a scheme, a court-appointed expert or panel has

---

[64] By the Litigation Reform Commission of Queensland. And cf. 'Tort Law Reform in New South Wales', para. 17.7.

been appointed and an opinion given by that expert or panel on the issue on which its opinion required, that opinion will generally, for all practical purposes, resolve that issue; it is highly unlikely that the judge will not accept it and, for that reason, so also will the parties. Consequently this is yet another means by which, in effect, an issue may be resolved expeditiously.[65]

A more radical solution is for experts, rather than a judge, to decide rather than merely advise on such issues. This would overcome rather than merely ameliorate the problem of judges' lack of comprehension or sufficient comprehension of complex scientific or technological questions. There are, however, two serious impediments to this solution. One is constitutional; that it may be to confer judicial power upon other than a judicial officer.[66] The other is a practical one; the consequent loss of power would, I think, be generally opposed by judges.

4.2. Simplifying and accelerating the litigation process

In a somewhat arbitrary way the division of state trial courts into the Supreme Court with unlimited jurisdiction, the District Court with jurisdiction generally up to $250,000, and the Magistrates' Court with jurisdiction generally up to $50,000, with a procedural system in the District Court a little more complex than that in the Magistrates' Court and a procedural system in the Supreme Court a little more complex again than that in the District Court, has the effect of creating procedural regimes which are, in complexity and consequently cost, generally related to the complexity of disputes. That this division has had some limited success in this respect can be seen by comparing the cost of small federal actions, in which system there are no courts below the level of the Federal Court of Australia, with those of the same size heard in a state Magistrates' Court or a state District Court. The latter are very much cheaper.[67] Nevertheless there are aspects of the procedural systems in all of our courts which encourage the expenditure of too much time and money. Reforms to remedy these defects have been made and are proposed in respect of almost all stages of the litigation process.

The first problem sought to be resolved has been the definition of essential issues and the elimination of irrelevant ones and those which, though marginally relevant, are kept primarily for forensic advantage. In some jurisdictions general allegations and general denials have been eliminated. A party must make specific allegations and a party against whom an allegation is made must now either admit it or state positively that it is untrue or that the party does not

---

[65] So may be referees' reports, for example in building cases. However referees' inquiries sometimes take the form of court hearings in which case there is little saving in cost.

[66] *Harris* v. *Caladine* (1991) 172 CLR 84; *Brandy* v. *Human Rights and Equal Opportunity Commission* (1994) 183 CLR 245; *Kable* v. *Director of Public Prosecutions (NSW)* (1996) 70 ALJR 814.

[67] There is currently a proposal to create a federal Magistrates' Court.

know whether it is true or not. A second means adopted to narrow issues has been to require appearances before a judge immediately upon the close of pleadings in order to isolate the real issues. That course is often desirable in complex cases. But there is a danger, especially in smaller cases, that it may increase rather than reduce costs.

A third, usually as an addition to the first, has been to require pleadings to be sworn by parties and to require each party's legal adviser to certify that there is evidence to support the factual allegations and denials in the pleading and that those factual allegations and denials, in his or her opinion, establish a reasonable cause of action or defence as the case may be. It would be reasonable to require a similar certification in respect of each application and the trial;[68] it would do no more than certify performance of the lawyer's existing ethical obligation.[69]

Together those requirements tend to narrow the issues to those genuinely in dispute. So also do notices to admit facts or documents' failure to admit which may have adverse cost consequences.

In more complex cases discovery has, in the past, been the single most expensive part of the litigation process. This has been, in part, because the common law test of what documents are discoverable, those which relate to any matter in question in the action, has been given a very wide meaning.[70] Another reason has been the ease with which, with electronic systems, extensive written records and frequent written communications are generated. This may and, particularly in commercial cases, often does require disclosure and consequent perusal of large numbers of documents which have, at best, only marginal relevance to the issues in dispute. The result is a huge expenditure of time and money with very little benefit. Moreover, as I have already mentioned, discovery can be used oppressively to waste time and an opponent's financial resources.

One solution to the problem is to limit disclosure to only those documents which are directly relevant to an allegation in issue. Rules providing for this have been in force in Queensland now for three years and appear to be having the effect of substantially reducing the cost of discovery in such cases with no noticeable increase in judgment error.[71]

---

[68] Cf. United States Federal Rules of Civil Procedure, r. 11 (b).

[69] Some professional ethical rules are general in this regard and simply prohibit lawyers from knowingly deceiving or misleading the court (for example, Queensland Solicitors Handbook, r. 4.07.1 (2)); other professional rules are more specific in requiring lawyers to have evidence in support of allegations they make: Australian Bar Association, Code of Conduct (1993), r. 5.8; Barristers Rules (Qld), r. 37; Professional Conduct and Practice Rules (NSW), r. 37; Bar Association Rules (NSW), r. 37; Professional Conduct Rules (NT), r. 16.13. See also *Clyne* v. *New South Wales Bar Association* (1960) 104 CLR 186 at 200–1.

[70] Those that may, not must, either advance a party's own case or damage an opponent's case, or would lead to a course of enquiry which would do so: *Compagnie Financière et Commerciale du Pacifique* v. *The Peruvian Guano Co.* (1882) 11 QBD 55 at 63; *Mulley* v. *Manifold* (1959) 103 CLR 341 at 345.

[71] See n. 35.

An alternative adopted in New South Wales has limited entitlement to discovery in three ways. First, a discovery notice may require production only of documents referred to in pleadings, affidavits, or witness statements or where the total is no more than fifty. Secondly, where an application is made to a court for discovery it will be ordered only in respect of classes of documents. And thirdly it will be ordered only in respect of relevant documents.[72]

I mentioned earlier a curious ambivalence in our system with respect to the disclosure of information; that it has, at least in the past, required excessive disclosure of documentary evidence, favourable or unfavourable; yet it has required no disclosure of oral evidence except to the extent to which that could be elicited by interrogatories. Moreover interrogatories became enmeshed in technicalities and the advent of the computer enabled the generation of multiple marginally relevant interrogatories. The process consequently became time-consuming, expensive, and sometimes oppressive. Sterile but expensive interlocutory arguments proliferated. In many jurisdictions in Australia interrogatories are now permitted only by leave and are rarely used.

One means of mutual disclosure of oral evidence has been the exchange of witness statements. Initially used in complex commercial actions, orders for exchange of witness statements are now common in some jurisdictions in Australia. In my opinion they have not been an unqualified success. There are a number of reasons for this.

The first is that it is by no means clear that, in all or even most cases in which exchange is ordered, the saving of court time results in a net saving of cost to the parties after expenditure of the extra cost involved in preparation and exchange of these statements. The preparation of such statements has become a new legal industry. Having in mind that they will be the witness's evidence-in-chief, the lawyers spend a great deal of time in presenting them in their best light, rephrasing them to subtly alter shades of meaning, and omitting unfavourable aspects of them. This work comes at considerable cost.

The second is that this work is likely to present the witness's evidence in a form much more partisan to the party for whom he or she is called than if the witness gave oral evidence. Involvement of the witness in this process is also likely to make the witness more partisan when cross-examined.

A third defect, already endemic in our system, is that, unlike disclosure of documentary evidence, it results in disclosure by a party only of the oral evidence favourable to that party, the evidence which that party intends to adduce. It still permits the party to conceal from his or her opponent known unfavourable witnesses.

I do not mean to imply by what I have said that exchange of witness statements should never take place. But I think that there is a tendency to overuse the practice because, I suspect, judges naturally think of saving court

---

[72] A test which is narrower than the common law test referred to in n. 70.

time without perhaps paying sufficient regard to the cost of that to the parties. Their use may illustrate two points which I made at the commencement of this essay: that a process used to reduce cost in complex actions may, if used in simpler actions, actually increase costs; and that reducing trial costs may come at the expense of unnecessary pre-trial costs in actions which may never come to trial. At least until there is some useful statistical evidence on these questions the cases in which witness statements are ordered to be exchanged should be carefully selected.

Another proposal is that, like the continuing obligation of disclosure of relevant documentary evidence, there should be a continuing obligation to disclose the names and addresses of relevant witnesses, favourable or unfavourable, known to the party.[73] This is a low-cost process which would give all parties the opportunity of interviewing all relevant witnesses, thereby ensuring that none are concealed and increasing the likelihood that those who are called will be objective. However, to achieve this result may require rules which prohibit a party or lawyer from preventing or discouraging witnesses from speaking to an opposing party or lawyer, and which otherwise ensure that the opportunity of doing so is facilitated. Requiring disclosure of known relevant witnesses is likely to increase the prospects of resolution of a dispute by fully informed agreement; and it is likely to reduce costs and increase fairness by sharing rather than duplicating the evidence-gathering workload.

Except where questions in dispute are likely to be finally resolved, interlocutory hearings tend to increase costs disproportionately to the benefit to the parties. One solution has been to prohibit applications for interlocutory relief until attempt has been made by correspondence to obtain the relief, or some solution satisfactory to the parties, by agreement. Rules in at least one jurisdiction[74] and proposals in another[75] provide for this.

Case management is the other major tool now used in most jurisdictions in Australia to simplify and accelerate the litigation process. It has been widely used for more than a decade in the pre-trial process[76] but only recently, and so far only in one jurisdiction,[77] for case management at trial.

There are now numerous different case management systems operating in Australia for management of the pre-trial process; in Supreme Courts, in the Federal Court, and in District Courts. This diversity would be of advantage if there were some regime in place for monitoring and comparing their effectiveness, if any, in reducing the cost and time of dispute resolution; but there is none.

---

[73] As proposed by the Litigation Reform Commission in 1995. And cf. United States Federal Rules of Civil Procedure, r. 26 (a) (1).   [74] Western Australia.

[75] Queensland.

[76] I use the term 'case management' in the pre-trial process to include control of the pace (sometimes called caseflow management) and shape (sometimes called individual case management or an individual docket system) of litigation. And, except where I specifically say so, when I refer to case management I mean pre-trial case management.

[77] Supreme Court of Western Australia. The system is explained below.

Case management is another illustration of the two points made at the commencement of this essay to which I referred when discussing exchange of witness statements; that a process used to reduce costs in complex actions may increase costs in simpler actions and that reduced trial costs may come at the expense of increased pre-trial costs. The first of these is also a specific application of my more general proposition that the complexity and cost of process should be closely related to the complexity of, and amount involved in, a dispute.

Here and in the United States, from which our systems of case management are derived, case management has been a judge-driven reform. Two consequences, not always fully appreciated, flow from this.

One is that judges, because of their concern to reduce delay, or to ensure that the issues are sufficiently defined and reduced for trial, may pay insufficient regard to the cost to the parties of case management; to whether that cost may exceed the cost benefit of an earlier or cheaper trial; or to its cost benefit in that vast majority of cases which settle before trial. The other is that they may transpose a process appropriate to complex and expensive actions, because it reduces their labour intensiveness, to simpler and less expensive actions without sufficient regard to whether it reduces, or perhaps increases, their labour intensiveness.[78] Even case management schemes which have attempted to differentiate, in the intensiveness of their management, between classes of cases[79] may have failed sufficiently to have regard to their cost to the parties.

Case management at its most intensive may involve individual control of an action by a judge from its commencement to trial; that is where a judge, often the judge who is assigned to hear the case if it comes to trial, monitors and controls its progress and the form it takes, usually by a series of directions hearings. At those hearings the judge will try to narrow and define issues, resolve some by adjudication, where appropriate refer the dispute to ADR, and set and require adherence to a timetable for the progress of the action. This form of case management, because it tends to be labour intensive, and consequently expensive,[80] should generally be reserved for complex and expensive cases or, at least in other cases, strictly controlled as to both number and length of hearings and kinds of orders which may be made.

Many simpler cases can be managed through their pre-trial phase[81] by a system into which, without any court hearing, actions are entered on commencement, in which specified milestones for an action are expected to

---

[78] Cf. J. Resnik, 'Changing Practices, Changing Rules: Judicial and Congressional Rulemaking on Civil Juries, Civil Justice, and Civil Judging' (1997) 49 (1) Alabama Law Review 133 at 192–5.
[79] Sometimes called differential case management.
[80] It also tends to be idiosyncratic depending, of course, on the extent to which the frequency of intervention and the kinds of orders which may be made are left to the discretion of individual judges. Individual variation has been reduced, but not eliminated, in one jurisdiction (Supreme Court of Queensland) by a series of standard form orders. [81] This occurs in Queensland.

be reached by specified times; and the failure of a stage of an action to be completed by its specified time may trigger a warning or even an immediate sanction. Such a system requires either no or few court hearings.[82] Between these extremes there is a variety of systems including those which contain elements of each, cases being 'streamed' into a regime appropriate to their complexity and amount involved. In theory a streaming process is ideal for it should match the complexity of the procedure to the complexity of the dispute. But there remains a danger that the case management process into which a case is streamed, or even the streaming process itself, may be unnecessarily costly. There is a tension here between the need for refinement in order to stream different kinds of cases and the containment of cost. Empirical studies are badly needed in this area.[83]

The system, to which I have referred, for case management at trial enables the trial judge to control the manner and extent of evidence; for example whether it should be given orally or in writing, how many witnesses may be called on any issue, and whether examination-in-chief or cross-examination should be limited. And it permits control over the manner and extent of submissions. Proposed reforms of this kind have been welcomed by the profession, at least in some jurisdictions in Australia, and I expect that they will shortly be widespread. To have maximum effect these powers should be used, as much as possible, before a trial commences. It is remarkable how often, when time limits are set, lawyers are capable of adhering to them without any loss in fairness or efficient preparation of the case.

There are also evidentiary provisions in some jurisdictions enabling judges to dispense with the rules of evidence in proof of any fact. In some of these the only limitation upon the exercise of the judge's discretion in this respect is an opinion either that strict proof might cause unnecessary or unreasonable expense, delay, or inconvenience or that the fact was not seriously in dispute. It has had some success in ensuring that litigation is confined to issues genuinely in dispute.

Rules in several jurisdictions in Australia also permit the taking of evidence and oral submissions by telephone or video communication and this is now widely used with substantial cost saving in many cases.

Whatever the complexity of a dispute, where it is necessary to decide a procedural question before trial, the means should be provided for an application to be made and the question determined entirely in writing without the need for either party or their lawyers to attend; either party should have the right to elect, in any such proceeding, to give evidence and make submissions entirely in writing. Reforms have been proposed[84] to achieve this.

---

[82] It must be accepted, I think, that the cost of case management is generally a reflection of the number and length of court hearings.

[83] Some lessons may be learned from the Report by the RAND Institute for Civil Justice, *Just, Speedy and Inexpensive? An Evaluation of Judicial Case Management under the Civil Justice Reform Act* (Santa Monica, Calif.: RAND Corporation, 1996).   [84] In Queensland.

4.3. Changing the costs system

The main concern here is not that lawyers' fees are generally too high for the work which they do. I do not believe generally either that the rate at which lawyers are paid is too high or that the incomes of lawyers are too high. Indeed surveys in Australia some years ago showed that the incomes of lawyers were generally no higher than those of other professionals such as accountants, engineers, doctors, or dentists.[85] My main concern is rather that our system in general and our costs system in particular discourage efficiency and, on the contrary, offer incentives to inefficiency and over-servicing. The related features to which I referred earlier, the encouragement which our system gives to the adversarial imperative and the encouragement which it gives to leaving no stone unturned, are powerful disincentives to efficient and economical conduct of a case. Those disincentives are exacerbated by the way in which lawyers generally charge for their services in litigation, which is either on the basis of time spent or on the basis of items of work completed. Costs should, in my view, be chargeable on the basis of the amount of work which should be done, that is the work which would be done by an efficient, competent, and honest lawyer, or best practice, rather than on the basis of the amount of work in fact done. Moreover, in our existing system, a litigant has no way of judging how much of the work actually done was worthwhile or, indeed, how much of the work charged for was actually done.

My second concern is that, under the existing costs system, costs are very difficult to predict. Because, at the present time, the supply of legal services exceeds the demand, sophisticated repeat litigants can and do obtain firm quotes for litigation. But the less sophisticated litigant, who is perhaps litigating for the first and only time in his or her life and who does not think of doing this, has generally little means of knowing what the total cost of his or her lawyer's fees will be. In some jurisdictions lawyers abide by and have even made rules requiring greater disclosure by them, upon first obtaining instructions, of the likely cost of litigation.[86] But I do not think that any of these go far enough. Litigants, especially first-time litigants, need to be much better informed, at the commencement of the dispute resolution process and continuously thereafter, of the likely outcomes of resolution of their dispute, the options open for its resolution, and the cost and likely time of completion of each.

The first of these concerns would be answered by a system under which, prima facie, costs, both between parties and between client and lawyer, are fixed by a scale. Such a scale, which has analogues in earlier scales in some courts of

---

[85] Submissions of LCA, 53.

[86] The Queensland Law Society requires principals in private practice to have a procedure in place whereby, at the outset of a matter, the client is informed of 'the basis upon which costs will be charged and if reasonably possible, an estimate of costs', Council Resolution, 11 Feb. 1993. See also Legal Profession Act 1987 (NSW), part 11 which imposes more stringent requirements.

limited jurisdiction in Australia and in the German system, would classify actions into categories by reference both to amount involved and complexity with a separate scale for each category; the scale in each case fixing a lump sum fee for each stage of the action, from instructions to sue or defend to issue of proceedings, from issue of proceedings to close of pleadings, from close of pleadings to trial, and for trial. Because a scale of this kind would have broad categories and stages, it would sometimes result in fees which were either unfairly high or unfairly low. There should therefore be a mechanism by which application may be made in any action, by any party or party's lawyer, to a court assessor for variation of the amount allowable under the scale for a stage in the action, either up or down, because of the greater complexity (or simplicity) or the greater (or lesser) volume of work. The court assessor should be a person skilled in costs assessing such as a practising or retired litigation lawyer or a practising or retired cost assessor.

Between lawyer and client the parties should be able to contract out of the scale. Although costs recoverable from an opponent should be limited there should generally be no limit on the freedom of contract between lawyer and client. The only qualification which I would make to this would be that the client should first be fully informed of what the scale would be, told that there are other lawyers who would conduct the litigation at the scale fee, and told who those lawyers are. And where a client agrees to pay on an hourly or item basis he or she should be given an estimate of the total cost with a right to a review of costs charged if they are substantially in excess of the estimate.

Scales such as I have envisaged would not result in any reduction of fees earned by honest, competent, and efficient lawyers. Nor should they. What they would do, primarily, is ensure that the incompetent or inefficient lawyer, or the lawyer who over-services, is not paid for incompetence, inefficiency, or over-servicing.

Together with the disclosure obligation to which I have referred, such scales would also answer my second concern by making costs more predictable and enabling a lawyer to give, and more importantly the client to receive, a firm quote at the time instructions are first given. And they would reduce the number and extent of subsequent disputes and misunderstandings over costs. The disclosure obligation should be a recurring one, with costs penalties on lawyers who fail to perform it; for it is only with the benefit of knowledge and of constant objective reappraisal that a client may make a realistic choice as to the manner and timing of resolution of a dispute.

My third concern is that without some limited provision for speculative fees by a lawyer to his or her own client, a person of average means may not be able to contest a difficult case, that is a case where either there is a serious risk that that person will not recover anything or costs and disbursements are likely to be very high. Class actions are only a partial answer to this problem. I would not ordinarily favour such fees being fixed as a percentage of the amount involved or recovered but I think that consideration should be given, in any such case, to allowing an agreement for a contingent fee, perhaps up to 200 per cent of scale fee for a successful conclusion in order to ensure representation for such litigants.[87]

4.4. Changing mind-sets

If it is correct, as I have urged, that, in order to substantially reduce the cost of dispute resolution, our system must be less labour intensive, there are a number of mind-sets shared by many lawyers and judges which inhibit that change. Two of the most pervasive and strongly held of these are a belief that our traditional system delivers near perfect justice and that an essential element of that is the adversarial system as we know it.[88] Even a superficial knowledge of other systems, such as the French or German systems, should at least cause us to wonder whether ours delivers more perfect justice than theirs. My purpose here is not to compare our system with some others. But it seems to be a corollary to these beliefs that a less labour intensive and less adversarial system (much the same thing) would reduce the quality of justice. I propose to expose some of the imperfections of our system and to demonstrate, I hope, that a substantial reduction in its labour intensiveness and adversarial intensiveness is unlikely to result in a significant reduction in the quality of justice which it delivers.

Those who hold these traditional beliefs about our system would also define systemic justice in a traditional, and in my view too narrow, way, restricting it to accuracy of result and fairness of procedure between the parties. But even on that traditional and, as I shall later endeavour to show, too narrow view of systemic justice, our system does not score highly.

As to accuracy of result, the more adversarial our system is, the more it is likely to distort or even suppress facts; objective witnesses will be discarded in favour of partisan ones, unfavourable witnesses will be concealed from an opponent, and witnesses generally will feel greater pressure, at least un-consciously, to shade their evidence in favour of the party who calls them. Increasing economic pressure on litigants and their lawyers is likely to result in a continuing decline in ethical standards of the latter. Moreover a system, such as ours, which relies so much on assessment of oral evidence is bound to be subject to error. Memory is notoriously defective, witnesses vary greatly in their capacity to express themselves clearly and convincingly, and, contrary to the

---

[87] This was proposed by the Litigation Reform Commission of Queensland in 1995, but not adopted by government. A similar but more limited scheme has existed in the United Kingdom for some time: Courts and Legal Services Act 1990 (UK) s. 58. However such an increased fee should not be recoverable unless the amount of the settlement or judgment is paid.

[88] See, for example Wigmore, *Treatise on the Anglo-American System of Evidence in Trials at Common Law* (3rd edn., 1940), vol. v, para. 1367; *Jones v. National Coal Board* [1957] 2 QB 55 at 63–4 per Denning LJ.

received view,[89] it seems unlikely that we can tell, from the demeanour of witnesses, where the truth lies.[90] In the end the fact finder, generally a judge, is left with a choice and the exercise of that choice may be affected by some unconscious bias. A similar choice also presents itself in the application of a legal principle, or one legal principle rather than another, to the facts found.

For these reasons both fact finding and application of law are far from accurate sciences and less labour intensive and less adversarial procedures are, in many cases, likely to enhance rather than reduce the accuracy of fact finding. Ensuring that each party has, from the outset, knowledge of and consequently access to all relevant witnesses known to the other is likely both to reduce duplication of the search for relevant witnesses, and consequently its cost, and ensure that no relevant witnesses are concealed from the court.[91] Similarly the greater use of non-partisan experts[92] is likely both to reduce the cost associated with a battle of experts and to increase the objectivity of the evidence given.

As to fairness of procedure, we all know that lawyers are not equal in ability and that generally those who are perceived to be better command higher fees. So the richer litigant can afford the better lawyer. That litigant can also afford to pay for more time to be spent on the preparation of his or her case. Up to a point, which is well beyond the means of most, under our existing system the more time and money spent by a litigant on the preparation of his or her case the greater is the chance of winning. Moreover a richer litigant may compel a poorer one to expend more money than he or she can afford by engaging in time- and cost-wasting procedures, thereby compelling the poorer litigant either to compromise unfairly or to give up. Fairness of procedure in our system assumes equality of bargaining power, a situation which rarely in fact exists.

Reducing the labour intensiveness and the adversarial intensiveness of our system is likely to increase procedural fairness for it will eliminate or at least reduce the opportunities to use and abuse time- and cost-wasting procedures to the disadvantage of a poorer litigant. The virtual elimination of interrogatories, the reduction of the discovery obligation to documents directly relevant to an allegation in issue and the reduction of opportunities for time- and cost-wasting interlocutory applications are examples of this.

In any event to confine the concept of systemic justice to accuracy of result and procedural fairness is too narrow a view for two reasons. First it ignores cost, not just the unfairness of cost between parties of unequal wealth but cost

---

[89] It is a legal truism that not to have seen and heard witnesses puts appellate courts in a permanent position of disadvantage, as against the trial judge, in assessing their credibility.

[90] O. Wellborn, 'Demeanor' (1991) 76 Cornell Law Review 1075; J. Blumenthal, 'A Wipe of the Hands, a Lick of the Lips: The Validity of Demeanor Evidence in Assessing Witness Credibility' (1993) 72 Nebraska Law Review 1157; see also C. Fife-Schaw, 'The Influence of Witness Appearance and Demeanour on Witness Credibility: A Theoretical Framework' (1995) 35 Medicine Science & the Law 107.   [91] See the text at n. 73.

[92] See the text at n. 64.

which, in most cases, puts litigation beyond the means of a person of average wealth. Secondly it ignores the interests of those litigants waiting to have their cases heard and those potential litigants who are deterred from attempting to vindicate their rights because of cost and delay. And if, as I also think, the reality is that the judicial system will remain a scarce resource,[93] there is, in addition, a public interest in the best use of that resource which cannot be ignored.[94]

The adversarial imperative and the consequent compulsion to leave no stone unturned in order to ensure victory are the most important aspects of the mind-set which I have just discussed. It is these which are the direct causes of the labour intensiveness of our system. And, in turn, both our procedural system and the way in which costs are at present assessed encourage that labour and adversarial intensiveness.

Once it is accepted, as I think it must be, that a person of average means cannot afford to litigate cases of average size because of the risk of financial ruin, it is plain that the justice of a system cannot be determined in terms only of accuracy of result and fairness of procedure. And even if, contrary to my view, substantially reducing the labour intensiveness of the system would significantly increase the risk of inaccuracy, that is a risk which has to be taken if persons of average means are to have genuine access to the system.[95]

I believe that I have demonstrated that our system is far from perfect either in accuracy of result or fairness of procedure, that because of its cost and delay it is unfair, especially to the poorer of competing disputants, and that less labour intensive procedures, whilst undoubtedly reducing cost, may also increase rather than reduce the accuracy of result and the fairness of procedure. It requires more than that, however, to change the mind-sets to which I have referred. That is because they are emotional rather than rational mind-sets, the adversarial imperative is strong, and resistance to change among lawyers and judges is institutionalized. Moreover economic pressures upon litigants and lawyers are making them more adversarial. And proposals which, because they reduce the cost of litigation, also have the effect of reducing the amount of money which ends up in lawyers' pockets are unlikely to be welcomed by many in a profession which, in Australia, is already too large for the work available. At least whilst that disproportion between the number of lawyers and

---

[93] Current indications in Australia are that governments are prepared to accept less, not more, of the cost burden of litigation. The 1996 federal budget reduced funds for legal aid by $33 million and governments are raising the issue of 'user pays' for court fees.

[94] That matters of this kind must now be considered was accepted by the High Court of Australia in *Sali v. SPC Ltd.* (1993) 116 ALR 625 at 629, 636. And cf. J. Newman, 'Rethinking Fairness: Perspectives on the Litigation Process' (1985) 94 Yale Law Journal 1643. See however *State of Queensland v. J.L. Holdings Pty. Ltd.* (1997) 141 ALR 353 where the majority appear to have adopted a narrower view of justice. The difference in the views expressed, rather than the results reached, in those cases, appears to show some judicial uncertainty as to the extent to which such factors should be taken into account. [95] That is, not as in access to the Ritz Hotel.

the amount of work available continues, the economic interests of lawyers under our present system will remain inconsistent with those of their clients.

Changing the procedural system and the way in which lawyers are permitted to charge in the ways I have indicated will assist in changing those mind-sets. But lawyers always seem to be able to circumvent changes they do not like and some judges, comfortable in an existing system, will tend to construe rule and legislative changes in a restrictive way.

What is needed to change these mind-sets, in addition to changes to the rules and to the system by which lawyers charge, is to provide incentives both to lawyers and their clients to resolve disputes by less labour intensive means than litigation and sanctions upon both for alleging or persisting with untenable claims or defences and for engaging in cost- or time-wasting procedures. What I have in mind, in terms of incentives, are tax incentives to disputants[96] and costs incentives to lawyers. And I have in mind sanctions against lawyers and their clients which would require them to pay costs, or additional costs, to their opponents for instituting or maintaining untenable claims or defences or for engaging in time- or cost-wasting procedures; and professional sanctions against lawyers for breaching ethical rules aimed at reducing cost and delay.[97]

I do not mean to imply by what I have said that, without incentives and sanctions, lawyers will never change. But without them change is bound to be slow because of the innate conservatism of the profession and the mind-sets to which I have referred. In the long term, with changes in legal education, those mind-sets will change. But can we afford to wait? I doubt it.

5. APPEALS, JUDGMENTS, AND ENFORCEMENT OF JUDGMENTS

5.1. Appeals

Delay, and consequent indirect cost, rather than direct cost, is a problem in appeals. A substantial cause of this, as I indicated earlier, has been the failure of

---

[96] The provision of tax deductions to repeat litigants for litigation costs, as now exists in Australia, is counter-productive to reform for two reasons. First it encourages litigation, rather than some less costly alternative. Secondly it unfairly advantages a repeat (usually corporate) litigant in disputes with a one-time (usually individual) litigant. Litigation against insurers and financiers is an example of this. A rough estimate made by the Australian Law Reform Commission is that about $700 million a year may be claimed as deductions from assessable income for legal costs incurred in litigation by businesses each year: 'Review of the Adversarial System of Litigation', Australian Law Reform Commission Issues Paper 20, Apr. 1997, 107.

[97] Cf. United States Federal Rules of Civil Procedure rr. 11, 16, and 37. In July 1996, Judge Cote in *Little* v. *Twentieth Century Fox Film Corp.* (No. 89 CIV 8526, 1996 WL 376971, SDNY 5 July 1996) imposed the largest reported sanction in the Southern District of New York under r. 11 since the 1993 amendments: New York Law Journal, 5 Sept. 1996, p. 3, c. 1. The judge assessed attorneys' fees and costs as against the plaintiffs' attorneys in the amount of $150,000 and against the plaintiffs in the amount of $30,000.

governments to appoint sufficient appeal judges in proportion to the number of judges from whom appeals are heard. A cause of delay in delivery of judgments has been the failure to factor in extra-judicial reading time because of the increase in the written content and reduction in the oral content of argument.

This last problem is being addressed and other steps have been taken to expedite the appeal process. In some courts some appeals may be heard by two judges only[98] and an application for leave to appeal may be heard by one judge or considered on the papers. Grouping of categories of appeals before panels of judges has tended to expedite their hearings. Requiring counsel to give realistic estimates of the length of oral hearings after submission of written argument has increased their reliability, particularly as counsel have become more familiar with the practice of appellate courts of discouraging repetition of written submissions. Case management of complex appeals has tended substantially to reduce their length. And requiring written submissions to be in a form suitable to assist the giving of *ex tempore* judgments has increased the incidence of such judgments. There is room for the extension of that process and, in some cases, for abbreviated reasons for judgment.[99]

ADR should also be considered at an appellate level. It appears to have had some success in the USA[100] although, for obvious reasons, mediation is unlikely to be as readily accepted at this level. A proposal in the New South Wales Court of Appeal[101] is that a process like case appraisal[102] be offered to the parties; a single judge would informally consider the appeal and express an opinion; if that opinion were accepted by the parties it would become the judgment of the court; but if either party were dissatisfied with that opinion that party would be entitled to a full appeal. It is not clear whether that would involve the risk of incurring indemnity costs if the judgment is more favourable than the opinion.

Although, because appeals are generally heard and decided on the written record of evidence at the trial, direct costs are not high, appellate courts are experimenting with electronic records of such evidence to reduce the cost of its reproduction.

---

[98] For example, damages appeals and appeals in interlocutory matters. But there is merit in extending this to all appeals on fact involving no question of general principle: see Clarke, 'Delay Reduction in the New South Wales Court of Appeal', at 93.

[99] In the USA these are called 'memorandum decisions'; Court of Appeal, Queensland, Annual Report 1995, 111; Clarke, 'Delay Reduction in the New South Wales Court of Appeal', at 103–4.

[100] See papers presented at 'Alternative Dispute Resolution Symposium', published in University of Memphis Law Review, 26, 3 (1996), 957–1228.

[101] Clarke, 'Delay Reduction in the New South Wales Court of Appeal', at 167–8.

[102] See the text at n. 57.

5.2. Judgments

Generally there is no substantial delay between hearings and judgments either at trial or appellate level. Some courts have published performance standards[103] for delivery of judgments within specified periods and that is likely to become more common.

5.3. Enforcement of judgments

Enforcement of judgments is a process which is still partly governed by ancient law and which is generally in an unsatisfactory state notwithstanding numerous inquiries and reports here and overseas. There is currently new legislation being prepared in Queensland aimed at modernizing procedures for enforcement of money judgments. The main features of the proposed changes are the abolition of any distinction between the kinds of credit accounts moneys in which may be attached, enabling the attachment, in the hands of an employer, of an employee's future earnings and enabling a court to order payment of a debt by instalments. In both the second and third of these cases the court must be satisfied that what is proposed will not impose unreasonable hardship on the debtor.

6. CONCLUSION

The starting point of civil justice reform in Australia must be the acceptance by lawyers and judges of a new concept of just dispute resolution; one which involves greater frankness between disputants, which is less adversarial, and which accepts that costs, the rights of others, and the public interest are relevant considerations. It is only if this is accepted that a system will evolve which resolves disputes without undue delay, at a reasonable cost, and with little or no diminution in the quality of result.

If lawyers accept this their clients will also do so. And if lawyers and judges accept this they will welcome and themselves initiate procedures of the kind to which I have referred; and those procedures will be fully utilized rather than given limited operation or even evaded. But if lawyers do not provide their clients with quicker and cheaper dispute resolution the clients will go elsewhere. And if courts do not provide quicker and cheaper dispute resolution they will cease to be used and will consequently lose both their authority and their status.

[103] For example New South Wales District Court.

Part III
Civil Law Countries

6

Civil Justice Reform:
Access, Cost, and Expedition.
The German Perspective

Peter Gottwald

The German Code of Civil Procedure (*Zivilprozeßordnung*) of 1877 was inspired by the French *Code de Procédure Civil* of 1806. Following the French example,[1] the German Code was geared towards the principles of orality and immediacy, and, at the same time, gave wide scope to liberal moral concepts. Party control over litigation extended not simply to procedural materials and the subject matter of the proceedings, but also to the course of the proceedings themselves. The judge was largely passive. Almost no precautions were taken to prevent the parties from drawing out cases over an unreasonably long period of time.

However, towards the end of the nineteenth century, and in association with the Austrian Code of Civil Procedure of 1898, the view that proceedings are not purely the private business of the disputing parties, but a social duty of the state, began to be increasingly asserted in Germany.[2] The relationship between the judge's power and party freedom was altered accordingly. This social conception of procedure (*soziale Prozeßauffassung*), as it is called, has arisen alongside the pre-existing liberal conception of procedure, without completely relegating the liberal conception to a secondary role. As well as this change, civil proceedings now increasingly appear to be a mass phenomenon. The legislature repeatedly tries to accelerate the judicial process and to relieve the courts of superfluous work, so that the increasing number of pending proceedings can be dealt with within a reasonable time.

1. ORGANIZATION OF CIVIL JURISDICTION IN GERMANY

For a party who wishes to assert a liquid pecuniary claim of any size, a popular and extremely simple procedure available in Germany is the so-called 'dunning procedure'. This is a summary procedure for an order to pay debts, called *Mahnverfahren*. The creditor submits an application for a court order for payment of a debt (*gerichtlicher Mahnbescheid*) by filling out a form at the local court

---

[1] See *Begrundung des Entwurfs einer Deutschere Civilprozeßordnung* (Berlin, 1872), 9 ff. (§§ 3–6), notwithstanding the fact that, according to the French system, written pleadings have always been of high importance. [2] See R. Wassermann, *Der soziale Zivilprozeß* (1978), 27 ff., 49 ff.

(*Amtsgericht*) nearest to his or her place of residence. If the form is filled out correctly, the order is granted without any review of the validity of the claim. If the debtor does not pay within two weeks after receiving notice of the court order, and does not raise any objection, then the creditor can apply for a writ of execution to be issued. This writ may be executed against the debtor in the same way as a preliminary executable judgment by default (§§ 699, 700 ZPO). In 1996, over 8.1 million dunning proceedings were pending in local courts.[3] From earlier research, it is known that objections against payment orders are raised in little more than 10 per cent of all cases. In cases where objections are raised, the process must be continued by the creditor in accordance with the general rules of procedure (§ 696 ZPO).

The option of making an ordinary claim is open to parties in all cases. For disputes worth up to DM 10,000,[4] the claim can be pursued at the local court (*Amtsgericht*), with no statutory requirement that parties have legal representation. Disputes of higher value are pursued at the regional court (*Landgericht*) (§§ 23, 71 GVG). For family and child cases, the local court has sole responsibility, with legal representation being compulsory (§§ 23a, 23b GVG).

The proceedings in the local court can scarcely be differentiated from those of the regional court.[5] However, in the local court only a single judge sits, whereas at the regional court a civil chamber of three judges sits, at least when the case initially comes to court. However, the civil chamber regularly transfers legal disputes to one of its members sitting as a single judge. Where this occurs, the following differences remain:

1. The local court judge has a greater duty to assist parties who are not legally represented (§ 504 ZPO).
2. In proceedings involving claims of up to DM 1,200,[6] the local court judge can deviate from the procedural rules, structuring the proceedings according to his or her discretion, reasonably exercised (§ 495a ZPO).
3. Since proceedings in the local court are mostly more straightforward, the local court judge has a higher workload to deal with, and therefore has less time to devote to individual cases than a regional court judge.[7]
4. Appeals against local court decisions are made to the regional court only. No further legal remedy is available. An appeal can be made to the regional appeal court (*Oberlandesgericht*) against regional court decisions and, if necessary, a further appeal on a point of law lies to the Federal Court of Justice (*Bundesgerichtshof*). In family cases, the appeal lies from the

---

[3] Statistisches Bundesamt, 'Fachserie 10 Rechtspflege Reihe 2' (1996), 14 f.
[4] At the rate of DM 2.92 to the pound, and DM 1.75 to the US dollar (as on 3 Sept. 1998) this figure represents roughly £3,425, or $US5,715.
[5] See L. Rosenberg, K. H. Schwab, and P. Gottwald, *Zivilprozeßrecht* (15th edn. 1993), § 111 I.
[6] Roughly £410, or $US685.
[7] Cf. Report 'Der aktuelle Pensenschlüssel', DRiZ 72 (1994), 396.

local court to the regional appeal court and, with the latter's permission, under certain circumstances to the Federal Court of Justice.

The Code of Civil Procedure provides a uniform process for the course of the proceedings. After the statement of claim and defence have been exchanged, in principle the judge should prepare the proceedings so that the case is ready for adjudication after one main oral hearing. Preparation for a main hearing can be carried out in an oral hearing (early first hearing) or in written proceedings.

The law only provides for express handling of cases through the *Urkundenprozeß* (§§ 592 ff. ZPO), a summary procedure where the plaintiff relies entirely on documentary evidence, and through special bill of exchange, and cheque proceedings. In these cases, an executable judgment can be issued on the presentation to the court of the documents, bill of exchange or cheque. Any objection by the defendant which is not capable of being proved by documentary means will be heard in full subsequent proceedings.

In addition, the Code of Civil Procedure provides for measures of temporary legal protection, generally via attachments and injunctions and, in family cases, through special interim orders. The basic purpose of these orders is to ensure that, in due course, execution of the judgment on the main issue will be possible and effective. In practice, however, injunction proceedings frequently operate as summary proceedings. In competition law cases in particular, a practice has developed of the parties agreeing to accept an interim injunction decision as final, by the use of a so-called 'closing letter'. By this letter, the defendant waives all possible further defences or appeals,[8] and submits himself or herself to the injunction through an unlimited and unconditional declaration of the obligation to refrain from the act complained of, secured by a contractual penalty.

Over and above these mechanisms, German procedural law recognizes that, in particularly urgent cases, an order to perform or satisfy (*Leistungs*—or *Befriedigungsverfügung*) may be required pending final resolution of the legal relationship between the parties through a decision in ordinary proceedings. In practice, the order to refrain (i.e. injunction) is used in competition cases, employment law, for the protection of personal privacy, for the surrender of possession of property after unlawful interference with possession, counter-statements in media law, temporary injunctions to ensure disclosure, the withdrawal of assertions, delivery of essential goods, payment of maintenance in an emergency, or partial payment of a wage to avoid someone having to live below subsistence level.

Generally, the plaintiff does not have to provide the defendant with any security that he or she can pay the costs incurred in the action. Only foreigners (those from outside the European Union) are obliged to provide security insofar as no exemption exists due to a state treaty or mutuality (§ 110 ZPO). In a first

---

[8] See H.-J. Ahrens, 'Die Abschlußerklärung', WRP 43 (1997), 907; V. Emmerich, *Das Recht des unlauteren Wettbewerbs* (4th edn. 1995), 423 ff.

instance decision, an order up to the value of DM 1,500, or an enforcement of costs up to a limit of DM 2,000,[9] is provisionally enforceable without providing security. The same applies for consent judgments, judgments by default, summary judgments in proceedings based on documentary evidence, and judgments involving landlord–tenant relationships and maintenance obligations (§ 708 ZPO). All other decisions are, in principle, only to be declared provisionally enforceable upon provision of security (to the value of the main issue and the costs of enforcement). However, a creditor may attach goods for his own protection without providing security, but he may only satisfy his claim from an attached item after providing security (§ 720a ZPO).

At present, each party can appeal as of right against any first instance decision involving a claim for over DM 1,500 (§ 511a I ZPO). In principle, such an appeal will lead to a repeat of the original process, reopening both the questions of fact and of law in the next instance. It is not just legally admissible but also common practice for new evidence to be raised at second instance, or for evidence raised at first instance to be viewed in a new and different light. A bill in favour of simplifying civil procedure, which was introduced into Parliament in July 1998 and is currently pending, was originally intended to raise the minimum sum required for appeal to DM 2,000.[10] However, the legal committee of the Bundestag dropped this rule and inserted a new one, according to which the court of appeal may reject appeals without any oral hearing by unanimous order if they appear to have no chance of success, provided that the amount in dispute is under DM 60,000[11] or the claim is a non-pecuniary one (§ 519c ZPO as amended by the bill).[12]

Access to the Federal Court of Justice is regulated in a somewhat more complicated manner. In disputes not involving property rights, and disputes involving property rights with claims of up to DM 60,000, access is only available when the regional appeal court allows for a further appeal on a point of law in its decision (§ 546 ZPO). In disputes with a gravamen of over DM 60,000, either party can appeal on a point of law without regional appeal court permission, although the Federal Court of Justice may refuse to accept such an appeal after a preliminary examination of the strength of the case (§ 554b ZPO). In practice, this acceptance procedure represents the main workload of the Federal Court of Justice in larger economic disputes. There have accordingly been regular attempts over the years to reduce the amount of work expended by the Federal Court on examining whether or not to accept appeals,

---

[9] Roughly £514 or $US860 for the order (DM 1,500), and £684 or $US1,140 for the costs figure (DM 2,000).

[10] 'Entwurf eines Gesetzes zur Vereinfachung des zivilgerichtlichen Verfahrens', BT-Drucksache 13/6398 of 4 Dec. 1996.   [11] Roughly £20,550 or $US34,285.

[12] 'Beschlußempfehlung des Rechtsausschusses', BT-Drucksache 13/11042 of 17 June 1998.

so that the Court can devote itself more intensively to deciding cases of general significance.[13]

2.1. First instance claims: local and regional courts

With small fluctuations, the number of claims brought before local and regional courts has risen constantly for many years. In 1965, only 276,750 new claims were filed in regional courts. In 1980, the number was already 328,080, and in 1988 it rose to 357,216. In 1993, after the monetary jurisdiction of the local court was increased to include claims of up to DM 10,000,[14] slightly fewer claims (357,020) were filed in the regional courts. However, by 1995 this figure had risen again to 418,807 and, by 1996, to 422,995.[15]

In 1996, 414,579 cases were dealt with in the regional courts, of which 114,739 ended in judgment on the merits; 64,399 in settlement; 91,946 by consent or default judgment; 5,731 by order on the costs (after formal declaration of settlement of the claim); 47,873 by withdrawal; 2,651 by non-payment of the advance (a payment which has to be made by plaintiffs before service of their claims); 31,320 by suspension of proceedings; 28,646 by transfer to the competent local court; and 2,748 by joinder and all other types of disposition.[16]

Of the regional courts' 1996 caseload of 414,579 cases, 349,125 cases were disposed of by the general civil division of the regional court; 64,166 by a commercial division; and the rest by the building law division and the reparation division.

A comparable growth can also be observed in relation to local courts. In 1965, 863,621 new claims were filed in the local courts. In 1984, the number had risen to 1,217,076, and by 1993 to 1,455,094. In 1995, 1,751,448 new claims were filed, and in 1996 the figure was 1,686,690.

Of the 1,737,202 cases dealt with by local courts in 1996, 497,871 were disposed of by judgment on the merits; 103,146 by judgment on the merits in a simplified small claims procedure; 152,526 by settlement; 461,032 by consent and default judgment; 56,599 by order on the costs; 184,019 by withdrawal; 8,775 by non-payment of the advance; 79,213 by suspension of proceedings; and 115,556 by transfer to another (the properly competent) local court. The remainder were dealt with in other ways.

In terms of the duration of proceedings, before the regional courts of first

---

[13] See W. Stichs, 'Für welchen Personenkreis und für welche Rechtsfragen leisten wir uns derzeit den BGH?', ZRP 31 (1998), 1. The new German government has indicated an intention not to present a bill for the reform of appeals until the end of 1999; see H. Däubler-Gruektin, 'Schwerpunkte der Rechtspolitik', ZRP 32 (1999), 81, 82.   [14] Roughly £3,425 or $US5,714.
[15] See Statistisches Bundesamt, 'Fachserie 10 Reihe 2' (1996), 14 ff.   [16] Ibid. 28 ff.

instance in 1996, 38.9 per cent of proceedings were dealt with within three months; 26.5 per cent within six months; 21.7 per cent within twelve months; and a further 9.6 per cent within twenty-four months. The average duration of all regional court proceedings, from filing to final settlement or final decision, was 6.5 months.

In terms of the value of claims, 36.5 per cent of cases before the regional courts in 1996 involved a claim of between DM 10,000 and DM 20,000; 32.3 per cent between DM 20,000 and DM 50,000; 13.5 per cent between DM 50,000 and DM 100,000; and only 13 per cent over DM 100,000. The average value of all claims up to DM 100,000 was approximately DM 30,000.[17]

In the local courts in 1996, 48.2 per cent of cases were dealt with within three months; 28.5 per cent within six months; and 17.5 per cent within twelve months. The average duration of all local court proceedings, from filing to final settlement or final decision, was 4.6 months.

In the local courts in 1996, 17.9 per cent of cases involved a claim of up to DM 500; 25.6 per cent between DM 500 and 1,500; 18.8 per cent between DM 1,500 and DM 3,000; 20.5 per cent between DM 3,000 and DM 6,000; and 17 per cent over 6,000 DM. The average value of all claims before the local courts was DM 3,170.[18]

2.2. Appeal business of the regional courts

The number of new cases admitted to the regional courts on appeal from the local courts rose from 72,047 in 1983 to 96,418 in 1988. The number then fell slightly to 82,455 in 1993, but subsequently climbed again to 91,317 in 1994, to 98,217 in 1995, and to 101,394 in 1996.[19]

Of the appeal cases dealt with by the regional courts in 1996, 97,015 were handled by the civil chambers, and only 715 by the chambers for commercial cases.

Of the 101,394 cases dealt with by the regional courts on appeal in 1996, 49,857 ended in judgment on the merits; 12,358 in settlement; 1,363 in consent or default judgment; 1,197 by order on the costs; 3,532 by formal dismissal order; 25,168 by withdrawal of the appeal; and the rest were dealt with by other means.

In 55 per cent of these cases, the appeal was fully dismissed as insufficiently well founded. In 35.9 per cent of these cases, the appeal led to a change in the first instance decision through a judgment on the merits from the appeal court. In 5.2 per cent of the cases, the first instance decision was simply repealed and the issue referred back to the lower court.

---

[17] Each DM 10,000 is roughly equivalent to £3,425 or $US5,714.
[18] Each DM 1,000 is roughly equivalent to £340 or $US570.
[19] Statistisches Bundesamt, 'Fachserie 10 Reihe 2', 28 ff.

Of the regional courts' appeals in 1996, 29.7 per cent were settled within three months; 39.1 per cent within six months; and 25.4 per cent within twelve months. The average duration of appeals was 5.3 months.

2.3. Appeals to the regional appeal courts

Likewise, a large rise in the number of cases is noticeable in the regional appeal courts. In 1983, 56,454 appeals were filed in the regional appeal courts. In 1989, the figure was 60,678. Despite the change in jurisdiction noted above, which shifted claims of up to DM 10,000 from the regional court to the local court in 1993, thus removing them from the appeal jurisdiction of the regional appeal courts, regional appeal court case numbers rose to 64,269 in 1995, and reached 66,696 in 1996.[20]

Of the appeals made to regional appeal courts in 1996, 686 were directed against a judge's decision in the local court in family issues; 17,838 against the judgment of a single judge in the regional court; 37,543 against the judgment of a civil chamber in the regional court; and 7,637 against the judgment of a chamber for commercial issues.

Of the cases dealt with by the regional appeal courts in 1996, 27,610 ended in judgment on the merits; 11,371 in settlement; 1,631 in consent or default judgment; 1,251 in formal dismissal orders; and 17,933 in withdrawal of the appeal. Of these appeals, 49.4 per cent were held to be completely unfounded; 42.5 per cent led to a material change in the first instance decision; and 5.2 per cent led to a revocation and referral back to the first instance court.

In terms of duration, 18.9 per cent of the regional appeal courts' cases in 1996 were completed within three months; 25.4 per cent within six months; 33.8 per cent within twelve months; and 18.1 per cent within twenty-four months. The average duration of appeal proceedings was 8.7 months.

2.4. Appeals to the Federal Supreme Court

The Federal Supreme Court has suffered most from the general increase in German court business over recent years. In 1983, 2,564 final appeals on a point of law were brought. In 1988 the number rose to 3,121; in 1994 to 3,490; in 1995 to 3,883; and, in 1996, to 3,888. Of the appeals on a point of law, on average only about 210 were *zugelassene Revisionen* (appeals allowed to be brought by decision of the regional appeal court). All others were appeals where at least DM 60,000 was in dispute, which meant that the Federal Supreme Court had to decide whether the final appeal was of general importance or, on a prima facie basis, justified on the merits (§ 554b ZPO). In such a case, the Federal Supreme Court is obliged to accept the appeal for

---

[20] Ibid. 46 ff.

a decision on the merits (*Wert/Annahmerevisionen*). Only 600 to 700 cases were disposed of by way of a decision on the merits. By contrast, 1,500 cases were dealt with through an order of the Court refusing the appeal (*Nichtannahmebeschluß*).[21]

2.5. The court system

In 1996, there were 706 local courts, with an average number of inhabitants of 116,000 per local court district. There were 116 regional courts, 24 regional courts of appeal, and one Federal Court of Justice. In the regional courts, there were a total of 1,529 civil chambers for civil matters, in the regional appeal courts 492 senates for civil matters, and, in the Federal Court, 12 senates for civil matters.[22]

Within the European Union, Germany has by far the highest number of judges *per capita* of population, with one judge for every 3,600 inhabitants.[23] In 1995, 16,338 judges were employed in courts of law under the civil services of the *Länder* (the states of the German Federal Republic), and 262 were employed in the German Federal Supreme Court. The latter judges deal with all civil issues, including proceedings with voluntary jurisdiction, and all criminal trials. The total number of judges has been constant for years.

By contrast, the number of lawyers admitted has grown considerably in recent years. In 1983, a total of 44,526 lawyers were admitted in the former West Germany. In 1996, 78,810 lawyers were admitted in all of Germany (East and West). The number of lawyers grows by an estimated 5 per cent per year.[24]

3. MAIN PROBLEMS IN THE ADMINISTRATION OF CIVIL JUSTICE IN GERMANY

Since the number of cases to be processed continually rises, but the justice system cannot be expanded, a dilemma has been created. How can an effective and efficient administration of justice be maintained, which properly fulfils its social role on behalf of the people of Germany?

---

[21] Statistisches Bundesamt, 'Fachserie 10 Reihe 2', 57; NJW-Dokumentation, NJW 50 (1997), 14, p. xxx; and 52 (1999), 13, p. xxiv.

[22] Ibid., 13. A 'chamber' (Kammer) is a panel of the regional court, which consists of three judges when sitting. The regional appeal courts also sit in benches of three, but these are known as 'senates' (Senate). The Federal Court of Justice also sits in 'senates', but these consist of five judges.

[23] H. Eylmann, 'Wandel durch Beschränkung und Konzentration: Überlegungen zu den Zielen einer Justizreform', Rpfleger 106 (1998), 45.

[24] Sachverständigenrat 'Schlanker Staat', Abschlußbericht (of 6 Oct. 1997) (2nd edn., 1998), 182.

3.1. Structural changes in the administration of justice

Political parties would like the administration of justice to fulfil the tasks required of it in a modern, social 'constitutional state', effectively and in line with citizens' wishes and their future expectations.[25] At the same time, though, the justice system must be put in such a position that it is able to carry out these new tasks as well as its existing functions. Although one might expect that serious structural suggestions would now be made in Germany to facilitate expansion of the courts' role, the steps which are most discussed, or which are being put into action, only amount to smaller attempts to relieve the problems, or to mobilize better the existing resources of the justice system.

(*a*) Courts have been given power to omit stating the facts of the case and the reasons for the decision when giving judgment in cases in which no appeal can be made against the judgment. Some relief can be expected from the courts' use of this power, which is provided for in § 313a I and in § 495a II ZPO. By giving shorter judgments, judges, preferably at local court level, can save time in disposing of contentious cases.[26]

(*b*) Further streamlining can be expected from the local court's extensive use of the opportunity presented by § 495a ZPO, which creates a simplified procedure for certain cases not capable of being appealed.[27] The area of application of this rule is supposed to be raised beyond its present scope and to be brought into line with the appeal boundary.

(*c*) Extension of the possibility of assigning a single judge to cases would enhance the system's ability to keep taking on cases and process them.[28] Traditionally, a single judge decides civil cases in the local court. The number of single-judge cases can be raised by extending the jurisdiction of the local court. The legislature finally did this in 1993, by raising the local court's jurisdiction from dispute values of DM 6,000 to DM 10,000.[29] The new bill to 'simplify civil proceedings'[30] leaves the local court's juridiction at this level, but extends the possibility of assigning a single judge to cases in the first instance in the regional court and in the regional appeal courts as well.

In 1993, the legislature extended the previous scope for a chamber to delegate the hearing of a case to a single judge at first instance in the regional court. Under this extension, the civil chamber 'should' transfer the legal dispute to one of its members to decide (without any limitation as to the dispute value),

---

[25] See Große Anfrage der SPD 'Bürgernahe und leistungsstarke moderne Justiz', BT-Drucksache 13/4262 of 26 Mar. 1996 and Antwort der Bundesregierung, BT-Drucksache 13/7992 of 18 June 1997.   [26] See U. Boysen, 'Alle Jahre wieder . . .', ZRP 29 (1996) 291, 294.

[27] See H. Rottleuthner, 'Rechtspflegeentlastung', in *Festschrift für E. Schneider* (1997), 25/34 f.

[28] See 'Straffung der Justizstrukturen', DRiZ 75 (1997) 192; Boysen, 'Alle Jahre wieder . . .', 291.

[29] From roughly £2,054 or $US3,428 to roughly £3,425 or $US5,714.

[30] See 'Rechtspflegevereinfachungsgesetz', DRiZ 76 (1998), 49; 'Beschlußempfehlung und Bericht des Rechtsausschusses', BT-Drucksache 13/11042 of 17 June 1998.

provided that the issue presents no particular difficulties of a legal or factual nature, and it has no fundamental significance. Despite this formulation (using 'should'), there is still a wide variation in the transferral rates between regions. For 1995, transferrals rates ranged from 6.1 per cent in Bremen up to 56.8 per cent in Baden-Württemberg and 65.1 per cent in Schleswig-Holstein. Even though a higher capacity to handle cases by deploying single judges to a greater extent cannot be statistically proven, and an increased deployment of single judges does not shorten the duration of proceedings, the legislature nevertheless believes that increasing the power of single judges to hear cases would create a certain amount of extra capacity.

Under the bill to simplify civil proceedings introduced in July 1998, the civil chamber will theoretically remain in existence. However, it will decide claims with a value of under DM 30,000[31] through a single judge. That judge may only transfer disputes to the chamber in difficult cases. If this reform is passed, more than half of all regional court claims will automatically fall within the competency of a single judge. In future, the civil chamber should therefore be able to transfer to a single judge cases with a greater amount in dispute than before, if the issue presents no particular difficulties and has no fundamental significance (§ 348a ZPO). The use of the three-judge chamber is maintained only for more difficult proceedings or proceedings of general significance.[32]

The bill also proposes increased resort to single judges in appellate courts. Presently, a single judge can only prepare the case in the court of appeal for the chamber's or senate's decision, if the issue arising for consideration in the course of that preparation can be dealt with in an oral hearing. In addition, a single judge can only decide upon formal arrangements, and can only adjudicate with the consent of both parties. After the 1998 bill to simplify procedure passes into law, the civil chamber of the regional court, sitting as an appeal court to the local court, will be competent to transfer cases to one of its members for decision—that is, such cases as present no particular difficulties and have no fundamental significance (§ 524a ZPO n.F.).

(*d*) Proceedings can be further simplified if courts do not have to hold oral hearings, but instead can determine cases on a documentary basis. Up until now, this has only been possible in principle with the agreement of both parties according to § 128 Abs. 2 ZPO. Such written proceedings can be arranged officially before the local court only when the value of the matter in dispute is below 1,500 DM, and one party cannot be expected to appear because he or she is too far away or for some other important reason (§ 128 subs. 3 ZPO). As claims with a value under 1,500 DM are regularly brought to the local courts, this rule is now to be transferred to the local court procedure (§ 495b ZPO) and,

---

[31] Roughly £10,270, or $US17,140.

[32] Critically F. Busse, 'Sog. Rechtspflegeentlastung, ein Angriff auf den Rechtsstaat?', *Festschrift für Odersky* (1996), 1003, 1008 ff.

at the same time, generalized. In future, the local court will be able to arrange written proceedings, so long as no statutory requirement that the parties be represented by a lawyer (*Anwaltszwang*) is in force in the local court, and one party cannot be expected to appear. There is no limitation on the value of the matter in dispute.

The State Ministries of Justice expect to make financial savings in future through the possible use of video conferences to examine out-of-town parties, witnesses, or expert witnesses. At present, the real cost of such techniques has yet to be ascertained.[33] In criminal proceedings, however, video conferences may take place in the near future. Organized for protective rather than cost-saving reasons by an amendment of April 1998, victims or other witnesses may be examined while they are not physically present at the trial. The examination then is recorded on video tape or via another, similar technology.[34]

(*e*) Since the procedural rules for proceedings at the local court and the regional court barely differ from one another, and in most cases now a single judge decides in both courts, the proposal to merge the local court and regional court together to form a unified court of first instance has been revived. This would transform the traditional German four-tier civil court structure into a three-tier system.[35] However, in June 1996, a ministerial working group came to the conclusion that the proposed three-tier model (*Dreistufenmodell*) was not realizable in the near future.[36] The reasons given for this were the projected high costs for new court buildings and difficulties in moving a high percentage of the judges. What seems to the writer to be a more probable explanation is that those within the justice system feared that, with the abolition of 706 independent local courts, just as many leading positions for directors and presidents of the local courts would be eliminated. Certainly, the three-tier model will remain on the agenda.[37]

(*f*) Admittedly, an advisory council set up by the Minister for Home Affairs, chaired by the law professor Rupert Scholz and with the objective of achieving a 'streamlined state', has recently suggested a rationalization of courts on an

---

[33] See T. Block, 'Herbstkonferenz der Justizministerinnen und -minister', ZRP 29 (1996), 26, 29.
[34] See §§ 168e, 247a Code of Penal Procedure (StPO) as amended by Zeugenschutzgesetz of 30 Apr. 1998 (BGBl. I, 820); for the bill see BT-Drucksache 13/7165 and 'Beschlußempfehlung des Rechtsausschusses des Deutschen Bundestages', BT-Drucksache 13/8990 of 12 Nov. 1997.
[35] See U. Boysen, 'Alle Jahre wieder . . .', 291, 296; Gottwald, 'Civil Procedure Reform in Germany', AmJCompL 45 (1997), 753, 754 f. The PDS even initiated legislation in this respect; see 'Entwurf eines Gesetzes zur Demokratisierung und Vereinfachung des Gerichtsverfassungs- gesetzes', BT-Drucksache 13/8598 of 25 Sept. 1997.
[36] DRiZ 75 (1997), 445, 449; critically H. Bartels, 'Effektivierung des Zivilverfahrensrechts', ZRP 29 (1996), 297.
[37] See H. Eylmann, 'Wandel durch Beschränkung und Konzentration', 45, 47 and DRiZ 76 (1998), 231; F. Behrens, 'Modernisierung der Justiz in Zeiten knapper Kassen', in *Festschrift für Posser* (1997), 419, 426; R. Faupel, 'Zur Dreigliedrigkeit in der ordentlichen Gerichtsbarkeit', DRiZ 75 (1997), 69; R. Wassermann, 'Alte Reformforderungen—neu belebt', Recht und Politik 34 (1998), 22, 23.

administrative level.[38] At present, the federal and state courts are divided up into five jurisdictions (general, administrative, labour matters, fiscal matters, and social). Each jurisdiction is the primary responsibility of a different ministry. After smaller states have led the way, standardized ministerial departments for the administration of justice for all jurisdictional divisions should now be established everywhere. The promised result is not only a more effective, economical court administration, but also the ability to move judges between the various jurisdictional divisions more easily.[39]

(g) The same working group also wishes to make the courts more effective and ease proceedings by standardizing the codes of procedure to a greater extent, and by reducing the number of court divisions. The long-term goal is a reduction to two 'jurisdictions': the general courts (for civil and penal matters including the labour courts); and administrative courts (for administrative, tax, and social matters).[40]

At present, a separate code of procedure exists for every branch of the court system. In the labour courts, this code refers to the general Code of Civil Procedure to a considerable degree, but in the other branches reference to the general Code is subordinate to particular rules peculiar to the individual jurisdiction. Previous attempts during the 1980s to create a standard code of procedure, at least on the administrative side, failed.[41] The advisory council believes, however, that this process of standardisation must be started anew, in order to increase the effectiveness of the system.[42]

(h) Since the advisory council would like to strengthen the first instance and reduce the frequency of appeals,[43] it also goes on, like many others before it, to suggest changing the structure of the judiciary. Currently, a German judge begins legal practice as a judge, entering the judicial branch of the profession after the second state exam as a junior judge in the regional or local court. If he or she is promoted, he or she will move to the next court up, or receive a managerial office in a lower court. So that future first instance decisions are more readily accepted by the parties, the advisory council would like highly qualified judges with several years' vocational experience to be installed as

---

[38] See Sachverständigenrat 'Schlanker Staat', Abschlußbericht, 181, 185; 'Leistungsstarke Justiz erhalten', DRiZ 76 (1998), 133.

[39] S. Franke, 'Wieviele Gerichtsbarkeiten brauchen wir?', ZRP 30 (1997), 333, 335; Eylmann, 'Wandel durch Beschränkung und Konzentration', 45, 47; 'Thesen zu einer Justizreform (Ein Diskussionspapier des Deutschen Richterbundes)', DRiZ 76 (1998), 264, 265.

[40] S. Franke, 'Wieviele Gerichtsbarkeiten brauchen wir?', 333, 336; Sachverständigenrat 'Schlanker Staat', Abschlußbericht, 188; S. Heitmann, 'Möglichkeiten der Justizentlastung', DRiZ 76 (1998), 123, 128.

[41] See 'Entwurf einer Verwaltungsprozeßordnung' of 13 July 1982, BT-Drucksache 9/1851 and 10/3437 of 31 May 1985.

[42] Sachverständigenrat 'Schlanker Staat', Abschlußbericht, 188.

[43] Ibid. 191; same opinion Heitmann, 'Möglichkeiten', 124, 127; Eylmann, 'Wandel durch Beschränkung und Konzentration', 45, 48. Opposed to structural reforms K. Geiß, 'Wieviele Rechtsmittel brauchen wir?', BRAK-Mitt. 28 (1997), 46.

judges sitting alone at first instance.[44] This would require that increased numbers of higher grade judicial positions be set up in the local courts; as has been the case in the Netherlands for a long time.

Finally, noting that courts in England with a bench of several judges at the appellate stage frequently decide with only two judges instead of three, the advisory council wished to ascertain whether this model could be transferred to Germany.[45]

3.2. Improvement of court management

Internal justice system resource consumption could be economized not only by improving the management of the courts' administration, but also by organizing work within each court according to modern business administration principles, using modern computer technology.[46]

(*a*) A recently published draft law to change the organization of the courts has begun this process. This law seeks to modernize the law governing the presiding committee of the court (which distributes all court business) and to establish rules for distributing cases within panels (§ 21g (2) GVG), thereby reducing the power of presiding judges.[47]

(*b*) Traditionally, judges' officers have been some distance away from central court administrative offices. These administrative offices, in turn, have been far away from filing departments, so that files have had to be transported in large numbers, taking up a lot of time and resources. New conceptions for organizing the courts are based on the idea that judges and court administrative offices, as well as clerical offices, form one integrated service unit. They should accordingly be located together.[48] The clerical offices should use integrated data processing systems to deal with all duties, under the supervision of, or with the support of, the judges, in the form of a management board. For every panel or *senat* a unified service should be set up.[49] What is promised as a result is a substantial simplification of the working processes in court, and an increase in employee motivation.

---

[44] Sachverständigenrat 'Schlanker Staat', Abschlußbericht, 186; same opinion Deutscher Richterbund, 'Thesen zu einer Justizreform', DRiZ 76 (1998), 264, 265.

[45] Sachverständigenrat 'Schlanker Staat', Abschlußbericht, 191.

[46] See A. Koetz and L. Frühauf, *Organisation der Amtsgerichte* (1992).

[47] See M. Wiebel, 'Effizienz und Gerichtsverfassung', ZRP 31 (1998), 221.

[48] See J. Stock, H. Wolff, and P.-I. Thunte, *Strukturanalyse der Rechtspflege* (1996), 19 ff.

[49] See G. Schedler and C.-J. Hauf, 'Strukturelle Veränderungen in der Justiz des Landes Baden-Württemberg', DRiZ 74 (1996), 53; W. Viefhues and K.-H. Volesky, 'Neue Konzepte zur Gerichts- und Arbeitsorganisation in Verbindung mit dem Einsatz moderner Informationstechnik in der ordentlichen Gerichtsbarkeit', DRiZ 74 (1996), 13; Sachverständigenrat 'Schlanker Staat', Abschlußbericht, 193; Heitmann, 'Möglichkeiten', 123, 128; Deutscher Richterbund, 'Thesen zu einer Justizreform', DRiZ 76 (1998), 264, 265; K. Röhl, 'Vom Gerichtsmanagement zur Selbstverwaltung der Justiz', DRiZ 76 (1998), 241.

(*c*) A prerequisite of this development is that word processing programs and special software suitable for the needs of the justice system must be developed, and the same system must be used throughout all of Germany.[50] Up to the present day, different courts and administrations have used different information technology systems. As a consequence, exchanging data between courts, and receiving data stored digitally upon referral or upon transfer to a court of appeal, has not usually been possible.

The adoption of such structures would also require that public officials and judges in managerial positions be trained for the corresponding administrative tasks, and that they be familiar with administration procedures on taking up office. In this respect, there is a willingness to learn American methods of court management.[51]

3.3. Relief of the strain on the justice system through out-of-court settlement

The Germans have the dubious reputation of being a nation of quarrelsome people. In percentage terms, the courts here are made use of to a greater extent than anywhere else in the world. Although this speaks for the quality of the courts and for the citizens' trust in the institution, nevertheless it is still desirable to tame the German public's enthusiasm for litigation.

(*a*) One possibility for achieving this end is to facilitate out-of-court settlements through lawyers before parties seek redress in court. Lawyers' fees are regulated by statute in Germany. In order to sweeten the idea of a settlement to lawyers (given that settlement entails them relinquishing any hope of earning more fees from bringing court cases through more of the statutorily recognized fee stages or appeals), the legislature has raised the statutory settlement fees for lawyers according to § 23 BRAGO 1994 from a full fee to 150 per cent of a full fee. Moreover, together with the new order covering arbitration proceedings which came into force on 1 January 1998, the legislature has eased the completion of lawyer-assisted enforceable settlements by allowing lawyers to sign settlements on behalf of the parties (§ 796a I ZPO n.F.). Previously, the parties had to countersign settlements personally.

(*b*) Beyond this traditional settlement through lawyers, consideration is being given in Germany, as in many other states, to whether disputes in which questions of fact are to be resolved, or which involve personal resentment, could be dealt with by an out-of-court conciliation body.[52] Such institutions

---

[50] See Project Inter Ius of June 1997, 'Studie über das Potential der Internet-Technologie zur Unterstützung der Justiz in Nordrhein-Westfalen', which was completed in April 1999; additionally see F. Behrens, 'Modernisierung der Justiz in Zeiten knapper Kassen', in *Festschrift für Posser* (1997), 429, 432 f.   [51] Sachverständigenrat 'Schlanker Staat', Abschlußbericht, 184.

[52] See W. Gottwald and D. Strempel, *Streitschlichtung* (1995); R. Schütze, 'Alternative Streitschlichtung', ZVglRwiss. 97 (1998), 117; Büchner, Groner, Häusler, Lörcher, et al., *Außergerichtliche Streitbeilegung* (1998).

exist in Germany in many areas on a voluntary basis. For example, conciliation bodies act in various categories of trade disputes, including vehicle
garages, building enterprises, and architects. Conciliation boards have also
been set up within doctors' associations, and in respect of third party liability
insurance.[53] Although proceedings before these conciliation boards are to a
large extent free for clients, and, as a rule, the mediators/conciliators are
equipped with good trade and specialist knowledge, these conciliation bodies
do not enjoy any great popularity with the public. In particular, because the
conciliators come from the same industry as the alleged wrongdoers, many
people have reservations about their impartiality. Even if these reservations
are unjustifiable, they produce, as a consequence, a low frequency of resort to
these institutions. They are only very seldom accepted by the public, despite
all the efforts of the Justice Minister and state governments to encourage their
use.

(c) What is particularly unsatisfactory is the cost–benefit relationship involved
in seeking legal redress in disputes over small amounts. To illustrate, in 1996 the
amount in dispute in over a third of cases (almost 600,000 proceedings) was
under DM 1,000. In these cases, the court fees (without including expenses and
evidential costs) were DM 210. The lawyers' costs per lawyer, excluding the
taking of evidence, were at least DM 240. Accordingly, the costs were at least
DM 700. On taking evidence, the costs per lawyer rose to at least DM 365.
Thus, the total costs of the proceedings, including evidential costs, exceeded the
amount in dispute.

For these proceedings and neighbour disputes, the legislature wishes to grant
German states (*Länder*) the authority to make bringing such actions before the
court conditional upon the prior failure of a compulsory attempt at a dispute
settlement before a conciliation board (§ 15a EG-ZPO).[54] Alternatively, an
obligatory dunning procedure (summary proceedings for order to pay debts)
should be immediately introduced. Even before this rule was enacted, there
were protests that the legislature should have extended this option to rental and
building disputes (at least as far as disputes on the statement of account or
settlement are concerned)[55] or, alternatively, that it should have authorized the
local courts to set up specific local rules.[56] Others have argued that the

---

[53] See 'Entlastungspotential weiter ausschöpfen', DRiZ 75 (1997), 445, 449.

[54] In favour: Eylmann, 'Wandel durch Beschränkung und Konzentration', 45, 49; H. Prütting,
'Obligatorische Streitschlichtung im Zivilprozeß', paper presented to the 62nd German Juristentag
in Bremen on 24 Sept. 1998; crit. K. Eichele, 'Obligatorische vorgerichtliche Schlichtung?', ZRP 30
(1997), 393; A. Dembinsky, 'Das Schlichtungsverfahren—eine sinnlose Zwangsinstanz?', BRAK-
Mitt. 29 (1998), 66. For the last period of legislature the bill, however, finally failed in the mediation
committee between Bundestag and Bundesrat. The CDU party has introduced the bill into the
Bundestag again; see B7-Drucksacke 14/163 of 8 Dec. 1998.

[55] See H. Bartels, 'Effektivierung des Zivilverfahrensrechts', ZPR 29 (1996), 297, 298.

[56] See W. Gottwald, 'Alternativen in der Rechtspflege', BRAK-Mitt. 29 (1998), 60, 64 f.

legislature should have empowered the local courts to refer parties to concilia-tion boards in all appropriate cases.[57]

How these conciliation boards, which are still to be created, should be staffed, and what they will cost, are still open questions at present. What is probably being considered is having both legal and non-legal experts sit on conciliation boards.

Conciliated proceedings should, in addition, be clearly cheaper than court proceedings. A reimbursement of expenses of DM 100 per settlement, in addition to reimbursement for outlays, is being considered. If a conciliation is successfully concluded, the settlement reached should have effect as an execut-able title.[58] To what extent this reform will succeed in increasing the popularity of out-of-court settlements through lawyers or conciliation bodies in the run-up to court proceedings remains to be seen. Any significant success would require a conscious change in society. Mere government publicity through brochures alone may not suffice.

3.4. Improving the extent to which the justice system covers costs

(*a*) Guaranteeing legal protection is, on the one hand, one of the classic primary tasks of the state. The administration of justice ensures peace under the law and legal certainty in the general interest and in the interest of individual citizens. For the economy, legal certainty and effective legal protection also enhance the security of investments, thereby promoting the willingness to invest, both from abroad and domestically. Therefore, the state must ensure a high standard of performance from the justice system.

On the other hand, the civil justice system is also a service undertaking that offers and carries out a wide range of services in the interests of the parties involved. This seems to suggest that the system should cover its own costs via fees charged to its users.[59] Non-contentious matters already work with full cost coverage. Fees required for the issuance of certificates of inheritance, entries in the land register, and entries in the commercial register cover the costs in full. By contrast, in contentious litigation the percentage of system costs which fees cover is scarcely over 50 per cent.[60] What is being considered is simplifying the final settlement of costs by standardizing court fees (including expenses) and, at the same time, raising fees with the intent of reducing the court's

---

[57] R. Greger, 'Diversion statt Flaschenhals: ein Alternativkonzept zur Etablierung des Gütegedankens im Zivilprozeß', ZRP 31 (1998), 183.

[58] See 'Außergerichtliche Streitschlichtung fördern', DRB-Modell für ein obligatorisches vorgerichtliches Schlichtungsverfahren, DRiZ 76 (1998), 226.

[59] See P. Marqua, 'Modellskizzen für eine "Justiz 2000"', DRiZ 76 (1998), 134.

[60] H.-B. Schäfer, 'Kein Geld für die Justiz: was ist uns der Rechtsfrieden wert?', BRAK-Mitt. 27 (1996), 2, 5, holds that this percentage is already too high.

caseload.[61] However, these changes must be accomplished without making access to the courts impossible for parties with lower incomes. The system of legal aid (for court costs and lawyers' fees) should be retained. The level of cost cover in the courts' social jurisdiction is particularly bad. No court fees are demanded in disputes between registered doctors on the National Health Insurance Scheme and health insurance scheme organizations.[62] It is clear that a privilege of this sort is not justified.

(*b*) A party who cannot cover the cost of his or her proceedings because of his or her personal and economic circumstances may apply for legal aid. Legal aid is granted towards the proceedings costs, if the claim or defence can reasonably be expected to result in a favourable decision (§ 114 ZPO). The former *Armenrecht* (literally translated 'law for poor people') was replaced in 1976 by a relatively generous legal aid scheme. Whilst the parties previously had to prove their 'poverty' by a certificate from the social authorities, now judges competent to resolve the main issue consider applicants' circumstances, and decide whether or not to grant legal aid applications. So long as parties willingly make the necessary details of their income and financial circumstances available, the courts are relatively generous in granting legal aid. In family law cases, in which the parties can only receive legal protection through a legal action, the courts are willing to presume the 'prospects of success'. For legal aid applications to be accepted, parties need only contribute something meaningful to the course of the proceedings.

Since the German states' expenditure for legal aid had grown enormously, the law was changed in 1980. The links between the legal aid scheme and social security law were improved. At the same time, the possibility of a later revocation of a grant of legal aid for misleading the court was made easier. The award of legal aid temporarily frees a party from court costs and, in proceedings where legal representation is obligatory, a lawyer is assigned to the aided party. In other proceedings where legal representation is not compulsory, a legally aided party is assigned a lawyer if the opposing party is represented by a lawyer, or if legal representation seems necessary, as in relatively difficult cases.

Although the lawyers assigned to legally aided parties receive a lower remuneration from public funds (according to § 123 BRAGO), in 1984 approximately DM 350 million were paid out of German state funds (*Länderkassen*) to lawyers assigned in this way.[63] More precise statistics on the present total expenditure for legal aid do not exist, because the statistics available do not

---

[61] A first step in this direction can be found in the bill 'Entwurf eines Gesetzes zur Änderung des Gerichtskostengesetzes', BR-Drucksache 538/97 of 18 July 1997. Objecting: Eylmann, 'Wandel durch Beschränkung und Konzentration', 45, 49; Schäfer, 'Kein Geld für die Justiz', 2, 7. As to the selection effects of different cost calculation models see D. Schmidtchen and R. Kirstein, 'Abkoppelung der Prozeßkosten vom Streitwert?', in *Festschrift für G. Lüke* (1997), 741.

[62] See Heitmann, 'Möglichkeiten', 123, 127.

[63] Roughly £119 million, or $US200 million.

include payments to witnesses and expert witnesses and any advance payments for travel costs; and do not allow for the court fees which are not charged after a party is legally aided. No official statistics exist on a federal level giving the number of applications for legal aid and the number of grants of aid made. The official figures for Bavaria are, however, likely to reflect the general trend. From these figures, it appears likely that the number of grants has generally continued to increase in the last few years. In 1996, Bavarian local courts granted legal aid in 9,224 general civil cases (a 9.5 per cent increase on 1995) and in 38,254 family cases (15.4 per cent more than 1995). Bavarian regional courts (in first instance matters) granted legal aid for 1,973 civil cases (7.6 per cent more than 1995). In 1996, the total Bavarian spending on assigned lawyers was approximately DM 64.6 million (15.8 per cent more than 1995), and in 1997 a total of about DM 73 million was spent (a 13 per cent rise).[64] It is estimated that the total annual expenditure on legal aid of the Federation and the *Länder* is approximately DM 500 million at present.[65]

Of the legal aid approvals made in Bavaria, 80 per cent were instalment free. In just under 20 per cent of cases the parties had to repay the aid granted in instalments. These contributions flowing back through instalments were estimated to be from 15 per cent to 20 per cent of expenditure in 1985. The effects of the alterations in the legal aid rules in recent years are not known in terms of figures. As the Bavarian figures clearly demonstrate, legal aid has a greater significance in family law than in general civil cases.

Since the association of legal aid with social legislation leads to an enormous amount of work in calculating disposable income and assets, there is a tendency to transfer the responsibility for determining the economic requirements for legal aid approval back to the social welfare offices.[66]

3.5. Strengthening the court of first instance

In 1996, appeals were filed against 11 per cent of the local court judgments capable of being appealed. These appeals were successful in 36 per cent of cases. Of the regional court judgments capable of being appealed, appeals were filed in 16 per cent of cases. These appeals were successful in 42.5 per cent of cases. It is difficult to say whether these figures are, objectively, too high or not. Either way, it would be better if more first instance judgments were accepted by the parties, and the accuracy of the first instance judgments were beyond doubt in a greater number of cases. For many years it has been a matter of concern for all German procedural reformers to improve the first instance court and to increase its significance. No one puts the case for restricting the judge's share of

---

[64] I am indebted to the Bavarian Ministry of Justice for this information. DM 64.6 million is about £22.1 million, or $US36.9 million. DM 73 million is about £25 million, or $US41.7 million.

[65] Roughly £171 million, or $US286 million.

[66] See G. Meister, 'Einsparmöglichkeiten bei der Prozeßkostenhilfe', ZRP 31 (1998), 166.

responsibility for the outcome of cases by way of judicial control over proceedings. But what is discussed is whether, and to what extent, the obligations on parties to give each other information and to disclose all relevant data before the oral hearing should be increased.[67]

(*a*) One possibility would be to introduce a general procedural duty of disclosure on the parties after commencing an action. If necessary, this duty could also apply beforehand, following the example of discovery in common law countries and in other states.[68] However, there is a lot of resistance to the idea of introducing discovery proceedings into the German system. This appears to be generated primarily by some horrifying reports from large product liability cases in the USA.[69] In practice, the consequences of the lack of any discovery process in Germany are bearable only because the courts work to a great extent in favour of the party having suffered damage. Presumptions are used, or a generous view is taken of prima facie evidence. In part, the courts will recognize substantive bona fide claims for disclosure; and, in any case, they do recognize a limited duty of disclosure, amounting to a minor burden of proving assertions by evidence, on the party without the overall burden of proof. This ensures that the party having the better knowledge of the course of events must account for its conduct, if the opposing side is not in a position to have any evidence of the relevant events. If a party refuses reasonable disclosure, then he or she will lose the case, although actual disclosure will not be compelled.[70]

(*b*) Under the present law, the parties are obliged to present their means of attack and defence at the proper time (§ 282 ZPO). Whoever does not produce their means of attack and defence by the deadline laid down by the court is excluded, if the hearing would be delayed by the late introduction of new material, and the party does not have an adequate excuse for being late (§ 296 (1) ZPO). If the defaulting party can file an appeal against the judgment, it can overcome its exclusion. If it immediately presents its means of attack and defence along with its grounds for appeal, acceptance of this new evidence cannot delay the completion of the appeal proceedings, and so the new material will be accepted. The July 1998 Bill simplifying civil proceedings intends to block this 'escape' to the appeal court. Under the new law, new means of attack and defence which were not presented in the first instance court within the deadline will only be admitted on appeal when the party has an adequate excuse for being late. The exclusion of late arguments will no longer depend upon a possible delay of the termination of the appeal proceedings (§ 528 ZPO

---

[67] Gottwald, 'Civil Procedure Reform', 753, 759 ff.; Heitmann, 'Möglichkeiten', 124, 127.

[68] See R. Greger, 'Vom "Kampf ums Recht" zum Zivilprozeß der Zukunft', JZ 52 (1997), 1077, 1080; Gottwald, *Gutachten für den 61. DJT* (1996), A15 ff; Gottwald, 'Civil Procedure Reform', 753, 760.

[69] See V. Vorwerk, '"Verfahrensvereinfachung" im Zivilprozeß zu Lasten der Justiz und der Parteien', MDR 50 (1996), 870.

[70] See Rosenberg, Schwab, and Gottwald, *Zivilprozeßrecht*, § 117 VI.

as amended by the Bill).[71] To what extent this change will lead to appeals becoming more of a legal review, by forcing the parties to conduct the enquiry into the facts seriously at first instance, remains to be seen.

(c) Even though the detailed arrangements for the appeal system are still unsettled,[72] the 'streamlined state' advisory board has spoken out in its final report in favour of a unified means of legal redress with one trial on the facts, and one appeal.[73] The appeal proceedings would be a legal review only, in contrast to the present position. The appeal on a point of law to the German Federal Supreme Court would no longer be a general, liberal means of legal redress, but would only be possible when admitted by that Court in cases of general importance. Previous reform proposals tending in this direction have failed because of resistance from the bar, and also, on many occasions, because of resistance from law professors, judges, and commercial lawyers.[74] Whether such reforms can be realized in future, under the diktats of poor finances and further state streamlining, remains to be seen.

4. HISTORICAL PERSPECTIVE OF REFORM

The German Code of Civil Procedure was created in 1877 as a product of a specialist bureaucracy influenced by the Digest. It was a codification in accordance with a purely liberal model, which followed the principles of pure freedom of the parties, orality, and immediacy in their entirety. It originated in a time of economic and political boom. The proceedings it created were geared towards the middle class, who were able to spend a bit of money on a legal action, not towards litigation as a mass social phenomenon. In the first years after the Code of Civil Procedure came into force, the pure principles of orality and party freedom were disapproved of, on the ground that parties and their legal representatives culpably delayed the settlement of legal disputes by frustrating discussion of the facts in hearings or wantonly causing adjournments. As early as ten years after the Code of Civil Procedure came into force, it was obvious that the parties themselves did not have a corresponding interest in settling cases quickly.

---

[71] See Gottwald, 'Civil Procedure Reform', 753, 763 f.

[72] For family cases see K. Schubert, 'Reformvorschläge zu Verfahren und Rechtsmitteln in Familiensachen', FPR (1997), 185.

[73] Sachverständigenrat 'Schlanker Staat', Abschlußbericht, 186, 189; 'Straffung der Justizstrukturen', DRiZ 75 (1997), 192, 193; of same opinion: Heitmann, 'Möglichkeiten', 124, 127; Eylmann, 'Wandel durch Beschränkung und Konzentration', 45, 48; critically P. Marqua, 'Nichts Neues zur Justizentlastung', DRiZ 75 (1997), 187.

[74] In favour of reforms, however, P. Gilles, 'Rechtsstaat und Justizstaat in der Krise', Neue Justiz 52 (1998), 225.

(*a*) Under the influence of the social proceedings model of the 1898 Austrian Code of Civil Procedure, awareness of these weak points grew ever stronger.[75] A significant number of practitioners and academics called for the breakdown in public confidence in the German administration of justice to be resolved by bringing German procedure into line with Austrian procedure. The reform debate in those years did not quieten down until the 1930s. It was ruled to a large extent by political faction disputes, between those espousing liberal and moderate social principles. The classical school of German procedural law specialists occupied a liberal camp, and rejected any renunciation of freedom of the parties and any weakening of fundamental liberal principles. The practical consequences, however, were so unsatisfactory that the Austrian Code of Civil Procedure's fundamental ideas regarding the role of judges and the order of proceedings were taken up piece by piece, and were finally put through Parliament.[76] Admittedly, all provisions constraining party freedom met with bitter resistance from the legal profession.

In 1902, the procedure 'experts' (reporters) at the 26th German *Juristentag* (*Neukamp* and *Wach*) identified party freedom as harmfully excessive, and spoke out in favour of introducing judicial case management and giving judges greater powers to give directions to litigants. However, the majority of the German *Juristentag*, dominated by advocates, did not want to interfere with party control over proceedings as a basic principle of the German Code of Civil Procedure, and so it rejected the experts' proposals. Only the local court amendment of 1909 introduced elements of judicial case management into the local court, despite the repeated and sharply formulated resistance of the legal profession. The parties retained the right to agree on a suspension of proceedings. Only a wartime decree of 1943 extended judicial case management to all other courts. This solution was retained after the Second World War.

The 1909 amendment gave the local court, for the first time, the power to discuss the facts and the disputed relationship with the parties, to prepare the enquiry into the facts, to obtain official information, and to summon witnesses, experts, and parties to appear.

(*b*) Subsequent discussions of reform and additional reforms have been shaped from that time until the present day by the tension between liberal procedural dogma and problems caused by increasing case numbers and delays. The liberal ideal is intent on restricting party freedom as little as possible. However, the increase in case numbers and procedural delays can only be fought by strengthening judges' powers, and by the parties accepting corresponding obligations. Be this as it may, the first reforms of 1909 helped establish the principle that civil proceedings cannot be based purely on party freedom,

---

[75] See P. Gottwald, 'Simplified Civil Procedure in West Germany', AmJCompL 31 (1983), 687.
[76] See P. Gottwald, 'Die österreichische Zivilprozeßordnung aus deutscher Sicht', in P. Mayr (ed.), *100 Jahre österreichische Zivilprozeßgesetze* (1998), 179.

and do not have to adhere strictly to the liberal ideal, but that the adversary system is a rule of expediency which must be subject to restraint in furtherance of the social purpose of the proceedings.

A substantial step in the direction of a system of social civil proceedings was made by an emergency order of 1924, known as the *Emminger* order. This order finally ended party control over deadlines and hearings. At the same time, it limited orality by referring to all previously exchanged pleadings and documents in the hearing. As these papers no longer needed to be read aloud at oral hearings, the hearings could concentrate on the real contentious issues. In addition, the court were given the general power to set hearing dates and to refuse to admit means of attack and defence submitted late with the intention of protracting litigation. Admittedly, in practice, little use was made of this power, presumably because the judges were afraid of issuing a wrong judgment. At that time, the aim was already to deal with legal disputes in one hearing (prepared by a judge sitting alone). But, in practice, this ideal was rather more remote.

(*c*) The 1933 amendment incorporated the parties' duty to tell the truth into the rules of procedure (§ 138 ZPO). This amendment was made on the basis of the 1931 draft of a new code, but the reformers of the day rejected the opportunity to follow the Austrian example and give courts the power to summon witnesses and request the transmittal of documents which the parties had not referred to. From then on, courts could exclude all means of attack and defence which were not communicated in prepared pleadings at the correct time. An automatic exclusion was not, however, imposed.[77]

(*d*) After the Second World War, Germany's economy flourished again, and the old problems of the civil courts being overloaded, proceedings being protracted by the parties, and legal redress taking an excessive amount of time all returned. After extensive reform work, a new model was introduced in 1977 through an amendment to simplify proceedings (a so-called *Vereinfachungsnovelle*). The new model was based on the Stuttgart model for compact proceedings in civil cases.[78] Critics have expressed the opinion that only a joker could have thought this name up, as the law is anything but simple. Essentially, it requires the judge to prepare proceedings either in writing or in one preparatory hearing (§§ 275, 276 ZPO), so that in one main hearing the case can be brought to a stage where it is ready for adjudication (§ 278 ZPO). In addition, the parties are required to produce their means of attack and defence at the correct time (§ 282 ZPO). If the judge sets deadlines, means of attack and defence which are brought late are excluded if their admission would delay settling the legal dispute and there is no excuse for their being late (§ 296 (1) ZPO). If the judge has not set any deadlines, the judge can exclude the parties if they have acted

---

[77] The reform debate between 1934 and 1944 did not lead up to official drafts, see W. Schubert (ed.), *Zivilprozeß und Gerichtsverfassung*, Akademie für deutsches Recht 1933–1945, VI (1997).

[78] See R. Bender, 'The Stuttgart Model', in M. Cappelletti and J. Weisner, *Access to Justice*, ii/2 (1979), 431.

with gross negligence (§ 296 (2) ZPO). Evidence presented which is rejected at first instance is also incapable of being brought afterwards in the appellate instance (§ 528 ZPO). While in theory this rule has relatively severe effects, certain technical defects in it were exploited in practice in the following period. Moreover, it was weakened further by precedents of the German constitutional court (*Bundesverfassungsgericht*) regarding the court's duty to grant a fair hearing. Thus, its effect, which was probably strong initially, has fallen at least partly flat after twenty years.[79]

The success and the fundamental correctness of the 1977 amendment to simplify proceedings (*Vereinfachungsnovelle*)[80] should not be cast into doubt by the comments made above. It is simply the case that, over the course of time, a certain fatigue set in. At the same time, the number of proceedings rose and, under the diktats of poor finances, the call for state streamlining became loud, especially on the part of the German *Länder*. Accordingly, the reform discussion of the last ten years has been characterized by calls to increase parties' duties in proceedings further, simplify the appeal system, and limit appeals. The details of the reforms proposed have already been discussed above in the course of describing the present system's problems.

(*e*) Perhaps in contrast to other countries, the financial aspects of access to justice in Germany no longer play a role, at least since the introduction of the new legal aid scheme in 1980. Only in the 1970s was it suggested that appeals should, in principle, be free, since they primarily serve to correct mistakes in the previous instance.[81] However, this discussion was terminated swiftly as being unrealistic. Appellate proceedings are carried out in the interests of the parties in the German system, so it is justifiable to impose the costs on those parties.

Through the statutory tariffs for courts and lawyers, the costs of German civil proceedings are kept within limits (in normal cases) which are a little more economical than in a free market system (such as applies to a normal civil suit in England or the USA), where lawyers charge by the hours worked, and set their hourly rates freely. Traditionally, there has been an understanding in Germany that, in practice in today's society, proceedings cannot be conducted without involving advocates on both sides. Lawyers' services have their price, however. In contrast, in the last few years, the view has intensified that the costs of bringing or defending proceedings must be increased, in order more effectively than before to prevent parties from thoughtlessly seeking redress in court. Therefore, an improvement in the justice system's level of cost-effectiveness is being considered, as explained above.

---

[79] See W. Lüke, '20 Jahre Vereinfachungsnovelle', JuS 37 (1997), 681.

[80] See R. Greger, 'Rechtstatsächliche Erkenntnisse zu den Auswirkungen der Vereinfachungsnovelle', ZZP 100 (1987), 377; Gottwald, 'Simplified Civil Procedure', 687, 700.

[81] See W. Grunsky, 'Empfehlen sich im Interesse einer effektiven Rechtsverwirklichung für den Bürger Änderungen des Systems des Kosten- und Gebührenrechts?', *Gutachten für den 51. Deutschen Juristentag* (1976), A22 ff.

The 61st German Juristentag looked into, among other things, steps to simplify, standardize and limit appeals in the interests of improving the effectiveness of legal protection.[82] Since then, some of the measures suggested have been adopted in the July 1998 Bill simplifying civil proceedings. Others, like the introduction of a general duty to disclose, the transition to a three-tier system, and the abolition of appellate review of the facts, are not supported by the majority of German legal experts at present.[83] Should the official policy continue to be aimed towards the realization of a 'streamlined state', our administration of justice will presumably continue to be cautiously developed step by step in the coming years in the direction of these goals.

5. ALTERNATIVE METHODS OF DISPUTE RESOLUTION

In recent years it has also become fashionable in Germany to consider and encourage alternatives to court proceedings.[84] However, conciliation proceedings tend to meet with a negative legal-political and social environment in this country.

(*a*) First, the justice system has constantly incorporated social elements into court proceedings themselves. Although the procedure is a legal action between parties, it is conducted under judicial direction, and the judge has to take care that a party does not lose the action as a result of making obvious mistakes while submitting their application or on presenting facts (§ 139 ZPO). The court has the duty to mediate between the parties and to try to settle claims (§ 279 ZPO) at any stage of the proceedings. Parties quite often accept judicial proposals to settle their cases. Under the 1998 Bill, parties may accept a judge's proposal in writing, thus terminating the proceedings without any further oral hearing (§ 279 (2) ZPO). Furthermore, after the filing of a petition for legal aid, the court may summon the parties to appear for a hearing with the intent of mediating a settlement of the case between them (§ 118 (1) 3 ZPO).

Thus, as the court is frequently engaged in mediation or settlement proceedings, the German system of justice does not encourage parties to search for means of redress through alternative dispute resolution methods.[85] Besides, although the financial burdens of contentious proceedings are not low, they

---

[82] See P. Gottwald, 'Empfehlen sich im Interesse eines effektiven Rechtsschutzes Maßnahmen zur Vereinfachung, Vereinheitlichung und Beschränkung der Rechtsmittel und Rechtsbehelfe des Zivilverfahrensrechts?', *Gutachten A für den 61. Deutschen Juristentag* (1996).

[83] See P. Gottwald, 'Civil Procedure Reform in Germany', AmJCompL 45 (1997), 753.

[84] See W. Gottwald and D. Strempel, *Streitschlichtung* (1995); H. Prütting, 'Verfahrensrecht und Mediation', in Breidenbach and Heussler (eds.), *Mediation für Juristen* (1997), 57; W. Gottwald, 'Alternativen in der Rechtspflege', BRAK-Mitt. 29 (1998), 60; F. Behrens, 'Außergerichtliche Streitschichtung in Zivilsachen', Recht und Politik 33 (1997), 73.

[85] Schütze, 'Alternative Streitschlichtung', 117, 121 ff.

are seen as reasonable by commercial litigants. Private parties can obtain financial support if needs be through legal aid, or they may bring suits with the help of legal protection insurance (very frequent in proceedings for damages after accidents and in other cases of tortious liability etc.).[86]

(*b*) More importantly, German litigants generally have great trust in the independence and capabilities of their judiciary. By contrast, they tend to distrust conciliation boards because they are, as a rule (at least at present), brought into being and organized by the interested trade, industrial, architectural, medical, and so on. Conciliators are thought either to be completely on the side of the organizers, or to sympathize with them. Correspondingly, people's tendency to submit voluntarily to the final ruling of conciliation boards is rather low. Therefore, the use made of the various conciliation bodies in numerical terms remains within extraordinarily narrow limits.[87]

In addition, in Germany the administration of justice has always been organized by the state, exercising its sovereign power. Establishing dispute settlement regimes socially, through conciliators or laymen of any kind, has accordingly never enjoyed popularity. In the German *Länder* which still have conciliators, their use in recent decades has radically declined. A typical citizen's thought process is quite straightforward: why use a layman if there is also a specialist available, and this specialist is easily reachable?

A certain exception has to be made with regard to the settlement boards at Chambers of Industry and Commerce, which mediate in competition cases between the parties (§§ 27a; 13, 13a UWG), and in respect of the settlement boards which mediate in disputes between employers and works councils (§ 76 BetrVG).[88]

(*c*) In the new *Länder* belonging to the former East Germany, other factors must also be considered. The demands made on the courts there are comparatively low. This phenomenon definitely results from the present poor economic conditions. It is also based on the fact that citizens there must gradually learn and develop a conventional culture of dispute resolution again. While the GDR (E. Germany) was still in existence, the courts there were also active as societal organs guided by the state. For smaller disputes there were 'social courts', in the form of conflict and conciliation commissions.[89] In 1978, there were over 25,000 conflict commissions and 5,000 conciliation commissions in the GDR. These commissions were supposed to protect social order and were, according

---

[86] See Jagodzinski, Raiser, and Riehl, 'Sind die Rechtsschutzversicherungen die Ursache für die "Prozeßflut"?', DRiZ 69 (1991), 189.

[87] As to the theoretical filter effect of ADR see: J. Stock, 'Der Geschäftsanfall der Zivilgerichte und die Filterwirkung außergerichtlicher Konfliktbearbeitung', in W. Gottwald and D. Strempel, *Streitschlichtung* (1995), 113.

[88] See G. Grotmann-Höfling, *Strukturanalyse des arbeitsgerichtlichen Rechtsschutzes: Konfliktlösung durch eine Betriebliche Einigungsstelle* (1995).

[89] See H. Kellner, 'Gesellschaftliche Gerichtsbarkeit in der DDR', Keio Law Review, Commemorative Issue 6 (1990), 227.

to the statutory conception, the citizens' bodies for education and self-discipline. The conflict commissions decided virtually all employment law disputes. Only 3.5 per cent of their judgments were later altered or repealed by state courts. The conciliation commissions decided issues involving residential areas and socialist co-operatives. Upon the demise of the GDR, these 'social courts' were mostly disbanded. What were preserved, however, were the conciliation bodies in the districts and the employment conciliation bodies.[90] The district conciliation boards were disbanded directly after Germany's reunification, because no demand was made on them by the public whatsoever. Given this background, it is understandably difficult to persuade the public in the east that they should look to new conciliation boards to remedy legal disputes from now on.

(d) As illustrated above, the Bill simplifying court proceedings of July 1998 gives the German *Länder* the power to introduce compulsory conciliation procedures (court-annexed arbitration) for small disputes, property issues between neighbours, and claims concerning insults and defamation in private (§ 15a EGZPO as amended). Whether the Bill will survive after the elections to the Bundestag, to what extent the German regions will make use of this authorization, and how far the public are prepared to reach a settlement before a conciliator, are still completely open questions at this point in time.[91]

In any case, some thought is being given to how the compulsory dispute conciliation procedure should actually be enforced.[92] One suggestion is that plaintiffs could have recourse to a conciliation board in an unstructured way, whereby the conciliator must formally summon the defendant to the hearing. The conciliation is considered to have failed if the defendant is not prepared to become involved or if no settlement is achieved within three months. In any case, the conciliation proceedings should be conducted independently of the court, so that the court merely supervises the conciliator and issues the execution clause for a settlement between the parties. The conciliator should work free of charge and receive a DM 50 package for reimbursement of expenses, in addition to reimbursement of any direct extra outlays. In each case no legal claim should be allowed before the conciliation proceedings are carried out. Any actions instituted nonetheless should be suspended until the end of the conciliation.

---

[90] See P. Rieß and H. Hilger, *Das Rechtspflegerecht des Einigungsvertrages* (1991), Rdn. 102c.

[91] The 62nd German Juristentag 1998 in Bremen was discussing within an actual forum 'Obligatorische Streitschlichtung im Zivilprozeß'; see P. Macke, NJW 51 (1998), Suppl. to 23, 28; H. Prütting, 'Obligatorische Streitschlichtung im Zivilprozeß', paper presented to the 62nd German Juristentag (1998).

[92] See H. Renk, 'Außergerichtliche Streitschlichtung als Entlastung der Justiz', DRiZ 76 (1998), 57, 58.

6. ASSESSMENT OF THE PRESENT STATE OF AFFAIRS

Taken as a whole, the German system of civil justice is probably not in a bad way. If one looks at the average data for the period of time required to deal with a civil dispute, they are quite satisfactory. Admittedly, the appearance given by the statistics comes under pressure when looked at in more detail. Above all, in some cities there is an enormous backlog of work and a build-up of pending cases. Waiting times of a year and longer until a case is heard in court are not unusual there. Likewise, postponements by the court are frequently made 'for professional reasons', without the case having been dealt with in between times. However, taken as a whole, the justice system is capable of settling the present amount of business fairly satisfactorily.

As explained, huge steps have been considered and partially introduced. These moves are planned to accommodate successfully a future growth in the amount of business; but, above all, to allow for the emergence of other tasks within the justice system (e.g. consumer insolvency proceedings; growth of supervision of carers).

The justice system is certain to take consistent advantage of the opportunities for internal rationalization, by improving court management, and easing technical operations through the improved use of data processing instruments in the next few years.[93] One could, therefore, be quite content and refer to the constant reforms of the German law of civil procedure which have had the effect of keeping it practicable, modern, and in a good condition.[94] Yet, if this evaluation is broadened to include the success rate in the realization of ideas to reform the court system, one must be more pessimistic. To what extent court administration can successfully be rationalized through the organization of ministries for the administration of all branches of jurisdiction remains to be seen. It is fully open whether, on another attempt, the codes of procedure of the five jurisdictions could be unified more strongly than before, or even whether part of these jurisdictions could be merged again.

Finally, there is the fully open question of to what extent the legal culture in Germany can be modified so that parties accept first instance decisions in principle and appeals, which (at least as a rule) deal only with questions of fact, become the exception. Such an alteration would not just require an increase in parties' obligations. It would also: call for a rethink on the part of advocates and within the administration of justice; require a reorganization of law firms specializing in appeals (which operate in around half of the German regions); and require replanning so that experienced and more highly qualified judges are not appointed to the court of appeal but to the local courts.

---

[93] See F. Behrens, 'Modernisierung der Justiz in Zeiten knapper Kassen', in *Festschrift für Posser* (1997), 419; for labour courts see A. Pieper, 'Justiz im Wandel', in *Festschrift für Posser* (1997), 479.
[94] Thus W. Gerhardt, '100 Jahre Entlastung der Zivilgerichte', JR (1998), 133, 139.

Such long-term strategies have no chance of success in the short term given the existing German legal culture. Looking back over the 100-year reform history of the present Code of Civil Procedure gives little cause for optimism. Such changes could only be implemented in moderately small steps, over the long term. For many years, the style of legislative reform in Germany can be characterized as reflecting a fear within the Ministry of Justice that far-reaching plans for reform would only be blocked by the Committee on Legal Affairs of the German Bundestag, with the consequence that those plans remained wishes or dreams. Only urgent reforms seem to be achievable, with the effect that there is no final change of conditions. In addition, many reform proposals are not based on empirical data.[95] Several experts believe that serious procedural reform will always fail due to the conservatism of lawyers and the phenomenon of group psychology.[96] Thus, the only hope remaining is that, in the near future, politicians will engage more with the problems of reform and modernization of the justice system.

[95] See H. Rottleuthner, 'Rechtspflegeentlastung: Neue Tendenzen in erster Instanz', in *Festschrift für E. Schneider* (1997), 25, 30 ff.

[96] See E. Schneider, Entlastung der Gerichte: Eine Sisyphusarbeit', MDR 50 (1996), 865, 867.

7

Civil Justice Reform:
Access, Cost, and Expedition.
The Japanese Perspective

Yukiko Hasebe

1. INTRODUCTION

In Japan the new Code of Civil Procedure was enacted in 1996 and came into effect in January 1998. The 1996 Code (which I will refer to as 'the New Code') replaced the former Code, which dated from 1926 (which I will refer to as 'the Old Code'). The aim of the reforms was to offer ordinary citizens plain and accessible civil justice.[1]

The main reforms of the New Code are as follows:

1. the establishment of pre-trial procedures for identifying genuine issues;
2. the improvement of the method for obtaining evidence;
3. the introduction of a small claims procedure; and
4. the restriction of appeals to the Supreme Court.

The overall objective is to achieve expeditious and efficient civil justice. This, in itself, is no doubt desirable. However, if it sacrifices fairness in justice, we should think it over again. What is justice? What are its most fundamental and essential elements? And how should we seek to realize them? It is against the background of these questions that I will describe the recent reforms and the present situation in Japanese civil justice.

2. OUTLINE OF THE JAPANESE CIVIL JUSTICE SYSTEM

2.1. Historical background

The first Code of Civil Procedure in Japan was enacted in 1890. It was based on German law. Most of the technical terms now current in Japanese procedural law were created through translation of the corresponding German terms.

---

[1] For the reforms, see *Homusho-Minjikyoku-Sanjikanshitsu* (Counsellors Office, Civil Affairs Bureau, the Ministry of Justice), *Ichimon-Itto Shin-Minjisoshoho* (Q & A on the New Code of Civil Procedure) (1996) (in Japanese); Masahiko Omura, 'A Comparative Analysis of Trial Preparation: Some Aspects of the New Japanese Code of Civil Procedure', in *Toward Comparative Law in the 21st Century* (The Institute of Comparative Law in Japan, 1998).

Since then, German law has strongly influenced the development of Japanese civil justice theory.

In 1926, the Code was entirely revised. This reform established the basic form of the Old Code, which was retained throughout the subsequent period, up to the enactment of the New Code in 1996. The Old Code maintained the German style of Japanese procedural law but, after the Second World War, introduced certain ideas from Anglo-American law. Cross-examination and the summary court as a forum for simple and accessible justice are examples.

The civil justice system was faced with fierce criticism in the 1980s. The critics said that civil justice was slow, expensive, and hardly comprehensible to the ordinary person. In July 1990, the Law Commission, an advisory body to the Justice Minister, started working on the reform of civil justice.[2] After a five-year debate among Ministry of Justice officials, the judiciary, the Japan Federation of Bar Associations, and scholars, the Civil Procedure Bill was submitted to the Diet in 1996. A controversy ensued over the immunity of official documents from orders for production, and all except that part of the Bill was passed by the Diet in June 1996.

2.2. The court system

There are two types of first instance court: summary courts and district courts. The summary courts are courts of limited jurisdiction, hearing both civil and criminal cases. For civil actions, their jurisdiction is limited to claims not exceeding 900,000 yen.[3] New small claims procedures, which have been established for monetary claims not exceeding 300,000 yen, are also conducted in the summary court.[4] Both summary court civil proceedings and small claims proceedings are conducted by a single summary court judge. However, summary courts deal with far more cases by way of conciliation, or under the special procedure for application for a payment order. A payment order (ss. 382 ff.) is issued on the application of a monetary creditor against the debtor without giving him or her an opportunity to be heard. It is frequently used by the credit industry or moneylenders.

The district courts handle claims that are not within the jurisdiction of the summary courts. They also hear appeals from summary courts. Most district court cases are dealt with by a single judge. A few important cases and appeals are heard by a three-judge collegiate court.

The family courts are specialized courts dealing with family matters and

---

[2] The Law Commission has so far engaged in making a draft proposal for reform of basic codes such as the Civil Code, Commercial Code, and Code of Civil Procedure. Through debate in the Law Commission, interested groups exchange their opinions. When they reach a consensus, the reform proposal is submitted to the Justice Minister. A new bill on the proposal is subsequently introduced into the Diet.   [3] 900,000 yen is roughly £5,064, or $US8,286.
[4] 300,000 yen is roughly £1,687, or $US2,762.

juvenile cases. They offer family conciliation and adjudicate on various matters, such as declarations of disability and the appointment of a guardian. However, divorce actions are not within their jurisdiction. Divorce actions are commenced in district courts.

The high courts hear appeals from district courts or family courts, and 'leapfrog' appeals from summary courts. The 'leapfrog' or 'jumping' appeal from the summary court is made only if both parties agree to jump the district court (ss. 311 (2), 281 (1) proviso). For those cases commenced in summary courts, the high courts are the courts of final appeal. Appeals are heard in the high court by a three-judge bench.

The Supreme Court stands at the top of the hierarchy of the courts. It deals with appeals from high courts, and 'leapfrog' appeals from district courts. Here again, the 'leapfrog' appeal is made only when both parties agree to jump the high court (ss. 311 (2), 281 (1) proviso). Hearings are held before either the Grand Bench, consisting of all fifteen justices, or by the Petty Benches, which normally consist of five justices (the quorum of the Petty Bench is three: s. 9 (2) of the Courts Act 1947).

In an ordinary civil action, the case goes up from a summary court through a district to a high court, or from a district court through a high court to the Supreme Court (Fig. 7.1).

2.3. The legal profession

A would-be lawyer has to pass the National Bar Examination. It is one of the most difficult national examinations. Over the last ten years, the success rate has only been 2 per cent to 3 per cent. The few candidates who do eventually pass have usually spent several years trying. In 1998, for example, just 812 out of 30,568 candidates passed the Examination. Their average age was 26.90. Most candidates start preparing for the Examination when they are undergraduate students and give up trying by this age.

A person who has succeeded in the National Bar Examination then has to complete two years of training at the Legal Training and Research Institute, a state-funded institution. At the end of the two years, he or she has to pass the final qualifying examination. Then, he or she is appointed as an assistant judge or a public prosecutor, or starts practising as an attorney. An assistant judge is

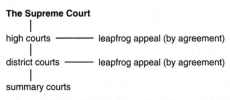

Fig. 7.1. Judicial system in civil cases

restricted to hearing cases as one member of a three-judge panel. He or she is normally promoted to judge after ten years. At this point, he or she is qualified to hear cases as a single-judge court. Thereafter, some judges are promoted to the high court bench, and a small number of them become Supreme Court justices.

Thus, the judiciary of the district court, family court, and the high court is largely composed of so-called 'career judges'. Supreme Court justices are recruited from judges, prosecutors, attorneys, and others, including law professors and ambassadors. Summary court judges are often retired judges.

An attorney (*bengoshi*) has to enrol in one of Japan's local Bar Associations. Together, the Bar Associations constitute the Japan Federation of Bar Associations, which represents the interests of attorneys all over the country.

It should be noted that there is another tier of professionals who deal with legal matters. Judicial scriveners (*shihoshoshi*) are qualified to handle conveyancing and to draft forms to be filed in courts. Although they are not allowed to act as legal representatives in any courts, in summary court cases they are involved to help litigants in person (see s. 2.4.1 below).

2.4. Civil proceedings

2.4.1. *Commencement*

The choice of venue between summary court and district court is determined by the Courts Act 1947. If the value of a claim is up to 900,000 yen, the case should be commenced in the summary court (s. 33 (1) (i) of the Courts Act 1947). A case involving a claim valued at more than 900,000 yen, or a claim to immoveable property, should be commenced in the district court (s. 24 (i) of the Courts Act 1947).

In a district court case, the plaintiff has to file a written complaint with the court (s. 133 (1) of the New Code). The complaint must contain the following matters:

(i)   the names of the parties (plaintiff(s) and defendant(s)) and, if any, their statutory
        guardians (if a party is a minor, his/her parents; if a person is under a disability,
        his/her guardian appointed by the family court); and
(ii) (a) the plaintiff's 'demand', and
(ii) (b) the 'cause of action'. (s. 133 (2) of the New Code)

The plaintiff's 'demand' is the plaintiff's request for a certain judgment. It might be, for example, 'P claims a judgment, ordering D to pay P 1,000,000 yen.' The demand sets the maximum amount which the judge may order in the judgment. In the above example, if the judge were to order D to pay P 1,200,000 yen, this would contravene the law (s. 246 of the New Code) and the appellate court would reverse the judgment.

The plaintiff's 'demand' gives no information as to why the plaintiff sues the defendant, or whether the plaintiff has a valid claim. Therefore in addition a 'cause of action' must be stated. 'Cause of action' means facts that are required to identify the plaintiff's claim against the defendant. According to the traditional view, the cause of action differs depending upon whether the plaintiff relies on a claim under contract or a claim in tort.

The complaint is then served on the defendant (s. 138 (2) of the New Code). Court officials are responsible for service, and the commonest method of service is by post (ss. 98 and 99 of the New Code). When the defendant receives the complaint, the action is deemed to be commenced.

The court in which the action is commenced must immediately set the first hearing date. This date must be within thirty days of the commencement of the action, except where special reasons apply (r. 60 of the New Rules). Once the defendant has received the complaint, he or she must prepare his or her reply, a written statement of defence. This document must be filed with the court in advance of the first hearing (r. 79 (1) of the New Rules). The defendant must also send a copy of the reply to the plaintiff before the hearing, so that the plaintiff can prepare for the arguments which the defendant will raise before the court (r. 83 (1) of the New Rules).

In the summary court, no written complaint need be filed. The plaintiff may go to the court office and commence an action by an oral presentation (s. 271 of the New Code). Under the Old Code, this oral commencement was rarely used. A plaintiff usually filed a complaint, which was often drafted by a judicial scrivener. One of the reasons for this practice was that the Old Code required plaintiffs in the summary court to make clear exactly the same matters as those required in the district court; namely, the names of the parties, their statutory guardians, the demand, and the cause of action. Because it was difficult for an ordinary citizen to state the cause of action clearly, court officials often suggested that the plaintiff see judicial scriveners. Under the New Code, the plaintiff need not state any cause of action, but must make the essence of the case clear (s. 272 of the New Code). This reform was based on the idea that the summary court should be accessible and familiar to ordinary citizens.

2.4.2. Hearings

In the Japanese civil justice system, there is no distinct demarcation between the pre-trial and trial stages. The following features of our civil justice may be noted.

First, a hearing is any occasion on which parties conduct oral argument before the court. In giving judgment, the judge may only take into account facts which the parties presented orally in court. Facts stated only on paper cannot form the basis of a judgment. However, this 'principle of orality' is eroded by the bulk of papers brought into court. In the district court, written statements are compulsory as part of the preparation for hearings (s. 161 of the New Code). Some complicated matters, such as calculations, may be most usefully presented in writing. In addition, since the parties are required to exchange written statements and also file them in court in advance (rr. 79, 83 of the New Rules), it may seem a waste of time to repeat the arguments which are written out in the statements orally at the hearing. For these reasons, it has become common for both parties at the hearing just to say, 'I will state as stated on the written statement.' In practice, neither counsel reads the written statement aloud. The oral reference is sufficient to allow reliance on the written document, without it being read out. Some commentators have complained that this practice reduces hearings to mere rituals for exchanging written documents.

Secondly, the same judge (or judges) should take charge of an action from commencement to final disposal. In principle, the judge conducts all of the hearings and, if necessary, gives the final judgment. In other words, only the judge who conducted the hearings can give judgment (s. 249 (1) of the New Code). If the judge is replaced during the action, perhaps because of a transfer to another court, the parties must state the result of former hearings before a new judge (s. 249 (2) of the New Code; this process is called 'renewal of hearings'). This principle (called 'principle of immediateness', translation of the German *Grundsatz der Unmittelbarkeit*) ensures that the judge can give judgment based on his or her own understanding and direct impression of the case. However, there is another evasion of principle. Although parties are expected to state the summary of former hearings, they never do so. One explanation is that they need not do so because the new judge has already read records of the former hearings. It should also be taken into account that judges and assistant judges usually move to another court every three years or so. It is not infrequent to have a judge changed before judgment is given. Judges may well feel it troublesome to have parties state the summary of former hearings every time a change of judge occurs. The bulk of judicial caseloads puts pressure on judges to dispense with anything that seems dispensable. Thus, in practice, parties make no oral presentation of former hearings before a new judge. A new judge simply says, 'we will renew former hearings' and the parties agree to do so.

Thirdly, hearings must be open to the public. This is required by the Constitution,[5] and is regarded as important for securing fairness in civil justice and maintaining public confidence in the administration of justice. Actually, however, except for a few cases of considerable public concern, only very few people attend civil hearings. Those who do come to court are likely to be friends or relatives of the parties.

At any hearing, the parties present their view of the issues, their arguments,

---

[5] Article 82 states: 'Trials shall be conducted and judgment declared publicly. Where a court unanimously determines publicity to be dangerous to public order or morals, a trial may be conducted privately, but trials of political offenses, offenses involving the press or cases wherein the rights of people as guaranteed in Chapter III of this Constitution are in question shall always be conducted publicly.'

and the facts on which they rely. They may apply for the examination of evidence in order to prove the facts they allege. Evidence consists of testimony (of witnesses, expert witnesses or parties), documentary evidence (e.g. contracts and wills), and real evidence (e.g. goods). Taking account of the importance of the evidence, the judge decides whether or not the examination should be carried out. If the judge thinks fit, even at the earlier hearings, witnesses are called to testify and to be cross-examined. After the examination, the parties may raise new issues and apply for the examination of further evidence. If the judge so orders, another piece of evidence will be examined. Through such repeated presentations of fact and examinations of evidence, the case becomes clearer.

This is the time-honoured method for conducting hearings, and is typical in Japanese civil proceedings. However, this traditional style has proven to be inefficient and time-consuming. For example, in an action P brings against D for payment of debt, suppose P and D argued about whether P lent money to D or to someone else (issue 1). On P's application, witness A was called and testified that A saw D borrow money from P (issue 1 proved). If, at a later hearing, D now agreed that he had borrowed the money from P, but asserted that he had repaid the money through B (issue 2), it would be necessary to call B or someone else to testify. Since issues 1 and 2 give rise to claims by D in his defence which are incompatible, if they were raised at the same time one issue would have had to be dropped. In that event, only one examination would have been required.

The main cause of the problems under the Old Code was that there were no effective methods of cutting down irrelevant issues. Therefore, one of the aims of the recent reform was to establish such apparatus and enable an intensive examination of evidence. For this purpose, the New Code has introduced three modes of procedure for cutting down irrelevant issues and identifying genuine ones (see s. 5 below). It may no longer be so true to say that there is no sharp demarcation between trial and pre-trial stages in Japan, now that the stages of examination of evidence, and preparation for it, are to be distinguished. The Japanese civil justice system may have become closer to that of the common law jurisdictions.

2.4.3. Default

Before 1926, if either party failed to attend the hearing, a default judgment was given against him or her. The unfavourable judgment against that party was a sanction for his or her failure to appear in court. It could be given at any hearing, even if the case up to that point was favourable to the absent party. However, the sanction for default was not very strict. The defaulting party could have the judgment set aside by making application within fourteen days. Then, the action reverted to the state it was in just before the default occurred; and it was simply hoped that the defaulting party would appear in court. Nevertheless, the defaulting party often failed to do so. If another default judgment was given, the party could apply to set it aside once again. Such repeated default judgments and applications for setting aside hindered progress of actions.

This scheme of default judgments was abolished by the 1926 reform. Since then, the following rules have been applied to cases in the district court.

1. If either party fails to attend the first hearing, the action will continue as if the defaulting party were present and had orally stated the contents of any written statements presented to the court in advance (s. 158 of the New Code). In practice, when the defaulting party, especially the defendant, has presented no statements, that party is assumed to have admitted the facts stated by the opposite party (s. 159 (3) of the New Code). On that basis, a judgment against the defaulting party is delivered. This is also called a 'default judgment' but it is distinguished from the 'default judgment' which was abolished, because the modern form is not a sanction against failure to appear.

2. If it is the second or a subsequent hearing that either party fails to attend, the presented written statements of that party, if any, are not taken into account. If they were to be considered, the 'principle of orality' would be almost completely undermined. If the appearing party applies for it, judgment may be given on the present state of the action (s. 244 of the New Code). This possibility was newly created by the recent reform as a means of tackling the delaying tactics of defaulting parties.

2.4.4. *Summary disposal of the action*

The principle of 'party autonomy' carries with it the corollary that the parties may voluntarily dispose of their action. There are four ways in which the parties may choose to end the case, namely:

1. withdrawal of the action;
2. waiver of the claim;
3. admission of the claim; and
4. settlement in court.

The plaintiff may withdraw the action at any time before the final judgment becomes conclusive, provided that the court is notified of the plaintiff's intention to withdraw and, where the defendant has already taken steps to defend the action, his or her consent is obtained (s. 261 of the New Code).

If the plaintiff waives his or her claim, or the defendant admits the plaintiff's claim, the waiver or admission is entered on the official record. Then, the action is terminated and the entry has the same effect as a judgment (s. 267 of the New Code).

In practice, a substantial number of actions are disposed of by way of settlement in court (see s. 3.2). The settlement is reached with the court's involvement, but the degree of its intervention varies from case to case. However, it should be noted that at any stage of the proceedings the court may promote a settlement between the parties (s. 89 of the New Code). The court often offers proposals for compromise and persuades the parties to settle. It was formerly said that a judge should give a judgment rather than a settlement. However, recently, settlement in court has been regarded as one of the most important methods of resolving disputes.

2.4.5. *Judgments and decisions*

Judgments may be interlocutory or final. An interlocutory judgment decides an intermediate issue, such as whether the liability of the defendant in a tort action is established or not (s. 245 of the New Code). In this case, if the interlocutory judgment declares the defendant's liability, the amount of damages is determined by the final judgment later on. No appeal lies against the interlocutory judgment itself. Only if the final judgment is entered, in their appeal against the final judgment, may the parties argue against the interlocutory judgment.

A final judgment determines the principal matter in question and disposes of the whole or part of action (s. 243 of the New Code). In this sense, a default judgment (s. 2.4.3) is a final judgment.

A judgment is prepared in written form, and contains: (i) the order of the court or the conclusion of the court; (ii) the facts on which the judgment is based; (iii) the reasoning which leads to the order; (iv) the date of the final hearing; (v) the parties and their statutory guardians; and (vi) the name of the court (ss. 252, 253 of the New Code).

The order of the court (i) is the court's conclusion in response to the plaintiff's demand. It cannot exceed what the plaintiff claimed as his or her demand in the complaint (as amended up to the conclusion of hearings) (s. 246 of the New Code, see also s. 2.4.1). It is only this part of the order that operates as *res judicata* between the parties or their successors (s. 114 (1) of the New Code).

Final judgments become conclusive when they become unable to be overruled by appellate courts. For example, if no further appeal lies against the judgment, or if it is possible to appeal but the parties have not appealed within the statutory time limit, the judgment becomes conclusive. Conclusiveness is an important concept, because in the Japanese civil justice system a judgment may not be enforced until it becomes conclusive. The only exception arises where the court declares in the judgment itself that the judgment is to be enforced 'temporarily' (s. 259 of the New Code). Such enforcement is 'temporary' in the sense that, if the appellate court overrules the judgment, its enforcement will become void. This declaration of temporary enforcement is compulsory in giving judgment on a money claim based on a bill of exchange or cheque (s. 259 (2) of the New Code). For other claims, the court has discretion (s. 259 (1) of the New Code). Under such a regime, a losing defendant is likely to make a fruitless appeal with a view to delaying enforcement.

'Decisions' are also orders of the court, but are distinguished from judgments.[6] Decisions are given when objections are raised to the judge who is hearing the case, or when incidental matters are in question. For example, an order for immediate examination of evidence (e.g. of a witness who is seriously ill and unable to attend hearings later on) or an order for production of documents is given in the form of a decision. In principle, judgments are given after hearings in open court, whereas decisions may be given without such hearings (s. 87 of the New Code). This is because, in dealing with such incidental matters, a simple and speedy process is considered to be more appropriate.

2.4.6. *Appeals*

The discretionary nature of the declaration of temporary enforcement tends to encourage delay. In addition, the appeal system itself contains causes of delay.

First, parties may appeal twice as of right against a judgment at first instance. The first appeal (*koso*) lies from a summary court to a district court, or from a district court to a high court, as the case may be. Grounds for the first appeal are questions of fact or law. It is an established principle that parties should have a second chance to be tried on questions of fact. If the value of the claim is under a certain amount, no restrictions are imposed on the appeal.[7]

Secondly, the second and final appeal (*jokoku*), which may be made only on legal questions, has raised controversies over the role of the Supreme Court from time to time. The Supreme Court is the court with ultimate responsibility for determining the constitutionality of law,[8] and is also the highest court to provide a unified authoritative interpretation of the law. However, it has not performed its function satisfactorily, because too many cases are brought in the Supreme Court every year (see Table 7.1). As far as civil cases are concerned, one of the reasons for this is that, under the Old Code, the grounds for appeal were too broad. Parties could appeal to the Supreme Court against a judgment of a high court at second instance, or, in the case of a leapfrog appeal, a judgment of a district court at first instance, for violation of the Constitution, for contravention of fundamental procedural rules, or for legal errors that apparently affected the judgment (ss. 393, 394 of the Old Code). For the purpose of alleviating the caseload of the Supreme Court, the recent reform has limited appeals. Under the New Code, parties may no longer appeal as of right to the Supreme Court just on legal errors. An appeal based on error of law in the

---

[6] The distinction between a judgment and a decision was also imported from German law.

[7] By contrast, under the newly introduced small claims procedure, no appeal lies against a judgment (s. 377 of the New Code). However, if the claim is within the jurisdiction of the small claims procedure and the plaintiff wishes to be tried under that simple and speedy procedure, an ordinary procedure is to be commenced immediately upon such an application of the defendant or after a decision of the court on its own motion (s. 373 of the New Code). In that case, an appeal could be made twice against a judgment on a monetary claim not exceeding 300,000 yen.

[8] The Supreme Court is the court of last resort, with power to determine the constitutionality of any law, order, regulation, or official act (Art. 81 of the Constitution).

Table 7.1. *Cases handled by the Supreme Court 1992–1996*

	Civil or administrative cases			Criminal cases		
	Started	Disposed of	Pending	Started	Disposed of	Pending
1992	2,632	2,544	1,760	1,320	1,243	686
1993	2,720	2,778	1,702	1,220	1,251	655
1994	2,984	2,802	1,884	1,339	1,295	699
1995	3,027	2,854	2,057	1,331	1,426	604
1996	3,144	3,112	2,089	1,429	1,443	590

Source: Supreme Court of Japan, *Justice in Japan* (1998), at 21.

lower court's decision will only be heard if, on the application of the intending appellant, the Supreme Court finds that the case involves important matters of the interpretation of the law and accepts the case (s. 318 of the New Code). In establishing this scheme, both the *certiorari* system of the United States Supreme Court, and the appeal with leave of the court of second instance system used in German law, were taken into consideration. The pros and cons of both systems were discussed and, finally, the *certiorari* model was adopted. On the other hand, a second appeal or a leapfrog appeal to a High Court may still be made even for simple legal errors that apparently affect the judgment (s. 312 (3) of the New Code).

The first appeal against a 'decision' (as opposed to a 'judgment') may be made, only when the appeal is statutorily permitted, to the appropriate appellate court. A second appeal lies only if the decision of the appellate court violates the Constitution or the law, and the violation apparently affects the outcome of the decision (s. 330 of the New Code).

Under the Old Code, it was not possible to appeal from a High Court to the Supreme Court purely on legal issues in the decision of the High Court. After the recent reforms, however, parties may appeal against a decision of a high court to the Supreme Court, if the high court permits the appeal on the grounds that the case involves important matters of the interpretation of the law (s. 337 of the New Code). This is because decisions of high courts have recently come to involve important legal matters. Between High Courts there have been conflicts of decisions on important legal questions, which have required authoritative, unified interpretation by the Supreme Court.

2.4.7. Provisional remedies

Provisional remedies help to protect the plaintiff against the risk that an enforceable judgment of the court might come too late, in that the defendant might have become insolvent or might have transferred the property in question to a third party in the meantime. To protect himself or herself from such a risk, the plaintiff is able to use the provisional remedies of temporary attachment (*kari-sashiosae*) and interlocutory injunction (*kari-shobun*). These remedies enable the court to freeze particular assets of the defendant, or to maintain the status quo between the parties. Temporary attachment is used for securing monetary claims; interlocutory injunction is used for non-monetary claims.

The Japanese forms of temporary attachment and interlocutory injunction were originally based on their German equivalents; namely, *Arrest* and *einstweilige Verfügung*. However, in 1989 a new statute of provisional remedies was enacted, and the schemes were remodelled. One of the main objectives of the 1989 Act was to speed up the process of issuing orders for provisional remedies. Under the old regime, if an order for an interlocutory injunction might have serious consequences for the opposite side, the court must hold hearings in open court, give the opposite party an opportunity to be heard, and issue the order in the form of a judgment. This caused delay and reform was required. Under the 1989 Act, on the other hand, all orders are issued in the form of a decision, and hearings in open court are not compulsory. Due to this change, the process is said to have become faster than before.

2.5. Costs

The cost rule is that the loser pays the winner's costs (s. 61 of the New Code). However, it should be noted that the costs so payable do not include lawyers' remuneration. Recoverable costs include court fees, travel allowances for witnesses, expert witnesses, or parties, and so on. The so-called 'American rule' applies; i.e., each party pays their own lawyers' fees.

The court fee which the plaintiff must pay on filing a complaint is fixed by the Costs Act 1971 according to the value of the claim (see Table 7.2). If he or she fails to pay it, the complaint is rejected, unless the court grants to him or her an exemption on the grounds of very limited means (s. 82 of the New Code). When the plaintiff wins, the court orders the defendant to pay the plaintiff's costs in the judgment. The plaintiff is then able to recover the costs through the court process. However, the amount of costs is usually too small to make the troublesome process for recovery worthwhile. Thus, in general, the winner will not recover costs from the loser.

The remuneration of lawyers is regulated by the remuneration code of the Japan Federation of Bar Associations. Under the code, time charging is permitted, but lawyers should normally be paid a fixed fee by reference to the value of the claim. The fixed fee consists of two parts. One is to be paid initially, regardless of the outcome of the case, and the other is to be paid at the end, only if the party wins (see Table 7.3). A partly contingent fee system is thus created.

Legal aid is available for citizens with inadequate means. The legal aid schemes are administered by the Japan Association of Legal Aid, a body set

Table 7.2. *Table of court fees*

For each part of the claim	Fee
For the first part of claim, up to 300,000 yen	500 yen for every 50,000 yen or part thereof
For the part of the claim over 300,000 yen, up to 1,000,000 yen	400 yen for every 50,000 yen or part thereof
For the part of the claim over 1,000,000 yen, up to 3,000,000 yen	700 yen for every 100,000 yen or part thereof
For the part of the claim over 3,000,000 yen, up to 10,000,000 yen	1,000 yen for every 200,000 yen or part thereof
For the part of the claim over 10,000,000 yen, up to 100,000,000 yen	1,000 yen for every 250,000 yen or part thereof
For the part of the claim over 100,000,000 yen, up to 1,000,000,000 yen	3,000 yen for every 1,000,000 yen or part thereof
For the part of the claim over 1,000,000,000 yen	10,000 yen for every 5,000,000 yen or part thereof

Note: At roughly 178 yen to the pound sterling, and 109 yen to the US dollar, 300,000 yen represents about £1,687 or $US2,762. Thus, the fee on the largest case permissible under the small claims procedure in the summary court (300,000 yen) would be 3,000 yen or about £16.87 or $US27.62. The fee charged to file the largest case permitted in the ordinary civil jurisdiction of the Summary Court (900,000 yen or roughly £5,064, or $US8,286) would be 7,800 yen or about £43.82 or $US71.56.

Table 7.3. *Table of attorney's fees by value of the claim* (%)

Part of the claim	Paid regardless of the outcome[a]	Paid if case won[a]
For the first part of claim, up to 3,000,000 yen	8	16
For the part of the claim over 3000,000 yen, up to 30,000,000 yen	5	10
For the part of the claim over 30,000,000 yen, up to 300,000,000 yen	3	6
For the part of the claim over 300,000,000 yen	2	4

[a] Each can be increased or reduced by up to 30%. The minimum amount to be paid, regardless of the outcome, is 100,000 yen. However, if the value of the claim is less than 1,250,000 yen, the fee can be reduced, depending on the circumstances.

up by the Japan Federation of Bar Associations, with subsidies from the state. However, the budget is so tight that eligibility is very limited. In addition, the assisted person must repay the costs, whether he or she recovers money through the action or not. Insufficiency of legal aid, together with the American rule on lawyer remuneration and the lack of legal expenses insurance, has discouraged claimants of modest means from starting litigation.

3. CIVIL JUSTICE VIEWED FROM STATISTICAL DATA

3.1. General information on statistical data

The following data are mainly extracted from *The Annual Report of Judicial Statistics*, i: *Civil Cases*, which is published every year by the General Secretariat of the Supreme Court, based on monthly reports from all the courts. Other statistical data are shown with their sources.

The *Annual Report* includes various information on court activities. The most fundamental information is the number of actions started in the year, actions carried over from the previous year, actions disposed of within the year, and actions carried over to the next year. The aggregate of actions started in a certain court in a certain year and actions carried over from the previous year in the court gives the total actions that were handled by the court during the year. Comparing the number of actions handled and those disposed of by the same court during the same year gives the measure of that court's performance, in terms of disposal of actions, for the given year. The General Secretariat of the Supreme Court is thus well informed of the performance of each court every year. Since the Supreme Court exercises a supervisory power over the inferior court judges and officials, including the power to make personnel appointments and transfers (s. 80 (i) of the Courts Act 1947), judges and court officials might well be encouraged to improve their performance.

Data available at the time of writing all pertain to practice under the Old Code. However, the data of the last ten years of the old practice are of significance. From the late 1980s, commentators were warning that civil justice was not accessible to the public in Japan. Various campaigns for speedy and satisfactory civil justice were launched, including the movement which led to the recent reforms. For this reason, as far as court activities are concerned, data between 1988 and 1997 are listed below.

3.2. Actions started and disposed of between 1988 and 1997

Figs. 7.2 and 7.3 show how many actions the district courts and summary courts handled between 1988 and 1997. The number of actions started in the year is

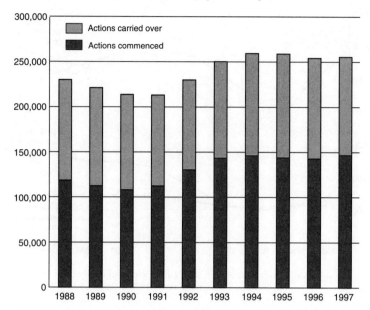

Fig. 7.2. Actions commenced and carried over in district courts 1988 to 1997

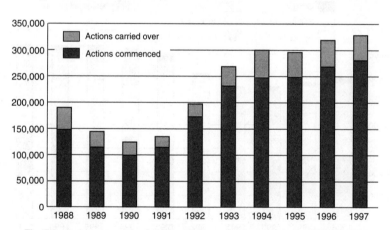

Fig. 7.3. Actions commenced and carried over in summary courts 1988 to 1997

counter-cyclical to economic fluctuations. In the 1980s business was brisk, but the number of actions brought into court was decreasing. Since 1991, when the economic boom came to an end, civil actions have been increasing. This trend is especially apparent for civil actions in summary courts, and applications for payment orders there (see Fig. 7.4).

Figs. 7.5 and 7.6 show how actions were disposed of during the ten years in question. It should be noted that the number of actions started in the year (see

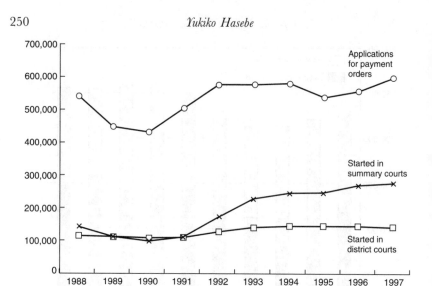

Fig. 7.4. Actions commenced in district courts and in summary courts and applications for payment order 1988 to 1997

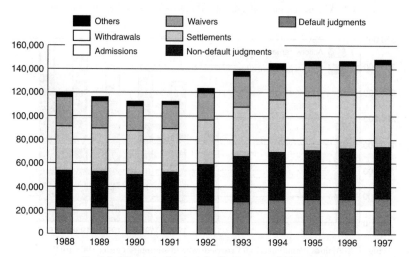

Fig. 7.5. Disposal of actions in district courts 1988 to 1997

Figs. 7.2 and 7.3) tends to be almost the same as the number of actions disposed of within the year (see Figs. 7.5 and 7.6). This is remarkable, given that the number of judges remained almost unchanged during the period. The courts seem to make an effort not to allow a backlog of actions to develop.

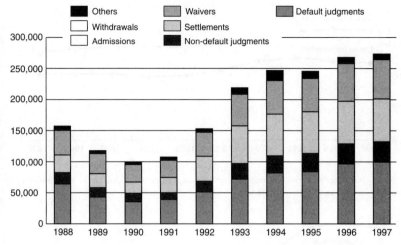

Fig. 7.6. Disposal of actions in summary courts 1988 to 1997

3.3. Average duration of actions at first instance

Figs. 7.7 and 7.8 show the average duration of actions in district courts and summary courts.[9] The time taken from commencement became shorter both in cases disposed of within the year and those carried over to the next year. This could be the result of campaigns for speedy trials and/or a consequence of the need for quicker disposal being acted on by the courts, as the number of actions increased.

3.4. Number of appeals

Figs. 7.9–7.12 show the numbers of appeals. Appeals from district courts, as courts of first instance, to high courts were increasing in number (see Fig. 7.9). The appeal rate was between 20 per cent and 25 per cent. (Compare the number of appeals started in Fig. 7.9 and the number of judgments in Fig. 7.5.)

As for appeals from summary courts to district courts, see Fig. 7.10. The appeal rate has fallen since 1991. In 1997, the rate was 1.5 per cent (compare the number of appeals started in Fig. 7.10 and the number of judgments in Fig. 7.6).

As for appeals from high courts to the Supreme Court (see Fig. 7.11), the appeal rate was between 30 per cent and 35 per cent.[10] 'Special appeal' means

---

[9] The data on the average duration of actions are taken from Civil Affairs Bureau of the General Secretariat, Supreme Court, 'A Survey of Civil Actions in the Year of 1997', *Hoso Joho* (Lawyers' Association Journal) 50/11 (Nov. 1998) (hereinafter cited as 'Survey').

[10] See Survey at 45.

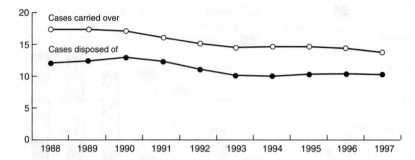

Fig. 7.7. Average duration of actions in district courts 1988 to 1997
Note: Showing average time since commencement for cases disposed of during the year, and average age of cases carried over into the next year.

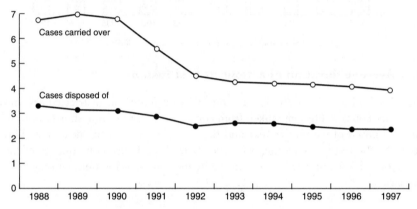

Fig. 7.8. Average duration of actions in summary courts
Note: Showing average time since commencement for cases disposed of during the year, and average age of cases carried over into the next year.

an appeal from a high court as a court of third instance (hearing an appeal of a case commenced in a summary court) to the Supreme Court on the grounds of violation of the Constitution (ss. 409a, 409b of the Old Code; s. 327 of the New Code). Normally, a high court is the final court for a judgment given in a summary court.

As for appeals from district courts to high courts as courts of third instance (where the high court is asked to hear a second appeal from the judgment originally given in a summary court), see Fig. 7.12. The appeal rate was over 30 per cent until 1995, but since then has been just below 30 per cent.[11]

---

[11] Survey at 49.

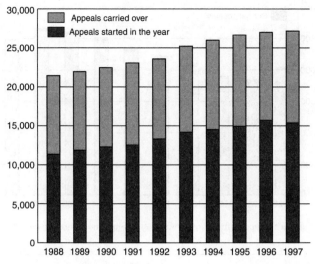

Fig. 7.9. Number of appeals from district courts to high courts between 1988 and 1997

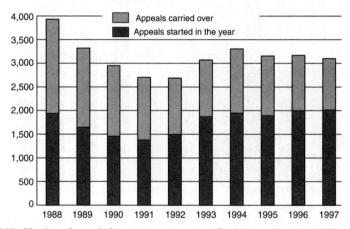

Fig. 7.10. Number of appeals from summary courts to district courts between 1988 and 1997

3.5. Average duration of appeals

Fig. 7.13 shows the average duration of appeals from summary courts to district courts.[12]

As for other appeals, available data are limited. In 1997, the average duration of appeals from district courts to high courts as courts of second instance

---

[12] For the data, see Survey at 57–8.

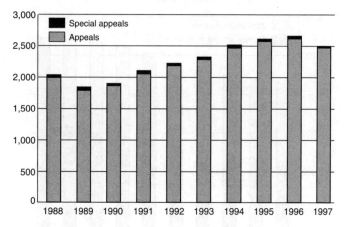

Fig. 7.11. Number of appeals from high courts to the Supreme Court between 1988 and 1997

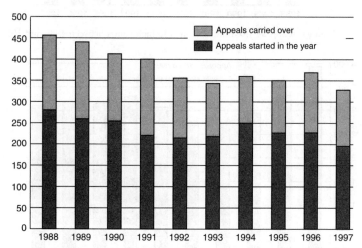

Fig. 7.12. Number of appeals in summary court cases against the result of district court appeals, brought up in the High Court (as a court of third instance) between 1988 and 1997

was 9.9 months and, as courts of third instance, was 7.6 months.[13] In the same year, the average duration of appeals from high courts to the Supreme Court was 9.5 months.[14]

3.6. Number of judges

As of November 1997, the numbers of courts and judges are as shown in Table 7.4.[15]

[13] See Survey at 51.   [14] Ibid., at 46.
[15] See Supreme Court of Japan, *Justice in Japan*, at 30, 31, 33, and 36.

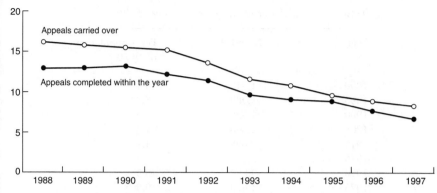

Fig. 7.13. Average duration of appeals from summary courts to district courts 1988–1997
Note: Showing average time since commencement for cases disposed of during the year, and average age of cases carried over into the next year.

Table 7.4. *Numbers of courts and judges*

	No. of courts	No. of judges
Summary courts	438	*c.*810 summary court judges
District courts	50 (with 203 branch offices)	*c.*910 judges, 530 assistant judges
Family courts	50 (adjunct to district courts); 203 branch offices (adjunct to branch offices of district courts); 77 local offices	*c.*200 judges, 150 assistant judges
High courts	8 (with 6 branch offices)	*c.*280 judges
Supreme Court	1	15 justices

3.7. Number of practising lawyers

Table 7.5 and Fig. 7.14 show the number of practising attorneys has changed over time, since the late nineteenth century. It has been pointed out that the number of attorneys is too small compared with other countries. At the end of 1997, the number of attorneys in Japan was 16,340. Since the population of Japan in 1997 was 126,166,000, there were approximately 13 attorneys for every 100,000 people in Japan in that year. In response to the criticism, the number of candidates who pass the National Bar Examination has gradually been increased. In 1991, the number was raised from 500 to 600, and in 1993, from 600 to 700. In 1999, the number is to be increased to 1,000. At the same time, the training period will become shorter, from two years to eighteen months.

Table 7.5. *Number of practising lawyers since 1890*

Year	Number	Per a population of 100,000
1890	1,345	3.4
1895	1,589	3.8
1900	1,590	3.6
1905	2,008	4.3
1910	2,008	4.1
1915	2,486	4.7
1920	3,082	5.5
1925	5,673	9.5
1930	6,599	10.2
1935	7.075	10.2
1940	5,498	7.6
1945	—	—
1950	5,883	8.2
1955	5,909	6.6
1960	6,327	6.8
1965	7,108	7.2
1970	8,520	8.2
1975	10,146	9.1
1980	11,494	9.9
1985	12,937	10.7
1990	14,173	11.5
1995	15,498	12.3
1997	16,340	13

Source: Kaneko and Takeshita, *Saiban hou* (Administration of Justice)
(3rd edn., 1994), Yuhikaku; Jiyu to Seigi (Liberty & Justice, Journal of
Japan Federation of Bar Associations) 2 (1996) and 2 (1998).

4. MAJOR PROBLEMS

Some of the problems encountered in the administration of civil justice have already been mentioned above. These include the delaying tactics used by losing parties under the present system of enforcement of judgments (see ss. 2.4.5 and 2.4.6) and the unsatisfactory legal aid system (see s. 2.5). In this section, another fundamental issue needs to be discussed; namely, the restrictive practices of the legal profession.

As shown in section 3.7, the number of practising lawyers is small in proportion to the population. In addition, they are concentrated in several large cities. Consequently, people in rural areas have difficulty in finding lawyers.

Even in large cities, such as Tokyo, it is not easy for an ordinary citizen to

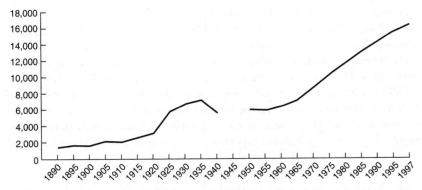

Fig. 7.14. Number of practising attorneys

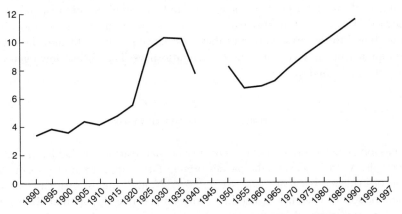

Fig. 7.15. Number of practising attorneys per 100,000 of population

retain his or her lawyer. Practising lawyers do not take on the case of a stranger without a reference. Therefore, in order to retain a lawyer, it is necessary to have friends or relatives who are lawyers, or at least who know lawyers.

Practising lawyers also hold a statutorily secured monopoly on legal affairs. The Attorneys Act 1949 provides that a person who is not an attorney shall not deal with legal affairs, including representation in litigation (s. 72). Violation is punished by imprisonment or a fine of up to 1,000,000 yen (s. 79). Therefore, judicial scriveners (see s. 2.3) who are legally trained and qualified for conveyancing and preparing forms to be filed in courts are excluded from legal representation. A company has to retain a practising lawyer to take or defend civil proceedings, even if it has a group of excellent in-house legal staff who read law in prestigious universities and have expertise in company law.

Owing to the scarcity of practising attorneys, and their monopoly, ordinary citizens have no choice of legal representatives. Further, because advertisement by attorneys is restricted by their code of practice, clients have little information on their specialities and remuneration. Uncertainty about legal fees prevents ordinary citizens from going to law.

The restrictive practices of attorneys have also affected conduct in civil proceedings. First, the rate of litigants in person is substantial. In 1997, cases including litigants in person on either or both sides amounted to 58 per cent of all district court civil cases.[16] As for summary court civil cases, the figure was 99 per cent, and, in 90 per cent of all summary court cases, both parties were litigants in person.[17] Judges are expected to intervene to assist litigants in person where necessary.

Secondly, incompetent attorneys survive because they have no competition. Judges should also sometimes intervene to assist them. This is because, without their intervention, parties represented by inadequate attorneys are at a disadvantage, through no fault of their own, and the administration of justice is harmed. However, it is also true that judges' paternalistic intervention has contributed to the preservation of these restrictive practices. Behind the delay and inefficiency in civil justice lie inactive attorneys. They bring down general standards of practice.

5. HISTORICAL PERSPECTIVE OF REFORM

It has long been a tradition of our civil justice that hearings are held at monthly intervals. At each hearing, the parties present facts and, if necessary, examination of evidence is carried out (see s. 2.4.2). Neither intensive discussion nor examination of evidence is feasible. However, no one doubts that this is inefficient and causes delay. Several attempts have been made over the last few decades to cut down irrelevant issues, and to achieve intensive trials. There have been repeated attempts to find an effective device for identifying genuine and relevant issues in the case.

1. The Old Code provided for a special procedure (*jumbi-tetsuzuki*), which may be translated as 'pre-hearing conference'. However, despite repeated attempts to facilitate this procedure, it was rarely used in practice. Frequently suggested causes are as follows:

   (*a*) Under the Old Code, if a party failed to present some facts and evidence in this procedure, he or she was not allowed to produce them in later hearings. Therefore, parties tended to present too many facts in this procedure just in case. As a result, management of the case became even more difficult.

---

[16] *The Annual Report of Judicial Statistics for 1997*, i: *Civil Cases*, table 31.   [17] Ibid., table 18.

(*b*) Under this procedure, the judge had no power to make examinations of evidence. He or she was obliged to grasp the case just from the facts stated by the parties on the complaint and defence. This prevented him or her from deciding with confidence which facts were really relevant.

(*c*) Because of the difficulties mentioned in (*a*) and (*b*), it required much experience to manage this procedure. Nevertheless, the judges assigned to this procedure were relatively young and inexperienced. The underlying idea was that the courts were too busy to spare experienced judges to do such preparatory work. This proved to be a fatal mistake.

2. In the late 1980s another attempt was made. This time, no new statutory provisions were passed. Instead, the judges invented a new procedure in their daily practice. Courts in large cities first took the initiative. Following their success, similar movements spread nation-wide. The new procedure, called *benron-ken-wakai*, which means 'hearing and conference for settlement', was literally a hearing but also a conference for settlement. It aimed to cut down facts and evidence to what was most relevant and/ or to promote settlement between the parties. Despite being a hearing, it took place in private, outside the courtroom. The reason was that a private and informal atmosphere was appropriate in this procedure. It was said that, in this informal procedure, the judge, parties, and their counsel were able to have a frank and fruitful discussion and easily reach settlement. Further, because the procedure had no statutory basis, judges could make flexible use of it. Its practical use could vary from court to court and from judge to judge. In one court, for example, this procedure might be used mainly for settlement, and in another court the purpose could be either promoting settlement or preparing for intensive hearings. This pragmatic approach was so popular among judges that the new procedure spread rapidly.

However, some academics were cautious about this thriving practice. They argued that, behind closed doors, judges are likely to become more dictatorial and force the parties or their counsel to accept the judges' settlement proposals. They also pointed out that in this procedure the judges often met separately with each party. In the common style, the procedure was as follows. First, only one party was called in and talked about his or her case to the judge. After he or she left the room, the other party came in and told his or her case to the judge.[18] During this process, neither party was informed of what the other party had told the judge. This method is commonly used in settlement, but, if it is used in a hearing, the academics argued, procedural fairness could be eroded.

---

[18] This style is similar to a 'caucus' in mediation.

As the critics claimed, most judges until then did not distinguish two different facets of the procedure: a hearing for narrowing down facts and evidence; and a conference for settlement. They preferred their hybrid procedure because it enabled them to grasp the whole picture of the case, get rid of irrelevant issues, and promote settlement, all on the same hearing date. The informal atmosphere, they thought, was an essential factor for all of these purposes. It was more important for judges to dispose of each case quickly than to respect formalities.

In any event, it was apparent that the lack of any statutory provisions to govern this procedure allowed judges to use it arbitrarily. Therefore, the New Code has introduced three modes of preparatory procedure to identify genuine issues of the case, namely:

(*a*) preparatory hearing (ss. 164–7);

(*b*) preparatory procedure for hearing (ss. 168–74); and

(*c*) preparatory procedure by written statements (ss. 175–8).

3. It is for the court to decide which procedure is suitable for the case, after consulting both parties. Features of the three procedures are as follows:

(*a*) The 'preparatory hearing' is held in public, because it is designed for matters of public concern. A typical example is an environmental pollution case. A labour dispute is also considered to be suitable, because in such a case a large number of people are interested in the court process. What the employee (plaintiff) claims, and how the employer (defendant) responds to it, are important to the group of employees supporting the plaintiff. Therefore, the procedure should be open to them. This is the basic idea on which this procedure is framed.

(*b*) The 'preparatory procedure for hearing' takes place in a closed room. It may be seen as a statutory version of the former 'hearing and conference for settlement'. However, equipped with statutory provisions, the new procedure has now avoided most of the criticisms that its predecessor was faced with.

One of the most significant provisions is s. 169 of the New Code. It states in its subsection 1 that the procedure takes place at the date when both parties are able to appear in court, which means that two-party face-to-face talks are ensured. This should be compared with the 'hearing and conference for settlement' which, not infrequently, took a separate meeting style.

Further, subsection 2 allows the opening of the closed door to non-parties in certain situations. This subsection should be noted, because it is the outcome of fierce debate during the forming of the legislation. In the consultation paper on the reform of civil procedure published in

December 1991, there were no proposals for making this procedure open to non-parties. At this stage, the Ministry of Justice designed the procedure as a revised version of the failed 'pre-hearing conference' (see 1). Since the pre-hearing conference was a procedure held in private, the Ministry of Justice did not refer to the possibility of opening the procedure to other persons.

By contrast, the Bar Associations insisted that the procedure should be open to the public. They also argued that the examination of documentary evidence should not occur in this procedure. The reason for this was that the examination of documents is an important process, through which the judge's view of the case is formed. If the procedure takes place in private, they argued, the judge should not examine documentary evidence. However, this is unreasonable because, in order to identify genuine issues, it is often necessary to read documents such as a contract. As we have seen in (1), the 'pre-hearing conference' failed partly because no examination of evidence was permitted there. Therefore, it was natural that the bar later conceded the examination of documents issue. In its stead, they came to press the principle of publicity more and more.

However, the bar had to make another compromise on the publicity issue. The Ministry of Justice and the judiciary favoured proceeding in private, for the sake of frankness in discussion. The idea of holding the preparatory procedure in open court did not win much support. Instead of absolute openness, openness with leave of the court was finally adopted.

As a consequence of the above debate, s. 169 (2) clearly states two points. First, the court may permit such a person as it thinks fit to come into the closed room and observe the court process. Secondly, if either party nominates someone as such a person, the court shall accept it, unless it might hinder the smooth progress of the procedure. The second point was inserted at the request of the Bar Associations as a proviso to the first point.

(*c*) If the parties or their legal representatives live far away from the court and it is difficult for them to appear in court, the court refers the action to the 'preparatory procedure by written statements' (s. 175 of the New Code). When this procedure is used, the court may identify genuine issues and cut down irrelevant ones without the parties' appearance, based solely on the written statements submitted to the court. The court may also consult both parties by holding a telephone conference, which takes place by using a tripartite telephone apparatus (s. 176 (3) of the New Code).

6. ASSESSMENT OF THE PRESENT STATE OF CIVIL JUSTICE

The reader may wonder why the Bar Associations insisted on the principle of publicity so persistently. As we have seen in section 2.4.2, very few people in Japan attend court proceedings. Does that principle really contribute towards securing fairness in civil justice? Is it not anachronistic to adhere to a principle that was developed in the French Revolution? If the parties are discouraged from discussing their case in public, the process need not be open to the public. Behind closed doors, the parties can express themselves better, the judge and the parties can more easily reach a common understanding on the case, and, consequently, the dispute can be resolved expeditiously. No one is harmed. On the contrary, everyone is satisfied.

It seems that this utilitarianism was the keynote of the recent reform. Certainly, as far as the statistical data show, the disposal of civil cases had become faster in the last ten years, during which time the 'hearing and conference for settlement', the procedure in private, spread nationwide. As far as utilitarianism prevails, another version of informalization, such as the 'preparatory procedure and conference for settlement', which takes place in private, could be possible. Even the 'hearing and conference for settlement', which, some commentators claim, should not currently be used, could persist under the New Code.

But, when all the proceedings become informal, and no longer bound by formalities written in law, is the quality of justice really unharmed? Is it the accessible and plain justice which the reform aimed at? I am afraid that such informality and secrecy will in fact cause people to lose confidence in civil justice in the long term.

It should be also noted that, in Japan, it is the pre-trial judge himself or herself who delivers the eventual judgment. Therefore, if the parties feel that the judge is unfair, they may not point it out for fear of receiving an unfavourable judgment. When the party is a litigant in person, or is represented by an incompetent attorney, the gap between the party and the judge in terms of ability to manage will be even wider. The parties will be placed in the most vulnerable situation. In Japan, therefore, it is all the more important to recognize and appreciate the real significance of traditional procedural principles.[19]

---

[19] In June 1999, a bill to set up a Commission on Reform of the Judicial System passed the Diet. The Commission's terms of reference include ensuring speedier civil justice and expanding the present legal aid system. The Commission is supposed to submit its report to the Cabinet within two years. It remains to be seen what will happen to access to justice for ordinary Japanese people in the future.

8

Civil Justice and its Paradoxes: An Italian Perspective

Sergio Chiarloni

1. ACCESS TO JUSTICE: AN UNRESOLVED PROBLEM

In Italy there seems to be a sharp contrast between the law as it is written in the books and its operation in reality. Article 24 of the Italian Constitution (*Costituzione*) gives every citizen the right to take legal action in the courts to protect his or her rights and interests. Further, Article 24 requires the state to provide legal aid to those who cannot otherwise afford legal proceedings. Yet, the reality is very different from these declamations. In practice, whenever the provision of access to justice proves difficult, the state fails to take adequate measures to overcome the difficulties.

To begin with, one of the major obstacles to access to justice is a lack of information. In Italy few measures have been taken to overcome this problem. In certain other EC countries greater efforts have been made in this regard. For example, in France a law dated 10 July 1991 promotes the dissemination of information about citizens' rights and duties through the establishment of citizens' rights bureaux. Such bureaux not only offer information about rights, they also give advice about the most suitable means for individuals to protect their interests. Help is given with the making of applications and with simple transactions. Similarly, in the UK the Lord Chancellor's Department provides help with forms and brochures written in simple language, so as to enable citizens to conduct cases themselves in the small claims court.[1]

In Italy the lack of information is partially due to strong resistance from members of the legal profession, a powerful lobby, to sharing their forensic knowledge with members of the general public. The lack of information about the operation of the law has one inevitable consequence. Access to justice is only available through lawyers, even in those cases where citizens could potentially

This paper was initially translated into English by Marita Freddi and subsequently revised by Sue Gibbons, to both of whom the author is grateful.

[1] In Italy, despite parliamentary lack of interest, in a few places judges have taken measures to improve the quality of the administration of justice. In the Court of Turin, for instance, we have recently witnessed the birth of an organization devoted to informing couples who intend to separate or divorce about their legal position and assisting them with resolving matters so as to reach a mutually agreed solution. In this way, couples are enabled to protect their rights without expensive legal representation. In Turin, for instance, about 25% of separations by mutual consent take place without the involvement of lawyers.

represent themselves, as in 'small claims' cases and divorce proceedings by mutual consent.

In such a situation, one might at least expect that poor citizens would be granted access to justice by way of legal aid from the state. But this is not the case. Formerly, in Piedmont a so-called 'poor person's lawyer' existed, structured as a civil servant like the public prosecutor. This office was introduced in the unified territories, but suppressed soon after Italian unification during the 1860s, due to claimed budgetary constraints. From unification until 1973, poor people wishing to litigate had to rely solely on the goodwill of lawyers, all of whom had a duty to represent them for free. Needless to say, the quality of the representation they received was typically very poor. In 1973 and 1990 laws were enacted providing for legal aid in the form of state payment of lawyers' fees. But the criteria for eligibility to receive legal aid are so stringent that very few indeed have been able to benefit. Legal aid today is available only to those who earn less than £3,500 a year. It is accordingly not surprising that the public expenditure on legal aid in Italy is less than one-hundredth of that in England.

2. THE DETERIORATION OF ORDINARY PROCEEDINGS IN CIVIL JUSTICE

In modern society, civil justice is a service which the state offers to citizens. In Italy, however, civil justice contrasts sharply with other state services. Its quality has increasingly deteriorated since Italian unification in the 1860s. Judicial statistics show that the total number of proceedings has vastly decreased since the 1860s, while the proportion of abandoned proceedings has progressively increased.

The Italian civil process is largely useless to citizens who ask for justice. As an Italian Senate Committee itself admitted, the original mechanism of the civil process has been replaced by 'a complex celebration of obscure and often indecorous rituals'[2] which delay justice. The party in the wrong may hide behind the extremely long duration of the process. The party whose claim is right has one sole weapon: appealing to the European Court of Human Rights in Strasbourg for the condemnation of the Italian government for failing to provide a process of reasonable duration.[3] Ironically, so many hundreds of applications are pending before the Strasbourg Court by Italian citizens that the reasonable duration of that Court's process is now at risk.[4]

---

[2] See *Rivista trimestrale di diritto e procedura civile* (1986), 318 ff.

[3] Art. 67(1) of the European Convention for the Protection of Human Rights and Fundamental Freedoms confers a right to trial 'within a reasonable time'.

[4] See B. Capponi, ' "Giudice di pace" e "arbitrato" nella reforma del processo civile', *Giustizia civile*, 2 (1989), 360. See also, by the same author, 'Giustizia civile: nuovi modelli verso l'Europa?', *Foro italiano*, 5 (1993), excerpt, 8–9.

Civil justice difficulties are spreading in many countries.[5] The volume of litigation is exploding while, inevitably, budget constraints preclude the introduction of adequate measures to cope with this explosion by increasing personnel and structures. In Italy, however, the causes of civil justice difficulties are different and must be sought elsewhere. Striving to find them means focusing our attention first upon the past.

3. THE EVOLUTION OF PROCEDURAL SCIENCE

Italian civil procedure has progressively evolved into a modern procedural discipline, influenced by principles developed in German jurisprudential thought since the second half of the nineteenth century. The starting point of this evolution was the 1865 Italian Code of Civil Procedure. The 1865 Code (an improved version of the French Napoleonic Code) was clearly inspired by the concept of minimal state intervention. Under this Code, control over the litigation process was left entirely to the parties, i.e. to their lawyers. Parties were left free to struggle within the judicial arena in front of a judge whose passivity was considered to be a guarantee of impartiality. At the same time, the 1865 Code was encumbered with procedural formalities, remnants of the ancient origins of its French model.

For instance, within the so-called *rito degli incidenti*, '*sentenze interlocutorie*' (judgments on interlocutory issues) were misused to produce separate decisions on the upcoming issues in a proceeding. The result was a fragmentation of proceedings, which might become delayed by appeals from these interlocutory judgments at many different stages. This complication survived even the 1901 reform, which greatly extended the application of summary proceedings as an alternative way to solve disputes.[6]

Inevitably, jurists started to oppose such a discipline, regardless of its functional effectiveness. The academic culture, indeed, had begun to consider various foreign models. Many jurists were influenced by the German juridical renaissance. A single charismatic intellectual, Giuseppe Chiovenda, is recognized as the father of modern civil procedure in Italy. Chiovenda elaborated a system which was based on German procedural concepts. The first and most important of these was the principle of orality, which carried with it many other innovations: the attribution to the judge of strong powers to direct proceedings and to find the truth; the simplification of procedural formalities; the concentration in the same judge of the functions of gathering evidence and giving judgment; the organization of parties' arguments and evidence into stages; and

---

[5] See G. C. Hazard, 'Per un approccio manageriale al problema dei ritardi nell'amministrazione della giustizia', *Rivista trimestrale di diritto e procedura civile* (1989), 961 ff.

[6] See M. Taruffo, *La giustizia civile in Italia dal '700 a oggi* (Bologna, 1980), 150 ff.

the abolishing of appeals against interlocutory judgments. The orality principle introduced strong features of publicity into civil proceedings, contributing to the transformation of our country from a purely liberal state into a welfare state.

Giuseppe Chiovenda's work influenced Italian civil procedural culture deeply, leaving a significant mark on the new Code of Civil Procedure. The new Code was introduced in 1940 and came into effect in 1942. This period, right in the middle of the Second World War, turned out to be the worst possible time to introduce a reform aimed at radically changing the consolidated traditions of the legal profession. Immediately after the war, the new Code was denounced as authoritarian and fascist, and its abrogation was requested.

In 1950 certain changes were partially introduced by the legislature. The importance of orality was diminished by allowing the written exchange of pleadings. In practice, this has become the standard procedure. The parties were permitted to present further allegations and defences and new evidence until the final decision. The concentration of proceedings was jeopardized by allowing the parties to appeal immediately against decisions upon issues arising within the proceedings.

The legal academics disapproved of these modifications. In the 1970s new legislation concerning labour suits was introduced, due to the increasing slowness of the ordinary civil justice mechanism. The new labour dispute procedure revived Chiovenda's proposals. Its principles are, once again, those of orality, simplification, rigid ordering of party activity, concentration, and immediacy.

This reform also presented an opportunity to begin a more general reform, including an amendment of the rules relating to ordinary proceedings, the rationalization of the courts, and the reform of the system of honorary judges. More than twenty years have been required to achieve these goals. New *justices of the peace* took office in 1993, superseding the old *giudice conciliatore* (discussed below). The minor courts were rationalized in 1989, abolishing those with a minimal caseload. The new version of the Code of Civil Procedure was finally completed in 1995, after a long and tortuous course. The length of time taken to introduce this revised Code was mainly due to the violent opposition of lawyers. The profession objected to the introduction of strict timetables designed to control the progress of litigation and to combat dilatory practices.

4. THE PARADOX OF CIVIL JUSTICE

If we shift our attention from procedural reforms in theory to an empirical view of the administration of justice, we must face a paradox: quality of service has fallen following procedural modernization in Italy.

4.1. The drastic reduction in first instances cases

Since the 1890s, the administration of justice has been changing in Italy. Judicial statistics show a startling reduction in the number of disputes. In 1894, Italian citizens brought nearly 2.5 million civil actions. In 1994 they went to law in only 1.3 million cases. Such a great change is even more surprising if we consider that the Italian population has approximately doubled since 1894.[7]

This reduction in civil actions is a consequence of the progressive elimination of small claims from the courts. From the 1860s until 1990, when the office was abolished, the so-called *conciliatore* (an honorary judge who was chosen from among the bourgeoisie) dealt with small claims. At the beginning of the twentieth century, he was at the height of his importance, judging about 80 per cent of civil cases. Thereafter, the role of the *conciliatore* slowly declined. His jurisdiction, based on the nominal value of the case, was not increased in line with inflation. After the Second World War, the importance of the *conciliatore* declined to the point where he was hearing a mere 5 per cent of civil cases, leading to a disappearance of small claims from court.[8] In the meantime there has been, especially in the last twenty years, an increase of proceedings before the professional judges, especially due to the introduction of divorce and of a new discipline in labour disputes.

4.2. The increase in appeals to the *Corte di Cassazione*

The *Corte di Cassazione* is the Italian Supreme Court. This court oversees the uniform interpretation of the law throughout Italy. The number of appeals to the *Corte di Cassazione* has increased dramatically over the last thirty years. Just over 3,000 appeals were submitted annually during the 1960s. The number has now grown to more than 17,000 per year. This increase in workload has had two consequences: decisions are delayed; and, importantly, the uniform interpretation of the law is lost, due to the large number of judges required. Thus, the *Corte di Cassazione* is no longer able to guarantee the equal treatment of parties throughout the country, the predictability of its decisions, and the high prestige of its members as supreme judges. Instead, the court has become a sort of judicial supermarket, wherein lawyers can often be sure to find any precedent they need to plead the case of their client.[9]

---

[7] Data up to 1974 in G. Cecchi, *Analisi statistica dei procedimenti civili di cognizione in Italia* (Bari, 1975), most recent data in ISTAT annual reports.

[8] On the serious consequences of this, see A. Rossi, 'Giustizia minore e giudice laico nell'emergenza del settore civile', *Questione giustizia* (1988), 1 ff.

[9] See S. Chiarloni, 'Efficacia del precedente giudiziario e tipologia dei contrasti di giurisprudenza', *Rivista trimestrale di diritto e procedura civile* (1989); id., *Formalismi e garanzie* (Turin, 1995), 52 ff. G. Moneta, *Conflitti giurisprudenziali in Cassazione: i contrasti della Cassazione civile dal settembre 1993 al dicembre 1994* (Padua, 1995).

4.3. The increase in the duration of proceedings

Between 1865 and 1942, under the discipline of the 1865 Code, proceedings lasted a shorter time than the comparable proceedings since 1942. The brevity of proceedings under the old 1865 Code seems incredible when compared to the present duration of civil proceedings. In 1900, *pretura* proceedings (minor court proceedings) lasted, on average, 55 days, while higher court proceedings lasted, on average, 116 days. By 1940, the duration of both proceedings had increased, but only up to 176 and 215 days respectively.

Proceedings before the *conciliatore* were even shorter. At the beginning of the twentieth century, they lasted only a few days on average. By 1940 they lasted a little more than two months. In many ways, the old *conciliatore* procedure was 'modern' already. The procedural rules were particularly simple, free of formalities, and more adaptable. Moreover, there was a *conciliatore's* office in each municipality, and people could appear in front of a *conciliatore* on their own behalf.

Immediately after the Second World War, under the new Code of 1942, the duration of ordinary proceedings increased dramatically. The latest available statistics date back to 1994. At this time, the average duration of first instance civil proceedings was estimated as 1,204 days.

4.4. The low number of judgments on the merits

Another singular feature of the Italian civil justice system is the small proportion of actions which end in a judgment on the merits of the case. Most proceedings are abandoned, generally due to party inactivity. Thus, in 1994, of 1,080,933 concluded cases, only 376,546 proceedings (about 35 per cent) ended in a decision on the merits.

Even more peculiarly, during the first decades of the application of the much-maligned 1865 Civil Procedure Code, the proportion of proceedings which ended with a judgment was much higher: 76.3 per cent from 1891 to 1990; and over 60 per cent in the years 1931–40. Under the new Code, the proportion fell to 35.4 per cent in the years 1951–60, with a slight improvement in succeeding years.[10]

4.5. The inefficienty of the enforcement of judgment

The creditor to whom an execution judgment has been granted must seek help from the state if the debtor does not agree to pay the debt. The ordinary execution process is weak.[11] In 1987, out of a total adjudicated debt of 1,600

---

[10] See Cecchi, *Analisi statistica*, 90, table 23.

[11] See M. Taruffo, 'Note sul diritto alla condanna e all'esecuzione', *Rivista critica di diritto privato* (1986), 635 ff.

billion lire, the amount recovered by execution processes was only about 300 billion lire.[12]

The sum awarded in proceedings concerning moveable goods was 770 billion lire, with an average duration of proceedings of 335 days. However, the proportion of debt actually recovered was only 6.21 per cent. The amount awarded in proceedings concerning real estate was 815 billion lire, with a higher recovered proportion of 37.03 per cent, but with the almost incredible mean proceedings duration of 1,508 days (over four years).

5. A FIRST LESSON COMING FROM THE PARADOX

The emerging truth is surprising. At the end of the nineteenth century, under the much-maligned 1865 Code, the administration of civil justice was conducted according to standards which now appear far out of reach. Paradoxically, the modern 1942 Code, although inspired by the most advanced ideals of procedural reform, has permitted the progressive decay of the administration of justice to levels which are intolerable in a civilized country. The recent and acclaimed reform concerning labour disputes seems headed for a similar fate in many areas of our country.

This result is of grave consequence. The considerable amount of intellectual energy which has been spent studying the art of procedural science certainly deserves much respect. Nevertheless, the hard lesson of history should compel those jurists who are concerned with the concrete consequences of their work at least partially to reorient their aims.[13]

6. THE INDIVIDUAL 'INTERNAL' EXPLANATIONS

A straightforward explanation for each deformation of Italian civil procedure might be useful.

6.1. Increased backlog, and increase in the duration of proceedings

In the 1950s the number of actions commenced increasingly exceeded the number of concluded actions. This has resulted in consistent increases in the number of cases on each judge's cause-list, creating a large backlog.

Such an endless increase seriously affects the duration of proceedings. To use

---

[12] Data in the *Annuario n. 35 delle statistiche giudiziare per l'anno 1987* (Rome, 1989), drafted and published by ISTAT.

[13] See A. Proto Pisani, 'Verso la riforma del codice di procedura civile? Prospettive in tema di processi a cognizione piena e sommaria in un recente disegno di legge delega', *Foro italiano*, 5 (1981), col. 227.

a simple example, if a court completes only 80 per cent of the disputes that it begins to deal with every year, e.g. 240 disputes out of 300, after twenty years, starting from zero, there will be 1,200 unfinished proceedings on its cause-list. The cumulative effect of this backlog ends up considerably prolonging proceedings.[14]

6.2. Decrease in civil litigation as a consequence of the spread of self-enforcement

As we have seen, there has been a decrease in the total amount of civil litigation in Italy this century. In smaller claims, excessive duration makes cost intolerable, preventing citizens from seeking legal protection. Even the recent increase in claims for higher amounts could well have been greater had proceedings been shorter. While no detailed information is available, the common belief is that the increase in larger-scale litigation involves mainly 'mass-litigation' or common type litigation, such as claims for car accident damages, divorces, separations, and standard labour disputes.

As far as other kinds of disputes are concerned, there has been a noticeable movement away from in-court dispute resolution towards alternative modes of dispute prevention and resolution. A new set of rules has developed in order to protect creditors. These rules might be referred to as 'self-help'.[15]

The Italian civil justice system forbids self-enforcement on principle. Nevertheless, some forms of self-help are allowed, such as the enforcement of sale or purchase agreements (Arts. 1515, 1516, Italian Civil Code). Other forms of self-help, such as assignment for the benefit of creditors, require the consent of the other party. In short, creditors are entitled to self-help only in exceptional cases explicitly provided for by law. The general veto on self-help to enforce one's own rights, and the specific prohibition of agreements of forfeiture, express the Italian law's general hostility towards the subjection of debtors to creditors' power, even where that subjection is voluntary and contractual. This hostility seems reasonable, as contractual consent often conceals inequality of party contractual power, and is open to abuse.

New trends in international trade law demonstrate indifference to such principles. Indeed, the present trend towards the 'devolution' of the administration of justice, which is particularly apparent in the new types of commercial relations, involves methods which almost totally disregard the law's traditional hostility towards penalties and forfeitures. New structures often involve contractually granting to creditors rights of self-help which are not expressly permitted in the general law, and which give great advantages to the stronger party.

---

[14] See S. Chiarloni, *La riforma del processo del lavoro: profili dall 'esperienza* (Milan, 1988).
[15] See G. Bongiorno, *L'autotutela esecutiva* (Milan, 1984).

It is easy to recognize in such mechanisms new instruments of private self-help. These have been developed in order to provide creditors with a workable remedy for debtor non-compliance, in the face of the present situation of delay and ineffectiveness within the justice system. Such developments reflect a belief that the decay of civil justice has no remedy, and therefore certain forms of self-help can be justified.[16]

However, the problems raised by most such forms of self-help arguably render them inappropriate. First, in cases where debtors are insolvent, there is a risk of subversion of the principles which underlie the right of all creditors to be treated equally. Secondly, there is an even worse risk of the abuse of self-help in order to overwhelm weaker parties, as the experience of commercial relations between first and third world countries very often shows. In such cases, the law is deprived of its fundamental function of balancing economic power in relationships to protect the weaker party's interests.

6.3. The rarity of judgments on the merits as a result of the tendency to settle

Almost two-thirds of claims are waived. It is important to understand what this means. Party inactivity causes most of the waivers. Usually, there is an out-of-court settlement, reached through the intervention of the parties' counsel. Certainly, agreement between litigants is preferable to a third party's decision, which is necessarily more traumatic for the parties. Nevertheless, the situation as a whole cannot be explained merely by inferring that the Italians have become more virtuous over the course of time and that, over the generations, they have grown more disposed to end their quarrels by 'laying down their swords'.

It seems more realistic to relate the decrease in the number of judgments given on the merits to the increase in case duration. Many litigants would rather accept any available settlement, however unfair, than wait for years to have their claims heard. It is now clear that creditors with monetary claims prefer to obtain even a small portion of their claims promptly through settlement, rather than endure a long wait to recover the whole amount through litigation.

6.4. Enforcement of judgment: coercive function and inefficiency

Where there has been an attachment in execution of judgment, the debtor becomes custodian of the attached property, and is entitled to use and enjoy it until it is seized and sold. The debtor is likely to want to pay off the debt and avoid the sale entirely, but he or she may not have enough money available to

---

[16] See id., 'Profili sistematici e prospettive dell'esecuzione forzata in autotutela', *Rivista trimestrale di diritto e procedura civile* (1988), 444 ff.

do so until the threat of immediate sale forces the debtor to pay at least something towards the debt. The debtor often pays regular instalments to the creditor's counsel towards extinguishing the judgment debt. Typically, creditors prefer to get cash in hand, and debtors prefer to keep holding and using their goods. Actually, the debtor is under a constant threat of the denial of post-ponement, and the sale of the property still in his or her possession. It is this threat, rather than the reality of actual seizure and sale, that creditors prefer to use in order to press debtors into paying as much as they can afford.

7. SPECIAL PROCEEDINGS TO PROTECT PRIVILEGED INTERESTS

Up to this point we have considered only the crisis concerning ordinary proceedings. But in order to gain a correct appreciation of the true state of affairs in Italy, we must also examine a few of the 'special' proceedings contained in the fourth book of the Italian Code of Civil Procedure. We will then see that the crisis is partial, and involves mainly the middle classes who need to use the ordinary proceedings to protect their rights. The special proceedings we will consider are in fact capable of offering rapid, and some times even very rapid, protection to particular privileged categories of interests.[17]

7.1. The injunction procedure for the summary recovery of commercial credit

Measuring by number of proceedings issued, the injunction procedure is the most important of the special procedures. Every year in Italy courts issue more injunctions than judgments after ordinary proceedings (617,179 injunctions as compared to 350,936 judgments in 1992).[18]

By means of an injunction, the creditor can achieve an award *ex parte* in a few days. If the debtor does not oppose the injunction by asking for an ordinary judgment, the injunction can be directly enforced. In order to obtain an injunction order, the creditor is supposed to produce 'written evidence' of the credit. If the creditor is an entrepreneur or a freelance professional, the so-called 'written evidence' can be the creditor's own document, such as an invoice or a fee note. Such documents would not normally be admitted as evidence in ordinary Italian proceedings.[19]

It is easy to perceive a procedural privilege here, aimed at protecting the

---

[17] For a previous, more detailed analysis, see S. Chiarloni, *Introduzione allo studio del diritto processuale civile* (Turin, 1975), 20 ff.

[18] Source: tables attached to the Report of the *procuratore generale* at the *Corte di Cassazione* for the inauguration of the judicial year 1993, in *Documenti giustizia*, 1–2 (1993), cols. 204 and 205.

[19] In fact, a situation of ancient privilege towards freeland professionals can be found even in non-procedural discipline. See F. Galgano, *L'imprenditore* (Bologna, 1970), 23 ff.

profits of entrepreneurs and the payment of money due to certain professionals, such as lawyers, notaries, physicians, commercial law consultants, architects, and the like. For justice to be properly served, the injunction procedure should be extended to other categories of creditors, such as all self-employed workers. It is plainly unfair that certain professionals are the only ones who can obtain an injunction simply by producing a note of their expenses and services. This injunction procedure should also be extended to cover employees' claims for wages.

7.2. The eviction procedure for the rapid protection of real estate owners' rights

The eviction procedure is a special procedure that allows a landlord rapidly to obtain an eviction order following contract expiry or tenant default. The structure of this procedure differs greatly from the injunction procedure, as it starts with a summons rather than an *ex parte* application, and the *inter partes* proceedings is accelerated rather than conditional and delayed. However, these two procedures are essentially similar for present purposes. In each, the defendant has to make the case against judgment for the plaintiff. (This in itself may not be sufficient to stop execution, since in many cases judges are empowered to give interlocutory orders for eviction.) Moreover, both procedures allow plaintiffs to obtain execution in a few days, rather than after several years as with the ordinary procedure.

Certain safeguards exist to protect tenants. The legislature has intervened both in substantive law, with several laws protecting tenants in relation to rent, and in procedural law. For instance, in proceedings for eviction for default in payment of rent, the judge can order an extension (the so-called *termine di grazia* or 'grace period') for the payment of arrears (Art. 3, Law no. 833 of 26 November 1969). Moreover, in some cases the effectiveness of the eviction order is abated, as the execution judge can delay its enforcement for a period of months, possibly up to two years.

The legislature's willingness to protect tenants' rights as against landlords' interests contrasts with the stronger position of creditors *vis-à-vis* debtors discussed in the previous section. This can be explained in economic terms. The legislature gives greater protection to entrepreneurs, as they generate *profitto* (profits made using labour, machinery, etc.) which contributes to the country's economic development. By contrast, landlords' contribution to the economy is passive. Accordingly, in relation to housing matters the legislature is more concerned to prevent social unrest than to protect landlords' economic interests. A good example is the legislative rent freeze after the Second World War, when housing was very scarce and inflation was very high.

7.3 Urgent or provisional relief

Article 700 of the Code of Civil Procedure provides for provisional relief when delay might cause the plaintiff irreversible damage. This procedure is similar to the French *référé*, but there is an important difference.[20] The plaintiff has to commence and prosecute the ordinary proceedings in order to preserve the effects of the remedy.

Urgent relief is common in commercial law, e.g. in intellectual property protection or in unfair competition cases, and in labour disputes, e.g. in cases of reinstatement of a fired employee. However, as the duration of ordinary proceedings becomes more and more unbearable, the number of applications for urgent relief is growing, thus jeopardizing the swiftness of the procedure.

7.4. Arbitration as a form of private justice for *beati possidentes*

Arbitration is a *sui generis* special proceeding, which allows private citizens to give judgment over disposable rights. Even if this cannot be said to be a global alternative to ordinary proceedings, arbitration is frequently used for the resolution of disputes between wealthy parties, especially within the business community, because it is efficient, fast, and discreet.

The prevalence of arbitration cannot be precisely quantified, as it escapes from statistical surveys. However, arbitration is commonly recognized as the preferred means for the resolution of disputes between *beati possidentes* (wealthy parties). Since ordinary proceedings between large companies turn out to be very few and far between, we can infer that such companies usually turn to other forms of dispute resolution. This is probably because the interests involved cannot wait for the slow rituals of ordinary proceedings to come to completion. Furthermore, the popularity of arbitration can also be deduced from the presence of a standard arbitration clause in national and international contracts involving relevant economic interests.

However, two points must be kept clear. First, arbitration presupposes a substantial balance of power between the disputants. By contrast, the present pattern of concentration of capital tends to produce hierarchical relationships in commerce, e.g. between the large manufacturer and its smaller agents and supplying firms. It will often be impossible for smaller commercial enterprises to obtain agreement from larger bodies to arbitrate individual disputes, or to obtain the inclusion of an arbitration clause in contracts. What agent would risk losing its commercial relationship with its supplier, an asset which may not be replaceable in the present market environment, in order to achieve an award in a particular dispute?

---

[20] Further considered in S. Chiarloni, 'Prime riflessioni sui valori sottesi alla Novella del processo civile', *Rivista di diritto processuale* (1991), 672 ff.

8. INTERESTS SERVED BY ORDINARY PROCESS DELAYS

As we have seen, certain powerful interests have been granted the privilege of access to special proceedings which allow swift, efficient, and economical recovery. This might lead us to suspect that the slow, 'inefficient', and expensive working of ordinary proceedings also serves certain powerful interests somehow.

Delaying the conclusion of proceedings surely brings advantages to the party who is in the wrong. However, this observation is too generic and needs further investigation in order to define the *idealtypus* of the deliberately dilatory defendant. Moreover, the slow bureaucratic stages of ordinary proceedings are preferred, for different reasons, by the majority of those who operate the justice system.

In summary, three different categories of interests are served by the present structure and, within certain limits,[21] the present situation of ordinary proceedings: the interests of insurance companies; the interests of the bar; and the interests of the judiciary.

8.1. Ordinary proceedings and defendants who resist even in clear cases: damages actions against insurance companies

Car accident cases made up nearly one-third of the civil cases which are dealt with using ordinary proceedings.[22] In such cases, the defendant is usually an insurance company, since Italy's compulsory insurance system has provided for the so-called 'direct action' since 1969. The general attitude of scholars is to consider only the positive aspects of insurance.[23] However, if we were to limit ourselves to this perception, we would fail to see that insurance companies in fact trade on the duration of proceedings.

If we were to consider insurance companies only as an example of human social solidarity in an economic democracy, as the scholars do, we would not see the connection between the present state of justice and their interests. We would only make the superficial observation that the extreme duration and cost of proceedings sharply contrasts with the institutional aims of these companies: the solidarity principle is greatly diminished if the insured needs years to be indemnified. But we must look deeper.

The insurer, like any entrepreneur, aims at increasing the value of the capital employed. Complex, costly, and lengthy proceedings help to maximize profit. When the amount of money is significant, it is economically appropriate for the insurer to resist, regardless of the merit of the case. The insurance company can

---

[21] See the remarks made below in s. 8.2.

[22] The problem of overcrowding roles within simple controversies such as car accidents is typical of developed countries. See A. Tunc (ed.), 'Traffic Accidents Compensation, Law and Proposals', in *International Encyclopaedia of Comparative Law*, vol. xi.

[23] See A. Donati, *Manuale delle assicurazioni* (Milan, 1956), 5.

speculate on the difference between legal interest and costs, and the investment interest that the company earns on the amount withheld.

In small cases (which are the majority), it ought to be economically inappropriate for the insurer to fight to the bitter end. With the final defeat, costs would outweight the advantages. However, maintaining a general state where proceedings to enforce even small claims are disproportionately costly and lengthy serves the long-term interests of the insurer. The knowledge that it will be too expensive to fight the insurance claim all the way through the court system contributes to the burdens on individual plaintiffs. Plaintiffs often prefer to settle on unfair terms rather than wait for years, and spend huge sums of money, to get their full awards. Moreover, lawyers are often tempted by insurance companies to induce their clients to settle. During the negotiations between the lawyer (on behalf of his client) and the insurer, the insurer will make a settlement proposal which includes a substantial sum for the lawyer. The lawyer will then put the settlement offered to his client, but without disclosing his own part of the bargain.

These considerations apply mainly when the opponent is a third party who has been injured, or whose property was damaged, by the insured. When the opponent is the insured, e.g. an entrepreneur whose factory has been destroyed by a fire, resisting the case may prove to be detrimental to the insurance company. The company might lose its client. Experience shows that the choice between paying and resisting is made on the basis of overall economic appropriateness.

The evident dilatory inclination of insurance companies has induced the legislature to intervene. Italian Law no. 990, dated 24 December 1969, deals with compulsory car insurance. It empowers the judge to award interim payments limited to four-fifths of the prospective damages on account of final judgment. Had such a provision been broadly applied since its inception, speculation by insurance companies would have been greatly reduced. But the conditions for applications for interim payments are too strict: the victim must be shown to be in financial need, and serious fault must be shown on the part of the driver.

8.2. Dramatis personae in the ordinary proceedings: lawyers

The modern Italian legal profession has moved a long way away from the fine ethical ideals which still notionally underpin its status as a profession. Lawyers too often conduct the proceedings to suit only their personal interests and schedules. Many years ago, a famous jurist noted that lawyers had turned out to be a stimulus to litigation instead of a restraint over it.[24] Subsequently,

---

[24] See P. Calamandrei, 'Troppi avvocati', now in id., *Opere giuridiche*, ii (Naples, 1966), 65 ff.

another jurist stated that proceedings in Italy were no longer 'a private question between the parties', but 'a private question between the parties' lawyers'.[25]

This movement away from ethical practice[26] is due to several factors. First, in Italy there are a large number of practitioners (almost 100,000). There are more lawyers in the Lazio region than in the whole of France. Moreover, an army of more than 100,000 lawyers-in-training are eager to join the profession. In the meantime, the social role of lawyers has greatly decayed. Apart from a lucky minority of specialists in such fields as business law, family law, administrative law, and consumer protection, most lawyers must make what income they can out of handling large numbers of cases in low-value fields, such as car accidents, credit recovery and labour cases.

The increasing number of lawyers has caused the profession to assume an unpleasantly parasitic aspect. The very survival of lower and lower-middle level practitioners depends on them conducting lengthy and complicated proceedings and increasing costs. If one has only a few cases, it is necessary to make them last as long and cost as much as possible.

Such a situation also contributes to the judicial burden. The courts are overloaded with futile controversies run by the lower strata of the legal profession. The lawyers conduct their cases so as to enlarge their incomes, which would be too low if ethical rules were followed.

The present organization of civil justice also serves the interests of upper and upper-middle level practitioners. The Italian written proceedings, lacking deadlines and based upon long delays, allow large law firms to organize a huge amount of work. In such hierarchically structured firms, a chief with managerial and representative functions supervises the work of a large number of employees. The lower level employees are often beginners, employed at the level that their talents allow. Some apprentices carry out jurisprudential and doctrinal research; others carry papers to and from the court.

The present slow procedures allow practitioners to manage an increasing caseload while keeping the same number of employees. Most work can be performed in the office. Thanks to postponements, work can be scheduled in order to allow the most cost-effective employment of staff.

These factors explain the fierce opposition of most lawyers to the innovations of the 1942 Code of Civil Procedure, the institution of justices of the peace in 1993, and the 1990 reform of ordinary proceedings.

It does not necessarily follow that lawyers benefit from the present parlous state of civil justice administration. Up to a certain point, lawyers are responsible for it. However, now that Pandora's box is open, the extreme duration of proceedings harms lawyers as well. Such harm arises especially when they have

---

[25] See M. Cappelletti, *Giustizia e società* (Milan, 1972), 36.

[26] This is not only an Italian problem. For the role of lawyers in the USA, see T. Veblen, *The Theory of the Leisure Class: An Economic Study of Institutions* (1st edn. New York, 1899) (It trans. *Teoria della classe agiati* (Turin, 1949), 181–2).

to wait for years, after the evidence has been gathered and the final written submissions exchanged, before judgment is issued and costs are awarded.

8.3. Dramatis personae in ordinary proceedings: judges

In Italy judges are civil servants, employed by the state. Law graduates become judges by way of a public examination. The fact that judges are civil servants causes the inefficiency problems typical of a bureaucracy lacking a tradition of excellence and hard work.

The bureaucratic spirit prevalent among the judiciary has even deeper consequences for civil justice. A cult of authority, passive obedience, and routine activity characterizes the bureaucratic individual. Excessive importance is given to formalities. In the judicial context, this leads to an environment where diligence is proportional to the juridical complexity of questions, rather than to their substantive weight. Judges prefer a written handling of cases to establishing personal contact with the parties. Moreover, they support their decisions with *obiter dicta* that have nothing to do with the case at hand, to show off their judicial learning with the aim of achieving progress in their careers.[27]

Certainly, much of this unfortunate state of affairs is due to the peculiarities of Italian history, such as the persisting influence of prolonged foreign domination and the economic and social differences between northern and southern Italy. But certain considerations are peculiar to the judges. The judiciary jealously guards its independence, in all its facets. This is appropriate under the high values of our *Costituzione*. However, it has brought with it pernicious consequences. For instance, while it is appropriate to resist hierarchical controls over judges' discretionary powers, in the present debate 'independence' has been used to justify the renunciation of any attempt to control judicial productivity by the senior judges. Individual responsibility has progressively decreased. Personal dedication, although frequent, is not enough to achieve an acceptable level of service.

Things are slowly improving. Improvement is occurring mainly at the ideological level. There is a real 'battle of ideas' under way. The social costs of parasitic incomes are starting to look more and more intolerable. Concern is growing about the troubles suffered by the administrative branches of the state. Even the autonomous 'separate bodies' of the state are feeling the change of wind. Their leaders are promoting reorganization efforts. The *Consiglio Superiore della Magistratura* (the body which governs the judiciary) has recently analysed and strongly denounced the poor service given by the courts (although the causes identified and remedies proposed are debatable). Finally, small 'quality clubs' are spreading among first instance judges. These groups are struggling,

---

[27] See the analysis carried out by G. Gorla in various essays published by *Quaderni del foro italiano* from 1966 to 1968.

often successfully, to improve matters through the better organization of judicial work.

9. PROSPECTS FOR CHANGE

The situation of civil justice in Italy, with its tangle of conflicting interests and different rules, is complex and contradictory. It is now essential to investigate the prospect of future changes to improve the current situation.

The fact that ordinary citizens have to wait for almost ten years before achieving the final resolution of their disputes through ordinary proceedings has led to public awareness of the necessity for change. Problems within the civil justice system are becoming popular topics in the media.

As for lawyers, although they might gain certain advantages from the slow, formal pace of written proceedings, that slowness is not always profitable. Lawyers risk seeing their clients give up taking court action, frightened by intolerably long proceedings. Growing concern about their professional incomes has caused lawyers to worry about the state of civil justice; although the solutions they have suggested seem rather poor.

Among judges, there is a growing consciousness that public unease could turn into hostility, threatening the courts' independence and their power within society.[28] An improvement in civil justice is necessary to resolve the contradiction between the strong efforts taken in Italy against political and administrative corruption, and the failure to address the endless inefficiency of 'everyday' justice.

The disincentive effect faced by lawyers, whereby potential litigation clients are deterred by too much delay, also applies to insurance companies. As typical 'resisting defendants', insurance companies increase their profits by refusing to pay out money which they owe under insurance policies until they are forced to do so by a judgment of the court. However, this hurts their image. In the free market, a company which is known to pay claims swiftly, and which does not speculate on the duration of proceedings to resist payment, may have a stronger appeal to clients.

9.1. Reforms affecting the structure of proceedings

Changes to procedural rules are not sufficient to solve the crisis in ordinary civil proceedings. Only a wide range of reforms, involving access to justice, legal

---

[28] For discussion of intervention by the judicial power in other countries, see N. Tate and T. Vallinder (eds.), *The Global Expansion of Judicial Power* (New York, 1995). On the evolution of democracies towards an increasing influence exercised by judges over political life, see C. Guarnieri and P. Pederzoli, *La Puissance de juger* (Paris, 1996), 177 ff.; A. Garapon, *Le Gardien de promesses* (Paris, 1996), 21.

practice, judges' recruitment, and reorganization of the Supreme Court (*Corte di Cassazione*), can lead to an effective result. Nevertheless, some reforms to the structure of proceedings could be of help.

More attention could usefully be given to summary proceedings, in order to make them more fruitful. One simple reform would be to separate the granting of urgent remedies from the procedure for interlocutory remedies (*Procedimento cautelare*), to create an urgent procedure for obtaining a final judgment. This reform would require two modifications to the existing procedural framework.[29]

First, the availability of an urgent remedy should not depend on irreparable damage. Urgent relief should be granted on the ground that the claim has been evaluated as being well founded. Such an evaluation should be based upon an informal examination of the parties and affidavits. In fact, judges are already moving down this path. They are already willing to find the requisite irreparable damage.

The second, and more important, modification would involve distinguishing urgent remedies from interlocutory remedies. The urgent remedy, granted *ante causam* under a summary procedure, should be able to become final. This would mean reversing the relationship between interlocutory judgments and judgments on the merits. If, due to the defendant's inactivity, the proceedings do not progress further, so that no final judgment is established after a full hearing on the merits, the preliminary judgment should be considered final. Moreover, as the summary judgment would be a product of the judge's consideration of the case, the remedy should be enforceable immediately, notwithstanding the defendant's opposition.

Such a reform should not completely substitute summary proceedings for the ordinary procedure in all civil cases. Instead, a sort of 'fast track' procedure should be established. This would be suitable for many categories of cases, chosen by judges according to their level of simplicity and urgency.[30]

9.2. Reforms affecting the structure of the professions

Reforming the structure of the legal and judicial professions could contribute greatly to improving the civil justice situation.

9.2.1. The need to mend the fracture between judges and lawyers

The conflict between lawyers and judges in Italy has reached a quite alarming level. Endemic antagonism characterizes both legal workplaces and public

---

[29] See S. Chiarloni, 'Prime riflessioni sui valori sottesi alla novella del processo civile', *Rivista di diritto processuale* (1991), now in id., *Formalismi e garanzie: studi sul processo civile* (Turin, 1995), 387 ff., esp. 403 and 404; G. Costantino, 'La lunga agonia del processo civile (Note sul d.1. 21 giugno 1995, n.238), *Foro italiano*, 5 (1995), cols. 321 ff., now in id., *Scritti sulla riforma della giustizia civile (1982–1995)* (Turin, 1996), 419 ff., esp. 437; R. Conte, 'Per un'autonomia del processo cautelare', *Questione giustizia* (1996), 369 ff.

[30] See also A. Proto Pisani, 'La tutela giurisdizionale dei diritti della personalità: strumenti e tecniche di tutela', *Foro italiano*, 5 (1990), excerpt, 20 ff.

debate. Recently, the conflict has worsened, and has assumed a political dimension.

In spite of official declarations of goodwill, the two professions stand more and more frequently in opposition to one another. For example, judges fought hard against the recent law reducing custody pending trial, which the lawyers strongly favoured. On the other hand, lawyers persistently oppose the reform of civil procedure, resorting even to strikes. In late 1998 they went on strike against a judgement of the Constitutional Court concerning the right to silence of a defendant who made declarations before the public prosecutor. Lawyers in Naples also went on strike in 1998 against the chief public prosecutor's policy in conducting cases.

The consequence of this animosity is paradoxical. Conformity to the law, and the right to a defence, are commonly accepted as concurrent and complementary values in our society. However, those professionals most responsible for each aspect, the judges and the lawyers respectively, risk coming into opposition in court practice.

The borderline between the use and abuse of both judicial control and the right to a defence is very thin and easy to cross. This is particularly true where criminal justice is concerned. In spite of this danger, impatience between judges and lawyers is common, even when they remain within the proper ambit of their respective roles.[31] Such a conflict fundamentally undermines the administration of justice. The debate lingers on points which may be important for the professions, but which are of minor relevance to the general public.

As long as the two professions keep focusing simply on their own particular interests a constructive dialogue is impossible. Neither profession will accept a solution which, although good for the public, reduces the privileges enjoyed by that profession while leaving those of the other intact. Both will regard every proposal coming from the other camp with profound suspicion.

9.2.1.1. The need to find a common background

A solution to this conflict could be found in a fundamental reform of the training processes of both professions. The present procedures for the selection of future lawyers and judges are highly unsatisfactory.

The examination for admission to the judicial profession does not test the candidates' real attitude to doing justice at all.[32] The most important part of the selection is the written examination. Success in this is essentially a matter of luck. Candidates have to absorb huge texts and study recent court decisions. It is also helpful to prepare for the exam by attending costly schools. Some of these schools are owned by former judges. The higher rate of success of candidates

---

[31] See E. Bruti Liberati, 'Deontologia del pubblico ministero nei rapporti con la difesa', *Rassegna forense* (1996), 40.

[32] See also the remarks by V. Chiusano, 'Il magistrato e l'organizzazione giudiziaria', in *Atti della prima conferenza nazionale dell'avvocatura italiana* (Milan, 1993), 174.

from these schools may cause some eyebrows to be raised. Candidates are at the mercy of the mood and attention of the examination committee members. After the oral examination, future judges enter a career in which there are effectively no further tests or checks.

The situation is not much better in respect of admission to the legal profession. The compulsory two-year training period appears to represent an improvement over the training of judges. However, senior practitioners do not commonly fulfil their duty to teach and transmit experience to the young.[33] Furthermore, there is great inequality in the regional administration of examinations. The data are astonishing. In certain districts, especially in southern Italy, 80 per cent of candidates pass the exam. In other districts, especially in northern Italy, the pass rate is lower than 15 per cent.

Some proposals contained in a draft law concerning the legal profession seem likely to be beneficial. The duration of the apprenticeship is to be extended from two to three years. Compulsory courses are to be introduced. However, in order to improve the selection system significantly, its present structure should be inverted. An examination should regulate the admission of a limited number of trainees, both intending lawyers and judges, to a common training period. This should last at least two years, with compulsory courses, seminars, and internships at law firms, courts, and in the public administration.[34] Access to the separate professions should be granted on the basis of the results achieved during the different training stages, together with a final examination.

Law no. 127 of 15 May 1997 empowered the governement to modify the rules for access to the judicial profession according to two principles: simplification of admission exam procedures; and gradual introduction of a two-year, postgraduate school as a prerequisite for admission to the bench or bar. The two-year, postgraduate specialization school for aspiring lawyers and judges represents a radical change. It has been introduced in a draft law, now approved by the government. However, the draft law still has some weak points, which have been highlighted by the *Consiglio Superiore della Magistratura*. In particular, the *Consiglio* has rightly criticized the fact that the school is not compulsory for entry into the legal profession. Aspiring lawyers can choose between training in a law firm and entering a specialization school. It is easy to foresee that internships in law firms will be preferred as the easier way. The *Consiglio* also rightly remarks that:

A two-year period of common postgraduate school for aspiring lawyers and judges might favour a deeper common perception of proceedings' values and principles, of citizens' rights and guarantees, and of the role of law and legality. An improved and widespread

---

[33] The internship period is often reduced to a modest subordination. See V. Siniscalchi, 'La formazione deontologica e professionale dell'avvocato', in *Atti della prima conferenza nazionale*, 79.

[34] I prefer a postgraduate professional education. My views on this differ from those of C. Consolo and L. Mazzarolli, 'L'università', in *Atti della prima conferenza nazionale*, 55 ff., who propose a graduate 'forensic jurisprudence' course.

cultural awareness of the common basic values of their respective functions is perhaps the only way of improving and spreading, in the two professions, the aptitude for recognizing and respecting each others' point of view, comparing their cultures, perceiving the complementary function of their roles, and creating the capacity for mutual enrichment.

The *Consiglio* has asked the legislature to make the specialization schools compulsory for those intending to join the legal profession. It hopes to be supported in this request by the *Consiglio Nazionale Forense* (lawyers' ruling organ), and to work together with the lawyers' body to plan admissions and define the study curriculum.

9.2.1.2. The opportunity of a pathway between the two professions

Understanding between the two professions would be improved if it were possible for lawyers, under certain conditions, to become judges. However, this does not mean that an extraordinary, one-off recruitment of a large number of judges should take place from among the members of the bar, as has been recently proposed.[35] Such a solution would create a danger of a fall in the quality of the judicial service. It is probable that the best practitioners would be unwilling to leave their successful careers to become civil servants.

The participation of lawyers in the honorary judiciary, e.g. as justices of the peace, would not suffer this effect. Here, their contribution to judicial service in the courts would only be part-time or temporary. However, at present these honorary judicial positions are inferior to the positions of ordinary judges. Being under the supervision of a full-time judge, possibly a very junior one, and dealing only with small claims, might not attract the best and most successful lawyers either. Some doubts might also remain about the possible conflicts of interests that such 'part-time' judges might encounter.[36] In most cases, however, lawyers have performed honorary judicial functions with great dedication and service.

Interestingly, a new type of judge-lawyer has been introduced in France. In 1995 the position of temporary judge was instituted. Such judges can exercise the functions either of a *juge d'instance* or of a member of the *tribunaux de grande instance*. The judges must be under the age of 65, and are appointed for a non-renewable period of seven years. Their judicial remuneration is set by the State Council. Civil servants, apart from university professors, cannot assume this role. Practising lawyers who become temporary judges cannot have been working in the district of the *tribunal de grande instance* to which they are appointed.

Finally, putting Article 106, s. 3 of the Italian Constitution into effect should be warmly welcomed. This article makes it possible for the *Consiglio Superiore della*

---

[35] See also V. Aimone and D. Donella, 'Il reclutamento straordinario', in *Atti della prima conferenza nazionale*, 127 ff.

[36] On the incompatibility between the functions of an honorary judge and of a lawyer, see A. Pizzorusso, 'Giudice onorario e giudice monocractico nel progetto ministeriale e nelle prospettive di riforma', *Rivista di diritto processuale* (1977), 261.

Magistratura (judges' ruling organ) to appoint university professors or lawyers with fifteen years' experience in practice to the office of Supreme Court judge, on the basis of personal merit.[37]

9.2.2. *The need for a legal cultural revolution and radical reform of the rules concerning compulsory legal representation*

As we have seen, stricter selection and better training of lawyers might well improve the quality of civil justice. A consequent reduction in the number of lawyers would automatically lead to tighter observance of the profession's ethical rules. Less frantic pursuit of sources of income by lawyers would end the clogging of courts with useless cases. Greater security would allow lawyers to face the question of compulsory legal representation with a more open mind.

In England, where the number of practitioners is far smaller than in Italy, legal representation is not compulsory in any court. Appearing in person is even encouraged in small cases where legal costs would rapidly overtake the value of the claims. This is done quite simply, by providing that the usual principle that 'costs follow the event' does not apply to small cases. In such cases, each party, even when successful, must pay for his or her own lawyer.

In Italy, proposing a similar rule would give rise to violent opposition. Any proponent would be accused of violating the citizen's right to a defence. Recent introduction of the possibility of appearing without legal representation before a justice of the peace, when authorized by him, is causing just such an uproar.

9.2.3. *Reform of the judicial profession*

Rationalizing the civil justice system requires many different changes to the judicial profession. Just as for the lawyers, the starting point is to improve the mechanism of selection and training. Other reforms are also necessary.

9.2.3.1. The abolition of automatic career progression and the introduction of productivity incentives

Under the old system, judicial career progression was based on qualification exams set by senior judges. This system was abolished in the 1960s for two good reasons. First, the practice threatened judicial independence. Secondly, the examination was based on a review of the candidate's decisions. Using judgments as a means of assessing a judge's learning and the correctness of his judicial technique led to judgments becoming long and time-consuming to prepare, full of unnecessary *obiter dicta*. However, the substitution of length of service for qualification examinations has not turned out to be a good alternative. The absence of checks over judges during their careers, together with the

---

[37] See E. Gallo, 'L'attuazione dell'art. 106 della Costituzione', in *Atti della prima conferenza nazionale*, 105.

lack of a true hierarchical judicial structure which we have already discussed, produce the worst of bureaucratic defects.

Between these two extremes, a preferable option would be to set up a career structure assessed by intermediate checks which do not threaten the judge's independence. (There are benefits to judicial independence. It is not inextricably linked to irresponsibility.) Objective evaluation criteria should be devised. The final decision on career progression should be left to collegiate bodies comprising representatives of the various categories of judges.

Secondly, further mechanisms should be introduced in order to increase judges' productivity by eliminating those patches of indolence which characterize state bureaucracies. Productivity indicators would be more precise than merely counting the yearly number of decisions.[38] There is no reason why productivity-based competition, even among judges, should not be used to reward economically those who work the hardest.[39]

Money appears to be a useful, if inelegant, motivator. Lawyers' incomes are proportional both to the amount of work which they obtain, and the amount which they do. A judge's salary, though higher than most other state employees' salaries, is independent of personal effort. Obviously, to protect judicial independence, judges' salaries must be stable. Yet nothing requires that salaries should be equal for all judges at a given stage of the judicial career. A judge of an urban court may achieve productivity levels which are twice those of a judge working in a country court. It is only rational to provide economic rewards for behaviour which we wish to encourage, taking into account the amount of work available within a given court.

However, there are some possible objections. First, some argue that the introduction of productivity criteria is incompatible with the dignity of the judicial role. This is not persuasive. The remuneration of justices of the peace is wholly calculated on the basis of numbers of hearings, judgments, and agreements. The dignity of these judges does not seem to be unduly affected. Secondly, an economic incentive for greater judicial productivity need not reduce the quality of judicial decisions. The productivity measure could be linked to the number of decisions not appealed by the parties, and/or those appealed but left unaltered by the higher court.

The real objection is the difficulty of objectively measuring productivity in such a heterogeneous field as judges' decisions. However, the social sciences should be able to construct objective criteria for evaluating the efforts of a single judge, allowing for all the widely varying manifestations of judicial activity.

---

[38] See 'La giustizia degli anni ottanta: le riforme possibili', *Foro italiano*, 5 (1984), col. 225.

[39] Judges' associations have started to discuss the matter. The *Associazione Nazionale Magistrati* organized a meeting held in Abano Terme, 14–16 June 1996, on the topic: 'Judges' career and work quality evaluation'. Some comments and the concluding speech have been published in *Questione giustizia* (1996), 329 ff.

9.2.3.2. Restructuring districts and introducing a sole judge at first instance

It has been known since the 1960s that Italian judges are inadequately distributed around the country. Judicial distribution conforms to an obsolete pattern of territorial subdivision. According to a survey from 1967,[40] more than 550 out of 900 *preture* (minor courts) did not have enough work to keep a single judge busy (i.e. they had a productivity index below 1). A slightly better situation emerged in tribunals, where 45 out of a total of 156 had a productivity index below 1.[41]

The situation has now improved. An important reform process has almost been completed. The process began with Law no. 30, dated 1 February 1989, which abolished the *preture di mandamento*. These *preture* have been transformed into local sections of new *preture* with a larger territory, corresponding to the jurisdictional areas of the tribunal.

This law had three main goals, one explicit, and two implied. The explicit goal was to avoid an excessive territorial dispersion of the new prosecutors' offices, which were attached to the *preture* after the reform of the Code of Criminal Procedure. One of the implicit goals was to establish a geographical distribution that would favour the future introduction of sole judges at first instance. The other implicit goal was to prepare for the abolition of unproductive *preture*. In order to prevent opposition from parliamentarians, the local *preture* could be abolished by simple administrative acts. Indeed, after the issue of the law, 272 local *preture* with a productivity index below 0.49 were abolished.

The last step in the process was to merge the new *preture* with the corresponding tribunals, in order to achieve the introduction of the sole judge at first instance.

The process still has some obstacles to overcome, including the abolition of the managerial posts of some hundred 'directors' (judges and public prosecutors who hold directorial posts) who at present work in the *preture*. Hopefully, after the process is complete, characteristics of the *preture* such as pragmatism, swiftness, and informality will not be lost.

9.2.3.3. The creation of special courts for certain civil matters

Ending the ordinary courts' monopoly over private litigation could greatly assist the rationalization of civil justice.[42]

This idea implies the introduction of a wide range of special jurisdictions, covering those particular fields where court protection may be needed. Such

---

[40] Report of the *Consiglio Superiore della Magistratura* on the state of justice, published as an appendix in M. Cervi, *La giustizia in Italia* (Milan, 1967), 189 ff.

[41] Ibid. 77 and 82, quoting data elaborated for the *Consiglio*.

[42] See, for instance, V. Denti, 'Tre interventi sul disegno di legge governativo di provvedimenti urgenti per l'accelerazione dei tempi della giustizia civile: una difesa d'ufficio', *Foro italiano*, 5 (1987), col. 172; S. Chiarloni, 'Nuovi modelli processuali', *Rivista di diritto civile* (1993), now in id., *Formalismi e garanzie*, 12 ff.

courts, in most cases, could be made up of representatives of the opposing interests, as in the French *Conseil de prud'hommes*[43] which has jurisdiction over labour disputes.

The specialist courts, however, should not be limited to labour disputes. They should extend to the fields of housing, health, essential services, consumer protection, and civil liability. An easily accessible and low-cost court, together with the right to appear without legal representation, could speed up the resolution of controversies and allow conflicts which currently go unresolved to be addressed. Specialist courts for distinct types of private litigation constitute a fundamental feature of many European systems, including France and England.[44]

9.2.3.4. Filtering access to the *Corte di Cassazione*

As we have seen, there are too many appeals to the *Corte di Cassazione*. Before discussing possible remedies for this problem, it is necessary to consider the current debate about uniform application of the law. Some commentators have suggested that uniformity is not essential for all the decisions of the *Corte di Cassazione*. According to a widely held position, the growing complexity and manifold interests of an increasingly regulated and evolving society endanger the effectiveness, and reduce the desirability, of the *Corte di Cassazione*'s efforts to ensure uniformity. Thus, the argument goes, the judges of the Court should be content to allow non-uniform, or 'pluralistic', interpretations to emerge.[45]

There are good reasons to reject this position. Let us consider the kind of rules that are subject to the Court's uniformity/legitimacy control. While detailed statistics are unavailable, it is likely that most appeals concern the rules of the codes and of a few fundamental special laws (e.g. divorce and bankruptcy law). Private litigation seems mainly to concern an established and limited set of rules. Given this fact, a plurality of interpretations is especially undesirable.

But, even if appeals concern a wider range of laws, this does not mean that the law is not to be applied uniformly any more. Certainly, we face manifold changing sources of law, with a permanent output of poor-quality laws. Often, identifying the *ratio legis* of statutes is difficult, and the laws are obscure, contradictory, or self-contradictory.[46] This, however, is the very situation that most strongly demands the intervention of the *Corte di Cassazione*.

Obviously, nobody argues that such authoritative interpretation of the law must occur once and for all. The uniform application of the law is a continuous,

---

[43] See H.-F. Herman, *Répertoire général alphabétique du droit français*, xxxi (Paris, 1906), 978.

[44] See R. Cranston, *Legal Foundations of the Welfare State* (London, 1985), 189 ff.

[45] See N. Irti, 'L'età della decodificazione', *Diritto e società* (1978), 613 ff.; V. Denti, 'L'idea di codice e le riforme del processo civile', *Rivista di diritto processuale* (1982), 100 ff.; S. Senese, 'Funzioni di legittimità e ruolo di nomofilachia', *Foro italiano*, 5 (1987), cols. 262 and 264; M. Franceschelli, 'Nomofilachia e Corte di Cassazione', in *Giustizia e Costituzione* (1986), 39 ff.

[46] For a discussion of similar problems in England, see W. Twining and D. Miers, *How to Do Things with Rules* (London, 1991), 309 ff.

sometimes even a tortuous, process.[47] In this situation, the lower judges' interpretative work, producing non-uniform interpretations, may make a valuable contribution to legal development.

Nevertheless, there is no place for such interpretative freedom in the *Corte di Cassazione*. Some have argued that the *Corte di Cassazione*'s traditional uniformity function should be relaxed. They approve of the behaviour of the present judges of this Court, who increase legal disorder by giving contradictory decisions. This approval is based on two implicit assumptions: a radical conception of the creative function of jurisprudence; and a belief that the interpretative discretion of the lower court judges should be matched by the same discretion within the *Corte di Cassazione*.

These assumptions produce untenable results. Pluralism in the interpretation of laws by the Supreme Court is not acceptable. The existing pluralism of the Court is only an accident, due to its large number of judges (approximately 450).

In order for the *Corte di Cassazione* to fulfil the task of ensuring uniform application of the law, there is only one way. There must be a drastic reduction in the number of appeals, and a concomitant reduction in the number of judges. This solution concerns both the *Corte di Cassazione* and the courts of appeal. Detailed statistical data are not available. However, as any court professional in Italy knows, the chances of successfully appealing to the courts of appeal depend more on questions of law (such as improper application or incorrect interpretation of laws) than on questions of fact. Thus, it would be entirely reasonable to restrict the ambit of appeals, as in common law countries, to questions of law only. In this way, appeals to the *Corte di Cassazione* could be confined to new and/or controversial questions.

Such a drastic change would require a profound reform of the Supreme Court, and in particular the way that its judges are appointed.

10. THE SPREAD OF ALTERNATIVE DISPUTE RESOLUTION

There is a growing awareness in Italy that the traditional court system is no longer adequate to meet the needs of a complex modern society. Citizens need faster, easier, and more economical ways to resolve their disputes.

In certain situations, it is now more convenient not to use the courts. In many disputes, alternative dispute resolution techniques bring great advantages to both citizens and the courts. The advantage to the courts lies in allowing them to concentrate only on those matters which require authoritative resolution by a judge.[48]

---

[47] See S. Chiarloni, 'Efficacia del precedente giudiziario e tipologia dei contrasti di giurisprudenza', *Rivista trimestrale di diritto e procedura civile* (1989), 124–5.

[48] See S. Roberts, 'Alternative Dispute Resolution and Civil Justice: An Unresolved Relationship', *Modern Law Review*, 56 (1993), 452 ff.

In the United States, 'alternative dispute resolution' comprehends many heterogeneous procedures, which sometimes have only their independence from the jurisdictional power of the state in common.[49] In the USA, ADR institutions deal with a wide range of controversies. In Italy, as in much of Europe,[50] apart from arbitration,[51] the development of 'informal justice' systems has been much slower. There are many restraining factors. First, there is the weight of a long tradition of ritual justice. Secondly, there is a long-standing myth of jurisdictional unity, which generates great suspicion of any attempt to lessen the judges' dominance. Lastly, in civil law countries, ordinary proceedings do not generate the enormous costs and difficulties that they do under the common law adversarial system.[52]

The protection of workers and consumers appears to be the fastest growing sector of ADR in Europe. In Italy, experimental conciliation and arbitration services are provided by *Telecom Italia*, the banking ombudsmen, conciliation and arbitration chambers established by the chambers of commerce, and conciliation offered by labour and employment offices.[53] What is their position in the framework of ADR and what is their future development? Some answers appear from an analysis of the situation.

In this context, it is necessary to mention the general power given to justices of the peace by the legislature, without value limits, to settle any dispute. In practice, this power is not used. Experience shows that conciliation bodies only succeed if they are located within the community, and if they specialize in the types of disputes for which members of each community want conciliation. Consequently, extra-judicial conciliation should be left to private or semi-public institutions, like the chambers of commerce. The state should focus its efforts on encouraging the impartiality of conciliation bodies and the effective participation of citizens.

We can now examine which categories of litigation fit best into the conciliation-mediation procedure. The relationships between companies, and those between companies and consumers, are the places where we can foresee a sharp development of conciliation in Italy. In respect of the former, the most promising field is that of small and medium-sized companies. Here, the relative

---

[49] See W. Twining, 'Alternative to What? Theories of Litigation, Procedure and Dispute Settlement in Anglo-American Jurisprudence: Some Neglected Classics', *Modern Law Review*, 56 (1993), 380 ff.

[50] See R. Coulson, 'Will the Growth of Alternative Dispute Resolution (ADR) in America Be Replicated in Europe?', *Journal of International Arbitration*, 9 (1992), 211 ff.

[51] The Centre for Dispute Resolution, London, treats arbitration separately from other ADR institutions. See *ADR Route Map* (London, 1992).

[52] See E. Blankenburg and Y. Taniguchi, 'Informal Alternatives to and within Formal Procedures', in *Justice and Efficiency*, Proceedings of the VIII World Congress of Procedural Law (Anversa, 1989), 335 ff.

[53] See F. Carpi, 'Settlement of Disputes out of Court in Italy', paper presented at the International Symposium on Civil Procedure in the Globalisation Era, Waseda University, Tokyo, 25–7 Aug. 1992.

equality of power between these companies can favour a friendly settlement with the help of an impartial third party, mostly in those cases where arbitration would be too expensive and court action too inefficient.

Even large companies may be interested in conciliation, especially of disputes with consumers. In the near future, we can expect to see very stiff competition between large companies, based not only on prices, but also on the quality and quantity of services offered. For instance, we can already see increasing contractual transparency, the extension of warranties, and increases in customer assistance.

In such a context, the possibility of settling customers' claims easily, rapidly, and economically represents an important weapon within a company's marketing strategy. Success can produce an imitation effect among similar companies, which can bring about a generalization of mediation services across an industry sector. Within this framework, the new law allowing the chambers of commerce to establish conciliation and arbitration bodies could be of great importance. Presumably, the establishment of such bodies could achieve great success if properly designed; especially as regards cost and ease of access. Obviously, they would have to be advertised among company and consumer associations, and establish strong and persisting relationships with them.

One last consideration. Conciliation should be distinguished from mediation. In addition to seeking to persuade the parties to reach agreement (conciliation), a mediator must also make a proposal on the basis of the facts disclosed and the parties' legal rights. If the parties do not accept such a proposal, this circumstance must be taken into account in any subsequent court proceedings. If the refusal comes from the plaintiff, he should be required to pay costs if he does not achieve a better result from the court. If the proposal is rejected by the defendant, her responsibility will be aggravated if the plaintiff is awarded an equal or greater measure than that which the mediator proposed.

It is superfluous to note that the establishment of such links between mediation and litigation proceedings, as already experimented with in the United States, would surely increase the number of successful recourses to mediation, with the benefit of alleviating the congestion of courts.

9
Civil Justice Reform: Access, Cost, and Delay. The French Perspective

Loïc Cadiet

1. INTRODUCTION

For many years, French justice, like all other systems, has faced the dramatic consequences of the exploding volume of litigation. The long delays and high costs which this explosion causes are, to a certain extent, the counterpart of democratized access to law and justice. Although several reforms have been initiated, one should not forget that the current difficulties originate largely from the fact that the resources of the justice system have not risen proportionately to the sharp increase in the volume of litigation with which courts have been faced. The solution to the crisis is essentially financial.

2. DESCRIPTION OF THE FRENCH SYSTEM OF CIVIL PROCEDURE

2.1. French justice in general: Jurisdictional dualism

The organization of different jurisdictions in France is characterized by a dualism between the judicial jurisdictions, organized under the authority of *Cour de Cassation*[1] and the administrative jurisdictions, under the authority of the *Conseil d'État*.[2] This dualism is an important source of complications. As in any borderline situation, it gives rise to conflicts of jurisdiction and opens the possibility for procedural dispute.[3] A second distinction, between civil and criminal jurisdictions, adds to the complexity of the French judicial system.

The author wishes to thank Michael Haravon, LL B (London), BCL (Oxon.), for his invaluable assistance with the translation of this paper.

[1] The highest court of the French hierarchy of 'judicial' courts.
[2] The highest court of the French hierarchy of 'administrative' courts; see below App. 9.1.
[3] On the origins of, and the problems caused by, this jurisdictional dualism, see L. Cadiet, *Découvrir la justice* (Paris, Dalloz, 1997), 100–3.

2.2. The hierarchy of the civil courts

Civil jurisdictions are organized like a three-level pyramid: the first instance jurisdictions; the appeal jurisdictions; and the *Cour de Cassation*.[4]

2.2.1. First instance jurisdictions

The first instance level is characterized by a wide diversity of jurisdictions.[5] Traditionally, a distinction is made between the *tribunal de grande instance*, of unlimited general jurisdiction, and other, specialized, courts, only competent in those particular matters in which their jurisdiction is expressly recognized in law. These first instance courts of special jurisdiction vary greatly, in their composition, powers, and procedure. We shall describe the main characteristics of each of the main first instance courts in turn. There are some other, minor, courts which we will not deal with.

2.2.1.1. *Tribunal de grande instance*

The *tribunal de grande instance* is the foundation of the French court hierarchy.[6] In addition to its general jurisdiction, based in French 'common law' or 'principle', many specific areas of jurisdiction have been expressly granted to the *tribunal de grande instance* by statute.[7] In total, France has 181 *tribunaux de grande instance*, including those in French overseas territories.[8] It is a court of regional jurisdiction, based on the *département*.[9]

Procedure before the *tribunal* usually takes the form of written exchanges. Representation by a local advocate is compulsory. The jurisdiction of the *tribunal de grande instance* is usually exercised by a bench of its three professional judges. This is strictly mandatory in certain areas of the law, including disciplinary matters, and disputes as to capacity. However, a single judge can also sit for the *tribunal de grande instance*, either in a particular case under a decision of the president of the court, or in certain matters under a procedure authorized by statute. Such procedures are prescribed by statute in the case of road accidents, and for the recognition and enforcement of foreign judgments.

Within a *tribunal de grande instance*, special powers are reserved to particular judges. One judge is in charge of family matters,[10] another is the judge for children. There will be a commission for the compensation of victims of

---

[4] See below App. 9.2.
[5] See L. Cadiet, *Droit judiciaire privé* (Paris: Litec, 2nd edn., 1998), nos. 188–244.
[6] See Arts. L. and R. 311-1 ff. of the Judicial Organization Code.
[7] See Art. L. 311-12 ff. of the Judicial Organization Code: capacity, property, licences and trademarks, civil companies, disciplinary proceedings.
[8] See below Apps. 9.2, 9.3, 9.6, and 9.14.
[9] Roughly equivalent to English counties or shires.
[10] See L. Cadiet, 'A la recherche du juge de la famille', in M.-Th. Meulders-Klein, *Familles & justice: justice civile et évolution du contentieux familial en droit comparé* (Brussels: Bruylant, and Paris: LGDJ, 1997), 235–70.

offences. The president of the court is put in charge of enforcement matters, with special power to deal with difficulties of enforcement of judgments, including both executable final judgments, and provisional measures. The president of the court also sits as the judge for all interlocutory and *ex parte* orders.[11] In recent years, the president of the court has been given quite a number of special powers in summary or accelerated proceedings.[12] There is a noticeable trend within the French procedural system towards hearings before a single judge for the purposes of saving time and costs.[13]

2.2.1.2. *Tribunal d'instance*

The *tribunal d'instance* has jurisdiction over small claims. In general, its territorial jurisdiction spreads among many cantons (or districts). Today, there are 473 *tribunaux d'instance*, including those located in the French overseas territories.[14]

Their history is one of increasing standardization. The *tribunal d'instance* is often presented as an 'emanation', or a 'local branch', of the *tribunal de grande instance*. Indeed, although it has its own exclusive jurisdiction in certain matters (for example, possession proceedings, electoral litigation, private and commercial rent litigation), the *tribunal d'instance* also shares much of its jurisdiction with the *tribunal de grande instance*. Both courts have jurisdiction in personal and real matters, that is, in all actions having their source in what French law considers a debt, be it contractual, delictual, or legal. The *tribunal d'instance* hears matters not exceeding F. Frs. 30,000 in value.[15] The jurisdiction of the *tribunal de grande instance* only covers claims beyond this limit. Proceedings in the *tribunal d'instance* take the form of mainly oral exchanges, and legal representation is not compulsory.

The jurisdiction of the *tribunal d'instance* is exercised by a single judge. Since 1970, its judges are appointed from the judges of the *tribunal de grande instance*, for renewable three-year terms. Any judge of the *tribunal de grande instance* can sit in the *tribunal d'instance*. What then is the point of having a separate *tribunal d'instance*? This court's place in the French hierarchy would come into question should the *tribunal de grande instance* become a jurisdiction with single judges for hearings, as is currently proposed.[16] The main distinguishing characteristic of the present *tribunal d'instance* would be gone.

The *tribunal d'instance* also has power to grant interlocutory and *ex parte* orders.[17]

---

[11] See below ss. 3.9.1. and 3.9.2, at text to nn. 47–51.
[12] As in new proceedings designed to settle speedily the status of illegal entrants, or people subject to a psychiatric hospitalization.
[13] See L. Cadiet, 'Le Juge unique en question', in Ch. Bolze and Ph. Pedrot (eds.), *Les Juges uniques: dispersion ou réorganization du contentieux?* (Paris: Dalloz, 1996), 5–22.
[14] See Arts. L. 321-1 ff. of the Judicial Organization Code, and below Apps. 9.1, 9.7 and 9.14.
[15] Approximately £3,000, or $US6,000. See below, the addendum.
[16] See below s. 10 at text to nn. 130–1.
[17] See below ss. 3.9.1 and 3.9.2 at text to nn. 47–51.

2.2.13. Commercial court[18]

The commercial courts are the oldest jurisdiction in the French judicial hierarchy. In spite of the sporadic examinations and reviews to which they have been subjected,[19] the commercial courts have never ceased to grow. They have remained largely unaffected by judicial reforms. Today, there are 227 commercial courts.

The commercial court is a collegiate body, exercising its jurisdiction through benches of an uneven number of judges, usually three. In certain cases, prescribed by statute, a single judge may sit as the court. Like all French court presidents, the president of the commercial court has his own special powers. Within the limits of the competence of the commercial court, he can grant interlocutory relief, and *ex parte* or payment orders.[20] A single judge acts as *juge-rapporteur*, playing, *mutatis mutandis*, the role of the *juge de la mise en état* (preliminary investigation judge) of the *tribunal de grande instance*[21] and the *juge-commissaire* in insolvency law. The proceedings are mainly oral and legal representation is not compulsory.

The commercial court is exclusively made up of professionals elected by their peers.[22] The commercial court has jurisdiction over commercial cases, defined largely as cases between commercial entities, but also including cases relating to commercial acts (even though not necessarily done by commercial entities, e.g. letters of credit), corporate law, insolvency, and winding up. These courts will be reformed in a few months.

2.2.1.4. Labour court[23]

The labour courts have jurisdiction over individual litigation born out of employment or training contracts. The jurisdiction is exercised in two stages: conciliation, followed by adjudication. The court sits as the court of first and last resort for litigation up to F. Frs. 22,000.[24] In cases above this threshold an appeal lies to the Court of Appeal. Today, there are 270 labour courts. The labour court is made up of elected magistrates,[25] who are chosen in equal numbers to represent employers and employees.[26] An election is held every five years.

---

[18] Called *tribunal de commerce*.

[19] A parliamentary commission is currently working on the subject, following scandals in some liquidation proceedings.   [20] See below s. 3.9.2 at text to nn. 50–1.

[21] See below s. 3.6 at text to nn. 39–40.

[22] See Art. L. 411-1 of the Judicial Organization Code and below Apps. 9.2 and 9.8.

[23] Called the *conseil de prud'hommes*.

[24] Approximately £2,100, or $US4,200. The court is described as sitting 'in first and last instance' when, due to the low value of the amount at issue, no ordinary appeal to the Court of Appeal by way of rehearing may be brought against its decision. Appeal by way of cassation, to the *Cour de Cassation*, is still possible, however.   [25] Called *conseillers prud'hommes*.

[26] See Arts. L. 511-1 ff. of the Labour Code, referred to in Art. L. 420-1 of the Judicial Organization Code, and below Apps. 9.2, 9.9, and 9.14.

Its mode of operation is unique. The conciliation bureau is made up of one magistrate representing employers and one magistrate representing employees, who preside in turn. The conciliation bureau's task is to try and solve disputes by conciliation between the parties, behind closed doors. Nevertheless, it has the power to grant provisional orders. If conciliation fails, the action is brought before the judgment bureau. This bureau is also composed of an even number of magistrates, with balanced representation of employers and employees, including at least one of the president or vice-president, sitting in turn. In practice, two employers' representative magistrates sit with two employees' representative magistrates. The judgment bureau has to decide the dispute on its merits. Applications for interlocutory relief are heard by a differently composed court, made up of one magistrate representing employers and one magistrate representing employees.

This equal judicial representation, a characteristic of this court, often leads to deadlock. When no majority can be found in support of one side or the other, a professional judge is called upon to resolve the situation. The judge is called the *juge-départiteur* and belongs to the *tribunal d'instance* in the area in which the labour court is located.

2.2.1.5. Social security and agricultural leases courts[27]

These two courts are highly specialized. The social security courts have jurisdiction over non-administrative litigation in social security matters (such as payment of a benefit etc.). There are 116 social security courts. A president, usually belonging to the *tribunal de grande instance*, sits with two lay magistrates, appointed by the first president of the court of appeal. Once again the magistrates represent employers and employees, and are balanced on the tribunal. An appeal is possible to the social chamber of the court of appeal.

The agricultural leases courts were instituted in 1944 to hear disputes between agricultural landlords and farmers. Today, there are 413 such courts. The president is a judge from the *tribunal d'instance*, assisted by four lay magistrates, two representing lessors and two representing lessees, elected by their peers. Since 1958, appeal lies to the court of appeal. Litigation volume is low. Each court deals with only about ten cases a year.[28] It very often happens that the court cannot sit due to the absence, recusal, or resignation of one or more of its members. The French court hierarchy could easily do without these minor specialized courts.

2.2.2. *Appeal jurisdictions*

2.2.2.1. Judging disputes again: the appeal path

The two-tier jurisdiction principle is a major principle of French procedural law.[29] It allows a party who failed at first instance to have his case considered a

---

[27] Called respectively *tribunal des affaires de sécurité sociale* and *tribunal paritaire des baux ruraux*.
[28] See below Apps. 9.2 and 9.11.
[29] See *Justices*, no. 4, 'Le double degré de juridiction' (Paris: Dalloz, 1996), esp. the introduction by L. Cadiet and S. Guinchard, 1–8.

second time. Nevertheless, it is not absolute. Not all cases go through both tiers. Sometimes an appeal is not possible. The party might not want to exercise it. The law may forbid it: either because of the low amount involved;[30] or because of the specific nature of the claim.[31] Conversely, the court of appeal sometimes hears dispute that have not been aired before. In certain circumstances, the first instance level may not be open to the parties. For example, when the trial has been held, and the lower court has rendered a decision, that court cannot reconsider the matter. Nevertheless, the parties may wish to present new arguments, or new evidence, which were not presented to the judge at first instance. The court of appeal may decide to hear those arguments. It is also possible to force a party to intervene in the dispute at the appeal stage.

2.2.2.2. Courts of appeal (*cours d'appel*), ordinary appeal jurisdictions

The court of appeal is the ordinary court for first appeals. Appeals are normally brought to one of the thirty-three courts of appeal (*cours d'appel*).[32] In very rare circumstances an appeal may be brought before another court.

The courts of appeal are formed exclusively of professional judges, who usually sit in benches of three. The proceedings normally take the form of written exchanges. It is mandatory to be represented by a specialist appeal lawyer, called an *avoué*.[33] The ordinary advocate only draws up the pleadings.

However, in certain specific types of dispute, such as those coming from the labour courts, the proceedings take the form of oral exchanges. In these proceedings, there is no mandatory representation either by *avoué* or advocate. This causes difficulties, because it tends to flood the court of appeal and, consequently, the *Cour de Cassation* with labour cases, and other cases brought under the easier procedure.

The judgments of the court of appeal can be revised by the *Cour de Cassation*.

---

[30] Such is the case for civil claims below F. Frs. 13,000 (£1,300 or $US2,600) or below F. Frs. 21,000 (£2,100 or $US4,200) for labour claims. The figure which defines the value below which no appeal can be made is referred to as the 'jurisdiction rate'. For cases below this threshold, the *tribunal d'instance* is the court of first and last instance. Thus a *tribunal d'instance* has 'jurisdiction', in the sense of 'competence to hear' cases worth up to F. Frs. 30,000; but has 'jurisdiction' in the sense of exclusive first instance jurisdiction, from which no appeal lies by way of rehearing, over cases worth up to F. Frs. 13,000. Appeal by way of cassation, however, still lies in every case. See below, the addendum.

[31] For example, the *tribunal d'instance* has exclusive jurisdiction in electoral matters, and gives its decisions in such cases as a court of first and last resort.

[32] See below Apps. 9.2, 9.3, 9.5, 9.12 and 9.14. App. 9.4 indicates the number of first instance courts per court of appeal, and App. 9.5 the population per court of appeal. The combination of these data makes it possible to determine the number of inhabitants per first instance court. The French judicial geography and the regional inequalities of the jurisdictional map can thus be assessed.

[33] An *avoué* has the exclusive monopoly on appearing before the court of appeal and is in charge of all administrative acts in that court, while the advocate pleads the case.

It is also possible, for cases which may not be appealed to the court of appeal, to bring an appeal directly from the first instance court to the *Cour de Cassation*.[34]

2.2.3. The Cour de Cassation (the highest court of the French judicial hierarchy)

2.2.3.1. Function of the petition to the *Cour de Cassation*: judging judgments again

Whereas the two-tier jurisdiction principle allows a party to ensure that his case is judged a second time, his subsequent petition to the *Cour de Cassation*, after his two chances, guarantees that the law as applied by the lower courts was correct and rightly applied. The Court is located in Paris.[35] It is exclusively made up of experienced professional and learned judges at the peak of their careers. The Court sits in different chambers: the criminal chamber for criminal cases; the civil; the commercial and fiscal; the social chambers. Ordinarily, three judges of one chamber form a bench to hear any particular case, but it is possible for more judges of a single chamber to sit together (*la plénière de Chambre*), or for judges of different chambers to sit in order to resolve conflicting decisions (*Assemblée Plénière* or *Chambre Mixte*).

2.2.3.2. Scope of the appeal to the *Cour de Cassation*

A double distinction must be highlighted. First, the *Cour de Cassation* is not a third level of jurisdiction. The facts as found by the lower courts are taken as fixed. It is not possible to argue new facts or new interpretations of facts already dealt with. Secondly, because the *Cour de Cassation* is only judging the law applied by the lower court, it can only say whether judgments are legally acceptable or not. It cannot deal with the merits of the case. Consequently, if the decision is wrong in law, the *Cour de Cassation* cannot substitute its own judgment. It must send the case back to a new lower court (usually a different court of appeal) which is to decide the case again, in conformity with the law as found by the *Cour de Cassation*.

3. AN OUTLINE OF PROCEDURE

3.1. General and particular rules

The new Civil Procedural Code does not provide for 'the trial' to be the same in every case. All actions must comply with certain rules, contained in the first book of the Code and called 'dispositions common to all jurisdictions'.[36] However, different groups of specific rules apply to specific types of action.

---

[34] Probably comparable to the English leapfrog appeals (the image is quite well chosen).
[35] On the activity of the *Cour de Cassation*, see below App. 9.13.
[36] See Arts. 1–749 of the new Civil Procedural Code.

Also, different courts organize the trial process along quite different lines. Nevertheless, there is an ordinary model of litigation, the *litigation plerum que fit*, otherwise called the contentious and adversarial procedure.[37] Specific proceedings which do not share these features, such as *ex parte* orders, interlocutory relief, and non-contentious hearings, comply with a different legal regime.

3.2. Commencement of ordinary proceedings

In principle, initiating the trial is up to the parties. However, the court only becomes *seized* of the case once a judge is in charge of the dispute. There needs to be a distinct act which can be recorded on the books (*rôle*) of the court.

3.2.1. Requests which do not seize the court: writs and 'common requests'

The issue of a writ is an act of the public officer of the court (*huissier*). By a writ, the plaintiff summons his opponent before the court. The common request[38] is an act of both the parties by which they indicate to the judge their respective claims, the points on which they disagree, and their legal arguments. Designed like a courteous substitute for a writ, the common request is an innovation of the new Civil Procedural Code. It is very rarely used, as it demands at least minimal co-operation between the parties. This is often impossible in contentious matters.

3.2.2. Requests which do seize the court: request, declaration, and voluntary appearance

The initial request and the moment when the court is seized merge into one and the same operation when the initial request itself necessitates the intervention of the court. This happens in the case of the voluntary appearance of the parties before the judge. Thus the *tribunal d'instance* and the commercial court are seized when the parties sign the record testifying their voluntary appearance.

3.2.3. Effects of the court being seized

Although seizing the court has different specific consequences for each jurisdiction, it also entails some general procedural consequences.[39] First, the case is

---

[37] This expression could be highly misleading, especially to common law readers. The French text reads: 'procédure contentieuse contradictoire'. 'Adversarial' is appropriate as a translation of 'contradictoire' in this context, but it should not be allowed to mislead. It is not used here as a term of art with its full common law legal signification. Although the French civil process is far from purely inquisitorial, it is not 'adversarial' in the common law sense. 'Adversarial' is used here simply to denote the presence of both parties (or their absence if they have been duly called) and hence at least the possibility of an exchange of argument on points of law and fact under the control of the judge. It is more akin to the English rule of natural justice providing that both parties must have the opportunity to be heard (*audi alteram partem*), than it is to the common law term of art for party-driven trial procedures.   [38] Called *requête conjointe*.
[39] And has some effects on the substance of the case, such as: interrupting the prescription attaches to every initial request, including *référé* orders; and starting interest running.

entered on the list of cases with which the court is seized. Each case on the list takes its turn on a specific assigned date. Secondly, the court clerk opens a procedure file for each case so listed. This file is the official record of the case. It will be referred to in case of an application, or an appeal. It is especially important in oral proceedings.

3.3. Preliminary investigation of the case (*l'instruction de l'affaire*)

The preliminary investigation of the case is an important step in the French civil process. It is within this period that the necessary procedural steps are completed to put the dispute into shape for hearing and decision (*mise en état*).

The form of the preliminary investigation differs between different courts. The Code contains the specific rules for each jurisdiction. Sometimes a specific investigation is undertaken before trial by a designated judge, as happens in the *tribunal de grande instance* and the court of appeal. These two courts have a mainly written procedure. Sometimes the case is investigated at the trial itself, as in the commercial court, the *tribunal d'instance*, and the labour court. These courts have a largely oral procedure. The key is the level of complexity of the case at the time when the court is seized. Accordingly, even before the *tribunal de grande instance* there are 'fast tracks', cases which are sent directly for hearing on the merits (*l'audience*). Conversely, especially in complex commercial cases, the case may go through a full separate preliminary investigation, under the authority of the *juge-rapporteur*.

Whatever the jurisdiction seized, the preliminary investigation phase always has the same object: putting the case into shape for decision. Most often, while the preliminary investigation is under way, parties will tend to narrow down the object and the grounds of their claim in their respective statements. More importantly, during the investigation, they will exchange, and present the judge with, the factual basis of their claim.

The rules of evidence are the same in all courts. On the whole, evidence may be adduced in two ways: by 'written materials', or by 'investigation measures'.[40] In this context, 'written materials' means evidence which existed before the judicial intervention, whereas 'investigation measures' means those created for the purposes of the court case, using the procedures of the court. In theory, there is a hierarchy between these different means of gathering evidence. An investigation measure ought to be ordered only if the party making an allegation does not have sufficient materials to prove it without the investigation measure. In practice, this is not the case. Investigation measures are quite easily ordered, especially the appointment by the court of an expert. This is not quite

---

[40] These comprise mainly: personal verifications of the judge; personal attendance of the parties; declarations of third parties, by way of either investigation (*enquête*) or statements (*attestations*); and technical measures, such as consultation, verification, and expert opinion.

in the spirit of the new Code and it does, of course, increase delay and costs. This is especially true for the *tribunal de grande instance* and the commercial court. Other jurisdictions do not face quite the same difficulty, especially the labour court, where the amount of litigation is high, and therefore few investigation measures are ordered.

3.4. Hearing and argument

Hearings are characterized mainly by publicity and orality. Orality of hearings is a trait common to all civil courts in France, even the *tribunal de grande instance* where the preliminary investigation takes a mainly written form. Even the *Cour de Cassation* has recognized the parties' right to an oral hearing. This is all very well, but both practice and theory tend to minimize the importance of orality. In practice, oral hearings have tended to lose their importance before the civil courts. Most often they take the form of no more than brief oral observations, either made spontaneously, or in answer to questions from the judge. The president of the court has a discretionary power to end the oral hearing when he thinks fit. Sometimes, the hearing is dispensed with altogether, in favour of the *dossier de plaidoirie*.[41] The development of preliminary investigation of cases, the congestion of the courts, and the weight of judges' preliminary hearings tend to explain this development, for which advocates must also bear responsibility. The new Civil Procedural Code emphasizes this trend, with its decrease in orality.

Publicity of hearings does not call for much discussion. Part of the right to a fair trial, under Article 6 § 1 of the European Convention on Human Rights,[42] the principle of publicity cannot be dispensed with, except in cases prescribed by statute. Statutory provision has been made in the case of non-contentious matters, and in certain matters relating to capacity (divorce, for example).

3.5. Chronology

In principle, it is always possible to fix a date for the hearing in advance. This date is normally known as soon as the initial request is made in oral proceedings. In written proceedings, a date is set on completion of the *mise en état*. The hearing must then take place on the date fixed. Hearings generally take any time from a few minutes to several hours.[43] If the parties agree, or if there is a legitimate reason, of greater significance than a mere personal circumstance, it

---

[41] This is a written report, drafted by the party's counsel, which presents the whole proceedings, including points of fact and law, and responds to the opponent's arguments.

[42] Directly enforceable in French law.

[43] Here the difficulty of using the word 'trial' in the context of the French civil process becomes apparent. There is clearly nothing very much like an English-type trial about the hearing in the French civil context.

is possible to ask the judge to postpone the case to a later date (*remise/renvoi*). The decision to postpone is regarded as a matter of judicial administration, and is in the discretion of the judge. Once oral argument begins the hearing may not be interrupted.

The hearing is conducted before the president. In addition, the clerk keeps the record of the hearing (the *plumitif*).[44] Speaking order during the hearing is determined by law. The plaintiff puts his or her case first, then the defendant, and then the public prosecutor (if he is involved). The president and judges may decide to hear the parties again, if they require further argument on the facts or on the law. The hearing is closed by the president, as soon as he or she considers the court is sufficiently well informed.

3.6. Special types of 'ordinary' proceedings

Not all contentious proceedings lead to a final adversarial[45] judgment, extinguishing the claim between the parties. Ordinary proceedings are not the only form of procedure in use before the courts. The Code also contains provisions governing specific types of proceedings which lack one or other of the elements of the contentious and adversarial proceedings.[46] The two main forms are: *référé* proceedings; and *ex parte* proceedings.[47]

3.6.1. Référé *proceedings*

3.6.1.1. Increase and diversification

While the 1806 Code only envisaged a *référé* before the president of the *tribunal civil* (the ancestor of the *tribunal de grande instance*), who could order urgent measures where there was no serious defence to be made on the merits of the case, the new Code now recognizes other purposes for the *référé* and opens the way to *référé* proceedings before any court (apart from the *Cour de Cassation*, of course).

Traditionally the *référé* was a means of rapidly obtaining a provisional measure pending a decision on the merits of the claim. Conservatory measures, such as a provisional prohibition (on the sale of a book alleged to infringe copyright, or to contain defamatory material, for example), or a provisional

---

[44] Keeping this record, which is signed by the president and the court clerk after each hearing, allows those concerned to check whether all the legal requirements have been complied with.

[45] In the sense of the parties having been present or having been duly called.

[46] Sometimes proceedings are brought to court in which even the contentious element is lacking. The proceedings may be needed as a formal or even substantive requirement for the validity of a consensual arrangement. This is the case where there is a strong public interest, as in: adoption; changing one's matrimonial status; or a divorce on a joint application. This question needs no particular development in this context. It must, however, be mentioned, as French law has a tendency to favour friendly settlement of disputes. Yet the agreement of the parties may be subject to approval of the judge and this approval is of non-contentious nature. A judicial control is therefore implemented. [47] Called *procédure sur requête*.

suspension (prohibiting the opening of a new shop alleged to be in breach of restraint of trade agreements, for example), do not affect the final decision of the judge. This classical *référé* is maintained by the new Code as the general type. However, new and specific types of *référés* slowly appeared. These do not necessarily share the features of the ordinary *référé*, especially the requirements of emergency and absence of serious objection on the merits. Thus a 'new' *référé* proceeding may be taken with the aim of obtaining: (*a*) a preliminary investigation, outside the context of a full court case (*référé in futurum*); (*b*) the provisional payment of a sum of money as damages, even up to the whole of the sum claimed; (*c*) conservatory measures (like the English injunction) to prevent impending damage or to force a troublesome interference to cease immediately. The *référé* judge also has the power to order somebody to fulfil his obligations, as by performing a contract, or delivering or replacing goods (the *référé-injonction*).

3.6.1.2. *Référé* procedure

The court is normally seized of a *référé* by way of a writ for a specific hearing at a certain time and date, usually on a day set aside for such cases. If the situation is urgent or, for some reason, the nature of the dispute requires it, the judge may make an order that the writ be served for a specific hour of a day, even a bank holiday or a Sunday (the 'hour to hour' *référé*).[48] Access to such urgent procedures is granted (or refused) on the *ex parte* application of the party concerned.

In most such cases, the judge will sit alone to decide the *référé* claim presented to him. However, the law gives the judge two other options. He may adjourn the case for consideration as a *référé* by a collegiate bench of the court at a specific future date. He may also decide that the case is not suitable for determination under the *référé* procedure, but is urgent, in which case he has the power to authorize the plaintiff to serve his writ for hearing on a specific day. These two techniques are different, even though they tend to merge in practice. In the latter case, the procedure leads to a judgment on the merits. In the former case, the resulting order is still a *référé* order, which is provisional by nature, rather than final and conclusive. The judge who will consider the merits of the case does have not any obligation to follow the order. Yet, the *référé* order does have legal effects. Binding, albeit provisionally, it can be immediately enforced, even if an appeal is lodged at the court of appeal. However, conditions such as provision of security or a guarantee can be attached to its enforcement.

Référé orders tend, in fact if not in law, to have the effect of a final, definitive

---

[48] *Référé d'heure à heure.*

decision on the merits of the case in hand.[49] In practice, the *référé* procedure has become the normal summary procedure for resolving uncomplicated civil claims.

3.6.2. Ex parte *applications*

3.6.2.1. *Ex parte* procedure

Ex parte applications are governed by Articles 493 to 498 of the new Civil Procedural Code. The resulting decisions are classified as neither 'adversarial'[50] nor final. The *ex parte* procedure may be used when the court can be persuaded that there are good reasons why the plaintiff should not call his opponent to court in opposition to the application before the order is made. It is sometimes necessary to maintain a degree of discretion for a provisional measure to be effective.

3.6.2.2. Special regime for interlocutory injunctions

The Code also creates certain specific interlocutory injunctions, which are obtained using the *ex parte* application procedure. The injunction to pay a sum of money (*injonction de payer*) is available from the *tribunal d'instance* and the commercial court, for a civil or commercial debt. The mandatory injunction (the order to do something) is available from the *tribunal d'instance* in cases where the complaint is made of a failure to perform obligations (*injonction de faire*). The *injonction de faire* has not really been used at all.[51] The procedure might as well be abolished. However, the *injonction de payer* is far more popular.[52] The *tribunal de grande instance* may well adopt a version of the procedure, for application in claims for civil debts over F. Frs. 50,000. Although the injunction is initially granted *ex parte*, an opportunity is allowed to the debtor for him to explain the reasons for his failure or refusal to pay. At this stage, the case is effectively sent back to the court on the merits, like any other claim for payment (in apparent contradiction of the essentially summary and *ex parte* nature of the initial procedure). The key to understanding the popularity of the procedure is to realize that the option of opposing the injunction is often not exercised,[53] and therefore it does not affect the efficiency of the whole scheme. If the defendant

---

[49] It is not inconceivable that a bold litigant might apply for a *référé* order which grants a creditor the whole of his claim for money! Given in first and last resort, it would be doubtful whether an appeal to the *Cour de Cassation* would be attempted. Granted in first resort, it may be appealed before the court of appeal, but because of its immediate and enforceable character, it cannot firmly be said that the sum provisionally paid could be restored in the appeal, in which the order to make provisional payment would be overturned, but the merits of the payment (which are the merits of the substantive case) would not be explored.

[50] See n. 37 above for comment on the meaning of 'adversarial' in the French procedural context.

[51] The official statistics of the Ministry of Justice do not even mention them.

[52] See s. 4 below at text to nn. 55–62 and in Apps. 9.6–9.15.

[53] Thus, in 1995, the *tribunaux d'instance* have granted 731,055 injunctions to pay and there has been an opposition in only 48,149 cases. *Annuaire statistique de la justice 1991–1995* (Paris: La Documentation Française, 1996), 73–4.

does not oppose the injunction within the legal period, the injunction produces all the effects of a properly 'adversarial' judgment on the merits,[54] without any possibility of appeal to the court of appeal.

4. STATISTICAL DATA

4.1. General observations

The official data assembled in the following pages are those of the Ministry of Justice, and are extracted from the *Annuaire statistique de la justice 1991–1995*[55] and from *Les Chiffres-clés de la justice: octobre 1997*.[56] Not all the statistical data which the editors of this book have requested are available for France. Information relating to the number of claims settled should be looked at carefully. Many settlements are not made known to the court or the judge. For the sake of clarity, the different data sets listed here are grouped in the different appendices at the end of this essay.

4.2. Activity of the *tribunaux de grande instance*[57]

Activity in these 181 courts has increased markedly since 1991. In that year, 492,391 ordinary actions were commenced. By 1996, the number rose to 673,664 actions commenced (roughly a 26 per cent increase). Nonetheless, average case duration has diminished slightly: from 10 months in 1991 to 8.9 months in 1996. This improvement is due to two major factors. First, the number of completed cases has risen over the same period: from 462,326 to 655,315 (an increase of about 29 per cent). Productivity within the *tribunaux de grande instance* has improved. Secondly, the number of *référé* proceedings commenced over this period rose from 96,184 to 126,501 (a 24 per cent increase). *Référé* proceedings are a highly attractive summary alternative to ordinary proceedings. However, due to their increasing popularity, their average duration has increased: from 0.9 months in 1991 to 1.2 months in 1995 (figures for 1996 are not yet available).

4.3. Activity of the *tribunaux d'instance*[58]

The activity of the *tribunaux d'instance* has not undergone similar changes. Rather, activity here has decreased significantly. This trend has affected:

---

[54] Once again, attention is drawn to n. 37.

[55] Published by La Documentation Française, 29–31 quai Voltaire, 75344 Paris cedex 07 (Tel: +33-1-40-15-70-00, Fax: +33-1-40-15-72-30).

[56] *Sous-direction de la Statistique, des Études et de la Documentation* (SIDESC), located at 7 rue Scribe, 75009 Paris (Tel: +33-1-44-77-66-27 and fax: +33-1-44-77-66-50).

[57] See below Apps. 9.6 and 9.14.   [58] See below Apps. 9.7 and 9.14.

- the number of proceedings decided on their merits;
- the number of actions commenced (which has fallen from 547,890 to 479,500, a decrease of 12.48 per cent);
- the number of terminated claims (which has fallen from 518,732 to 456,081, a decrease of 12.07 per cent); and
- the number of *référé* proceedings (which has fallen from 91,596 in 1991 to 83,962 in 1995, a decrease of 8.33 per cent).

An explanation can be found in the numerous transfers of jurisdiction from the *tribunaux d'instance* to the *tribunaux de grande instance* which occurred during the relevant period (including jurisdiction over contested alimony cases, and over matrimonial over-indebtedness). However, as the number of concluded cases has decreased less rapidly than the number of new cases commenced, and as the number of *référé* cases has not increased, the average duration of cases before the *tribunaux d'instance* has increased. Average duration has gone from 4.5 months in 1991 to 5 months in 1996 for ordinary proceedings; and from 1.6 months to 1.8 months for *référé* proceedings.

4.4. Activity of commercial courts[59]

Data available for the commercial courts are more limited. The only figures concern the number of completed cases, and the average duration of ordinary proceedings and *référés*. With regard to completed cases, numbers seem to be quite stable: 259,062 in 1991 and 263,682 in 1996. The same applies to *référé* proceedings with 54,370 claims in 1991 and 51,007 in 1996. Perhaps surprisingly, the average duration of ordinary proceedings has increased: from 4.9 months to 6.2 months; whereas average duration of *référé* proceedings has remained quite stable: 0.9 months in 1991 compared to 1 month in 1995.

4.5. Activity of labour courts[60]

The labour courts have experienced a sharp increase in the number of cases, and in average duration. Efforts have been made to improve efficiency. These have led to an increase in the number of cases concluded each year of about 7 per cent. However, the number of new claims brought each year has also grown (increasing by 7 per cent for claims on the merits and by 19 per cent for *référé* proceedings). This has resulted in an increase in the average duration of labour court proceedings: from 9.2 to 9.4 months for ordinary proceedings, and from 1.1 to 1.4 months for *référés*. The increase in volume of cases in the labour court also has adverse effects on the higher courts (courts of appeal and *Cour de Cassation*). Judgments of the labour courts are subject to a high rate of appeal.

---

[59] See below App. 9.8.   [60] See below Apps. 9.9 and 9.14.

4.6. Activity of social security courts[61]

Trends in the activity of these courts are difficult to identify, because they do not come within the general reporting framework of the Ministry of Justice. Available figures are limited. However, these courts are of very little practical significance. Claim numbers are relatively low. There are only about 100,000 new cases in total each year, in the 111 courts.

4.7. Activity of agricultural leases courts[62]

The comments made above in respect of the social security courts apply even more strongly to the agricultural leases courts. These 413 courts see a total of only about 4,000 claims each year.

4.8. Activity of courts of appeal[63]

The courts of appeal have been adversely affected by the increase in litigation at first instance. The 26 per cent increase in new appeals between 1991 and 1996 has overtaken the 21 per cent increase in concluded cases. The backlog of appeals has grown, causing an increase in average appeal duration: from 13.9 months in 1991 to 15.6 months in 1996. This increase is considerable, as these are cases which have been tried once already, and should, in theory, be ready to be tried a second time immediately.

4.9. Activity of the *Cour de Cassation*[64]

Available statistics do not give much information. The *Cour de Cassation* is known to be in a state of crisis (especially in the criminal law and labour law fields). However, the average duration of cases in this court is not documented. With a few exceptions, the *Cour de Cassation* concludes as many cases each year as are commenced before it. However, the stock of pending cases remains large and stable. Its situation cannot be said to be improving.

4.10. Judicial activity in 1996[65]

These data supplement the information provided for the period 1991–6.

4.11. The legal/judicial professions[66]

Three remarks must be made. First, in addition to the judges appointed by the Ministry of Justice, one must take into account the 3,000 elected judges sitting in

---

[61] See below App. 9.10.   [62] See below App. 9.11.
[63] See below Apps. 9.12 and 9.14.   [64] See below App. 9.13.
[65] See below App. 9.14.
[66] See below App. 9.15, which allows assessment of the relative importance of each profession and the links between each of them. It is possible to compare them with the French population.

the commercial courts and the 12,000 elected labour court judges. These judges are not professional magistrates, but are lay persons who simultaneously pursue their primary career.

Secondly, not all advocates litigate. About a third of them work as in-house lawyers for commercial companies, where their primary task is the giving of legal advice. Thirdly, judicial experts and conciliators are not working on a permanent basis for the justice system.

5. DESCRIPTION OF THE MAIN PROBLEMS ENCOUNTERED IN THE ADMINISTRATION OF CIVIL JUSTICE

5.1. The different interpretations of 'the justice crisis'

Paradoxically, although the French crisis has been described, its origins analysed, and its causes specified, all in the most careful and scientific manner, French justice is still ill. The crisis has three aspects: a crisis of confidence; a crisis of growth; and a crisis of conscience.[67]

5.1.1. Crisis of confidence

Public surveys consistently highlight the low confidence French people have in the justice system. In a 1991 survey, 97 per cent of the persons surveyed saw justice as being too slow; 85 per cent too difficult; 84 per cent too costly; 83 per cent too unequal. In 1995, a survey conducted by the Ministry of Justice showed justice came last in the ranking of public services. In 1997, surveys still show that 77 per cent of people find the justice system too costly, and 87 per cent too old-fashioned. Its overall image was bad for 66 per cent of people.

5.1.2. Crisis of growth

Above all justice is the victim of its own success. There has been a continual expansion of litigation since the end of the nineteenth century, which has accelerated even further in the last twenty years. Numerous factors have contributed. Population has grown. Legislative and executive inflation respond to the demand for more and more legal regulation. An increasing ideology of compensation has arisen, transforming any trouble into a claim for damages against someone else. Familial, professional, and institutional (school, village, church) solidarities have eroded. There has been a considerable democratization of access to justice as legal aid has been reformed. All these factors contribute to the perception that France is moving slowly towards an American-style litigation society.[68]

---

[67] F. Terré, 'Crise du juge et philosophie du droit: synthèse et perspectives', in J. Leadble (ed.), *La Crise du juge* (Paris: LGDJ, 1990), 157 ff.

[68] See L. Cadiet, 'Le spectre de la société contentieuse', in *Écrits en hommage à Gérard Cornu* (Paris: PUF, 1994), 29 ff.

The resources of the justice system have not increased proportionately to the increasing demand for justice. In the middle of last century, France had about 6,000 judges for a population of 37 million. The size of the judiciary is approximately the same today, although there are now 58 million people living in France.[69]

The justice budget has doubled since 1981. However, at 1.5 per cent of the national budget the French justice budget is higher than the budget for culture, but lower than the budget for veterans. At F. Frs. 270 per capita (in 1991), French justice is a poor relation compared to Great Britain (F. Frs. 492) or Germany (F. Frs. 495).[70] Moreover, much of the French justice budget is allocated for prisons and judicial protection of young people. How could this situation lead to anything but a crisis of confidence among the parties, and a crisis of conscience among justice professionals, especially judges? These two crises reinforce one another.

5.1.3. Crisis of conscience

The French judge is responsible for more than just the application of the law to cases in the sacred and reassuring confines of his courtroom. The judge in the modern welfare state is required to take charge in a vast range of difficult individual or collective situations. This calls for qualities beyond the traditional qualities of a lawyer and a judge. He or she must now become a social facilitator, expert in all fields.

When the welfare state is in crisis, the judge must resolve the same difficult social situations without the resources or the authority. Disrespect for the state is spreading to its servants. At the same time, the judge sometimes has the feeling of being dispossessed of more and more of his traditional purview, as more and more disputes of all types are entrusted to extra-judicial organs. This is especially true of economic and financial disputes, for which non-judicial means of resolution, such as conciliation commissions and independent administrative authorities, have emerged. The present situation thus leads to a profound feeling of dissatisfaction not only among judges, who are deeply affected in their traditional role, but also among those who work for justice and who are faced with fierce competition, hitherto unknown.

5.2. Delay: the paradox of timetabling a case

The timetable for trial is paradoxical in that the right measure is the result of a balance. Time taken must be long enough to assess the case, gather the evidence, and prepare for its presentation. However, it must also be short

---

[69] A contemporary comparison: today there are 6,000 judges in Poland for 39 million inhabitants, as opposed to roughly the same number in France for more than 58 million people.

[70] See M. Cantat, 'L'administration de la justice', in *La Justice*, Cahiers français 251 (Paris: La Documentation Française, 1991), 49–55.

enough for the judgment to be of use, and for the system to be seen to work promptly and wisely.[71] Unfortunately, parties' and lawyers' inertia tends to ensure the first consideration outweighs the second. Cases are delayed 'for preparation' for long periods when no preparation actually occurs. This means that, in spite of long delays to prepare, the judge is not actually in any better situation to assess the dispute presented to him than if the case had come on more quickly. In the end, the inflation of time becomes extreme, and the system is clogged with delayed cases, causing further delay.

5.2.1. Delay at first instance

On the whole, the official statistics reveal an increase in the average time taken between a full hearing on the merits and delivery of judgment across the first instance jurisdictions. There is also a correlation between this increase and increasing numbers of new cases. This is so, despite an increase in terminated cases over the same period (1991–6).[72] Thus, for the *tribunal d'instance* the average time to judgment after a full hearing on merits rose from 4.5 months in 1991 to 5 months in 1996. It went up from 8.3 to 9.6 months in 1995 for the court of agricultural leases, and, worst of all, from 9.2 to 10.1 months for the labour court. It is possible to show an improvement in the situation before the *tribunal de grande instance* with a decrease from 10 months in 1991 to 8.9 months in 1996. This figure is deceptive, as the same period showed a large increase in the number of *référés*. This suggests that a large number of cases have been diverted from hearing on the merits to *référés*, in accordance with the evolution of their role discussed above. The increase in *référés* and in the average time of these summary proceedings is observed in all courts: 1.6 to 1.8 months for the *tribunal d'instance*; 1.1 to 1.4 months for the labour court; and 0.9 to 1.0 for the commercial court.

5.2.2. Delay on appeal

This general deterioration can also be observed at the second level of jurisdiction. From 1991 to 1996, the average time for a dispute to be resolved on the merits went up from 13.9 to 15.6 months. This may be compared with the increase in new disputes before the courts of appeal, which went from 173,177 to 219,335 over the same period. The official figures do not indicate the average time of appeal for *référés* coming from first instance. However, it appears likely that it increased considerably. The appeal rate for *référés* rose from 13,436 to 16,176.

5.2.3. Delay before the Cour de Cassation

Each year, the official reports[73] of this jurisdiction show a considerable increase in number of petitions.

---

[71] J.-M. Coulon and M.-A. Frison Roche (eds.), *Le Temps dans la procédure* (Paris: Dalloz, 1996).
[72] See below, Apps. 9.6 to 9.15.
[73] See for example *Rapport de la Cour de Cassation 1995* (Paris: La Documentation Française, 1996), esp. 435–56.

5.2.4. *Perspective*

Recent official figures from the Ministry of Justice tend to show that civil justice will probably be paralysed, especially at the appeal level, by the year 2000. From 1975 to 1995, the number of claims before civil and commercial courts rose by 122 per cent. Terminated disputes have increased at the same pace (+128 per cent). The number of pending claims is increasing, and is projected to reach 2 million by 1 January 2000.[74] This would constitute an increase of roughly 300 per cent since 1975. As a side effect, the average time for liquidation of the stock of claims, at least before the *tribunal de grande instance*, could rise from 10 months in 1994 to 12 months in the year 2000.[75]

The greatest increase in claims has been seen by the court of appeal (+208 per cent). Despite a rise in terminated claims of 219 per cent, the stock of pending claims increased by 730 per cent over the reference period. At this pace, the number of pending claims on 1 January 2000 could reach 400,000, which is eleven times as large as in 1975. This would lead to an increase of the average period for liquidation of the stock from 17.3 months in 1994 to 24 months in the year 2000. Average statistics do not paint the full picture, as there are great disparities between the different courts of appeal. Some, among them the largest, are already full and cannot grant any appeal a hearing date before the year 2000.[76]

Can this be 'reasonable', as required by Article 6 (1) of the European Convention on Human Rights?

5.3. Cost: the ambiguity of so-called 'free' justice

The principle of free access to justice means parties must be freely able to have resort to the courts to obtain a resolution of their claims.[77] All parties must be allowed this right. This principle was restated on 30 December 1977, in a statute whose Article 1 reads: 'Justice shall be free, and given in accordance with the conditions laid down in this law.' This provision must be properly understood. Justice necessarily has a cost. This cost is even higher when justice of a high quality is to be provided. The state cannot meet the whole of this cost. As justice is a service, rendered to private parties, it would not be abnormal for

---

[74] This estimate was produced by projecting the current rates of new and terminated disputes up to the year 2000, based on observations over the period 1980–95. Backlogs have been extrapolated as at 1 January of each year, on the basis of the difference between these two estimated values (J.-M. Coulon, *Réflexions et propositions sur la procédure civile* (Paris: La Documentation Française, 1997), 14–15).
[75] The average time for liquidation of the stock of claims is the relation between the stock of pending claims on 31 December and the monthly number of terminated claims. This pointer has a prognostic value: when it increases, the average time for determination of individual claims, which takes into account past activity, follows the increase with a slight shift in time.
[76] Coulon, *Réflexions*, 15.
[77] See M. Capelletti (ed.), *Accès à la justice et état-providence*, preface by René David (Paris: Economica, 1984).

parties to bear some of the cost. No tax has been levied on procedural acts since 1977. Nevertheless, the costs of a trial involve more than the costs of the functioning of the judicial administration. A trial requires the involvement of professionals such as lawyers, *avoués*, process servers, and expert witnesses, ordinarily chosen by the parties, who must be paid. These costs must be borne by the parties.

5.3.1. *Cost to the state: receipts increasing slowly, spending increasing rapidly*

The budget for justice has already been dealt with.[78] For those who like figures, recall that between 1991 and 1997, the Ministry of Justice budget rose from F. Frs. 18.17 billion (1.42 per cent of the general budget of the state) to F. Frs. 23.90 billion, an increase of roughly 31 per cent. This increase does not match the rate of increase of costs in civil and commercial matters and of legal aid. For the same period, the total amount of costs in civil and commercial matters rose from F. Frs. 256.49 million to F. Frs. 484.09 million, an increase of about 89 per cent. The total amount of sums distributed in the legal aid context rose from F. Frs. 367.72 million to F. Frs. 1072.21 million, an increase of 191 per cent. These figures do not call for any commentary. As far as the legal aid figures are concerned, the spectacular increase can be explained by the reform of the legal aid system in 1991, the budgetary effects of which made themselves apparent as early as 1992. Legal aid spending soared to F. Frs. 859.39 million that year. One of the objectives of the reform was to increase access to justice. These figures show that, on the whole, this goal has been achieved.[79] These sums, however, do not represent the real cost of French justice, as part of the cost is borne by the parties and is unknown to us.

5.3.2. *Cost to the parties: principles and qualifications*

In principle, the parties have to bear the costs of the trial. This creates the risk of restricting access to justice for those who are not fortunate, and infringing the principle of equality of access to public services. Thus, society makes a financial contribution to the least fortunate parties.

5.3.2.1. *Les Dépens*

The professionals' costs are twofold. Certain costs come within what are called *les dépens*. These are the costs legally necessary to pursue the trial. These costs are regulated, either via an administrative scale of charges, as in the case of process servers, or by judicial decision, as in the case of experts. The exhaustive list of costs within *les dépens* is given by law.[80] These costs must be borne by the

---

[78] See above s. 6.1.2. at text to nn. 69–70.
[79] For details, see below s. 6.4.6 at text to n. 82.
[80] See Art. 695 of the new Civil Procedural Code. *Les dépens* consist of fees for technicians in charge of a preliminary investigation measure (e.g. expert witnesses), indemnities for witnesses, process servers' fees, and lawyers' fees in proceedings where representation is mandatory.

parties. Usually the losing party must pay both his own costs and those of the other party, although the judge may reallocate this burden, where there is reason to do so.

5.3.2.2. *Les Frais irrépétibles*

The second category is made up of those costs not comprised within *les dépens*. It corresponds to all costs not strictly necessary to the pursuit of the trial, especially lawyers' fees. These costs are known as *frais irrépétibles*, because they originally had to be borne by the party who incurred them. In practice, incurring such costs at quite a high level is all but unavoidable. The new Code now gives the judge a wider discretion.[81] The judge can order a party to pay a sum of money, not necessarily amounting to the full costs incurred by the other, described as an 'indemnity'. The judge can take the economic situation of the party into consideration. Experience proves that the indemnities awarded by judges only compensate for a very small fraction of the costs incurred as *frais irrépétibles*. It is therefore necessary for lawyers to justify the sums charged precisely, something which they often forget.

French law prohibits both fixed and contingency fees as impeding competition, and prohibits the agreement on a *quota litis* contract. Fees must be determined case by case, at the beginning of the trial with a fee agreement, or at the end of the trial, depending on different criteria, including the duration of litigation, the difficulty of the case, the experience of the lawyer, and the resources of the client. An advocate, will, as a matter of practice, ask his client for a provision during the trial. The practice of determining fees by reference to an hourly scale is growing, especially in commercial litigation. This method is still not really widespread. The new Civil Procedural Code contains a procedure for contesting an advocate's fees. The claim is brought, in first instance, before the head of the Bar Council (*Le Bâtonnier*).

The above arrangements also apply to advocates' work on appeals, where representation by an advocate is not compulsory, but employment of an *avoué* is. The *avoué* is a public officer and his fees come within *les dépens* already described above.

5.3.3. *Social assistance with the costs of litigation: two types of contribution*

The state organizes legal aid, enabling those with modest means to obtain access to justice without having to bear the whole cost of the trial. The legal aid system is designed with sharp cutoff. No help is given to those whose incomes, although still modest, are above the legal aid limit. This has particular impact on the middle classes. The cost of a trial will be very difficult for them to bear. A divorce petition, for example, without any particularly special applications or appeal, costs approximately the equivalent of the minimum monthly

---

[81] See Art. 700 of the new Civil Procedural Code.

wage, about F. Frs. 7,000. Legal expenses insurance may be the only realistic alternative source of finance.

5.3.3.1. Legal aid

It has always been seen as necessary to allow those with modest resources free access to justice. The first French law for this purpose was passed on 22 January 1851, and related to judicial assistance. A new law of 10 July 1991 instituted a new mechanism for access to justice, called legal aid. This is aid for legal advice and assistance with out-of-court proceedings (non-contentious administrative proceedings or conciliation proceedings before certain commissions, such as that dealing with the affairs of over-indebted households).[82] The reform has achieved most of its objectives. The number of persons benefiting from legal aid in 1995 was 581,829. This was an increase of 66 per cent compared to 1991. The increase was higher in criminal matters (+90 per cent) than in civil matters (+55 per cent). The scope of legal aid is wide. It is given before all courts: civil; administrative; criminal; disciplinary; contentious; and non-contentious; to plaintiff or defendant, for all or part of the trial, including interviews in police stations and proceedings for the enforcement of judgments. However, the fraction of parties benefiting from legal aid varies from one matter to another. Rather low before the labour court (10 per cent) and before the *tribunal d'instance* (7 per cent), it is approximately 30 per cent for proceedings before family judges and 35 per cent for divorces.

The grant of legal aid is usually made for claimants with a monthly income below a certain limit, determined by the law. On 1 January 1992 the limit was F. Frs. 4,400 per month for a complete award, and F. Frs. 6,600 per month for a partial award. Since 1 January 1997, the limits have been increased to F. Frs. 4,848 and F. Frs. 7,273 respectively. (The minimum wage in France is F. Frs. 6,406 per month.)

Where only partial legal aid is granted, the beneficiary must pay for the help of professionals other than the advocate (process servers and the like) and, usually, must also pay all the fees involved for a trial in which an award of damages is won. In principle, the professionals employed on legal aid are chosen by the applicant. If not, the head of the profession involved will make the choice (e.g. the head of the Bar Council will select an advocate for the party, if the party does not choose one for herself).

5.3.3.2. Legal protection insurance

For an important number of households, especially those just above the income limit for partial legal aid, the cost of a trial is an steep expense, but one which nevertheless must sometimes be faced. For annual premiums of about £30 to £50, legal protection insurance is available to cover the fees involved in a trial.

---

[82] See below s. 8.5 at text to nn. 107–10.

This particular variety of insurance is a valuable supplement to legal aid. Following a Directive from the Council of the European Communities, a statute was promulgated on 31 December 1989 implementing legal protection insurance.[83] The law established a principle of freedom of choice of the advocate, who will be in charge of 'defending, representing, or serving' his interests. If there is a disagreement between insurer and insured regarding measures to be taken in the main dispute, the problem is referred to an external person, appointed in common by the parties, or by the president of the *tribunal de grande instance* by way of *référé*. The person appointed acts more as a mediator, and his opinion does not bind the contracting parties. Indeed, the contracting party always retains the right to commence litigation, paying his own costs, against the opinion of the third person and the insurer. Should the ultimate solution of the main dispute be more favourable than that proposed by the insurer, the insured party is compensated for all of the fees paid in his action.

6. HISTORICAL PERSPECTIVE OF REFORM

6.1. From one Code to another

The new Civil Procedural Code seeks to ensure the more efficient handling of civil proceedings. Without going too far back in time, it is necessary to examine the innovations of the new Code against the background formed by the old one, to see how reform has been undertaken, and to examine its effects.

6.2. Civil trial under the 1806 Civil Procedural Code: nobody's business but the parties'

France began the twentieth century under the 1806 Code which was, on the whole, a copy of the Great Royal Charter on Civil Procedure drawn up in 1667 and initiated by Colbert under the reign of Louis XIV.[84]

This Code adopted very extreme liberal principles of party control of their own proceedings. Despite sporadic attempts at limited reform, the position remained largely unchanged right up until 1958.

6.3. The Fifth Republic: rationalization

In 1958, under the Fifth Republic, procedural law-making power was transferred from Parliament to government, enabling real progress to be made on reform. The court structure was rationalized, modifying the territorial

---

[83] See Arts. L. 127-1 to L. 127-7 and L. 321-6 of the Insurance Code.
[84] See N. Picardi and A. Giuliani, *Code Louis*, i: *Ordonnance civile, 1667* (Milan: Giuffrè edn., 1996).

competence of the different courts, and simplifying the hierarchy. The *tribunal de grande instance* replaced *tribunaux civils* and the *tribunal d'instance* replaced the justices of the peace. The court of appeal was established as the ordinary jurisdiction at the second level. This reform created substantial savings, as 172 *tribunaux de grande instance* replaced 353 *tribunaux civils*. Even more radically, 455 *tribunaux d'instance* replaced 2,092 justices of the peace.

At the same time, along the lines of today's reforms, mass litigation was either withdrawn from the judge, as in the case of motor accidents,[85] or allocated to specialized judges,[86] as, for example, divorces were allocated to a judge for matrimonial matters[87] and matters of enforcement to an enforcement judge.[88] A new procedure before a single judge was often adopted, together with new simplified procedures. These were usually oral, without the mandatory involvement of an advocate. In this way, rules of judicial organization and rules of procedure are linked in the state's response to the justice crisis.

6.4. The new Civil Procedural Code, 1975

The new Civil Procedural Code, launched by Jean Foyer,[89] was progressively developed, section by section, by a reform Commission instituted in 1969.[90] The new Code came into force on 1 January 1977. It was not until 1981 that it reached its definitive form. The 1975 Code was new in both its form and content.

6.4.1. Theoretical reform under the new Code: co-operation between the parties and the judge
There are several possible conceptions of the civil trial. Depending on the perspective adopted, different roles will be allocated to the different actors concerned. The new Code was designed according to a particular conception of the civil trial, a more co-operative conception, at odds with the independent, party-driven viewpoint of the 1806 Code. This innovation can be seen right from the start in the 'guiding principles of the trial' (*principes directeurs du procès*)

---

[85] For which the law organizes the settlement of compensation for victims, made possible by compulsory insurance in this area. See Ph. le Tourneau and L. Cadiet, *Droit de la responsabilité* (Paris: Dalloz, 2nd edn. 1998), 3785–904.

[86] See Cadiet, 'Le Juge unique en question', and see above s. 2.2.1.1 at text at nn. 6–12.

[87] See Cadiet, 'A la recherche du juge de la famille', and see above s. 2.2.1.1 at text at nn. 6–12.

[88] See J. Le Normand, 'Le Juge de l'exécution', in R. Perrot (ed.), *La Réforme des procédures civiles d'execution* (Paris: Sirey, 1993), 31–47; J. Héron, 'Le Juge unique et l'exécution en droit privé', in Bolze and Pedrot, *Les Juges uniques*, 35–43.

[89] Then Professor of Law, and president of the Law Commission of the National Assembly after having been Charles de Gaulle's Minister of Justice.

[90] See G. Cornu, 'L'élaboration du Code de procédure civile', in B. Beigner (ed.), *La Codification* (Paris: Dalloz, 1997), 71–80. See also *Cour de Cassation, Le nouveau Code de procédure civile: vingt ans après* (Paris: La Documentation Française, 1998), esp. contributions of Mr Cornu and Mr Parmentier, who were members of the Commission in charge of drafting the new texts.

which open the Code (Arts. 1 to 24)[91] and which express the 'quintessence of the civil trial'.[92] The whole spirit of the civil trial is contained in this core of the first twenty-four first articles. It is possible to read here an intended balance between the prerogatives of the parties and the powers of the judge in the unfolding of the trial and the resolution of the dispute. This 'charter of the division of roles between judges and parties' is not the implementation of an inquisitorial, authoritative and administrative, trial model, as some feared immediately after the Code was promulgated.[93]

The Code is essentially a work of compromise, endeavouring to mitigate the extremely liberal principles of the French tradition. The trial is still to 'belong to' the parties, but the judge is given extended powers, and the responsibility to promote the public interest in the justice of the case, by reaching the fairest possible solution to the dispute. Justice is a public service. Impartiality does not mean passivity. Important powers have been given to the judge, for conducting the trial: power to grant adjournments; power to order investigation measures, including, sometimes, under the threat of a civil fine (Art. 3); power to take into account all relevant facts, even if the parties have not specially raised them in argument (Art. 7); power to order the production of materials (Art. 11); and, even on his own motion, power to order any legally available preliminary investigation measure (Art. 10). This 'emphasis on the prerogatives of the judge'[94] was a big change from previous practice, involving a rethink of the entire basis of the French trial, right from square one.

The Code also retains certain of the previous practices.[95] The parties keep the power to initiate proceedings. They are also given the power to modify the extent of the prerogatives of the judge, either to limit or to extend them, by restricting him to the consideration of evidence and points of law they wish to have considered, or, conversely, by giving him the power to judge as a referee (Art. 12). The position is balanced by limiting the powers of the judge, making it necessary at all times to consider the object of the claim (Arts. 4 and 5) and, above all, requiring the judge 'under all circumstances to comply with the "adversarial" principle'.[96] Twenty years on, the growing opinion is that Articles 1 to 13 of the new Code create a balanced and appropriate theoretical frame-

---

[91] See G. Cornu, 'Les principes directeurs du procès civil par eux-mêmes: fragments d'un état des questions', in *Études offertes à Pierre Bellet* (Paris: Litec, 1991), 83–100. See also L. Cadiet, 'Le Code', in *Cour de Cassation, Le Nouveau Code de procédure civile: vingt ans après*, 45–73.

[92] Cornu, 'L'Élaboration du Code de procédure civile', 250.

[93] According to the confession of those who drafted the new Code, there is one real inquisitorial point in the whole scheme. Art. 222 para. 2 allows the judge to determine the appropriate facts to be proven in the investigation. G. Cornu, 'Les Principes directeurs du procès civil par eux-mêmes', 87.

[94] Cornu, 'L'Élaboration du Code de procédure civile', 251.

[95] Cornu, 'Les Principes directeurs du procès civil par eux-mêmes', 90–1.

[96] Art. 16, para. 1 of the new Civil Procedural Code. As to the meaning of 'adversarial' in the context of French civil procedure, see above n. 37.

work, based on a useful principle of co-operation between the judge and the parties in the process of reaching a judgment.[97]

6.4.2. *Reform of practice: simplification*

The legislature hoped its reforms would simplify the trial process and increase its flexibility. The procedure has been simplified, by the suppression of exceptions and of the numerous irrational variations in procedure before each different court, most of which were inherited from history. Numerous rules became common to all jurisdictions. Simplification has also come from a harmonization and improvement of procedures. It is now possible to seize a court by mere declaration to the clerk, even orally. The ordinary form of notification of procedural acts is by means of a simple letter. Some decisions of judges can be recorded by simple inscriptions on the file.

6.4.3. *Flexibility*

The task of simplification goes hand in hand with the willingness of the government to make procedure more flexible. Above all, flexibility enables better management of the time spent on the trial. The ideal is that each case should be treated according to its own needs. Emergency situations require rapid decisions; hence the development of *référés* or *ex parte* orders. Complex cases call for more care within the preliminary investigation; hence the implementation of 'tracks' having different timetables, with judges of varying degrees of specialization (*juge de la mise en état, juge-rapporteur, conseiller rapporteur, conseiller de la mise en état*).

Better management of courtroom resources, both human and physical, is also possible. The use of single judges is developing. There is a more rational treatment of human resources within courts. Multiple passages between courts, or within the same proceeding, allow changes from one procedural option to another. As far as preliminary investigations are concerned, the powers of the judge have diversified.

6.4.4. *A balanced evaluation*

The reforms have not been altogether successful. The best reforms of procedure are of limited use if the judicial system does not acquire the human, material, and financial resources to implement them properly. More resources would give the judge and his partners the necessary time to do justice.[98] Progress in improvement of the civil trial process is constrained by this crisis of judicial resources. When one looks carefully at the history of French justice during the twentieth century, one sees a picture of repeated attempts by the state to improve the judicial system. The courts are rationalized, adapting them to demographic changes, and to economic and social developments. Single-judge

---

[97] See Cadiet, *Droit judiciaire privé*, nos. 1100–37. [98] See above s. 6.2 at text to n. 71.

courts grow in significance. Alternative modes of dispute resolution develop. These changes are all responses to the increase in litigation. The standardization of speedy proceedings, such as the *référé*, and the increased efficacy of judgments through provisional enforcement, are responses to the slowness of proceedings caused by overcrowded courts.

Yet recent projections produced from official statistics show all of this is insufficient.[99] This produces two tendencies, which we shall examine in the next two sections. On the one hand, there is an increasing temptation to take disputes out of the judicial system for an alternative mode of resolution; and, on the other hand, there is continuing pressure to reform the rules of civil procedure.

7. ALTERNATIVE MODES OF DISPUTE RESOLUTION

7.1. Value

The current taste for amicable settlements is a change which can be described as the passage from an imposed legal order to a negotiated one. As courts have become more congested, they have tended to lose authority. The public's respect is reduced for courts which cannot deliver timely justice.

The alternative modes raise a central question, that of respect for the fundamental 'defence' rights of the parties (*droits de la défense*). Alternative modes like arbitration, conciliation, and mediation offer speedy, non-violent, and non-formalistic proceedings. But the parties involved are not necessarily equal. They do not necessarily have the same technical ability or the same economic power. Guarantees are necessary to prevent unfair advantage being taken of the possible imbalance. Respect for minimal guarantees of procedure, like the 'natural justice' of the 'adversarial' principle[100] and the possibility of recourse to a judge, are extremely important.

These conditions mean that any alternative solutions should develop as part of the state's judicial system, as, for example, arbitration has developed as an institutionalized alternative. In the French conception, amicable settlements do not exclude the recourse to a judge, and recourse to a judge does not exclude amicable settlements.[101]

---

[99] See below, Apps. 9.6 to 9.15.

[100] See n. 37 above as to the meaning of 'adversarial' in the French procedural context.

[101] For a general view, see Ch. Jarrosson, *Les Modes alternatifs de règlement des conflits: présentation générale* (Paris: Revue Internationale de Droit Comparé, 1997), 325 ff.; L. Cadiet, 'Solution judiciaire et règlement amiable des litiges: de la contradiction à la conciliation', in *Mélanges offerts à Claude Champaud* (Paris: Dallloz, 1997), 123–47.

7.2. The amicable settlement of disputes without the judge

7.2.1. Spontaneous conciliation

'Spontaneous', as opposed to 'instituted', conciliation is where parties seek conciliation on their own initiative, rather than seeking to use the justice system, which then offers or requires recourse to conciliation. Spontaneous conciliation may take two forms depending on whether or not a third party intervenes to help the parties find a way to settle their dispute.[102]

7.2.1.1. Without the intervention of a third party

Parties can choose to launch negotiations directly, with a view to finding a settlement. Sometimes, conciliation is even planned by the parties in advance of any trouble. A clause may have been inserted into their contract favouring the settlement of any claim which might arise. For example, clauses of good faith, or clauses for amicable settlement, are frequently inserted in contracts for the transfer of technology or commercial distribution. Attempts at amicable settlement can be a prerequisite to other modes of resolution for the dispute, such as arbitration. These clauses do not oblige parties to sign a compromise. They only create an obligation to negotiate in good faith, with a view to finding a solution to the claim.

Often, conciliation is organized by the parties' respective lawyers. This practice is on the increase. It is said that litigation before the commercial courts is decreasing in favour of such alternatives.

7.2.1.2. With the intervention of a third party

A third party may be called in to assist the parties to come to an agreement. Sometimes the third party stays passive. He may not be asked to find a solution to the dispute himself. Expert clauses may appoint an expert to follow the implementation of a contract so as to avoid performance problems. In the case that difficulties arise, the expert is called upon to give an independent technical solution for the parties to consider.

Sometimes the role of the third party is more active. He may be expected to try to reconcile each party's point of view and to find a solution to the dispute by proposing the terms of an agreement. Such is the role of conciliation or mediation clauses, which, as opposed to arbitration clauses, do not give the mediator the power to impose a solution. Recourse to a contractual mediator may be the compulsory prerequisite to a claim before a judge or an arbitrator.

---

[102] See L. Cadiet, 'Les clauses contractuelles relatives à l'action en justice', in J. Mestre (ed.), *Les Principales Clauses des contrats conclus entre professionnels* (Aix-en-Provence: Presses Universitaires d'Aix-Marseille, 1990), 193–223.

7.2.2. Instituted conciliation

The examples of instituted conciliation are manifold. Quite early on, individual conciliation was given legislative sanction. Recently, collective conciliation has grown drastically.

7.2.2.1. Individual conciliation: the conciliator before the *tribunal d'instance*

The institution of individual conciliation is the result of a decree promulgated on 20 March 1978, and amended many times since then. This conciliation is made possible by a special category of professionals, called *conciliateurs de justice*, who are appointed temporarily to carry out their functions, free, under the jurisdiction of the *tribunal d'instance*.

The conciliator is not a judge and does not exercise any judicial authority. At least three years' legal experience is necessary to be appointed as a conciliator. It is possible for any person to require the assistance of a conciliator. No particular form is required and no consequences are attached to the request for assistance of a conciliator. In particular, it does not suspend the prescription or appeal period.

The conciliator does not pronounce any decision. His sole function is to 'facilitate, outside the context of judicial proceedings', the friendly settlement of disputes relating to rights of which the parties have free disposition.[103] If he achieves even partial conciliation, the agreement may take the form of a statement of agreement. This statement, which is a purely private document, is optional. However, the conciliator must lodge a copy with the clerk of the *tribunal d'instance*. The parties can reinforce the authority of their agreement by submitting it to the judge of first instance so as to give it the binding force of a judgment of the court.

The institution has not been a great success. The recruitment of conciliators was stopped in 1982 and started again in 1987. A 1993 reform launched the integration of conciliators into the judicial system. It was confirmed by a pluriannual plan for justice contained in a law promulgated on 8 February 1995. Now the *tribunal d'instance* can order reference to a conciliator.[104] It is in doubt whether the resources devoted to this scheme will be sufficient to enable it to live up to its express goals.

7.2.2.2. Other sorts of conciliators and mediators

The conciliation model has quickly become popular. Conciliators have been established for consumers, with exclusive charge of disputes between professionals and consumers. The medical profession has developed a conciliation structure. Insurance conciliators were instituted in 1993 by the liaison committee for insurance (a pool of the main French insurance companies) to solve disputes

---

[103] Decree 78-381 of 20 Mar. 1978, JO, 23 Mar. 1978, Art. 1.
[104] See Arts. 831–5 of the new Civil Procedural Code.

between insured persons and the insurer companies. These conciliators have been more or less successful.[105] These developments will certainly continue.

7.2.2.3. Collective conciliation: diversity of collective conciliation

French law also has examples of collective conciliation. Collective agreements have grown rapidly in all sectors in France. Collective conciliation has proven to be more effective in some areas than in others. It is very useful for insurance or lease disputes, but is almost ineffective in labour disputes.[106] Conciliation can also be collective in another sense, when multiple parties are involved, as, for example, where a debtor must negotiate with his numerous creditors. The procedure for dealing with the economic difficulties of business firms offers a perfect illustration. Its main characteristic is its strong link with judicial proceedings.

7.2.2.4. Amicable settlements and businesses in financial difficulties

A law promulgated on 1 March 1984 established a procedure for the amicable settlement of the difficulties of commercial business firms. These proceedings are instituted under the authority of a conciliator appointed by the president of the commercial court, for commercial businesses and workshops, and by the president of the *tribunal de grande instance* for any business having an economic activity but not subject to the commercial courts.

It allows a debtor firm to negotiate a scheme with its main creditors for payment of its debts in order to save the business from liquidation. The conciliator has no power to decide anything or bind anyone. His mission involves favouring the smooth operation of the business and looking for agreement between the debtor and the main creditors for cancellation of debts or more time to pay. If agreement is reached, it is a binding private contract, but its submission to the judge reinforces its authority. This conciliation takes place out of the context of proceedings, but in their shadow. The judge and his numerous powers of investigation are always present in the background. A judge could order an expert opinion on the economic situation of the company and its prospects. He could decide to suspend individual claims, or could order delays for debts not within the agreement. While still just conciliation, and dependent upon obtaining agreement, this form of intervention is closely integrated with judicial proceedings, much more so than individual conciliation.

7.2.2.5. Amicable settlements and over-indebted households

A conciliation process for indebted households has been instituted by a law of 31 December 1989, called *loi Neïertz*.[107] The procedure has been reformed by a

---

[105] See Cadiet, *Découvrir la justice*, 72–3.   [106] See Cadiet, *Droit judiciaire privé*, no. 937.
[107] The name of the then Secretary of State for consumers, Ms Véronique Neïertz.

law of 8 February 1995 which also implemented judicial mediation.[108] This law is unlike any other in France.

The proceedings come before local commissions of indebted households, which conduct a preliminary investigation, and define a possible solution. The civil judge intervenes as enforcement judge[109] supervising the application of the decided measures. The commission must endeavour to 'conciliate the parties with a view to coming to an agreement approved by the debtor and his main creditors'.[110] It has important fact-finding powers.

If the plan is agreed upon by the parties, it acquires the binding effect of a contract. If the commission fails in its task of conciliation, it then recommends to the judge complete or partial enforcement of the proposed measures. These recommendations, described by the law as mere 'opinions', can only be made at the request of the debtor, parties having been put in a position to express their points of view. If the recommendations are disputed by the creditors, the court is seized of the claim which it solves by way of a contentious order. The economic situation of the debtor is thus dealt with by the judge who can impose a kind of judicial plan for resolving over-indebtedness. If the recommendations are agreed upon, they are given binding force by the enforcement judge, after having been checked by the judge, who does not enter into their merits. Thus the judge can help to find friendly settlements. Proceedings of this type are numerous.

7.3. The amicable settlement of disputes by the judge: arbitration

The essential characteristic of arbitration is the agreement of the parties to submit their dispute to the decision of a person they have chosen, rather than to the decision of the judge selected by the state. Seen as a desirable and amicable alternative mode of dispute resolution, there is pressure to extend the scope of arbitration in France. Under the 1806 Code, the scope of arbitration was doubly limited. Arbitration was only possible for rights which the parties themselves could freely dispose of (which excluded separations between husbands and wives, state questions, and disputes involving information of the Public Prosecutor). More importantly, no advance commitment to arbitration was possible.

Since 1925, however, at least in commercial disputes, arbitration clauses have been recognized as binding. Yet the situation is still too rigid. The administration could benefit from access to arbitration in its own disputes. A reform is needed to open the way for arbitration in all civil matters, including some family cases.

---

[108] See below s. 8.9 at text to nn. 111–13.
[109] This function is taken on by the president of the *tribunal de grande instance*. See above s. 2.2.1.1 at text to nn. 6–12.   [110] See Art. L. 331-6 of the Consumer Code (*Code de la Consommation*).

7.4. Tendency to institutionalize the arbitration regime

The popularity of arbitration might be undermining its success. More and more organizations are offering arbitration services, with standardization of forms and timetables. The courts are called upon more and more to adapt their procedures to allow or require reference to arbitration. Such arbitrations lack the friendly, freely chosen aspects of the standard ideal of spontaneous arbitration. They lack its flexibility, economy, and speed. All this leads to a backlash, involving the re-judicialization of disputes, especially where the litigants can take the benefit of access to specialized courts, in which the commercial courts tend to be most highly regarded. The movement back to state judges is potentially a simpler alternative than opening up state courts to conciliation.

7.5. Development of the amicable settlement of disputes before the judge

The treatment of litigation by the judge is not as one-dimensional as the Civil Procedural Code suggests. In practice, his role is not limited to 'solving the disputes according to applicable rules of law' as laid down in Article 12, paragraph 1. Besides the numerous instances in which the judge has the task, in law or at the request of the parties, to rule according to equity or as a friendly *compositeur*,[111] the judge must always favour conciliation of interests. The development of judicial conciliation is part of a larger movement towards the promotion of a contractual or consensual type of justice in which the final step is the recognition of judicial mediation.

7.5.1. Judicial conciliation

Judicial conciliation is an amicable mode of resolution by the judge of disputes among private parties. This conciliation is enshrined in the Civil Procedural Code as a principle on par with the rights of defence and the principle of publicity of debates. The guiding principles of the trial are established at the beginning of the Civil Procedural Code. Article 21 lays down that 'It is part of the judge's task to conciliate the parties'. The new Code has implemented a very old position of French judicial law.

7.5.2. Scope of judicial mediation

Civil mediation now seems wide open. 'A judge seized of a dispute' can, at any moment of the proceedings, appoint a third person 'in order to hear the parties and confront their points of view in order to offer them a solution to their

---

[111] See for example Art. 12, para. 4 of the new Civil Procedural Code. See L. Cadiet, 'L'Équité dans l'office du juge civil', in *Justices*, 9 (Paris: Dalloz, 1998).

dispute'.[112] In the absence of any limiting definition, the 'judge' referred to here must be any civil judge.

Access to judicial mediation is doubly limited. First, mediation leading to a compromise between the parties is necessarily limited to rights of which parties have free disposition. Mediation is thus not available for divorces or separations or for issues relating generally to status and capacity. Secondly, the judge can only use mediation if the parties agree. He cannot impose it.

7.5.3. Regime

The parties bear the cost of the mediation. If an equitable agreement cannot be reached, the costs are allocated by the judge. Although an amicable mode of dispute resolution, mediation nevertheless does have a cost. Where mediation does not succeed, the mediator's tasks cease and the trial goes on in the ordinary way, as if nothing had happened. In case an agreement is reached, the parties can present it to the judge who gives it binding force. Whatever its success, failures or disadvantages, the development of judicial conciliation is part of a larger phenomenon, the birth of a negotiated or consensual type of justice.

8. THE PRESENT STATE OF AFFAIRS

8.1. The Haenel and Arthuis Report and its aftermath: the Méhaignerie Plan

In 1994, the French government received a report from two members of the Senate, Messrs Haenel and Arthuis,[113] and formulated a national and pluriannual plan for justice. This plan was launched in three laws passed at the beginning of 1995: an organizational law;[114] an organic law relating to judges;[115] and another law[116] which encompassed court organization and civil, criminal, and administrative procedures. The mountain gave birth to a mouse, as the allocated funds were mostly reserved for prisons and the judicial protec-

---

[112] Art. 131-1 of the new Civil Procedural Code.

[113] Close to the then Minister of Justice, Mr Pierre Méhaignerie, president of the *Centre des Démocrates Sociaux*, a party orientated to the right of centre. See H. Haenel and J. Arthuis, *Rapport de la commission de contrôles chargée d'examiner les modalités d'organization et les conditions de fonctionnement des services relevant de l'autorité judiciaire* (Journal Officiel de la République Française, Documents du Sénat no. 357, 1990–1).

[114] Law no. 95-9, 6 Jan. 1995, relating to justice (JO 8 Jan., p. 381): planning financial resources for the duration of the plan.

[115] Law no. 95-64, 19 Jan. 1995, relating to the status of judges (JO 20 Jan., p. 1042). In French law, an organic law lays down, according to the Constitution, rules relating to public powers. It is submitted, as far as its adoption is concerned, to a specific procedure. This law was thus needed because of the constitutional framework of the status of judges.

[116] Law no. 95-125, 8 Feb. 1995 (JO 9 Feb., p. 2175).

tion of young people.[117] From the perspective of civil procedure, the changes introduced were essentially designed to relieve the judge of tasks for which he ought not properly to be responsible. The new law created judicial assistants, and transferred functions to the head clerks of courts. It reformed judicial conciliation before the *tribunal d'instance*, so that it could be implemented by a third person, appointed by the judge, and recognized judicial mediation.[118]

8.2. The Coulon Report

At the end of 1995, the Minister of Justice appointed a learned judge, Jean-Marie Coulon,[119] to formulate proposals on civil procedure. M. Coulon launched a vast consultation among leading members and representative organizations of the different legal professions. This consultation led him, at the end of 1996, to make thirty-six precise proposals for reform,[120] which the reader can find in Appendix 9.16.

Beside some measures tending to favour recourse to ADR,[121] the most spectacular proposals consisted of: (*a*) generalizing single judges before the *tribunal de grande instance*;[122] (*b*) imposing mandatory representation by an advocate in the labour and social chambers of the courts of appeal; (*c*) introducing the speedy proceedings of the injunction to pay before the *tribunal de grande instance*;[123] (*d*) simplifying the procedure for divorce applications by common request;[124] (*e*) asking parties to formulate their claims in fact and in law;[125] and (*f*) transforming first instance judgments into immediately enforceable judgments.[126] In M. Coulon's view, these proposals should not be conceived of as a reform of the Civil Procedural Code, but, rather, as 'directly in conformity with the spirit of the authors of the Code'.[127]

However, the best reforms are of limited use if the judicial institution does not

---

[117] On these laws, see L. Cadiet, 'Montagne ou souris? Les Réponses du plan pluriannuel aux problèmes de la justice française', *Chronique de droit judiciaire privé, La Semaine jundique* (1995), gen. edn., I, 3846, nos. 1, 2, 5, 7, 8, 15, and 29.   [118] See above s. 8.9 at text to nn. 111–13.

[119] Then president of the *tribunal de grande instance* of Nanterre, who became the president of the *tribunal de grande instance* of Paris.

[120] See Coulon, *Réflexions*, 119–21. For an interpretation of the philosophy of this report, see A. Garapon, *Vers une nouvelle économie politique de la justice?* (Paris: Recueil Dalloz, 1997), 69 ff.

[121] See above s. 8 at text to nn. 99–113.

[122] Except in disciplinary matters and capacity matters such as marriage and divorce.

[123] Which at present is only possible before the *tribunal d'instance* and the commercial court, for debts below F. Frs. 30,000.

[124] By reducing delays for reflection currently imposed on the spouses.

[125] It is not currently necessary to detail, or even to mention, legal arguments.

[126] Apart from certain legally excepted cases, and subject to the power of the judge to hold otherwise, on his own motion or at the request of the parties. This system would reverse the current position. *De lege lata*, provisional enforcement is an exception to the principle of the suspensive effect of appeal, and entails a special provision in the law (which is the case for *référé* orders, for example) or a decision of the judge (if imposed by the necessity and when compatible with the nature of the case). See Arts. 514 and 515 of the new Civil Procedural Code.   [127] Coulon, *Réflexions*, 24.

have sufficient resources to implement them. M. Coulon noted that the success of these modifications entailed the implementation of two other conditions. First, a reform of the judicial map was called for, in order to spread the resources for justice in a more appropriate way, including a merger of the *tribunal de grande instance* and the *tribunal d'instance*. Secondly, an increase in the state's justice budget is essential.

As soon as they became public, these proposals led to various reactions by those concerned, including, of course, those contradictory and self-interested corporatist reactions which render any judicial or procedural reform so difficult to implement.[128]

8.3. The commitment of the President of the Republic and the change of parliamentary majority

As M. Coulon made the result of his mission known, by delivering his report to the Ministry, the President of the Republic made some strong public pronouncements, affirming the regime's commitment to improving the justice situation. However, coming as they did so soon after M. Coulon's report, and repeating the need to act, investigate, and improve things which was trumpeted so loudly when M. Coulon was appointed, the statements call into question the depth of the government's understanding of its own programmes, and the sincerity of the expressed commitment. At the very least, some more co-ordination is needed between the high officers of state. Since the latest French parliamentary elections returned a left-wing-dominated Parliament, who will have to work with a right-wing President, hope of increasing co-ordination seems small.

Nevertheless, a new reform project on justice was presented to the French Council of Ministers on 29 October 1997[129] and tabled in Parliament. As far as civil justice and trial are concerned, the proposed measures are not up to the problems encountered. They consist essentially in a strengthening of the *conseils départementaux de l'aide juridique* (departmental councils for legal aid), an increase in the monetary limits to the jurisdiction of the *tribunaux d'instance*, and the further development of ADR.

9. THE WAY AHEAD?

The problems are now well known, and the solutions too, it seems. A substantial increase in resources for justice and a profound reform of judicial organization seem more effective than radical modification of the rules of procedure. This

---

[128] See in particular the *États Généraux de la profession d'avocats sur la réforme du Code de procédure civile autour du Rapport Coulon*, published under this title in *La Revue juridique d'Île-de-France*, 48–9 (1997).
[129] See Press Release of the Ministry of Justice, *La Semaine juridique* (1997), gen. edn., nos. 45–6.

presupposes, in both cases, a strong political willingness, and an even stronger capacity to resist local or corporatist pressure groups. Civil justice reform needs a will, more than a bill.

As far as resources are concerned, it will not be possible to stop short of a significant increase in the justice budget, allowing justice to enter the twenty-first century. However, this increase presupposes a reorganization of the French judicial landscape. Before increasing the resources for justice, it would be important to use existing resources more efficiently by:

1. revision of the judicial map, as a matter of course, which is the nodal point of any ambitious reform;
2. rationalization of the judicial organization, in order to suppress courts which are no longer necessary (*tribunal d'instance*, agricultural leases court);
3. simplification of the divisions between courts which are a useless source of complications and costs.[130]

As far as strictly procedural reforms are concerned, those proposed are all of interest, but only if they come on the top of the reforms noted above. On their own, they would be of limited use. Before the standardization of single judges before the *tribunal de grande instance*, particular attention must be devoted to the commercial and labour courts. Too often, these jurisdictions suffer what the *tribunal de grande instance* suffered under the former Civil Procedural Code. Comparable solutions, *mutatis mutandis*, to those implemented by the new civil procedure before the *tribunal de grande instance* would probably produce the same effects in these other courts, providing they are properly resourced.

The quest for amicable solutions through ADR must be favoured. The present provision is still too restrictive. Recent government projects contemplate taking divorces by common request out of the judicial context.

On the other hand, within the civil trial, an increase in the judges' powers is not absolutely incompatible with a parallel contractualization of the procedure. From a more general point of view, it can also take the form of collective conventions, covering each type of proceeding, formulated between the officers of each court (judges, clerks) and their normal partners (advocates, process servers, etc.). Some such agreements are already in force.[131] It is up to the justice professionals to become aware of their responsibilities, show some imagination, and the courage needed to accept mutual concessions. Without this type of action, there will be no future.

---

[130] See above s. 2.1 at text to nn. 1–3.

[131] See agreement, concluded in spring 1997, between the Paris Court of Appeal, its clerks, and the heads of the competent bars so as to improve the treatment of labour cases, *La Semaine juridique* (1997), gen. edn., Act, no. 22, V° *Échos et opinions*.

Addendum

Since this contribution was written, some of the propositions of the Coulon Report have been implemented. These modifications are contained in a statute published in the *Official Journal* of France on 20 December 1998 (Statute no. 98-1163, 18 December 1998) and a regulation of 28 December 1998 both revising the French Judiciary Organization Code and the New Code of Civil Procedure (*Official Journal*, 30 December 1998, 19904) and relating to access to justice and peaceful settlement of disputes.

These texts target two aims: rationalizing judicial work and favouring peaceful solutions of disputes (see L. Cadiet, *Chronique d'actualité: Droit judiciaire privé*, in *La Semaine juridique*, gen. edn. (1999) i, 130).

The main modifications are as follows:

- The competence rate rose from F. Frs. 30,000 to F. Frs. 50,000 and the jurisdiction rate from F. Frs. 13,000 to F. Frs. 25,000, except with regard to labour disputes (F. Frs. 22,000) and commercial matters (where it stays at F. Frs. 13,000).

- Before the *tribunal de grande instance*, the *tribunal d'instance*, the commercial courts and the Court of Appeal, parties are invited to formulate legal arguments and not just facts.

- Before the *tribunal de grande instance* and the Court of Appeal, parties must disclose all of their arguments. Those which are not included in their briefs or those which are advanced at an early stage but subsequently withdrawn will be disregarded by the judge.

- Before the *tribunal de grande instance* and the Court of Appeal, the powers of the preliminary investigation judges are extended, as they are now in a position to rule on procedural exceptions (irregularities etc.).

- Interlocutory injunctions are improved, before the *tribunal de grande instance* and the Court of Appeal.

- Before the *tribunal d'instance*, the judge now has the possibility of committing all proceedings to conciliation.

- The benefit of legal aid is extended to peaceful settlement of disputes as soon as an agreement is reached and even though the competent court has not yet been seized.

- Simple proceedings for enforcing peaceful settlements are instituted before the president of the *tribunal de grande instance* who can confer upon them a binding force through a mere declaration to the court.

These modifications are not of major importance but should not be overlooked. It is likely that they will lead to other reforms in the months or years to come.

A critical reform is under review at the moment. Under this reform, first instance judgments would be immediately enforceable even though an appeal has been lodged and even though the principle is that of a suspension of enforcement nowadays. A decrease of appeal proceedings could follow.

Appendix 9.1
General Organization of French Justice[a]

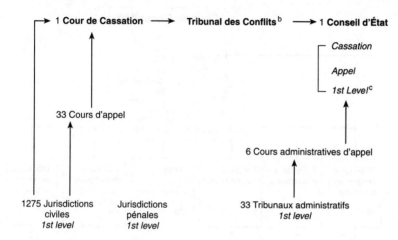

Courts of the judicial order ... **Courts of the administrative order**

1 Cour de Cassation ⟶ Tribunal des Conflits[b] ⟶ 1 Conseil d'État

┌ *Cassation*

│ *Appel*

└ *1st Level*[c]

33 Cours d'appel

6 Cours administratives d'appel

1275 Jurisdictions   Jurisdictions   33 Tribunaux administratifs
civiles   pénales   *1st level*
1st level   *1st level*

[a] This schedule does not take the Constitutional Council into account as it is not a court as such, except in electoral matters. Its role is mainly to ensure the conformity of laws voted by Parliament (National Assembly + Senate) with the Constitution and with the rules applicable thereto.

[b] The Conflicts Court is not a permanent jurisdiction. It sits occasionally in order to solve a conflict between the judicial and administrative jurisdictions. It is made up of judges of the *Cour de Cassation* and judges of the *Conseil d'État* in equal representation. If no solution is found, the conflict is resolved by the Minister of Justice, who is the *ex officio* President of the Court.

[c] The situation of the *Conseil d'État* is not exactly parallel with that of the *Cour de Cassation* in respect to the administrative courts. Although it is sometimes the ultimate judge, it can also rule in appeal and even in first and last resort. The tendency of recent years is to transform it into a supreme court.

Appendix 9.2

Organization of the Civil Courts of the Judicial Order

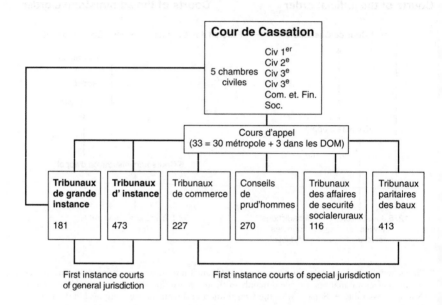

First instance courts of general jurisdiction   First instance courts of special jurisdiction

Appendix 9.3
Map Showing the Regional Jurisdictions
of the Civil Courts of the Judicial Order

Regional boundary
Department boundary
■ Capital City
● Regional capital

Departments of the Paris Region

VAL-D'-OISE
HAUTS-DE-SEINE SEINE-SAINT-DENIS
YVELINES Paris VAL-DE-MARNE
SEINE-ET-MARNE
ESSONNE

Regions

1 Alsace
2 Aquitaine
3 Auvergne
4 Bourgogne
5 Bretagne
6 Centre
7 Champagne-Ardenne
8 Franche-Comte
9 Languedoc-Roussillon
10 Limousin
11 Lorraine
12 Midi-Pyrénées
13 Nord-Pas-de-Calais
14 Basse Normandie
15 Haute Normandie
16 Pays de La Loire
17 Picardie
18 Poitou-Charentes
19 Provence-Alpes-
   Côte d'Azur
20 Rhône-Alpes
21 Ile-de-France

Appendix 9.4

Number of Courts per Court of Appeal (as at 1 January 1997)

Jurisdiction of the courts of appeal	Tribunaux de grande instance	Tribunaux d'instance	Conseil de prud'-hommes	Commercial jurisdictions			Tribunaux des affaires de sécurité sociale
				Tribunaux de commerce	Tribunaux de grande instance à compétence commerciale	Chambres commerciales	
Agen	4	11	5	5	—	—	3
Aix-en-Provence	8	21	14	16	1	—	5
Amiens	9	14	13	10	2	—	4
Angers	4	12	5	6	—	—	3
Bastia	2	5	2	3	—	—	2
Besançon	7	13	8	6	3	—	5
Bordeaux	5	17	6	8	—	—	3
Bourges	3	12	5	5	—	—	3
Caen	7	16	10	16	—	—	3
Chambéry	5	9	7	1	4	—	2
Colmar	4	16	10	—	—	4	2
Dijon	4	14	9	14	—	—	3
Douai	11	21	21	10	3	—	5
Grenoble	5	12	10	5	2	—	4
Limoges	4	10	4	3	1	—	3
Lyon	7	11	11	5	2	—	5
Metz	3	9	5	—	—	3	2
Montpellier	7	17	11	15	—	—	4
Nancy	6	13	9	7	—	—	4
Nîmes	6	14	8	5	2	—	4
Orléans	4	10	5	5	—	—	3
Paris	9	52	12	11	—	—	7
Pau	5	12	6	7	—	—	4
Poitiers	8	18	9	10	1	—	5
Reims	4	13	7	6	—	—	3
Rennes	12	25	14	11	2	—	6
Riom	7	16	8	13	—	—	4
Rouen	5	11	9	13	—	—	3
Toulouse	6	14	7	6	—	—	4
Versailles	4	24	14	5	—	—	4
Metropolitan territory	175	462	264	227	23	7	112
Basse-Terre	2	4	2	2	—	—	1
Fort-de-France	2	3	2	2	—	—	2
Saint-Denis	2	4	2	1	1	—	1
Overseas departments	6	11	6	5	1	—	4
Both	181	473	270		263		116

Appendix 9.5
Population per Court of Appeal[a]

[a] Numbers in thousands. Population of France: 58,073,600.

Appendix 9.6

Activity of *Tribunaux de Grande Instance* between 1991 and 1995

	1991	1992	1993	1994	1995
Number of *tribunaux de grande instance*	181	181	181	181	181
New cases (ordinary proceedings)					
Total number	492,391	523,026	566,723	658,042	660,189
Terminated cases after full hearing on the merits					
Total number of cases	462,326	475,775	532,494	610,234	645,319
Nature of the decision					
Decision on the merits	333,402	344,310	390,644	449,537	479,237
Complete or partial acceptance					
of the claim	284,326	296,011	338,015	383,475	407,208
Dismissal of the claim	49,076	48,299	52,629	66,062	72,029
Other decisions (of which:)	128,924	131,465	141,850	160,697	166,082
Radiation (striking out)	56,779	57,673	65,292	72,387	69,854
Lack of jurisdiction	2,909	3,046	4,487	5,439	7,013
Conciliation of the parties	1,632	1,394	1,165	1,298	1,850
Withdrawal of the plaintiff	22,394	23,377	26,297	29,383	31,776
Average time of terminated cases					
(months)	10.0	9.5	9.6	8.9	8.!
Proportion of decisions on the merits					
with presence of the parties (%)	68.1	68.2	68.6	70.1	71.♦
Référés					
Total number	96,184	110,132	125,752	120,999	126,501
Nature of decision					
Decisions on the claim	70,606	80,713	82,855	87,603	98,968
Partial or complete acceptance	61,901	70,490	73,976	78,306	88,389
Dismissal	8,705	10,223	8,879	9,297	10,579
Other decisions	25,578	29,419	42,897	33,396	27,533
Radiation (striking out)	8,075	9,959	12,555	11,697	11,299
Withdrawal of the plaintiff	3,215	3,285	3,142	2,794	3,388
Lack of jurisdiction	2,821	2,743	2,829	2,522	2,292
Conciliation of the parties	115	146	188	212	238
Average time (in months)	0.9	1.0	1.1	1.2	1.!

Appendix 9.7
Activity of *Tribunaux d'Instance* between 1991 and 1995

	1991	1992	1993	1994	1995
Number of *tribunaux d'instance*	473	473	473	473	473
New cases (ordinary proceedings)					
Total number	547,890	609,190	563,300	513,490	483,909
Terminated cases after full hearing on the merits					
Total number of cases	518,732	588,126	556,189	505,690	491,021
Nature of the decision					
Decision on the merits	406,591	459,351	440,742	394,984	377,988
Complete or partial acceptance					
of the claim	362,675	409,872	391,291	346,448	331,523
Dismissal of the claim	43,916	49,479	49,451	48,536	46,565
Other decisions (of which:)	112,141	128,775	115,447	110,706	113,033
Radiation (striking out)	37,589	40,277	37,927	36,090	34,911
Lack of jurisdiction	3,112	3,719	3,850	3,722	8,983
Conciliation of the parties	4,369	4,909	5,003	3,919	3,154
Withdrawal of the plaintiff	46,531	51,591	46,871	44,388	41,879
Average time of terminated cases					
(months)	4.5	4.4	4.9	5.2	5.1
Proportion of decisions on the merits					
in presence of the parties (%)	38.8	36.5	45.8	49.0	50.3
Référés					
Total number	91,596	93,178	90,918	89,032	83,962
Nature of decision					
Decisions on the claim	73,577	74,278	73,917	71,803	67,828
Partial or complete acceptance	68,850	67,573	68,387	66,966	63,392
Dismissal	6,727	6,705	5,530	4,837	4,436
Other decisions	18,019	18,900	17,001	17,229	16,134
Radiation (striking out)	5,934	6,032	5,586	5,402	5,176
Withdrawal of the plaintiff	8,066	8,798	7,679	7,601	6,810
Lack of jurisdiction	1,272	1,406	1,274	1,058	1,016
Conciliation of the parties	323	335	335	322	276
Average time (months)	1.6	1.7	1.8	1.8	1.8
Special proceedings					
Injunctions to pay	818,610	867,472	832,397	777,184	731,055
Ex parte orders	88,492	87,108		36,221	35,145

Appendix 9.8
Activity of *Tribunaux de Commerce* between 1991 and 1995

	1991	992	1993	1994	1995
Number of *tribunaux de commerce*	229	229	229	229	229
Terminated cases after full hearing on the merits					
Total number of cases	259,062	266,305	297,746	254,858	282,070
Nature of the decision					
Decision on the merits	196,082	201,444	223,563	191,107	209,534
Complete or partial acceptance					
of the claim	185,617	190,266	210,784	178,881	196,539
Dismissal of the claim	10,465	11,178	12,779	12,226	12,995
Other decisions (of which:)	62,980	64,861	74,183	63,751	72,536
Radiation (striking out)	48,847	50,571	56,864	46,900	52,465
Lack of jurisdiction	1,156	1,197	1,371	1,140	1,363
Conciliation of the parties	63	71	60	63	70
Withdrawal of the plaintiff	2,848	3,287	3,527	3,172	3,578
Average time of terminated cases					
(months)	4.9	5.0	5.5	5.9	6.2
Proportion of decisions on the merits					
in presence of the parties (%)	45.5	46.2	50.4	53.4	54.2
Référés					
Total number	54,370	56,853	62,945	55,066	54,158
Nature of decision					
Decisions on the claim	44,063	45,826	49,698	42,166	42,374
Partial or complete acceptance	40,090	42,826	46,020	39,205	39,120
Dismissal	3,973	3,654	3,678	2,961	3,254
Other decisions	10,307	11,027	13,247	12,900	11,784
Radiation (striking out)	7,370	8,018	10,027	9,210	9,201
Withdrawal of the plaintiff	455	475	533	599	577
Lack of jurisdiction	1	1	5	4	9
Conciliation of the parties	10	5	18	9	14
Average time (in months)	0.9	0.9	1.0	1.0	1.0

Appendix 9.9

Activity of Labour Courts between 1991 and 1995

	1991	1992	1993	1994	1995
Number of labour courts	281	281	281	270	270
New cases (ordinary proceedings)					
Total number	156,298	172,883	172,001	167,809	157,542
Terminated cases after full hearing on the merits					
Total number of cases	148,547	161,128	163,073	168,250	166,593
Nature of the decision					
Decision on the merits	80,916	85,018	89,799	96,187	94,514
Complete or partial acceptance					
of the claim	60,757	65,174	67,896	72,668	72,020
Dismissal of the claim	20,159	20,744	21,903	23,519	22,494
Other decisions (of which:)	67,631	75,210	73,274	72,063	72,079
Radiation (striking out)	21,457	25,359	23,860	24,050	24,157
Conciliation of the parties	13,289	13,993	13,045	12,526	12,362
Withdrawal of the plaintiff	13,427	14,153	13,964	13,387	13,739
Average time of terminated cases					
(months)	9.2	9.7	9.5	9.7	10.1
Proportion of decisions on the merits					
in presence of the parties (%)	84.9	85.0	84.5	84.8	84.6
Référés					
Total number	43,078	49,268	52,155	51,856	51,384
Nature of decision					
Decisions on the claim	24,615	27,362	28,663	28,240	27,136
Partial or complete acceptance	17,987	19,439	20,258	20,476	19,635
Dismissal	6,628	7,923	8,405	7,764	7,501
Other decisions	18,463	21,906	23,492	23,616	24,248
Radiation (striking out)	6,977	8,478	8,880	9,044	9,142
Withdrawal of the plaintiff	4,511	5,086	5,524	5,468	5,399
Conciliation of the parties	1,760	1,769	1,922	1,967	1,936
Average time (months)	1.1	1.2	1.2	1.4	1.4

Appendix 9.10
Activity of Social Security Courts between 1991 and 1995

	1991	1992	1993	1994	1995
Number of social security courts	111	111	111	113	113
New cases (ordinary proceedings)					
Total number	94,046	103,050			
Terminated cases after full hearing on the merits					
Total number of cases	93,860	83,741	87,132		

Appendix 9.11
Activity of Agricultural Leases Courts between 1991 and 1995

	1991	1992	1993	1994	1995
Number of agricultural leases courts	413	413	413	413	413
New cases (ordinary proceedings)					
Total number	4,566	5,605	3,778	3,664	3,614
Terminated cases after full hearing on the merits					
Total number of cases	4,590	6,042	3,686	3,720	3,807
Nature of the decision					
Decision on the merits	2,581	3,398	2,085	2,089	2,089
Complete or partial acceptance					
of the claim	1,951	2,611	1,575	1,551	1,511
Dismissal of the claim	630	787	510	538	578
Other decisions (of which:)	2,009	2,644	1,601	1,631	1,718
Average time of terminated cases					
(months)	8.3	8.7	10.1	9.9	9.6
Proportion of decisions on the merits					
in presence of the parties (%)	83.3	83.9	84.7	82.6	86.0
Référés					
Total number	297	541	213	216	209

Appendix 9.12
Activity of the Courts of Appeal between 1991 and 1995

	1991	1992	1993	1994	1995
Number of courts of appeal	33	33	33	33	33
New cases (ordinary proceedings)					
Total number	173,777	182,794	204,935	218,880	220,066
Originating jurisdiction					
Court of appeal	5,948	6,578	8,530	7,717	12,219
Tribunal de grande instance	69,636	69,502	79,101	89,467	87,756
Commercial court	30,181	32,052	35,236	33,179	35,128
Tribunal d'instance	29,955	30,809	34,088	33,533	28,368
Labour court	28,900	32,734	35,385	38,069	36,016
Social security court	5,269	5,211	5,605	6,981	7,635
Agricultural leases court	1,017	1,035	924	877	856
Terminated cases after full hearing on the merits					
Total number of cases	168,011	171,082	179,585	187,246	198,754
Nature of the decision					
Decision on the merits	114,142	116,584	119,957	126,920	135,023
Complete or partial acceptance of the claim	86,117	87,926	90,881	96,197	102,720
Dismissal of the claim	28,025	28,658	29,076	30,723	32,303
Other decisions (of which:)	53,869	54,498	59,628	60,326	63,731
Radiation (striking out)	20,781	21,951	23,681	23,543	22,615
Ill-founded claims	1,941	2,174	2,345	2,345	2,766
Conciliation of the parties	1,059	1,034	722	700	938
Withdrawal of the plaintiff	13,843	14,232	15,721	16,518	18,011
Average time of terminated cases (months)	13.9	13.8	13.5	13.9	14.7
Proportion of decisions on the merits in presence of the parties (%)	87.9	85.7	84.6	86.1	83.7

Loïc Cadiet

Appendix 9.13
Activity of the *Cour de Cassation* between 1991 and 1995

	1991	1992	1993	1994	1995
New cases (ordinary proceedings)					
Total number	19,386	18,841	19,962	19,115	19,969
Terminated cases after full hearing on the merits					
Total number of cases	18,427	18,049	18,569	18,456	21,499
Nature of the decision					
Overruled decisions	3,563	3,778	4,064	3,777	5,300
Dismissal of the claim	7,554	7,040	7,094	7,691	8,475

Appendix 9.14
Judicial Activity

Number of decisions in civil matters

	1996	Change 1995/6 (%)
New cases (ordinary proceedings)		
Common jurisdiction	1,335,813	−1.8
Cour de Cassation	20,420	−5.0
Court of appeal	203,997	+2.6
Tribunaux de grande instance	655,315	+1.5
Tribunaux d'instance	456,081	−7.8
Specialized jurisdictions	678,390	−1.3
Children's matters (assistance in education)	138,944	+4.1
Commercial courts	263,282	−6.7
Social security courts	116,675	+11.1
Labour courts	159,489	−4.3
Référés		
Tribunaux de grande instance	124,052	−1.9
Tribunaux d'instance	81,911	−2.7
Labour courts	51,226	−0.3
Commercial courts	51,007	−5.8

New cases (ordinary proceedings) in 1996

	1996	Change 1995/6 (%)
Overall	1,540,091	+1.0
Courts of appeal	219,335	−0.3
Tribunaux de grande instance	673,664	+2.0
Tribunaux d'instance	479,500	−1.6
Labour Courts	167,592	+6.4

Nature of the Case	Court of appeal		*Tribunaux de grande instance*		*Tribunaux d'instance*		Labour courts	
	Number	%	Number	%	Number	%	Number	%
Overall	219,335	100.0	673,664	100.0	479,500	100.0	167,592	100.0
Capacity law	924	0.4	20,008	3.0	103,256	21.5		
Family law	36,202	16.5	385,703	57.2	3,200	0.7		
Business law	28,075	12.8	43,704	6.5	21,850	4.6		
Contract law	68,468	31.2	82,391	12.2	268,012	55.9		
Tort law	8,626	3.9	25,863	3.8	15,378	3.2		
Real and personal property	7,842	3.6	15,255	2.3	22,327	4.6		
Labour relations and social security	50,745	23.2	5,306	0.8	21,410	4.5	165,653	98.8
Other cases	6,818	3.1	12,688	1.9	6,887	1.4	1,797	1.1
Specific proceedings	11,635	5.3	82,746	1.9	17,180	3.6	142	0.1

Average Time of Proceedings (in months)

	1995	1996
Courts of appeal	14.7	15.8
Tribunaux de grande instance	8.9	8.9
Tribunaux d'instance	5.1	5.0
Labour courts	10.1	9.4

Note: For each civil case terminated during the year, the time is the interval between the commencement of the proceedings and the date of judgment. For a court or for a group of courts, the average time is the arithmetical mean of all the cases terminated during the year.

Cases in progress on 31 December

	1995	1996
Overall	1,281,916	1,347,125
Courts of appeal	291,640	306,978
Tribunaux de grande instance	558,750	577,099
Tribunaux d'instance	296,628	320,047
Labour courts	134,898	143,001

Appendix 9.15
Legal Profession

Total number of professionals on 1 January 1997	86,101
Professionals belonging to the Ministry of Justice	27,053
Judges	6,287
Working in the central administration and in the common services	1,763
Judges	170
Working in jurisdictions	25,290
Judges	6,117
Public servants	19,173
Chief clerks and clerks	7,810
Professionals not belonging to the Ministry of Justice	59,048
Advocates	33,005
Avoués (counsel with right of audience in the courts of appeal)	391
Avocats au Conseil (counsel with right of audience in *the Conseil d'État* and the *Cour de Cassation*)	85
Clerks of commercial courts	265
Process servers	3,228
Judicial administrators	144
Company liquidators	343
Judicial experts	20,250[a]
Judicial conciliators	1,337[a]

[a] On 1 January 1996.

Appendix 9.16

Jean-Marie Coulon, *Réflexions et propositions sur la procédure civile* (Report to the Ministry of Justice, La Documentation Française, 1997)

M. Coulon's Proposals

A. Judicial organization

1. Increase the 'jurisdiction rate' from F. Frs. 13,000 to F. Frs. 25,000[a] and the 'competence rate' from F. Frs. 30,000 to F. Frs. 50,000.[b]
2. Transfer jurisdiction over commercial lease matters to the *tribunal de grande instance*.
3. Certain *tribunaux de grande instance* and certain courts of appeal should specialize in trademark law.
4. Single judges should be established as the norm before the *tribunal de grande instance*.
5. Reinforcement of the collegiate rule before the court of appeal.

B. Representation and legal aid

6. New rules governing assistance and representation before the *tribunal d'instance* should be adopted.
7. Conditions for representation before the commercial court should be modified.
8. The principle of mandatory representation before social chambers of the court of appeal and the *Cour de Cassation* should be extended.
9. The powers of the president of legal aid bureaux should be increased.
10. The delegation of powers to the president within legal aid bureaux should be organized.

---

[a] The 'jurisdiction rate' refers to the value up to which cases are not subject to appeal by way of full rehearing in a second instance court. Such decisions are said to be given in 'first and last instance'. A dissappointed litigant who wishes to challenge the decision has access only to the procedure for cassation before the *Cour de Cassation*. The *Cour de Cassation* can quash the decision of the lower court for error of law, but, as noted in the text, cannot substitute its own substantive decision. Where the cassation appeal is upheld, the *Cour de Cassation* must refer the case back to the court whose decision was challenged for substantive determination in accordance with the correct law.

[b] The 'competence rate' refers to the borderline between cases which are to be heard in the *tribunal d'instance*, and those which will be heard in the *tribunal de grande instance*.

11. The regime for withdrawal of legal aid proceedings should be clarified.

C. *Alternative modes of dispute resolution*

12. A distinction must be introduced, between withdrawal of the records of the court (pronounced at the request of the parties pending a compromise) and *radiation* (or 'striking out'). The punitive character of *radiation* should be reinforced.

13. *Ex parte* orders proceedings before the president of the *tribunal de grande instance* should be created, so as to give binding force to compromises reached outside the context of a pending claim.

14. The benefit of legal aid payments should be granted to justice professionals for their services in arranging the settlement of a dispute without bringing proceedings in court.

15. Where conciliation results in settlement of a matter before the courts, legal aid fees should be payable to the lawyers, up to the maximum applicable rate.

D. *Optimized management of mass litigation*

16. The injunction to do something (*injonction de faire*) should be suppressed.

17. Injunctions to pay (*injonction de payer*) should be introduced before the *tribunal de grande instance*.

18. The procedure for obtaining a divorce on a common request should be simplified.

E. *Emergency management*

19. It should be possible for the judge seized of *référé* proceedings to fix a date to hear and resolve the dispute on the merits.

20. A new procedure should be introduced for appeal of a *référé* order, based on the procedure for a fixed date appeal before the Court of Appeal.

21. There must be some reinforcement of the efficacy of Article 910 of the new Civil Procedural Code.

F. *A better management of cases by way of a greater formalism for writs and statements of claim*

22. The legal and factual grounds of the writ; the facts; the evidence; and the applicable rules of law for each claim should be set out in statements of claim.

23. There should be an obligation to recapitulate claims and legal arguments by the parties beyond statements of claims.

24. Attachment of a sheet recapitulating evidentiary documents to each formal document presented by the parties should be compulsory.

25. The preliminary investigation judge should have the jurisdiction to rule on any procedural exceptions.

26. The rules of preliminary investigation before the *tribunal de grande instance* should be adapted to suit the new system of single judges. . . .

29. Where there is no statement of claim on appeal filed within the prescribed time, the appeal should be treated as in default.

30. The appeal judge should have the power, on his own motion, to refuse to accept new claims at the appeal stage.

31. New legal argument and new evidence should be prohibited in appeal proceedings coming back from the *Cour de Cassation*.

32. Judges should be put in charge of controlling expert reports.

33. There should be better management of delays and costs in obtaining judicial expert reports.

G. Judgments and enforcement

34. The drafting of judgments should be simplified, including:

making it possible for the judge to explain the parties' claims and legal arguments by reference to writs and statements of claims; and

making it possible to respond to rejected legal arguments in brief.

35. Judgments of the first instance courts should be immediately enforceable, unless there is a legal exception, or the judge decides against it (on his own motion or at the request of the parties).

36. The range of causes of suspension of the enforceable decision given in first instance by the first president of the court of appeal should be increased.

10
Administration of Civil Justice in Brazil

Sergio Bermudes

1. SIGNIFICANCE

Although Brazil has a federal constitution (the Constitution of the Federal Republic of Brazil of 5 October 1988), the Brazilian Code of Civil Procedure (in Portuguese, *Código de Processo Civil*, frequently abbreviated as CPC) governs procedure in courts throughout the whole country. This makes the Brazilian system, covering as it does the whole of the fourth largest country in the world, one of the very largest anywhere. The population of Brazil is increasing, and is expected to reach close to 200 million people by the turn of the century.

2. THE BRAZILIAN COURTS

2.1. State and federal jurisdictions

Brazil has a dual system of civil jurisdiction. Under Article 109 of the Constitution, some cases, such as those to which the Federal Union or some entities of the federal administration are parties, are reserved for the federal courts. These cases are tried at first instance by a single federal judge. Decisions of such federal courts may be appealed to a regional federal tribunal, whose jurisdiction may cover more than one state of the Union.

A civil case will generally start before one of the state or federal courts of first instance having civil jurisdiction. 'Civil cases' in this context comprises all cases which are neither criminal, labour, nor electoral. Labour cases are those arising from conflicts between employer and employee, for which Brazil has a separate system of courts. There is also a separate electoral court system, which is in charge of matters involving political parties, candidates, and elections generally. The term 'civil cases' thus goes beyond the standard definition of disputes between private parties, to encompass all cases involving: the Federal Union; the states and the municipalities; their agents and authorities; and all commercial cases, including bankruptcy proceedings and tax cases.

The court before which a civil case commences has a single judge, who presides over the proceedings from commencement through to final judgment. As well as the final decision (*setença*), all interlocutory decisions can also be appealed to the court of appeals. Appeals are tried in chambers of three justices at state courts, or five justices at federal courts. If there is a dissenting opinion at the trial of an appeal against a final decision, the losing party may apply for a retrial of the appeal before another chamber.

All other cases are handled by the two-tier court system of the member states or of the federal district (corresponding to the federal capital of Brasília, of the same political nature as Washington DC).

2.2. First instance or trial courts

In Brazil, first instance courts with jurisdiction (*rectius*, or competence) to try civil cases are unipersonal. A single judge sits to hear a case at any given time. However, judges may succeed one another throughout the proceedings until the hearing. The general rule (CPC, Art. 132) is that the judge presiding at the hearing for the collection of oral evidence should decide the case. However, this provision does not apply if that judge leaves the court, in which case the decision will be handed down by his or her successor.

3. OUTLINE OF PROCEDURE

3.1. Commencement

Under Article 262 of the CPC, a civil action commences by the initiative of the parties but, once commenced, develops by official impulse. Under Article 263, an action is deemed to have been commenced as soon as the initial petition is presented to the court.

Both the Code of Civil Procedure of Brazil and Brazilian procedural doctrine distinguish between the *process* and the *proceeding*. While the process is a juridical relationship linking the opposing parties and the state, via the judge as an agent of the state, the proceeding is the manner in which the process develops.

3.2. Proceedings subdivided

Article 272 of the CPC divides proceedings between *common* and *special* forms. The *common* form is further subdivided into *ordinary* and *summary* proceedings. The ordinary proceeding is the standard form.

Summary and special proceedings are each used in those cases where the CPC has made particular provision for this. For example, under Article 275. II. d of the CPC, a lawsuit for damages caused by a motor vehicle (whether for personal injury or material loss) should be brought under the summary form of proceeding. Conversely, the special nature of a suit for the division or demarcation of private land means that such a suit should be brought under the special proceeding prescribed in Articles 946–81 of the CPC.

3.3. Ordinary proceedings

The ordinary proceeding is the standard procedural form given to the civil judicial process before the Brazilian courts. The provisions governing ordinary proceedings also apply to all other proceedings in a subsidiary manner, as provided for in Article 272, sole paragraph.

The plaintiff's claim is presented by means of a written document, called *petição inicial* (literally, 'initial petition'), which is filed before the court that has jurisdiction to rule on the case. The court has to admit the petition, and order the summons of the defendant. The defendant may then present a response (CPC, Art. 297) in the form of an answer to the claim (*contestação*), a counter-claim (*reconvenção*), or an exception (*exceção*). An exception is an objection to the proceedings taking place before the present judge, in the form of an application to disqualify the judge on grounds of lack of territorial jurisdiction or suspicion of partiality.

The plaintiff is generally entitled to reply to the defendant's answer. Afterwards, the court will either:

- dismiss the case for lack of jurisdiction (as, for example, where it finds that the plaintiff before the court is not the person legitimately entitled to make the claim presented to the court); or
- immediately try the case (as, for example, where production of evidence is unnecessary: say, because of the absence of the defendant's response; because the documents produced by the parties suffice as evidence; or because the dispute involves only a purely legal issue); or
- order a conciliation hearing (if the case involves a claim that could potentially be settled amicably).

If a settlement is not achieved at the conciliation hearing, the judge will decide any procedural questions pending resolution. He or she will determine what evidence is necessary for the trial, including whether expert evidence needs to be produced, and will designate a hearing date. At the hearing, the judge will take the depositions of the parties, witnesses, and court experts, and will listen to the oral argument of parties' counsel, who may apply for substitution of written briefs for oral argument (CPC, Arts. 329–31; 444–7). The court will then produce its decision at the end of that hearing or within a further ten days (CPC, Art. 456).

3.4. Interlocutory and other appeals

Brazilian civil courts are composed of a single judge at the first tier of jurisdiction. There is no trial by jury in civil cases. All interlocutory decisions are subject to an appeal, called *agravo* (CPC, Art. 522). *Agravo* differs from the appeal from a first-tier final decision, called *apelaçao*. Under Article 162 §2 of the CPC, an interlocutory decision is one which resolves an incidental question, i.e. any question which arises during the proceedings and which must be decided so that the proceedings can follow their due course. Examples of interlocutory decisions include: dismissing one or more of the plaintiff's claims, but not all of them; declaring that the defendant has failed to produce his or her defence within the time allowed by law; dismissing the defendant's counter-claim; denying the defendant's application for a declaration that the court lacks jurisdiction to hear the plaintiff's claim; dismissing the request of a third party to join the proceedings; and granting or refusing the admission of expert or other evidence.

Interlocutory appeals do not affect the progress of the case (CPC, Art. 497). The interlocutory appeal comes to the court of appeals in a separate file of its own. If the appeal succeeds, and the interlocutory decision is overturned, in most cases acts in the main action subsequent to the interlocutory decision will be considered null and void, and the proceeding will have to start again from the point at which the overturned decision was made. A second type of inter-locutory appeal, the *agravo retido* (CPC, Art. 523), has the same effect. In the case of this interlocutory appeal, the appeal is not immediately presented to the court of appeals, but is registered on the file of the lower court, and is tried, at the appellant's request, as a preliminary matter in any appeal against the final decision brought in the same case.

Thus, interlocutory appeals do not normally delay or stop the proceedings, unless the appellant obtains a stay. A stay may be granted by the court of appeals under special circumstances, such as where there is a risk of irreparable damage to a party's rights or interests (CPC, Art. 527. II, and 558). All final decisions are subject to appeal to a court of appeals, except for a few cases when the first-tier court itself tries the appeal, or it is tried by a three-judge chamber at the same level of jurisdiction.

3.5. Summary proceedings and 'small cases courts'

Both the Brazilian Code of Civil Procedure, dating from 1973, and Federal Law 9.099 of 26 September 1995, provide for summary procedures to be applied to cases of a lesser economic value or a simple nature. These proceedings are predominantly oral and informal, and are designed in such a way that a final decision should be reached within a rather short period of time from commencement.

Special courts have been, and are still being, created throughout the country in order to try cases in accordance with the proceeding set forth in Federal Law 9.099 of 1995. Federal Law 9.099 has given effect to Article 98. I of the Brazilian Constitution of 5 October 1988. Under this constitutional provision, the Federal Union, the federal district and territories, and the states shall create special courts, presided over by judges or laypeople, to promote settlement, trial, and execution of decisions in civil cases of a lesser complexity and minor criminal offences.

Such courts have been created in both state and federal court hierarchies. They provide conciliation, try cases, and execute judgments in those cases which come under Article 3 of Federal Law 9.099. Their jurisdiction is subject to a monetary limit (currently about $US 4,000), and they have special jurisdiction in cases of certain types, such as the eviction of a tenant by a landlord who intends to live in the premises as his or her own residence, and certain criminal matters of lesser importance.

The courts are located in the main courthouses, and are also at certain other locations, especially in the more populous cities. They may hold night sessions, and they are required always to proceed in an informal manner. The plaintiff presents his concise request for trial, containing the facts, his reasoning, his plea, and the amount of his claim, in written or oral form. If it is presented orally, the court clerk must prepare a written summary of it, in plain layperson's language, to ensure that the defendant can understand the matter. The defendant is then summoned, mostly by mail, to appear in court on a fixed date, for conciliation and presentation of written or oral defence and counter-claim.

On the assigned date, if the defendant does not appear, the court will accept the case stated by the plaintiff as being true, unless the judge is convinced otherwise. If the defendant does come to court, the judge or layperson presiding over the session (which may be dealing with one or more cases) will stress the advantages of an amicable settlement. If settlement is not achieved, the parties may choose a layperson to settle their case as arbitrator. The arbitrator will preside over an immediate hearing, at which each side will produce its evidence. A decision will be handed down either on the spot or within five days.

If arbitration is not adopted, there is an immediate court hearing, although this may be postponed for up to fifteen days if the court deems it necessary in order to allow the parties to exercise their right to a proper defence. At the hearing, the judge takes the depositions of the parties and witnesses, and decides the case. No record is produced of the depositions, which the judge simply refers to in his or her decision. At the hearing, the judge may take the depositions of experts appointed by the court, and the parties themselves may produce expert witnesses. The hearing may be conducted by laypersons, under the supervision of the judge. Parties need legal representation only if they appeal the decision. Up to the level of appeal, they may appear in court themselves. An appeal will be tried by a three-judge bench at the same level of jurisdiction. Further appeal to the Federal Supreme Court is only possible where a constitutional issue is at stake.

These special courts have succeeded in bringing justice closer to the Brazilian people. People can litigate at a very low cost, in an informal manner, and see immediate results from their judicial initiative. Paradoxically, the highly successful experience of these special courts, also called 'small cases courts', is highly likely to have a positive impact on traditional proceedings. Sooner or later, the principles governing summary proceedings will be largely adopted in ordinary and special proceedings. It could well be said that the system of special courts has been by far the best improvement in the administration of justice in Brazil ever.

4. PROVISIONAL RELIEF BY INJUNCTION AVAILABLE BY SEPARATE ACTION

Provisional relief by injunction is not available as a matter of course from the courts in most forms of proceeding. Only in special proceedings, where the law has specifically granted the court the power to make particular forms of interim or provisional orders, can provisional remedies be obtained in the same action as the main relief sought. For example, the action for eviction of squatters follows a special procedure established in Articles 920–31 of the CPC, whose Article 928 allows the judge to grant an injunction.

However, when the law does not allow an injunction to be granted in the main proceeding, the party concerned can file a specific action for an injunction (*ação cautelar*). Such a supplementary proceeding may be used to obtain, on a preliminary or final basis, the injunction needed to protect the interest at stake, and to assure the effectiveness of the decision ultimately handed down in the main proceeding.

5. COSTS

5.1. Fees and expenses of counsel and witnesses

According to Article 19 of the CPC and its two paragraphs, each party must pay the court costs of those judicial acts which they initiate. Payment is made on an advance basis, in the expectation that the winning party will be reimbursed the court costs which they have paid by the loser. The rule of payment in advance by the initiating party applies unless they lack the means to cover court expenses, and have been granted the benefit of 'gratuity'. The plaintiff should not only pay for the costs of acts of his or her own initiative, but also for those ordered by the court on its own motion or requested by the Public Ministry. Article 20 of the CPC establishes that the final decision shall require the defeated party to pay to the winner the expenses anticipated by him or her, plus attorneys' fees in an amount set by the court (which is not necessarily the same amount that the party has paid to counsel).

5.2. Security

Security is not generally given for costs, which are to be collected after the final judgment. In a few cases, the CPC and other statutes determine that security for costs must be provided. For example, Article 835 of the CPC establishes that if the plaintiff, native or alien, is domiciled outside Brazil or becomes absent from the country during the proceeding, and has no real estate in the national territory the value of which suffices to cover costs, he or she should give a guarantee for court expenses and attorneys' fees for which he or she may be liable.

5.3. Court fees and taxes

Litigation can become expensive in Brazil. In order to file a civil action, the plaintiff must pay a judiciary tax. In actions before state courts this tax can equal 2 per cent of the value of the case, either established in accordance with the economic value at stake, or merely estimated when there is no monetary value involved. In the state of Rio de Janeiro, the judiciary tax is limited so as not to exceed approximately $US8,200. The plaintiff must pay a fee for the service of papers on the defendant, and other fees at certain stages of development of the proceeding. Experts must be paid by the parties. Most appeals are subject to a tax, and will be dismissed if this tax is not paid. Of course, each party must pay their counsel's fees. These fees are often much higher than the fees granted by the court to the winner.

Although there are no statistical data available to allow an estimate to be made of average costs, it certainly costs money to litigate in Brazil. It has been said that the judiciary in many states of the Union collect more money than they spend. However, even on this point, reliable evidence is lacking.

Fees are also payable for some interlocutory applications and for all appeals. Fees are set at a level which takes into account both the value of the case and the nature of the judicial procedure initiated. Lawyers' fees are not fixed by law. Lawyers are free to charge what they can persuade their clients to agree to pay. Generally, lawyers charge a fee which reflects the amount of work which they are required to do, the benefit to the client, and even the prestige of their law firm. They may charge up to 20 per cent of the economic benefit to be obtained by the client through litigation (with the percentage diminishing as the benefit to the client increases). Most lawyers will charge a modest initial fee at the beginning of a case, and substantial contingency fees, the amount of which will depend upon them obtaining victory for their client and the extent of that victory. To give some idea of the level of fees charged, in a lawsuit for the collection of a debt of $US1 million, a lawyer might charge an initial fee of $US30,000, plus a contingent fee of 10 per cent of what the client recovers, reduced by any fees received directly from the losing party. Under such schemes, the level of the fee tends to stabilize at about 10 per cent of the economic benefit of court proceedings. In a simple lawsuit for the collection of a debt, about 50 per cent of the fees are likely to be recovered from the losing debtor. In other types of cases, the percentage will vary between 5 per cent and 20 per cent.

Litigation lawyers, particularly those belonging to large firms, might prefer to charge by the hour. Although widely accepted in extra-judicial work, this system of billing is still infrequent in litigation, because of client fears that lawyers will protract or complicate cases if they are paid on a time-sheet basis.

6. OUTLINE OF APPEAL PROCEDURE

6.1. Appeal courts and appeals

The relevant state or federal appellate court, acting in panels of three justices, will try the appeals filed against interlocutory and final decisions. Uniquely to the Brazilian system, if an appeal against a final first instance decision (*sentença*) is not unanimously decided at the appellate court, the losing party is entitled to file another appeal. Such an appeal (*embargos infringentes*—CPC, Art. 530) is tried at the same court, but by a panel of five justices.

6.2. Extraordinary appeals

The final decisions of the appellate courts may still be subject to extraordinary appeals. Extraordinary appeals may be of two different kinds: a special appeal (*recurso especial*) to the Superior Tribunal of Justice, when interpretation of a federal law is at stake; and an extraordinary appeal (*recurso extraordinário*) to the Federal Supreme Court (*Supremo Tribunal Federal*), when there is a constitutional issue involved.

Parties may choose to file only a special appeal, or only an extraordinary appeal, or they may bring appeals of both types. If appeals of both types are brought, trial of the special appeal before the Superior Tribunal of Justice must precede trial of the extraordinary appeal before the Federal Supreme Court.

With a few exceptions, the extraordinary appeal and the special appeal are tried by chambers of five justices in both the Supreme Court and the Superior Tribunal of Justice. If a decision rendered by one chamber dissents from a previous decision of the court, then another appeal, called *embargos de divergência* (CPC, Art. 546), may be filed for trial by the full court.

It should be pointed out that, in Brazil, all but one type of appeal is filed before the court which rendered the first instance decision, and not before an appellate court. The lower court may deny the right to appeal. In such a case, another appeal must be filed to decide the question of admission of the appeal that has been denied.

Both the Superior Tribunal of Justice and the Federal Supreme Court are extremely strict in deciding which appeals to hear. Even so, although most attempts to bring appeals before either of these two courts fail, parties insist on trying all they can. Indeed, in most cases an appeal is made to these highest courts. This results in incredible numbers of applications for the hearing of appeals being lodged with the courts, all of which have to be individually dealt with. Even if the answer is a stock 'No', considering the case, and answering the request for an appeal hearing, takes up the time of the judges and clerks of the courts. This phenomenon explains how the Federal Supreme Court, with only eleven justices, and the Superior Tribunal of Justice, with just thirty-three, manage to hand down thousands of decisions each year. This level of judicial performance might seem incredible to someone unfamiliar with the Brazilian system, but it is largely explained by the fact that the vast majority of these decisions are denials of extraordinary or special appeals. Such decisions are taken by individual justices of the two courts on the papers, without any hearings.

6.3. Procedure on appeal

An immense proportion of cases in Brazil goes to appeal. This is especially true in the southern states, where it is customary to appeal simply in order not to lose the chance that the first instance decision might be overturned, or to gain time (as appeal prevents the decision becoming *res judicata*, and fully enforceable). It is interesting to observe that appeals are less frequent in less developed states, and among poorer parties. In those cases, a final first instance decision is more likely to become firm without first having to be upheld on appeal. More than 75 per cent of the cases tried before the two highest courts of justice, the Federal Supreme Court and the Superior Tribunal of Justice, come from the seven wealthiest of Brazil's twenty-six states.

All appeals in all appeal courts are assigned to a specific justice, the reporter (*relator*), who prepares appeals for trial. Some appeals have to be examined by a second justice, called the reviewer (*revisor*). The justice acting as reporter may strike out an appeal which is evidently inadmissible (for example, filed late), groundless, or contrary to declared precedents of the court of appeals or of a higher court. The appellant may request review by the appellate panel of a decision by the reporter to strike out an appeal.

The date scheduled for an appeal hearing must be announced in advance by the judicial press. At trial, the reporter will present an oral summary of the case to the other justices sitting with him or her in the same chamber, and announce his or her opinion. Both the appellant and the respondent are entitled to present oral argument for fifteen minutes, except in an appeal against an interlocutory decision. The other justices will announce either a concurring or a dissenting opinion, based on what they have heard and on oral argument by counsel. Any justice, including the reporter and the reviewer, may request postponement of the hearing, so that he or she can examine the files or study aspects of the case. Appeals are tried in public, before parties, counsel, and whoever desires to attend the session, with the exception of a few cases, such as family matters, when attendance is restricted to parties and their lawyers.

As the reader can see, the appeal system in Brazil is rather complex. A large number of appeals of different types are possible in any given case. The resulting complexity is made worse by the fact that a large number of groundless appeals are filed, simply because a case becomes closed and the doctrine of *res judicata* applies to a decision only when it is no longer subject to any kind of appeal whatsoever.

7. STATISTICAL DATA

7.1. Inadequate data

The lack of statistics on civil justice in Brazil is simply shocking. For the most part, no statistical data are available at all. Where data are available, they are unreliable. Therefore, it is impossible to ascertain the number of actions started each year, the number of actions disposed of by summary procedures or default judgment, and the number of actions settled or resolved by judgment on the merits after a full hearing.

According to the National Association of Magistrates, at least 25 per cent of the actions filed before the Brazilian judiciary are not processed, and simply sit in the courts.

7.2. Estimate of performance

It could be said, although this is little more than our best guess, that, at least in the developed southern states, the average duration of a civil action before the first instance courts is between two and three years. The situation drastically changes in the north-eastern and northern states of the Brazilian Union, where an action may crawl for years and years and not be tried at all!

7.3. Performance varies regionally

For the better administration of justice, federal courts are grouped into five different regions. However, this makes it even more difficult to make a proper assessment of the overall Brazilian situation. For example, a case before the federal courts of the 4th Region may be tried at first instance within one year or less. However, a case before the federal courts of the 2nd Region may take five years or more to be decided. The same difficulty arises in respect of the state courts. The Tribunal of Justice is the name given to each state's supreme court (*Tribunal de Justiça*). In the states of São Paulo and Rio de Janeiro (which are the two most populous areas in the Brazilian federation), a civil case may be tried by a first instance court within two or three years of its commencement. However, this uniform standard of performance in comparable states' first instance courts breaks down at the appeal level. At the Tribunal of Justice of the state of Rio de Janeiro, an appeal may be tried within a year from the commencement of the appellate procedure. By contrast, at the Tribunal of Justice of the state of São Paulo, or at one of that state's two civil intermediate courts of appeals (*tribunal de alçada*, in charge of certain appeals), an appeal may have to wait for two years until it is assigned to a justice who will act as its reporter.

It ought to be no surprise that the reality of Brazilian administration of civil justice matches the variability and complexity of the social and political dimensions of the country itself. There are vast regional differences in this enormous country. Brazil's land mass is larger than the continental part of the United States. The Brazilian Union is made up of 26 states plus a federal district. Its total population should be close to 200 million by the turn of the century. While the five southern states (Rio de Janeiro, São Paulo, Paraná, Santa Catarina, and Rio Grande do Sul) are more developed than the rest of the country, the north-eastern and northern states (the latter comprising the Amazonic region) still lack the development which is indispensable for the adequate working of social and political institutions, including the courts. With one exception (Minas Gerais), the central and western states still need to be properly developed and organized. The prevailing social, economic, and political conditions interfere with the administration of justice, making it rather precarious in the country at large.

7.4. Workload

Most courts are unbearably overloaded. According to available data, in 1997 the eleven justices of the Federal Supreme Court, which is predominantly in charge of constitutional issues, handed down the incredible number of 40,000 decisions. This total includes all decisions taken by justices of the court, who may sit either in panels of five, in the full court of eleven, or individually as justices of the court. The Superior Tribunal of Justice is the court in charge of protecting federal laws. If one adds up all individual and collective decisions of its justices, it appears that the Superior Tribunal of Justice rendered more than 100,000 decisions in the same year (1997). According to the recently inaugurated Chief Justice of the Superior Tribunal of Justice, in just the past five years the federal branch of the judiciary alone has handed down 2,000,000 final decisions.

7.5. The legal profession

According to the National Association of Magistrates, there are a total of 10,637 judges in the various courts in all tiers of jurisdiction in Brazil. This means that there is one judge per 20,000 inhabitants. Brazil has less than one-third of the number of judges who are needed for a reasonable administration of justice.

There are about 300,000 lawyers registered in the twenty-seven sections of the Brazilian Bar Association. Although Article 133 of the Constitution declares that the legal profession is essential to the administration of justice, it is estimated that no more than 100,000 lawyers are actually in practice. Further, many of the lawyers in practice are not fully dedicated to the profession, but work on a part-time basis.

There is a system of public defenders for those persons who cannot afford to pay counsel's fees. The Constitution of Brazil (Art. 134 and sole paragraph) establishes that this institution, maintained by the Federal Union, the federal district, and the states, is essential to the administration of justice. Unfortunately, despite its constitutional position, the public defence system (*Defensoria Pública*) lacks defenders, supporting personnel, and infrastructure. It remains working at far below the minimum desirable conditions to enable it to perform its constitutional role adequately.

The Public Ministry (*Ministério Público*) is another institution, maintained by the Federal Union, the federal district, and the states, deemed essential to the administration of justice (Constitution, Art. 127). The Public Ministry has to act in the civil process whenever the interests of minors and other persons without legal capacity, and certain public interests, are at stake (CPC, Art. 82). The Public Ministry is a prosecuting body, whose role in civil cases is to represent or assist parties who lack full legal capacity, or to plead for the correct application of the law (as *amicus curiae*). In such cases, the Public Ministry prosecutors act as guardians of the law (*custos legis*), and take an impartial approach to the wishes of the parties. In their representative capacity, of course, they have to advance the interests of the party whom they represent.

The Federal Union is represented in the judicial process by the General Advocacy of the Union, the states by the State Attorney-General's Office, and municipalities by their attorneys.

8. MAIN PROBLEMS ENCOUNTERED IN THE ADMINISTRATION OF CIVIL JUSTICE

Problems encountered in the administration of civil justice in Brazil can be divided into three groups. There are: (*a*) personnel problems (i.e. problems concerning the operators of the jurisdictional mechanism, namely judges, lawyers, Public Ministry prosecutors, public defenders, and supporting personnel); (*b*) infrastructural problems (i.e. problems arising from the structure of the courts, their organization, equipment, etc.); and (*c*) procedural problems (i.e. problems with the legislation regulating civil jurisdiction).

8.1. Personnel problems: the poor skills base

Legal courses in Brazil are very precarious, as is the training of those who are responsible for the administration of justice, including not only judges and lawyers, but also all others who operate the system. Of course, this lack of any proper legal education and adequate training for all persons connected in any way with the administration of civil justice causes immense problems. If a lawyer does not plead a case properly, and if judges do not conduct the judicial process in an adequate manner, this inevitably affects the administration of justice. To a great extent in Brazil, the low skill level of the persons with roles to play in civil justice disturbs the good development and proper outcome of the judicial process.

8.2. Infrastructure problems: under-resourcing

In addition to the problem of a poor skills base, the lack of adequate infrastructure delays the judicial process and creates all sorts of obstacles to its development. Most courts of justice in Brazil lack essential equipment to accomplish their tasks. Many tasks are performed manually which, in more developed systems, would be automated or simply obsolete. The pages of files of proceedings are still numbered and stamped by hand. Every new piece of paper is actually sewn to the files of the case with needle and thread. Stenography and recording are rarely used. Court offices generally do not have any document reproduction facilities. They lack trained personnel, and seem always to be short of basic instruments for the work at hand.

8.3. Procedural problems: of lesser significance

Erroneous interpretation and application of the law by judges, lawyers, and supporting personnel is a much bigger problem than difficulties arising from deficiencies in the legislation. Of course, Brazilian laws regulating jurisdiction have their loopholes and defects and must be improved. However, if existing laws were correctly applied, undoubtedly the quality of justice in this country would be much more satisfactory. One of the problems faced when a new procedural law comes into effect is the very strong conservatism of those in charge of the administration of justice, who tend to react adversely to changes, or who seek to apply new laws and practices according to obsolete principles.

9. THE PROCEDURAL LAWS

The basic statute governing the administration of civil justice in Brazil is the Code of Civil Procedure (Federal Law no. 5869, of 11 January 1973, effective 1 January 1974). Strongly inspired by continental codes, the Brazilian CPC is a modern statute, of the same level of sophistication as modern European codes. The Constitution of the Federal Republic of Brazil, of 5 October 1988, also has a number of very important provisions about the administration of justice.

There are numerous laws outside the CPC governing different aspects of civil jurisdiction. Most of these laws date from before the 1988 Constitution but have been absorbed by it. Examples include: the bankruptcy law, dated 1945; the law regulating the *mandado de segurança* (a special constitutional injunction to protect indisputable rights from violation by public authorities), dated 1951; the laws regulating the popular lawsuit (*ação popular*) (instituted by the Constitution for citizens to plead the annulment of Acts which cause damage to public goods or offend administrative morality), dated 1965; and the more recent law regulating the civil public action (of a similar nature to the popular lawsuit), dated 1985. The civil public action (*ação civil pública*) has the same aim as the popular lawsuit (i.e. to protect public goods and proper administration), but can be brought by different parties. Only individual citizens can bring the popular lawsuit. The civil public action can be filed by the Federal Union; the states, municipalities, or their agencies; the Public Ministry; or by private associations which have been in existence for at least a year, and which have as their aim the protection of the environment, or of public goods in general.

Among the special laws dealing with the administration of civil justice (called 'extravagant' laws in Brazil because they are not included in a code), special reference should be made to the procedural part of the modern Law of Protection of Consumers (Law 8.078, dated 1990) and, above all, to Law 9.099, of 26 September 1995. As has already been pointed out, Law 9.099 organizes the special courts provided for by Article 98. I of the Constitution to promote conciliation, and trial and enforcement of civil cases of a lesser complexity and minor criminal offences.

Again, these laws are generally workable and appropriate, but they are often inadequately applied due to the personnel problems outlined above. It is the writer's firm opinion that, although the statutes could always be improved, most problems with the administration of justice in Brazil do not arise from the laws but from those in charge of applying them, and from the infrastructural problems facing the judiciary.

10. REFORMS OF THE PROCEDURAL LAWS

Over the past few years, the CPC has been subject to reforms which have made significant improvements. Four laws passed in 1994, and two others from 1995, have introduced separate and very important alterations. These changes were intended to make the CPC more apt to accomplish its aims, and appear to have been successful. These six laws have attempted (successfully) to expedite the administration of justice, by suppressing unnecessary acts, emphasizing conciliation, and simplifying the procedures for interlocutory appeals and summary proceedings. The possibility of anticipating judgment where the plaintiff's claim seems indisputable or the defendant unreasonably protracts the proceedings, by granting the plaintiff provisional early access to the fruits of his or her coming victory, is one of the highlights of these reforms. The other highlight is a new possibility for obtaining orders for specific performance, requiring a party to do, or to refrain from doing, some thing in particular, rather than providing only monetary compensation. All of these reforms are inspired by the principle of effectiveness of the process, which provides that the proceedings shall be conducted in such a manner as to achieve the best and fastest results.

Unfortunately, it takes more than reform of the CPC to change the administration of civil justice in Brazil. Court costs remain a significant obstacle to access to justice. The fact that a party must pay to litigate, and pay again to appeal, often prevents people from litigating. Costs can be high. Only those who can show that they are unable to meet these costs are granted relief, by being allowed the privilege of 'gratuity'. The system of public defenders is still very inefficient. In many states it does not operate at all, or it exists only by way of token public legal assistance to persons most in need. It is evident that, if a party cannot obtain official legal assistance, he or she will have to hire a lawyer on his or her own, knowing that the attorney's fees provided for in the final decision are usually insufficient to reimburse fully the remuneration of counsel.

Last but not least, the fact that Brazil has not yet adopted the *stare decisis* principle means the system suffers from unnecessary repetition of cases. Individual fact situations have to be tried by the courts even though many similar cases may have already been determined, all in a similar way. Such repetition wastes time and money, in the obviously sterile activity of parties trying once again, over and over, an issue that has already been tried. There is no hope for the administration of justice in Brazil in any jurisdiction, be it civil, criminal, labour, or otherwise, unless the country adopts the proposed binding precedent system. According to this system, a court will be obliged to apply precedents which have been established and announced. A proposition reflecting the understanding of the court about a certain legal issue can then be reliably formulated, and used to guide both advice given by lawyers to litigants and court decisions in subsequent cases.

11. ALTERNATIVE MODES OF DISPUTE RESOLUTION

ADR methods are very little practised in Brazil. It seems that lack of experience with, and a certain suspicion of, ADR methods make them very unpopular in the country. Arbitration is scarcely used. The recent arbitration statute of 23 September 1996 (Federal Law no. 9.307) does not seem to have been successful. Mediation, as practised in countries like the United States, is unknown in Brazil. Extra-judicial settlement of disputes is still carried out in most cases by lawyers. Such legal negotiation is especially common in cases in which the conflicting parties face significant losses if their cases do not come quickly to an end.

The CPC and other procedural laws, especially the statute of special courts, emphasize conciliation between the parties. They allow the judge to call parties to court for the purpose of settling the case at any point in the proceeding (CPC, Art. 125. IV).

Perhaps it would not be wrong to say that Brazilians have not yet become aware of the advantages of amicable settlement, either in court or out of it.

12. ASSESSMENT OF THE PRESENT STATE OF AFFAIRS

Although this brief report on the administration of civil justice in Brazil (inevitably vague given the palpable lack of statistical data) may look rather sombre as it depicts the existing conditions, the truth is that there are reasons for optimism. History shows that the administration of civil justice in Brazil has always, slowly but surely, improved.

Past legal reforms, especially those which began with the Code of Civil Procedure of 1939 and the statutes subsequent to it, have been successful. They have modernized the legislation, better enabling it to meet the needs of the justice system. The study of civil procedure has flourished, at least in the past three decades. This fact has had direct and positive effects both on the procedural legislation and on practice. The tremendous ongoing efforts of institutions like the Brazilian Bar Association, the Association of Magistrates at national and state levels, the Institute of Brazilian Lawyers, the Public Ministry, and entities in charge of trans-individual interests, are highly positive factors, contributing strongly to the improvement of the administration of justice in Brazil.

It is amazing how Brazil has grown, particularly in the second half of this century. Brazil has evolved from being a backward country to being a modern one, eager to pass quickly through all the various stages of development. Since there have been so many accomplishments in other areas, there is strong reason to believe that Brazil will also develop a better system for the administration of justice in the near future.

11

Civil Justice Reform:
Access, Costs, and Delay.
A Greek Perspective

K. D. Kerameus and S. Koussoulis

1. INTRODUCTION: THE GREEK SYSTEM OF CIVIL PROCEDURE

1. Article 26 III of the Greek Constitution of 1975 stipulates: 'The judicial powers shall be exercised by courts of law, the decisions of which shall be executed in the name of the Greek People,'[1] and Article 94 III of the Constitution provides especially for civil justice: 'Civil courts shall have jurisdiction on all private disputes, as well as on cases of voluntary jurisdiction assigned to them by law.'[2]

Thus, pursuant to constitutional provisions, only the ordinary civil courts have jurisdiction to rule on private disputes.[3] In all cases, courts are comprised of professional judges enjoying guarantees of personal and functional independence (Art. 87 I of the Constitution). There is no provision for a jury in civil cases; the participation of jurors-assessors is only allowed in certain serious criminal cases.

2. The Code of Civil Procedure of 1967 provides for three types of civil courts of original jurisdiction: justices of the peace; single-member district courts; and three-member district courts adjudicating at first instance. Subject-matter competence of each of these first instance courts normally depends on quantitative criteria, e.g. on the amount in dispute.[4] The subject-matter competence is, in addition, defined in a qualitative way according to the nature of the dispute at hand or the complexity of the legal or factual issues arising therefrom.[5] Recent press announcements have indicated that the justices of the peace may be eliminated as separate courts and may merge with the single-member district courts. Interestingly, similar announcements are coming forth from France.

3. The three-member district courts have general jurisdiction and also hear

---

[1] *The Constitution of Greece*, trans. by E. Spiliotopoulos, X. Paparrigopoulos, and S. Vassilouni (Athens, 1995), 33. [2] Ibid., 79.
[3] For the distinction between civil and administrative courts see P. Yessiou-Faltsi, *Civil Procedure in Hellas* (Sakkoulas/Kluwer, 1997), 127–9.
[4] See K. D. Kerameus, 'Civil Procedure', in K. D. Kerameus and P. J. Kozyris (eds.), *Introduction to Greek Law* (Kluwer/Sakkoulas, 2nd edn. 1993), ch. 15 III B, 270.
[5] For further details see Yessiou-Faltsi, *Civil Procedure in Hellas*, 134–9.

appeals from the justices of the peace. Appeals from the other district courts go to the courts of appeal, which hear cases *de novo*, both in law and on the facts. The Supreme Court (*Areios Pagos*), comprised of sixty judges, is solely a court of cassation which confines its extraordinary review to questions of law, having in principle no authority to review findings of fact.

4. In the Greek appellate system, one has to distinguish between ordinary and extraordinary methods of appeal. Regardless of this distinction, all methods of appeal are exercised by a writ registered with the court that issued the decision appealed against (*iudex a quo*). The first group comprises:

(i) The *reopening of a default judgment*, which is premissed on the right to be heard in court (Art. 20 I of the Constitution): it is only permitted when a party is not summoned at all or not duly or timely summoned, or when the absence of the defaulting party can be attributed to *force majeure* (Art. 501 of the Code of Civil Procedure, as amended);[6]

(ii) The most important and frequent method of attack on first instance judgments is the *appeal*, which aims to re-adjudicate the case *in toto* at second instance.[7] Even so, new claims are not admissible at this second instance, and new allegations of the parties may only be taken into consideration under specific conditions.[8] Grounds for appeal may refer to simple questions of fact, including the assessment of evidence, to legal questions of a substantive or procedural nature, or to alleged procedural mistakes of the lower court.

5. Extraordinary methods of appeal are:

(i) The *reopening of contested judgments*, modelled on the French *requête civile* and the German *Wiederaufnahme des Verfahrens*. Based on very narrow grounds of a purely procedural or both a procedural and substantive nature, this attack purports to overturn a judgment which has already acquired a *res judicata* effect, regardless of the availability of cassation before *Areios Pagos*.[9]

(ii) Based on the distinction between fact and law,[10] the *cassation* is intended to review judgments having *res judicata* effect for breach of either any rule of substantive law or of some specific rule of procedure. It is also allowed

---

[6] The previously existing form of 'unjustified' reopening of default judgments is no longer applicable; see below para. 19(*b*).

[7] The doctrinal controversy concerning the object of appeal was finally decided by the *Full Bench of Areios Pagos* 12/1989, *HellDni* 1989, 1313–16, which held that the appeal does not constitute a new trial matter but, rather, the means for the full realization of the claim within the scope of the first instance trial through its re-examination on appeal.

[8] See Yessiou-Faltsi, *Civil Procedure in Hellas*, 270.

[9] For an overview of the appellate procedure see ibid. 281–4.

[10] See G. Mitsopoulos, 'Die Unterscheidung zwischen Tatfrage und Rechtsfrage im Kassationsverfahren', *ZZP* (1968), 251 ff.

for lack of legal basis (*manque de base légale*),[11] which is upheld when the facts of the case necessary for the application of a particular norm do not clearly appear on the face of the record, or when there is inconsistent or insufficient reasoning as to the facts which have been admitted.[12] Thus, cassation is considered as a method of attack dealing purely with questions of law. Article 580 I, II, as amended by Law 2172/1993, sets out as a general rule that, upon reversal, no further adjudication on the merits is allowed by an *Areios Pagos* Chamber. The case must be remanded for re-adjudication to the court which rendered the reversed decision.[13]

6. In Greek law, provisional remedies, applicable only in order to temporarily settle an urgent situation or to avoid an imminent danger (Art. 682 I CC Proc.), are divided into two main categories:

(i) *conservatory measures*, tending to secure the future satisfaction of a substantive right; and

(ii) *regulatory provisional remedies*, which aim at the provisional regulation of a disputed legal relationship.[14]

Conservatory remedies include judicial security in order to allow the eventual satisfaction of the plaintiff after adjudication on the merits; pre-notice of mortgage, i.e. a mortgage registered as a provisional measure only with the purpose of securing priority, albeit subject to the final award of the claim; conservatory attachment; judicial custody; and sealing, unsealing, inventory, or public deposit of property. The regulatory measures for the provisional settlement of disputes are not enumerated in the Code of Civil Procedure. Moreover, the judge is entitled to order any measure that he or she thinks appropriate, with no reference to a statutory list.[15] Nevertheless, according to Article 692 IV CC Proc., a provisional remedy may not lead to the full satisfaction of the right to be secured or protected. Despite the doctrinal fluctuations as to the scope and the real function of this provision, it is generally accepted that provisional remedies should prevent an irreparable situation from occurring before a final decision on the underlying substantive right is rendered.[16]

---

[11] See P. Yessiou-Faltsi, 'Ist der "manque de base légale" ein Kassationsgrund, der über die Unterscheidung des materiellen Rechts und des Zivilprozessrechts hinausgeht?', in *Festschrift W. Henckel* (1995), 923 ff.

[12] This is the definition of *manque de base légale* according to the *Full Bench of Areios Pagos* 5/1994, *HellDni* 1994, 1252–3. [13] See below para. 19.

[14] See K. Kerameus, 'Der einstweilige Rechtsschutz vom Standpunkt der neuen griechischen Zivilprozessordnung', *Studia iuridica*, 1 (1980), 427 ff.; K. Kerameus and K. Polyzogopoulos, 'Les Mesures provisoires en procédure civile hellénique', in G. Tarzia (ed.), *Les Mesures provisoires en procédure civile* (Milan, 1985), 55–86 = IDME (ed.), *Justice and Efficiency*, i (Athens, 1987), 243–85.

[15] Yessiou-Faltsi, *Civil Procedure in Hellas*, 243–4.

[16] Kerameus and Polyzogopoulos, 'Les Mesures provisoires', 75–6 = 270–2.

7. Three types of actions are known in the Greek legal system:

(i) action for performance,
(ii) action for declaratory judgment, and
(iii) action for judicial modification of a legal relationship.[17]

Regardless of the type of action, ordinary proceedings in the courts of first instance follow the same pattern. A civil action commences by filing a complaint with the clerk who appoints a day and time for the first hearing of the case. He or she then enters the action in the docket. The defendant will then be served with a copy of the complaint, also indicating the day and time fixed. Service takes place on the plaintiff's initiative, usually at the defendant's home or at his or her place of business. Service must be made at least thirty days before the first hearing. Once service is completed, the action is considered as having been brought (Art. 215 I CC Proc.). Failure properly to serve the action can be remedied by the actual appearance of the defendant, to the extent that he or she does not raise the relevant objection.[18]

8. Formal preparation for litigation is not necessary for either plaintiff or defendant.[19] Generally, the plaintiff may bring an action as the first step in the proceedings against the defendant. The defendant is not required to answer the complaint immediately, but may wait until the first hearing of the case, when both parties set out their factual and legal positions in their pleadings. Written pleadings other than the complaint are never required to be served or even sent to the other party. They may be filed with the court clerk as late as the date of the hearing.

The first hearing of the case is the most important phase of the entire proceedings. Indeed, it belongs to the traditional characteristics of litigation under Greek law that, as a rule, no exchange of written pleadings takes place before the hearing. Naturally, the introductory document must have been served to the defendant ahead of time. By contrast, the plaintiff is not at all aware of the arguments to be presented by the defendant. Even the judges do not usually know in advance what any given suit is about. Thus, the first hearing of the case gives to all persons concerned a first glimpse of the subject of the suit, rather than a concluding consideration.

Both parties articulate their statements of fact, which also delimit the evidence to be produced. Regarding the proceedings before justices of the peace or one-member district courts, the first hearing is, for all practical purposes, the only one. Such proceedings are mostly oral. The parties are required to produce all their means of proof at the first hearing, after which it is expected that judgment will be given. Only in exceptional cases may the

---

[17] See Kerameus, 'Civil Procedure', ch. 15 IV B, 273–4.

[18] See, for instance, *Athens Court of Appeal* 4367/1988, *HellDni* 1990, 591. The whole presentation follows the text by Kerameus, 'Civil Procedure', ch. 15 VI, 276–9.

[19] See, however, below para. 10, on compulsory attempts at conciliation.

court order further evidence to be taken. The same procedure has been followed since 1994 before the three-member district court as well, unless the president orders otherwise (below para. 17(*b*)).

9. A particular characteristic of Greek civil procedure is the coexistence of several procedural models. Apart from the normal proceedings, applicable in principle in all cases, there also exist a number of special proceedings, corresponding to actions of a particular nature. According to the prevailing opinion, the type of proceedings to be followed does not constitute a condition for the action to be admissible. Therefore, the submission of the dispute to the wrong type of proceedings does not entail inadmissibility or any other procedural sanction.[20] The *raison d'être* for such special proceedings is to provide a more flexible framework for the adjudication of disputes. The special proceedings are characterized by simpler and speedier procedures (oral pleadings and concentration of evidence) coupled with wider powers for the adjudicating judge.[21]

There are special proceedings for the adjudication of matrimonial disputes (Arts. 592–613 CC Proc.); of disputes involving the relationship between parents and children (Arts. 614–22 CC Proc.); of disputes involving negotiable instruments (Arts. 635–46 CC Proc.); of disputes between landlords and tenants (Arts. 647–62 CC Proc.); of labour disputes (Arts. 663–76 CC Proc.); of disputes involving the remuneration of certain professionals (Arts. 677–81 CC Proc.); of disputes arising out of the use of cars (Art. 681A CC Proc.); of disputes on maintenance and parental care (Arts. 681B–681C CC Proc.); of disputes involving compensation for damage caused by the press or other mass media (Art. 681D CC Proc.); and, finally, for granting orders of payment (Arts. 623–34 CC Proc.).[22] It must be noted, however, that the flexibility inherent in such special proceedings made them an attractive model for the normal proceedings as well. As a result of recent amendments, the ordinary procedure is now generally patterned after the special proceeding for labour disputes.

10. A legislative attempt to alleviate the resolution of disputes was made through the enactment of Law 2298/1995. This law amended the Code of Civil Procedure, adding a new Article (214A CC Proc.). This requires the parties to a private dispute which is susceptible to conciliation to attempt such conciliation as a condition for their appearance before the three-member district courts. Should this examination of the dispute by all available means result in a settlement, the agreement reached would be subsequently approved by the court (before which the action is already brought, and is still pending) and vested with the power of *exequatur*. If, on the other hand, the attempt at

---

[20] See *Areios Pagos* 315/1986, *HellDni* 1987, 608–9: it is not a ground for cassation that the case has been adjudicated in proceedings other than those provided by law; *Thessaloniki Court of Appeal* 347/1990, *HellDni* 1990, 1320.   [21] Kerameus, 'Civil Procedure', 288–90.

[22] For an overview of such special proceedings, see ibid.; Yessiou-Faltsi, *Civil Procedure in Hellas*, 367–72.

conciliation fails or one of the parties refuses to take part, then the hearing may proceed as usual.

This mandatory attempt at conciliation (an obligation of conduct rather than an obligation of result) met with a strong reaction from the bar, who drew attention to the practical difficulties that might arise. As a result, the entry into force of Article 214A CC Proc. has been repeatedly postponed. It is currently, by virtue of Article 6 of Law 2479/1997, scheduled to come into force on 16 September 1999. This conciliation procedure is 'mandatory' only in the sense that no judicial hearing of the case may take place unless conciliation has been attempted. The parties cannot be compelled to appear at the conciliation procedure, nor is conciliation itself bound to be completed.

2. STATISTICAL DATA

11. In Greece, in a total population of around 10.5 million, there were, in spring 1998, about 3,600 judges and 26,000 practising lawyers. Statistical data on the cases pending before the courts may be found in a publication of the National Statistical Service: *Judicial Statistics*. The most recent edition (Athens, 1997) contains data for the year 1995. These data, however, may be taken as indicative of the present situation, since they largely correspond to the data for the previous years 1991–4.

12. Thus, in the year 1995, 168,568 cases were pending before the justices of the peace, of which 38,861 had already been brought in the previous year. Among them, 43.4 per cent of the cases were not tried for various reasons, e.g. the parties opted for conciliation or the hearing was cancelled. The remaining 56.6 per cent of pending cases were tried, and 75,399 decisions were issued. Of the issued decisions: 35.9 per cent were rendered in regular proceedings; 11.9 per cent in petty disputes proceedings; 2 per cent in proceedings for negotiable instruments; 3.6 per cent in proceedings for the return of rented property; and 25.1 per cent in all other kinds of special proceedings; while 21.3 per cent referred to orders granting provisional measures.

13. During the same year, 1995, 203,116 cases were pending before the sixty-three courts of first instance (in both their single-member and three-member formations), of which 26,044 had already been brought in the previous year. Among them, 20.4 per cent were not tried for various reasons, e.g. the parties opted for conciliation, the hearing was cancelled, or the parties withdrew the suit. A further 3 per cent were granted a postponement. The total number of decisions issued by the courts of first instance was 289,717. Among them, 77,856 were rendered in regular proceedings (37 per cent of these were in the framework of voluntary jurisdiction), while the other 211,861 decisions were issued in all kinds of special proceedings.

There were 4,656 decisions of the three-member court of first instance dealing with appeals against decisions by the justices of the peace. Out of the total of 49,061 first instance decisions of the three-member district courts issued in regular proceedings, 25.7 per cent were non-final decisions ordering evidence, 70.9 per cent addressed the merits, while the remaining 3.4 per cent dismissed the suit on procedural grounds, i.e. lack of some procedural prerequisites. Among the decisions issued in special proceedings, 12.3 per cent referred to landlord and tenant disputes; 10 per cent to disputes involving negotiable instruments; 6.3 per cent to labour disputes; 52 per cent to provisional measures; and the remaining 19.4 per cent to other kinds of special proceedings.

Out of the totality of final decisions issued by the courts of first instance in regular proceedings, 63.1 per cent were concluded within one year of the suit being first filed, while the remainder extended to more than one year. Unfortunately, statistical data do not offer any further indication of the time eventually required.

14. Greece has thirteen courts of appeal, before which, in 1995, a total of 52,325 cases were pending, 14,399 of them already brought in the previous year. Of these cases, 63.4 per cent were not handled for various reasons, e.g. the parties opted for conciliation, the hearing was cancelled, or the appeal was withdrawn. During this same year, 10,289 decisions were issued in regular proceedings. Of these, 15.5 per cent covered decisions ordering evidence, 83.6 per cent addressed the merits, while 0.9 per cent dismissed the appeal on procedural grounds. There were also 20,656 appellate decisions dealing with cases adjudicated at first instance in the framework of special proceedings.

In 50.8 per cent of their final decisions, the courts of appeal confirmed the decisions issued at first instance. The same happened in 66 per cent of the decisions issued by the three-member courts of first instance on appeal from the justices of the peace. Moreover, 69.1 per cent of appellate cases were concluded within one year from the time when the appeal was filed, while, at the courts of first instance, 75.5 per cent of appeals from the justices of the peace were concluded within one year.

It is worth pointing out that the vast majority of first instance judgments are appealed against, so much so that no specific statistical data exist.

15. During 1995, a total of 3,628 cassation cases were brought before *Areios Pagos*, of which 44.3 per cent were struck from the record or cancelled. That same year, 2,093 decisions were issued, of which 22.8 per cent reversed the judgment of the lower court.

3. MAIN PROBLEMS ENCOUNTERED IN THE ADMINISTRATION OF CIVIL JUSTICE

3.1. The first instance procedure

16. The basic cause of the overloading of courts and the long time required for a final decision is considered to be the large number of cases filed every year. In

Greece, this phenomenon is often attributed to sociological reasons. Parties seem unwilling to reach a settlement, since neither the present law (see, however, above para. 10) nor their lawyers encourage them to do so. The financial state of debtors often does not allow them willingly to carry out their obligations. Finally, mostly in family disputes, the militant attitude of the parties, who, by bringing a case before the court, wish at the end of the day for their opponent to suffer rather than for their own right to be vindicated, makes litigation inevitable and settlement impossible.[23]

17. However, important as they may be, these psychological parameters do not seem to be the decisive reason for the congestion of the courts. The statistical data indicate that approximately 85 per cent of the actions tried during the year 1995 resulted in decisions in favour of the plaintiff. It is obvious, therefore, that resort to courts is induced by a true need for justice rather than by purely superficial reasons. Thus, one should look elsewhere for the 'root of the evil'. It is perhaps the structure of the trial itself that makes it last such a long time. Lately, the legislature has repeatedly intervened in order to accelerate the administration of justice, particularly at the first instance level.

(*a*) Before the justices of the peace and in the one-member district courts the proceedings are conducted orally and the parties are required to produce all available means of evidence at the first hearing (Art. 237 I CC Proc.). At the same time, the judge assumes a more active role: by asking questions, he or she may assist the parties in accurately identifying the crucial facts and providing the necessary clarifications on the relevant points (Art. 236 CC Proc.).[24] Thus, the judge obtains a clear picture of the case at the first hearing, so that he or she may issue a final judgment forthwith. Additional evidence, however, may be ordered, should the judge deem it necessary (Art. 270 VI CC Proc.; see also above para. 8).

(*b*) The procedure before the three-member district courts was different in the past. The principle of orality was abandoned in practice, and procedure was based mainly on written pleadings and on taking evidence either before the court or, usually, before one member of the chamber (judge *rapporteur*), following a non-final decision to that effect (Art. 341 CC Proc.). The examination of witnesses takes place before the judge *rapporteur*, although his or her intervention is restricted to technical questions, leaving the initiative to counsel for the parties.

Law 2207/1994 attempted to simplify the procedure before the three-member district court after the model adopted for single-member courts. As a result, the rule at present is that the procedure followed before the three-member district courts is the same as the one followed before the justices of the

---

[23] See N. K. Klamaris, 'Ursachen gegenwärtiger Probleme der Überlastung von Gerichten: soziologischer Überblick', in IDME (ed.), *Justice and Efficiency*, 104–5.

[24] See K. D. Kerameus,' Judicial Activism in Greece', *Studia iuridica*, 3 (1995), 155 ff., 163.

peace and the single-member district courts. However, if, at the time of filing the suit, the president of the court thinks that the case presents difficulties requiring a more detailed investigation, he or she may order the hearing to be held according to the full procedure, i.e. on the basis of evidence ordered by a non-final decision and taken usually before the judge *rapporteur.*

(*c*) As a result of these legislative initiatives, the procedure before the first instance courts presents the following picture. The bulk of cases, whether in regular proceedings or in any kind of special proceedings, are adjudicated in a flexible procedural framework characterized by: the oral elaboration of arguments; the taking of evidence at the first hearing; and the issuing of the final decision within a reasonable period of two to five months from the day of the hearing. Only in those cases falling under the original jurisdiction of the three-member district court which are deemed to be of particular importance due to their factual or legal complexity is a more strict procedure followed, under which no real oral hearing is conducted. If the court, based on the written pleadings of the parties, considers the action admissible and well founded in law, a non-final decision is issued ordering evidence to be taken (Art. 341 I, II CC Proc.). The same decision also indicates the subject matter to be proved, the party bearing the burden of proof, the means of proof allowed, and the time limit within which the procedure must be completed. The non-final decision on evidence-taking is issued at least two months after the first hearing of the case. The taking of evidence follows by all available means but usually by two witnesses on each side. Although in principle the whole process may not exceed six months in duration (Art. 341 III CC Proc.), in fact, depending on the case and mostly due to successive extensions of the relevant deadline, it may last in total from one to two or even more years. Thus, the time elapsed from the initial hearing of the case before the three-member district court until the final decision is rendered may reach approximately two or three years.

Regarding in particular the allocation of the burden of proof, Greek law follows the principle of *Tatbestand*: each party must prove the prerequisites for the application of the legal norms that he or she invokes in support of his or her claim (Art. 338 I CC Proc.). For instance, in a sales claim, the plaintiff must prove that a sale contract was concluded and that it has not succumbed to limitation; whereas the defendant must prove that he or she justly refused to pay the price as the object sold was defective in a manner destroying or significantly diminishing its value or fitness for ordinary use (Art. 534–53 CC Proc.).

18. The time required for the final decision in the two kinds of procedure followed before first instance courts is often extended due to the tactics of counsel. Counsel have the procedural capability to delay the progress of the trial, should they wish to do so (occasionally as a tactical move on behalf of their clients).

(*a*) The basic means of delaying the progress of the trial is the postponement of the hearing, at a party's request. According to Article 239 CC Proc., any party is entitled to appear at the hearing and ask orally for a postponement, invoking serious reasons that prevented him or her from submitting his or her written pleadings in time, namely before the first hearing. A party may do this only once. The same may happen even if a party has submitted his or her pleadings in time but, nevertheless, requests a postponement with good cause (Art. 241 CC Proc.). The court has the discretionary power to grant such a postponement, but only for a period that does not exceed two months. Should this prove impossible, the trial is set as soon as possible thereafter. Although the relevant provisions explicitly state that the reason for postponement should be evaluated before postponement is granted, judicial practice shows that cases brought before the court for the first time are usually granted a postponement simply by a party asking for it, without any evaluation by the court of the grounds for postponement alleged by the party. It is clear that, in this way, the progress of the trial is significantly delayed, particularly since courts overloaded with cases, such as those of Athens, Piraeus, and Thessaloniki, tend to grant a postponement for a period of time longer than two months, usually even longer than six months. Consequently, the statutory scheme for the normal period of time required for the first instance courts to give a final decision is severely undermined.

(*b*) The final first instance decision may also be seriously delayed by the ability of the parties to prolong the initial six-month time limit provided for the taking of evidence to be completed. This deadline can be extended twice, by four months each time, making eight months in total (Art. 149 I CC Proc., as amended). Once the fourteen-month (6+4+4) period has elapsed and the first round of evidence is complete, a new six-month extension may still be granted by the court (Art. 149 IV CC Proc., as amended). The courts tend to favour such extensions, interpreting the relevant provisions in a broad way. Case law holds that the aim of such a prolongation is to offer a new timetable for taking evidence, thus avoiding the disadvantageous results of precluding the right to present evidence after the initial time limit has expired.[25] The extension of the time limit is generally entrusted to the discretion of the court,[26] provided that a good reason for the delay is offered by the parties,[27] or because the new time limit is considered necessary for the further examination of the case and does not amount to an abuse of the right of evidence.[28] Nevertheless, this attitude encourages the submission of requests for new time limits for taking evidence even after the initial period and both extensions have expired. It is obvious that, in such a way, the completion of the first instance procedure (although excep-

---

[25] *Areios Pagos* 399/1983, *Dike* 1984, 392.   [26] *Areios Pagos* 587/1989, *Dike* 1990, 849.
[27] *Athens Court of Appeal* 4490/1992, *HellDni* 1995, 1540.
[28] *Athens Court of Appeal* 6358/1984, *Dike* 1985, 310; *Larissa Court of Appeal* 182/1993, *Harmenopoulos* 1993, 1069.

tionally: see above para. 17(*c*)) is unduly prolonged, particularly if one takes into account that the new time limit may also be twice extended. The ensuing delays prompted the legislature to abolish the relevant provision by adopting Article 8 IV of Law 2145/1993. Nevertheless, the possibility of further extensions was reintroduced through Article 3 V of Law 2207/1994, which is currently in force.

3.2. Appellate procedure

19. As already mentioned, there are ordinary and extraordinary methods of appeal. The existence of no less than four modes of appeal presents the parties with a variety of choices as to the mode they will use, should they wish to appeal. In any event, Greek law stipulates that a decision acquires *res judicata* effect only after the exhaustion of the ordinary modes: *reopening of default*; and *appeal* (Art. 321 CC Proc.).

As a matter of principle, no appeals are allowed against interlocutory decisions. Eventual complaints by a party against them may only be availed of in the appeal against the final judgment itself. Particularly with regard to provisional remedies, these are subject to a motion for modification or revocation rather than to a regular appeal (Art. 699 CC Proc.). By way of exception, provisional determinations of possession or detention of things are subject to appeal, which, however, does not as such suspend the enforcement of the determinations.

(*a*) The distinction between ordinary and extraordinary modes of appeal does not correspond to how frequently these methods are used. Ordinary appeal and cassation are usually the methods of choice. The use of the other two methods is rather limited. Reopening of default presupposes the existence of a default decision as the object of attack. The reopening of contested judgments is not a popular method, since the grounds available are rather limited.[29] Thus, the ordinary appeal and, on a smaller scale, the request for cassation make up the body of options generally available. Under one or other of these two modes of appeal, every case could, as a matter of law, proceed further after the procedure at first instance is concluded, should one or other of the parties so choose.

There are various reasons for resorting to these methods of attack. First, the natural inclination of the parties is to avail themselves of all available means of review.[30] Furthermore, the legislature, albeit not constitutionally or otherwise required to create two levels of jurisdiction,[31] is reluctant to restrict appeals. Although Article 20 I of the Constitution, which guarantees access to courts in general, does not safeguard a right to appeals as well,[32] it is unusual to

---

[29] See P. Kargados, 'Das Überlastungsproblem der höheren Gerichte in Griechenland', in IDME (ed.), *Justice and Efficiency*, 132–3. [30] Ibid. 188.

[31] *Council of State* [Supreme Administrative Court] 2614/1993, *Dike* 1994, 623.

[32] *Areios Pagos* 866/1995, *HellDni* 1996, 1572.

encounter legal restrictions to appeal or cassation, e.g. by setting financial limitations as a condition for admissibility.[33] The most important factor accounting for the frequent resort to appellate proceedings is the rule according to which the filing of an appeal has a suspensive effect *vis-à-vis* the judgment appealed from, thus conferring an *ex lege* stay of execution until the final decision is rendered on appeal (Art. 521 I CC Proc.). There is some support for the abolition or at least restriction of this suspensive effect, since it is expected that this would prevent parties from filing unmeritorious or abusive appeals.[34] This point of view is corroborated by statistical data. While almost 44 per cent of the cases filed with the first instance courts are not tried, e.g. due to withdrawal or settlement, this percentage rises to 63.5 per cent in the courts of appeal. The suspension of both the *res judicata* effect and enforceability of the judgment under attack are often the very reasons for initiating an appeal.

By filing a regular appeal, the defendant-appellant may postpone the evil day of payment. But, of course, the fact that there has already been a suspension, either by operation of the law or where specifically ordered by the appellate court, does not prejudice the outcome of the appellate case. In other words, suspension of the first instance final judgment may well have been ordered but, at the end of the day, the appellate court is totally free to dismiss the appeal and confirm the judgment appealed against.

(*b*) One of the most important recent legislative interventions in civil procedure was the abolition of the 'unjustified' reopening of default judgments through Article 9 I of Law 2145/1993. In the past, all default judgments rendered after the first hearing of a case, at first or second instance, could be attacked as of right by way of *opposition*. The attacking party had to show neither a good ground of opposition nor a good reason for the default. As a result, default judgments were always vulnerable, and had to be examined on their merits on the application of the defaulting party. The availability of this method of attack provided the parties with much scope to engage in dilatory tactics at first or second instance.[35] The abolition of this 'unjustified' reopening (i.e. in English procedural terms, the end of the setting aside of default judgments as of right), and the introduction instead of a system of 'justified' reopening of default (i.e. its replacement with a more limited setting aside for cause shown), was combined with the right of the party defaulting at first instance to appeal immediately from the default decision, thus bringing the case directly before the second instance court. Article 528 CC Proc., as amended by Article 3 § 21 of Law 2207/1994, provides that, once an appeal is launched against a default judgment, the latter is reversed and the appellant may present at the second instance all the allegations that he or she could have presented at first instance,

[33] It was held by the Council of State (2614/1993, *Dike* 1994, 623) that it is in principle acceptable to set a minimum value limit for the dispute to be allowed to go to appeal.

[34] See Kargados, 'Das Überlastungsproblem', 191.

[35] Kerameus, 'Civil Procedure', 283–4.

if he or she had not defaulted there. In such a way, the defaulting party may in essence bypass first instance adjudication. The percentage of default judgments has radically decreased since the abolition of the 'unjustified' reopening of default.

20. As already indicated by the statistical data presented, almost 31 per cent of the cases pending before the courts of appeal take more than one year before the final decision is reached. This delay may also be due, among other factors,[36] to the specific structure and purpose of the ordinary appeal as a method of attack. We have already indicated that 15.5 per cent of the appellate decisions in the year 1995 were non-final ones, ordering the taking of evidence. This involvement of the court of appeal with evidence is due to two main reasons. First, in principle, parties are allowed to produce new evidence at the appellate level (Art. 529 II CC Proc.). The court of appeal may exceptionally turn down such evidence only if it considers that the party did not produce it at first instance out of severe negligence or bad faith (Art. 529 II CC Proc.). Second, the subject matter of appellate adjudication coincides with the substantive right that underlay the subject matter of the first instance trial.[37] It is therefore held that the court of appeal may order the taking of new or additional evidence, even before the judgment under attack is quashed, in order for the appellate judges to be able to decide whether the grounds for appeal are well founded or not.[38] It has also been held that the decision granting the appeal and remanding the case to the court of first instance for further consistent consideration is not a final one.[39] It may thus be revoked if the same court should subsequently change its mind as to whether the grounds for appeal were well founded. The possibility of repeated review of the grounds for appeal, and repeated reversal of decisions on appeal, may result in a better judgment on the merits, but it is not conducive to a speedy completion of the appellate stage of adjudication.

21. The recent amendment, through Law 2172/1993, as to the procedure of cassation also impedes the rapid final conclusion of adjudication. Under the previous rule, the *Areios Pagos* could, when granting a request for cassation, remand the case to one of its chambers for a new adjudication on the merits. The provision currently applicable stipulates that, once cassation is granted, the *Areios Pagos* is required to remand the case for further adjudication to a court of the same level as the *iudex a quo*, or even to the same court if that court can be composed of different judges (Article 580 III CC Proc., as amended),[40] for the appeal remains pending before the *iudex a quo*. The Supreme Court thus maintains its status as a pure court of cassation, addressing only questions of law. However, this amended procedure certainly delays the final conclusion of

---

[36] Other causes of delay are mentioned by Kargados, 'Das Überlastungsproblem', 156–61.
[37] See above n. 7.   [38] *Full Bench of Areios Pagos* 1285/1982, *NoB* 1983, 219–21.
[39] See, e.g., *Areios Pagos* 1541/1997, *Dike* 1998, 246.
[40] See Yessiou-Faltsi, *Civil Procedure in Hellas*, 272–3.

the case. Indeed, the decision of the court to which the case was remanded may itself be subject to cassation on other grounds. Should such re-cassation be granted, the new decision after re-remand would also be subject to further cassation, and so on. Having to choose between the speedy administration of justice and the quest for a correct final judgment on the merits, the legislature clearly opts for the second alternative.

3.3. Cost of litigation

22. As the administration of justice is generally considered to be a duty of the state, the citizens are not directly burdened with the costs required for the existence, maintenance, and operation of the machinery of justice. However, as a contribution towards the necessary expenditure, the state asks those seeking judicial protection to pay dues, including stamp duty and suchlike. They also pay for the services of judicial agents not remunerated by the state, namely counsel and bailiffs. Thus, litigation costs can be divided into court fees and out-of-court expenses (including counsel's fees).[41] This bifurcation corresponds in general to state dues, on the one hand, and the private expenditure of the parties, on the other.[42] Generally speaking, the cost of litigation in Greece is low and courts rarely order full payment of the expenditure incurred.

23. In Greece there is no uniform method of calculation, nor any maximum limit on fees, for the remuneration of counsel. The Code of Attorneys (Legislative Decree 3026/1954, as amended) provides for a specific fee for each type of procedural activity to be calculated as a percentage of the value of the subject matter of trial (as a rule, between 1 per cent and 2 per cent). However, these percentages are the lowest permissible fee for counsel, who may negotiate and contract for a higher fee in a particular case. Contingency fees are also allowed. Counsel may arrange with his or her client that the fees payable shall depend upon the favourable outcome of the trial or the completion of a specific task. The contingency fee may not exceed 20 per cent of the subject matter of the trial (Arts. 92 III–VI, 95 of the Code of Attorneys).[43]

A network of provisions safeguards the payment of fees to counsel. Apart from imposing minimum fees, Greek law provides several procedural means for the speedy adjudication and the privileged satisfaction of claims relating to counsel's fees. The relevant actions are tried according to the flexible proceedings on the remuneration of certain professionals (Art. 677 no. 1 CC Proc.).[44] At the enforcement stage, claims for counsel's fees, remuneration, and expenses effected during the last six months before the day of the public auction of the debtor's property and already finally determined, i.e. claims fairly recent and

---

[41] See G. Rammos, *Manual of Civil Procedural Law*, i (Athens, 1978), § 217, pp. 599–601 (in Greek).
[42] See K. D. Kerameus, *Civil Procedure: General Part* (Athens, 1986), no. 133, p. 342 (in Greek).
[43] See, for instance, *Areios Pagos* 164/1996, *HellDni* 1996, 1329–30.
[44] See above para. 9.

firmly established, are considered privileged claims (Art. 975 no. 3 CC Proc. as amended by Art. 6 § 16 of Law 2479/1997).[45]

24. The issue of counsel's fees and litigation costs in general was addressed by the Special Supreme Court in its judgment no. 33/1995,[46] which ruled on the constitutionality of Article 96 II of the Code of Attorneys, following conflicting opinions by the *Areios Pagos* and the *Conseil d'État* (the Supreme Administrative Court). This provision requires the parties to pay a percentage of the minimum fees for counsel, fixed by statute (as a rule 10 per cent of the amount of fees), in advance before each court hearing or other procedural act. Indeed, Article 96 VI of the Code of Attorneys provides that, unless the relevant document of payment is presented to the court, the party shall be considered in default, and shall suffer all the ensuing procedural sanctions. The Court, construing Article 20 I of the Constitution, which safeguards the right of access to the courts, delineated the outer limits of the financial burdens that may be imposed upon resort to the courts. The legislature may link the admissibility of certain legal acts to the payment of dues, but, for such dues to be constitutionally tolerable, they must be connected with the administration of justice and they must not exceed certain limits beyond which the right of access to courts is directly or indirectly denied. Applying this basic position, the Court held that the provision declaring in default a party who does not present the court with a document for part payment of his or her counsel's fees does not relate to the operation of courts or the administration of justice at large. It simply purports to facilitate and ensure the collection of counsel's fees, or, at least, a percentage of them, and also restricts tax evasion on those fees. The payment of counsel fees, however, does not relate to the operation of courts or the administration of justice at large. Thus, the Court held that Article 96 VI of the Code of Attorneys is contrary to Article 20 I of the Constitution. The *Areios Pagos* 1601/1992,[47] upholding constitutionality, had previously decided that the contested provision was simply part and parcel of a web of provisions aiming to safeguard the legal profession. Refuting this particular point, the Special Supreme Court held that, at any rate, the protection of the legal profession may not be achieved through measures affecting the fundamental human right of access to courts.

25. According to Article 173 I, II CC Proc. the party instigating the main trial or challenging a judgment has to pay all court dues before the first hearing. If such payment is not effected, the party is considered to be in default at the hearing of the case (Art. 175 CC Proc.).[48]

---

[45] Previous case law held that a lawyer's recurrent remuneration arising from a permanent contract for services is not covered by such privilege. See *Full Bench of Areios Pagos* 13/1990, *NoB* 1990, 1334–5 with a strong dissenting opinion by fourteen justices; *Athens Court of Appeal* 10008/1991, *NoB* 1993, 297–8.

[46] *NoB* 1995, 908–9 with a dissenting opinion. On the function of the Special Supreme Court in the Greek legal order, see P. D. Dagtoglou, 'Constitutional and Administrative Law', in Kerameus and Kozyris, *Introduction to Greek Law*, 21 ff., at 29.   [47] *HellDni* 1994, 115–16.

[48] See Yessiou-Faltsi, *Civil Procedure in Hellas*, 303.

The advance payment of court dues in case of an action for performance serves mostly tax purposes. The dues are about 1 per cent of the pecuniary subject matter of the trial. Non-payment of the dues before the judgment is handed down means that the party is in default, with all the procedural sanctions that this entails. It is a usual practice, however, for the plaintiff to file an action for performance and then, at the first hearing, to change his or her plea to an action for a declaratory judgment only, thus evading payment of the said dues. Although the plaintiff will not eventually have a decision vested with *exequatur*, he or she nevertheless succeeds in procuring a final decision on the dispute without paying an inordinate amount by way of fee for such judicial protection. Case law seems recently to encourage such practice even in respect of interest. Thus, it was held that the claim for default interest due from the time when the action is served on the defendant is not affected by the subsequent transformation of an action for performance into an action for a declaratory judgment. This is so because the transformation is only a partial waiver of a procedural situation, leaving the underlying substantive rights of the plaintiff unaffected. The right to default interest arose from the initial submission of the action for performance, and this is enough to bring the defendant into default.[49] Irrespective of the doctrinal discussion to which this decision gave rise, its importance extends to all financial parameters of the trial. The plaintiff who filed an action for performance, and then changed his or her plea into an action for a declaratory judgment, neither has to pay the court dues nor does he or she sustain any financial loss, since default interest will nevertheless be running. This decision follows the present general trend of Greek case law, not to let financial burdens affect unduly the effective exercise of the right of access to courts.

26. Litigation costs are allocated after the trial, following the 'defeat principle'. According to this principle, each losing party is charged with his or her own costs as well as with the costs of the opponent (Art. 176.1 CC Proc.). The definition of defeat depends on whether a motion was upheld or rejected. The defeated party is the one whose motion was rejected, as to the part not confessed or admitted by the opponent (Art. 176.2 CC Proc.). The defeated party is considered, at the end of the day, as the party responsible for the trial, and he or she bears the totality of litigation costs. The defeated party does not receive any restitution for his or her own costs and, in addition, he or she is obliged to compensate the opponent for the latter's court expenses as well.[50]

This principle of defeat may be departed from in two instances. As a rule, the court is allowed to take into account whether a party's behaviour has caused the initiation of the suit unnecessarily. The costs are thus charged to the (victorious) plaintiff whenever the defendant has not provoked the initiation of the trial and

---

[49] *Full Bench of Areios Pagos* 13/1994, *NoB* 1996, 33–4, with a dissenting opinion by nineteen justices.   [50] See Kerameus, *Civil Procedure*, no. 133, p. 343.

has at once confessed or admitted the action (Art. 177 CC Proc.).[51] Litigation costs are also charged to the victorious party if he or she did not comply with the duty of truth, belatedly presented an allegation, belatedly offered evidence, or was responsible for the invalidity of a procedural act or hearing (Art. 185 CC Proc.). In such cases, the court is authorized to charge costs to the victorious party for this procedural misbehaviour, even though this was not enough to deprive him or her of the final favourable outcome.[52] According to the scarce case law, charging the court costs or part of them to a victorious party who is found in breach of the duty of truth remains the only sanction imposed upon him or her, since other sanctions, such as an obligation to pay damages, are in practice unavailable.[53]

Of much greater practical importance is the second exception to the principle of defeat. When there are justified doubts as to the outcome of the trial, the court is allowed to order that no costs will be recovered from the defeated party. Thus, each party can be left, at the end of the day, to bear his or her own litigation costs (Art. 179 CC Proc.). This exception, grounded on equity, is applied by the courts in a rather haphazard way within the general tendency to make access to courts widely available, with no hindrance due to financial considerations, either initially or *ex post facto*.[54] The lack of any established and consistent criteria applicable on the matter may be seen from the fact that the court may decide that each party shall bear his or her own costs, even if the losing party has lost the case by virtue of unanimous decisions at all levels of adjudication (e.g. first instance, court of appeal, court of cassation).[55] On the other hand, *Areios Pagos*, in applying the principle of defeat, has charged court costs to the party who finally lost the suit, although he had won at the panel of the Supreme Court but the case was necessarily referred to the Full Bench because the decision was taken by a margin of one vote (Art. 563 II 2 CC Proc.).[56] Although, strictly speaking, the party concerned would justifiably have had some doubts as to the outcome of litigation in this case, since two justices out of five espoused his point of view, the Court preferred not to depart from the principle of defeat in allocating litigation costs at the highest level of civil adjudication.

27. Generally speaking, in Greece, litigation costs have never been a means for avoiding court overload. On the contrary, the trend seems to have been that costs remain low so that access to courts may at least be unencumbered, if not encouraged. A reasonable increase in costs has repeatedly been suggested, corresponding partially to the expenditure globally involved and as a means to reduce the number of cases, in particular before appellate courts.[57] However,

---

[51] Yessiou-Faltsi, *Civiel Procedure in Hellas*, 303–4.   [52] Kerameus, *Civil Procedure*, 343.
[53] *Athens Court of Appeal* 7752/1991, *HellDni* 1993, 1637.
[54] Kerameus, *Civil Procedure*, 347.   [55] Ibid.
[56] *Full Bench of Areios Pagos* 28/1993, *Dike* 1994, 522–4, comments by Beys, ibid. 529–34.
[57] Kargados, 'Das Überlastungsproblem', 196–7.

no intention to adopt this position may be perceived on the part of the legislature, and the bar is firmly opposed to it.[58]

At any rate, keeping court costs at a low level and reducing the applicability of the principle of defeat do not seem to be the appropriate means for securing easy access to justice. This is because, once litigation costs are borne by each party, the victorious party remains still charged with the expense required for the full implementation of his or her substantive claim. On the other hand, it is generally considered in Greece that a substantial increase in litigation costs would offer a serious disincentive against judicial inflation. However, this disincentive is too general and abstract, as it is not tailor-made to the content, needs, and specifications of each individual case, and therefore may well end up precluding meritorious yet impecunious litigants from vindicating their claims. In general, *ex post facto* allocation and recovery of costs should relate to the merits of the particular case rather than serve as a vehicle connected with accessibility of justice. The appropriate means for the latter is the provision of state benefits for impecunious litigants, better known nowadays as legal aid.[59]

28. The Code of Civil Procedure devotes a special chapter to the 'benefit of poverty' (Arts. 194–204), thus indicating a strong interest in the institutional assistance of impecunious litigants. Any party who proves that he cannot pay the costs of litigation without unduly restricting the necessary means for supporting himself and his family (Art. 194 I CC Proc.), and, moreover, that the case is not manifestly unjust, hopeless, or pointless[60] (Art. 194 IV CC Proc.), may be relieved from the obligation to pay, in whole or in part, litigation costs including counsel's fees (Art. 199 CC Proc.). The benefit is granted through special proceedings (Arts. 196–7 CC Proc.) and is available at all instances, including enforcement proceedings (Art. 198 CC Proc.). At the request of the party concerned, the order of the court granting the benefit also appoints a counsel, a notary, and a bailiff, in order for them to offer the necessary legal assistance without being remunerated in advance (Art. 200 I CC Proc.). The granting of the benefit does not interfere with the *ex post facto* allocation of court costs. If such costs are charged to the party enjoying the benefit, liability for payment thereof will only be effective when the conditions warranting the benefit no longer exist (Arts. 202, 203 II 2 CC Proc.). The benefit of poverty may also be accorded under similar conditions to legal entities (Art. 194 II, III CC Proc.), to aliens upon condition of reciprocity (Art. 195 I CC Proc.),[61] and to stateless persons (Art. 195 II CC Proc.). In such cases, counsel offer *pro bono*

---

[58] Kargados, 'Das Überlastungsproblem', 196 n. 141.   [59] Kerameus, *Civil Procedure*, 348.
[60] See, for instance, *Single-Member First Instance Court of Mytilini* 62/1988, *Dike* 1988, 780: the suit should not be inadmissible or unfounded in law and its purpose should not be achievable through simpler or less costly means.
[61] According to G. Mitsopoulos, *Civil Procedure*, i (Athens, 1972), 80 (in Greek), the requirement of reciprocity for granting legal aid to aliens does not conform to the general judicial protection accorded by Art. 20 I of the Constitution.

work and may only be paid if a substantial recovery of costs and fees is ordered by the court.

This legal aid framework is very narrow in theory; in practice, it is almost non-existent. This is due to the restrictive interpretation developed by the case law, the reluctance of the parties to bear the label of 'destitute' with its accompanying social stigma, and the unwillingness of counsel to accept *pro bono* work.[62] Judicial protection of all legal rights is safeguarded by the Constitution. This safeguard is neither marginal nor reducible so as to limit state assistance only to those at the subsistence level, as Article 194 I CC Proc. in effect provides.[63]

4. ALTERNATIVE MODES OF DISPUTE RESOLUTION

29. As already stated, over the past decade there have been several legislative interventions concerning civil procedural rules with a view to accelerating the pace of adjudication. Among these, only one constituted an attempt to avoid further suits by requiring the use of alternative dispute resolution, and it is not yet in force.[64] Thus, it seems that the legislature is more interested in reducing the factors conducive to delays in the administration of justice than in setting out attractive and effective dispute avoidance mechanisms. One cannot state with any degree of certainty the underlying reasons for this tendency. However, case law clearly indicates that there is in the Greek legal system an intense and penetrating sensitivity towards the constitutionally safeguarded right of access to courts. Only such sensitivity would justify the statutory dislike of anything that could remotely be construed as a limitation over the exercise of this right. The example offered by the treatment of methods of appeal is characteristic in this respect. Although their existence is not safeguarded by the Constitution, the extremely limited and exceptional restrictions on their exercise[65] testify as to the inherent value accorded to a full-blast and multi-tier administration of justice.

30. In this context, one may understand why arrangements for a dispute avoidance system have never belonged among the legislative priorities. Nevertheless, the Greek legal order as such is not unfavourable to alternative modes of dispute resolution.

31. Within the existing procedural framework, the most general alternative means of dispute resolution connected with the court system is conciliation.[66] Among the several kinds of conciliation,[67] judicial conciliation available at any

---

[62] See Yessiou-Faltsi, *Civil Procedure in Hellas*, 302. [63] Kerameus, *Civil Procedure*, 349.
[64] See above para. 10.
[65] See above para. 19(*a*). Cf. also G. Orfanides, 'Alternativen zu und in der Justiz', in IDME (ed.), *Justice and Efficiency*, 202. [66] Ibid. 207–11.
[67] K. D. Kerameus, 'The Function of Conciliation as a Means of Avoiding Litigation and Settling a Dispute', *Studia iuridica*, 3 (1995), 167–82.

stage of the proceedings seems to be the most comprehensive, provided that the substantive terms and conditions are met. This conciliation is effected by means of a declaration before the court or a notary public, and automatically results in the termination of the trial (Art. 293 I CC Proc.). The court minutes containing such conciliation are vested with the power of *exequatur* and may be used for the enforcement of the underlying claim (Art. 904 II c CC Proc.). However, in spite of its purported efficiency, judicial conciliation remains rare in practice. Only 3.5 per cent of the cases pending before the courts of first instance in 1995 were terminated by judicial conciliation or by a waiver of action. The reasons relate not only to the amount of the conciliation dues,[68] namely 6 per cent of the claim when the conciliation is effected before a notary public or 3.5 per cent of the claim when effected in court, but also to the mentality of the parties. Indeed, the Greek example gives rise to the observation that, in such marginal legal phenomena as conciliation, greater importance is to be attributed to the litigants' attitudes than to institutional elaboration. Conciliation assumes a deliberate disregard of legal constraint and addresses itself more to internal disposition than to any particular institutional framework. Society at large may profit from the idea and practice of conciliation to the extent that it no longer adheres to the omnipotence of law in remedying social conflicts.[69]

32. The stance of the domestic legal order today is favourable towards arbitration. Articles 867–903 of the Code of Civil Procedure set up a regulatory system allowing the parties to resolve their dispute by recourse to arbitration.[70] All private law disputes may be submitted to arbitration, provided that they are subject to free disposition by the parties (Art. 867.1 CC Proc.).[71] The case *AED* 24/1993 is indicative of this favourable approach towards arbitration. In this case, the Special Supreme Court held that even tax disputes may be submitted to arbitration, if an investment agreement between the Greek state and an investor importing foreign capital so provides.[72] At the core of the Court's reasoning is the consideration that such arbitration does not result in formally setting aside administrative acts and, therefore, does not interfere with the jurisdiction of administrative courts. This judgment, further expanding the scope of arbitration, is consistent with the generally favourable stance adopted by Greek law towards arbitration.

The same favourable stance is taken with regard to international arbitration. Although there is no specific legislative context in Greek law for international arbitration, Greek case law consistently promotes international arbitration as a

---

[68] Orfanides, 'Alternativen zu und in der Justiz', 211.

[69] Kerameus, 'The Function of Conciliation', 182.

[70] See in general K. D. Kerameus, 'Probleme des griechischen Schiedsverfahrensrechts aus rechtsvergleichender Sicht', *ZZP* (1979), 419–31.

[71] Labour disputes are expressly exempted from the possibility of recourse to arbitration (Art. 867 (2) CC Proc.), whereas arbitrators have no jurisdiction to decide on disputes arising from provisional measures.   [72] *HellDni* 1994, 314–16.

privileged method for the settlement of international private disputes.[73] It is significant that *Areios Pagos* has accepted since 1965 that the prohibitions or restrictions imposed on public law legal entities, which prevent them from submitting their disputes to arbitration, apply to national arbitration only. The restrictions do not apply to international contracts which address the needs of international commerce,[74] since such restrictions belong to the body of national rather than international public order. The same viewpoint was upheld the following year by the French *Cour de Cassation* in the well-known *Galakis* case,[75] generally hailed as being favourable to international arbitration.[76]

33. Finally, the order of payment should also be mentioned here as a quasi-alternative method of dispute resolution (Arts. 623–34 CC Proc.). Once a creditor's money claim is proven by means of a private or public document, he or she may request that an order of payment be issued without any prior hearing of the debtor. This order of payment is vested with the power of *exequatur* (Art. 631 CC Proc.). On the basis of such an order, the creditor may request provisional remedies, such as pre-notice of mortgage[77] or conservatory attachment of debtor's assets (Art. 724 I CC Proc.). The debtor may protect his interests by challenging the issuance of such an order and, in addition, may request a stay of execution (Art. 632 I, II CC Proc.). If, however, no opposition is forthcoming, even after a second service on the debtor, the order becomes *res judicata* (Art. 633 II 3 CC Proc.).

Thus, the order of payment constitutes a speedy and effective means for the enforcement of money claims, providing the creditor with a title vested with the power of *exequatur* within a short period of time and also taking into account the debtor's defences,[78] to the extent that the latter has filed an opposition against the order of payment. This easy method of reaching execution has recently been used as a model for the institution of similar proceedings for the return of rented property (Art. 6 XII of Law 2479/1997, adding Arts. 662A–H to the Code of Civil Procedure). On the basis of experience accumulated in respect of orders of payment, the new Article 662A allows an order of eviction to be issued provided that there is evidence in writing as to the existence of the rent agreement and the payment of rent is withheld in bad faith.

---

[73] See in general K. Kerameus, 'Arbitrage international et ordre juridique hellénique', *Revue de l'arbitrage* (1987), 35–48; S. Koussoulis, 'Actual Problems of International Arbitration: The Greek Law in Comparison with the UNCITRAL Model Law', *RHDI* 49 (1996), 479–99.
[74] Koussoulis, 'Actual Problems of International Arbitration', 484. This was later accepted and expanded by the legislature as well: Art. 49 I of the Introductory Law to the Code of Civil Procedure. See also *Full Bench of Areios Pagos* 8/1996, *HellDni* 1996, 1052–4.
[75] *Trésor Public v. Galakis*, *JDI* 1966, 648.   [76] See, for instance, Level, *JDI* 1966, 649–53.
[77] See above para. 6.
[78] Orfanides, 'Alternativen zu und in der Justiz', 231–3. Statistical data show that justices of the peace were presented in the year 1995 with 81,263 petitions for the issuance of orders of payment.

34. Greek experiences with civil justice reform since the introduction of the Code of Civil Procedure (1967) show a mixed picture of legislative innovation and practical inertia. Parliament and government have been unusually active, and, in recent years, at an accelerated pace, in continuously amending, sometimes even at the price of increased complexity and short-lived impact, large parts of the Code in an effort to improve the administration of justice. But the actual improvements achieved have fallen short of both ambitions and expectations. Among the several reasons that may explain this unsatisfactory result, three viewpoints deserve particular attention. First, legislative amendments have been too frequent, too piecemeal, and too speedy for them to be allowed the benefit of thoughtful consideration *ex ante facto* and prudent implementation *ex post facto*. Second, no real improvement, or, for that matter, any legislative modification in the field of civil justice, can be effectively brought about without previous preparation of, and, at least, tolerance by, both the bar and the bench. These are the two true addressees of any procedural rules. Their participation and consent seem, therefore, to be in practice required. No code of civil procedure can by itself overcome well-entrenched and cherished judicial traditions. Successful procedural reform relies on a special type of mutual understanding and support from the main adjudicative actors. But support needs education and education needs time. Lastly, the dispensation of justice in a modern democratic state affects a highly valued human right but, at the same time, constitutes an important societal phenomenon, whose function depends on economic and general social parameters. One may perceive here a juxtaposition of ideal and real conditions in the administration of justice. No matter what terms are used, no purposeful legislation may ignore any of these constraints. Whoever aspires to draft meaningful and effective procedural rules should be aware of the fact that one is not drafting, particularly here, in a social vacuum.

12

Civil Justice in Spain: Present and Future. Access, Cost, and Duration

Ignacio Díes-Picazo Giménez

1. CHARACTERISTICS OF SPANISH CIVIL PROCEDURE

Spain has the continental European system of law, known as the 'civil law' system. I shall therefore limit this introduction to a consideration of the most relevant peculiarities or characteristics of the Spanish civil justice system.[1]

The *jurisdicción ordinaria* (ordinary jurisdiction)[2] in Spain is divided into four 'orders' or branches: civil; criminal; contentious-administrative; and social. The civil branch deals with litigation related to civil and commercial law. The criminal branch deals with conduct classified as a crime or a misdemeanour. The contentious-administrative arm is charged with controlling the public administration, subject to administrative law. Finally, the social branch covers labour and social security litigation.

This structure means that some matters which form part of 'civil justice' in other countries (e.g. labour law actions) are entrusted to specialist courts in Spain within the *jurisdicción ordinaria*. On the other hand, some matters which are commonly dealt with by specialized courts in other countries, e.g. commercial matters, have not been allocated to specialist tribunals in Spain. In this discussion, the expression 'civil justice' will be given the same meaning as in the current Spanish legal system. Thus, with the exception of isolated references to labour or administrative law, this analysis of Spanish civil justice refers exclusively to courts which are charged with the resolution of civil and commercial litigation.

---

[1] I would refer a reader who is interested in gaining more detailed knowledge and understanding of this subject to the following general textbooks: principally those of Oliva Santos and Fernandez López, *Derecho procesal civil* (Civil Procedure Law), 4 vols. (4th edn. Madrid, 1995); Montero Aroca Ortells Ramox Gómez Colomer and Montón Redondo, *Derecho jurisdiccional* (Jurisdictional Law) (Barcelona, 1996); Cortés Dominguez, Gimeno Sendra, and Moreno Catena, *Derecho procesal civil* (Civil Procedure Law) (2nd edn. Madrid, 1997).

[2] Together with all the courts of the ordinary jurisdiction, the Spanish Constitution provides for certain special courts, such as the courts martial, or the Court of Accounts (*Tribunal de Cuentas*). In addition, at the top of the legal system, although not part of the judiciary, the Constitutional Court (*Tribunal Constitutional*) is entrusted with a combination of functions, namely: control of the constitutionality of the laws; the resolution and determination of legal disputes between the state and the autonomous communities; and the protection of the fundamental rights and freedoms recognized by the Constitution, exercised through the procedure of the *recurso de amparo* (the procedure of appeal to the Constitutional Court for the protection of fundamental rights).

2. THE SPANISH HIERARCHY OF THE COURTS

Spain has a large number of different civil courts and tribunals. There are: the *juzgados de paz* (magistrates' courts);[3] the *juzgados de primera instancia* (first instance courts) and the *juzgados de primera instancia e instrucción* (first instance and magistrates' courts);[4] the *audiencias provinciales* (the county courts);[5] the *tribunales superiores de justicia* (the high courts of justice);[6] and the *Tribunal Supremo* (the

---

[3] The *juzgados de paz* (magistrates' courts) are 'unipersonal' courts, i.e. composed of a sole judge. They exist in all of the municipalities except for those which are situated in the seat of a *partido judicial* (Spanish judicial district) that has a *juzgado de primera instancia e instrucción* (court of first instance and instruction). These courts are served by lay judges, who perform their function voluntarily and do not have any formal legal qualification. They are appointed to serve by the relevant *ayuntamiento*, (municipal town council) for a term of four years. Their civil jurisdiction is currently limited to claims for less than 8,000 pesetas (roughly £33, or $US56). Clearly, their jurisdiction is more symbolic than real, since in practice there are no legal proceedings brought for such small amounts.

These courts are also competent to hear conciliation proceedings prior to the main proceedings. However, such conciliation is voluntary, at the discretion of the parties involved. Currently, the debate which centres around these courts is concentrated on abolishing these *juzgados de paz* or, alternatively, granting them more effective powers and strengthening their legal competence.

[4] The *juzgados de primera instancia* and the *primera instancia e instrucción* courts are also 'unipersonal' courts, i.e. composed of a single judge. They are served by professional judges and their jurisdiction covers a special legal district (*partido judicial*) which consists of one or more adjoining municipalities within the same province. There may be various courts within the same legal district (in Madrid, for example, there are seventy courts of first instance). In the very active and busy legal districts which process a great number of legal cases and proceedings, the courts are separated into two divisions: that of civil jurisdiction (*juzgados de primera instancia*) and that of criminal jurisdiction (*juzgados de instrucción*)—'instruction' here refers to the investigation of a criminal case. However, in most cases it is normal that the same court has both civil and criminal jurisdiction (hence the *juzgados de primera instancia e instrucción*). In practice, the jurisdiction of these courts includes all first instance cases.

[5] The *audiencias provinciales* (the principal courts of each Spanish province) are collegiate courts and their jurisdictional powers are limited to the particular province where they are located. In Spain there are fifty provinces. Each *audiencia* is divided into divisions composed of three *magistrados* (senior judges). In some *audiencias* there are divisions which are exclusively dedicated to civil matters and others to criminal matters. In other *audiencias*, however, the same division has both civil and criminal jurisdiction (known as 'mixed courts'). The civil jurisdiction of the *audiencias provinciales* includes appeals against decisions of the *juzgados de primera instancia* of that province. However, they do not have jurisdiction at first instance. As a general rule, all of the first instance judgments can be appealed, except for those cases whose value is less than 80,000 pesetas in which credit rights are in issue (roughly £330 or $US560).

[6] The *tribunales superiores de justicia* (high courts of justice) are collegiate courts and their jurisdictional limits cover the autonomous community. (Since the passing of the Constitution, Spain has carried out a thorough and wide-reaching process of political and administrative decentralization. The result is the division of the country into seventeen so-called 'autonomous communities'. However, it must be emphasized that, although the limit of the *tribunal superior de justicia* is the territory of the autonomous community, each *tribunal* is a legal organ of the State and not an organ of the autonomous community. The autonomous communities do not have their own independent judicial power.) Nowadays, the civil jurisdiction of the *tribunales superiores de justicia* is greatly reduced. Apart from certain cases of civil liability of senior government officers, they only have power in those autonomous communities which maintain their own civil institutions, such as Catalonia, the Basque Country, Aragón, Galicia, the Balearic Islands, and Navarra. In these autonomous communities, where a *casación* appeal (a special appeal to quash a decision of an inferior court on grounds of an error in application of the law) is based on the breach of the regulatory rules of these special *forales* institutions (*forales* comes from *fuero* or customary law—historically special laws containing certain

Supreme Court of Justice).[7] Because the jurisdiction of the *juzgados de paz* and *tribunales superiores de justicia* is so extremely limited, practically all cases are dealt with at first instance by the *juzgados de primera instancia*. In the vast majority of first instance cases, judgment may be appealed to the *audiencia provincial*. Certain appeal judgments (as a general rule, where the amount involved is more than 6 million pesetas) are subject to further appeal, by way of *casación*, to the *Tribunal Supremo*. Accordingly, the normal civil action takes place: (1) at first instance before the *juzgados de primera instancia*; (2) on appeal to the *audiencia provincial*; and, (3) in certain cases, final appeal to the *Tribunal Supremo*.[8]

3. SOURCES OF CIVIL PROCEDURAL LAW

Possibly the most noticeable feature of Spanish civil procedure is the antiquity and dispersion of its regulatory sources. This is also the key to understanding much of the present situation.

The *Ley de Enjuiciamiento Civil* (Civil Procedure Act) was passed in 1881.[9]

different privileges, i.e. various rules about economic rights in marriage, inheritance, and legacy, etc.), the court which is competent to try such matters is the *tribunal superior de justicia* and not the *Tribunal Supremo* (Supreme Court).

[7] The *Tribunal Supremo* is also a collegiate court. It has jurisdiction throughout all of Spain. It is composed of eleven *magistrados* (senior judges) who act either in *Pleno* (Full Chamber) or, depending on the case, in chambers of three or five. Its basic purpose is to hear and determine appeals of *casación*. Without going into detail, as a general rule any judgment issued by the *audiencia provincial* may be appealed through the *casación* appeal procedure, provided the amount in question is more than 6 million pesetas (roughly £24,800, or $US41,750). In keeping with tradition, the Spanish *casación* appeal procedure does not allow review of the facts of the case in issue. *Casación* is only a review of the substantive and procedural legal correctness of the appealed judgment. What is unusual about the Spanish *casación* appeal procedure is the treatment of the merits of the case. The Spanish appeal of *casación* has always been a non-transferable appeal procedure. This means that, when the *casación* appeal succeeds, and the Supreme Court finds that there has been a wrong application of the law in the judgment under appeal, it does not transfer the case on to another court. It actually resolves the case itself once it has quashed the judgment (*casada*).

[8] Although, once the parties involved have exhausted all other legal remedies available to them, they can still lodge an appeal, called *el recurso de amparo*, to the Spanish Constitutional Court. This is a special appeal procedure designed for the protection of the fundamental rights which are guaranteed in Arts. 14–30 of the Spanish Constitution. Amongst these fundamental rights are those found in Art. 24, which are dedicated to a wide range of basic legal procedural guarantees. Most of them are applicable to civil procedures. These include: the right to justice; the right to be defended; the right of access to the ordinary courts as predetermined by the law; the right to legal assistance through the services of a lawyer; the right to a public trial; the right to a fair and proper trial; and the right to present relevant evidence. A very high percentage (nearly 70 per cent) of the appeals which are brought before the Constitutional Court are based on breaches and infringements of fundamental rights as set out in Art. 24 of the Spanish Constitution. However, constitutional case law concerning these fundamental rights has often given rise to very different and radical interpretations of many facets of Spanish procedural law. For further information in this area, I suggest the reader consult Diez-Picazo Giménez, 'Artículo 24: Garantías Procesales' (Article 24: Procedural Guarantees), in Alzaga Villaamil (ed.), *Comentarios a la Constitución española de 1978* (Commentaries on the Spanish Constitution of 1978) (Madrid, 1996), ii. 19–123.

[9] Hereinafter referred to as 'the 1881 Act'.

Hence, the principal body of law governing civil procedure was enacted in an era in which scientific elaboration of procedural law had hardly been born. The 1881 Act is an archaic code, in both system and terminology. Many basic concepts and institutions of procedural law are neither contemplated nor regulated by the 1881 Act. Therefore, in Spain, throughout the twentieth century, doctrine and precedent have been much more significant sources of procedural law than in other civil law countries which have more modern civil procedure codes.

Indeed, the 1881 Act was already an antiquated law at the time it was passed. It did not represent a modernization of civil procedure as at 1881. Rather, it represented a maintaining of the Roman/canon/civil procedures. The common civil procedure (the so-called *juicio de mayor cuantia*), created by the 1881 Act, was a direct heir of the medieval *solemnis ordo iudiciarius*. This procedure is character-ized, amongst other things, by: an emphasis on written procedures rather than on oral hearings; the lack of judicial intervention; the almost total absence of discretionary powers for the judge to control procedure; and the dispersion of the elements of the process, accentuated by the proliferation of motions and interlocutory applications. As well as this procedure, the law provides for other types of procedure in which there *is* provision for maximum oral intervention and concentration (as opposed to dispersion). Also, the 1881 Act has been reformed on various occasions. Important partial reforms were made in 1984 and 1992. However, this has not represented a general reform, and the ancient spirit of the law remains strong.

As a consequence of the antiquity and the archaism of the 1881 Act, throughout this century there has been what is termed an 'escape' from the 1881 Act. Through a series of partial reforms and extravagant regulations, contained largely in substantive laws pronounced with neither plan nor harmony, the Spanish civil legal system has become a jungle of localized rules and special proceedings.

4. THE BASIC SPANISH PROCEDURE

All of this makes it difficult to provide a simple outline of the basic declaratory process. In the Spanish system there is no single declaratory process. Rather, there are four: the *juicio de mayor cuantia*;[10] *juicio de menor*

[10] The *juicio de mayor cuantia* is the civil procedure for large claims. Throughout the system of the Civil Procedure Act 1881 it is known as the *juicio tipo* ('typical procedure'). This means that the *juicio de mayor cuantia* is the procedure in which all procedural issues are regulated in detail, and whose rules are of secondary application in all the other procedures. Furthermore, for a century, the *jucio de mayor cuantia* was the procedure most frequently used in practice. Nevertheless, since the 1984 reform it has been maintained only for large claims. Currently, large claims are those which are greater than 160 million pesetas (about £660,000 or $US1.11 million).

cuantia;[11] *juicio de cognición;*[12] and *juicio verbal.*[13] As well as these procedures, there is a wide range of special procedures for matters of particular types.[14] For decades, it has been apparent that this abundance of procedures does not make sense. The reason for the proliferation of procedures is that the lawmakers,

The procedure is considerably drawn out, expensive, and practically all written. It consists of the following basic steps: the *demanda* (writ/statement of claim); the response to the initial claim; the reply and rejoinder (*réplica* and *dúplica*); the presentation and proposals of evidence; pre-trial discovery regarding the means of evidence; the writs of conclusions (opinions); and the decision. But, apart from these formal steps, the parties may submit further issues during the proceedings that may require separate proceedings and consequently a separate decision. Examples include: questioning the appropriateness of the procedure; challenging the territorial jurisdiction of the court; or raising one of the so-called *excepciones dilatorias*—the dilatory exceptions—whereby the parties challenge some or all of the legal and formal requirements of the process.

[11] Since the 1984 reform, the civil procedure for lesser claims, *el juicio de menor cuantia*, has been the most widely used type of ordinary civil procedure, or, to put it another way, the typical procedure. Nevertheless, the model civil procedure continues to be the civil procedure for large claims as previously explained. The civil procedure for lesser claims is applied to cases where the amount in question is between 800,000 and 160 million pesetas (roughly £3,300–660,000 or $US5,500–1.11 million), as well as to cases and claims concerning the capacity and civil status of natural persons and any other case for which there is no special type of proceedings determined by the law, such as for example any case in which it is impossible to fix the quantum (i.e. proceedings of affiliation, paternity, or maternity). Since the 1984 reform, the procedure basically comprises the following stages: the issue of the writ (statement of claim) which is served on the defendant; the defendant's reply (defence) in response to the claim; the first appearance in court by the parties (the purpose of which is threefold: (i) the parties attempt to settle; (ii) to examine and rectify any possible procedural defects; and (iii) to determine the factual and legal terms of the conflict); the presentation of the evidence; the conclusions (the parties submit their arguments or opinions on the case); then finally the decision. As one can appreciate, although it is a procedure which is less complicated than the civil procedure for large claims, it is nevertheless a procedure which is predominantly written.

[12] The *juicio de cognición* is the civil procedure for small claims. It was not originally a part of the 1881 Act, but was created by a decree law of 1952. Currently, it is applied to cases in which the quantum of the claim is between 80,000 and 800,000 pesetas (roughly £330–3,300 or $US550–5,500), as well as to certain areas such as urban leases. Its structure is simpler. After the writ of claim is served and a written response to the claim by the defendant is returned, the parties may be called to an oral hearing. At this hearing, the other steps and formalities necessary are carried out, such as rectifying points which were raised in written allegations and requesting the presentation of evidence etc., and the final decision is given. This is a more modern procedure in which the judge is given greater powers of direction over the whole procedure. It is characterized by its oral nature, its speed in resolving a case, and its thoroughness. However, in practice, these positive characteristics of many of the procedures of this type are no longer true. The courts have become slower and less effective.

[13] The oral procedure for minor claims, *el juicio verbal*, is the least complex of the Spanish civil procedures (claims up to 80,000 pesetas). It starts by way of a simple writ, which does not have to comply with the normal formal requirements of a writ. This is so that it can be drafted by a layperson or by the interested party himself, without him having to use the services of a lawyer. The parties are then summoned to a hearing. During this hearing other steps are carried out, such as the pleadings and the submission of evidence and argument. Finally, the decision is issued. As can be appreciated, it is a procedure which is extremely simple and straightforward. However, like the *juicio de cognición* (small claims procedure) noted above, these procedures are losing in practice the advantages of speed and thoroughness they should have. Today they are much less effective and slower than they were in the past.

[14] For example: the exercise of a right of pre-emption or first refusal; eviction; protection from summary possession; maintenance orders; urban leases; rural leases; the right to personal dignity and privacy; matrimonial proceedings; intellectual and industrial property; unfair competition; illegal advertising; public limited companies and corporations; traffic accident damages claims.

instead of undertaking a global reform and enacting a new Civil Procedure Act, have continually elected to carry out partial reforms and establish special procedures instead.

In spite of this variety of procedures, it is possible to identify characteristic features of Spanish declaratory proceedings. These are: (1) the prevalence of written submissions over oral; (2) a considerable dispersion of the procedural stages over time; (3) the lack of judicial intervention; and (4) a rigid principle of preclusion (or 'estoppel')—i.e. the impossibility of taking procedural steps after the expiry of the stipulated time periods.

5. THE SPANISH LEGAL PROFESSION

Another aspect which one ought to bear in mind is the difference in the Spanish system between the *procurador* and the *abogado*. The *procurador* represents the litigant before the court. The *abogado* is the advocate/solicitor. The *abogado* has the main role in the judicial process. Although in practice the *procurador* is limited to being a kind of agent (he lodges the relevant litigation documents with the courts, receives summonses, etc.), under the law he is technically the litigant's legal representative. Therefore, the *abogado* cannot act without him. Furthermore, both professions are incompatible, i.e. you cannot practise at the same time as both an *abogado* and a *procurador*.[15] Except in proceedings for a limited amount, the involvement of both *abogado* and *procurador* is obligatory.[16]

---

[15] This is something which is peculiar to Spain. To practice as an *abogado* or as a *procurador*, it is necessary only to be a law graduate. There are no other requirements, such as further legal qualifications or professional vocational experience within the legal world. Any law student, on the day after obtaining his or her law degree from the Law Faculty, can enrol as a member of the *Colegio de Abogados* or the society of the *Procuradores* (Spanish Law Society/Bar Association). Furthermore, he or she can begin practising law from that very day, which includes appearing before any Spanish court, even the Constitutional Court and the *Tribunal Supremo*. This situation is absurd and alarming. For many years commentators have argued for the need to establish a filter or screening system for access to both professions. However, any proposal which is put forward regarding this issue, apart from other difficulties, is always met by head-on opposition from the students. In any event, the European Community rules concerning the free movement of professionals within the European Union will certainly lead to new rules regarding access to the legal profession.

[16] The active participation of the *procurador* does not especially increase the costs of the legal procedure, basically because his professional fees are fixed by official regulations and are low in comparison with those of the *abogado*. Although it has been constantly debated whether it is appropriate to maintain the division between the professions, or whether the functions of the *procurador* could be absorbed by the *abogado*, currently there seems to be a consensus of opinion in favour of the continuance and maintenance of the *procurador* within the legal system. The most recent reform proposals are even in support of strengthening the functions of the *procurador* rather than reducing them.

6. APPEAL PROCEDURE

As we have already seen, practically all judgments of the *juzgados de primera instancia* can be appealed to the *audiencia provincial*. Even within the appeal system, procedures vary. The most characteristic feature is that, at second instance, there is no full appeal rehearing. Spanish appeals are not a second chance to fight the whole case again. The appeal is limited to a *revisio prioris instantiae* as opposed to a *novum iudicium*. The litigants cannot present new claims or defence arguments, and even the pleading of new facts is limited to those which have newly arisen or those which the litigants demonstrate were previously unknown.

Appeals to the *Tribunal Supremo* (*casación*) are essentially limited by the *summa gravaminis* (as a rule, 6 million pesetas). In accordance with its French roots, the *Tribunal Supremo* appeal is limited to a consideration of the law. It is not a third instance hearing. There is no review of the facts as found by the inferior courts. The function of the appeal to the *Tribunal Supremo* is *nomophilactic*.[17] The *Tribunal Supremo* creates judicial precedent (which, in the Spanish legal system, does not bind the inferior courts).

To conclude this review of the essential characteristics of Spanish civil procedure, it is necessary to mention certain protective procedures, both summary and provisional. With regard to summary protective procedures, there are 'protective possession processes' (injunctions). In addition, there are certain documents to which the law gives enforceability (*fuerza ejecutiva*). These allow the creditor to instigate enforcement proceedings directly, without needing a prior declaratory process. Likewise, there is a wide range of injunctive procedures (regulated in a notoriously unsystematic manner). Finally, Article 1428 of the 1881 Act regulates indeterminate injunctive procedures, i.e. it allows the applicant to request the judge to apply what he or she considers to be the most appropriate remedy to the case.

7. THE NATURE OF CIVIL LITIGATION IN SPAIN: STATISTICS

It is not a simple task for a Spanish jurist to furnish statistical details about civil justice in Spain. The lack of reliable legal statistics has been denounced as a serious deficiency on behalf of the Spanish administration of justice.[18] The

---

[17] Literally, concerned with the protection of the law. In this context, ensuring the proper development of the law through the adoption only of the right/best interpretations as precedents—judging the law as applied by the lower courts.

[18] V. Pastor Prieto, *¡Ah de la justicia! Política judicial y economía* ('Ah! That's Justice! Legal and Economic Policy') (Madrid, 1993), 59–64; Diez-Picazo Giménez, 'Reivindicación de la estadística judicial' (Restoration of Legal Statistics), *Tribunales de justicia*, 1997/5, 725–6. The *Consejo General del Poder Judicial*, the General Council of the Judiciary, which is the governing body of the judiciary, has come to recognize this deficiency. Recently (in September 1997), the *Consejo* published the *Libro blanco*

statistics that are available are scarce and of poor quality. In addition, the continuity necessary to produce statistical patterns, from which accurate conclusions can be drawn, is lacking. Nevertheless, there have been some recent data made available which are worth considering.[19]

First, in global figures for initiated proceedings, in 1996, 770,727 matters were filed with the civil courts. For the first time in a long while, this figure was lower than the figure for the previous year. However, it does not seem that this marks a continuing trend, as, over the last fifteen years, the quantity of civil litigation has seen an average 10 per cent annual increase. There is no reason, therefore, to conclude that litigation is on the decline. I venture to suggest that the future growth rate of litigation will be less than in recent years. It is relevant to note that 2,032 judges dealt with the 770,727 matters aforementioned.[20]

Secondly, with regard to the litigants, the *Libro blanco de justicia* (White Book of Justice) shows that, in 92 per cent of cases, there is a single plaintiff and, in these cases, 56 per cent of plaintiffs are natural persons with corporate plaintiffs representing 43 per cent. If the above data are considered together with data reflecting the quantitative or qualitative importance of the litigation, one can draw the conclusion that 'companies occupy the top place in the list of litigants', particularly in debt recovery actions.

Both a *procurador* and an *abogado* are involved in 82 per cent of cases, either

de la justicia (White Book of Justice). This volume contains details of, reflections on, and diagnoses of numerous aspects of the legal system and justice in Spain—not only civil justice. There are also proposals for the courses of action that should be taken to improve the current legal situation. As regards legal statistics, the *Libro blanco de la justicia*, after recognizing that 'reliable statistics which are based not only on quantitative and qualitative criteria are the essential starting point . . . for all policy in matters of justice', affirms that 'the General Council of the Judiciary must recognize and acknowledge that this is one of the most important tasks that must be developed in the short term, as it must be accepted that the current statistics—which moreover are within its exclusive competence and thus, it is these statistics which equally serve the rest of the Public Administration—are not the reliable and qualitative statistics that are necessary for the Administration of Justice' (*Libro blanco de la justicia* (Madrid, 1997) 67).

[19] The information incorporated in the *Libro blanco de la justicia*. This volume also notes the lack of reliable legal statistics, as indicated above. It contains a body of information that is very revealing about the current state of civil justice in Spain. For the very first time we are provided with a complete and thorough insider's examination of our civil jurisdiction. Most of the information in the *Libro blanco de la justicia* is taken from a study which was requested by the General Council of the Judiciary from the Madrid University of Carlos III and which was prepared and written by Moreno Catena, Professor of Law, and Pastor Prieto, Professor of Economics, entitled 'A study concerning the civil litigation proceedings conducted before the courts of first instance and the courts of first instance and instruction. A sample examination of the duration and other characteristics of the civil procedures' (Madrid 1997). Although the *Libro blanco de la justicia* makes reference to this study as a supplementary source of information, in actual fact it has not yet been published. I would therefore like to express my gratitude to the authors who have provided me with an advance copy. The following details are taken accordingly both from the *Libro blanco de la justicia* and from this work of Professors Moreno Catena and Pastor Prieto.

[20] The only difference between judges and *magistrados* (senior judges) is their category within the body of the legal profession. The *magistrado* is a judge who sits in the higher courts such as the *Tribunal Supremo*, the *tribunales superiores de justicia*, or the *audiencias provinciales*. The figure of 2,032 court judges only includes professional judges and does not include the 'judges' of the *juzgados de paz*.

because such involvement is legally obligatory or, even when not legally obligatory, the litigants have decided to engage the services of both. The statistics show that the percentage of cases in which a *procurador* and an *abogado* are involved is higher than the percentage of cases where such involvement is required by law, leading to the conclusion that litigants prefer to instruct both even where not so required by the law. On the other hand, in only 3 per cent of civil matters involving both a *procurador* and an *abogado* are the lawyers appointed under the free legal assistance system ('legal aid'). It is interesting to note that, in 38.6 per cent of cases, the procedure is *en rebeldía* (where the defendant fails to appear). The majority of cases are dealt with by the court for the locality in which the defendant resides. The cases where the defendant has to litigate outside the locality where he or she is domiciled vary, according to the type of procedure, between 34 per cent and 48 per cent.

Thirdly, with respect to the frequency of different types of proceedings, it is difficult to disassemble and interpret the data. This is due to the fact that, in some cases, the procedure followed depends on the nature of the claim, whilst in other cases it is the amount or the economic value of the claim which dictates the procedure. Nevertheless, there are some significant statistical data: the *juicio de cognición* (the procedure for small claims) accounts for 22.1 per cent of litigation; the *juicio ejecutivo* (debt enforcement proceedings) 16.3 per cent;[21] the *juicio verbal de tráfico* (traffic cases) 12 per cent;[22] the *juicio de desahucio urbano* (landlord and tenant/eviction proceedings) 9.8 per cent;[23] the *juicio de menor cuantía* (small claims) 8.7 per cent; the *juicios verbales ordinarios* (ordinary oral) 7.7 per cent; and matrimonial cases—annulment, legal separation, and divorce (including cases where the proceedings are not contested)—8.9 per cent. It is significant to note that these seven types of civil proceedings account for 85.5 per cent of litigation. Likewise, it is interesting to note that three matters alone (damages for traffic cases, landlord and tenant, and matrimonial actions) account for 30.7 per cent of proceedings. Of further significance is the fact that the *juicio de cognición* and the *juicios verbales ordinarios*, including small claims litigation (up to 800,000 pesetas[24]), represent 29.8 per cent of litigious matters. It is not difficult to draw the conclusion that a considerable percentage of civil

---

[21] The *juicio ejecutivo* is a special summary procedure for the enforcement of liquidated monetary claims in which the creditor has an extra-judicial enforceable right contained in a written instrument or deed (such as a public deed, mortgage, bill of exchange, etc.) which certifies the existence and enforceability of the debt which he or she is owed. In these cases, the creditor may directly initiate enforcement without bringing prior declaratory proceedings, and the debtor may challenge the enforcement on the basis that the debt is disputed or enforcement is unfair.

[22] The oral procedure for minor traffic offences is a special oral procedure in which claims for compensation for loss and damage caused by traffic accidents are processed. As can be appreciated, it is a procedure which is often used in practice and whose special characteristics are intended to obtain a swift and rapid recovery of compensation for the injured party.

[23] The urban eviction procedure is intended to obtain the discharge of an urban leasing contract, normally in the case of default in payment of the rent, or for the natural expiry of the term of the lease. [24] Roughly £3,300 or $US5,500.

litigation is made up of claims of a routine nature or small claims. Moreover, although there may be no direct relationship between the type of matter, or the amount involved, and its complexity, it is not difficult to believe that the majority of cases involve matters of small factual or legal difficulty.

In this sense, it is particularly noteworthy that in 73 per cent of cases the judgments are completely in accordance with the plaintiff or applicant's claim. In 10 per cent of cases judgments are partially in accordance with the claim; and 6 per cent of cases involve orders as to procedure with no in-depth consideration of the cause of the litigation. Only 11 per cent of cases involve complete rejections or dismissals. The percentage of successful plaintiffs increases in enforcement proceedings, where 95 per cent of judgments are in favour of the plaintiff/applicant's claim and only 1.75 per cent result in complete rejection or dismissal. With respect to costs, in 70 per cent of cases the costs order is made in favour of the plaintiff; and in only 15.8 per cent of cases are the costs split between the parties.

8. SOME CONCLUSIONS ON THE NATURE OF SPANISH CIVIL LITIGATION

In the light of these figures, it is not preposterous to state that civil litigation consists of small claims in which the courts find for the plaintiff. Neither is it difficult to believe that in Spain the increase in litigation has been produced because a large number of cases that previously did not reach the courts now do so. There are various reasons for this: the increased purchasing power of litigants; people's greater legal awareness; a larger number of lawyers; the lower cost of justice (as will be seen later); etc. Having viewed the statistics, it appears that, in recent years, there has been a huge influx to civil justice. On the one hand this movement ought to be regarded as positive. However, on the other hand, large numbers of 'new' claims cause serious problems with the legal system.

Fourthly, in what are referred to as general considerations about the burden of matters and the duration of the cases, the *Libro blanco de la justicia* states that the number of matters pending is approximately equal to those which are dealt with in any given year. The logical conclusion is drawn, namely that the average waiting period for matters to be resolved is one year. Studies show that, in most ordinary civil proceedings, the average duration is just short of a year at first instance but, for higher instances (where the number of matters falls considerably), the duration of the appeal processes is excessive. For example, for an appeal to the *Tribunal Supremo*, the average duration is almost three years and, in the absence of legal reform, this increases each year by four months. Hence, ·should this trend continue, by the year 2000 an appeal to the *Tribunal Supremo* will take four years. From 2000 onwards, the wait will increase by one year every three years, meaning that, by 2003, an appeal to the *Tribunal Supremo* will take five years before it is resolved.

8.1. Delay

If the average duration of a first instance proceeding is just less than a year, it is clear that all proceedings have an average duration which is greater than the procedural timetable provides, i.e. greater than the sum of the time limits established by the law. Hence, a *juicio de menor cuantía* (small claims procedure), which should last 100 days, lasts on average 436 days. A *juicio de cognición*, which should last 65 days, lasts 320 days. A *juicio verbal*, which should take a maximum of 36 days, takes 207 (and 300 if the case concerns damages resulting from a road traffic accident). Debt enforcement proceedings, which ought to last no more than 20 days (where the debtor is not involved), take more than 250 days when the debtor does not contest the proceedings, and 550 days when the debtor does contest the action.

With regard to the duration of appeals, the only thing revealed by the statistics is that there are large discrepancies between different *audiencias provinciales*. Hence: in certain *audiencias* the average appeal takes 3 months (for example in Extremadura); or 5 months (Aragón). In others, the average can be as much as 16 months (Comunidad Valenciana); and up to 19 months (Madrid). What is certain is that there seems to be a link between the duration of appeals and the incidence of litigation; i.e. there is more litigation in the provinces in which we find the greater delay, and the longer delays are proportional to the higher incidence of litigation. Thus, unless measures are established to reduce the number of appeals, the only possible option is to increase the number of senior judges.

Delays in judgment enforcement proceedings are also significant. The average duration of a judgment enforcement proceeding is 9.16 months. With enforcement matters, data as to the types of property charged or seized are important, as there is a connection between the charged property and the duration of the enforcement proceeding. In the largest group of cases, 38 per cent, the property is real property. In 13 per cent of cases the property is earnings or pensions. The remaining cases concern other types of property. When enforcement is sought against real property, the enforcement proceedings can take up to 13.38 months for rural property, and up to 17.48 months in the case of urban property. On the other hand, when the enforcement proceedings are by way of an attachment of earnings, pensions. or other liquid income, the duration is approximately one month.

9. PRINCIPAL PROBLEMS OF CIVIL JUSTICE IN SPAIN

There is little doubt that the principal problem with civil justice in Spain is the excessive duration of litigation. The reasons for this are numerous and varied, ranging from flaws in court organization through a shortage of court personnel and judges to complicated and cumbersome procedures.[25]

The excessive duration of litigation is caused, therefore, by a combination of factors. Although it is difficult to assess the respective importance of these factors, attention should be drawn to the following three categories: the insufficient number of judges; the lack of material or personnel resources; and the chaotic nature of the procedural legislation.

9.1. Insufficient number of judges

In recent years, an enormous effort has been made to increase the number of judges in Spain. In 1985, the total number of professional judges in all jurisdictions was approximately 1,500. There are currently in the region of 3,500: i.e. in thirteen years the number of judges has more than doubled. Yet, in comparison with the number of judges in other European countries, this figure would still seem to be insufficient in proportion to the population. As the population of Spain is approximately 39.2 million, there is one judge per 11,200 people. This phenomenon is not, however, without serious inconveniences. Whilst, on the one hand, there has been a considerable increase in the number of judges, there has also been a spectacular rejuvenation of the Spanish judiciary.[26] This has had the effect of forcing the appointment as judges of persons who might not, in other circumstances, have passed the examinations. In some cases, judges attain positions of great responsibility, having to deal with matters of great magnitude, after very little experience.

9.2. The lack of resources

Although impressive efforts have been made over recent years in Spain in this respect, there is still a long way to go. The lack of personnel and, above all, the lack of material resources continue to be matters in need of attention. Given that current economic policy demands economic austerity, for the sake of the convergence required by European Economic and Monetary Union, it would seem that the coming years are not going to permit significant changes in this respect.

The administration of justice in Spain is notorious for suffering from a chronic lack of material resources. Justice is the forgotten area of the annual budget, and the comparative inequality between the Justice Department and others is clear for all to see. Even from a purely economic point of view, the politicians responsible ought to realize that the proper functioning of a

---

[25] As the *Consejo General del Poder Judicial* (General Council of the Judiciary) indicates in the *Libro blanco de la justicia*, 150–1.

[26] It should also be highlighted that this has produced a huge increase in the number of women becoming judges. In the last few years, two out of every three new judges have been women.

country's justice system influences its ability to compete. As I have mentioned on earlier occasions, we live in an age in which the principal political aim seems to be to win the 'competitiveness' battle. In the name of this buzzword we have faced a series of structural reforms. The goal of globalization of the economy, and supranational economic, monetary, and political integration, can appear a long way from the world of the courts. However, that is not the case. As economists know, when it comes to analysing competition between the economies of different countries, one of the factors taken into account is what is somewhat enigmatically referred to as the 'bureaucratic differential'. This is the difference in the level of development of the countries, reflected in the efficiency of their respective administrations. The work of the law courts needs to be included in this differential.

9.3. The chaotic nature of the procedural legislation

While other causes of delay seem to be common to the majority of countries, the chaotic nature of the procedural legislation seems to be peculiar to the Spanish legal system. Spanish civil procedure requires total reform, not only because current legislation contributes to and causes delay, but also for many other reasons. We continue living with nineteenth-century legislation, which was to a great extent already archaic when it was passed. The laws enacted in the twentieth century have represented nothing more than merely papering over the cracks.

9.4. The cost of justice in Spain

It is necessary to consider the cost of justice. As things stand, I do not believe that the cost of civil justice is a serious problem in Spain, especially if we compare cost with the problem of delay and its causes, the need for more material and personnel resources, the need for total procedural reform, etc.

9.5. Court taxes

The service provided by the courts is not subject to any form of taxation. The state receives no direct financial contribution for the administration of justice.[27] This has been the case since Act 25/1986, of 24 December 1986, abolished both judicial duties and the taxes/fees to which certain procedural steps were subject. The stated justification for this measure was to move towards free justice, insofar as Article 119 of the Spanish Constitution provides that 'justice shall be free of charge when the law so provides and, at all events, for those with

---

[27] Obviously the state collects VAT for fees charged by *abogados* and *procuradores*. But, strictly for using the court, there are no elements of state taxation by way of court fees or whatever.

insufficient means to litigate'. In fact, it is clear that this constitutional rule does not actually prevent the state from assessing the administration of justice for the purposes of taxation. What the rule does is to ensure that there is a system of legal assistance for those without sufficient resources.

In reality, the removal of judicial taxation was a measure against corruption. Insofar as the taxes were assessed and charged by the courts themselves, this provided an opportunity for the payment of bribes to court officials. Because money was already circulating in court, it was not strange or suspicious to see an *abogado* or a *procurador* giving money to a court officer. By removing the need to pay money into the courts, such temptations were removed. This does not mean that there was corruption on a grand scale within the Spanish justice system. Rather, small payments were made to civil servants in order that, for example, the progress of matters could be speeded up, or they should work beyond office hours to carry out an enforcement process or a court summons. These circumstances, provoked by low salaries, were both widespread and well known. The 1986 Act put an end to this and, in this respect, in actual fact our courts have changed radically. The Inland Revenue (*Hacienda*) has not lost much, as the total taxation revenue generated from the legal system did not amount to any significant sum.

A different question is whether the removal of court fees will be judged, over time, to have been a wise decision. The 1986 Act was enacted on the basis that the previous taxes were unfair, in that everyone was treated as equal. They were not progressive taxes, nor even proportional to the value of the litigation. Nevertheless, this inequity could have been removed by establishing fees that were proportional to the value of the claim, or even to the economic capacity of the subject. Furthermore, the tax could have been collected outside the courts. It is also clear that a system in which the wealthiest can use the courts without contributing a single peseta is unfair. It has not been possible to gauge the effect that the removal of court fees has had, although it has, without doubt, increased litigation. Above all, court fees operated to dissuade unscrupulous and unfounded claims.

9.6. Parties' liability to pay the costs of their opponent

Since 1984, there has been a general rule in Spanish civil procedure called the *sistema objetivo o de vencimiento* governing costs orders. This means the losing party must pay the other party's costs. Among the disbursements necessary to the conduct of litigation, the law establishes those which are considered proper costs, and which are included in a costs order. Although at the outset there seemed to be a certain reticence from the courts in applying this rule, now the rule is generally applied. Costs awarded include: the *abogado*'s fees; the *procurador*'s fees; fees and allowances for witnesses and expert witnesses; expenses arising from announcements or publications; registry filing costs; and any necessary notaries' fees or judicial support processes.

9.7. The fees of Spanish lawyers

Of the elements which constitute procedural costs, the most significant, as a percentage, are the *abogado*'s fees. In principle, the *abogado*'s fees are unrestricted. Any *abogado* can charge what he or she considers appropriate. The only limit that the *Colegio de Abogados* (the Bar Association/Law Society) has established is certain criteria for the calculation of fees. These criteria are simply guidelines and, as a last resort, are regarded as minimum fees, so as to try to avoid unfair competition through the provision of a very cheap yet poor-quality service. In any event, the parties can always refer the *abogado*'s bill to the court if it is considered to be excessive. In such cases, before deciding the dispute, the court must hear the opinion of the *Colegio de Abogados*. It is also interesting to note that the *Colegio*'s guidelines establish 'regressive fees', i.e. they are proportionally lower the greater the amount involved in the dispute. This means that litigation is proportionally more expensive when smaller claims are involved.

For example, the *Colegio de Abogados de Madrid* establishes that, for a claim of 10 million pesetas, the *abogado*'s recommended fee (whether representing the plaintiff or defendant) would be 1.185 million pesetas. For a claim of 100 million pesetas, it would be 6.385 million pesetas. As already noted, these are recommendations only. It is not usual for an *abogado* to work for a fixed fee, agreed in advance. However, it is quite usual for the client to ask for an estimate budget. Only very large firms charge by the hour, and this practice is clearly a recent foreign influence. The rules of professional ethics expressly prohibit what is referred to as a *quota litis* agreement between lawyer and client. Under such an agreement, the lawyer charges the client a percentage of the award, but only in the event of winning the action. The reason for this prohibition is that such remuneration would imply a kind of association between the lawyer and the client, which could cause the former to compromise his independent standard of judgment. Despite the prohibition, such agreements occasionally occur in practice.

The *procurador* charges by way of a tariff system, i.e. there is a binding rule (not a guideline as in the case of the *abogados*) which stipulates the precise amount to be charged with regard to the nature and amount of the matter. One might think that having two sets of lawyers' fees would increase the cost of litigation. It does not seem, however, that this is the case. First, the tariff is regressive; i.e. the greater the amount of the claim, the cheaper as a proportion the *procurador*'s services become.[28] Secondly, on average the *procurador*'s remuneration represents approximately 10 per cent of the *abogado*'s remuneration (although, given that the *abogado*'s fees are not fixed, this percentage cannot be accurately established). Bearing in mind that the *procurador* effectively

---

[28] To give a rough idea, the basic tariff of the *procuradores* is as follows. For claims of 100,000 pesetas, the tariff is 8,000 pesetas; for a claim of 1 million pesetas, it is 25,000 pesetas; for a claim of 10 million pesetas, it is 115,000; and for a claim of 100 million it is 233,000 pesetas.

performs a representative role and conducts the procedure, it cannot be said that his presence renders the litigation particularly more expensive. In fact, as has already been mentioned, the current trend is to promote the *procurador* and his functions.

10. LEGAL AID

The Spanish legal process has a system of free legal assistance. This system, which had already been considerably widened by reform in 1984, was further reformed recently in the Free Legal Assistance Act 1/1996, of 1 January, which applies to all jurisdictions.

Essentially, the 1996 Act extends the right to free legal assistance to those persons whose annual income is lower than double the minimum wage.[29] In exceptional cases, according to certain financial and family circumstances of the applicant, the relevant Commission may grant free legal assistance to those persons whose annual income is between double and four times the minimum wage; although in such cases the assistance may be limited in certain respects. When full legal aid is granted, it covers all procedural costs, including all defence costs and free representation during the judicial process by an *abogado* and a *procurador.* The lawyers are paid a stipulated amount by the state. The 1996 Act includes important new provisions, such as extending the right to free legal assistance to prior legal advice, and to receiving expert opinions.

The fundamental problems of the free legal assistance system are the quality of the legal professionals providing the services and the low fees paid by the state to the aforementioned professionals. In recent years, measures have been taken in both respects. On one side, steps have been taken to ensure the prompt payment of fees. On the other, the *Colegio de Abogados* has imposed more and more requirements on *abogados* who wish to provide services via the *turno de oficio* (duty solicitor scheme). These requirements normally consist of professional development courses, and the requirement of prior experience for certain types of case.

Legal aid fees payable to lawyers are currently fixed by a *Decreto* (a rule passed by the Spanish government) dated 20 September 1996. In the civil jurisdiction, the general rule is that the lawyer is paid 24,000 pesetas for defending a party during the whole process. As we have seen, these legal aid fees paid by the state are significantly lower than normal fees. I would say that they are almost ridiculous.

---

[29] The minimum wage is set annually by the government.

11. A BRIEF CONSIDERATION OF ALTERNATIVE DISPUTE RESOLUTION
UNDER THE SPANISH LEGAL SYSTEM

The Spanish legal system provides alternatives to the judicial process to resolve civil disputes, such as conciliation (which can result in a settlement) and arbitration.

11.1. Conciliation

With regard to conciliation, despite the fact that this can be carried out outside the legal system, the 1881 Act (Art. 460 onwards) provides for judicial conciliation. Before proceedings are instigated, the potential plaintiff may request the judge to issue a summons against the other party, in order to seek to reach a settlement, so as to avoid litigation. The other party, however, is not obliged to appear. Until the 1984 reform of the 1881 Act (the most important during its existence), it was obligatory to make an attempt at conciliation, i.e. as a rule, one could not present a civil claim without having attempted the conciliation process. The awareness that, in the vast majority of cases, such attempts at conciliation were useless led to the requirement being abolished in 1984. At present, therefore, any prior attempt at conciliation is purely optional. Nevertheless, in certain cases conciliation continues to be attempted, as it is a simple and cheap method of prolonging the limitation period.

Once the writ has been issued and the proceedings instigated, nothing prevents the parties from reaching an out-of-court settlement and putting an end to their proceedings. Such an out-of-court settlement can be effected before a judge (*transacción judicial*) or privately between the parties (*transacción extra-judicial*). In general, judges do not force the parties to arrive at a settlement. Only in small claims cases have the legislators introduced the precautionary measure that, at the first appearance of the parties before the judge (which takes place once the statement of claim has been presented and the defence served), the judge ought to commence by attempting to promote settlement between the parties. There are no reliable data as to the success of this measure. The commonly held view is that this conciliation attempt is successful in those cases where the judge is well informed as to the reason for the dispute, and this depends definitively on the judge's own character and workload.

Clearly, this attempt at conciliation with the proceedings having already commenced carries the risk that a certain coercion is implied on the judge's behalf towards either or both parties, in the sense that parties might feel forced to settle, as they assume that the judge has already formed an opinion about the case. Nevertheless, there may be cases in which the judge, being already aware of the facts of the dispute, can make it clear to the parties that what is under discussion is only a minimum part of the facts, or that it consists of merely a legal question, or even that the costs of the pleading and trial process (for example, expert evidence) may exceed the difference between the positions of the two parties. Given this fact, and assuming active participation from judges who, at the same time, respect the liberties of the parties, this process can be extremely useful.[30]

11.2. Arbitration

With regard to arbitration, both domestic and international arbitration is thriving in Spain. The Spanish legal system has a modern Arbitration Act (passed in 1988) and, since 1977, Spain has been a party to the 1958 New York Convention. The 1988 Act opened the door to institutional arbitration. In the last decade, a good number of institutions have flourished, creating arbitration courts which have had notable success.

In my opinion, arbitration is a mechanism the usefulness of which is limited to large disputes and litigation deriving from international commerce. It is inconceivable that arbitration could operate as an ordinary means of resolving domestic civil disputes and those of small economic value. Nevertheless, in Spain a network of arbitration courts for consumer disputes has been created. This consists of arbitration courts, normally with a municipal scope, comprising a representative of the administration, a consumers' representative, and a representative of the business community. Conceived of as a means for resolving small disputes between consumers and businesses, it does not appear that, since their implementation at the beginning of the current decade, the arbitration courts have been successful. Their performance has been uneven, however, and in some cities there have been appreciable numbers of cases.

In any event, my impression is that an institutionalized arbitration system, intended to resolve a great mass of small claims cases, would end up becoming a parallel jurisdiction. Thus, arbitration runs the risk of dying because of its own success. It is logical therefore that arbitration should be used for economically large disputes, disputes between large companies, disputes where there is a special legal difficulty, or, finally, in litigation deriving from international commerce in which neither party wishes to litigate before the courts of another state.

As with conciliation, there is no statistical information as to the level of

---

[30] Although, as I have already stated, there are no data or information regarding the success rate of this attempt at conciliation, I note the direct testimony of a senior judge (*magistrado*) whom I have heard comment that he was obtaining an extremely high success rate of conciliation at this stage in proceedings. His success rate was obviously based on thorough prior study of the cases. However, the picture is quite different in labour law cases where it is compulsory to attempt conciliation before proceeding to a full trial. Unlike in the civil procedure, there is a much lower rate of success in conciliation attempts. This is for two reasons. First, as a general rule, it is necessary to have attempted to reach a settlement before bringing proceedings before the administrative service which is expressly charged to deal with such matters of conciliation; and secondly, once the procedure is initiated, the hearing must be preceded by an attempt at conciliation by the parties before a judge.

recourse to domestic or international arbitration. Nevertheless, it would seem to be a well-founded impression that institutional arbitration in particular is thriving.

12. REFORM: CIVIL PROCEDURE BILL (DECEMBER 1997)

Since the enactment of the Civil Procedure Act in 1881, many reforms have been made. Many of these reformed small details of the system. Some had greater amplitude. The most important of the reforms was made in 1984, more than a century after the 1881 Act came into force. Innumerable statutory rules affecting civil procedure have been created in the last 117 years. The idea has already been put forward that all of this has brought with it a pernicious proliferation of diverse rules. Until recent years, the view that it was necessary to create a new Civil Procedure Act was not the dominant opinion amongst procedural law experts, the Spanish legal profession, or those responsible for the administration of justice. Today, however, the general opinion seems to be that there is a need to draft a new Civil Procedure Act (or at least, that this will be the most convenient way forward).

This trend produced a response from the Ministry of Justice. In April 1997, a draft Civil Procedure Bill was announced. The draft Bill[31] was debated and discussed for months by public and private institutions and, in December, it was approved as a Bill.[32] During 1998, the Bill has been the subject of a report by the *Consejo General del Poder del Estado* (General Council of the Judiciary) and it is currently awaiting the report of the *Consejo del Estado* (Council of State). In any case, it seems that, before long the Bill will be approved by the government as a *Proyecto de Ley* and presented before Parliament for debate and approval in turn. It seems, therefore, that complete reform of the Spanish civil legal system is well under way. In my opinion, from all points of view, the political decision to put an end to emergency and partial reforms, and inaugurate the age of global reform, ought to be hailed as a wise one.

Obviously, the simple creation of a new Civil Procedure Act is not going to be the immediate cure for all of the problems associated with our civil justice. Improvement of civil justice depends on many factors, which are not all connected with the deficiencies of the procedural legislation. Even with technically deficient procedural laws, civil justice could, in the past, have adopted a different course of action. Equally, even with technically perfect procedural laws, it could continue into the future on the wrong track. It is best not to

---

[31] A more detailed examination of the general characteristics of the Bill can be found in my study: 'Approach, System and Features of the Draft Civil Procedure Bill', in *The National Debates Regarding the Draft Civil Procedure Bill* (Murcia, 1997), 9–45.

[32] The Bill has been published in the *Boletín de información del Ministerio de Justicia* (Official Information Journal of the Ministry of Justice), year II (Dec. 1997).

believe in the miraculous power of laws. A new Civil Procedure Act is not going to change those causes of deficiencies in the system which are not connected with the procedural legislation. Furthermore, some of these problems are not easy to solve by legislation, but are related to our legal tradition and, in particular, the culture of our legal professionals. In particular, in practice Spanish civil procedure is almost exclusively written, with very few oral hearings before the courts. For many *abogados* this is a very comfortable situation. The *abogado* litigates from his legal office without having to appear before the court, and has time enough to elaborate the written pleadings. Changing this is not only a matter of legislation, but of culture.

A new Civil Procedure Act will not change the difficult position of civil justice by itself, although it may serve as a guiding instrument. On the other hand, a Civil Procedure Act cannot be made in the abstract, without giving attention to time and space considerations. The legislative work must be guided by the sincerity and economy of resources relevant to Spain at the end of the twentieth century and beginning of the twenty-first century, not in some other time or some other place. Having made this initial reflection, let us proceed to consider what are the most important characteristics of the Civil Procedure Bill (hereinafter referred to as 'the Bill').

12.1. Scope of the Bill

The Bill, although it is intended to be a single, uniform civil procedure code, does not include all of the individual institutions of civil justice. It is useful to note which institutions are not covered.

First, the Bill does not include strictly organic regulation; that is, that which concerns the types of courts, their composition, the legal status of the judges, etc. Such regulation can be found in the *Ley Orgánica del Poder Judicial 1985*. Secondly, the Bill does not include the regulation of bankruptcy law. Bankruptcy law is sufficiently autonomous and has sufficiently particular features for it to be governed by a separate Act. Since the 1950s there have been attempts to reform bankruptcy law. All such attempts have been led by the idea of having a single regulation so that the same institutions can be applied both to business people and to private individuals. Furthermore, there is a draft Bankruptcy Bill, which is currently being studied.

Thirdly, the Bill does not include the so-called 'voluntary jurisdiction'. In the European-continental legal systems, the term 'voluntary jurisdiction' is used to describe all those matters in which a judicial decision is required, but where there is no conflict or opposition between the parties. For example, the adoption of a child, or a guardianship for an incapable person, must be authorized by a judge. Once again, there is a consensus of opinion that a separate law is most appropriate for this area. The attribution of voluntary jurisdiction matters to judicial organs is contingent, i.e. it is based merely on reasons of convenience.

Hence, it will be necessary carefully to appraise what voluntary jurisdiction matters ought to continue in the hands of judicial organs, and to omit those matters in which judicial intervention would not be entirely justified or which could be dealt with effectively by other non-judicial institutions.

Fourthly, unlike other civil procedure codes, it has been decided not to include arbitration in the Bill. Fifthly, questions of international civil procedure have not been included in the Bill. Hence, the acknowledgement and enforcement of foreign judicial decisions or the process of international judicial co-operation are not covered in the Bill. Such matters will be dealt with in a future International Legal Co-operation Act for civil matters. In the meantime, the existing legislation will remain in force.

The Bill will radically simplify the Spanish civil procedure. Whilst it does not amount to a complete unification of the civil procedure system in one legal text, it has an excellent codifying effect. All of the Spanish civil procedure law will be contained in five Acts: the Civil Procedure Act (*Ley de Enjuiciamiento Civil*), the Bankruptcy Act (*Ley Concursal*), the Voluntary Jurisdiction Act (*Ley de Jurisdicción Voluntaria*), the Arbitration Act (*Ley de Arbitraje*), and the International Legal Co-operation Act for civil matters (*Ley de Cooperación Jurídica International en materia civil*). It is also to be hoped that, if the codifying and simplifying effect is achieved, this will radically dissuade future legislators from introducing procedural precepts into the substantive law.

With regard to content, given the obvious impossibility of analysing it in this discussion, I will limit myself to covering what are, in my view, the inspirational ideas of principle and the most important new features.

12.2. Content of the Bill: Principles

The Bill is clearly inspired by the adversarial principle (*Dispositionsmaxime* and *Verhandlungsmaxime*). Although there is a basic requirement that the state, as a social state, provides the legal system and determines its requirements, private autonomy remains a general principle within the legal system. The civil procedure system has to reflect the substantive system. It also has to serve as a means for the protection of legal status and property, subject to the power to change status and dispose of property vested in each individual citizen. The only places where the adversarial principles, of party control and autonomy, logically give way are those areas in which civil procedure does not serve as a means for the protection of legal powers of disposition. In some cases, civil procedures are designed instead primarily for the protection of legal status, and the substantive system has identified a greater public interest overriding the private interest. Examples of procedures where the parties logically ought not to be in control include capacity, affiliation, and matrimonial proceedings.

12.3. Procedural Simplification

In general the Bill attempts to rationalize the system and reduce the number of different types of proceedings: declaratory, enforcement, and injunctive. Thus, the Bill establishes two ordinary declaratory procedures (as opposed to the four which currently exist): the *juicio ordinario* and the *juicios verbales*. It only retains those special procedures which are absolutely necessary. On the one hand, the capacity, affiliation, and matrimonial procedures are retained. This is necessary because of the different principles which inspired them. (Basically, unlike pure private law cases, these areas involve considerations of public interest, as noted above.) On the other hand, the processes for the enforcement of judgment debts (*proceso monitorio*) and bills of exchange (*juicio cambiario*) are retained. These are summary proceedings for certain types of credit. The procedural simplification is also reflected in the appeal process. A single procedure is established, as opposed to the large number that are currently in existence.

The new declaratory procedure is characterized by greater oral argument and concentration. In contrast with the previous prevalence of written procedures, the Bill seeks to establish a basically oral civil procedure in Spain. But it is not intended that the change be swift. As already noted, the culture of the legal profession in Spain has been based for centuries on civil justice in which litigation has basically consisted of the exchange of written documents prepared by law firms.

The *juicio ordinario*, with certain exceptions, is envisaged for litigation where the amount involved is more than 3 million pesetas.[33] After the presentation of the written claim and the written defence, the parties attend a preliminary hearing before the judge. This hearing has the following features: first, the parties can settle the matter and end the process; secondly, it must be shown that the process has been initiated in compliance with the procedural requirements; thirdly, the parties must confirm their respective claims and indicate the facts over which there is disagreement. Once this is admitted as acceptable and relevant, the parties are summoned to another appearance before the court where the evidence is heard. After this, the parties put forward their final arguments and judgment is given. As can be seen, the *juicio ordinario* consists of a procedure created so that, after the initial claim and defence, everything is covered in two court appearances.

There are two types of *juicio verbal*. The first is provided, with certain exceptions, for claims between 300,000 and 3 million pesetas. The difference from the *juicio ordinario* lies in the fact that, after the presentation of the written claim and the written defence, the parties are summoned to a hearing at which all further procedures must be presented (complementary pleadings, evidence, and conclusions) in one single hearing or in consecutive sessions. The second type of

---

[33] Roughly £12,400 or $US20,800.

juicio verbal is even simpler (and similar to the existing *juicio verbal*). It is envisaged that, for certain cases, particularly claims for less than 300,000 pesetas, the court's involvement ought to be especially swift. In this case, there is no requirement for the presence of either *abogado* or *procurador*. The plaintiff commences the action with a *demanda sucinta*, that is, a written claim in which it is not necessary to provide a complete statement of the facts or the law. It is sufficient, instead, to identify the parties and succinctly explain the claim (remember that this is designed to be done without a lawyer). The judge, without further steps, summons the parties to a hearing. At the hearing all of the additional procedures are covered.

As can be observed, although there are important differences, the proceedings which are envisaged by the Bill attempt to create greater reliance on oral argument and concentration than exists at present.

12.4. A system of control for the procedural prerequisites

The Bill introduces new features of considerable importance under what is referred to as the 'control system for the procedural prerequisites'. The Bill endeavours to reduce the incidence of judgments being given on the basis of procedural rather than substantive points. Its aim is to promote justice on the merits. To this end, the Bill uses three techniques. First, the judge is given discretionary powers of judicial control, allowing him or her to give directions to ensure that the majority of procedural prerequisites have been complied with. Secondly, a general rule is established for the rectification of procedural defects that are not by their very nature insoluble. Finally, the streamlined nature of the first hearing is emphasized (or the initial phase of the hearing in the case of the *juicios verbales*), to enable the determination of the outstanding procedural issues.

In fashioning a control system for procedural prerequisites, any system faces a dilemma. Should the structure allow for a prior examination of the case for compliance with the procedural prerequisites, or should it simply provide that compliance be confirmed in the final judgment? The first alternative has the advantages that, if the examination is passed, the risk of a merely procedural judgment is avoided, and, if the examination is not passed, then a useless trial has been avoided. However, there is the disadvantage that a delay is inherent in the two-stage nature of the overall proceeding. The second alternative has the advantage and the inconvenience absolutely inverted. The proceeding is not delayed for the examination of procedural questions, but there is the risk that the trial will be wasted. These two alternatives are pure and extreme models, like two poles between which procedural legislation is situated, nearer to one or the other. To combine the advantages and eliminate the inconveniences completely is impossible. Hence, it is necessary to choose a reasonable and realistic combination. If the rule of prior examination at the hearing or at the outset of the *juicio oral* is combined with the judge being given discretionary powers to give procedural directions, an appropriate balance seems to be struck. This is especially so when combined with a principle of rectification of procedural defects. Then, as long as there is no possibility of a separate appeal against the procedural rulings, the result is a system which promises to deliver a substantive, and not merely a procedural, judgment in the vast majority of cases, once the pleading period is finalized, without great cost in terms of delay.

12.5. Rationalization of the Appeal System

The Bill maintains the existing system by which, at first instance, practically all cases are dealt with by the *juzgados de primera instancia*.[34] The decisions of the *juzgados de primera instancia* can be appealed to the *audiencias provinciales*. The Bill establishes that the non-definitive (interlocutory) decisions of the judge at first instance cannot be directly appealed. Only the final judgment will be able to be appealed and, in this appeal, the appellant will have to establish good reason to appeal, with regard to what happened at first instance. All first instance judgments can be appealed against, whatever the matter or the amount involved. As we shall see, the Bill establishes measures to dissuade appeal; basically, by providing that the first instance judgment is provisionally enforceable. The Bill clearly favours a strengthening of the importance of first instance. The second instance still figures, in accordance with Spanish tradition, as a limited appeal in which the parties cannot introduce new points and in which only exceptionally can new evidence be adduced.

The major new feature of the appeal system, and one of the principal new features of the Bill, is the articulation of the further remedies that exist after the first appeal. The litigant must make a choice between the so-called *recurso extraordinario por infracción procesal* and *casación*. The two remedies are alternatives. The *recurso extraordinario por infracción procesal* is brought before the *tribunal superior de justicia de la comunidad autónoma* (which approximates the High Court in England and Wales). In this appeal, the litigant may invoke any type of procedural grounds for appeal, but may only raise procedural grounds. *Casación*, on the other hand, is the appeal to the Supreme Court (the *Tribunal Supremo*).[35] In this application, the litigant may not invoke any procedural arguments, but is restricted to substantive grounds for appeal only. Furthermore, for the application to be admissible it will be necessary that: (1) the litigation relates to a

---

[34] The *juzgados de paz* retain a symbolic power for claims which are less than 15,000 pesetas (roughly £62 or $US104). With regard to this point, the reformers have not dared to make any significant changes. There would be two options: (i) to abolish these courts which are served by non-professional judges; or (ii) to grant them more effective and far-reaching powers.

[35] As noted above, the *tribunales superiores de justicia* exceptionally hear and determine *casación* appeals, when the appeal is based on the breach or infringement of civil law which is particular to the relevant autonomous community.

fundamental law (except those which are recognized by Article 24 of the Constitution which are procedural in content); (2) the judgment being appealed from contradicts another or other judgments based on substantially similar circumstances from the same or another *audiencia provincial*; or (3) the rule that is considered to have been infringed was created less than five years ago and, thus, there has not yet been uniform precedent established.

The central point is that these appeals become alternative remedies. The litigant must elect one or the other. If both appeals are presented simultaneously, the appeal to the *Tribunal Supremo* is taken to be waived. If the appellant elects to lodge the appeal in the *Tribunal Supremo*, then he will not subsequently be able to bring a *recurso extraordinario por infracción procesal*. Equally, if he elects the *recurso extraordinario por infracción procesal*, he will not subsequently be able to present an appeal to the *Tribunal Supremo*. One or the other is the stark choice that the appellant must make.

Given that the primary function of the *Tribunal Supremo* is the creation of judicial precedent, the function of protection of *ius litigatoris* and the *nomophilactic* function must be subordinate to this primary role. If this premiss is accepted (and many do not accept it), then the prerequisites from which the organic and procedural design of the *Tribunal Supremo* must start are clear. A supreme court can really only create effective judicial precedent if it consists of a small number of judges and deals with a small number of matters. Any other combination would lead irrevocably to contradictions, the antithesis of precedent. A small or large group of senior judges deciding a large number of cases, or many senior judges deciding a few matters, would make it impossible to create clear and consistent *rationes decidendi* which the other courts and the legal profession could understand and follow. The answer is not simply to remove matters from the *Tribunal Supremo* so that it has as few as possible to decide. Reducing numbers presents the danger of becoming an end in itself. This seems to have been the theme of some recent reforms. We must seriously consider the question and resolve the role of the highest court of appeal.

Further, in deciding the role of the *Tribunal Supremo*, it should be remembered that it must be able to deal with litigation related to all areas of the legal system. This is not only common sense, but is also a constitutional requirement. Article 123.1 of the Spanish Constitution establishes that, with the exception of matters concerning constitutional guarantees, in which the *Tribunal Constitucional* (Constitutional Court) has supremacy, the *Tribunal Supremo* is the supreme jurisdictional organ for all branches of law. Within the legal system, it is legal methods which allow the interpretation and application of the law. These methods must be sustained by the supreme judicial organ and followed by the inferior organs. Such methods can be very varied, and can range from the *stare decisis* rule of Anglo-Saxon systems to the unconditional possibility of access to the supreme court appeal existing in the Italian legal system. Without such methods, supremacy would be worthless.

Combining these premisses, I conclude that there is a need to limit access to the supreme court through appeal. Such a limitation could be articulated in a number of ways. The most radical is the current system in the United States, the so-called *certiorari* system. This gives the US Supreme Court the discretionary power to decide which matters it will hear, on the grounds of importance, interest, or novelty. The draftsmen of the Spanish Bill have decided to reject this possibility, presumably because it is so totally foreign to our legal tradition. Nevertheless, with this possibility discarded, the option chosen in the Bill seems to be more than reasonable. The *Tribunal Supremo* will deal with all types of civil and commercial litigation by way of a pure *casación* appeal. One of the following must be established. There must be either an infringement of the regulatory provisions of fundamental rights, or infringements of the legal system or precedent. In the latter case, it will be necessary for there to be a conflict between judgments of the *audiencias provinciales* as to a controversial legal question, or for the appeal to concern a law that has recently been enacted. The *tribunales superiores de justicia* will undertake to oversee infringements of procedural law.

12.6. Strengthening the protection of credit

The Spanish civil procedure is a paradise for defaulting debtors. The Bill intends to strengthen the procedural position of creditors. Three aspects of the reform reflect this change: the facilities for the provisional enforcement of judgment; the new facilities in the enforcement proceedings of the physical location of the debtors' goods and the means for restraining them; and the introduction into our legal system of a 'monitoring procedure'. Each is considered in turn.

Under the Bill, first instance judgments are provisionally enforceable even if they can be appealed. The respondent who wishes to avoid the provisional enforcement of a judgment against him must prove that obtaining redress, or the recovery of his goods in the event of revocation of the judgment, would be impossible or extremely difficult. The Bill itself creates measures designed to avoid this situation, by providing that the applicant cannot dispose of the goods obtained through the provisional enforcement (for example, selling them to a third party) during the appeal. As a general rule, a defendant who has lost at first instance, and seeks to avoid provisional enforcement, must provide a deposit or guarantee. This is bound to dissuade defendants from launching unmeritorious appeals. The new regime of provisional enforcement is the most radical change introduced by the Bill. Although it obviously has its risks, it represents a strong reliance on the quality of justice granted by the courts of first instance.

Secondly, the Bill attempts to strengthen the position of the applicant creditor and seeks methods which will guarantee a greater effectiveness of the mandatory enforcement procedure. It introduces into the Spanish legal system a duty of disclosure, whereby the debtor must reveal his goods. This means that, at the time when the goods are restrained, the debtor is the person who has the duty to provide the court with a list of his goods. In the event that he does not provide such a list, or he makes a false declaration, he will be criminally penalized. Likewise, the Bill provides for a coercive fine system for breach of these obligations. It is also worth mentioning the possibility that the compulsory seizure of the arrested goods may be done either in the way that the parties have agreed upon or through specialized persons or entities. Both provisions create methods which are very untypical of the normal methods for the compulsory seizure of goods, and they introduce into this area a great amount of much needed flexibility.

Thirdly, the Bill attempts to introduce the so-called 'monitoring procedure' into the Spanish legal system. This change is of prime importance. This type of procedure has been needed for a long time. If the Spanish experience is similar to that of other countries where monitoring procedures exist (for example, the *Mahnverfahren* in Germany, the *procédure d'injonction de payer* in France, the *procedimento d'ingiunzione* in Italy), the monitoring procedure will fundamentally change the court protection of credit. This can be a decisive factor in reducing the number of declaratory proceedings.

The essence of the monitoring procedure is the provision of a procedural channel to create summarily an instrument which is enforceable against the debtor if, after having been summoned to make payment by the court, he neither pays nor appears in court to allege grounds for not paying his debt. If the debtor alleges grounds for not paying the debt, then the monitoring procedure is finished and the creditor must initiate a normal procedure. If the debtor does not appear in court alleging grounds for not paying, then the debt is directly enforceable. The same characteristic procedure is known under various guises, including those procedures which require an initial document of a particular type, such as a negotiable instrument, to prove the existence of the debt, or those which provide for minimum and maximum amounts for their use. The Bill opts for a model of the monitoring procedure which is of a documentary nature. The application must be attached to a document that proves and certifies the existence of the debt, albeit that documents which are solely prepared by the creditor will be accepted (for example, an invoice). The procedure will be limited to debts under 3 million pesetas. Although debatable, this quantitative limitation is based on experience that shows that the monitoring procedure is normally used for demanding the payment of small debts, above all those owed to non-professional creditors (fundamentally tradesmen and independent professionals). For larger debts, the normal procedure is required, and it will continue to be required, especially for professional creditors (banks and financial entities). These must establish the existence of an enforceable instrument.

12.7. Rationalization of the system of Provisional Remedies

In the Spanish civil procedure there are different kinds of pre-emptive measures or interim relief. The main kind is the provisional attachment of goods—*embargo preventivo*—which operates *in rem* and not *in personam* like English *Mareva* injunctions. There are other typical measures, such as the inscription of the statement of claim in the Real Estate Registry Office—*anotación preventiva de la demanda*—or in other public registry offices. Finally, there is Article 1428 of the 1881 Act, which allows the courts to decide the interlocutory injunction most adequate to the case. Some recent Acts, passed in the 1980s and the 1990s, such as those relating to intellectual property, industrial property, and unfair competition, contain special regulations concerning interim relief. In recent times, there has been a noticeable increase in the actual use of provisional remedies in judicial practice.

The system of provisional remedies contained in the Bill is a complete and systematic reconstruction. The Bill puts an end to the dispersal, fragmentation, and lack of formal organization of the current system of provisional remedies. But not only this. The Bill also provides a unitary regulation of the provisional remedies. It provides a set definition of the normal characteristics that all provisional remedies must have, and produces a characteristic list of examples of the more common provisional remedies. The complete, systematic, and unitary nature of the regulation of provisional remedies in the Bill is worth adopting, especially in view of the growing importance of the protection provided by such provisional remedies.

13

The Portuguese System of Civil Procedure

Maria Manuel Leitão Marques,
Conceição Gomes, and João Pedroso

1. DESCRIPTION OF THE PORTUGUESE SYSTEM OF CIVIL PROCEDURE

1.1. The judicial system

One of the foundation principles of the Portuguese legal system is the independence of the courts. The Constitution of the Portuguese Republic expressly declares that the courts, whose essential function is to administer justice, are sovereign entities of the state, as are the President of the Republic, and Parliament (*Assembleia da República*). The courts are independent of both of these entities, and are subject to the law alone.

The Constitution establishes the following courts: Constitutional Court; Supreme Court of Justice and judicial courts of first and second instance; Administrative Supreme Court and other administrative and fiscal courts; Court of Auditors and military courts. The Constitution also anticipates the possibility of creating maritime and arbitration courts, as well as nominating justices of the peace.

The Constitutional Court is responsible for constitutional matters. Administrative matters are dealt with in the separate administrative court hierarchy. This leaves ordinary civil matters to the 'judicial' courts.

The judicial court hierarchy consists of courts of first and second instance and the Supreme Court of Justice. The division between courts of first and second instance is related to the system of appeals. The courts of second instance are called *tribunais da relação*. There is one such court for each of the four judicial districts. The Supreme Court of Justice (*Supremo Tribunal de Justiça*) is the highest entity in the hierarchy of the judicial courts. It is possible to appeal to this court for a third evaluation of a case. In some situations, an appeal can come to this court directly from the first instance court.

The courts of first instance are organized according to subject matter and territory. The courts of general jurisdiction, such as the county courts (*tribunais de comarca*), have power to decide on all cases not reserved by law to another court. The courts of specialized jurisdiction are: the civil (including small claims courts); criminal; criminal investigation; family and children; employment; and judgment-execution courts. Specialized courts exist only in the most important cities.

As for their territorial organization, the courts of first instance are divided into county courts and courts with jurisdiction over a judicial circuit, which includes several counties. The circuit courts have jurisdiction over civil cases of a value exceeding the limited monetary jurisdiction of the second instance courts, and when the intervention of the collective court (consisting of three judges) is requested.[1]

1.2. Basic principles of civil procedure

The Portuguese legal and procedural system is founded on a set of general procedural principles. Some of these principles, because they concern fundamental rights, are enshrined in the Constitution of the Portuguese Republic. Principles found here include the principle of publicity of trials, the principle of legality, and the right of access to courts.

The Portuguese Constitution expressly states that 'everybody is guaranteed access to the law and the courts for the defence of their legitimate rights and interests, justice never being denied because of insufficiency of means'. This article concerns both the right to bring an action and the right to defend an action brought against you. The right of access to justice also means that judicial decisions should be given within a reasonable time.

Other basic principles are established in the Civil Procedure Code.[2] The principle of self-responsibility of the parties; the principle of co-operation; the principle of free appreciation of evidence; the principle of search for material truth; and the principle of procedural economy are all to be found here.

1.3. Forms of civil procedure

The Civil Procedure Code establishes two main forms of procedure: common procedure and special procedure. The form of the procedure is adapted to the claim laid in the lawsuit. The special procedure applies to cases expressly stated in the law (such as, for example, child custody, inventories and bankruptcies). Employment disputes are dealt with in specialized courts using a special procedure.

The common procedure is applicable to all cases for which there is no special procedure. The common procedure may be ordinary, summary, or very summary, according to the value of the claim. As a rule, the ordinary procedure is used when the value of the case exceeds the jurisdiction of the second instance

---

[1] See Miguel Pedros e Rocha Machado and João Luís de Moraes, *Organização judiciária e estatutos das profissões forenses* (Lisbon: Edições Cosmos, 1994).

[2] See Manuel de Andrade, *Noções elementares do processo civil* (Coimbra: Coimbra Editora, 1956); Anselmo de Castro, *Processo civil (declaratório)* (Coimbra: Almedina, 1982); Abílio Neto, *Código de processo civil anotado* (Lisbon: Ediforum, 1997); José Lebre Freitas, *Introdução ao processo civil* (Coimbra: Coimbra Editora, 1996); and Manuel Leal Henriques, *Recursos em processo civil* (Lisbon: Vislis Editores, 1998).

court (PTE 2,000,000).[3] Otherwise, the summary procedure is used. However, where the value of the case is not greater than half of the limit of the jurisdiction of the county court (half of PTE 500,000),[4] and the action is one to enforce a purely pecuniary obligation, such as a claim for compensation for damage caused, or for the surrender of personal property, the very summary procedure applies.

Procedural law also distinguishes between declaratory actions and actions for execution. The declaratory action is the general civil action. The action for execution is one for the enforcement of a judgment, or of an obligation supported by an appropriate bond, such as a bill of exchange or a cheque.

This essay deals only with the common declaratory procedure. This procedure is the basic form, of which the other forms of procedure are modifications. Summary and very summary procedures, as their names suggest, are both simplifications of the ordinary declaratory procedure.

1.4. Common declaratory procedure

The proceedings are initiated by the complaint, and comprise five stages: articulated pleadings; remedies and condensation; determining the facts; final hearing; and final judgment.

In the pleading stage, the parties define the disputed issues. The main pleadings are the statement of claim, the defence, and the reply. In exceptional cases, other pleadings may be accepted, such as the defence to a counter-claim.

In the statement of claim, the plaintiff must indicate the names of the parties, the form of procedure, and the factual basis for the action. The value of the case must also be specified. When the court has received the statement of claim, it examines it for compliance with the formal requirements only. If the statement of claim complies, the court must send a copy to the defendant. The defendant should present his or her defence within thirty days.

After this stage comes the stage of remedies and condensation. At this stage, the judge intervenes in the procedure in order to perfect the pleadings or remedy defects. The facts are discussed in a preliminary hearing, and the judge decides which ones are verified and proven, and which ones still lack evidence and so must be considered at the fact-finding stage.

Eventually, there is the final hearing stage. At this hearing, the matters of fact are discussed and the witnesses and experts or other participants in the proceedings are heard. The evidence is given orally, and it may be tape-recorded upon request.

The court is constituted at the commencement of the hearing. It consists of

---

[3] PTE 2,000,000 (Portugese escudos) is approximately £6,666 or $US11,111 (at PTE 300 to the pound, or PTE 180 to the US dollar on 2 Sept. 1998).
[4] PTE 500,000 is roughly £1,666 or $US2,777.

three judges in cases using the ordinary procedure (a collective court), but only one judge in the other forms of procedure. Thereafter, witnesses and experts, as well as the lawyers, are summoned. The absence of any of the people summoned may justify the postponement of the hearing. The law states, however, that the hearing cannot be postponed more than once.

When the hearing begins, the judge tries to reconcile the parties and make them come to an agreement. If this attempt fails, evidence is called, starting with the depositions of the parties and concluding with the witnesses. Then submissions are made orally on the facts by the parties' barristers. Once these submissions are over, the court decides the facts. Once the facts have been found, the law is argued. This may be done orally if the parties' barristers agree. The legal argument takes place before the judge, who also gives the final judgment.

Not all proceedings end in a final judgment. The lawsuit may come to an end during an earlier stage of the procedure for various reasons. A preliminary order for dismissal may be made if the judge finds that the claim is groundless. The plaintiff may waive its claim. A settlement (known as a *transaction*) may be reached between the litigants. Finally, events outside the procedure may supervene to render the proceedings useless.

1.5. Appeals in civil procedure

Appeals may be extraordinary appeals or ordinary appeals. The extraordinary appeal, an appeal from a final and conclusive decision which has become *res judicata*, is only allowed in very specific circumstances. These commonly involve rehearings, or appeals by third parties in opposition to decisions reached.

Ordinary appeals are those brought from decisions which are not yet final and conclusive, not yet having become *rem judicatum*. These appeals may be by way of appellate review, revision, or by a bill of exceptions.

1.5.1. Appellate review

Appellate review is a form of ordinary appeal. It is used when the appellant seeks to achieve an alteration in the judgment as a whole. The appellate review consists of a second examination of the case, this time before a superior court. In an appeal from a decision reached after applying the ordinary procedure, this type of appeal usually leads to the suspension of the effectiveness of the decision of the court below. An appeal from a decision reached after applying the summary procedure does not usually suspend the effectiveness of the decision appealed from.

This ordinary appeal process begins with a petition, which is lodged with the court that decided the suit. Next, the judge of that court issues an order accepting or rejecting the appeal. If the appeal is accepted, this order sets out its consequences. Once the appeal is accepted, the parties are summoned to produce their arguments. After the time allowed for arguments has expired, the appeal is sent to the superior court.

As soon as it gets to this court, the suit is allotted to one of the judges, who becomes its *juge rapporteur* (*juiz relator*). This judge becomes responsible for the conclusion of the process. The *juiz relator* examines the appeal (preliminary examination) to check for any irregularity. He or she may also summarily decide the appeal, if he or she deems the issue to be a simple one (for instance, because it has been repeatedly and uniformly decided by previous courts), or if the appeal has no basis. Next, any documents still not attached may be joined, if they are indispensable to the fair hearing of the suit. After this, two other judges analyse the file and, later, the *juiz relator* hands down a proposed decision, which is voted on by the court at the trial.

1.5.2. Revision

The second type of ordinary appeal, the appeal by way of revision, is limited to issues of law. It is addressed to the Supreme Court of Justice. Revision is especially designed to detect and correct errors of law in judicial decisions. The appeal by way of revision is possible from decisions of the court of second instance (*tribunal da relação*) and, in some situations, from decisions of the courts of first instance (*appeal per saltum*). The procedure is similar to the procedure for appellate review. However, as the purpose of revision is to obtain uniformity of case law, the judges from all civil sections of the Supreme Court decide the appeal. Revision does not usually lead to the suspension of the decision of the court below.

1.5.3. Exception

The bill of exceptions is available in all situations in which an appellate review is not possible. Its procedure is similar to that of the appellate review. The law stipulates the cases in which exception suspends the decision of the court below.

2. STATISTICAL DATA

2.1. Number of judges, public prosecutors, court clerks, and lawyers

In 1996, Portugal had 1,231 judges, 939 public prosecutors, 7,185 court clerks, and 13,809 lawyers for 9,934,110 inhabitants (Apps. 13.1 and 13.2). The number of judges, public prosecutors, court clerks, and, particularly, lawyers rose significantly in absolute and relative terms between 1970 and 1996 (Fig. 13.1). In the case of judges, public prosecutors, and court clerks, the increase reflects the system's response to the growth of both civil and criminal litigation. Some procedural and structural reforms (the creation of new courts and specialization) have also contributed to the same trend.

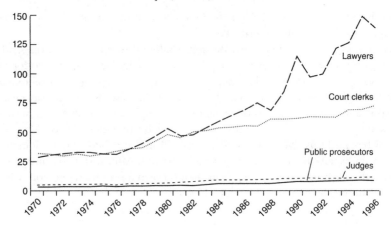

Fig. 13.1. Evolution of the number of judges, public prosecutors, court clerks,
and lawyers 1970–1996 (per 100,000 inhabitants)
Note: For an extended analysis of statistical data on justice, see *Relatório do Observatório Permanente da Justiça Portuguesa*, 2 vols. (Coimbra: Centro de Estudos Sociais, 1998), vol. i.
Source: Department of Studies and Planning of the Ministry of Justice.

The growth in the number of lawyers is, in great part, a variable independent of the variation in the demand for judicial services. It is due to the creation of new law schools in private universities. In addition to the two existing state law schools, more than twenty private law schools have been created in a short period of time. Although the *Ordem dos Advogados* (Lawyers' Association) has tried to control access to the profession through an examination, this system has not yet proven to be very selective. If Marc Galanter's hypothesis is correct, then this growth in the number of lawyers will itself lead to an increase in the demand for judicial services.[5]

2.2. Variation in judicial demand and supply of civil litigation

Fig. 13.2 shows the evolution of the total number of civil cases entered, pending, and disposed of in the period between 1970 and 1996, including all the different types of civil procedure except the employment procedure.[6] The number of cases entered provides a measure of the actual demand for the services of the judicial system. There has been a sharp growth in demand throughout the period under consideration, especially noticeable in the period immediately after the 1974 revolution and in the 1990s. Social, economic, and legal factors explain this variation. The increase is mainly due to the increasing numbers of

---

[5] Marc Galanter, 'Direito em abundância: actividade legislativa no Atlântico Norte', *Revista crítica de ciências sociais*, 36 (1993), 103 ff.   [6] See also App. 13.3.

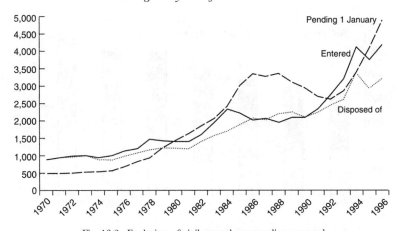

Fig. 13.2. Evolution of civil procedures pending, entered,
and disposed of 1970–1996 (per 100,000 inhabitants)
Note: See Salvador da Costa, *Código das custas judiciais anotado* (Coimbra: Almedina, 1997).
Source: Department of Studies and Planning of the Ministry of Justice.

three types of litigation: debt claims; torts related to traffic accidents; and divorce.[7] The number of cases disposed of corresponds to the supply of judicial services. We can see that the volume of cases disposed of has also increased, but not as much as the volume of cases entered. Pending procedures gives us the measure of unfulfilled demand. The period between 1975 and 1988 saw considerable accumulation of pending cases, due to the increase in cases entered. Since 1988, there has been a clear tendency for the number of pending cases to decrease. This situation may mean that the growth of litigation has been accompanied either by growth in the material and human resources of the judicial system, or by an increase in the system's productivity, influenced, for instance, by changes in substantive or procedural law.

2.3. Type and evolution of civil actions (1942–1996)

A more detailed study of civil litigation shows the most important types of litigation and the principal litigants. The study deals only with declaratory actions, which are the most important type of action in civil litigation (Fig. 13.3 and App. 13.4). Taking 1996 as a year of reference, debt recovery is by far the most important type of civil litigation, representing 68 per cent of all actions disposed of. This type of litigation is followed by divorce, which represents 8 per cent of all cases disposed of, by evictions (4 per cent), by

[7] For an extended analysis of delay of justice, see *Relatório do Observatório Permanente da Justiça Portuguesa*, ii.

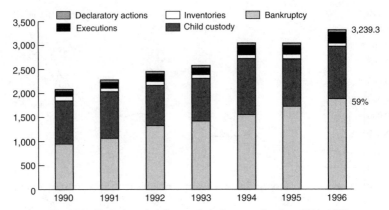

Fig. 13.3. Evolution of civil procedures by type of actions 1990–1996
(per 100,000 inhabitants)
Source: Department of Studies and Planning of the Ministry of Justice.

actions relating to property rights (4 per cent), and by torts (4 per cent) (Fig. 13.4 and App. 13.5).

Claims for debt were also the most important claims in the period between 1942 and 1996, although their relative significance has varied throughout the period (Fig. 13.4). In any one of these years, debt actions were the most important type of litigation. Their relative importance increased substantially, from 38 per cent of all declaratory actions disposed of during 1942, to 68 per cent during 1996. Economic crisis at the beginning of the 1990s, and the dramatic expansion of credit, partly explain the growth of debt claims.

Divorces increased substantially after 1974. Before the revolution of that year, divorce was forbidden to Roman Catholic marriages. A new law over-turned this rule in 1975.

The importance of evictions is due in part to a law established after 1974 which 'froze' urban rents, forbidding landlords from increasing them periodic-ally. Low rents made tenants interested in keeping houses even when they did not live in them. On their part, landlords were interested in taking advantage of all of the legal possibilities to break their contracts, and to remove tenants from their houses by eviction. If the tenants could be removed, the landlord would have the house back, and could live in it or sell it. This was a much more lucrative investment, considering the high interest rates.

Torts registered the most significant growth during the period under analysis, mainly due to the increase in litigation arising from traffic accidents. From 1942 to 1996, traffic accident cases increased 4,378.6 per cent (168 lawsuits disposed of in 1942; 7,524 in 1996). The rise in average family income, the increase in the number of cars, and compulsory insurance have caused the growth of this type of litigation.

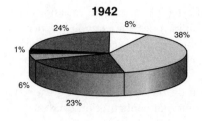

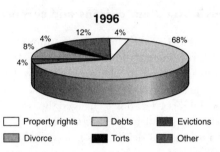

☐ Property rights ▨ Debts ▧ Evictions

▨ Divorce ■ Torts ▨ Other

Fig. 13.4. Evolution of the principal declaratory actions disposed of 1942–1996
(per 100,000 inhabitants)
Source: Department of Studies and Planning of the Ministry of Justice.

On the other hand, the least pronounced growth occurred in actions relating to property rights, a fact related to the expansion of urbanization. Our research confirmed that these actions are more frequent in rural areas, especially in the central and northern parts of Portugal, which are areas characterized by large numbers of small, rural properties.

Perhaps surprisingly, several types of lawsuit are insignificant in Portuguese civil litigation. For some types, the number of lawsuits brought to court is considerably inferior to the number of actual or potential conflicts. This means that there are factors either diverting conflicts away from the courts into alternative mechanisms of resolution, or simply preventing them from coming to court. Little propensity to litigate, especially by individuals, is a sign of the passivity which may be a trait of the Portuguese national character. The difficulty of access to the judicial system, and hostility in principle against resorting to the courts, also contribute to this situation. As a matter of fact, in a survey that we launched in 1992, the majority of people answered that, without a lot of money, especially to hire a good lawyer, it was not possible to obtain an advantageous decision from the courts.

Among the cases which are of little significance in Portuguese civil justice statistics are bankruptcies, actions relating to corporations, breach of contract (except debts), and actions concerning 'new rights' (consumer or environmental protection).

We have also observed that certain kinds of civil dispute are relatively stable, while others are more affected by short-term variations in social and economic conditions. The first group includes, for example, property and inheritance; the second group includes debts. An intermediate group includes divorce, evictions, and torts. In these cases, changes occur either through liberalizing or restricting the law, or through long-term structural change external to the judicial system.

The civil justice system on the whole displays great stability, and has maintained the same kind of internal configuration over the years.

2.4. Plaintiffs in civil litigation: citizens and corporations

Plaintiffs in a civil action may be individuals or institutions (associations, unions, professional societies, firms, corporations, or the state). Fig. 13.5 shows the distribution of civil suits according to whether the plaintiff is an individual or an institution, and compares it with the distribution of defendants.[8] We observe that institutions, particularly corporations, engaged the courts in more than half of the civil procedures disposed of in 1996 (60.6 per cent).

The proportion of institutional defendants is less significant (31.9 per cent), which means that most actions in which the plaintiff was a corporation had an individual as a defendant. We have verified that 41.4 per cent of the declaratory actions in 1996 had a corporation as plaintiff and an individual as defendant. In 26.7 per cent of cases, both of the litigants were corporations.

2.5. Sporadic and frequent litigants

We can also group litigants according to the frequency of their recourse to the courts; that is, by taking into account the number of actions per plaintiff during a certain period of time. As Galanter has shown,[9] due to differences in size and financial resources, as well as differences in the law, some plaintiffs repeatedly resort to the courts, getting involved in similar kinds of suits throughout a period of time ('repeat players'), while others use the courts only occasionally or sporadically ('one-shot players').

One-shot players are mainly individuals. Typically, therefore, in the absence of experience of using the justice system, a one-shot player's suit will involve greater costs, greater risks, and greater interest in resolving the problem.

On the other hand, repeat players, who are usually corporations, have better access to resources that allow them to litigate frequently. This does not mean that they engage in every type of action. Their demand for the courts is very selective. It concentrates on frequent litigation against sporadic partners; that is, on debt collection, mainly when the debtors are individuals or less economically

---

[8] See also App. 13.6.
[9] Marc Galanter, 'Why the "Haves" Come out Ahead: Speculations on the Limits of Legal Exchange', *Law and Society Review*, 9/1 (1974), 95.

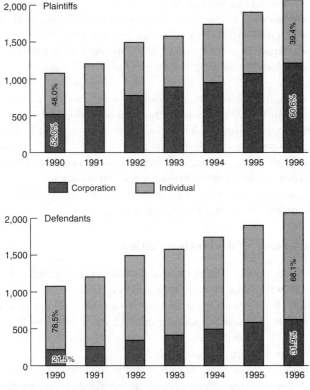

Fig. 13.5. Distribution of declaratory civil actions by individual or corporate
plaintiffs and defendants 1990–1996 (per 100,000)
Source: Department of Studies and Planning of the Ministry of Justice.

powerful corporations. Repeat players resort less to the courts for disputes involving the internal affairs of corporations (conflicts between partners) or for disputes with suppliers, either subcontracted or usual clients. In these cases of non-routine conflict, special resources need to be made available, and the probability of winning the case is smaller. Hence, corporations prefer a negotiated solution.

This hypothesis was validated through case studies undertaken in the two main Portuguese civil courts (Lisbon and Oporto). We have observed that a large number of civil actions during any given year, almost exclusively debt claims, involve a small number of corporations. While some corporations bring only two actions to court every year, there are others that bring as many as 22,000 (as was the case in 1996 with each of the two cellular phone companies operating in the Portuguese market). We also noticed that insurance companies, banks and consumer credit companies, and the public administration are among the principal plaintiffs.

Insurance companies are frequent plaintiffs because of debt claims for unpaid insurance premiums. These debts mainly concern compulsory automobile insurance and employment-related accident insurance. In the case of banks and other consumer credit companies, the number of debt actions is a result of the increasing indebtedness of consumers, largely through the use of credit cards.

In most cases, the value of these lawsuits is not great. Fig. 13.6 represents the relative importance of debt claims in the total of all declaratory actions, isolating the debt actions with a value equal to or less than PTE 250,000.[10] We observe that these debts represent 38.5 per cent of the declaratory actions disposed of in all of the courts, and 56.9 per cent of the actions disposed of in Lisbon. They are low-intensity procedures that do not require the mobilization of many court resources, usually being resolved by default and often without the defendant having hired a lawyer.

2.6. Termination of declaratory actions

In 1996, only 16.7 per cent of declaratory actions ended in trial. Of those which were resolved before trial, 1.2 per cent ended in preliminary dismissal, 3.9 per cent in waiver, 8.1 per cent in settlement (*transaction*), 7.2 per cent in impossibility or supervening uselessness of the suit, 42.7 per cent in judgment against the defendant, 1.9 per cent in judgment for the defendant, and 18.3 per cent in some other form of termination (Table 13.1).

What stands out from these figures is the limited number of trials, and the high percentage of cases (debt claims) in which there is no defence from the defendant, as a result of which judgment is given by default against the defendant for the whole of the plaintiff's demand. This might be called 'low-intensity' litigation, dominated by easily resolvable cases that consume little time in terms of hearing of evidence, selection, and interpretation of the applicable law and enforcement of judgments.

Besides the actions which are not replied to, there are those in which the court merely has a ratifying function, as in the case of divorce by mutual consent. The reduced number of trials is also influenced by the fact that many of the main high-intensity types of litigation (tort claims; evictions; property rights disputes) end by negotiated settlement.

2.7. Duration of declaratory actions

The duration of declaratory actions refers only to the time spent in the court of first instance, and does not include either the duration of the appeal, where there is one, or the duration of any execution process which may be necessary.

---

[10] £833 or $US1,388.

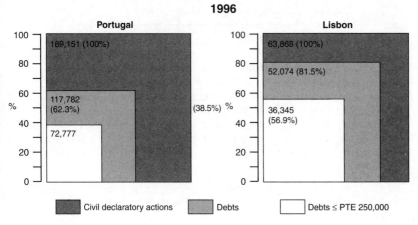

Fig. 13.6. Relative importance of debt claims according to their value

Table 13.1. *Termination of declaratory actions*

1996	Units	%
Before trial		
Preliminary order dismissal	2,183	1.2
Waiver	7,292	3.9
Settlement	15,286	8.1
Impossibility or supervening uselessness	13,642	7.2
Judgment against the defendant	80,595	42.7
Judgment for the defendant	3,631	1.9
Other form of termination[a]	34,588	18.3
In trial		
Judgment against the defendant for the full claim	21,031	11.1
Judgment against the defendant for part of the claim	4,766	2.5
Judgment for the defendant	5,823	3.1
Total	188,837	

[a] Includes divorce by mutual consent.

Source: Department of Studies and Planning of the Ministry of Justice.

Table 13.2 shows the distribution of declaratory actions disposed of in 1990 and 1996 according to their duration. Table 13.3 shows the duration of the main declaratory actions, by type of action. In fact, most civil actions are for debt collection, and these actions are solved relatively quickly, since the evidence is straightforward and they are seldom defended. This situation makes the average duration of declaratory actions shorter, concealing the fact that a high number of the remaining actions take much longer than the debt actions.

Table 13.2. *Duration of declaratory actions*

Duration (years)	1990		1996	
	Units	%	Units	%
0–1	58,555	62.3	124,540	65.8
1–2	17,805	19.0	42,592	22.5
2–3	6,967	7.4	14,533	7.7
3–5	5,891	6.3	5,710	3.0
> 5	4,731	5.0	1,977	1.0
Total	93,949		189,352	

Source: Department of Studies and Planning of the Ministry of Justice.

Table 13.3. *Duration of the main declaratory actions*

Type of action	1990		1996	
	Units	Avge. duration (days)	Units	Avge. duration (days)
Torts	4,994	841.65	7,524	595.31
Property rights	5,915	853.09	7,090	613.15
Divorces	11,110	465.62	14,597	350.00
Evictions	6,800	693.38	7,604	500.83
Debts	57,027	396.64	117,782	326.48
Total	85,846		154,597	

Source: Department of Studies and Planning of the Ministry of Justice.

In 1990, 58,555 civil actions lasting up to one year were registered. This figure rose to 124,540 in 1996. Over this period, there was a decrease in procedural delay, related to a reduction in the percentage of more protracted actions; that is, actions that take over three years to be decided in the first instance. For example, the number of actions lasting more than five years dropped by more than half over this period. This decrease reflects enhanced efficiency within the legal system.

Table 13.3 shows the average duration of actions, by type. We can see that there is a huge difference between the average duration of actions for debt collection and divorce on the one hand, and the average for the remaining actions on the other. This is explicable insofar as the latter demand a greater effort from the courts regarding the hearing of evidence and handing down of decisions. It can be observed that the progress seen in terms of shortening the duration of actions between 1990 and 1996 was reflected mainly in the slower actions, which means real progress in the efficiency of the judicial system.

2.8. Duration of appeals

In the court of second instance, 6,437 civil appeals were disposed of in 1990. This number rose to 10,523 in 1996. In the Supreme Court of Justice, 1,266 appeals were concluded in 1990, and 2,082 in 1996. The number of appeals is thus keeping pace with the growth in litigation recorded at first instance, although its variation is less significant. This is due to the fact that many of the new actions in first instance are debt collections of small value, without the possibility of appeal.

In 1996, the majority of appeals took between three months and one year to be decided in the court of second instance. The same situation applied in the Supreme Court of Justice (Table 13.4).

3. MAIN PROBLEMS OF CIVIL JUSTICE

3.1. Causes of delay

The inability of the Portugese state to create a judicial system capable of responding, in reasonable time, to the demand for legal protection has aggravated general dissatisfaction with the functioning and efficiency of judicial institutions. This poor performance shakes the credibility of the judicial system as a means for solving conflicts. The public, and those who operate the judicial system, are all concerned about delay. The issue of 'the delay of justice' directly affects the exercise and guarantee of rights.

In Portugal, despite improved court performance as regards duration of civil declaratory actions, the proportion of actions taking over three years to be resolved is still quite significant. This influences citizens' perceptions of the slowness of justice.[11]

In our research on case duration, we studied only the judicial time taken in respect of actions. However, in civil matters, the duration of litigation is not exhausted in the period of time between initiating the action in court and its transit in *rem judicatum*. Attention should also be paid to the duration of pre-judicial and post-judicial stages, including such questions as choice of time to bring an action, enforcement of judgment, and so on.

Several different factors delay the disposition of disputes in the courts, such as

---

[11] For an extended analysis of the delay of justice, see *Relatório do Observatório Permanente da Justiça Portuguesa*, ii.

Table 13.4. *Duration of appeals (1996)*

Duration	Second instance	Supreme Court of Justice
Up to 3 months	985	333
3 to 6 months	2,503	792
6 to 12 months	4,576	763
1 to 2 years	1,977	123
2 to 5 years	465	60
Over 5 years	17	11
Total	10,523	2,082

Source: Department of Studies and Planning of the Ministry of Justice.

the law itself, the behaviour of judicial actors, and the working conditions of the courts. The necessary duration, which means 'the reasonable time' needed for the protection and exercise of procedural rights, should correspond to the legal duration of the proceedings. Nevertheless, according to our research, excessive or unnecessary formalism in the law itself is responsible for delay in many types of action.

The judicial actors (including judges, lawyers, litigants, police, experts, and clerks) may also contribute to excessive case duration. Such delay may be unintentional or intentional. The former derives from involuntary negligent acts on the part of the judicial actors. The latter is caused by one of the litigants, or someone on their behalf, in pursuing their interests. The boundary between the unintentional and the intentional is hard to discern in a system with vast organizational defects.

Delay may also be endogenous to the system. It may result from the overloading of the system and adherence to routines developed over the years, as well as from the organization of the courts. Our analysis showed the main causes of endogenous slowness to be the following:

(*a*) poor working conditions (facilities and equipment);
(*b*) irrational distribution of court clerks;
(*c*) court clerks' lack of training and negligence;
(*d*) judges' lack of training and negligence;
(*e*) volume of work;
(*f*) the need to resort to outside experts for reports and tests to be brought as evidence in court (e.g. DNA tests in paternity suits);
(*g*) compliance with precatory and rogatory letters (i.e. requirements to render services to another court).

Our study has enabled us to state that the main characteristics of the aforementioned causes of delay are as follows.

(*a*) The more varied, intense, and cumulative the causes, the worse the delay. Consequently, measures to combat this delay will only be effective if they are taken in a co-ordinated manner by the various entities involved, and if they are directed towards all relevant causes of delay. Only in this way will it be possible to avoid the effect of transferring delay from one cause to another. One cause may inadvertently be aggravated by a measure taken in isolation to diminish another cause. For instance, some courts have benefited from the appointment of temporary or auxiliary judges and public prosecutors, in addition to established posts, because they have a backlog of cases awaiting attention. However, reinforcing the number of court clerks on the staff did not, as a rule, follow these measures. Consequently, there has been a transfer of delay from one cause to another. Procedures which were previously halted because of a lack of judges became paralysed by a lack of clerks.

The different causes of delay thus act in a feedback system, one over the other. Delay leads to the accumulation of a backlog of cases, which exacerbates staff inadequacy and poor working conditions, which in turn increase the delay and provides a justification for the delay itself. For example, lack of space is not a direct and necessary cause of delays, but there is a heightening effect on the irrational distribution of human resources when there is no space to accommodate staff. This aggravates the accumulation and duration of actions, leading to judges and clerks losing motivation to work and, at the same time, not feeling responsible for delays in judicial procedures.

(*b*) The irrationality in the distribution of clerks is found more frequently in those courts with poorer working conditions. When this irrationality is in itself a 'strong cause' of delay, the duration of actions and the volume of work in each division immediately increase. Added to all of this, poor working conditions cause a vast turnover of clerks, who request to be transferred to another court as soon as they have an opportunity. In fact, the most common irrationality factors are the unfilled vacancies, the insufficient number of staff recruited, and the great mobility of clerks.

(*c*) The lack of training or negligence of judges and court clerks is found in any type of court. This, by itself, has a strong impact on the increase in delays. This cause of delay is independent of the volume of work in the courts. It is essentially characterized by a judge or clerk not working on a case for months or years, and occurs frequently with the more complex procedures. These situations have often been registered in the reports of the periodical inspections, but, as far as we know, no serious consequence has resulted to the career of the negligent judges or clerks.

(*d*) The irrationality in the distribution of judges and public prosecutors is one of the better controlled causes of delay, but, when it does occur, the duration of actions increases immediately. Today it is still common for courts to go without judges for long periods of time, when the usual office-holders are on commission, prolonged leave of absence, or maternity leave, and are not replaced by other judges during that period. Backlogs accumulate during the resulting delays, and take years to overcome.

3.2. Costs of litigation

There are two types of legal costs that may be incurred by the parties: direct private spending on a lawsuit, including fees paid to lawyers and other expenses (such as producing and copying documents, travel expenses, telephone calls, etc.); and the payment of court fees. Taking into account only the court fees, civil justice in Portugal cannot be considered expensive. But, if we take into account all the litigation costs, resort to the courts is very expensive indeed.

Naturally, not all disputes are handled judicially. A dispute may never come to court. The 'non-judicialization' of a case may result from the mediation of lawyers leading to an out-of-court settlement, or from the plaintiff giving up his or her claim.

3.2.1. Lawyers' fees

Lawyers' fees vary according to the stage reached by the dispute and whether the case is settled extra-judicially or through the court. There are no absolute rules establishing either the methods of calculation or the level of lawyers' fees. The normative statute that introduced some regulation on the issue is the *Estatuto da Ordem dos Advogados*[12] (Lawyers' Association Act) approved by Decree-Law no. 84/84 of 16 March. However, the regulation on this subject is very vague. It is limited to the definition of the basic principles that lawyers should comply with when setting their fees.

Thus, according to this Act, lawyers should act with moderation when setting their fees, taking into consideration the time spent, difficulty of the matter, importance of the service rendered, income of the client, practices of the county, and outcome of the case. The Act also allows the prior settlement of fees, but prohibits 'success' or 'contingency' fees based on the result of the lawsuit or deal. Besides defining the framework for setting fees, there are schedules indicating the minimum fees in each county. These schedules are fixed at a meeting by the lawyers of each county, and are therefore different in the different counties. Their objective is, above all, to avoid competition at the lowest price between lawyers.

These schedules consist of a list of standard services rendered by lawyers and the related minimum fees. As a rule, they are divided into the following parts: general services; judicial actions up to the first instance; appeals; administrative law; judicial and extra-judicial collections; inventories; and extra-judicial partition. Under the heading of general services, the list includes: oral and written consultation; site inspection; draft contracts; judicial notice; petitions; and

---

[12] *The Ordem dos Advogados* is a statutory public body.

assistance with notarization. Under the heading of judicial procedures, a distinction is drawn between criminal and civil. In criminal matters, fees vary according to the procedure and whether trial is by single-judge, collective, or jury court. In civil matters, fees vary according to the type of procedure (very summary, summary, or ordinary). Fees for debt recovery and inventories vary in accordance with the amount to be collected or the value of the inheritance. For instance:

Where the claim is for PTE 150,000 the current fees are PTE 52,500.[13]
Where the claim is for PTE 1,500,000 the current fees are PTE 225,000.[14]
Where the claim is for PTE 3,000,000 the current fees are PTE 400,000.[15]
Where the claim is for PTE 30,000,000 the current fees are PTE 3,750,000.[16]
Where the claim is for PTE 150,000,000 the current fees are PTE 18,100,000.[17]

There is a specific fee for divorce cases. Where the divorce is by mutual consent, the fee is PTE 130,000[18] for both spouses. Where the divorce is litigious and defended, the current fee is PTE 200,000.[19] These fees do not include the fees for the division of marital assets.

The total fees for appeals are different according to whether the appeal is taken to the second instance court (*tribunal da relação*), the Supreme Court of Justice, or the Constitutional Court.[20]

As there are no rigid criteria for the setting of fees, each firm will take several parameters into consideration. As a rule, the matter in question, its complexity and value, and the time spent on it are of particular importance. But, according to the Ethical Code of the *Ordem dos Advogados*, the fees should never exceed the value of the claim. There may be some large firms which establish an hourly fee for oral consultation. However, this is not usually the rule at national level. Contracts of retainer, providing for advice in return for fixed periodic payments, are still very common, and are normally used by companies. Retainer payments are made monthly, and generally relate to providing legal assistance and accompanying judicial actions up to a certain amount.

The amount of the current lawyers' fees is the most relevant cost paid by the litigants. For individuals (sporadic litigants), fees have a deterrent effect on

---

[13] Thus, a claim for about £500 costs roughly £175 (or, for $US833.33, costs $US291.66).
[14] Thus, a claim for about £5,000 costs roughly £750 (or, for $US8,333, costs $US1,250).
[15] Thus, a claim for about £10,000 costs roughly £1,333.33 (or, for $US16,666.66, costs $US2,222.22).
[16] Thus, a claim for about £100,000 costs roughly £12,500 (or, for $US166,666.66, costs $US20,833).
[17] Thus a claim for about £500,000 costs roughly £60,333.33 (or, for $US833,333.33, costs $US100,555.55). [18] Roughly £433.33 or $US722.22.
[19] Roughly £666.66 or $US1,111.11. We took as reference the schedule of minimum fees of Aveiro county; Aveiro is a medium-sized city in the centre of Portugal.
[20] As a rule, the fees for appeal are 25 per cent of the fees paid at the first instance. The lawyers' fees do not include the expenses related to transport, lodging, and so on.

access to the court. Only very large claims are brought to court. Naturally, the litigant must also have enough money to pay the lawyer.

3.2.2. Court costs

The amount and the form of payment of legal charges, taxes, fines, and costs are settled in the Code of Court Costs.[21] For example, the legal tax to be paid for a debt claim at first instance in the amount of PTE 1,000,000 is PTE 46,000.[22] The basic principle for paying legal costs is that costs must be borne by the losing party. Consequently, responsibility for costs results from a judgment against the party with transit *in rem judicatum* or from a final unfavourable decision. In the case of a negotiated settlement, or when liability is shared, the costs and charges are borne *pro rata* by the parties to the extent to which each party was defeated in the action.

Payment of the legal tax is made gradually, according to the stage of the action, and is naturally made by both parties according to the extent of their intervention in the proceedings. Appeals to a superior court carry a specific legal tax. At the end, legal taxes paid are refunded to a party who is held not to be liable. When a party obtains part judgment, reimbursement is calculated on the amount exceeding the liability. The winning party, in due proportion, also has the right to receive an amount from the losing party by way of payment of lawyers' fees. However, this amount is a very insignificant one. For instance, where the claim is for PTE 3,000,000, the winning party would receive from the losing party between PTE 18,000 and PTE 36,000. As we have mentioned before, the winning party must pay to his or her lawyer the minimum fee of PTE 400,000.[23] This means that even the winning party must pay almost all of the fees owing to his or her lawyer.

3.3. Access to law and courts

The right of access to legal information and protection is constitutionally enshrined in Portugal. The state establishes a system of access to the law and to the courts, the aim of which is to encourage all citizens to get to know, claim, or defend their rights, regardless of their economic, social, or cultural situation. Access to the law and to the courts is the joint responsibility of the state and the Lawyers' Association through an agreement. Access to the law and to the courts takes on three different forms: legal information; legal consultation; and legal aid.

---

[21] See Salvador da Costa, *Código das custas judiciais anotado* (Coimbra: Almedina, 1997).

[22] £153 or $US256 tax on a claim for £3,333 or $US5,555 (4.6 per cent at this level). The total value of the court costs paid in the first instance and courts of appeals, including all the types of procedures and not only the civil ones, was PTE 18,726,895,000 in 1996 (£62,422,983 or $US104,038,305). The average value per procedure was PTE 33,200 (£110 or $US184). The average value per appeal was PTE 62,594 (£209 or $US348).

[23] Between £60 and £120, or $US100 to $US200, are reimbursed on a claim of roughly £10,000 ($US16,666) for which the minimum fee is £1,333 or $US2,222.

Legal aid may comprise a total or partial discharge from the payment of court fees or their postponement, and from the payment of the lawyers' fees. The system of legal aid is applied in all courts, whatever the form of procedure, and is independent of the position that the litigant holds in the procedure (whether plaintiff or defendant). It may also be requested at any stage of the procedure and is maintained for the purposes of appeal, regardless of the decision in the case. Competence to grant legal aid belongs to the judge in the action for which it is requested. When a lawyer is needed, the judge requests a nomination from the District Board of the Lawyers' Association. The lawyers are paid by the state, in accordance with a legally established schedule, taking into consideration the form of action in which they intervene. As a rule, lawyers appointed are either trainees or lawyers embarking on their careers. Consequently, legal aid does not work very well.

4. REFORMS IN THE CIVIL JURISDICTION

Recent civil justice reforms in Portugal have been of three types:

(*a*) 'de-judicialization';
(*b*) reform of civil procedure; and
(*c*) reform of the judicial system.

(*a*) 'De-judicialization' is the removal of certain disputes from compulsory reference to the courts. It was introduced in the area of family and inheritance litigation.

In 1995, a new law was introduced allowing divorces by mutual consent to be transferred to and decided by an administrative jurisdiction, the Civil Register Office. However, the need for judicial ratification of the regulation of children's custody has limited the effects of this reform. For example, in 1996 only 1,978 divorces by mutual consent were registered in the Civil Register. In the same year, 10,194 mutual consent divorce actions were disposed of in the courts.

The conditions for compulsory inventory of deceased estates were also altered, in the event of one of the heirs being a minor or lacking legal capacity. The inventory is obligatory only when the heirs and the public prosecutor do not reach an agreement regarding the division of property. This reform had an enormous impact, removing nearly all of the formerly compulsory inventories from the courts.

(*b*) The reform of civil procedure began in 1983 with the introduction of measures aimed at simplifying procedures, such as the elimination of some articulated pleadings, simplification of remedies, and provision for notifying litigants by registered letter instead of compulsory notification by the court clerks.

In 1997, the new Code of Civil Procedure came into effect, considerably

altering the relationship between litigants and the courts through the establishment of the co-operation principle.[24] Judges now have the duty to compensate
for the omissions of the litigants, in furtherance of the principle of the discovery
of the material truth. The judges protested against this reform because it meant a
substantial increase in their work and responsibility in conducting civil actions.

To simplify debt recovery, an injunction procedure was created in 1993. This
procedure is designed to allow summary enforcement of smaller debt claims. It
applies wherever a claim is made to enforce a pecuniary obligation arising from
a contract the value of which does not exceed half of the monetary jurisdiction
of the court of first instance (half of PTE 500,000, which is PTE 250,000).[25]
The injunction procedure enables an invoice not signed by the debtor to
become an executable instrument, if it is not contested. The injunction replaces
the need for a full declaratory action to be brought and won before execution
proceedings can commence. The aim of the reform was to introduce an alternative way of recovering debt, one complying with the principles of celerity,
simplification, and modernization which inspired the new civil procedure.

However, this reform has not met with great success. Its failure was partly the
result of bureaucratic errors in its conception. To begin with, the injunction
procedure was more difficult to manage and more expensive than the declaratory action.

The injunction was more difficult to manage because the plaintiff needs to
buy and fix a 'stamp' to each demand for an injunction. In the case of the
declaratory action, he or she can pay the legal taxes for a set of actions with only
one cheque. The injunction is also more expensive. The 'stamp' has a fixed
value (PTE 5,000) for claims up to PTE 100,000, and another fixed value (PTE
7,500) for claims higher than PTE 100,000.[26] The system of legal taxes is
different for declaratory actions and more variable. Normally, for the same
value of the claim, the legal tax is lower than the cost of the injunction stamp.[27]
Considering that the potential users of this procedure are frequent plaintiffs,
who bring to court as many as 200 cases per week, any small additional
complication is greatly enlarged. Our analysis of several law firms confirms
this effect. The gains achieved in terms of reducing the duration of actions were
not enough to justify the greater expense and difficulty of the new system, since
the declaratory actions for debt are usually relatively quick.

---

[24] See J. Pereira Batista, *Reforma do processo civil: principios fundamentais* (Lisbon: Lex, 1997); António
Santos Geraldes, *Temas da reforma do processo civil* (Coimbra: Almedina, 1997).
[25] The jurisdictional limit of the first instance court is roughly equivalent to £1,666 or $US2,777,
leaving the injunction procedure restricted to cases involving about £830 ($US1,350) or less.
[26] About £16.66, or $US27.77, for claims up to £333.33, or $US555.55; £25 or $US41.66 for
higher claims.
[27] An insurance company simulated the total court costs it would need to pay for a set of debt
claims whether it chose injunctions or declaratory actions. If it chose injunctions, it would pay PTE
2,020,000 (£6,733.33 or $US11,222.22). If it chose declaratory actions, it would pay PTE 902,000
(£3,006.66 or $US5,011.11).

The reduced impact of the injunction is demonstrated in the number of injunction applications made in 1995 and 1996. In 1995, 2,839 applications were made, a figure that dropped to 2,475 in 1996. In that year, around 70,000 declaratory actions for debt recovery were disposed of. According to our research, the majority of these actions could have been replaced by the injunction procedure if the plaintiffs had considered it more functional. Because of this, further reform of the injunction procedure is in progress.

(*c*) Over the past ten years the judicial system has undergone successive changes and adjustments to respond to the increase in the demand for court services. The main reforms are:

- Establishment of new courts.
- Establishment of courts with jurisdiction over a judicial circuit, covering the area of several counties, for more important or more serious suits. Lawyers and judges protested against the establishment of these courts, because it forced them to move frequently from their county to the seat of the judicial circuit. In 1991, the law was partly changed, enabling the panel of judges to move to smaller counties.
- Specialization of the courts (civil, criminal, small-claims) in the main counties. Considering the importance of debt recovery actions in civil litigation, special reference should be made to the establishment of the small claims courts. These were introduced immediately after the difficulty of solving, through the injunction procedure, the problem of the 'colonization' of the civil court by small debt claims was realized. Small claims courts have the power to decide very summary procedures; that is, cases having a value of equal to or less than PTE 250,000.[28] In 1996, 73,901 claims (declaratory and execution proceedings) entered the small claims civil court of Lisbon. This figure nearly doubled in 1997 (122,191 claims). The actions disposed of in these courts were practically confined to debt collection. Small claims courts have rapidly become overwhelmed by disputes between institutional creditors and consumers. Since consumer indebtedness tends to increase, it is foreseeable that small claims courts will soon reach breaking point.
- One of the last reforms has been the increase in the numbers of court staff, and the computerization of judicial services.

5. ALTERNATIVE MODES OF DISPUTE RESOLUTION

Alternative modes of dispute resolution are constantly referred to in speeches about the reform of the judicial system. However, in Portugal moves towards more alternative dispute resolution have been of little effect so far.

[28] Roughly £830 or $US1,350.

Family mediation took its first steps only in 1998, with the creation of two offices currently regulated by the Ministry of Justice.

Portuguese law allows the resolution of civil and commercial disputes by institutional or *ad hoc* arbitration, through arbitration conventions, and by arbitrators chosen by the parties. Over the last few years, the Ministry of Justice has certified sixteen institutional arbitration centres. Nevertheless, according to a survey that we conducted, only one of these centres has permanent and continuous activity. Non-institutional arbitration, according to our interviews with lawyers, is almost exclusively restricted to the commercial area, and to litigation over amounts in excess of PTE 100,000,000.[29] Arbitration centres for the resolution of consumer litigation—consumer disputes arbitration centres— were created in the main cities. These centres have been established by an agreement between the town hall, consumers' association, and trade associa- tion, with the support of the Ministry of Justice. They are able to resolve disputes of small and medium value up to PTE 500,000,[30] which corresponds to the first instance jurisdiction.

Procedure in the arbitration centres is relatively simple.

Following the consumers' complaints, there is a conciliation procedure. Parties are summoned to the conciliation procedure, by notice from the centre. The supplier of goods or services may contest either in writing or orally. Both parties may submit any evidence they wish. Only if the conciliation fails, and if both of the parties express the wish to have the dispute undergo an arbitration procedure, will the dispute be trans- ferred to the arbitration court. The arbitration court will resolve the dispute in compliance with the applicable law or by resorting to equity.[31]

The shopkeeper's agreement is unnecessary if he or she is a member of the centre, as this means that the shopkeeper has recognized the competence of the arbitration court to resolve all consumer disputes in which he or she might become involved.[32] In these arbitration centres, the arbitrators are normally judges. However, this is not a condition required by law. Such centres have been largely successful.[33] Nevertheless, they are not a real alternative to the courts. They seem to be providing a new way of resolving many minor disputes that were simply left unresolved in the past, and that constituted what we have termed the large zone of 'self-repressed litigation'. For this reason, they can be regarded more as a way of enforcing the right of access to the law than as a measure for reducing the number of actions coming to court.

---

[29] Roughly £333,330 or $US555,550.   [30] Roughly £1,666 or $US2,777.

[31] José Gil Roque, *Consumer Access to Justice* (Lisbon: Instituto do Consumidor, 1992), 119.

[32] In 1997, at least 550 shopkeepers joined the most important arbitration centre in Lisbon, the Lisbon Consumer Disputes Arbitration Centre.

[33] In 1997, the Lisbon Consumer Disputes Arbitration Centre resolved 467 disputes by concilia- tion and 242 by arbitration.

Appendix 13.1
Evolution of the Portuguese population

Years	Population
1942	7,830,026
1970	9,013,700
1971	8,967,200
1972	8,973,700
1973	8,978,200
1974	9,218,400
1975	9,633,100
1976	9,698,800
1977	9,773,000
1978	9,829,800
1979	9,883,200
1980	9,819,000
1981	9,852,000
1982	9,878,400
1983	9,894,300
1984	9,908,000
1985	9,909,100
1986	9,908,100
1987	9,897,500
1988	9,888,600
1989	9,878,200
1990	9,867,900
1991	9,855,400
1992	9,859,600
1993	9,887,560
1994	9,912,140
1995	9,920,760
1996	9,934,110

Source: Department of Studies and Planning of the
Ministry of Justice.

Appendix 13.2

Evolution of the number of judges, public prosecutors, court clerks, and lawyers 1970–1996

	Judges	Public prosecutors	Court clerks	Lawyers
1970	422	246	2,823	2,573
1971	422	246	2,768	2,677
1972	429	248	2,679	2,780
1973	443	249	2,774	2,870
1974	441	292	2,695	2,960
1975	482	327	2,983	2,965
1976	434	293	3,206	2,969
1977	555	359	3,441	3,394
1978	578	354	3,580	3,818
1979	578	423	4,156	4,476
1980	612	375	4,647	5,134
1981	688	439	4,441	4,550
1982	758	392	4,891	4,678
1983	840	519	5,037	5,234
1984	899	558	5,295	5,818
1985	875	597	5,360	6,287
1986	876	593	5,444	6,729
1987	907	580	5,429	7,376
1988	987	623	6,044	6,716
1989	1,004	708	5,994	8,278
1990	1,018	762	6,031	11,319
1991	1,028	793	6,161	9,526
1992	1,032	817	6,161	9,804
1993	1,059	850	6,194	12,022
1994	1,095	922	6,846	12,581
1995	1,165	942	6,900	14,836
1996	1,231	939	7,185	13,809

Source: Department of Studies and Planning of the Ministry of Justice.

Appendix 13.3

Evolution of civil procedures pending, entered, and disposed of 1970–1996 (per 100,000 inhabitants)

	Pending 1 January	Entered	Disposed of
1970	486.1	890.7	886.7
1971	492.6	949.9	941.7
1972	500.5	995.9	969.6
1973	526.6	996.3	986.6
1974	522.3	939.0	884.8
1975	551.6	988.9	864.4
1976	671.5	1,123.0	974.1
1977	814.2	1,185.5	1,082.1
1978	912.3	1,443.9	1,136.6
1979	1,213.0	1,413.0	1,218.7
1980	1,416.6	1,392.9	1,193.1
1981	1,611.0	1,393.5	1,179.8
1982	1,819.8	1,580.2	1,392.5
1983	2,029.0	1,926.5	1,556.0
1984	2,371.8	2,303.5	1,681.1
1985	2,989.4	2,192.5	1,852.5
1986	3,306.8	1,986.5	2,031.7
1987	3,237.5	2,030.0	1,985.7
1988	3,311.8	1,920.6	2,165.3
1989	3,070.7	2,040.4	2,199.3
1990	2,906.6	2,060.5	2,060.4
1991	2,642.8	2,292.7	2,205.9
1992	2,563.3	2,699.1	2,410.7
1993	2,828.1	3,157.9	2,563.0
1994	3,337.2	4,086.2	3,360.2
1995	4,056.8	3,719.1	2,906.4
1996	4,863.4	4,148.1	3,188.3

Source: Department of Studies and Planning of the Ministry of Justice.

Appendix 13.4

Evolution of civil procedures by type of action 1990–1996 (per 100,000 inhabitants)

	Declaratory actions	Executions	Inventories	Child custody	Bankruptcy
1990	952.1	849.1	109.3	90.3	1.8
1991	1,054.8	935.6	99.6	94.6	2.1
1992	1,312.2	816.5	107.3	112.2	3.4
1993	1,408.0	861.8	95.4	117.6	3.2
1994	1,549.1	1,142.5	96.4	156.3	4.3
1995	1,728.5	966.6	108.4	150.1	5.8
1996	1,911.8	1,056.3	77.7	186.5	6.9

Source: Department of Studies and Planning of the Ministry of Justice.

Appendix 13.5

Evolution of the principal declaratory actions disposed of 1942–1996

	1942		1996	
	Value	%	Value	%
Property rights	1,219	8	7,003	4
Debts	5,788	38	117,656	67
Evictions	3,432	23	7,604	4
Divorce	847	6	14,723	8
Torts	168	1	7,524	4
Other	3,587	24	20,048	11
Total	15,041		174,558	

Source: Department of Studies and Planning of the Ministry of Justice.

Appendix 13.6

Distribution of declaratory civil actions by individual or corporate plaintiffs and defendants 1990–1996 (per 100,000 inhabitants)

	1990		1991		1992		1993		1994		1995		1996	
	Value	%	Value	%	Value	%	Value	%	Value	%	Value	%	Value	%
Plaintiffs														
Corporation	534.18	51.95	606.34	52.92	771.09	54.31	878.70	57.98	941.13	56.41	1,061.74	58.17	1,209.22	60.63
Individual	493.99	48.05	539.51	47.08	648.77	45.69	636.75	42.02	727.29	43.59	763.62	41.83	785.36	39.37
TOTAL	1,028.16		1,145.85		1,419.85		1,515.45		1,668.42		1,825.36		1,994.58	
Defendants														
Corporation	221.37	21.54	257.77	22.52	347.56	24.51	407.75	27.01	496.12	29.88	583.71	32.15	633.23	31.87
Individual	806.31	78.46	887.03	77.48	1,070.33	75.49	1,101.71	72.99	1,164.49	70.12	1,231.85	67.85	1,353.94	68.13
TOTAL	1,027.69		1,144.79		1,417.89		1,509.46		1,660.61		1,815.56		1,987.17	

Source: Department of Studies and Planning of the Ministry of Justice.

14

Civil Justice:
Access, Cost, and Expedition.
The Netherlands

Erhard Blankenburg

1.1. The hierarchy of the courts

1.1.1. Courts of general jurisdiction

The Dutch court system is made up of four levels of courts of general jurisdiction: local; district; and regional courts; surmounted by the High Court for final appeals. Each level has its own separate civil and criminal sections.

Nationally, there are:

Sixty-two local courts (*kanton-gerecht*). Local courts handle petty crime and small claims. They also have jurisdiction in all tenancy matters, and family cases. In 1994, there were 139 judges in local courts. In 1999, local courts will be administratively integrated with the district courts. However, more than 50 local court offices will remain open, complete with judges and administrative staff, for the hearing of cases.

Nineteen district courts (*rechtbank*). These courts have original jurisdiction in those cases where more serious criminal charges or larger sums are at stake (presently Dfl. 5,000 or more). They also hear appeals from local court decisions involving a sum of at least Dfl. 2,500. Figures for 1994 showed about 850 judges in the district courts.

Five regional courts (*Hof van Justitie or Gerechtshof*). The regional courts hear appeals from the district courts. They also have original jurisdiction in fiscal matters, and certain other specified matters, regarded as of some symbolic importance, such as high treason, and matters involving threats to the security of the state. In 1994, the total regional court bench consisted of 224 judges.

The High Court (*Hoge Raad*). The High Court is the final court of appeal of general jurisdiction. The High Court is able to review cases only on their legal merits (cassation). It is divided into three divisions—civil, penal, and fiscal. Of its three chambers, the one dealing with fiscal matters is the biggest, having 11 members, as compared to 10 in the penal, and 9 in the civil chambers.

1.1.2. Courts of special jurisdiction

In a radical move (for a European jurisdiction, at least) the previously separate administrative courts were recently integrated into the district courts system. This involved doing away with the special courts for social security matters in 1992, and ending the traditional jurisdiction of the Council of State in matters involving judicial review of public administration in 1994. However, the highest level of appeal in each system of administrative courts does remain in existence, in the form of the Council of State for administrative matters, and the Central Social Security Appeal Council (*Centrale Raad van Beroep*) for social security appeals.

The number of judges has been rising recently, but unfortunately the Ministry of Justice would not provide us with exact data. Our estimate is that, in 1994, about 1,250 judges were employed (counting full-time judges and the time equivalent of part-timers). Relative to the population (15.5 million) this amounts to 8 judges per 100,000 of the population. Add to this about the same number of substitute judges who serve between a few times per year up to one day a week. Their recruitment from the advocacy, the universities, and other legal occupations is highly controversial as it casts doubt on the objectivity and independence of the bench.

The amalgamation of administrative chambers into the district court system brings to an end the very hesitant introduction of judicial review into the Dutch system. Social security review dates back to 1955, when special courts were established with their own court of appeal (*raden van beroep* with appeals to the *centrale raad van beroep*). It was not until 1974 that judicial review of other branches of public administration was introduced. The first system adopted was simply to entrust the next higher echelon within each provincial or municipal administration with the initial hearing of complaints; and to allow appeals from those decisions to a section of the Council of State (the *afdeling rechtsspraak* of the *raad van staate*). Acting as a court of justice, the Council of State was thus the court of both first and last instance for administrative matters.

The Council's traditional role is as an advisory body in the legislative process. There is, however, some tradition of entrusting the Council with judicial functions. As early as 1861, a section of the Council was formed to deal in a quasi-judicial manner with complaints to the Crown (*kroonberoep*). In 1985, however, the European Court of Human Rights in Strasbourg found that the purely advisory function of the *kroonberoep* did not satisfy the criteria for recognition of the *kroonberoep* as a judicial court.[1] The amalgamation of the Dutch administrative jurisdiction into the district court system in the early 1990s was achieved by the establishment of administrative chambers in each District Court. This might be seen as partly driven by a need to come into line with European developments. More directly, however, it is a natural consequence of rising

---

[1] *Benthem v. Staat der Nederlanden* EHRM 23 Oct. 1985.

caseloads in administrative matters which the Council of State could no longer manage.

This zealous judicial reform can be seen as a catch-up process, resulting from the relatively late development in the Netherlands of specialization within the court system. In most neighbouring countries, a multitude of specialist courts and tribunals developed much earlier. In some cases, judicial specialization began as early as the nineteenth century. Perhaps its greatest growth was in the years between the world wars. The majority of European judicial systems saw the emergence at that time of specialist tribunals and courts for labour disputes, administrative complaints, and social security matters. By contrast, until 1974, Dutch public agencies considered themselves 'open' to public complaints, and granted direct access to citizens to hear their concerns on an informal basis. Even today, this traditional informality is preserved by the institution of a system of local, as well as national, Ombudsmen who deal with complaints not covered by the jurisdiction of the courts.

2. DUTCH COURTS AND CASELOAD ISSUES

By comparison with neighbouring countries, the Netherlands can be seen, so far at least, to have avoided much of the caseload burden associated with debt enforcement and notary cases. Dutch courts developed a short-cut procedure to reinforce the use of the courts as a forum for mediation. Recent changes in divorce proceedings, as well as the innovative use which presidents of the district courts make of the preliminary injunction/*kort geding* procedure, provide further prominent examples of the way in which the Dutch system has managed to avoid an overwhelming flood of litigation.

2.1. Civil procedural codes

The foundation for Dutch civil procedural law was laid by the Procedural Code of 1838 (*wetboek burgerlijke rechtsvordering*=RV) and the law on the organization of the judiciary of 1827 (*Wet op de rechterlijke organisatie*=RO). Of course, both have often been amended, and they have been complemented by later statutes, such as the laws on the advocacy (first passed in 1952) and on legal aid (first passed in 1958, and subjected to major amendment in 1994).

The core rules concern procedures before district courts (*rechtbanken*). Chambers at first instance consist of one judge, although, exceptionally, chambers with three judges are possible. Representation by a lawyer is mandatory for both parties. Emphasis is laid on holding public hearings, unless reasons of privacy (family matters etc.) require the exclusion of the public.

In comparison with trials in common law countries, some basic differences in judicial management of procedure have to be kept in mind. In theory, continental procedures are oral and judges are 'passive'; leaving the initiative to the parties. However, the practice is not as absolute as the theory suggests. Both orality and party control are limited. Judges lead the hearings on the basis of a file which contains all relevant documents submitted by the parties. This offers the presiding judge the possibility of acting in an inquisitive role, as well as of encouraging the parties to settle. The formal possibility of certifying the settlement in court serves as a major incentive. Both parties have the right to an appeal *de novo*. Appeal courts (*gerechtshoven*) consist of chambers of three judges. Appeals on legal matters from both first and second instance courts can be brought before the High Court in cassation.

Though the basic institutions of Dutch civil procedure basically coincide with those of the French codes, some remarkable differences can be observed in practice. This is especially true of the preliminary procedure before the president of the district court (*kort geding*—Art. 289RV, in French *référé*). Leading to final disposal of the case in most of these instances, *kort geding* procedures replace a considerable part of the caseload of full civil procedures in both local and district courts. (See the sociological evaluation below.)

Simplified procedures apply to civil cases in minor tenancy and labour law matters (Art. 38 RO, monetary jurisdiction soon to be raised to Dfl. 10,000[2]). Appeal is possible only in cases with a value of Dfl. 2,500 or more. Legal representation is not necessary. These simplified cases are handled by single judges in local courts. Except for the initial claim (*dagvaarding*), arguments and pleas can be brought forward orally. Judges usually present only short written reasons for their decisions, while being more explicit in explaining them carefully to the parties (if they are present). Even more informal are request procedures, which can be initiated by notice to the court clerks, whose powers are outlined in special laws. The main areas are post-divorce issues (child support), rent adjustment, and labour dismissal cases.

2.2. The *kort geding*

The development of the *kort geding* is a prominent example of informality within the Dutch system. Technically, the *kort geding* is the procedure for a preliminary injunction, but it has developed largely informally into a type of summary proceeding. The presidents of the district courts technically have the power to decide only urgent matters using this procedure. It is intended for cases where the interests of one party might be damaged during the long period of time for which a full proceeding must remain pending. However, it has come to be commonly used as a summary procedure to decide vital matters of substantive law.

To decide a *kort geding* rarely requires more than one oral hearing. The parties

---

[2] About £3,100, or $US5,260.

present their respective case and reply immediately. The proceedings are informal enough for the president of the court to indicate to the parties what their chances of success in a full action are likely to be. The non-adversarial character of the Dutch proceeding renders it highly unlikely that the lawyers would (mis-)use the free and frank exchanges of views in the *kort geding* to argue for the disqualification of the judge as biased. On the contrary, the oral hearing very often ends in a settlement achieved between the parties. On the average, cases in *kort geding* are terminated within six weeks from start to finish. Even though they remain free to do so, few parties initiate ordinary proceedings afterwards.

The freedom which presidents of the district courts enjoy to organize summary proceedings as they prefer is quite remarkable. As the *kort geding* gained in popularity with litigants, presidents of the crowded big city district courts began to delegate part of the caseload to vice-presidents. In any given case, a decision is often taken in chambers, immediately after the public hearing, in consultation with a law clerk, who often will ghost-write the decision.[3]

Such injunction proceedings also exist in the French code of civil procedure. In fact, the Dutch provision is a literal translation of the provisions of the French code. However, in France the preliminary injunction procedure has not developed into an alternative short form of proceeding the way it has in the Netherlands. This development came about by slow evolution as a result of the activity of a few 'judicial entrepreneurs'. Some of the presidents, particularly those in Amsterdam and The Hague, have used these procedures for exemplary, innovative case law. Although only judges at first instance, they took the chance to formulate innovative doctrine which is now published in legal journals and cited in the law books. In addition, they have immensely enjoyed taking the opportunity to shape the legal consciousness of the public by commenting on the reasons for their decisions in the mass media.

3. SPECIFIC SOCIAL INSTITUTIONS AND THE RELATED PROCEEDINGS

3.1. Debt collection

Debt collection accounts for the biggest part of the civil caseload in developed countries. In most European courts, a summary debt collection procedure of some sort or another has developed, and is widely used. Examples include *Mahnbescheid* in Austrian and German courts, and *injonction de payer* in France. Such procedures allow creditors to make out their claims, without presenting more evidence than a contract, and a statement that payment is overdue. As such procedures are quick, cheap, and painless for the plaintiff, they lead to a

---

[3] Freek Bruinsma, *Korte Gedingen* (Zwolle, 1995).

high number of court procedures being brought in which debtors do not contest the claim.

In the Netherlands such a summary procedure (*betalingsbevel*) existed until 1992, when it was abolished for lack of use. The bailiffs (*deurwaarders*) are the key agents in Dutch debt enforcement. They simply preferred not to use the existing summary procedure. Unlike their French or German counterparts, Dutch bailiffs can combine business as a private debt collector with the public function of summonsing a debtor to court and, ultimately, executing a legal judgment. Judicial proceedings are used only as a last resort. The mere threat of court action is often effective to allow negotiation of terms of payment directly with the debtor. Moreover, in full proceedings in the local courts, competent for monetary claims of up to Dfl. 5,000, there is no need to be represented by an attorney. It is no wonder that two-thirds of all claims at local level are decided by default of the defendant. Most of these claims are by institutional creditors, such as housing agencies, mail-order firms, and consumer credit institutions.[4] They are commenced as full proceedings in the normal way.

3.2. Divorce

As in most European countries (except Denmark), divorce in the Netherlands must be by judicial decision. However, the procedure can be very simple. Unless one of the parties objects, or the Council for Child Protection claims that children will be adversely affected, the decision can be taken on the basis of written documents. A one-sided request is sufficient in more than 60 per cent of all cases. In 25 per cent the parties handle their own divorce, on the basis of a pre-court agreement negotiated with the help of only one attorney. The prospect of divorce mediators who are not qualified lawyers has even appeared on the horizon.[5] If, as announced, Parliament ends the attorneys' monopoly on representing clients in district courts, divorce mediators could become serious competition for lawyers. How effective such a threat can be at fostering the out-of-court handling of legal disputes can be seen in the precautionary steps taken by the chamber of advocates, which now offers mediation skills training to its members.

4. LITIGATION AVOIDANCE IN DUTCH SOCIETY AND CULTURE

Even though Dutch courts are less crowded than the courts of any of the neighbouring countries, many insiders still lament the 'unprecedented flood

---

[4] However, the process of establishing uniform civil procedures throughout the European Union has led to the reintroduction of the *betalingsbevel* being tabled by the Ministry of Justice. Cf. M. Freudenthal, *Incassoprocedure* (diss. Utrecht: Deventer, 1996).

[5] Cf. the Report of the Commission for the Reform of Divorce Procedures, *Anders scheiden* (The Hague, Oct. 1996); Statistics given are for 1995, from *CBS Kwartaalbericht 96/2*.

of litigation which is seeping into our courts'. The reasons are the same all over the world. Increasing credit facilities and housing problems, increasing divorce of families and mobility between workplaces, and the increasing tendency of people and organizations formally to claim their rights when breaking up relationships are responsible for the growth of litigation. The unprecedented mobility which shapes social relations fosters an attitude of calculating one's rights, and (especially younger) people are increasingly learning how to use legal instruments for claiming them.[6]

However, while growth rates for most types of civil litigation are high and positive (see Table 14.2), numbers of some types of case are falling. Jurisdictional changes appear to have been the cause. Increasing the jurisdiction of local courts has moved some of the former district court caseload down to local courts. The creation of the new request proceedings for divorce meant that more minor procedures could often be used, replacing what was formerly an adversarial procedure in every instance. Summary debt enforcement was abolished altogether in 1992, leaving it to bailiffs to collect small claims out of court, or have resort to full adversary procedures. Similar changes in jurisdiction and the introduction of simplified procedures are common in neighbouring countries as well. Such changes can be seen as a streamlining of the courts in reaction to massive caseload increases. In the long run, courts have repeatedly managed to limit growth by relieving their calendars of routine proceedings.

Within these general trends in litigation management, the Dutch are especially successful in keeping their judiciary small. It does not simply reflect the size of the country, but results from a national habit of treating litigation as a last resort. Neighbouring small countries like Belgium or Austria are far more litigation-happy. The Dutch pattern looks more like that of Japan (see Table 14.3), a country which is famous for its conflict-avoiding institutions—but a big country nonetheless. A historical observation tends to confirm that this is a remarkable trait of the Dutch national culture. The rank order of national litigation rates within Europe is constant over long stretches of time.[7]

The Netherlands and Japan are both highly regulated countries. Their relative success in avoiding litigation cannot rest on absence of legal regulation. Neither can it arise from an absence of conflicts. Rather, avoidance is achieved by having a plurality of institutions.[8] These may involve the parties concerned

---

[6] For survey evidence on instrumental legal attitudes, see E. R. Blankenburg, *Mobilisierung des Rechts* (Heidelberg, 1995).

[7] See especially Wollschläger, in Blankenburg (ed.), *Prozeßflut? Studien zur Prozeßtätigkeit europäischer Gerichte in historischen Zeitreihen und im Rechtsvergleich* (Cologne, 1989).

[8] Cf. Japan, which is among the highly developed countries lowest in litigation and attorney rates. In 1990, there were only 1.2 *bengoshi* per 10,000 inhabitants. 'Mentality' explanations have been doubted in the Japanese context by O. J. Haley, 'The Myth of the Reluctant Litigant', Journal of Japanese Studies, 4 (1978), 359–90. As we have done for the Netherlands, Haley traces litigation avoidance back to the availability of avoidance institutions.

Table 14.1. *Civil court litigation 1985–1995*

	Civil procedures	
	Absolute nos.	Growth rate (%)
Local courts		
Adversary (*dagvaarding*)	128,900–215,700	67
Requests (*verzoek*)	40,800–149,400	263
Summary debt enforcement	39,500–n/a	−100
District courts		
Adversary (*dagvaarding*)	56,300–34,800	−38[a]
Kort geding	5,400–13,200	242
Requests (*verzoek*)	48,400–94,100	95
Regional (appeal) courts	2,400–3,400	42
High Court	200–300	50

[a] Reduction due to increase in competence threshold.
Source: CBS, judicial statistics.

Table 14.2. *Civil litigation per 100,000 of the population 1984*

	Civil procedures		
	Default proceedings—including summary debt enforcement	First instance adversarial	Appeal courts
Legal cultures which are litigation prone			
Austria	10,800	5,020	430
Belgium	[a]	4,800	536
West Germany	9,400	3,561	251
Between the extremes			
France	3,640	1,950	250
Italy	2,400	1,640	14
Legal cultures which are litigation avoiding			
Denmark	[a]	4,800	64
The Netherlands	1,600	1,430	37
Japan (inc. summary/family courts	[a]	500	15

[a] No summary procedures.

Sources: E. R. Blankenburg and C. Wollschläger, in E. R. Blankenburg (ed.), *Prozeßflut? Studien zur Prozeßtätigkeit europäischer Gerichte in historischen Zeitreichen und in Rechtsvergleich* (Cologne, 1989), 104.

Table 14.3. *Functions of courts in civil litigation*

	Outcome	
	Unpredictable	Predictable
Interest configuration		
Zero-sum[a]	Adjudication	Enforcement
Common interests	Mediation	Notarial

[a] Zero-sum is a standard term from game theory, signifying a conflict situation in which party A loses what party B gains, and vice versa, so that each party can only make gains at the expense of the other's loss.

in more authoritative control; such as is usually the case with administrative regulatory agencies. They can also offer informal alternatives to a more formal judicial procedure. Such 'alternative' institutions may be out of court, helping to avoid the resort to litigation altogether. They may also be built into court procedures, as in the form of an offer to the parties to 'exit' after having filed a court case. Settlement in court is the typical result of such in-court exit opportunities, which help the parties to avoid the high costs of excessively adversarial behaviour.

5. PATTERNS OF LITIGATION IN A LITIGATION-AVOIDING SOCIETY

Parties who litigate to judgment have rejected the option of settling their dispute out of court. Particularly in the Netherlands, where there are many opportunities to settle out of court, where social pressures and the structures of litigation encourage such settlement in by far the majority of cases, and where there are numerous alternative forums, one might fairly assume that those who go through the court system right down to judgment have an extraordinarily hard case. We might then expect them to pursue their case obstinately to the bitter end, and even then, to appeal. This, however, happens in only a minority of all court cases.[9] Statistics on the patterns of litigation refute the common stereotype of litigation as adversarial conflicts that involve a zero-sum game where the outcome is uncertain. In most cases the outcome is perfectly predictable for both parties. Cases brought to judgment tend in fact to be easy-to-decide cases in which the plaintiff needs an executable title rather than a judgment over disputed facts. Moreover, many 'judgments' do not primarily involve an adversarial confrontation with the court imposing a

[9] E. R. Blankenburg and J. R. A. Verwoerd, 'The Courts as a Final Resort?', Netherlands International Law Review, 35 (1988/1), 7–28.

decision. Rather, they end up with settlements facilitated by court mediation. Shifting back and forth between their adjudicative and mediatory roles, judges often actively use the threat of their decision as an element in the negotiations about a possible settlement.

6. PROCEDURAL ISSUES: DELAY AND COSTS

6.1. Duration and costs of civil procedures

Simple comparisons show that summary procedures (*kort geding*—which are technically preliminary injunctions, but are often used as an equivalent to full procedures) count their average duration in terms of weeks. *Kort geding* make up 12 per cent of the civil caseload, here defined exclusive of divorce and family law. Ordinary procedures count duration in terms of months (if appeal is involved, in terms of years). Traditionally there is a big difference between local courts (*kantongerecht*), with an average duration of 133 days for an opposed case to come to final judgment, compared to 626 days at a district court (*rechtbank*),[10] but reforms bringing both courts under one administrative roof might lead to a redistribution of these distinctive patterns in the near future. In the context of reform plans, some interesting experiments are under way. Some district courts, in co-operation with local lawyers, offer parties the possibility of choosing an abbreviated procedure. If plaintiff and defendant lay their arguments on the table from the beginning, the court will strive for a settlement in an early stage and—in case this fails—will try to arrive at a final judgment within six to eight months. Indeed, the first evaluation[11] of this 'abbreviated regime' suggests 89 per cent of the cases adopting this procedure produce a final judgment within eight months (representing an average duration of 191 days). However, it also reports that a mere 4.3 per cent of all parties in civil proceedings chose the abbreviated procedure. It is evident that early consensus among the parties for laying all arguments open is an indication of a will to play it fair. Accordingly, those who choose this course are more willing to settle. Not surprisingly, private parties are over-represented in the group choosing the abbreviated procedure, compared with the frequency with which they appear in civil litigation generally, as compared to business firms.

For an informed interpretation of the average data given in official court statistics, breakdowns by issues at stake as well as by the kind of activities and termination of procedures are needed. Our own studies of court files at two district courts (Amsterdam and Groningen) show that:

---

[10] A. Klijn *et al.*, *De civiele procedure bij de kantonrechter*, WODC 134 (The Hague, 1994).
[11] R. J. J. Eshuis, *Haastige spoed, gaat dat wel goed?*, WODC (The Hague, 1997).

- in 1972 an average of 45 per cent of cases terminated within three months;
- in 1977 an average of 52 per cent of cases terminated within three months; and
- in 1982, an average of 52 per cent of cases terminated within three months.

Between 20 per cent and 25 per cent took more than nine months in each year surveyed. Fewer than 10 per cent of cases took more than two years in 1972 and 1977, whilst in 1982 there were no procedures which took that long.

Thus, even though caseloads of both courts rose considerably during this span of time, the duration of procedures fell. In order to interpret these figures, however, one has to add that only 45 per cent of all procedures went all the way to a verdict, all others ended by default or settlement. Appeal courts in the same years had to proceed to a verdict in more than 90 per cent of appeals. On appeal, an average of only 25 per cent of cases could be finalized within nine months, and two-thirds were terminated within two years.

Since those days, many complaints have been made about the increasing duration of procedures, mostly substantiated by no more than unintelligible average figures. However, in recent years the complaints led to a few studies by the research unit of the Ministry of Justice (WODC) on the duration of different stages of civil proceedings.[12] Restricted to small samples in a few selected district courts, they show no consistent trend towards longer duration between 1983 and 1994. Opposed proceedings took a *median* duration of 618 days in 1986, 497 days in 1986, and 522 days in 1994. Settlements took a median of 176 days in 1983, 380 days in 1986, and 392 days in 1994. Default judgments took 80 days in 1983, 142 days in 1986, and 84 days in 1994. The study demonstrates varying patterns of changes according to types of termination in different courts. The main overall effect, a longer *average* duration, might stem from the increase in opposed cases at the cost of a decrease in default judgments. The main shortening effect in some courts can be attributed to an increase in settlements in place of verdicts.

6.1.1. Costs

Costs of civil procedures have to be seen in context of the arrangements about who is paying for them. In general, the losing party has to pay the court fees of both sides and must pay its own lawyers' fees. The winning party may claim its lawyers' fees from its opponent, and the opponent must pay, unless the judge decides otherwise. As attorneys declare hourly fees, the amount may be subject to some negotiation. For very small claims, the costs easily exceed the value at

---

[12] E. J. M. Barendse Hoornweg, *Hoe worden civile zaken afgehandeld?*, WODC (The Hague, 1992); J. A. Wemmers, *Doorlooptijden in de civiele rechtsspraak*, WODC (The Hague, 1995).

stake. In legal aid cases, there is a set fee, depending on the work done, controlled by the Legal Aid Board.

My last study of court costs dates back to 1989. At that time a verdict for Dfl. 50 would cost Dfl. 126 in court fees alone, and about the same for the attorneys on each side. A default judgment on a claim for Dfl. 5,000 would cost Dfl. 458 in court fees. A verdict after trial would cost Dfl. 638 in court fees. An appropriate two-hourly fee for an attorney might be Dfl. 360. Of course, if both parties have lawyers acting the fee must be paid on each side.[13]

6.1.2. Legal expenses insurance

Private parties are sometimes covered for legal costs either by legal aid or by insurance. About 15 per cent of all Dutch households hold policies for legal expenses insurance. In Germany, the comparable figure is more than half of all households. Dutch legal expenses insurers appear to have taken a role in avoiding the high litigation costs which neighbouring German or Belgian insurance companies have to pay. Dutch legal insurance companies handle the legal problems of their clients in-house first, before they refer them to an attorney. Not being bound (unlike their counterparts in Germany) by a lawyers' statutory monopoly on giving legal advice, they negotiate a settlement in 96 per cent to 98 per cent of all conflicts.[14]

In the Dutch market (which has free competition in legal services, unlike the monopoly on legal advice granted to lawyers in Germany), legal insurers and attorneys arrive at a division of labour. Legal costs insurance covers the legal risks of respectable citizens, and the insurers render first-hand advice. This often prevents escalation to a full litigated case. Advocates are sought *after* legal information has been found elsewhere, legal first aid has been exhausted, and court litigation is seriously threatened. The first attempts to gain legal information and consultation can be satisfied routinely, and at low cost, especially if the social barriers to access are low. In the majority of cases, consultation leads to handling legal problems outside of the courts. This holds true for legal insurance services, just as for professional advocates.[15] They might still negotiate, *in the shadow* of the law, but once a case escalates under the threat of litigation, clients as well as first-line legal insurance agents are glad to resort to attorneys.

A Dutch survey illustrates this point. A representative sample of Dutch households was asked which legal problems they have encountered in the past two years, and, if they asked anybody for advice, who they went to (see Table 14.4). The result is striking as to the role played by the insurance companies in comparison to that played by the advocates. Insurance services

---

[13] See calculations included in Blankenburg (ed.), *Prozeßflut?*, at 318–20.

[14] E. R. Blankenburg, 'Access to Justice and Alternatives to Courts: European Procedural Justice Compared', Civil Justice Quarterly, 14 (1995), 176–89.

[15] As demonstrated even in Germany by Rainer Wasilewski, *Streitverhütung durch Rechtsanwälte* (Cologne, 1990).

Table 14.4. *Legal services sought from advocates and legal insurance agents according to household survey in the Netherlands 1988*

	Legal insurance services (%)	Attorneys (%)
Type of service sought		
Advice	43	27
Legal assistance	45	65
Others	12	8
Problem area		
Civil law, liability	61	5
Civil law, contract	11	8
Landlord–tenant	12	13
Labour law	7	18
Family law	—	24
Social insurance	4	12
Penal law	4	8
Tax law	—	8

Source: CBS enquête slachtoffer misdrijven/vraag naar rechtshulpverlening (1987).

are clearly more geared to advice in the first instance, while lawyers are more often consulted for action in a case (which does not necessarily include representation in court, however). Insurance claims are predominantly concerned with liability questions (mostly regulating traffic accidents) and contract law matters, to a lesser degree with landlord–tenant cases, and labour relations. Most insurance policies exclude family law and tax consultancy from coverage. Penal law coverage is usually restricted to negligence, not intent (thus covering drunken driving, but not theft or robbery).

The Dutch pattern of litigation avoidance is even more amazing, if seen in the light of the Netherlands' generous legal aid infrastructure. Furthermore, as pre-court procedures handle cases more informally and less adversarially than a court would do, such procedures lower the entry threshold which the judicial system presents to socially weak parties. Both of these elements of Dutch legal culture have a compensating effect on the usual unequal distribution of chances for access to justice. The occasional party can invoke the courts somewhat more easily for private problems, while organized repeat players are somewhat more reluctant to use the courts as a routine matter of their business.

6.1.3. *Legal aid*

Almost half of all Dutch households are eligible for legal aid. Roughly two-thirds of these have to pay contributions of their own, starting from Dfl. 50 and increasing up to Dfl. 1,200 per case. For legal aid clients, the attorney fees are paid by legal aid councils according to a fixed fee scheme. Where hourly fees are allowed under the legal aid scheme, they are set at around Dfl. 125. Privately paid attorneys charge two to three times that amount.

One might suspect that the competitive and open supply of legal consultation and representation in the Netherlands would increase the amount of litigation in court. Dutch taxpayers also contribute via a legal aid scheme which grants access to more than just the very poor. In the 1980s, more than 60 per cent of Dutch households were entitled to some form of legal aid. Austerity policies in the 1990s led to a sharp reduction in eligibility, and contributions to be paid by middle-income clients were raised. When consequently the level of eligibility dropped to 40 per cent of all Dutch households in 1994, the government corrected its regulations in order to raise it again to about 50 per cent.[16]

Table 14.5 shows that the government had some success in putting a ceiling on legal aid expenditure in 1994. Step by step the income thresholds of entitlement to legal aid were raised, contributions by those receiving legal aid were increased, and the extent of services was reduced. Attorneys' legal aid fees, which had been set by collective agreement between the government and the chamber of advocates, were not raised for ten years. Finally, in 1994, the fees were adjusted by a factor related to the inflation in lawyers' costs. At the same time regional auditing councils (*raden voor rechtsbijstand*) took over the administrative control of legal aid subsidies, including taking responsibility for the correctness of the means test (which, until then, had often been handled in a rather relaxed way).

Budgetary figures hide an adverse effect of this austerity policy. Since 1994, the increase in legal aid subsidies has stopped, but the cost has been that far fewer services have been delivered. While the overall amount paid to attorneys in subsidies has remained the same, more of it is used up on each job since the increase in allowable fees. For the same money, 30 per cent fewer clients can be served. In addition, the fastest increasing cost in the whole system has been the money paid to auditing councils.

For those who suspect that legal aid always increases the courts' caseload, it may come as a surprise that the Dutch, with their generous legal aid scheme, have to handle much less litigation than their neighbours. Legal aid does not necessarily mean that litigation is encouraged. The experience of the Dutch system shows that, apart from easing access to justice for people's private problems, legal aid stimulates handling problems outside of courts. The variety of access institutions available in the Netherlands helps to avoid the commencement of court cases as much as it facilitates initiating them.

---

[16] Cf. Albert Klijn and Sylvia van Leeuwen, *De Toegevoegde kwaliteit*, WODC 151 (The Hague, 1996).

Table 14.5. *Government spending on legal aid 1973–1995* (Dfl. million)

	1973	1978	1990	1993	1995
Legal aid paid to attorneys					
Civil law	28.5	75.0	156.0	191.9	207.3
Criminal defence	5.0	26.1	71.6	73.5	73.5
Subsidy for legal aid					
bureaux/councils	a	40.0	50.8	74.6	91.7

[a] Not yet in existence.

Source: Budget of the Ministerie van Justitie.

7. THE PROFESSION

On the other side of the desk from clients who pay are the lawyers who operate this litigation-minimizing system. In the Netherlands there are, at present, nine universities offering law. Law study begins at the undergraduate level, right after high school at the age of 18 or 19. The standard of education and of the examinations is supposed to be at the same level for the entire country, but implementation lies entirely with the law faculties. Examinations are taken after each course and accumulate up to the final degree. University education in the Netherlands should take four years, but the actual time required for legal studies is closer to four and a half years on average. After having received a master's degree (*meester in de rechten*) graduates are free to enter in-house training at an attorney's offices, with the court administration, in a government office, or with one of the private companies which offers a recognized professional training programme.

Each of the separate careers within the legal profession has its own distinct apprenticeship programme. Though this splits the profession into distinguishable occupational divisions, the practice of recruitment for the judiciary has traditionally emphasized mobility from all branches. It is not exceptional to be nominated for judgeship up to the age of 45 years (and even at a later age as far as the highest court is concerned).

As in all post-industrial countries, the Dutch legal profession has grown explosively since 1970. The principal cause has been the extension of higher education. While in 1970 only 8 per cent of the Dutch had received some university education by the age of 20, in 1990 the rate stood at approximately 25 per cent. As the growth of the educational system was accompanied by the formation of many new academic disciplines, the share of law students shows a long-term downward trend. However, in the 1980s legal education climbed in popularity among university students at the cost of the social sciences and pedagogical fields. This was clearly due to the pull factor of the labour market

Table 14.6. *Size and composition of the legal profession*

	1970 (%)	1989 (%)
Registered attorneys[a]	14	23
Judicial office	14	12
Government, notaries	28	25
Education	12	8
Private employment	32	32
Number (absolute)	14,600	28,000

[a] This figure includes all persons trained as lawyers who are not within one of the other categories. I estimate that only about 10% of these are not in fact active in legal practice—a low figure compared to other countries.

Source: Estimates based on: Staatsalmanak/unpublished survey of v.d.Berg and van Sapora (no more recent data are available).

which offers more chances for beginning lawyers than for teachers, social workers, or social scientists.

The annual number of Dutch law graduates rose from 716 graduates in 1970 to 3,601 in 1990. Part of the growth also stems from greater enrolment of women in universities and their changing career opportunities. At the universities the gender gap started to lessen from the beginning of the 1970s. Women's emancipation in the profession began late and grew slowly after the Second World War. The first woman judge took her oath in 1947. Today 72 per cent of the young judges-in-training are women. However, the existing gender imbalance is very slow in correcting itself further up in the judicial hierarchy. Comparing generation cohorts, women are still under-represented in the higher judicial offices (see Table 14.7).

With the public administration recruiting relatively openly from different legal backgrounds, one might also expect to see laymen and -women being appointed judges, or otherwise being integrated into judicial bodies. This expectation might be reinforced by a consideration of the history of the Low Countries. Here, the French revolutionary idea of lay members on the bench replaced an even earlier tradition of the democratic legitimization of local judicial appointments in the Dutch townships. After the separation of Belgium in 1830, however, the institution of lay judges in criminal courts was abolished in the Netherlands, never to gain ground again. (The one exception to be made has been social security courts which, until their abolition in 1992, had non-jurists sitting on the bench. However, these might more readily be called *experts* than *laypeople* as they were chosen on the basis of their expertise in social insurance matters.)

This leads us to characterize the Dutch approach to keeping justice receptive

Erhard Blankenburg

Table 14.7. *Representation of women in the judicial careers*

	1973/4	1990	1995
Women judges as a % in:			
All courts	11	28	31
Highest courts	1.3	5.5	7.4

Source: L. E. deGroot-van Leeuwen, *De rechterlijke macht in Nederland* (Arnhem, 1991), *ipso* 1997.

to social changes as professional rather than democratic. Judges receive thorough judicial training. Law graduates who begin their career in the judicial branch start with at least six years' professional experience, usually as court clerk (*griffier*). Clerks performs a variety of tasks in support of the judges on the bench, including even acting as a substitute judge. The training is monitored and accompanied by courses provided by the academy of magistrature. These courses can also be followed by jurists from other branches of the legal profession. After at least six years' experience as attorney, ministerial bureaucrat, or law teacher, the applicant from a non-judicial branch of the legal profession has an even chance of a place on the judicial training course.

The growth of the entire profession, and especially the enthusiasm of women lawyers, rendered careers in the judiciary so popular that, since 1983, the academy of the magistrature has increasingly screened the candidates, considering both professional achievements and social skills. In addition to legal expertise, candidates' ability to work in a large court organization and productively manage high caseloads is tested. Recruitment into full judicial positions is decided by magistrates' councils, which are dominated by presidents of the district courts.

Court presidents enjoy more privileges in allocating personnel. They commonly ask *substitute judges*, selected from among attorneys, university law teachers, and other legal professionals, to fill in during times of peak caseload, or to sit in on cases which afford specialized legal knowledge. Until recently, objections that such practices undermine the independent decision of the lawful judge were hardly raised. With the growth of the court system, however, the increased use of such informal practice has led to complaints of conflicts of interest arising.

There are other advantages of the small scale of Dutch courts which might be waning with organizational growth. Traditionally judges' careers developed through progress to better-paid echelons within the court system by either moving up from district courts to chambers of the regional courts or down to a local court. Being a single judge gave the 'judge-king' of a local court a desirable position.

Lately, many of the informal characteristics of Dutch courts are coming under pressure from organizational growth. Reorganization plans, which were implemented step by step throughout the 1990s, aim at integrating most first instance jurisdiction into the district courts, and concentrating all appeals at the regional court level. The system of local courts will not disappear, but the jurisdiction of these courts is likely to be restricted so that they become outposts for easy access procedures. As noted above, from 1999 local courts are to be administratively integrated with the district courts. Most court functions will be integrated into the management of district courts, forming big 'judicial supermarkets'.

7.1. Attorneys and law firms

It is not just in the judicial branch that present-day law graduates are entering a world of big organizations. Due to the uncertain labour market, about half of the law graduates register as attorneys. Only one-third stay with advocacy. Others move to salaried positions in insurance companies, or with the legal departments of corporations and associations. While previous generations were accustomed to choosing between tenure in the civil service and a position in the judiciary, nowadays law graduates look for careers with a law firm or as counsel for a business enterprise. Dutch law firms in Rotterdam, The Hague, and Amsterdam have increased in size, competing with mega-law firms in London or Brussels (see Table 14.8).

While there is much talk about big law firms rising up in Amsterdam, Rotterdam, or The Hague, statistics reveal that there is a solid layer of small partnerships and even solo lawyers underneath. Most attorneys still work as general practitioners for private as well as for business clients. The competition is tough. Advocates do not enjoy any monopoly on the giving of legal advice. This permits trade unions or other membership clubs to offer legal advice as part of their membership services, and it allows legal cost insurers to offer their own consultation and representation for lower court cases. If the government's present plans become law,[17] the privilege of representing parties in court might be extended to a number of salaried lawyers. According to these plans, in-house lawyers of big companies and staff lawyers of legal aid bureaus, trade unions, and legal insurance companies will be admitted to the bar. They are often highly specialized in certain fields of law.

Many people prefer to look for advice elsewhere than traditional law firms. Old age pensioners would often rather take their problems to social workers, who are employed by some big cities (*sociale raads lieden*). Small business people consult their accountant. Often the kind of legal problem is decisive. To the extent that the occurrence of problems is group-specific, there is an array of

---

[17] Report of the Government Commission Cohen, 1996.

Table 14.8. *Number and size of law firms*

	1978	1993	1997
Number of registered attorneys	2,694	7,595	9,252
Number of solo lawyers	645	923	1,188
Number of lawyers in firms with 2 to 9 partners	1,795	3,295 ⎫	6,943
10 partners or more	1,493	4,749 ⎭	

Source: Orde van advocaten, The Hague.

consultative professions, which—in addition to providing other advice—also deal with legal problems. Using a simplified scheme of the *social*, the *general*, and the *commercial* clientele, the market of lawyers and their competitors might be sketched as in Table 14.9.

The differentiation of the practice of law by clientele groups also means stratification and huge income differences among advocates. While contingency arrangements are considered unethical, hourly fees can vary between Dfl. 150 and Dfl. 600. Lack of a uniform fee scheme renders litigation for small amounts unattractive. The possibility that the winner will get only part of his own legal costs repaid makes the expense to the litigant largely unpredictable. Dutch litigants and attorneys therefore look more carefully at alternatives before starting a formal court procedure.

The same income stratification effect can be observed in the decline in the position of salaried lawyers who work at legal aid bureaux. The low-income work done by these *social advocates*, who work on a government-subsidized fee scheme, is quickly losing its attraction. While in the heyday of the legal aid movement, in the early 1980s, about 16 per cent of all attorneys worked predominantly for legal aid clients, twelve years later they count as a mere 8 per cent.[18]

8. ADR AND ALTERNATIVES TO DIRECT LEGAL ACTION

We have seen how court reforms, in the shape of the *kort geding,* and debt collection and divorce procedural changes have contributed to minimize court caseloads. The Netherlands also has a range of social institutions which provide alternatives outside direct recourse to the courts by the affected individual.

---

[18] Cf. research by Albert Klijn, *De balie geschetst,* WODC 24 (The Hague, 1981) and Sylvia van Leeuwen *et al., De toegevoegde kwaliteit,* WODC 151 (The Hague, 1996), 76 ff.

Table 14.9. *Stratification of the bar*

Clientele	Bar	Competitors
Welfare recipients Low-income groups	Social advocacy	Legal aid bureaux, trade unions
Private clientele Upper middle income	General advocacy	Legal cost insurance, automobile, and other notaries
Well-to-do clients Traditional business	Commercial advocacy	Tax advisers, accountants
International business	Mega-law firms	international accountants

8.1. Consumer groups

Consumer complaints everywhere face the dilemma of diffuse interests. Each individual case might be too trivial to risk litigation costs, while collectively they could be of great significance. Therefore, in the Netherlands, consumer associations follow a strategy of handling individual complaints by direct negotiation, campaigning publicly on major issues, and occasionally taking a few serious test cases to court. Their main impact is achieved by publicity. Furthermore, many service industries such as travel agencies, cleaners, the textile industry, and car repair garages have installed complaints boards to take up the bulk of cases. In the Netherlands such boards are usually set up with tripartite representation, including industrial representatives and consumer organizations, with a neutral person chairing.

8.2. Industry-specific arbitration bodies

Arbitration organizations exist in a number of industrial sectors. Most arbitration boards have their seat in Rotterdam or The Hague, and provide experts as arbitrators. A statutory arbitration code regulates the procedure. It opens the possibility of appeal to the civil courts, if the procedural rules have not been followed. Substantive appeal is possible only if parties have expressly allowed for it beforehand. The bimonthly *Tijdschrift voor arbitrage* publishes decisions with precedent value. In the course of time the boards have successfully compiled their 'code of arbitration', which is generally considered a binding source of law. Commercial arbitration in the Netherlands forms an externalized system of *private justice*, as opposed to the German tradition, which tends to *internalize* as much as possible of the justice function in the courts. In Germany, only a few sectors, such as shipping and international trade, have developed a tradition of arbitration similar to the Dutch.

The Dutch skill in handling conflicts before they escalate can best be seen in the construction industry, where the stakes are high. Problems between owners and contractors are always a risk, given the inherent conflict in their interests, and the long duration and complexity of the jobs. Contractors often work with a number of subcontract firms which may be hard to co-ordinate. Time schedules are regularly neglected. Materials may not be delivered in time and may have to be replaced. Changing conditions and new wishes may force a variation of the contract. Renegotiating is the rule, rather than the exception. The Dutch saying goes: 'Find a lawyer before you look for a contractor.'

However, in the Netherlands, construction contractors almost never see the inside of courtrooms. They always include in their standard contracts that disputes will be heard by the Council for Construction Firms. This is an arbitration service set up by the construction industry, and based in The Hague. Parties may choose an arbitrator from among the architects and engineers of the Council. The arbitrators decide the substantive dispute, without appeal. Appeal to a court can only be made on procedural grounds. The arbitrators' decisions can be formally executed if they are registered with the district court. A monthly journal (*Bouwrecht*) publishes all novel decisions and is used as an authoritative source of case law. A legally trained secretary guards the procedural fairness of the arbitration.

Landlord–tenant disputes provide yet another example. Before a claim against a rise in rent is admitted to court, a Dutch tenant has to file his protest with a landlord–tenant committee. Its decision becomes binding after two months. Before then both parties are free to take the case to court. However, only a small percentage do so. Here too, easy access to the committees encourages more tenants to complain in the Netherlands than in Germany, but at the same time keeps these cases out of court.

There is a similar out-of-court procedure for employment protection cases. Employers in the Netherlands need permission from the regional employment agency if they wish to dismiss an employee from a regular employment contract. Compared to procedures before courts, this administrative procedure has advantages for both sides. If the licence is given, the employer's fear of being confronted with extensive claims based on unfair dismissal is diminished, and the employee has had a chance to object and question the validity of redundancy or dismissal arguments.[19]

However, the days of the informal procedure before the labour bureaux may be numbered. More and more employment is under casual and temporary labour contracts, which escape the protection given to regular employment contracts. More and more employers use a request procedure before the civil

---

[19] Only 5% of the yearly 90,000 requests are refused, and 11% are withdrawn by the employer. Thus, the procedure is not effectively preventing dismissals, but it provides continuation of the labour contract until the request is properly assessed.

courts to terminate labour contracts. Recent figures show that in 1995 both procedures, applying for a permit before dismissal, and suing in court after dismissal, have reached about equal volumes.

8.3. An enlightened self-interest/co-operative industry approach

The last illustrative example is traffic tort. The problem of traffic accident damages usually comes down to distributing the losses among a limited number of insurance companies. Therefore, it makes sense for the companies concerned to settle such cases out of court. Dutch insurance assessors routinely inspect the damaged vehicle a few days before repair is begun. They try to assess fault by mutual understanding among the liability insurers.[20] There are very few exceptional cases, in which car accident liability is not agreed among those concerned without litigation. Such cases arise particularly where injury is involved.

9. CONCLUSION

Overall, the Netherlands experiences less litigation, and fewer problems with court congestion, than its neighbours, not because there is no demand for litigation, but because the supply side of the legal profession and social institutions have responded to the existing incentives to create alternatives to the court process that work better and faster at less cost to the litigant. Going to court has its costs, even for the winner. Lawyers serve their clients' interests by exploring and exhausting the alternatives first. Social institutions offer a number of effective alternatives for particular sorts of cases. Lawyers have no monopoly protection in the giving of legal advice. They must be able to anticipate the advice a potential client might receive about alternatives to court, and can only recommend court action if its cost is truly justified in all the circumstances.

This leaves the courts relatively free to concentrate on those cases which need judicial attention. Even in these cases, settlements may be possible, and are encouraged by the ability of the judges to urge them. Finally, the quick, simple *kort geding* procedure has proven to be a very popular and effective way to deal with a wide range of cases which need the decision of a judge, but which do not require the fullest exploration which a complete trial can provide.

---

[20] Ch. Simsa, 'Die gerichtliche und außergerichtliche Regelung von Verkehrsunfällen in den Niederlanden und der Bundesrepublik Deutschland' (diss., VU Amsterdam, 1995).

15

Swiss Civil Justice: With an Emphasis on the Laws of the Canton of Zurich

Isaak Meier

1. A BRIEF DESCRIPTION OF SWISS PROCEDURAL LAW

1.1. Bodies of law

1.1.1. In general

Since 1912, private law has been federal law (BV=*Bundesverfassung*/Swiss Constitution, Art. 64 II). Procedural law, however, is still cantonal (state) law. That is to say: Switzerland, a very small country of only 7 million inhabitants, has twenty-six different statutes of procedural law. Furthermore, there is a special federal statute for cases which take place in the Federal Court (*Bundesgericht*) as a trial court (*Bundesgesetz über den Bundeszivilprozess*, 4 December 1947). In a few cases, such as actions brought by private persons against the state, the Federal Court acts not as a court of appeal but as a trial court or court of first instance (OG=*Bundesgesetz über die Organisation der Bundesrechtspflege*, 16 December 1943, Art. 41).

Despite the fact that private law and procedural law are in the hands of different legislators, there is no exact separation of both laws. In the codes and statutes of private laws, such as OR (OR=Code of Obligations/*Obligationenrecht*), ZGB (ZGB=Code of Civil Law/*Zivilgesetzbuch*), UWG (UWG=trade law/*Gesetz über den unlauteren Wettbewerb*), and many others, you can find a vast number of procedural rules concerning such matters as venues, provisional measures, law of evidence (burden of proof etc.), declaratory judgments (*Feststellungsklage*), and the duty of courts to act ex officio in matters which the parties are not able to dispose of. Furthermore, in the last thirty years, the Federal Court has developed a body of unwritten federal principles of procedural law which have to be adhered to in the cantonal courts. These laws, made by judges, cover amongst other things: more or less all ·questions concerning *res judicata*, *lis pedens* (*Rechtshängigkeit*), declaratory judgments and provisional measures as long as they are not regulated by a federal statute, joinder of claims, and intervention of a third party in an action.

Since the end of the last century there have been efforts to achieve unification and harmonization of procedural law. Until recently these efforts have never been successful. Now, with a project for a new constitution, there is a realistic hope that—within the next two or three years—people and states will give the

Federation legislative power in relation to procedural law. But even seen from a very optimistic viewpoint a new federal code of civil procedure will not come into force within the next ten years.

Although international procedural law is not part of this report, it must be mentioned that there is a special federal statute in this matter, the IPRG (IPRG = International Private Law), which is always applicable if the case is not within the scope of an international treaty or convention. The most important body of law is the Lugano Convention.

1.1.2. Diversity of cantonal law

In relation to the very fundamental issues the twenty-six cantonal statutes of procedural law are similar. But in details there are uncountable differences which make going to court a risky undertaking for a lawyer in another canton. A party may also win a case in one canton and lose it in another canton because of differences on questions of evidence.

The most important differences concern the following issues:

- Law of evidence: duty to testify as a witness, such as attorney privilege, or to disclose documents; the right and duty of courts to act ex officio in taking evidence.
- Stage of procedure: some cantons have a very concentrated oral procedure (for example the canton of Glarus). Other cantons have a more sophisticated procedure with different separated steps (see especially the law of the canton of Zurich, section 1.4 below).
- The amount and scope of remedies are significantly different. In some cantons there is only an appeal with a limited possibility of introducing new facts and evidence. In other cantons, after appeal the parties have another cantonal remedy to a cantonal supreme court (*Kassationsgericht*).

1.2. Organization and scope of the cantonal courts and the federal courts

1.2.1. Cantonal courts

1.2.1.1. In general

Generally speaking, each case has to be commenced in a cantonal court. Despite the fact that private law is federal law, in the first instance the cases are—with some exceptions—handled by a cantonal court.

1.2.1.2. Ordinary courts

The ordinary courts consist of either a single judge or a bench of judges (normally three to seven judges). Small cases and matters of summary proceedings are typically heard by a single judge sitting with a clerk. In most cantons major cases and family matters are handled by a bench of judges.

Canton of Zurich. Single judges are competent for cases up to Sw. Frs. 20,000 (approximately £8,700) and summary proceedings (GVG ZH §§ 21 ff.). All other cases are heard by a court of three judges (so-called *Bezirksgericht/*district court) (GVG ZH §§ 26 ff.). There are twelve district courts.

In all the cantons, district courts handle both civil and criminal cases. But there are separate courts for administrative law litigation.

1.2.1.3. Justices of the peace

One of the major features of Swiss civil procedure is the important role of justices of the peace. In almost every case the parties have to undergo a mandatory settlement conference led by a justice of the peace before an action can be brought in court.

Canton of Zurich. Unless the law says otherwise, the plaintiff has to commence a case by asking the local justice of the peace to hold a settlement conference (ZPO ZH §§ 93 ff.). Each community has its own justice of the peace. If the meeting is not successful the action can be brought to court. A direct commencement at the court is provided by the law mainly in the following cases: matters of labour law and litigation between tenants and landlords (ZPO ZH § 105); summary proceedings (ZPO ZH § 205); and in some cases of family law, such as alimony cases (ZPO ZH § 196).

In the canton of Zurich, justices of the peace are also competent to decide a case if the amount in dispute does not exceed Sw. Frs. 500.

For litigation between tenants and landlords there are special courts of the peace (so-called *Schlichtungsbehörden*) in all the cantons (OR Art. 274 a). The main task of these courts is also to encourage the parties to settle their cases.

1.2.1.4. Special courts

Several cantons have, in addition to the ordinary courts, special courts for commercial law, labour law, and disputes between tenants and landlords.

Canton of Zurich. There are courts for labour law in the cities of Zurich and Winterthur (GVG §§ 8 ff.). These courts are headed by a district judge. The other two judges are proposed by the local organizations of employers and employees. Each district has a special court for disputes between tenants and landlords (GVG §§ 14 ff.). Finally, there is a commercial court in Zurich for commercial litigation in the canton. The bench of five judges is composed of a high court judge as chief justice, a high court judge as a member of the court, and three expert judges who are specialists in the field in question. For example, if the dispute concerns computer questions the judges would be highly qualified computer specialists.

1.2.1.5. High court/court of appeal

In every canton there is a cantonal high court/court of appeal (the so-called *Obergericht* or *Kantonsgericht*). Its main competence is to hear appeals from district, labour, and tenant–landlord courts. In a few cases the cantonal high court acts as a trial court.

Canton of Zurich. The high court deals with appeals (see in more detail section 1.6.1.1) against judgments of district courts (single judges and bench of judges), labour courts, and tenant–landlord courts (GVG § 43). As a first instance court it is responsible for cases in special matters such as disputes concerning business names and copyright law (GVG § 43 II). By an agreement the parties can also choose the high court as a first instance court if the cause of action is worth at least Sw. Frs. 20,000.

1.2.1.6. Cantonal supreme court

A few cantons have a (cantonal) supreme court (so-called *Kassationsgericht*) which deals with remedies against judgments of high courts and commercial courts (canton of Zurich: GVG §§ 66 ff.). But the scope of these remedies is limited (see section 1.6.1.3).

1.2.1.7. Judges

Job requirements/laypersons. To have studied law is not a requirement in order to be elected as a judge. Therefore the majority of judges in Switzerland are laypersons.

Canton of Zurich. With a few exceptions, justices of the peace are laypersons coming from all sorts of professions. On a bench of judges in almost all the district courts (except in the cities of Zurich and Winterthur) only chief justices are jurists. All the other judges are laypersons. High court judges are always jurists.

Elections/term in office. In Switzerland there is no lifetime tenure for judges. In most cantons they are elected for six years. The election body is either the local parliament or the people.

Canton of Zurich. District court judges are elected by the people of a district. High court judges and supreme court judges are elected by the parliament of the canton of Zurich. All the judges serve a term of six years. After this period their election has to be renewed.

Independence and neutrality. The right to an independent and neutral judge is guaranteed by the Constitution (Art. 58), Art. 4 EMRK (EMRK=European Convention for the Protection of Human Rights and Fundamental Freedoms), and the cantonal codes of civil procedure. Canton of Zurich: GVG 95 ff.

1.2.2. Federal court

The Federal Court, based in Lausanne, is, as a civil court, mainly a court of appeal against judgments of the cantonal high courts and commercial courts (see section 1.6.2).

Federal judges are elected by the Federal Parliament for a period of six years. Although there is no such requirement, all the judges are jurists.

1.3. Attorneys

As a part of the legislative power in procedural law the cantons are also competent to regulate all questions concerning attorneys. Therefore each canton has its own statutes in this field (canton of Zurich: *Gesetz über den Rechtsanwaltsberuf*, dated 3 July 1938). Apart from details the cantonal rules are very similar.

The general principles are:

- There is only one type of lawyer. There is no separation into solicitors and barristers as is the case in England.
- A lawyer who is a member of the bar in one canton is automatically also admitted in all the other cantons and at the Federal Court. This means that a Swiss lawyer can plead in all sorts of courts. The admission is not restricted to a certain court or to a certain level of courts.
- Requirements to become a lawyer are: studies in law at a university; apprenticeship at a law office or in court for one or two years; bar exam in front of a body composed of professors, high court judges, and experienced lawyers.
- The lawyers are supervised by a special commission of the cantonal high courts. In a case of breach of the rules of behaviour, such as acting in a conflict of interest or committing a criminal offence, a lawyer can lose his or her licence or receive a fine.

1.4. Commencement of civil proceedings, preparation for trial, and trial

In this section an overview of a civil action according to the law of the canton of Zurich is given. In most cantons the procedure is very similar. Features of the law of the canton of Zurich are mentioned.

1.4.1. Ordinary proceeding

Steps of procedure	Deadline to offer facts and/or evidence and for motions
Settlement conference: In general, as a first step the plaintiff has to ask the local justice of the peace to hold a settlement conference	The parties should disclose their evidence (ZPO § 96). But there are no consequences if they do not adhere to this rule.

Steps of procedure

Deadline to offer facts and/or evidence and for motions

(ZPO § 93). If agreement is reached the result is regarded as an enforceable court settlement.

If there is no settlement the justice of the peace delivers a special document, called *Weisung*, which describes the cause of action and the plaintiff's motions.

Commencement of civil proceedings:
If there is no settlement the plaintiff can start a real procedure within a period of three months by sending the *Weisung* to the court (ZPO § 101).

If a settlement conference is not required, an action has to be commenced by mailing a document to the court with the plaintiff's motions and detailed descriptions of the facts and arguments (ZPO § 103).

With this step the action is brought in the court in compliance with Art. 21 Lugano Convention. This means that the same action cannot be commenced in another forum. A change of action is only possible under the circumstances of ZPO § 61 (close connection of both actions).

Stage of pleadings (Hauptverfahren):
The next step is the main part of the procedure, the so-called *Hauptverfahren* (main procedure). This part is either oral or written or a mixture of both.

As a rule there is an oral session where both parties have a least two pleadings: statement of claim, defence, reply and rejoinder (ZPO § 121).

If the plaintiff wants to do so he can give a written statement instead of his first oral pleading. In this case also the defendant is asked to give a written answer. Only the rest of the pleadings would be given in an oral session (ZPO § 123).

In complex cases the court can allow the parties to give all the pleadings in written documents (ZPO § 124).

In the pleadings both parties have to submit the relevant facts and evidence. Legal reasoning is allowed but is not necessary.

With his or her last pleading, as a rule, a party is excluded from submitting new facts. New facts are only allowed under the circumstances of ZPO § 115 (facts which a party did not know before although he or she was acting carefully etc.).

There is no restriction over new evidence being introduced (see stage of proof).

NB: This is a feature of the law of the canton of Zurich. In the majority of cantons, with the last pleadings the evidence also has to be submitted in full.

Steps of procedure	Deadline to offer facts and/or evidence and for motions

Stage of evidence:
The next stage deals with evidence. In an interlocutory judgment the court decides which facts have to be proved and which party has the burden of proof (ZPO § 136).

The parties now have within a certain period of time (20 to 60 days) to call their witnesses, submit documents, or—if a document is in the hands of the opposing party or a third party—to ask the court to issue a disclosure order concerning that document.

Evidence which is not offered within this period of time is excluded from being heard (ZPO § 138). New evidence is only allowed under the circumstances of ZPO § 115.

Now it is time for taking evidence. Unlike the situation in England or the USA there is no cross-examination of witnesses and experts. Primarily they are interviewed by the court. The parties and/or their lawyers are only allowed to ask additional questions.

After the court has taken evidence the parties are invited for a final session (*Schlussverhandlung*) where they can express their opinions about the results of this stage (ZPO § 148).

Judgment:
The last step is the finding of the judgment by the court.

1.4.2. Special proceedings for consumer litigation and other disputes

There are slightly different proceedings for consumer litigation up to Sw. Frs. 8,000 and other disputes such as litigation about alimony, labour law, and tenant–landlord relationships. There is always an oral proceeding (ZPO § 119 Ziff. 3). At the stage of presenting proof there is no separate interlocutory judgment, which gives the parties the opportunity to complete their submissions of evidence. After finishing the main proceeding the court immediately steps forward to take evidence (ZPO § 141).

1.4.3. Summary proceedings

1.4.3.1. Scope of summary proceedings

In Swiss civil procedure summary proceedings play a very important role. There are five different types of actions which can be pursued in summary proceedings.

Money claims. There are very special summary proceedings to pursue money claims (so-called *Rechtsöffnungsverfahren* (ZPO § 213 Ziff. 2).[1]

Undisputed and clear cases. Instead of ordinary proceedings a plaintiff can choose summary proceedings if the facts are clear or not disputed and the legal situation is indisputable (ZPO § 222 Ziff. 2).[2]

Provisional measures. A party can ask for provisional measures before or after *lis pedens* of an action (ZPO § 222 Ziff. 3=before *lis pedens*, § 110=after *lis pedens*). Measures can be granted *ex parte* or after hearing both parties (ZPO § 224). For money claims the provisional measures are regulated entirely by federal law. The most important measure is the *Arrest*, an attachment/seizure of debtor's property (Art. 271 SchKG=*Schuldbetreibungs und Konkursgesetz*). This measure is always an *ex parte* decision.

Non-contentious jurisdiction (so-called *freiwillige Gerichtsbarkeit*) (ZPO ZH § 215 f.). *Actions concerning bankruptcy and single debt collection* (ZPO ZH § 213).

1.4.3.2. Form of procedure

In general summary proceedings are oral (ZPO § 206). Unlike the ordinary proceedings no settlement conference takes place before commencement of a procedure. Typically there is a restriction of evidence (ZPO § 209).

1.5. Costs

1.5.1. In general

In Switzerland going to trial is very expensive. The party who loses the case in general has to pay his or her own lawyer, the costs of the opponent's lawyer, and the court fees. Contingency fees are not allowed.

To give an example, a party who loses a case worth Sw. Frs. 100,000—after going from the district court to the cantonal high court and finally to the Federal Court—has to pay more than Sw. Frs. 90,000 (see the tariffs of the canton of Zurich for court and attorneys' fees and the federal rules in this matter.)

In general, the calculation of costs is not based on hours spent by lawyers and judges but on the estimated value of the claim.

---

[1] See details in Isaak Meier, *Rechtsschutz im summarischen Verfahren als Alternative zum ordentlichen Zivilprozess im schweizerischen Recht* (Cologne, 1997), 163 ff.　　[2] See in detail ibid. 43 ff.

1.5.2. Legal aid

In most cantons legal aid is only available for very poor people. Only a person with an income not exceeding a certain minimum level has a chance of getting legal aid (ZPO ZH §§ 84 ff.). A minimal standard of legal aid is also guaranteed by the constitution (Art. 4).

1.6. Remedies

1.6.1. Cantonal level

Generally speaking the law of the canton of Zurich provides three different types of remedies: an ordinary appeal (*Berufung*), a 'little' appeal (*Rekurs*), and an extraordinary remedy to the cantonal supreme court or high court (*Nichtigkeitsbeschwerde*).

Except for the remedy to the cantonal supreme court or high court, the remedy system of the canton of Zurich is typical of Swiss procedural law.

1.6.1.1. Ordinary appeal

The parties can appeal against a judgment of a district court, a single judge, a labour court, or a tenant–landlord court if the amount in dispute is Sw. Frs. 8,000 or more. Furthermore, the ordinary appeal is only possible with a case resolved by a judgment on the merits (ZPO § 259).

Procedure on appeal. Statements of appeal and defence are in writing (ZPO § 264/265). Further pleadings are made at an oral session (ZPO § 268). The high court can re-examine both legal and factual questions. But the parties are restricted in submitting new facts and evidence. It is only allowed within the scope of ZPO § 115 (see section 4.1.3).

1.6.1.2. 'Little' appeal

The 'little' appeal, according to ZPO § 271, can be filed against the following judgments if the disputed question is worth more than Sw. Frs. 8,000 (ZPO § 271):

- disposals because of formal reasons (lack of competence or capacity or other such reasons);
- interlocutory judgments, particularly concerning provisional measures, legal aid, or competence;
- disposals because of settlements;
- judgments in summary proceedings.

Procedure. There is only one exchange of a written statement from each party (ZPO § 275 ff.).

Also in a 'little' appeal the high court can re-examine both legal and factual questions. But the parties are also restricted in submitting new facts and evidence.

1.6.1.3. Extraordinary remedy

If neither the ordinary appeal nor the 'little' appeal is possible, a judgment can be attacked by an extraordinary remedy, the so-called *Nichtigkeitsbeschwerde*, according to ZPO § 281 ff. This remedy is heard by the high court if it is filed against a judgment of a district court, a single judge, a labour court, or a tenant–landlord court, and by the cantonal supreme court if it concerns a judgment of the high court or the commercial court.

This remedy is only successful if the judgment was rendered under a clear and obvious violation of law or a statement of facts which is clearly and obviously faulty (ZPO § 281).

Procedure. There is only one exchange of a written statement from each party (ZPO § 288/289).

1.6.2. Federal Court

At the federal level in civil matters there are mainly two remedies available: the appeal, the so-called *Berufung*, according to Arts. 43 ff. OG, and the constitutional complaint, called *Staatsrechtliche Beschwerde*, according to Art. 83 ff. OG.

1.6.2.1. Appeal

The appeal against a high court or commercial court judgment can only be filed if the amount in dispute is more than Sw. Frs. 8,000. The scope of re-examination is restricted to legal questions arising from federal law (Art. 43 OG). Factual and constitutional questions cannot be discussed.

Procedure. Basically there is only one exchange of written statements.

1.6.2.2. Constitutional complaint

The constitutional complaint is only possible if there is no other remedy at the cantonal or federal level. This means that, before a party can file this remedy, he or she has to file a *Nichtigkeitsbeschwerde* to the cantonal high court and supreme court.

The constitutional complaint is available against violations of the Constitution. Amongst other things, each statement of facts which is clearly and obviously wrong is regarded as a violation of the Constitution (Art. 4, guarantee of equal treatment of all citizens).

1.6.3. Concurrence of remedies

A serious problem for practitioners is the fact that the scope of the different remedies is overlapping and they are often extremely difficult to distinguish. For example, as is the case in many laws all over the world, it is very difficult to separate factual from legal questions. Furthermore, it is also difficult to say whether there is a violation of the Constitution or only a violation of law.

Consequently, a party who wants to attack a high court or a commercial court decision has to file at least two and often three remedies at the same time: the appeal to the Federal Court because of violations of federal law; and the extraordinary remedy to the cantonal supreme court because of wrong factual statements. Furthermore, if the latter remedy is not successful, the party often has to file a constitutional complaint at the Federal Court.

2. STATISTICAL DATA

For the canton of Zurich a large variety of statistical data is provided by the annual high court reports going back to the last century (1831). The following statistics—except those concerning attorneys—are extracted from the annual high court reports.

In 1995 the canton of Zurich had 1,178,854 inhabitants.

2.1. Case load in the last decade

Table 15.1. *Caseload in the last decade (number of actions started)*

	1988	1989	1990	1991	1992	1993	1994	1995	1996	1997
Single judge in ordinary proceedings	934	822	820	862	1,060[a]	1,247[a]	1,149[a]	925	1,320[a]	1,412[a]
District courts (excluding family law)	1,225	1,274	1,364	1,465	1,847[a]	1,837[a]	1,601[a]	1,546	920	806
District courts, family law	3,256	3,274	3,501	3,561	3,705	3,720	3,849[a]	3,801	3,976[a]	4,131[a]
Commercial court	451	459	466	589	739[a]	788[a]	685[a]	587	548	500
Labour court in Zurich	1,175	1,224	1,110	1,212	1,301	1,252[a]	1,118[a]	1,238	1,304[a]	1,104
Appeal	376	334	364	343	387	382	489[a]	455	465[a]	538[a]
'Little' appeal	794	803	936	935	1,034	1,179[a]	1,220[a]	1,140[a]	1,028	922
Extraordinary remedy to high court	475	415	472	429	530[a]	636[a]	639[a]	490	423	424
Remedy to the cantonal supreme court	333	303	273	286	307	353[a]	391[a]	345	367[a]	342

[a] Years of heaviest caseload.

Trends and remarks.

1. The big increase of cases of the single judges and the decline of cases in district courts (excluding family matters) in 1996 resulted from a shift of competence.
2. Since 1988 there has been a constant increase in divorce cases (see amount of cases at the district courts in family matters).
3. In 1992/3 and 1994 there is a remarkable all-time high of cases filed in commercial matters and civil matters excluding family cases. An obvious explanation is the fact that Switzerland experienced a serious recession at the beginning of this decade. As an indication of it, in 1992/1993 the real estate prices dropped dramatically. Average real estate prices per square metre for land to build family homes or apartment houses in the canton of Zurich are shown in Table 15.2.
4. All in all the amount of civil cases filed in this period of time did not increase significantly.
5. In comparison with 1988, today we have somewhat more appeals (ordinary and 'little' appeals).

2.2. Duration of litigation in 1997 and 1977

See tables 15.3–15.6.

Results:

1. All in all very few cases take more than one or even two years.
2. The numbers of 1977 are not significantly different from those of 1997. The only exception seems to be the ordinary appeal. Today there are quite a lot of cases which take more than one year, compared with 1977.

2.3. Settlement ratio for 1997 and 1996

See tables 15.7–15.8.

In this context a settlement means an agreement where both parties give in, but it also includes a waiver or an acceptance of a claim.

Results:

1. All in all a settlement is the most likely form of disposal of a claim. Concerning settlement in court, the percentage is between 44 per cent and 77 per cent (average 58 per cent). There is no doubt that one would find similar data in all the cantons.
2. If the settlements reached in front of justices of the peace and those in court are taken together, the average ratio of settlement is even higher, at 79 per cent.

Table 15.2. *Real estate prices per square metre in the canton of Zurich* (Sw. Fr.)

	1989	1990	1991	1992	1993	1994	1995	1996	1997
Price (Sw. Fr.)	604	740	745	701	600	667	635	602	592

Table 15.3. *Duration of litigation: single judges in ordinary proceedings*

	Less than 3 months	3 to 6 months	6 to 12 months	More than 1 year
1997 (3,092)	2,563	308	146	75
1977 (2,138)	1,609	368	126	45

Table 15.4. *Duration of litigation: district courts*

	Less than 3 months	3 to 6 months	6 to 12 months	1 to 2 years	More than 2 years
1997 (5,533)	3,087	1,080	711	446	209
1977 (6,150)	3,568	1,193	730	454	203

Table 15.5. *Duration of litigation: commercial court*

	Less than 3 months	3 to 6 months	6 to 12 months	1 to 2 years	More than 2 years
1997 (549)	117	141	159	56	76
1977 (371)	75	126	97	47	26

Table 15.6. *Duration of litigation: ordinary appeal*

	Less than 3 months	3 to 6 months	6 to 12 months	1 to 2 years	More than 2 years
1997 (537)	212	115	136	53	21
1977 (220)	99	72	25	8	6

Table 15.7. *Settlement ratio: justices of the peace*

Year (cases)	Settlement	Delivering of a *Weisung*	Ratio (%)
1997 (15,400)	5,429	9,971	35
1996 (15,957)	5,614	10,343	35

Table 15.8. *Settlement ratio: single judges in ordinary proceedings/district courts/labour court/commercial court (1996 in brackets)*

Court: cases	Settlement	Other forms of disposal	Ratio (%)
Single judges: 3,093 (3,033)	1,374 (1,449)	1,719 (1,584)	44 (48)
District courts excluding family matters: 855	442	413	52
Labour court in Zurich: 1,126 (1,357)	815 (1,026)	311 (351)	72 (77)
Commercial court: 549 (563)	335 (328)	214 (235)	61 (58)

2.4. Amount of remedies in 1997

See tables 15.9–15.10.

Results:

1. In 1997 against 26 per cent of all the judgments an appeal to the cantonal high court was filed. In the same year 33 per cent of the judgments were attacked by an appeal to the Federal Court.

2.5. Number of judges in the canton of Zurich in 1997

See table 15.11.

In the canton of Zurich, as is the case in most cantons, judges serve either full-time, part-time, or only in a few cases a year. In order to make it possible to compare the number of judges in the canton of Zurich with the situation in other countries, I will give an estimated number of full-time jobs. Furthermore, most judges hear both civil law cases and criminal cases. Therefore the number of full-time jobs in civil matters can only be estimated.

Results:

1. In the canton of Zurich there are an estimated number of 225 full-time jobs for civil law judges.
2. With approximately 1,178,854 inhabitants, the canton of Zurich has one judge per 5,239 people. This number probably is about the average number in Switzerland.[3]

---

[3] See also Richard Posner, *Law and Legal Theory in the UK and USA* (1996), 28. He suggests the number of 5,600 as a ratio of population to full-time judges for Switzerland. In my opinion this amount is too high.

Table 15.9. *Appeals to high courts against a district court or single court judgment*

	Number of judgments where an appeal is possible	Appeals (number of appeals started)
Single judges	800 (approx.)	343
District courts (except family matters)	252	
Labour courts	160 (approx.)	
Tenant–landlord courts	80 (approx.)	
Total	1,292	

Note: The amount of judgments where an appeal is possible can only be given approximately because the data do not specify how much money was at stake.

Table 15.10. *Appeals to the Federal Court against a high court or commercial court judgment*

	Number of judgments where an appeal is possible	Appeals (number of appeals started)
High court	316	176
Commercial court	214	
Total	530	

Table 15.11. *Number of judges in the canton of Zurich, 1997*

Courts	Number of judges	Full-time jobs	Civil law judges	Full-time jobs of civil law judges
Justices of the peace	183	60	60	60
District courts/single judges/labour courts/tenant–landlord courts	125	100	80	75
High court/commercial court	64[a]	55	45	40
Special commercial court judges	70	15	70	15
Special labour court judges	—	—	—	10
Special tenant–landlord court judges	—	—	—	20
Supreme court judges	20	7	12	5

[a] Ordinary and extraordinary judges.

2.6. Number of lawyers in Switzerland

See table 15.12.

Results:

1. Since 1988 the number of lawyers practising in Switzerland has increased constantly (average per year: 4.82 per cent). In ten years the number has risen by 48.34 per cent.
2. There is a certain tendency for the concentration of lawyers in cantons with a lot of business and industry. In 1988 23 per cent of all lawyers were practising in the canton of Zurich, the canton with the most business and industry in Switzerland. Today 27 per cent are working in the canton of Zurich.
3. The ratio of lawyers to the population of Switzerland is 1 : 1,228. In the canton of Zurich there is one lawyer for every 761 people. The canton of Glarus, a small canton with only 39,254 inhabitants, has one lawyer for every 1,636 people.

2.7. Costs of the judiciary branch in the canton of Zurich in 1997

See table 15.13.

Results:

1. In the judiciary branch in the canton of Zurich the court fees cover a reasonable part of the expenses. Criminal and civil courts have a ratio of

Table 15.12. *Number of lawyers domiciled in Switzerland, the canton of Zurich, and other cantons 1988–1998*

	1988	1989	1990	1991	1992	1993	1994	1995	1996	1997	1998
ZH	932	997	1,028	1,079	1,132	1,198	1,268	1,340	1,421	1,505	1,561
AG	137	141	152	162	171	184	191	203	202	205	218
BE	301	320	325	361	371	395	406	424	439	462	491
GE	508	519	539	577	601	634	643	657	672	668	699
GL	17	17	19	19	20	18	19	20	20	22	24
TI	366	375	379	415	448	470	487	502	527	543	557
CH	3,887	4,019	4,141	4,345	4,544	4,742	4,954	5,167	5,349	5,541	5,766
Increase	141	132	122	204	188	198	212	213	182	192	225
% of increase	3.76	3.4	3.04	4.90	4.58	4.36	4.47	4.3	3.52	3.59	4.06

Notes: ZH=Zurich (1,187,854), AG=Aargau (525,360), BE=Bern (951,804), GL=Glarus (39,254), GE=Geneva (395,876), TI=Tessin (300,446), CH=Switzerland (7,080,948) (population figures in brackets).
Members of the the Swiss Bar Association (the SBA is a federal association covering 24 independent cantonal bar associations. About 95 per cent of all independent lawyers practising in Switzerland are members of it.)

Table 15.13. *Costs of the judiciary in Zurich*

Courts and agencies	Expenses (Sw. Frs.)	Revenue (Sw. Frs.)	Ratio of revenue to expenses (%)
Judiciary branch in total	188,161,238[a]	143,782,124[b]	78
Judiciary branch excluding agencies/offices for registration of land and companies and bankruptcy administration	147,158,480	57,287,960	39
Civil and criminal court only	135,393,040	56,298,854	42

[a] Salaries, computers, continuing education, legal aid, etc. But without costs for buildings.
[b] Mainly fees and fines to a lesser extent.

42 per cent. Without criminal cases the ratio would probably go up to much more than 50 per cent.

3. DESCRIPTION OF THE MAIN PROBLEMS ENCOUNTERED IN THE ADMINISTRATION OF CIVIL JUSTICE

3.1. Duration of litigation

At least in the canton of Zurich duration of litigation is not a general problem (see section 2.2). But it allegedly is a problem in other cantons, for example in the canton of Tessin, the Italian-speaking part of Switzerland, or in the canton of Zug.

In the canton of Zurich only a few cases are not solved in good time or within a reasonable period of time. The main reasons for delay are, in my opinion:

- Inability of judges to handle complex cases and take decisions. According to my personal experience as a clerk at a district court (1.5 years) and the commercial court (2 years) this is a crucial point. Serving as a judge is a very demanding job. Many judges are just not good enough.
- Job-rotation. The career-ladder of a judge goes from district court, to single judge, to high court, and finally to the Federal Court. A judge moving to a higher level leaves behind him or her a large number of cases which have to be dealt with by a new colleague.
- Causes in the legal system itself. Some reasons for overdue cases of course are based in the legal system itself. In the canton of Zurich an important one is certainly the complex remedy system (see section 1.6).

3.2. The courts' reaction to delay and overload of work

3.2.1. Electing new judges and/or employing new clerks

In Switzerland the most common reaction of the courts to delay and overload of work is to demand additional judges and, if that is not possible, more law clerks. The number of law clerks in particular has increased a lot in the last few decades at all levels of court.

3.2.2. Improvement of 'trial management'

Judges of today are much more aware of the importance of 'trial management'. In the canton of Zurich a good example is organizing a settlement conference at an early stage of procedure. Now, as a rule in ordinary proceedings, judges organize well-prepared settlement conferences after the defendant's answer, as has been the practice in the commercial court for a long time. In the past, at district courts a settlement session took place at the end of the main proceedings. Furthermore, judges nowadays are much stricter in granting time limits in written proceedings than they used to be.

3.3. Costs of litigation

See in general section 1.5.

The enormous costs of litigation and the legal aid system of today are weak points of Swiss procedural law. As explained above (section 1.5) in general only very poor people get legal aid. In my opinion we have to move to a system similar to that existing in Germany: that is to say, people should get legal aid if, and to the extent that, they are not able to pay the estimated cost of litigation out of their disposable income in a short period of time.

3.4. Appeals

See in general sections 1.6 and 2.4 concerning frequency of appeals.

In general there are too many remedies and often their scope is extremely difficult to distinguish (see my criticism in section 6.1).

3.5. System costs

See section 2.7.

4.1. Piecemeal changes over the past decades

In the canton of Zurich the legislators enacted several piecemeal changes to the rules in order to make procedure more effective. The most important ones are as follows.

4.1.1. Shifting power from district courts to single judges

One successful method of accelerating litigation and reducing judges' work-load is to give single judges more power. Since 1987 a single judge has been competent to hear a case up to Sw. Frs. 20,000 instead of Sw. Frs. 8,000 as was previously the case. Since 1996 divorce cases have been handled by a single judge as far as, and so long as, they are not disputed (GVG § 31a). Furthermore, the single judges have been given more competence in bank-ruptcy matters.

4.1.2. Changes concerning consumer litigation and other actions

In the revision of 1996, the legislature made important changes to the rules concerning consumer litigation and other actions such as alimony and labour law action.

4.1.2.1. Default judgments

According to the law of the canton of Zurich, in general a default judgment can only be rendered after the defendant has been invited to the main hearing or to give a written defence twice (ZPO § 129 I). In this case one service of the writ is enough (ZPO § 129 II).

4.1.2.2. Submission of evidence

As already shown above (section 1.4.2), at the stage of proof there is no separate interlocutory judgment which gives the parties the opportunity to complete their submissions of evidence. After finishing the main proceedings, the court immediately steps forward to take evidence (ZPO § 141). This means that the parties have to call all their evidence at the stage of the main proceedings.

4.1.2.3. Hearings and time limits during the court vacation/recess

In this kind of case hearings and time limits also take place during court vacation (GVG § 140 II).

4.1.3. Restriction of submission of new facts and evidence in appeal

Before 1996, in an appeal the parties were allowed to submit facts and evidence without any restrictions. However, since the revision of 1996, a restriction over submitting new facts and evidence on appeal (ordinary and 'little' appeal) has been introduced, applicable to all cases. According to ZPO §§ 267, 278 and 115, new facts and evidence are only allowed under the following circumstances:

- if the parties were compelled to raise them by the ongoing procedure;
- if they can be proved definitely by documents which can be submitted immediately;
- if they concern facts and evidence which the parties were not able to submit at the first instance although they acted carefully;
- if they concern facts and evidence which the court has to examine ex officio;
- if they concern facts and evidence which the parties would have submitted at the first instance if the court had fulfilled its duty of questioning the parties because of obvious mistakes or incomplete submissions.

4.1.4. Criticism of piecemeal changes to the system

In my opinion the changes mentioned under 4.1.2 and 4.1.3 are very disputable. They make going to trial far more risky and tricky. At the same time, I have no doubt that, all in all, they have no significant effect on the duration of a procedure! For example, as to the restriction of submission of facts and evidence, the appellate court, instead of dealing with new facts and evidence directly, now has first to examine whether the new submissions meet the above-cited requirements.

4.2. Disputed revisions

4.2.1. Restriction of access to the Federal Court

For more than ten years there have been proposals to restrict and simplify access to the Federal Court. But it is still not clear when and to what extent these proposals will be realized.

4.2.2. Abolition of the cantonal supreme court

The abolition of the cantonal supreme court has been on the agenda of politicians in the canton of Zurich for a long time as a means of relieving judiciary resources and taxes. So far the supreme court still exists.

4.2.3. Justices of the peace

In all fundamental revisions of cantonal procedural law, one of the problems most intensively discussed is the role of justices of the peace. Although the settlement conference led by a justice of peace before starting a procedure has a long tradition in Swiss procedural law, people disagree over whether this institution makes sense or not. Lawyers often regard it as a waste of time and money, especially if on both sides business people are involved.

It is in fact not clear whether these settlement conferences contribute significantly to a more efficient procedure or not. It is possible that most cases settled by the justices of the peace would have been settled anyway before trial. One could also argue that this institution makes access to court easier and therefore attracts more cases. I personally think that one should not abolish, but rather renew, the settlement conference, by introducing more elements of mediation.

5. DEVELOPMENT OF EXTRA-JUDICIAL OR SUMMARY WAYS FOR PROTECTING RIGHTS

5.1. Importance of summary proceedings

In Swiss procedure, summary proceedings play, and always have played, a very important role. This is especially the case for money claims and cases where the facts and the legal situation are clear and/or indisputable (see section 1.4.3).

5.2. Consumer litigation

5.2.1. Increase of alternative dispute resolution
In consumer litigation ADR gets more and more important. In Switzerland there is an increasing number of ombudsmen and -women for disputes and complaints from consumers. This is the case in the banking, travel, and insurance sector. The ombudsmen and -women are employed by trusts founded by the companies of these branches. For example, the travel ombudsman, as far as I know, attracts almost all disputes in this area and solves them efficiently, mostly by 'phone call justice'.

5.2.2. Litigation of consumer organizations
According to Article 10 UWG consumer organizations have their own right to sue. In practice this right has rarely been used, allegedly because these organizations have no or little money.

5.3. Labour litigation

According to my observations, there is a tendency in labour litigation towards resolving it by negotiation between employers and the unions. For example, in a situation involving the solvency of a company, all problems are almost always resolved by agreement with the unions. Therefore employees no longer need to go to court.

5.4. Mediation

As is the case in all Europe, the mediation movement has also arrived in Switzerland. However, although there are a lot of seminars, congresses, and intensive education about mediation, in practice there are only a few cases in which it is used. This is at least the case in business matters. In divorce cases mediation gets more and more important.

6.1. Problem of remedies

In my opinion the main problems of Swiss procedural law lie in the remedy system. In general there are too many remedies and often the scope of each remedy is extremely difficult to distinguish.

There is a project to restrict and simplify access to the Federal Court. But—as is certainly the case in the canton of Zurich—the remedies at the cantonal level also need to be examined. The best way forward would be to create a new remedy system within a new federal code for procedural law. At a time when law is becoming increasingly supra-national, the confusion caused by twenty-six procedural laws in a small country is ridiculous.

In forming a new remedy system one may consider this: one of the only effective ways to cut the cost and duration of litigation is to reduce the available remedies. In civil matters one appeal to a federal court or a cantonal high court, which is competent to correct legal and factual mistakes, is enough. An extraordinary remedy is needed against the appellate court decisions and against some interlocutory judgments, such as provisional measures and decisions concerning legal aid. For small claims one extraordinary remedy would be sufficient.

6.2. Problem of piecemeal changes to the existing system

In my opinion small changes to the existing system, hoping to make procedure more effective, are often dangerous. More or less all these changes cut the parties' rights with little or no gain. In the canton of Zurich the revision concerning the so-called *einfaches und rasches Verfahren* for consumer litigation and other cases is a good example of this (see section 4.1.4).

6.3. Election and education of judges

As I pointed out above, delay is often caused by judges who are not able to handle complex cases efficiently (section 3.1). This means that it is important to optimize the election process for judges and also to have a closer look at the further education of elected judges.